Mohammed's Koran

Why Muslims Kill for Islam

Peter McLoughlin
and
Tommy Robinson

Fourth Edition 2019

The full persuasive power of the book *Mohammed's Koran* is to be found in the print edition.

ISBN-13: 978-0-995584921

cover art courtesy of:
https://en.wikipedia.org/wiki/Caucasus_Emirate#/media/File:Flag_of_Cauca sian_Emirate.svg

The black flag is known as the Raya ("the banner of the eagle").
The writing on the flag is the Shahada:
"there is no god but Allah and Mohammed is his prophet".
https://en.wikipedia.org/wiki/Black_Standard
The flag of Saudi Arabia is similar, but with a green background.
Anyone who believes that such flags are fake should read this:
http://www.khilafah.com/qaa-islamic-flags-and-banners/.

Published by McLoughlin

http://www.mohammeds-koran.com

The above website contains hundreds of five-star reviews deleted by Amazon when they banned the book. Also there are four side-by-side standard translations of different Korans, allowing you to compare the Pickthall translation with the others, showing that the Pickthall translation is more deceptive than some other translations.

It is not for any prophet to have captives [slaves] until he hath made slaughter in the land. — *Koran* 8:67

"Islam was never a religion of peace. Islam is the religion of fighting. **No-one should believe that the war that we are waging is the war of the Islamic State. It is the war of all Muslims**, but the Islamic State is spearheading it. It is the war of Muslims against infidels". — Abu Bakr al-Baghdadi, Leader of the Islamic State, *Newsweek*, May 2015

"Pope says Koran is a book of peace and Islam is a peaceful religion" — *Daily Mail*, August 2016

"ISIS jihadis blast Pope Francis and claim their war is sanctioned by Allah in the Koran" — *Daily Express*, August 2016

"Waging jihad – spreading the rule of Allah by the sword – is an obligation found in the Quran, the word of our Lord." — "Why We Hate You", *Dabiq* (official statement of the Islamic State) Issue 15, August 2016

"On the IRA we told the truth, on the Islamic problem, we lie." George Walden, UK Government Minister for Higher Education (1985–1987)

"Islam... is the most viciously sectarian of all religions in its heartlessness towards unbelievers" — "Just Don't Call It War", *The Spectator*, July 2005, **Boris Johnson, Prime Minister of The United Kingdom** (2019-)

ABOUT THE AUTHORS

Tommy Robinson has been campaigning against Islamic extremism since 2004. In 2009 a small protest group he set up in his home town in England became a national protest group: the English Defence League. After being hounded by the State for organizing this protest group, Tommy Robinson was imprisoned in 2013. In 2015 his best-selling autobiography *Tommy Robinson: Enemy of the State* was published by The Press News Ltd (ISBN 0957096496). Despite the police being given hundreds of documented death threats made against Tommy Robinson (and his entire family) police have not even prosecuted a single individual. Under laws which oblige the British police to warn potential victims of credible plots to kill them, police have been compelled to inform Tommy Robinson of more than six known plots to kill him. No-one has been prosecuted for any of these plots. In addition, Muslim terrorist groups such as Al Shabab have also threatened to kill Mr. Robinson. On a regular basis the British police continue to hound Mr. Robinson and even his small children. By February 2019 Tommy had been censored by internet companies such as Twitter, Facebook, YouTube, Paypal, etc. The media make programmes about him but do not allow him to speak for himself. The British state was to prove repeatedly that they have no regard for the rule of law, wrongfully imprisoning Tommy Robinson as a political prisoner.

Peter McLoughlin is a writer who lives in England. Brought up in a Communist household, he considered himself a Leftist Libertarian until mugged by reality in 2009. Whilst researching evidence that schoolgirls were systematically entrapped into prostitution by Muslim gangs in England, McLoughlin uncovered that the State had known of this grooming phenomenon for decades, but the agencies and the news media had concealed their knowledge of the phenomenon. After decades of cover-up the grooming scandal was broken open by *The Times* in 2011, following two years of protests across England by the English Defence League. In 2014 McLoughlin published the first book on the nation-wide cover-up, months before "Rotherham" became a byword for taxpayer-funded agencies turning a blind-eye to the rape of schoolgirls on an industrial scale. In 2016 an updated edition of his book *Easy Meat: Inside Britain's Grooming Gang Scandal* was published by New English Review Press (ISBN 1943003068).

The first edition of *Mohammed's Koran* was published in July 2017 and on release it rocketed to the No.1 spot on the Amazon best-seller chart for the UK (the first time in the internet age that a self-published book began life out-selling all other books in print). In February 2019 Amazon banned *Mohammed's Koran*, apparently under orders from the British government.

TABLE OF CONTENTS

PREFACE

Throughout this book phrases and paragraphs are emphasised using bold text. None of this emphasis should be assumed to occur in the original texts from which we quote. We render these parts of the book in bold text because this book attempts to undo decades of deception from politicians, religious clerics and journalists. The use of bold text is to enable the reader to quickly and easily grasp the core content of this book, whilst the rest of the text is there to supplement the core content.

A frequent ruse used to confuse people in coming to terms with the Koran is "what you have heard has been taken out of context". To destroy this ruse, this book contains the entire Koran, with the only significant difference being that this Koran has been put into the accepted chronological order (but in reverse, so that the latest – and most violent – commands spoken by Mohammed are the first thing the reader sees). As we explain in the Introduction, it is the normal Koran, the standard Koran which "takes things out of context" (insofar as the standard Koran is in no rational order), thus denying the reader the context provided by the chronology of what was said first and what was said last.

The reader need no longer be fobbed-off with lies such as "Islam is a religion of peace", or "Islam is opposed to all killing", or "Muslims only fight in self-defence". With the expertise gained from this book, the electorate can start to demand political change, before it is too late. In the eighteen months before Amazon banned the first edition of this book no-one claiming any expertise attempted to refute the arguments contained in the book, despite the book being a number one best-selling book. You will find in this edition an Appendix documenting the censorship of this book. This edition also contains an exensive Index which proves beyond doubt that the foundational document of Islam promotes nothing but hatred and violence towards non-Muslims.

Because of these features, our Koran allows the non-Muslim reader to grasp in minutes what might otherwise takes months or years of study. The reasons why Muslims kill for Islam will become readily apparent, and the reader will easily be able to convince family, friends and colleagues that these are the reasons. The Introduction proves that this view of Islam was the standard view among Western experts for centuries before Muslim terrorists brought down the Twin Towers on September 11, 2001.

We would like to thank the following for their assistance in providing *inter alia* advice, reference material, organisational guidance, proof-reading: Alex Felix, Andrew Bostom, Brian John Thomas, Gavin Boby, Kay, Jack Mitchell, Paul Collins, Robert Bor. Any defects which remain in this work are the responsibility of the authors.

INTRODUCTION

Following any horrendous terrorist attack by Muslims, an attack explicitly done in the name of Islam, we are immediately reassured by politicians, academics and clergy that Islam is "a religion of peace". If you are impatient to try and understand this contradictory situation, a situation in which most of us have found ourselves on a monthly or even weekly basis for many years, just **read to the end of this paragraph and then turn to the Koran which follows the Introduction and you will immediately see why Islam is the very opposite of a religion of peace.** You will see why Muslims kill, and you will see that those members of our own society who have a duty to inform us have been blatantly lying to us about Islam. The lies by those who we trust have had the populations of democracies confused for so many years. If you do not believe what you see after just a few minutes of reading the Koran contained in this book, then return to our Introduction for further evidence and explanation. **If you are a Muslim, please put this book down. We do not wish you to become a killer because this book leads you to understand the doctrines and history of Islam more thoroughly.**

⊞

Since the fall of the Twin Towers, a narrative has been pushed claiming that Islam is a religion of peace. But the truth is the opposite: Islam is a religion of war. Moreover, this truth about Islam was known by the educated class for centuries, right up until the end of the twentieth century. But just a decade after 9/11, the unimaginable became fact: the police in Britain would arrest those who dared to quote the views on Islam of such great historical figures as Winston Churchill. When the truth about the violence inherent in Islam is occasionally heard, the Left are to be found denouncing the speaker as "racist", "Islamophobic" or "far-right" - those who tell the truth being demeaned as holding uninformed and prejudiced views. Such denunciations are nonsense, as anyone looking at *only* the core texts of Islam will see that Islam is a religion of war. When a Muslim would explicitly articulate the Islam recognized by the companions of Mohammed, the Islam practised for over a thousand years, that Muslim would often be marginalized by our elite as "an Islamist extremist". This is an example of another deceit used to confuse the public, to claim that there is something called "Islamism" which is separate from Islam, and that there is even a violent version of Islamism. But there are no shades of grey in Islam. From the image of Mohammed portrayed by the core texts of Islam, if Mohammed was alive today, we would be unable to distinguish between the founder of Islam and a so-called "violent Islamist". The truth about Islam is black and white, and has been known for centuries, as we shall demonstrate.

Whilst your child is being deceived at school, the adult population in the West is deceived by the lies of politicians (lies supported by their allies in the media). Meanwhile, in homes and madrassas, in mosques and Islamic organisations, Muslims in the West are told the truth about Islam. One of the first things that Barack Obama did on becoming President of the United States was to visit the world's foremost Islamic university, to tell the world that in the Middle Ages, when Spain was ruled by Muslim invaders, it was a place of peace and tolerance.

> Obama hit many of the right notes. He conveyed to his audience that he is familiar with the vast and glorious history of Islam, such as the long periods of religious tolerance in Andalusia, where Muslims, Jews, and Christians lived together in peace under Islamic rule.[1]

The above quotation is taken from an article in the "Religion and Ethics Newsweekly" of the PBS website (PBS is the American equivalent of the BBC). The article cites numerous professors of Islam (some Muslim, some non-Muslim). If those experts have any criticism of Obama's speech, it is that he was not positive enough about the greatness of Islam. However, this **idea that there was peace and religious tolerance under Islam is a lie. The lie is so gross that those politicians who put it forward might as well say that there was peace and tolerance in Nazi Germany. This lie about Islamic tolerance is easily exposed based solely on Islamic scholarship from that period (although in recent years entire books have been published exposing this lie about the myth of Islamic tolerance).[2]** Obama's speech concluded by quoting portions from the Talmud and the New Testament that promote peace. The word "peace" appears twenty-eight times in this speech, yet the verse from the Koran with which Obama concludes has nothing to do with the promotion of peace.[3] Thus, in his key speech purporting that Islam was peaceful and tolerant the President of the United States (who says he comes from a long-line of Muslims and that he grew up in Muslim Indonesia), could not cite a single verse from the Koran which promotes peace.[4] Yet no journalist or academic thought to point out this discrepancy.

To expose this discrepancy further let us turn to a famous commentary on the Koran by Imam Qurtubi, a scholar who lived in this supposedly tolerant Islamized Spain over 700 years ago. In 2003 British convert to Islam Aisha Bewley translated the Imam's *Classical Commentary of the Holy Qur'an*.[5] Ms. Bewley is far from being some ignorant extremist when it comes to Islam, and in the small print of her translation it says that her husband Sheikh Bewley was the editor of the commentary. Between them these two converts to Islam have published dozens of books on Islam, including such books as *Islam: The Empowering of Women* (1999) and *Islam: Basic Practices and Beliefs* (2008). We can take it for granted that not only are the Bewleys considered to be very mainstream and respectable Muslims but also that they are highly knowledgeable about Islam. They have even published their own translation of the Koran.[6]

Ms. Bewley says that her translation of Qurtubi's commentary "is intended to give modern readers access to the immense learning of Imam al-Qurtubi in such a way that it will illuminate for them the meaning of Allah's words in the Qur'an".[7] Yet this learned, illuminating commentary on the Koran portrays Islam as anything but tolerant. **When it comes to discussing the key violent sections of the Koran, this classical commentary makes it clear not only that "the religion of peace" commands violence, but this violence is to be used against those who are doing absolutely nothing to harm Muslims:**

> permission to fight was revealed about fighting **in general** and **the instruction is to fight not only those idolaters who fight the Muslims but also those who do not fight.** [...] This is the position of the majority of scholars.[8]

This Islamic scholar goes on to clarify: Islam demands that all peaceful non-Muslims are to be killed purely because we have not submitted to the values of Islam.

> **It is an unqualified command to fight without any precondition of hostilities being initiated by the unbelievers [...] the reason for fighting is disbelief** because Allah says, "until there is no more fitna," meaning disbelief in this case. So **the goal is to abolish disbelief and that is clear.**[9]

We can forget the lie that Muslims are only acting in response to aggression. Is it any surprise that the world is plagued by Islamic terrorism, when these classical scholarly interpretations of Islam make it clear that the Koran instructs Muslims to kill unbelievers "without any precondition of hostilities being initiated by the unbelievers"? In the aftermath of devout Muslims slaughtering innocent people in the name of Islam, it is a lie of the greatest magnitude when leaders in the West describe Islam as "a religion of peace". As we will show, for at least 150 years before 9/11, the educated elite in the West were in no doubt that Islam was a religion of war.

Following repeated terrorist attacks by Muslims in the West it is not uncommon for Sheikh Bewley to publish a statement denouncing the actions of these Muslim terrorists.[10] In these denunciations it would be helpful if Sheikh Bewley explained *why* the actions of the Muslim terrorists are supposedly at odds with the Koranic commands to kill, commands such as those found in his wife's translation of the commentary from Qurtubi. Experts inform us that Qurtubi's commentary is among the greatest sources of inspiration for Muslim terrorists.[11] Are these modern, moderate, educated Muslims who translate such works oblivious to any connection between the texts they cherish and the violence performed in the name of those texts? President Obama could praise as "tolerant" the society which produced a scholar like Qurtubi, yet the liberal journalists who reported on Obama's speech (and the academic experts on Islam quoted by these journalists) had nothing even remotely critical to say about the texts or the doctrines from that society, doctrines which incite genocide.[12] What is going on?

The explanation is that Islam is completely unlike our normal expectations of a religion. Contrary to religions like Buddhism and Christianity, Islam sanctifies violence against unbelievers: the only reward guaranteed to Muslims is they will get to spend an eternity in Paradise *provided* they die fighting to impose Islam on others. Not only do those who die during jihad go to Paradise, they have the most honorific position in Paradise, and have the power to help get members of their family into Paradise.[13] Those Muslims who do not die in this way face the prospect of an eternity of torment in Hell. The body of scripture underlying Islam is very explicit in the violence perpetrated by Mohammed and his followers. The violence was aimed at conquest and such violence was committed even when the opponents of Islam were pluralist and offered no resistance. Islam is expansionist, instructing its followers to wage jihad on non-Muslims for all time (as Qurtubi says, the commands to kill are "general" and "unqualified"). The Islamic State we now see in Syria and Iraq is a new incarnation of the previous Islamic State, a state which only ceased to exist in 1924 (after enduring from the twentieth century all the way back to the seventh-century Arabia). Seeing Islam as a religion is less accurate than viewing it as an ideology committed to installing the most totalitarian regime imaginable. Compared to the centuries-old threat from Islam, the threat from National Socialism was over in the blink of an eye. Islam encompasses religion, politics, etiquette, morality, legality and even the conduct of war. Islam is so all-encompassing that truth itself is subservient to the total system.[14]

As the Koran contained in this book makes abundantly clear, the world-view of Muslims is based on a world that is divided in two parts: the world of peace (Dar al-Islam) where Islam reigns, and the world of war (Dar al-Harb), the lands of the people who have not submitted to rule by Islam. The process of converting Dar al-Harb to Dar al-Islam is called jihad. If we turn to mainstream scholarly works from the 1980s we see that this is made emphatically clear: the entry on Jihad in a thirteen volume encyclopaedia about the Middle Ages says that the world of war "must be brought under the rule of Islam by ceaseless jihad".[15] It is thus a holy duty for every Muslim to assist in increasing the area controlled by Islam, whether by preaching or by violence. As you will see for yourself in our Koran, the division into those two oppositions — peace and war, believer and unbeliever — permeates the book. But you are not to be allowed to know that these are the fundamental principles of Islam, you are to be deceived by schools and the media into believing that Islam is "a religion of peace" and that throughout history Muslims have been tolerant people.

It is only when the Koran has been arranged chronologically that the non-Muslim can see that Islam is constructed to bring the non-Muslim to kneel before Muslims and Islam. The book you have before you is the most overt attempt to display the chronological structure of

the Koran and to prove that the Koran commands war and subjugation instead of peace and tolerance. After so much deception by the elite, we hope that this book brings the problem with Islam into clear focus.

The Deliberate Deception Of The Public

"slay the idolaters [kill the non-Muslims]"

Koran 9:5

As soon as you start reading the pages of the Koran in the way in which devout Muslims know the Koran has been seen for over a thousand years, it will become immediately clear to you why Islam is a religion of war. In 1953 here is what the *Encyclopaedia of Islam*, the twentieth-century's single most authoritative account of Islam in English,[16] had to say about jihad:

> The spread of Islam by arms is a religious duty upon Muslims in general [...] Whether Muhammad himself recognized that his position implied steady and unprovoked war against the unbelieving world until it was subdued to Islam may be in doubt [...] Still the story of his [Mohammed's] writing to the powers around him shows that such a universal position was implicit in his mind, and it certainly developed immediately after his death, when the Muslim armies advanced out of Arabia.[17]

In the light of this, the most expert view on Islam in the West, how could any honest leader in a Western democracy have ever responded to a terrorist attack from devout Muslims by unequivocally describing Islam as "a religion of peace"? There are scores of books by academics in the West which document that Mohammed gave rise to a religion of war, and we will cite many of them in this Introduction as proof of this.[18] These books have made it clear that, from the very first claim by Mohammed that he had a revelation, Islam achieved almost no converts until it embraced violence. Yet between the scholars who write the books and the general public (whose votes are supposed to determine policy in a democracy) there is a wall of politicians, clergy and journalists who read these precise and informed academic books but then lie to the public and claim that "Islam is peace", "up is down", as if the scores of books published in the previous 150 years proving the contrary had never been written.

After 9/11 it was only those with no role officially sanctioned by the institutions of the state who would highlight once again the proof that there was a direct connection between violence and the doctrines of Islam. A couple of years after 9/11, in a book about religion and terrorism, a philosopher attached to no institution wrote:

On almost every page, the Koran instructs observant Muslims to despise non-believers. On almost every page, it prepares the ground for religious conflict. [...] Islam, more than any other religion human beings have devised, has all the makings of a thoroughgoing cult of death.[19]

Sam Harris' book received glowing reviews from many members of the educated elite and was praised as a best-seller. But in the decades following 9/11 this kind of information never found its way into public debates among the educated elite, despite Islam affecting the personal security and the rights to privacy and freedom of speech of all. **A wall of deception is maintained by politicians, clergy, schools and the media who want to maintain The Grand Lie that "Islam is a religion of peace".**[20] **They ensure that truly informed discussions about Islam are confined to a small group of intellectuals.** Such books as the one cited above might as well have never been written: they are like cogs turning inside a large machine, but cogs which connect to no other part of the machine. More than a decade later, and despite all the praise heaped upon the Sam Harris, politicians could still claim that "Islam is a religion of peace" and there would be no dissent heard by the general public. There would be no voice heard to contradict The Grand Lie, there would be no gruelling television interview where a journalist or some expert would challenge the politicians' lies.

In *Mohammed's Koran* we vividly demonstrate the point made by Sam Harris and show you that, seen in the context of expert opinion of the previous centuries, his claim was nothing new. **That the essence of Islam is permanent war with non-Muslims was the standard view of Islam held by Western scholars before 9/11.** The principle means of demonstrating to you why the world is plagued by violence from Muslims is by presenting the Koran in the correct chronological order. When you turn to the Koran which follows this Introduction, you will see for yourself that Islam views non-Muslims as the enemy, and that Islam rules that those believers who do not die in the fight to subjugate non-Muslims are Muslims whose destiny is an eternity of torture. If this book fails to show you the reasons why Muslims are violent towards non-Muslims, then we do not believe that you will ever understand what is happening. We do know the image of Islam presented here flies in the face of years of propaganda fed to people via television and what passes for education in schools and universities.

We non-Muslims in the West have been grossly deceived by the lies and omissions of an elite class.[21] As ordinary members of the public, whether we be atheists or Christians, conservatives or communists, we should not need to seek out the Koran and decipher it ourselves, we should not need to find our way to university libraries to discover the shelves of books going back centuries which proved to their readers that Islam was a violent and expansionist ideology. **This is a job which in normal life our society delegates to an elite class. But instead of telling us the truth, this elite**

class have constructed a wall of lies and misinformation. Whether they did this deliberately or from fear is irrelevant: the result is the same. Devout Muslims are murdering and slaughtering our countrymen, and all our lives have been affected in some way by the actions of these Muslims, yet no leader is offering us any explanation which makes any sense. From the Koran we present here, you will see for yourself that Islam is the absolute opposite of a religion of peace.

We hope that in seeing a Koran where *the last commands to come from the lips of Mohammed are the first things you read* will make clear to you that Islam is a religion of war, where the true believers are seen as the soldiers of Allah. It is only when the people of the West clearly see the nature of Islam that we can proceed to deal with this threat head on. That is not to say that there is complete agreement about the entire chronological ordering of the chapters of the Koran. Nevertheless, the authorities are agreed on one key fact: the last parts of the Koran which came from Mohammed, are the chapters commanding war, and certainly not any chapters extolling restraint.[22] Commands from Allah to kill the unbelievers are what dominate the later part of the Koran, and these commands cancel out those few earlier commands which might suggest that Islam is a peaceful and tolerant religion. **It is these cancelled, earlier commands which our leaders use to deceive us about the violent history of Islam and the commands to violence contained in the Koran. One of the most frequently cited verses used to claim that those Muslims who use terrorism are not Islamic is a verse which says "there is no compulsion in religion".[23] But as our chronological Koran shows, this is one of the parts of the Koran which experts say was cancelled by the commands to kill. Those who cite this verse about supposed religious tolerance are either lying or they are ignorant.** The book you are reading is peppered with references to historians and Islamic scholars so that we can prove the scale of the deceit. Anyone who remains unconvinced by our presentation should read the works referenced in the footnotes and reading list.

Decoding The Koran

"Let those fight in the way of Allah [Jihadis] who sell the life of this world for the other. Whoso fighteth in the way of Allah, be he slain or be he victorious, on him We shall bestow a vast reward [those who die imposing Islam get the greatest reward from Allah]."

Koran 4:74

For 1000 years Muslims, like most rational people, have decided that when faced with contradiction, instructions which come later should replace instructions which came earlier. When someone says "stop" and then subsequently says "go", rational beings naturally take the later command as over-riding the earlier command. By presenting the Koran in reverse chronological order, we can see that Mohammed's latest commands to Muslims about killing would countermand anything else that he said earlier about peace. Knowing that almost every Koran in existence has the commands jumbled-up in no particular order, permits those who would conceal the doctrines and history of Islamic genocide to make their false claim that Islam is a religion of peace. We expect that for most people seeing the Koran in chronological order will be an astonishing revelation, and the problems we face at the start of the twenty-first century will suddenly make sense.

From the 1860s onwards scholars of Islam in the West knew that it was vital that the Koran be understood in chronological order. One of Britain's foremost Islamic scholars in the twentieth-century was Richard Bell of Edinburgh University. In the late 1930s Bell produced a translation of the Koran marking the chronological position of various verses. In 1953 Bell's book *Introduction to the Qu'ran* was published, with a chapter devoted to the discussion of the work of Western scholars (from the mid-nineteenth century onwards) and the efforts of these scholars to put the Koran into chronological order.[24] Bell's book also has a table at the end of the book, where the traditional order of the Koran is contrasted with different translations of the Koran by Western scholars (you can see a similar table in *Appendix 1* of our book). **The one point on which all these scholars of the Koran agreed, is that it was not any chapter on peace and tolerance that came from Mohammed at the end of his life, but the huge Chapter 9 and Chapter 5, which are more concerned with genocide and apartheid against the Kuffar. 'Kuffar' (unbelief) is the term of hatred that Islam uses to describe all that is not Islam (this includes all beliefs which are not Islamic and all those people who are not Muslim – the term can also appear as 'Kafir').**[25] In Islam it is an offensive term, even more offensive than the word 'nigger' is in English - 'Kuffar' designates a systematic position, where non-Muslims are sub-human, meaning no true believer is going to ever be ashamed of their hatred and hostility towards unbelievers, because such hatred is sanctioned by the highest authority they know, Allah.[26] Our politicians and clergy promote Islam which considers us Kuffar to be sub-human, but they would not promote an ideology which designated Africans or Muslims as sub-human. Racists can be shamed out of their racism, Muslims cannot be shamed out of their kuffarphobia. You will see from our presentation of the Koran, that the supposed word of god is pervaded with hatred, hostility and violence towards the Kuffar.

If you show to Muslims the Koran contained in this book many of those Muslims may tell you it is not in the correct order. That is because the Koran they are accustomed to using is in no sensible order (in effect, it has been encrypted in a fairly simple manner). If you have ever tried to read a common Koran you will know that the book makes almost no sense.[27] The Koran printed in that traditional order makes no sense to you and it may make no sense to most Muslims (which is one reason why most Muslims are not directly involved in terrorism, although they may be involved in jihad indirectly, since the Islamic concept of "charity" considers funding jihad as an act of piety).[28] It might seem that horrific violence by Muslims has only occurred in the last few decades. However, the truth is that across 1400 years, Muslims have been killing non-Muslims (and Muslims) in the name of Islam. Throughout history, those who refused to be subjugated by Islam were killed. Those who tried to leave Islam were killed. As ex-Muslim Dr. Sookhdeo says, even the killing of non-conformist Muslims is a form of jihad.[29]

There are over one hundred places in the Koran where Hell and Paradise are contrasted. In Islam unbelievers are going to spend eternity in Hell, where we will have our skin burned off, only to have our skin grow back and be burned off again.[30] By contrast, obedient Muslims are going to spend eternity in the Gardens of Paradise, gardens which have flowing rivers of fresh milk and of wine (yes, wine), whilst the unbelievers are drinking boiling water in Hell.[31] **But not all Muslims are assured of going to Paradise: only those who die fighting to impose the rules of Islam are guaranteed entry to Paradise: "Allah hath bought from the believers their lives and their wealth because the Garden will be theirs: they shall fight in the way of Allah and shall slay and be slain".**[32] Devout Muslims have no doubt about the opposition Islam creates between believers and unbelievers,[33] nor any doubt about the eternal horrors of Islam's Hell, contrasted with the eternal pleasures of Islam's Paradise. Those who find the faith of religious people puzzling or even ridiculous should try to understand that to the religious their beliefs are not silly. If some Muslims really are believers, they really do believe in the eternal torment of Hell and the eternal pleasure of Paradise. Some of those believing Muslims may be terrified of war and violence and death; but if they really do believe that a short life on earth is to be replaced by an eternity of pleasure or an eternity drinking boiling water, why should we be surprised if they kill for Islam, as the Koran commands? Many of us in the West are even being compelled by law to respect the religious beliefs of Muslims, beliefs which declare us to be an enemy, a sub-human enemy who the Koran says is to be killed if we will not submit to rule by Muslims. So, if we sub-human Kuffar are supposed to respect an ideology that despises us, why would we not also respect their Islamic belief that unless they kill for Islam they risk spending an eternity having their skin burned off? If we are to respect Islam, then should we not also respect that they are commanded to kill? Muslims believe that what Mohammed recited were the eternal words of Allah, which is why Mohammed was not only known as "the Prophet" but also known as "the messenger of Allah". The Islamic belief is that the commands to kill in the Koran are the word of god, and to those who follow Islam there is no greater authority in the world than Allah.

If you read the Koran contained in this book *from back to front*, you will be reading the verses Mohammed *issued first*. You will also see in our Koran verses where we have put a line through the text: these are verses which

Muslim authorities recognize as having been "cancelled" by the later (violent) verses. When reading from the back of our Koran, you will see that the verses commanding violence do not start until you are more than half-way through the Koran – because in the first half of Islam that Mohammed revealed, Mohammed was not preaching violence. But **for the last half of the Koran recited by Mohammed, the god of Islam was commanding Muslims to fight the unbelievers (the Kuffar), to kill those who refuse to abandon their beliefs, to kill those who refuse to follow the rules of Islam.** By distracting you from the later, violent stage of Mohammed's commands and telling you that Islam is "a religion of peace" your leaders in the West are deceiving you about what the Koran says and deceiving you about the history of Islam for over 1000 years.

The chronology of the Koran (and the history of how Muslims have behaved based on their understanding of this chronology) is of vital importance to you and your family. **As a famous French philosopher said in 1883:**

> **Those liberals who defend Islam do not know Islam. Islam is the seamless union of the spiritual and the temporal, it is the reign of dogma, it is the heaviest chain mankind has ever borne [...] as soon as Islam had a mass of ardent believers at its disposal, it destroyed everything in its path. Religious terror and hypocrisy were the order of the day. Islam has been liberal when weak, and violent when strong.**[34]

Understanding this problem (and being able to convince those around you of the enormity of the problem) is the most important challenge facing the world today. We hope this book is the only tool you need to convince your family and friends of the threat from Islam.

Devout Muslims Kill, Our Leaders Lie

> *"whosoever killeth a human being for other than manslaughter or corruption in the earth, it shall be as if he had killed all mankind [...] The only reward of those who make war upon Allah and His messenger [Mohammed] and strive after corruption in the land will be that they will be killed or crucified"*
>
> *Koran 5:32 - 5:33*

It is famously said that a lie could travel half-way around the world before the truth had even got out of bed. The momentous horror when Muslims brought down the World Trade Center, killing 3000 innocent people, was followed by a lie that rushed around the world: "Islam is a religion of peace". This must be the biggest lie in history, since it turns upside-down the history of the last fourteen-hundred years, a history which has wrought horrific violence on the people of Africa, Asia and Europe. The lie has been used since 9/11 to cover up murder and terror that is fundamental to Islam. We can put the blame for this lie at the feet of American President George Bush Jr., who popularised the lie. After horrific Islamic terrorist murders in subsequent years, apologists for Islamic violence kept repeating the lie. As one of the few journalists to break ranks says: **"Never do politicians more loudly proclaim Islam a 'religion of peace' than when bombs are set off in its name"**.[35] But any Muslim who has memorised the Koran knows that what the apologists for Islam keep saying is not true. Any Muslim who has read the Islamic sayings (which record how Mohammed lived his life) knows how enormous is this lie. Any Muslim who has read the most authentic Muslim biography of Mohammed knows that describing Islam as "a religion of peace" is not a true account of that history. Moreover, there is ample evidence that in the nineteenth and twentieth-centuries, before countries like Britain or America had any sizable Muslim population, the truth about Islam was routinely expressed by academics in the West.[36]

When one searches a database of twelve million books published in the last three hundred years (all the content of these books having been indexed), it transpires that before 9/11 there was only one occurrence of the phrase "Islam is a religion of peace" in all those twelve million books. The singular book in which that phrase occurred was a Tom Clancy novel, that is, "Islam is a religion of peace" was a phrase spoken by a fictional character.[37] Not one factual, academic, scholarly book in the hundreds of years covered by this index had ever referred to Islam as "a religion of peace". But ever since September 2001 this fiction has been used repeatedly to deceive the electorate in Western democracies.

In the immediate aftermath of 9/11, President Bush issued this statement to the American people, a statement made with the authority of someone who professes intimate knowledge of the Koran:

> **These acts of violence against innocents violate the fundamental tenets of the Islamic faith. And it's important for my fellow Americans to understand that.** The English translation is not as eloquent as the original Arabic, but let me quote from the Koran, itself: In the long run, evil in the extreme will be the end of those who do evil. For that they rejected the signs of Allah and held them up to ridicule. **The face of terror is not the true faith of Islam. That's not what Islam is all about. Islam is peace. These terrorists don't represent peace. They represent evil and war.**[38]

In 2001 there was little reason why the American people should have known that much about Islam, after all, the first massive bomb attack on the World Trade Center in 1993 had failed,[39] and two major terrorist attacks against the USA in 1999 had also failed,[40] suggesting that Islam was not much of a real threat to Americans at home. However, following the massive escalation in the threat to Americans on 9/11, it was to be expected that ordinary people would look to their President (their Commander in Chief) for an explanation and contextualization of such shocking events. **President Bush was not only claiming expertise on the contents of the Koran but hammering that point home to the public by purporting to have read the Koran in Arabic:** there could be no clearer marker of expertise, than to have peppered his talk with claims about how much more eloquent was the message of Islam as found in the original Arabic Koran. This was the start of The Grand Lie.

For over a thousand years before the World Trade Center was brought down, those in the West who knew the doctrines or history of Islam knew that Islam was the opposite of a religion of peace.[41] **Yet in 2001 none of the educated elite spoke up to contradict this monumental lie from "the leader of the free world".** Here are some examples from previous centuries, proving how much this lie went against the known history of Islam. In 1919 the Foreign Office of the British government issued a handbook entitled *The Rise of Islam and the Caliphate*.[42] In World War I, Germany demonstrated their knowledge of Islamic doctrine by attempting to foment jihad against Britain in countries with large Muslim populations, even going so far as inciting Islamic genocide against Christians, and letting Muslims believe that the Kaiser had converted to Islam.[43] In the latter half of the nineteenth century, the British public knew that British General Gordon gave his life fighting the slave-taking jihadi war-mongers of the Sudan.[44] Outside the Palace of Westminster in London, the mother of Parliaments for so many countries, there is a statue of the twelfth-century Crusader King Richard the Lionheart, a statue which was installed there in 1860, memorializing the threat to Europe from Islam for over a thousand years.[45] The US Navy was created in 1794 with the attempt to stop Muslims from taking American sailors as slaves, the slavers justifying their actions by citing Islam's laws on continuous warfare against non-Muslims,[46] (these slave-raiding parties travelled far beyond the coast of Africa, as far as London, Ireland and even Iceland). Nearly a century before the creation of the US Navy, Englishman Joseph Pitts escaped from a life of enslavement as a soldier for Islam, and upon returning to England in 1704 he published the first account of the pilgrimage to Mecca (he had been able to go to Mecca on pilgrimage because he had undergone a forced conversion to Islam).[47] Across Europe the humble crescent-shaped croissant was supposed to remind people on a daily basis of the unceasing threat from Islam, after the centuries of military assault on Europe by the Caliphate was stopped in Vienna in 1683.[48] Cervantes published what is considered the first novel in literature and the most famous novel in the Spanish language. The novel contains several chapters on Christian slaves held by Muslims in Algeria, and this was written from personal experience, as from 1575 Cervantes himself was enslaved by Muslims for five years.[49] In Dante's *Divine Comedy* from 1320, one of the West's greatest works of literature, Mohammed is consigned to eternal torment in the eighth circle of Hell.[50] And of course, most famously of all, in 1096 the Pope raised the first Christian jihad against

Islam, in response to centuries of Islamic jihad against Christendom and the persecution of Christians in their own lands, lands which have mostly never been reclaimed for Christians since they were conquered and occupied by the soldiers of Allah.[51] It is thus demonstrable that for 1000 years the educated elite in the West have known that Islam was a religion of war, with the Koran being the fundamental instruction manual. **From the Crusades of the eleventh century to the creation of the US Navy, and from the poetry of Dante to the humble croissant, the people of the West were supposed to never forget that Islam was a predatory religion of war.** But following the attack on 9/11, an attack by the religion of war in the very heart of the West, **the educated elite did not contradict George Bush and his promotion of The Grand Lie. None of the educated elite drew attention to a thousand years of history which proved that the President of the United States was blatantly lying.**

This speech by George Bush at the start of the twenty-first century will be seen as the crucial point from which the elite in the West brazenly lied to those who had delegated authority to this elite. At the very time that the American public needed to grasp what was the cause of, and the implications of, this attack (the biggest single assault on the USA at least since Pearl Harbor), a Republican President gave the public not the truth, but lies.[52] Not surprisingly, President George Bush cited no chapter and verse from the Koran to substantiate his claim that "Islam is peace". The President did not even tell his audience if what he was saying was taken from the Koran or taken from some commentary on the Koran.[53] **The world's only superpower, a country whose entire national defence system failed, permitting an enemy to slaughter thousands of people in multiple simultaneous terrorist attacks, was blatantly deceived by its own Commander in Chief.** As is obvious from the warning signs about Islam listed above, signs which permeate the culture and institutions of so many countries in the West, Bush's Grand Lie could only work with the complicity of the elite throughout politics, journalism, academia and the clergy.

The deception around this pivotal event was not confined to President Bush. In the aftermath of the Islamic terrorism of 9/11, the British Prime Minister gave a speech where he insisted:

> **Islam is a peaceful and tolerant religion, and the acts of these people are contrary to the teachings of the Koran.[54]**

Thus, the President of the USA and the Prime Minister of Great Britain, two highly-educated men, world leaders who had access to the research and opinions of hundreds of civil servants and academics, both chose to emphatically deceive the citizens who delegated authority to these men. This deception has fatally framed the debate about Islam ever since.

Without Jihad There Would Be No Islam

"They [non-Muslims] long that ye should disbelieve even as they disbelieve, that ye may be upon a level (with them). So choose not friends from them till they forsake their homes in the way of Allah; if they turn back (to enmity) then take them and kill them wherever ye find them, and choose no friend nor helper from among them"

Koran 4:89

The people of the Western world have struggled to disentangle ourselves from this Grand Lie ever since 9/11. We are living through a time of near universal deceit. It is said, that in this situation, telling the truth becomes a revolutionary act. This book will prove to you that Islam is a religion of war and will show you that this doctrine of war is not only to be found in the texts of Islam but has also been implemented throughout the history of Islam. Moreover, you will see evidence that this was known not just by Muslims but also by scholars in the West. Once you have seen the truth, you will gape at how the elite have so consistently deceived the public,[55] and at how in just a few decades our academics and journalists have buried over one thousand years of knowledge and popular memory: for example, in the 1970s even the TinTin comics told the story of the rise of Islam, showing Mohammed leading his soldiers into battle, his sword aloft. That one image in a comic book for children represented the essence of Islam more adequately then most mainstream accounts of Islam since 9/11.

The Grand Lie has led to many attempts to mislead the Kuffar about the meaning of the word "jihad". In a book about the Koran published in 2007, shortly after the worst terrorist attack in Britain's history, a Professor of Islamic Studies in Scotland said jihad "denotes an inner struggle [...] of the individual over his own weaknesses and sins [...] and has nothing to do with war or warring of any kind".[56] In Britain this absurdly false claim about "inner struggle" was taken up by Muslims,[57] Christian clergy,[58] government departments,[59] news media,[60] and even judges.[61] Never mind that the view of Western scholars for over a century before 9/11 had been describing jihad primarily as warfare, and the Muslim terrorists themselves were using this meaning of the word "jihad".[62] The lie about the meaning of jihad became so commonplace that by 2008 even Muslims on trial for a terrorism plot to behead a British soldier used this ruse of "inner struggle" in their testimony before the criminal court.[63] But consult any dictionary of the English language before 1990, and if it contains the word "jihad" at all, the *only* definition offered is that of "religious war of Muslims against unbelievers".[64] None of these standard dictionaries of English have any mention of there being a primary or even a secondary usage, where jihad means "inner struggle". **In those core texts of Islam having chapters devoted to jihad, there is not one entry on the topic which is to do with inner struggle, as**

every single entry is about jihad as violence.[65] Yet as the above examples show, as late as 2014, government departments and even those testifying before Parliament were claiming that jihad meant "inner struggle". The idea that jihad is "inner struggle" is another form of the lie "Islam is a religion of peace". There is so much discussion of jihad (as warfare) in the core texts of Islam, that the deceivers tried to frame the mind of anyone who should start to look at the core texts of Islam. The terrorists were using the word "jihad" as it had always been used in Islam, and a fictional secondary meaning was conjured up to deceive the public in the West. The thirteen volume *Dictionary of the Middle Ages*, one of the world's two greatest reference works on that historical period, went so far as to say that "holy war" was so fundamental to Islam that it could even be considered one of the five "pillars of Islam".[66]

You will see from the highlighted verses of our Koran that this "struggle" or "striving" (a shortening for the allusive phrase "striving in the cause of Allah"), entails using any means necessary to enforce Islam on non-Muslims.[67] Here is what one of the mainstream experts on Islam had to say just a couple of years prior to 2001:

> The Arabic word jihad [...] means to strive, to exert oneself, to struggle. [...] The origin of the concept of jihad goes back to the wars fought by the Prophet Mohammed and their written reflection in the Koran.[68]

The destruction of the World Trade Center meant that the elite needed to sow confusion among the populace, in case the public started to voice criticism of the Islamization of the West, a project of the elite which had been under way for decades.[69] As the religion of war showed itself capable of killing on an industrial scale, right in the heart of the West, the Quisling elite set about lying for this genocidal ideology (Quisling is a term from World War II referring to someone who collaborates with the enemy).[70]

Variations on the phrase "striving in the path of Allah" mean promoting and implementing Islam, and when necessary fighting and losing one's life for Islam, with the reward of entering Paradise: "Those who believe, and have left their homes and striven with their wealth and their lives in Allah's way are of much greater worth in Allah's sight. These are they who are triumphant".[71] The word "jihadi" principally means "one who will kill and die for Islam", but since 9/11 this sustained campaign of deception was maintained: across the West in schools and in the media the non-Muslim would be told that the idea of jihad as war was some kind of peculiar misunderstanding by a tiny minority of Muslims. Meanwhile, in mosques and homes of Muslims across the West, many Muslims would continue to be told the doctrinal and historical truth concerning jihad as war. The deceit of the Kuffar worked and, instead of terrorist attack after terrorist attack leading to the public demanding an end to Muslim immigration, the number of Muslim immigrants increased like never before. Instead of allowing the public to learn that this modern terrorism from Muslims was simply a resumption of the murderous violence from Muslims which extended for over a thousand years after the death of Mohammed, the elite lied to the masses, ensuring that by the time the public does come to grasp the truth of Islam the problem will be almost impossible to solve. **It is thus urgent that the population of Western democracies should understand that violence is the true essence of Islam.**

More than ten years after 9/11 and on the other side of the Atlantic, the British were a nation in shock when, out of the blue, a man was beheaded on a sunny afternoon in London.[72] There had been many other Muslim terrorist plots in the West in the intervening decade (some of which succeeded and even more of which were foiled), but there was something particularly horrendous about this attack: an off-duty British soldier was murdered and nearly beheaded in his own country by people born in Britain but who had converted to Islam.[73] The killers chose to stand over the dead body courting publicity, demanding a passer-by take a video statement from the killers. The police arrived and kept their distance, until twenty minutes later when the armed police arrived. Then, brandishing a gun, the jihadis rushed at the armed police, presumably hoping to be shot dead by the police as "martyrs" for Islam. You might think that in the decade leading up to this, there would have been some critique of those politicians and journalists who repeated the lie that Islam was a religion of peace. But incredibly, the elite just became increasingly confident of their ability to lie to the public about Islam with no consequences.

A few days after the beheading of this soldier, Nick Clegg the Deputy Prime Minister made a public statement about the attack, and in doing so he too deceived the British public about the nature of Islam, but in a far more brazen way than even President Bush deceived Americans. This liberal British politician was no ignoramus: before entering politics, he had been a journalist and was a graduate of three prestigious universities: Cambridge University, Minnesota University and the College of Europe.[74] His speech was widely-quoted by the media and was placed on the website of his political party.

> Clegg cited verse 32 chapter 5 [of] the Koran, which says: "If anyone kills a human being it shall be as though he killed all mankind whereas if anyone saves a life it shall be as though he saved the whole of mankind".[75]

In espousing The Grand Lie, President Bush was vague about what part of the Koran he was supposedly quoting as proof that Islam was a religion of peace. But when the Deputy Prime Minister of Britain addressed a public meeting to explain why this beheading of soldier Lee Rigby was not Islamic, you will note that Clegg actually cited the chapter and verse of the Koran from which he was supposedly reciting.[76] What most non-Muslims would not realise from this speech, is that the Deputy PM could only "prove" that Islam is opposed to the

taking of human life by *omitting* **the central part of that very verse, the part of the verse which encourages Muslims to kill.** It was as if this politician stood up and claimed that one of the ten commandments of Christianity was "Thou Shalt Murder" instead of "Thou Shalt Not Murder". Judaism and Christianity both have commandments saying that murder is a sin.[77] Islam has no such commandment. On the contrary: **Islam explicitly commands Muslims to kill non-Muslims. So, the only way in which the elite can "prove" Islam is opposed to killing is by deliberately distorting what the Koran says.**

To make it completely clear how brazen was the deception by the Deputy Prime Minister, here is what the full verse of Koran 5:32 says.

> For that cause We decreed for the Children of Israel that whosoever killeth a human being for **other than manslaughter or corruption in the earth**, it shall be as if he had killed all mankind, and whoso saveth the life of one, it shall be as if he had saved the life of all mankind.[78]

If you compare the sentence we quote with what the Deputy PM claimed he was quoting, you can see that he removed the section about killing people for "manslaughter or corruption" (in bold in the quotation above). The section omitted by the Deputy PM, specifically *authorizes killing* (thus completely refuting the idea that the Islam opposes killing). And if one looks at the following verse (Koran 5:33), it spells out what is meant by "corruption" (the grounds on which someone may be killed):

> **The only reward of those who make war upon Allah and His messenger and strive after corruption in the land will be that they will be killed or crucified,** or have their hands and feet on alternate sides cut off, or will be expelled out of the land. Such will be their degradation in the world, and in the Hereafter theirs will be an awful doom.[79]

The "corruption" for which killing is the punishment authorized in Koran 5:32 is defined in the following verse as "making war against Allah and Mohammed", that is, attempting to implement some political, religious, moral or legal system other than Islam. Resisting domination by Islam is thus seen by Muslims as an act of war against Islam and for this death is sanctioned. So, **resisting Islamic domination (in order to practice your existing religion or lack of religion) is corruption, for which the penalty is death.** Koran 5:32 is the only part of the Koran which apologists for Islam ever cite as (supposedly) being some sort of proof that Islam opposes killing.

If you look out for this verse being 'quoted' by those defending or promoting Islam, you will find that without exception they omit the part of the verse which sanctions killing. Why do this unless they are intentionally trying to mislead their audience? Whilst frequently accusing critics of Islam of taking verses out of context, this is instead precisely what the Quisling elite does, with the pretence that Koran 5:32 supposedly condemns killing.[80]

So, in the simplest possible terms: the only verse of the Koran which is routinely cited as proof that Islam is "a religion of peace" is actually a verse which commands the killing of those who do not submit to Islam! Despite being found near the beginning of most editions of the Koran, chronologically this verse is among the very last things Mohammed ever said. This is another indicator of the need to put the Koran in chronological order.

Journalists: Allies Of The Grand Lie

"And the first to lead the way, of the Muhajirin [Immigrants] and the Ansar [Helpers], and those who followed them in goodness - Allah is well pleased with them and they are well pleased with Him, and He hath made ready for them Gardens underneath which rivers flow [Paradise] , wherein they will abide for ever. That is the supreme triumph."

Koran 9:100

What did the two converts to Islam give as their justification for killing the soldier Lee Rigby? The justification was that the soldier would have "killed Muslims in Iraq and in Afghanistan".[81] A Kuffar soldier who killed Muslims would undoubtedly fall into the category of those who waged war against Islam (whether or not the individual soldier these converts to Islam killed had even been sent abroad was irrelevant to the killers).[82] Reported interviews with one of the Muslims involved in the beheading of this British soldier show that the killer's understanding of Islam was in accord with the above unedited verses from the Koran, rather than the Deputy PM's garbled and deceptive account of Koran 5:32.[83] Not only did Lee Rigby's killers ask a member of the public to record a video statement for them, one of these killers had prepared a text which explained his actions as the obligation on Muslims to undertake jihad: **"To my beloved children, know that to fight Allah's enemies is an obligation".[84] These two converts to Islam had no racial or national identification with any supposed "victims" of this randomly chosen soldier (the killers were neither Iraqis nor Afghans). They were killing this soldier for ideological reasons, because they believed that this is what the Koran told them they must do.** As you will see from our chronological Koran, these Muslims had sound reasons to believe that jihad is an obligation in Islam. Lee Rigby would have been a schoolboy when Bush issued The Grand Lie in September 2001, with the schoolboy being told "Islam is a religion of peace". Meanwhile his killers would have had it proven to them by other Muslims that dying for Islam is their only guaranteed entry to Paradise, and (as believers) the killers would have taken this to have been a direct recitation of a command from Allah. Even when the media claimed to quote "the full text" of the letter one of the killers handed to a member of the public, the media omitted the long list of

Koran references at the end of the letter, most of which are commands from the Koran commanding Muslims to kill for Islam.[85]

At the meeting where the Deputy PM of Britain presented his "evidence" that the Koran opposed killing, the following prominent Muslims were in attendance: Labour MP Sadiq Khan (who subsequently became the first Muslim Mayor of London), Conservative peer Lord Tariq Ahmad, former officer of the British Army Afzal Amin,[86] and Islamic scholar Sheikh Shams ad-Duha Muhammad of Ebrahim College. Whilst the Deputy PM claimed the Muslims who beheaded the soldier were "perverting" Islam, in excising parts of a Koranic verse it was the Deputy PM who was perverting the message of the Koran! **The question must be asked: why were these Muslim pillars of the British establishment at this event, if not to confer authenticity on the Deputy Prime Minister's account of Islam? Yet there's no record of any of these educated Muslims objecting to the Deputy PM perverting the Koran and deceiving those Kuffar who would hear the speech or who would see reports of it in the media.**

Since the Deputy PM had explicitly stated which part of the Koran he was supposedly quoting, any journalist who was ignorant of the Koran could easily look up this verse on the internet in mere seconds and then challenge this deception. Yet this lie told by the Deputy PM of Great Britain was not exposed then (or at any time since) by any journalist, nor by any academic, nor by any Muslim. Our leaders can thus lie in full knowledge that the elite members of our society will help them sustain that lie: those whose job it is to correct mistakes, those whose job it is to scrutinize our politicians, are instead just amplifiers of the lies. Muslims who are presented to us as pillars of the establishment will stand by whilst our leaders lie for Islam. Imagine in the 1920s, after Hitler published *Mein Kampf*, politicians and journalists in Britain had just said "Hitler doesn't mean it, he's a man of peace". Imagine, after Hitler had attacked country after country, if Germans living in our country and on whom we had conferred the highest honours told us "this is nothing to do with National Socialism, Nazism is a doctrine of peace". Would we not rightfully suspect these leaders, these pillars of the establishment?

Following the Muslim terrorist attack on British holidaymakers in Tunisia a few years after the beheading of this soldier, Britain's Conservative Prime Minister David Cameron, once again declared that Islam was a religion of peace.[87] Some months later came the horrific terrorist attack in Paris at the end of 2015. This was one of the worst terrorist attacks in Europe's modern history, where Muslim "refugees" working for the new Islamic State butchered the audience at a rock concert, gunned-down people drinking at a bar, and attempted to set off a suicide bomb inside a packed football stadium (at which game the French President Hollande was in attendance). The enormity of this attack in Paris finally seemed to shake the British Prime Minister, leading to him stating: "it is not good enough to say simply that Islam is a religion of peace and then to deny any connection between the religion of Islam and the extremists".[88] But even then he still managed to make an indirect claim that Islam is "a religion of peace"! No matter how horrific the acts of terrorism by the followers of Islam, the lie that "Islam is a religion of peace" has been exploited again and again by world leaders. They could do this because virtually no member of the establishment ever offered even a whisper of criticism about the blatant contradiction between The Grand Lie and the tens of thousands of acts of terrorist violence by Muslims across the globe since 2001.[89]

Between 9/11 and these other landmark terrorist attacks nearly fifteen years later, came the worst ever terrorist attack in Britain, worse than anything seen in over a century of terrorism from Irish nationalists. A group of Muslims (brought up in Britain) became suicide bombers on the London transport network in 2005, killing 52 innocent people and injuring another 700. In the wake of this carnage, Tony Blair (the Prime Minister of the day), gave a speech about the events which simply implied that the Muslims who became suicide bombers must not have been real Muslims.

> The greatest danger is that we fail to face up to the nature of the threat we are dealing with. What we witnessed in London last Thursday week was not an aberrant act. [...] **Senseless though any such horrible murder is, it was not without sense for its organisers. It had a purpose. It was done according to a plan. It was meant. What we are confronting here is an evil ideology. [...] They demand [...] Sharia law in the Arab world en route to one caliphate of all Muslim nations.** [...] We must be clear about how we win this struggle. [...] In the end, it is by the power of argument, debate, true religious faith and true legitimate politics that we will defeat this threat. That means not just arguing against their terrorism, but their politics and their perversion of religious faith. [...] It means championing our values of freedom, tolerance and respect for others. [...] The spirit of our age is one in which the prejudices of the past are put behind us, where our diversity is our strength. It is this which is under attack.[90]

Despite claiming that we must "face up to the nature of the threat" and "it is by the power of argument" that Islamic terrorism will be defeated, nowhere in this speech does the Prime Minister explain to the British public what it is that could have motivated the Muslim terrorists. He does show that **as early as 2005 the political elite knew the key role that the Caliphate (Islamic State) played in the motivation of Muslim terrorists. Within a decade of this speech, the Islamic State had come back into existence.**

Britain's highly-educated Prime Minister Blair had been a lawyer after graduating from Oxford University. He claimed the problem with terrorism from Muslims is to be found in countries all over the world, and that these terrorists follow a "perversion" of Islam. But what he did not say is that this supposed perversion is nothing more than a literal

reading of what the Koran says, a reading supported by Muslim interpretations of the Koran which have been accepted as the standard interpretation for over 1000 years.[91] And this "perversion" was part of a plan to return the World of Islam (Dar al-Islam) to the state in which it had been from the time of Mohammed until the early 1920s. Unlike President Bush, the former lawyer Tony Blair didn't even bother to try and prove to his audience in what way Muslim fundamentalists have perverted Islam. The Prime Minister's entire speech is just smoke and mirrors, hand-waving to distract the public from the idea that this is a fundamental clash of civilisations. While the public are kept in the dark about the doctrines and history of Islam, the public will not understand that it is a clash of civilisations that goes back to the time before the USA existed, to a time before the British Empire existed. Islam was at war with Christianity and Judaism in the Middle East a thousand years before the Pilgrim Fathers landed in America. It is hard for us in the West to grasp the enormity of the historical and geographical scale of Islam's war on everything that is not Islam (Christianity, Paganism, Judaism, Buddhism, Hinduism and even atheism). As we will discuss below, from year one of the Islamic calendar, Islam has proven itself to be at war with everything that is not Islam.

What no-one will tell the public is that Muslims are still implementing the system of conquest initiated by the founder of Islam. Contemporary Muslims are still modelling their behaviour on the actions and sayings of the founder of Islam as recorded in the canonical scripture of Islam, just as Muslims 1000 years ago modelled their behaviour on those same recorded actions and sayings of Mohammed. Islam has collections of texts amounting to thousands and thousands of pages, texts which report the minutiae of what Mohammed said and how he behaved in different situations, texts which are accepted by virtually all Muslims on the face of the planet as the upright behaviour mandated by Allah. The Caliphate to which Blair referred was the name given to Mohammed's Islamic State following the death of Mohammed in 632 AD. This Caliphate did not disappear until 1924: that is, the Islamic State (the Caliphate) only ceased to exist at the same time as Hitler was preparing *Mein Kampf* for publication. Blair could pretend that jihad and a desire to re-create the Islamic State were some kind of perversion, but in the Islamic view of the world it is the short time since the Caliphate was abolished in the twentieth century which has been the perversion. As mentioned above, as late as 1919 the British Foreign Office thought that Islam and the Caliphate were of such significance to Britain's interests, that the British government produced a handbook entitled *The Rise of Islam and the Caliphate*. It is only by keeping the public in a historical vacuum that our leaders can get away with pretending the Caliphate is some ancient, exceptional part of Islam, something of no interest to most Muslims. This is not the case. Even after the Caliphate was abolished, throughout the twentieth-century Muslims in many different countries were working to bring it back (as we show below). **If Hitler and the Nazis are considered important political landmarks in the West, then the Caliphate should** be considered to be of even greater importance. Any acolytes of Hitler are considered lunatics on the fringe of society. But the acolytes of Mohammed are to be found in the very heart of government, universities and the media.[92]

You might think that any comparison between Islam and Nazism is tasteless and uneducated. But a few weeks after the 7/7 terrorist attack on London[93] (and after the now-forgotten 21/7 failed terrorist attack on the same city),[94] David Cameron, the future Prime Minister of the UK, compared Islamic extremists to Nazis.

> The driving force behind today's terrorist threat is Islamist fundamentalism. The struggle we are engaged in is, at root, ideological. During the last century a strain of Islamist thinking has developed which, like other totalitarianisms, such as Nazism [sic] and Communism, offers its followers a form of redemption through violence.[95]

In talking of National Socialism and Soviet Socialism, David Cameron presented himself as if he was Winston Churchill, battling those genocidal forms of European socialism from the first half of the twentieth century.[96] Just as our Leftist elite ensure that Socialism escapes any blame for Hitler's National Socialist German Workers' Party, so the Quisling elite ensures that Islam escapes all blame by being contrasted with "Islamism". **As one senior researcher on Islam says, the term "Islamism"**

> **reflects a reluctance to identify acts of terrorism with the bona fide teachings of one of the world's great religions or to recognize the derivation of the jihad phenomenon from the tenets of Islam...**[97]

As the global crisis of a resurgent Islam grows - with the rise of Islamic State in Syria, Al Qaeda in Afghanistan and North Africa and Boko Haram and Al Shabab in Central Africa – what we are witnessing is simply a Muslim vanguard[98] returning to the violent, supremacist, slave-taking ideology that Islam had been for over a thousand years of our history. But this vanguard is supported by virtually every Islamic organisation in the world – they all want the return of the Caliphate.

Why does the public keep swallowing The Grand Lie, a lie which makes no sense in the light of Muslim terrorist attacks like 9/11, or the Madrid bombing, or the 7/7 bombing, or the beheading of soldier Lee Rigby, or the Kenya shopping mall attack, or the Paris attacks, or the attack in Brussels, or the Dhaka massacre? The Grand Lie succeeds because *our* conception of religion does not encompass the idea of a supremacist ideology that will murder and enslave all those who do not join in with its attempt to dominate the world. In the West we are so accustomed to the idea that all religions are something like Christianity (a natural assumption for people who do not spend their lives immersed in the study of world religions), that we simply do not have the mental framework to grasp the idea of Islam-the-Religion-of-

War. **Our minds are receptive to the idea of a religion extolling peace (even if its adherents fail to live up to this principle) that we cannot make sense of the idea of a religion dedicated to war. It seems to be a contradiction in terms, like a round square. And it is this inability to comprehend the true nature of Islam which the elite exploit. Instead of explaining that this religion of war is not really a religion in our sense of the word, the elite instead exploit our incomprehension to pretend that there is no basis for warfare and murder in Islam, and that the jihadis are not "real Muslims", when according to the core texts of Islam the jihadis are the only true believers.** Accepting that Islam is a religion of war is such a horrendous idea to most of us, The Grand Lie persists because we do not want to believe that Islam is intrinsically violent and will be a relentless problem for our secular liberal democracies. Accepting the truth about Islamic doctrines and history fills any sane person with dread.

Hiding The Truth Causes Terrorism

> *"And He brought those of the People of the Scripture [Jews] who supported them down from their strongholds, and cast panic into their hearts [terrorised them]. Some ye slew [killed], and ye made captive [enslaved] some."*

> **Koran 33:26**

Christianity and Buddhism are belief systems which can rightly be regarded as religions of peace: they were both founded on an exemplary individual who did not command the killing of his opponents as a means of propagating the belief system. By contrast Islam is founded on an exemplary individual who not only commanded killing, but who personally took part in torture, mass slaughter and slavery (according to the core texts of the belief system itself).[99] The very idea of a religion of war seems to us like a contradiction, but this is narrow-minded of us: we are assuming that alien cultures are just like our culture, insisting that other value systems must be no different from our own. Yet as the doctrines of Islam and the history of Islam show, it is far more appropriate to consider Islam to be a religion of war than a religion of peace. But we in the West simply cannot put the idea of "monk" and "killer" into the same thought, yet many of those Muslims organising and instructing other Muslims to kill are Sheikhs (Muslim Bishops),[100] and the opinion of twentieth-century experts on Islam was that being a jihadi dedicated to killing the unbeliever is precisely the Islamic equivalent of being a monk in Christianity or Buddhism.[101] The most authoritative biography of Mohammed was known by Muslims throughout the following centuries as "the book of campaigns" i.e. the book of wars.[102] **That Islam promotes war and that Mohammed was a warlord is the single most distinctive feature of Islam as a "religion" - it is this which truly distinguishes Islam from all other religions in the last 3000 years.**

It is only while Muslims are a small minority in the West that they feel the need to conceal that Mohammed was a military leader. We will show some Muslim experts do not even bother to hide this.

The terrorist attacks discussed earlier are just a tiny fraction of the terrorist attacks by Muslims since 2001. And in the West the number of thwarted terrorism attempts by Muslims greatly exceeds the number of attempts where they succeeded. **It is no surprise that we have become accustomed to Islam-related terrorist attacks by Muslims. What is astonishing is that we do not notice the *absence* of Islam-related terrorist attacks by us Kuffar: no-one goes and kills Muslims in response to Muslims killing our countrymen.** Despite thousands and thousands of terrorist attacks and foiled terrorist attacks by Muslims, the Kuffar do not fight fire with fire. **In the West there is no political or religious group promulgating an ideology which commands and rewards terrorist attacks on Muslims.** If in a Muslim majority country some immigrant religion was used to justify attacks on Muslims, the response from Muslims would be swift and shockingly brutal. So why in the West are politicians and their cronies so intent on systematically and repeatedly deceiving the public about Islam? Is it because there are too many Muslims here for the truth to be told? Are we really going to allow an immigrant population to terrorise us? Or is it that our elite have been planning for decades that the West should submit to Islam? Praising Islam after every Muslim terrorist attack simply encourages more Muslims to become terrorists and ironically appears to bring fresh converts to Islam.

Under the Islamic conception of the world, there will only be peace when there is no belief other than Islam, when there will be no "Kuffar" (no people who manifest beliefs other than Islamic belief). That is, in Islam there will be peace when there is no difference of opinion concerning how life is to be lived. To the extent that we Kuffar are ever tolerated under Islam, we are tolerated provided the Kuffar acknowledge the supremacy of Islam and so long as we Kuffar pay for our own subjugation i.e. we pay money to Muslims to stop them from killing us (rather like the Mafia and the way they use threats of violence to extort protection money). So, **after the latest terrorist attack by Muslims, those political leaders who insist on telling us that "Islam is the religion of peace" are seeing the world from the very standpoint of the Muslim terrorists! These apologists are effectively telling us: *submit to Islam and Muslims will have no need to attack you.* They are in fact serving as vehicles for Islamic supremacism.**

Just as enslavement is seen within Islam as saving unbelievers from their erroneous ways of living,[103] so Muslim terrorists do not see themselves as criminals. They do not accept our laws and customs; they are implementing Islam, following the exemplary behaviour of the founder of Islam. The violence will end when the world only contains Muslims, dead bodies, or those subservient to Muslims. **That is the only meaning of the word "peace" in Islam. As Germany's most esteemed scholar of Islam said**

towards the end of the nineteenth century: Mohammed "preached war against unbelievers […] they have no choice but between acceptance of Islam and extermination".[104] Scholars such as these could hardly have made it clearer that Islam is a religion of war and genocide. Long ago our own experts in the West were warning our people over and over about the nature of Islam, yet this entire history of Western scholarship has been forgotten and concealed in recent decades. **The terrorism and violence from Muslims in the West will not stop, cannot stop, until there are no beliefs, no behaviours which contradict what Islam allows. This is the grim truth being concealed from you by the Quisling elite.**

In the speech where a future Prime Minister of Britain compared Islam to Nazism, he also made comparisons between Islam and Communism.

> They [Muslim fundamentalists] work, like Trotskyist 'transitional demands', to rally support among the disaffected and radicalise them for the greater struggle. [105]

But responding to these "transitional demands" is precisely what he and other British political leaders have done: they promote the idea of a transitional form of Islam, a "British Islam" or a "French Islam" that is somehow an Islam-lite,[106] a reformed low-calorie Islam, one (supposedly) without all the nasty murder and enslavement exposed by Western scholars throughout the nineteenth and twentieth centuries.[107] **In proposing a moderate Islam, an Islam-lite, the elite will not do anything that actually poses any challenge to Islamic demands or Muslim behaviour in the West.** Thus, we Kuffar are not to do anything that might challenge any of the principles of Islam (such as drawing Mohammed), and the history of Islamic domination and genocide is to remain concealed from the public; the population of Muslims is to continue increasing despite the terrorism and other threats; no laws are to be put in place to monitor what is said in the thousands of Mosques. **How the Muslims in the West have responded to events (such as depictions of Mohammed), would inform the public about how well the (supposed) process of moderating Islam has been going. If the public were to see huge demonstrations by Muslims in favour of freedom of speech, then there might be some reason for us to believe that "British Islam" was somehow different from the Islam in Pakistan or Iran. But there is no reason for anything other than pessimism. Submitting to Muslim transitional demands (provide halal meat, don't burn the Koran, respect Islam, etc.) simply emboldens the Jihadis.**

The elite, drawn from our own countrymen, have sided with the most fundamentalist forms of Islam - for example, the Islam where all images of Mohammed are banned. During the controversy over the Mohammed drawings in a Danish newspaper in 2005 (a controversy entirely manufactured by Muslim imams to stop the Kuffar having accessible visual accounts of the story of Mohammed's violent rise to power),[108] the number of western newspapers and TV channels who showed the cartoons at the heart of the controversy could be counted on the fingers of one hand. Out of thousands of news outlets in dozens of countries - countries not ruled by sharia law, countries which boast about freedom of speech - all the news outlets in those countries surrendered to the censorship demanded by the most extreme form of an immigrant religion, a religion followed by less than 10% of the population in any of those countries. And the elite who want to fob off the population with the ruse of an Islam-lite promoted the need for censorship in order to stop Muslims from being "offended" and resorting to violence! Yet, if there really was an Islam-lite that was not in conflict with the West, then there would have been no need for this censorship. The rest of us do not become murderous terrorists when we are offended.

What the elite are forcing on our societies is Islamisation by stealth and deceit: the rules of Islam are to be imposed not just upon the followers of Islam but also upon the majority non-Muslim population. The elite tell us to put our trust in a "transitional demand" (moderate Islam, Islam-lite), whilst the behaviour of the elite shows they are siding with the most extreme form of Islam, the form of Islam compared to Nazism. For example, between 9/11 and the 7/7 terrorist attack in London the left-wing British government was attempting again and again to pass a law criminalising anyone who offended a Muslim.[109] Thus, whilst telling us that Islam in our countries was somehow different from Islam in the Muslim world, our newspaper editors were opting for self-imposed censorship and our governments were passing laws protecting Muslims from being offended by the victims of Islam learning about our future fate. These laws punishing the Kuffar for "blasphemy" against Islam are the kinds of laws that exist in Muslim-dominated countries.[110] **Slowly but surely, through refusal to stand up for our rights (or through legislation taking away our rights), our countries are being Islamized. And the driving force behind all of this is the preparedness of Muslims to kill in the name of Islam.**

A mostly secular, increasingly atheistic public in the West is expected to believe that there is no point of contact between the Islam-lite in the West and the slave-taking Arab Muslims in the Islamic State, or the slave-taking African Muslims of Boko Haram in Nigeria.[111] In recent decades no attempt is made by our politicians, journalists or academics to explain just how it is that Islamo-Nazis could find anything in Islam, anything in the Koran itself, anything in the behaviour of the founder of Islam, which would serve as the basis for the terrorist violence which the world is enduring. Our educated elite would prefer to allow Islam to spread in the West, like Trotskyism, infiltrating organisations under the pretence that the infiltrators have the same morality and agenda as the majority of the population in our liberal democratic Western societies. In reality the infiltrators follow a doctrine which instructs them to overturn our society in order to subjugate the people around them. Thus, countries like the UK pass laws against Islamic practices like Female Genital Mutilation and then the UK never enforces those laws.[112] **The State pretends to oppose barbaric acts from seventh-**

century Arabia being applied in twenty-first century London, whilst ensuring that these laws are never enforced. The refusal to apply the law of the land shows to Muslims that we Kuffar are being transitioned into a country where sharia law applies. Here is another example: in general, people in Western countries are forbidden to wear clothing which hides the face, unless the people in question are Muslim (in which case such laws are not applied).

Muslims with all the benefits of citizenship in our country resort to murdering other citizens *en masse*, and we are both passively encouraged and actively coerced into avoiding anything which "provokes" violence from the followers of a doctrine which seeks our subjugation.[113] Our laws become subservient to Islamic law, just as if the country is 95% Muslim rather than 5% Muslim. And slowly but surely, people start to behave increasingly in ways that are compliant with Islam whilst the size of the Muslim population continues to grow, with no space in the national media to discuss the problems which Islam introduces into our countries nor to discuss how our society has been changed for the worse and where we are headed. The force propelling us along this trajectory is not that we Kuffar like Islam and want more of it. **The force driving this is that Islam is violent in the face of that which is not Islam, that which is Kuffar. If we do not stand up to the violence and the threats, then our societies will inevitably become Islamic (in 2004 the twentieth-century's greatest mainstream expert on the history of Islam predicted that in less than 100 years Europe will be Islamic).**[114] As our chronological Koran shows, the commands for segregation, supremacism and for violence towards the non-Muslim permeate the Koran, but are found in greatest density in the later chapters of the Koran, which are known to be the final commands of Mohammed. Non-integration is a form of jihad, a way of ensuring that more of Dar al-Harb becomes Dar al-Islam (land controlled by Muslims).

Can you imagine what it will be like when a country of the West is 20% Muslim? The Muslim population of France is thought to be around 11%, and France has been in a permanent State of Emergency for some years.[115] **Even with the army fully-deployed and with 15,000 reservists called-up, the government of France finds its Muslim population so unmanageable that the government has re-created the National Guard, a citizen militia which was disbanded in 1872.**[116] The National Guard was a large force of military police formed in the wake of the French Revolution of 1789. When this militia was abolished in 1872 it consisted of 300,000 soldiers[117] (considering the population of France was about half the size it is now, an equivalent citizen militia now would have over half a million soldiers). In adopting this symbolic move, it indicates that the French government fear that the very foundation of the French Republic is in a more perilous state than at any time during either World War I or World War II, as during those wars the French government saw no need to re-create this militia. Immediately after the Muslim terrorist attacks in Paris (November 2015), several of the mainstream French newspapers had headlines which said that France was at war (a few hours later these headlines had disappeared). Following the attack on Brussels by Muslim terrorists (March 2016), the Prime Minister of France said "We are at war and have been suffering for several months in Europe".[118] Since we in the West cannot rely on our leaders to give us anything like an honest assessment of the threat that Islam poses within our societies, we need to look elsewhere for information about the danger we are in. Our leaders pretend that Islam's 1400 years as a religion of war have nothing to do with our countries being "at war" with jihadis.

The Crime Of Quoting Winston Churchill

> *"the Mahommedan religion increases [...] the fury of intolerance [...] propagated by the sword [...] the hopes of plunder and the joy of fighting [...] The religion of blood and war is face to face with that of peace. Luckily the religion of peace is usually the better armed."*
>
> *Winston Churchill, 1898*

Below the surface of any debate, the true doctrines of Islam and the history of Muslim wars and slavery against Europe, Africa and Asia are concealed by the sugary and dishonest phrases of our own educated elite. Indeed, **in twenty-first century Britain, Paul Weston (the leader of a political party) was arrested for daring to publicly read some of Winston Churchill's comments on Islam.** Many of the British news media could not even bring themselves to repeat what it was that Churchill said about Islam that led to Mr. Weston being arrested. Instead the news reports about the arrest of Mr. Weston were filled with quotations from Muslim organisation after Muslim organisation, people who were not even witnesses to the event![119] That is how detached any debate on Islam is from reality: a respectable man seeking political office was arrested for quoting the most famous British Prime Minister of the last 100 years, and "serious" newspapers could not even bring themselves to inform their readers what it was that Churchill had written that was supposedly so outrageous. By act or by omission, politicians, journalists and educators will lie to you and your family about how Mohammed came to power, they will lie to you about what the Koran says, they will lie to you about the nature of Islam, and they will lie to you about the history of Islamic genocide, even as the devout soldiers of Allah are murdering people in New York, London, Paris, Madrid, Mumbai, Brussels, Dhaka, etc. **The Quisling class will dress themselves up as if they are fighting the same ideological battles as Churchill, whilst their police forces instead arrest those who dare to quote what Churchill actually said. The situation is dire.**

Even when Cameron sought to look Churchillian in his comparison of Muslim extremists with Nazis, this was but a pale imitation of Churchill's actual view of Islam. Here are the remarks by Churchill which resulted in Paul Weston's arrest in 2014:

> How dreadful are the curses which Mohammedanism lays on its votaries [followers]! Besides the fanatical frenzy, which is as dangerous in a man as hydrophobia [rabies] in a dog, there is this fearful fatalistic apathy. The effects are apparent in many countries. Improvident habits, slovenly systems of agriculture, sluggish methods of commerce, and insecurity of property exist wherever the followers of the Prophet rule or live. A degraded sensualism deprives this life of its grace and refinement; the next of its dignity and sanctity.[120]

Perhaps the above remarks by Churchill might sound impolite, but the book from which this quotation was taken was published in 1899. **Any upset at such harsh words from Churchill will be contextualized once you turn to the chronological Koran, and you see that the final words of Mohammed were that you and your family should be killed. We are sure you will agree that genocide is worse than some harsh language about Muslims.**

Harsh words or not, quoting Churchill is certainly not grounds for arresting the leader of a political party. Paul Weston continued quoting from Churchill's book, and here is where the text gets to the nub of the problem.

> The fact that in Mohammedan law every woman must belong to some man as his absolute property — either as a child, a wife, or a concubine — must delay the final extinction of slavery until the faith of Islam has ceased to be a great power among men. Individual Moslems may show splendid qualities. Thousands become the brave and loyal soldiers of the Queen: all know how to die. But the influence of the religion paralyzes the social development of those who follow it. No stronger retrograde force exists in the world. **Far from being moribund, Mohammedanism is a militant and proselytizing faith. It has already spread throughout Central Africa, raising fearless warriors at every step; and were it not that Christianity is sheltered in the strong arms of science — the science against which it had vainly struggled — the civilization of modern Europe might fall, as fell the civilization of ancient Rome.**[121]

In this latter part of the quotation, one can see precisely why Weston might have thought the remarks to be still relevant. Mr Weston is one of the handful of political party leaders across the world who has tried to offer an explanation as to why Muslims kill in the name of Islam. But rather than allow the British public to hear what one of the greatest leaders of the twentieth century thought about Islam, Mr. Weston was arrested to silence him. And **as with the controversy over the Mohammed cartoons in**

Denmark most of our Quisling journalists could not even bring themselves to let the public know what the quotation was that resulted in Mr. Weston's arrest.[122]

When comparing Muslim fundamentalists to Nazis, David Cameron was very vague about why the more Islamic a Muslim becomes, the more like a Nazi that Muslim would be. But in quoting Churchill, Weston made explicit what the British Prime Minister had only been prepared to hint at: namely, that Islam is a fanatical, proselytizing warrior religion, and the more that Muslims find out about the rules of their religion, the more likely they are to be violent. Churchill could see no force in the world that was more dangerous than this, with Islam capable of destroying European civilisation if not held in check by our superior technology. Churchill could see that throughout history Muslims are constantly held in bondage to the behaviour of Mohammed. The Churchill of 1899 would not be surprised by problems visited on the West by Islam in recent decades: terrorism, beheadings, female genital mutilation, Muslim rape gangs,[123] women dressing as if they were in a desert, the reliance of Muslims on taxes paid by the 'inferior' Kuffar.[124] **In all likelihood Mr. Weston was arrested precisely because Churchill's remarks are so relevant to the problems we see with Islam in the West. And for the same reason, the media could not bring themselves to repeat the words of Churchill.**

What was the context for these apocalyptic remarks from Churchill in his book called *The River War*? Fifteen years before Churchill published this book at the dawn of the twentieth century, Britain had seen the rise of "The Mahdi Army", a group of devout warrior Muslims in Sudan whom we would today classify as being "Islamists", comparable to Boko Haram in Nigeria or Islamic State in Syria and Iraq, or comparable to Al Qaeda and the Taliban in Afghanistan. **Thus the problems the West has seen with devout, murderous Muslims at the start of the twenty-first century is something that was also well-known to Churchill's peers at the end of the nineteenth century.**[125] **The apparent period of calm by Muslims on the world's stage between 1919 and 1979 only appears calm if we ignore the attempts of Muslims to wipe out the Jews of Israel in three different wars,**[126] or if we ignore hundreds of thousands murdered because of the demands of Muslims in India to have their own Islamic State (Pakistan) instead of being part of a secular, multi-faith India, as that sub-continent gained independence from Britain after WWII.[127] So let us have no doubt that our twenty-first century problems with Islamic terrorism and the slave-taking by Islamic State do not just reach back to the Sudan of the 1880s described by Winston Churchill, but these problems are a consistent pattern going back 1400 years to the Arabia of Mohammed in the Dark Ages. Thus, Churchill's view of Islam at the dawn of the twentieth century was entirely relevant to the events and policies of the twenty-first century, and Mr. Weston was doing the responsible thing in quoting the wise words of an elder statesman whose fame comes from standing up to National Socialism.

We have heard it claimed that Churchill's view of Islam in 1899 was that of an uninformed young man who knew nothing of Islam (after all, Churchill was in his early 20s when he wrote *The River War*). However, in the nineteenth century educated English people like Churchill knew far more of the truth about Islam than do our contemporary "experts". Moreover, as Churchill got older and wiser over the following fifty years and became one of our greatest statesmen, his nineteenth-century view on Islam remained unchanged. So Mr. Weston was quoting a view of Islam that was held consistently by one of Britain's greatest statesmen over a period of half a century. In his memoirs published in 1948, Churchill described the rise of National Socialism in the 1920s as a new, fanatical, religion of war, something more akin to Islam than to anything else in history:

> **When eventually he [Hitler] came to power, [in *Mein Kampf*] there was no book which deserved more careful study from the rulers, political and military, of the Allied Powers.** All was there – the programme of German resurrection; the technique of party propaganda; the plan for combating Marxism; the concept of a National-Socialist State; the rightful position of Germany at the summit of the world. **Here was the new Koran of faith and war: turgid, verbose, shapeless, but pregnant with its message.**[128]

Churchill equated *Mein Kampf* with the Koran, and like David Cameron sixty years later, Churchill equated Islam with Nazism. As Churchill indicates in describing *Mein Kampf* as "the new Koran of faith and war: turgid, verbose, shapeless", he considered the Koran likewise to contain the programme of war to enable Islam to take over the world. Churchill's complaint was that the political class ignored *Mein Kampf* and thus did not foresee the threat from National Socialism. The difference now is that our contemporary political class are Quislings, aligned with Islam and lying to the public about the contents of the Koran and lying about the history of Islamic violence against the world. As we will show, in recent decades, our Quisling elite cannot be truly ignorant about the doctrines and history of Islam.

If you have been indoctrinated by political correctness, you might be saying to yourself "comparing Muslims to Nazis is just anti-Muslim prejudice". But some twentieth-century Muslim commentators have themselves proudly seen Mohammed as a *greater* political and military leader than Hitler, Julius Caesar and Alexander the Great!

> If the social and political circumstances of his time are taken into account, he has no equal among the initiators of major historical change. Men such as Alexander, Caesar, Napoleon, Hitler [...] do not bear comparison with him. They all had the support of the armed forces and public opinion of their peoples, whereas Mohammad made his way into history with empty hands and in a hostile society. Perhaps Lenin can be rated the

most potent man of the present century and compared with Mohammad.[129]

Despite the parallels between Islam and National Socialism, in a European election campaign in Britain in 2014 (a year in which there were over three thousand Islamic terrorist attacks across the world),[130] the British public were not even allowed to hear Mr. Weston point out that politicians of just fifty years ago were warning the West about the perennial threat from Islam. **Mr. Weston was not comparing Mohammed to Hitler (the way some Muslim experts do). Mr. Weston was not comparing Islam to Nazism (as the serving Prime Minister David Cameron had done). Mr. Weston was simply trying to educate the British public about the way that Islam was seen in Britain before The Grand Lie meant that the truth could no longer be spoken.** In describing the Koran and *Mein Kampf* as "shapeless" Churchill clearly thought both books prove difficult to read, difficult even for those who most needed to understand what these books contain. **To Churchill it was the impenetrability of books like *Mein Kampf* and the Koran which meant that people could not see what was coming. The book you are reading has been written precisely to enable the general public to understand why Muslims are so much more likely to be killing people in the name of their religion than are Buddhists or Christians.[131]**

The Grand Lie Is Holocaust Denial

"They surely disbelieve who say: Lo! Allah is the Messiah, son of Mary. The Messiah (himself) said: O Children of Israel, worship Allah, my Lord and your Lord. Lo! whoso ascribeth partners unto Allah, for him Allah hath forbidden paradise. His abode is the Fire. [Christians are unbelievers, destined for Hell.] For evil-doers there will be no helpers."

Koran 5:72

A year after Mr. Weston was arrested for quoting Winston Churchill, the Prime Minister of Britain was no longer making Churchillian comparisons between Islam and National Socialism, but was instead proclaiming: "Islam is a religion of peace" and that Muslim terrorists are motivated by a "perverted ideology" rather than being motivated by Islam.[132] Yet as far as the Muslim "extremists" are concerned their aim is to copy the behaviour of Mohammed as closely as they can, based on the core texts of Islam (texts which for a thousand years Muslims have agreed are reliable accounts of the behaviour of Mohammed). The men who beheaded soldier Lee Rigby on the streets of London went out of their way to give the Islamic justification for their act. The man who leads Islamic State and calls himself the new Caliph has a doctorate in Koranic studies.[133] And the doctrines and history of Islam concord with the behaviour of the killers of Lee Rigby, as was known to Western experts on Islam for 150 years before President Bush provided Muslim terrorists with the cover of The Grand Lie. **If those proclaiming**

that "Islam is a religion of peace" are not promoting a perverted version of Islam (one with no basis in the texts of Islam nor in the history of Islam), then the alternative explanation is that this elite mean there will only be peace when everyone has been subjugated by Islam.

Yet a month after PM Cameron's much-hailed "counter extremism" speech, this man with the best education money could buy didn't seem to know if he was coming or going when he tried to explain Islamic terrorism:

> this is what we face – a radical ideology[...] that is overpowering moderate voices within the debate... **any strategy to defeat extremism must confront, head on, the extreme ideology that underpins it. [...] It cannot be said clearly enough: this extremist ideology is not true Islam. [...] But simply denying any connection between the religion of Islam and the extremists doesn't work, because these extremists are self-identifying as Muslims.** [...] To deny it has anything to do with Islam means you disempower [...] the voices that want to challenge the scriptural basis which extremists claim to be acting on.[134]

So, the ideology which motivates Islamic terrorism is not true Islam, but it is somehow connected with Islam because the terrorists "self-identify" as Muslims. What other way is there to be a Muslim other than to identify oneself as a Muslim? All that it requires to become a Muslim is to sincerely say "There is no god but Allah, and Mohammed is his Messenger". Stating that in front of two witnesses is enough to make someone a Muslim.[135] Being a Muslim is not a biological category. Being a Muslim is a commitment to implementing specific behaviours based on specific doctrines. And the source code for these doctrines is the Koran.

The British PM insisted that it is an "extremist" interpretation that's winning, but that this interpretation has some "scriptural basis". So where are Muslims getting this interpretation from? And just how much basis is there in the scripture of Islam for this "extremist" interpretation? If this is an "extreme ideology" which is "not true Islam" but is somehow "connected" to Islam, the British government seemed determined never to address how it was connected to Islam. Moreover, **how is this extremist ideology overpowering "moderate voices within the debate" if this debate is never taking place? Throughout the thousands of hours of television programmes every week, none of this television output is devoted to discussing which is the true form of Islam.** TV debates might pit the Kuffar against Muslims, but we see no TV debates between "moderate" and "extremist" Muslims, because the TV producers know that the latter would win such debates concerning what is the truth about Islam. Those state-funded schools in Britain which are following the national curriculum are not articulating some violent form of Islam. When the World Trade Center collapsed most people did not have internet access, so whatever this "extreme ideology" is, it was winning over Muslims before the internet was part of our lives. **There is thus no venue, no medium in general society where this debate takes place. This means the British PM must believe that Muslims are hearing (and believing) that their religion is one of warfare and deceit in the company of other Muslims.** So, Muslims are becoming routinely "radicalized" to hate the surrounding society by other Muslims (and this hatred is usually preached out of earshot of non-Muslims). Meanwhile, in total ignorance of the doctrines and the history of Islam, we Kuffar are being fooled into allowing Islamic Nazism to spread across the land and to infiltrate more and more of our society.

We Kuffar are being treated like sheep, whilst Muslims are being taught we are to be slaughtered. That is the implication of what the British Prime Minister has said. And yet no programme of keeping all mosques under surveillance was ever put into place by David Cameron. If this debate is being played out anywhere, it is in the Mosques and the homes of Muslims. In 1990 the concept of "extreme Islam" in Britain was the vision of women wearing the Burka or Niqab. But since "extreme" and "moderate" are only defined in terms of each other, as the Muslims in Britain become more extreme (for example, becoming suicide bombers), then what was previously extreme (wearing a Burka, the unmistakable uniform of Islamo-Nazism) becomes accepted as "moderate" and even "progressive".[136] So, **what does that say about the future of Britain, where the Muslim population doubles in size every decade, and where what was considered "extreme" one year starts to seem "moderate" a few years later? What does it say for the idea of Islam-lite, if what is extremist one year is considered moderate ten years later? If we listen to Muslim leaders like Erdogan, the Prime Minister of Turkey, we are told "These descriptions [such terms as 'moderate Islam'] are very ugly, it is offensive and an insult to our religion. There is no moderate or immoderate Islam. Islam is Islam and that's it."[137]**

What is truly shocking, is that the 2015 speech by PM Cameron was supposedly his landmark intervention on Islamic terrorism, the first major intervention in a decade by the politician who had previously compared Islamic extremists to Nazis. Yet this later speech is obviously feeble, stuttering, a nonsense of an intervention, showing less clarity of vision than he showed a decade earlier. Nobody who studied his later speech would be any the wiser about the connection between Islam and Islamic terrorism, nor what (if any) steps could be taken to stop this terrorism. When The Rushdie Affair began in 1990, there was more public debate about the nature of Islam than there is now. Indeed, if one looks at articles from the BBC website in 2005, it is clear there was more debate then about the nature of Islam than there is now. And **if we look further back into the twentieth and the nineteenth centuries, we would find educated people were far better informed about Islam than they are now. With each new terrorist attack or each new threat to those who want to openly discuss the problems with Islam, there is a reduction in what people feel we**

are able to say about Islam: most publishers will not publish books that are truthful about Islam,[138] **art galleries happy to offend any Christian will not show any work related to Islam, venues will not allow public debate within their walls, members of Kuffar families dare not even discuss Islam among themselves.** Geert Wilders, the leader of one of the largest political parties in Holland, underwent multiple criminal trials for publicly speaking about Islam,[139] that is, for publicly discussing the principle policies of his party. When a group of authors met in Denmark to discuss the ten-year anniversary of the Mohammed cartoon controversy, their meeting had to be held inside the Parliament building – the only building in Copenhagen that the police thought was enough of a fortress that it could protect such dangerous thought as a discussion about cartoons.[140] In February 2015 a previous meeting in Copenhagen to discuss the issues around these cartoons resulted in a terrorist attack on the gathering.[141]

It seems perfectly clear, the elite are not going to provide the public with any of the material needed to make informed decisions about the kind of immigrants we wish to permit into our countries, the true risks of Islamic terrorism,[142] or even what risks your daughter faces on her way home from school.[143] **If fundamentally important information is concealed from the public, then there is naturally a chasm between what the public believe about Islam and how members of the public can justify those beliefs with proof from the Koran itself (Muslims and their Quisling allies may dismiss all other forms of evidence except the Koran). It is bad enough when the basic text of Islam is turgid, verbose, and shapeless, as Churchill said. Yet whilst the doctrines of Islam remain beyond the grasp of the ordinary person, it is easier for Muslims and their helpers among the elite to confuse us, to stifle debate and to hinder the introduction of the necessary policies.** While there are no truthful television programmes or movies about the life of Mohammed or about the history of Islam's genocides against us unbelievers, then even the basic narrative of the rise of Islam can be concealed from the ordinary person.

In his landmark "counter-extremism" speech David Cameron brought up the example of the historian David Irving. Irving is described as a "revisionist" historian, which means that he does not accept some of the significant details of the account of the Holocaust that occurred in World War II. Cameron says

> When David Irving goes to a university to deny the Holocaust –
> university leaders rightly come out and condemn him. They
> don't deny his right to speak but they do challenge what he
> says.[144]

This is another part of the deceit played by Cameron: Irving is barred from speaking at academic institutions and is even considered a criminal in some countries for stating his views.[145] Cameron pretends that David Irving is given some gentlemanly invitation to state his position in universities, and that Irving's ideas are calmly and politely challenged and presumably defeated. But this is not so: Irving does not get into universities to make his case, such that most university graduates have no idea what it is he disputes about the Holocaust.[146] But **Islamic preachers, who are known to express "extremist" views, *are* going into universities to speak, invited to do so by Muslim students.[147] And in such situations it is even known for student unions to command that the student body put up no protest!** This even occurs when Parliament has heard evidence that Muslim students from those specific universities have been involved in major terrorism plots.[148] Should David Irving have ever been invited into a university to state his beliefs, it is absolutely unimaginable that he would have been allowed to do so with the students' union telling students not to protest against his presence. So, it is not just that Irving is barred from entering universities to be debated and refuted; Islamic extremists go into university to speak with clear evidence that their views are *not* allowed to be protested, let alone refuted. **Political leaders in the West are not only able to perpetuate The Grand Lie, but these leaders are also able to pretend that those with political views beyond the pale have those views openly and rationally refuted. This is the myth of how "the Open Society" works, but it is just another lie. When Islamic "extremists" visit UK universities, those non-Muslims in the audience are even instructed that they must not criticise what they hear** (they are only permitted to approve of what the "extremist" says). Once again, it is simply unimaginable that someone like David Irving would get this treatment.

Whilst Cameron was chastising university leaders for looking the other way when Islamo-Nazis came to speak in their institutions, Cameron did precisely the same, looking away from the doctrines of Islam and the Muslim account of how Mohammed rose to military power. The British PM lied to his Kuffar electorate, telling us Islam was a religion of peace, when there was not a shred of doctrinal nor historical evidence to support this ludicrous claim, and all evidence was to the contrary. Indeed, in making these claims it is people like David Cameron who should be accused of revisionism and Holocaust denial, since **The Grand Lie denies the slaughter of untold millions throughout history in the name of Islam. This revisionist account of Islam has become the standard position for all politicians in recent years, even as hundreds of Muslims were convicted in Britain in order to prevent further slaughter of Cameron's own countrymen.** Is this not a worse form of revisionism than even that of which David Irving is accused? National Socialism is not currently a threat to Jews. Indeed, whilst this revisionist account of Islam was being broadcast by those in the highest positions of authority, Jews were once again fleeing Europe because of the terrorist violence from Muslims.[149] So it is arguable that The Grand Lie is the worst form of revisionism of all, concealing the Islam-inspired genocides of the past[150] and the Islam-inspired anti-semitism of the present (the devout Islamic organisation Hamas has the extermination of the Jews as one of its founding principles)[151]

Appeasing Violent Supremacism

"Those who believe in Allah and the Last Day ask no leave of thee lest they should strive [Jihad] with their wealth and their lives [losing their lives in war]. Allah is Aware of those who keep their duty (unto Him)."

Koran 9:44

The public in Western democracies are kept in the dark about the true nature of Islam, but behind the closed doors of Mosques and Muslim homes, Muslim children are being taught the truth about the hatred the Koran has for us Kuffar, and what the violent history of Islam has been.[152] **The media join the politicians in lying to the public, telling you that it is hard to understand why followers of a religion of peace are becoming suicide bombers, when the book in your hands is able to explain the violence from Muslims with crystal clarity. The public are given no explanation why, in their thousands, Muslims in Europe are evading police and struggling to join the sex-slave rapists of Islamic State. Nor is the media narrative able to explain why other Muslims won't inform on those who are preparing for terrorism** (for example, a 2016 survey found only about one in three of the Muslims in Britain "would inform the police if they thought somebody they knew was getting involved with people who support terrorism in Syria").[153] Such survey results are not remotely surprising when one sees that Muslims are commanded to be violent towards us Kuffar[154], that the Koran commands Muslims to not have friendly relations with the unbeliever (with any Muslim who disobeys this command being classed as an unbeliever),[155] that the Koran says that aiding us Kuffar to resist the spread of Islam constitutes the "corruption" of opposing Islam[156] (the latter strictures both mean that other Muslims will kill those Muslims who align themselves with the Kuffar). Yet the politicians and the media in the West act as if such a lack of integration with Western values on the part of Muslims is untrue or is somehow inexplicable, or is even the fault of us, the indigenous population of Kuffar (the very people whom the Koran instructs Muslims to despise and to kill).

In the early 1930s, when Churchill's warning to the world that the National Socialists in Germany were already running their military and munitions factories as if they were at war, he was ignored.[157] Churchill predicted that London would be a target of fire-bombing from the air and warned that Britain was woefully unprepared. The British secret service seemed to know less than Churchill, and he was considered to be a war-mongering extremist. The government of the day might be forgiven for their folly. But in our own time, a future British Prime Minister was prepared to compare Islam with National Socialism whilst out of office. Unlike Churchill, when David Cameron became Prime Minister his warnings and actions against Islam did not intensify, but instead went into reverse. Yet there is no need to conjecture about the future of the West: the future has already been written, as the doctrines and the history of Islam have been known by our educated elite for over a thousand years. **There is simply no excusing the behaviour of political leaders in the West in recent decades. They have sold their people into a future of war, rape, slavery and subjugation. As the insightful writer Mark Steyn reiterates: demography is destiny.**[158]

Churchill warned that Islam is militant and proselytising, producing fearless warriors, threatening the very existence of European civilisation, and for decades this has been borne out by jihadist attacks on Western democracies (Israel was the canary in the coal-mine).   Churchill was informing the public about the true nature of Islam when there was barely a Muslim to be found in the West and when the risk was low. But with significantly larger Muslim populations in France, Holland, Germany, Britain, America, Sweden, Belgium — Muslims who are murdering and wreaking havoc in the name of Islam — our political leaders are lying to the public that the behaviour of these Muslims has nothing to do with Islam. Just as people in the 1920s and 1930s refused to pay attention to the threat posed by Hitler, so our Quisling elite are determined never to help the people of the West know what Muslims are saying at Islamic gatherings across our countries.

George Orwell's novel *1984* is one of the most famous novels of the twentieth century, so famous that many of the key ideas from the novel have passed into common usage, including the very title itself, representing a totalitarian future where the people are systematically deceived about political events. As you will know, the dictator Big Brother is even able to get the denizens of this world to think illogical thoughts, such as "War is Peace".

> To know and not to know, to be conscious of complete truthfulness while telling carefully constructed lies, to hold simultaneously two opinions which cancelled out, knowing them to be contradictory and believing in both of them, to use logic against logic...[159]

Orwell named this kind of indoctrination "Doublethink". Orwell has shown untold millions how Doublethink operates (his novel has been on the literature syllabus in schools for decades). Yet Doublethink has been routine across the West, in the form of The Grand Lie: all over the world Muslims kill in the name of Islam, and the elite in the West present a united front in their deception that "Islam is a religion of peace". **What enabled the elite to pull off this deception is that it is so hard to make any sense of the Koran. While the Koran is distributed as a jumbled-up series of chapters, the true structure of its commands to kill and subjugate you and your family are not evident. In our Koran, these commands are exposed, with the aim that readers can understand the threat in minutes, not months.**

Most of the population of the West have known nothing about Islam, and most of us have had no reason to take an interest in this strange, alien religion. Like children, we have allowed the elite in our societies to lie to us:

we have yielded to the authority of our highly-educated politicians, journalists and clergy, assuming they would tell us the truth. Yet for the sake of your own children and grandchildren, we all need to grow up and take responsibility for our own understanding of what is inevitable with the importation of Islam into our culture. **We are informed of some devout Muslim committing some horrendous violent crime against us in the name of Islam, and then we are immediately made to swallow the illogical claim that "Islam is a religion of peace". This Doublethink cannot be permitted to continue.**

Despite this near-universal attempt to deceive the public into considering Islam to be a religion of peace, surveys show that in most Western countries, the public view Islam with hostility. Without facts and evidence to hand the public can be duped into believing themselves prejudiced. In the USA between 2001 and 2015 public hostility towards Islam went from 39% to 61%.[160] In Britain in 2015, 55% thought that Islam was incompatible with British values (with a mere 22% answering that it was compatible).[161] A survey in 2011 subtitled "Muslim-Western Tensions Persist" showed that in Britain, France, Russia and the USA only a small majority of those asked had a favourable view of Muslims; whilst in Germany and Spain the majority of respondents had a negative view of Muslims.[162] Why is it that in democracies the hostility found in these surveys is not manifested *at all* in the national debate nor in public policy? We would argue that it is because individuals do not feel they can justify their hostility towards the followers of Islam the way they feel they can justifiably articulate their hostility to Nazis. **When people see the Koran in chronological order and see that it culminates in commands to kill non-Muslims, individuals should have no difficulty in justifying their hostility to Islam and to those who follow the doctrines of Islam.** Why is it that general hostility is not manifested in terrorist violence by us Kuffar towards Muslims? We would argue that is because our culture has at its basis the Christian ideal of universality and non-violence, the exact opposite of Islam. But the fear of Muslim jihad is now so great that a survey at the start of 2017 showed that a majority of Europeans want to close the borders to further immigration from Muslim-majority countries.[163] It is arguable that Britain's vote to leave the European Union was the closest approximation the British were given concerning the choice to close the gates to Islamic immigration. Over the previous six decades the electorate was never given a referendum asking if they wanted mass immigration and Islamisation.

Leftists will argue that hostility towards Islam comes down to prejudice on the part of the ignorant working-class. But it is the reverse: when people understand Islam, they should be as resolutely opposed to Islam as they are to National Socialism. However, no matter how negatively those in Western countries might view Muslims, in Muslim-majority countries the unfavourable attitudes of Muslims towards Westerners are nearly universal (in most of the Muslim countries sampled over 92% were hostile towards Westerners – see the

2011 survey mentioned above). The survey showed that however bad Western attitudes towards Muslims were, Muslims despised us Kuffar more (see the table below).

	Western View of Muslims	Muslim View of Westerners
	%	%
Selfish	35	68
Violent	50	66
Greedy	20	64
Immoral	23	61
Arrogant	39	57
Fanatical	58	53
From "Muslim-Western Tensions Persist", p.4		

When people in the West grasp that Islam is a doctrine of permanent war to subjugate all us Kuffar, perhaps our hostility will reach the levels of enmity with which they regard us. It is only in the characteristic of "fanatical" that we Kuffar regarded Muslims as worse people than Muslims regarded us unbelievers. **Despite the hundreds of terrorist attacks by Muslims in recent decades, we Kuffar still do not dislike Muslims anywhere near as much as Muslims dislike Kuffar.** In the same report, when it comes to asking Muslims and Westerners who was to blame for bad relations between Muslims and Westerners, Muslims blame us far more than we blame Muslims.[164] So, once again, Muslims have a far more negative attitude towards Kuffar than vice versa. In France, Germany, Spain, Russia, Britain and the USA a majority of respondents agreed that in their country Muslims do not want to integrate.[165] **When it came to asking which religion is most violent, Westerners overwhelmingly deemed Islam to be by far the most violent religion, yet those in Western countries who pass our laws and who are responsible for an increasingly Muslim population, tell us "Islam is a religion of peace".[166]**

Even if you skim through our chronological Koran, it is instantly clear that Islam teaches Muslims to be violent and teaches Muslims to despise Kuffar, and it teaches Muslims to view the world entirely in terms of "Muslim versus Kuffar". People in the West are very good at separating out the individual human Muslim from the ideology to which he or she subscribes and promotes. This ability almost certainly comes down to our Kuffar culture *not* being suffused with the idea of hating those who are different. **As the highly esteemed expert on Islam Professor Bernard Lewis said (in a book devoted to extolling the greatness of Islam): in Islam "unbelief is**

one nation", that is, to Muslims all the Kuffar (atheists, Christians, Buddhists, Jews, etc.) are a single group to be despised as a whole.[167]

When one considers how Muslims have treated non-Muslims throughout history, these negative attitudes from Muslims will be seen to have nothing to do with any action by Western governments in the recent or even distant past but have everything to do with Muslims being indoctrinated by Islam. Following on from Mohammed's wars in Arabia which gave him control of Medina and Mecca, the Muslim armies swept out to slaughter and enslave people in France and Spain (and even as far as India and China). As Prof. Lewis says "the historical tradition of the West acclaims the Frankish victors at Poitiers [in France] in 732 A.D. as the saviours of Christendom from Islam; Muslim tradition mentions the battle, if at all, only as a minor episode".[168] **Muslims do not hate unbelievers because our ancestors fought off their past invasions. The terrorism we see is just a manifestation of the commands in Islam to hate the Kuffar, a tradition which goes back to year one of the Islamic calendar.**

It is hard for us liberal Westerners to grasp just how much loathing there is in Islam towards the Kuffar. Mohammed Baqer Majlesi, a notable seventeenth-century Muslim scholar, highlighted how dirty the Muslims considered us Kuffar: "It would be better [...] if the ruler of the Muslims would establish that all infidels [non-Muslims] could not move out of their homes on days when it rains or snows because they could make Muslims impure".[169] The Leftist allies of Islam in the West will say this ancient prejudice and hostility towards us Kuffar is a thing of the past. Not true. Even in the twenty-first century, when Muslims in the West swear an oath of truth in a court of law, or where Muslims are sworn-in as politicians, those of us officiating these events are considered too dirty to touch the Koran. We must handle the Koran while wearing gloves, or the Koran is handed to the Muslim in a slip-case, so that the hands of the "dirty Kuffar" do not touch the Koran.[170] **In Muslim-dominated countries the Kuffar are forced to do the dirtiest work:**

> **In Pakistan and Egypt, this has included forcing Christians to take the worst jobs – such as collecting Cairo's garbage, repairing sewers and scavenging in trash dumps, professions shunned by Muslims.**[171]

Those jobs are shunned by Muslims because of Islamic supremacism, although often "experts" in the West seem to have adopted the servile position that Muslims are somehow essentially cleaner people than Christians, and therefore it is only right that we "dirty" Kuffar do the dirty work.[172] This idea that we Kuffar are essentially unclean did not just apply to the Sunni Muslims of Egypt and Pakistan, but also to the Shia Muslims of Persia. As late as the early twentieth-century Muslims in Persia had rules demanding that Jews did not leave their homes when it rained, in case rain-water that touched a Jew should touch Muslims and contaminate them.[173] This kind of institutionalised religious discrimination in Persia still continued after the "Iranian revolution", with the Iranian clerics passing fatwas saying that non-Muslims are unclean.[174]

That in Islam there is a dogmatic, doctrinal loathing towards non-believers may be shocking to most non-Muslims, but what is incomprehensible is that our elite should institute rules which re-affirm in Muslims in the West the idea that the host society is indeed essentially unclean in comparison to Islam and Muslims. This is an act of subservience by our leaders, who are maintaining and supporting the Islamic hostility towards all the Kuffar. Anyone in our liberal Western societies who insisted that all Muslims were essentially dirty and could never be clean would face criminal prosecution,[175] and possibly years of imprisonment.[176] This would be considered a serious crime: she could lose her job,[177] maybe have her children taken from her,[178] and she would perhaps even be murdered.[179] It is simply unimaginable that we would institute rules marking out all Muslims as fundamentally dirty, yet we have such rules in our own society protecting Muslims from us dirty Kuffar!

One must wonder: how many indicators are needed before people realise that our elite are in the process of subjugating us to an ideology whose followers will kill us if we do not bow down to them? When you see images of Kuffar children in the West being taken by teachers to Mosques where they are bowing down to Islam it is just a concrete instance of the future.[180] In Western countries no element of Islam is to be challenged, and your offspring are to be further subjugated to Islam. You will not see Muslim children being taken to a Christian church and praying there as though they were Christians, yet the opposite is a routine occurrence. **If the public had been informed of the true nature of Islam, then none of us Kuffar would permit our children to be taken to a mosque and made to behave as if they were Muslims.** What future lies in store for your children and grandchildren as the proportion of people in their society who despise them grows? What kind of violent future awaits your offspring?

Muslim Pride In Their Doctrine Of War

"wage war on all of the idolaters [non-Muslims]"

Koran 9:36

It would be bad enough if Muslims were only killing other Muslims, for example Muslims killing those Muslims who have perhaps agreed to be punished by this moral code (although one's heart still goes out to children born into this dogma). But our politicians and academics are mocking the concept of peace when they excuse those Muslims who are murdering and maiming us unbelievers who are innocently going about our daily lives. Why would the followers of a religion which prized peace,[181] be killing not just themselves but also others? Buddhist monks have been known to kill *themselves* as a form of political protest. But with Islam we have devout

Muslims killing themselves and others.[182] If Islam was anything like other religions why do Muslims make threats saying, "we love death as much as you love life", i.e. they will kill themselves in order to kill those of us who are not engaged in warfare?[183] This is a world-view that is totally alien to almost every other civilisation on the planet.

Those of us brought up as Christians or who were taught to follow a morality imbued with Christian values were never told of any time when Jesus cut off someone's head, we were never told of a martyr for Christianity who was praised for killing another person. Indeed, there are no texts by the followers of Christianity which show Jesus torturing someone or killing hundreds of people. There are *not even texts by the enemies* of Christianity which claim that Jesus behaved in this way. But in the core texts of Islam one not only finds Muslims being commanded to kill the Kuffar, one finds that for over 1000 years Muslims have glorified this violence in their own texts. These are not texts written by the enemies of Islam or those family relatives of the victims of Islamic violence. **These are the core Islamic texts which portray Mohammed as a torturer, a robber, a slave-monger, and a mass-murderer;** they are texts written by Muslims, preserved by Muslims, promulgated by Muslims. Even those throughout history who have most hated Christianity have never attributed to Jesus the kinds of horrendous violence and evil which Muslims have proudly attributed to Mohammed. It does not matter if some Muslims tell us that they only accept the Koran as a guide (as far as the vast majority of Muslims are concerned, such Muslims would constitute a tiny minority of heretics). It does not matter if contemporary Western scholars claim the evidence for Mohammed's existence is slight (Muslim death threats to such Western scholars are taken so seriously that television companies cancel scheduled events and will not dare tackle this subject again).[184] The idea of positing that Mohammed was not a real historical person is something that Muslims reject. When the despised Kuffar claim that the man who is the foundation of their religion did not exist, Muslims' only interest is the desire to kill the people who make this claim. Muslims have no doubt that Mohammed existed, his existence being the foundation of Islam: 'There is no god but Allah and Mohammed is his prophet'. And the Islamic texts which provide their most authoritative evidence for his existence show him as a killer and a slave-monger.

Christianity and Buddhism were founded by men who killed no-one and who never advocated that others be killed. Following the first few centuries of Christian thinking, even suicide, where one killed only oneself, was turned into a sin. We might validly describe Christianity or Buddhism as religions of peace. Ibn Ishaq's *The Life of Muhammad* is the most authoritative Muslim biography of Mohammed and was translated from Arabic into English in 1955. In the Table of Contents of this very highly-regarded scholarly translation of Mohammed's biography, it lists the battles (wars) fought by Mohammed. You don't even need to read this book to see that Islam is a religion of war, and not a religion of peace. You don't even need to buy this book: go to Amazon's website and use the "Look Inside" feature and look in the Table of Contents at Part III of the book, a section which is entitled "Muhammad's Migration To Medina, His Wars, Triumph, And Death". Does that sound anything like a religion of peace?[185] How have successive Presidents and Prime Ministers been permitted to get away with The Grand Lie, when less than one minute spent with the most authoritative Muslim biography of Mohammed portrays him as a warlord?

This core Islamic text tells of Mohammed commanding that a Jew be tortured over a fire to find out where his gold is hidden: "Torture him until you extract what he has".[186] The Muslim biographer records Mohammed's approval of assassinations of those people who warned their fellow Kuffar about Mohammed's plans for violence (including killing a woman asleep at night with her baby).[187] **Do you have any doubt that contemporary Muslims are copying Mohammed's Companions and assassinating those who warn the Kuffar about what is coming from increasing Islamization? In Holland artist Theo van Gogh was assassinated by a Muslim; the leader of the Party for Freedom (PVV) in Holland has been under 24x7 police protection for fear that he will be assassinated. In Germany, the ex-Muslim Hamed Abdel-Samed, author of** *Islamic Fascism*, **is also under 24x7 police protection to prevent Muslims copying the Companions of Mohammed and assassinating that author.**

The most shocking deed recorded in the Muslim biography of Mohammed is that in one day the founder of Islam personally beheaded 600 to 900 unarmed men and boys who would not convert to Islam:

> they surrendered, and [Mohammed] the apostle confined them in Medina [...] the apostle went out to the market of Medina [...] and dug trenches in it. Then he sent for them and struck off their heads in those trenches as they were brought out to him in batches. [...] There were 600 or 700 in all, though some put the figure as high as 800 or 900. [...] This went on until the apostle made an end of them [...] Then the apostle divided the property, wives, and children [...] among the Muslims [...] some of the captive women [enslaved by Mohammed] he sold them for horses and weapons.[188]

Remember: this information is coming from the most authoritative Muslim biography of Mohammed, the foundation of all other biographies of Mohammed. So, Muslims cannot say "these are lies made up by those who hate Mohammed or Islam". Indeed, these are the stories about Mohammed which Muslims have proudly told their children for 1000 years. **Are the parallels with the twenty-first century Islamic State terrorists not obvious?** We have never seen any Muslim provide evidence that Muslims have rejected the details in this biography. Anyone who tries to tell you to ignore this biography, is someone who is trying to deceive you.

Note that Mohammed's Muslim biographer does not try to diminish the scale of Mohammed's atrocity, but rather proudly boasts that "the apostle" might have beheaded as many as 900 men and boys in this one incident (other Islamic texts point out that in this attack, any boy with even one single pubic hair was beheaded).[189] Also, note these **boys and men whom Mohammed massacred were people who had** *surrendered* **after being attacked by Mohammed and his army, yet still the founder of "the religion of peace" killed them all!** Imagine the even worse account of these events that might have come down from any survivors of this massacre (for example, from the women and children whom the biographer reports were sold as slaves by Mohammed). But, of course, the stories by those whose families were massacred by Mohammed and his disciples have not been passed down as history is written by the victors, so the version we have is the one which portrays Mohammed in the most flattering light to his followers. **To Muslims, the killer who was the founder of Islam is seen as someone to admire above all other men and Muslims believe they are to live as Mohammed lived. Our Quisling leaders side with Mohammed and his followers against us unbelievers, the people whom Islam is committed to killing.**

Some Muslims might argue that Mohammed had declared war on those people whose beheading is described above and these Muslims would then try to use this supposed war to justify Mohammed's evil actions. Some Muslims or their apologists will try to argue that Mohammed and his followers only went to war after first responding to aggression with defensive violence. This claim can even be found in recent years in the work of some of the contemporary scholars on Islam:

> Muhammad and his followers tended to be quite moderate with regard to war or any kind of physically aggressive behaviour against their detractors, even in the face of aggression committed against them [...] aside from a very few individuals, they avoided physical aggression at almost any cost and suffered physical and emotional abuse as a consequence.[190]

This is a most extraordinarily subservient view and is not borne out by any objective analysis of the Muslim accounts of what happened. For thirteen years the Pagans in Mecca allowed Mohammed to create a new religion and to foment dissent in Mecca. These Pagans were tolerant multiculturalists. They offered to let Mohammed put an icon to represent his new god Allah in their pantheon, the Kaaba.[191] Let us compare how "abusive" these seventh-century Pagans were, with the subsequent history of Mecca - once Mohammed's religion had control of the Kaaba.

We can't examine what the original people of Mecca have to say about this, as *their* account of the rise of Islam is not known, so the history we have is that which came from the victors.[192] **The authoritative Muslim biography records that the Pagan Meccans were not hostile to Mohammed or Islam until Mohammed spoke disparagingly about the** gods worshipped by the Pagans: Mohammed mocked not just their gods but their customs and the ancestors of the Pagan people of Mecca.[193] Even with all this provocation, the first violent blow between a Pagan and a Muslim was struck by a follower of "the religion of peace".[194] And before Mohammed decided to leave Mecca with his handful of followers, this was not the only act of violence from the Muslims towards the tolerant Meccans.[195] In the authoritative biography of Mohammed, there is no record that the Pagan Meccans responded to these violent incidents with violence themselves. By the time he was ready to leave left Mecca for Medina the founder of Islam had *already* entered into an alliance with the people of Medina for "war against all and sundry".[196] It is astonishing that a Kuffar Westerner would claim that the Pagan Meccans were abusive and aggressive, when the most authoritative Muslim biographer of Mohammed (cited by that Western scholar himself) clearly shows that before Muslims left Mecca, the Muslims were the people who were rude, abusive, and aggressive. It was Muslims who were preparing for war against everyone else.

Ten years after making this alliance for "war against all and sundry", Mohammed returned to take Mecca with an army of 10,000 mercenaries. The transformation Islam underwent in Medina meant that Mohammed was able to go from 150 followers (men and women) to 10,000 (or more) male soldiers. With this huge military force Mohammed was able to take control of Mecca (and the Kaaba) from the Pagans. He achieved this phenomenal growth in Islam by making robbery and killing components of Islam: those involved in the attacks on non-Muslims could keep 80% of their booty (which included taking people as slaves), whilst 20% of the profits of these raids went to Mohammed (as a kind of tax to fund his Islamic State and to propagate Islam further).[197] Isn't it clear from the historical record preserved by Muslims for over 1000 years that politics and war are intrinsic parts of Islam?

The army with which Mohammed invaded and occupied Mecca was a huge army for the time. He was able to take control with no resistance from the Meccans, not just because of the size of this army, but because of Mohammed's already terrifying reputation for slaughtering those who offered him and his army of mercenaries any resistance, slaughtering people even when they had surrendered and were disarmed (as we have seen above). Once Muslims had control of Mecca and Medina, the patient and tolerant Pagans of Mecca were banned from Mecca (risking death should they return), and the Jews of Medina who had taken Mohammed and his Muslims to live with them were banned from their home-place.[198] Thus, by whatever standard apologists of Islam wish to use, the Pagans who were ethnically-cleansed from Mecca were far more tolerant than the Muslims who replaced them, yet even at the start of the twenty-first century, with Islamic State once again committing genocide and raping sex-slaves, in the West religious and political leaders portray the founder of

Islam as a victim of persecution.[199] The historical revisionism of the elite is beyond shameless.

The sheer terror of the Pagan population of Mecca meant that Mohammed was able to take the city with almost no resistance. In Islam, the Koran is not the only source of doctrine, but the Koran is the primary source. There are also the "hadiths": these are sayings about the behaviour of Mohammed traced back to loyal and devout contemporaries of the founder of Islam. The sayings collated by a Muslim named Bukhari are considered by believers to be among the most trusted. One of the books of hadiths is entitled "Fighting for the Cause of Allah (Jihaad)".[200] There it is reliably reported that Mohammed said, "I have been made victorious with terror (cast in the hearts of the enemy)".[201] Just **to confirm that instilling terror into those who opposed him was recognized by Mohammed as a key to his success, one of the other most trusted collections of hadiths has Mohammed expressing an almost identical sentiment, narrated by the same reliable source: "I have been helped by terror (in the hearts of enemies): spoils [gold, enslaved captives] have been made lawful to me" i.e. Mohammed and his followers had divine authority to rob and terrorise those whom they attacked.**[202] Thus, the idea that Islam is terrorism is not just to be found in the authoritative Muslim biography of Mohammed, but it is to be found in the statements of those Muslims who knew Mohammed and who went to war by his side.[203] Such ideas are also to be found in the Koran.[204] These ideas are thus found across the fundamental texts of Islam. But our Quisling elite still insist on portraying Muslims and Mohammed as the victims not the aggressors, and on portraying the religion of war as a religion of peace.

It seems almost impossible for the public to comprehend that Islam can endorse robbery, slavery, terrorism and yet be placed in the same category as religions like Christianity or Buddhism. It is even worse than that: no-one feels the need to keep championing Christianity and Buddhism as religions of peace. But this is what the educated elite in the West have maintained, repeating The Grand Lie whenever Muslims practice the terrorism that their religion sanctions. What our educated elite are not telling the public, is that Islam is only partly a religion: it is largely a political system and a legal system, and to informed Muslims these features are inseparable and go all the way back to the time of Mohammed.[205] The legal and political aspects of Islam are also instituted with the unquestioning, divine authority of a religion. **The morality of Islam (the religion) is inseparable from the laws and politics of Islam.** In terms that might make more sense to a Western reader: the Church and the State are one in Islam. Whilst it makes no sense in Christianity or Buddhism for the founder of each respective religion to have been a political and military leader, in Islam this is unquestionably the truth. Even if separation between Church and State is apparently championed by some Muslims, that does not mean that such a division is sanctioned within Islam, nor that such a separation would endure for very long.

Islam: The Most Totalitarian System

"He it is Who hath sent His messenger with the guidance and the Religion of Truth, that He may cause it to prevail over all religion, however much the idolaters may be averse."

Koran 9:33

From at least the time when Buddhism was created (around 2,500 years ago), Islam is the first and only world religion which makes war and murder into acts of devotion: it is through dying in a war for Islam that Muslims have the certainty of being rewarded within the framework of their beliefs. Killing to get an eternity in Paradise might seem stupid to atheists (obsessed with seeking pleasure in the here and now), but to those who believe in "the afterlife", giving up the pleasures of this short life for an eternity of pleasure might seem like the most rational decision in the world. If Islamic doctrine was such that those Muslims who died killing for Islam were guaranteed to go to Hell, then it might be reasonable to say that Muslim suicide bombers were insane. But since Islam says that dying in the process of killing for Islam is the only guaranteed way a Muslim is getting to Heaven, then Islam gives Muslims the best reason in the world to kill other people. It is this doctrine which our elite should be discussing most urgently with the citizens.

The idea that these "true believers" of Islam are "insane" or "fanatics" is really just an explanation from an atheistic, humanistic or materialistic point of view. Failing to explain the importance that dying to impose Islam on others has for Muslims, means **our Quisling elite have been concealing from the public that murder in the name of Islam is not just a part of Islam, but is the most fundamental aspect of a system which constantly pits Heaven against Hell, believer against non-believer, devout believer against hypocrite.** Those Muslims and Quislings who insist that Islam is a religion of peace can only "prove" this by concealing from those they would deceive all the commands in the Koran to kill, commands which our chronological Koran makes clear and obvious (which is why we do not want Muslims to read this book). In Islam, the killing of those Kuffar who refuse to submit to Islam is not murder; bizarrely, it is viewed within Islam as a kindness![206] The ordinary person cannot be expected to wade through the thousands and thousands of often jumbled-up and repetitive instructions to be found in the Koran and the hadiths to find those which explain why Muslims are killing in the name of Islam. It is the job of our educated elite to explain what is different about Islam. Yet for all their praise of diversity, the educated elite do not want the public to consider what it means for people to have beliefs which truly diverge from our own belief system, the way the beliefs of Islam diverge from those of Western civilisation, with Islam legitimizing the slaughter and enslavement of those who think differently.

The Quisling elite pass laws to force us non-Muslims to respect Islam. Of course, the Quislings must fall short of telling us to respect that Muslims are commanded to kill us unbelievers in order to get to Paradise.

The deception by Muslims and their Quislings is aided by the assumption of a humanist, Westernized public; the assumption that no religion would advocate murder, discrimination and deception.[207] We Kuffar are also distracted by a myriad of events (work, television, gossip, social events, family problems, etc.) which are infinitely more absorbing than the tedium of trying to make sense of the jumbled-up and incomprehensible Koran. That the most authoritative Muslim biography of Mohammed is simple and straightforward, showing how Mohammed became a belligerent, genocidal, torturing, slave-taking Islamic "Statesman" is something about which most of us Kuffar have no idea. Our Quisling elite ensure that the public know nothing about Islam except for the few selected deceptions which they filter through to your children in the process of the brainwashing described as religious education. Despite the decades of problems with Islam the West has experienced, we have seen no television documentaries, no television dramas, no movies about how Islam came to explode out of Arabia and in just one century managed to conquer lands from the Atlantic Ocean to the mountains of Afghanistan. Instead of teaching the public that the Islamic State survived from the Dark Ages to just after World War I, the public is kept in an ahistorical bubble. There are more movies about the Vikings, about ancient Greek myths, about space travel, about the romance novels of Jane Austen than there are about how Mohammed's religion of war spread across the world. The public are given no easy access to information about Islam, the biggest problem facing the future of the West.

The Islamic State is not something which came into being in the last few years. It is simply another name for the Caliphate, a pan-national Islamic empire, tracing itself back to the warrior (the 'Caliph', the 'deputy') who took charge following Mohammed's death. That warrior, the successor to Mohammed, led the armies of Islam to burst forth from Arabia. Since 2014 the BBC has been referring to "the *so-called* Islamic State" in Syria, as if this is somehow a bogus concept. Eight years earlier (and before any ordinary member of the public had heard the phrase "Islamic State"), a Harvard professor of law wrote a book called *The Fall and Rise of the Islamic State*.[208] Since his book was written years before the Islamic State in Syria was declared, it proves that this concept had been known to the educated elite for many years before. This Harvard professor's book is just one of many that discuss the Caliphate, the Islamic State which only ended in 1924 after enduring for 1300 years.[209] Rather than being some weird idea dreamt up in the twenty-first century by Muslims who supposedly knew nothing about Islam, ask yourself: what legal and political institution in the history of the world endured as long as the Islamic State did? Communism, National Socialism, Fascism, the British Empire, the Roman Empire and the Holy Roman Empire did not last as long as the Islamic State. It is no surprise that as soon as the Caliphate was abolished in 1924 Muslims began their efforts to bring it back.[210]

To Muslims, the political and legal authority of the Islamic State is found in the Koran and the example of Mohammed, who created the first Islamic State when he moved from Mecca to Medina:

> Allah hath promised such of you as believe and do good work that He will surely make them to succeed (the present rulers) in the earth even as He caused those who were before them to succeed (others)... [211]

Given that Muslims believe the existence of the Islamic State to be the will of Allah, it is no wonder they want to see it return. Before the Caliphate was abolished, a delegation (including Islam-collaborator Mahatma Gandhi) made the arduous journey by ship from India to Britain to solicit the Prime Minister's support in retaining the Islamic State.[212] In the 1920s the British elite had known of the risk of "a theocratic state" arising in the region of Iraq when the Caliphate was abolished.[213] In the 1960s, just decades after Pakistan was carved out of India, Muslim scholars and activists were agitating for Pakistan to be the Islamic State.[214] After "the Iranian Revolution" of 1979, when the Ayatollahs came to power in Iran, that country also provided a contender for the title "Islamic State".[215] Thus from Arabia, to India, to Iraq, to Pakistan, to Iran, and in our day in Syria, Muslims have sought the jurisdiction of a pan-national Islamic State. And the educated elite in the West cannot have been unaware of this as they saw the rise of pro-Caliphate political organisations across the West from the 1990s onwards. But rather than ensure the electorate understood what Islam was, when Muslims proved they could strike in the heart of the West on 9/11, the elite chose to disseminate and maintain The Grand Lie rather than admit that for decades this elite had failed their citizens and they had imported into the West a new form of Nazism.

As with other twentieth-century forms of totalitarianism, there is even an economics of Islam: throughout history the economies and armies of Islam have profited from the exploitation of untold millions of slaves, sanctioned by the behaviour of Mohammed.[216] Here is how the West's greatest experts in the twentieth century defined the core of Islam:

> the system of beliefs and rituals based on the Kur'an [...] a cultural complex, embracing specific political structures and legal and social traditions [...] In Europe [...] the influence of Islam continues to decline.[217]

It is clear from this *Encyclopaedia of Islam* definition that in the mid twentieth century the experts viewed Islam as an entire political and legal system (of which religion is but a part). There was no dispute that Islam was a political system. This all-encompassing, totalitarian system is now ignored by our elite, who separate "Islam" from "Islamism" (a conceptual distinction unknown to Muslims and unknown to Western

experts on Islam before the attacks on September 11th 2001).[218] **In the twenty-first century this new concept "Islamism" was invented to deceive the Kuffar public into believing "religious Islam" was separate from "political Islam". But in the 1950s it was clear that expert opinion knew no such variant of Islam as "political Islam". Islam was regarded as political in the 1950s and Islam was regarded as political in the 650s, 1300 years earlier, and throughout that 1300 years Islam was known to be inseparable from warfare.** We see from the final sentence in the passage quoted above, how much of a revolution has occurred in Europe in the last fifty years. As the influence of Islam has come to dominate the West, the populations of Western countries have been increasingly deceived into believing a false distinction, namely, that "Islam" is something different from "Islamism" and that "Islam is peace".

The combination of legal, political and economic structures which are inseparable in Islam are considered to be unchanging and eternal in the eyes of Muslims, because the Koran was the word of god and because Mohammed was the model of behaviour whom Muslims are to copy. Mohammed went to war, he committed genocide,[219] he took slaves and sold them, and he kept slaves (sometimes just for his own right to have sex with them).[220] If taking sex-slaves was un-Islamic one would expect that terrorist groups like Boko Haram and ISIS would be denounced as apostates by Islamic authorities across the world for their part in taking sex-slaves.[221] As Murray Gordon says in his book *Slavery in the Arab World* (1992),

> the most common and enduring purpose for acquiring slaves in the Arab world was to exploit them for sexual purposes. [...] These women were nothing less than sexual objects who, with some limitations, were expected to make themselves available to their owners.[222]

Throughout history no Muslim has denounced these things which we Kuffar regard as evil, because no Muslim would have had any shame in approving of these things, since such values were enshrined in the core texts of Islam, supposedly sanctioned by Allah, the ultimate authority.[223] It goes without saying, that if a human being is reduced to being a slave (an object, that is owned, a piece of property) her legally consenting to sex is immaterial.[224] In the 1960s, as Islamic states were being forced by the West to "outlaw" slavery, Muslim jurists were kicking back by publishing commentaries on the UN Declaration of Human Rights, in which they pointed out that in Islamic law slavery was legal.[225] When the Islamic State was again recreated in the twenty-first century, their scholars issued theological justifications for why they were taking sex-slaves.[226]

Not only is slavery legal in Islam, killing for Islam is not wrong to Muslims, because this is what Mohammed did in order for Islam to succeed, and Muslims are commanded to ensure that Islam succeeds. In the Muslim system of values, there could not possibly be any negative judgement of these things, provided they were done as Mohammed did them. As one Muslim professor says:

> Muslims believe that expansion through war is not aggression but a fulfilment of the Qur'anic command to spread Islam as a way to peace. The resort to force to disseminate Islam is not war (harb), a word that is used only to describe the use of force by non-Muslims. [...] those who resist Islam cause wars and are responsible for them.[227]

War in the name of Islam is thus not even considered as war by Muslims. The world is so entirely seen through the lens of Islam, that when Muslims go to war against us Kuffar it is the fault of the Kuffar for our intransigence in refusing to submit to Islam. As a violent husband blames his battered wife for speaking back, so Muslims kill the Kuffar for resisting Islam. The bully feels no guilt for his actions.

Whilst politicians and journalists tell the public that "Islamic State is not Islamic",[228] in truth Islamic State is far closer to following the behaviour of Mohammed than are all those Muslims who live in the West and who lie to us about the past, present and future victims of Islam, who lie to us about the nature of this unchanging ideology. As one of the mainstream non-Muslim experts of Islam said, five years before the hundreds of jihadi attacks in the West which followed the collapse of the World Trade Center:

> **The doctrine of jihad, as laid down in the works on Islamic law, developed out of the Koranic prescriptions and the example of the Prophet and the first caliphs, which is recorded in the hadith. The crux of the doctrine is the existence of one single Islamic state,** ruling the entire umma [pan-national community of Muslims]. It is the duty of the umma to expand the territory of this [Islamic] state in order to bring as many people under its rule as possible. [...] **Expansionist jihad is a collective duty [...] which is fulfilled if a sufficient number of people take part in it.**[229]

This shows how Muslims around the world are connected as a single network (the Ummah) to sharia law, to the Islamic State and to jihad. It also explains why not all Muslims need to become jihadis: provided enough Muslims are engaging in warfare to expand the territory of Islam, then the collective moral obligation of the Ummah is being met. **Your friendly Muslim colleague does not have any obligation to become a jihadi while enough of his Muslim brothers are killing to subjugate us Kuffar.**

1400 Years Of Jihad Against Non-Muslims

"Now when ye meet in battle those who disbelieve, then it is smiting of the necks [beheading] until, when ye have routed [defeated] them, then making fast of bonds [enslaving those not killed ...] And those who are slain in the way of Allah [die as jihadis], He rendereth not their actions vain [...] And bring them in unto the Garden [Muslims who die in battle will go to Paradise]"

Koran 47:4 -47:6

Before 9/11, before The Grand Lie became the only concept of Islam the elite in the West would allow to be publicised, the view of Islam we are putting forward in this book was common knowledge among the educated elite. **It is nothing short of amazing that the view of Western experts on Islam should have been so consistent over the centuries. In eighth century northern England, the monk Bede described Muslims as "shiftless, hateful, and aggressive",[230] whilst in the early nineteenth century the sixth President of the United States was able to accurately say:**

> **The precept of the koran [sic] is, perpetual war against all who deny, that Mahomet is the prophet of God [...] the command to propagate the Moslem creed by the sword is always obligatory, when it *can* [sic] be made effective. The commands of the prophet may be performed alike, by fraud, or by force.[231]**

But following the shock of the attack on America in September 2001, it would be almost impossible to find an academic expert who would concur with what had been the educated view of Islam in the previous centuries. Before 9/11 academic experts were prepared to tell the public the truth about the interconnectedness of jihad and the expansion of Islam. To the extent that the truth about Islam has been told to the general public in the past few decades, this has come mostly from people who are neither professional journalists nor professional academics.[232] Famous names in this regard are people like Bat Ye'or, Robert Spencer, Andrew Bostom, etc. These people have filled the gap left by journalists and academics. One name which is often overlooked in this regard is Paul Fregosi, whose publisher in the mid-1990s decided to cancel the contract for Fregosi's book on Islam's unending war against Christendom.

Fregosi's book *Jihad in the West: Muslim Conquests from the 7th to the 21st Centuries* was to be published by one of Britain's major publishers. The publisher

> accepted Jihad in the West, announced it [the book] in its spring 1997 catalogue, and copy-edited the work, only to turn it down under fear of fundamentalist Muslim pressure. [...] His [book] is,

as he rightly claims, "the first history of the Muslim wars in Europe ever published..."[233]

Just let that observation sink in for a moment. Here we have a religion of war, proudly proclaimed to be so by its own texts for over 1000 years, and despite all the hundreds of universities in the West, the first book to provide a narrative history of the different attacks on Europe by Muslims was not published until the end of the twentieth century! No wonder Fregosi's original publisher saw a gap in the market. Moreover, this history of Islamic holy war was written not by an academic in a publicly-funded university, but by a popular biographer of Napoleon. This was at a time when the few attacks on Western interests (such as embassies, etc.) were almost all taking place far away from our own countries, in parts of the world where we could be easily deceived that the problem was some local grievance rather than part of a systematic series of assaults dating back to the time of Mohammed. Apart from the wars and terrorism conducted against Israel, throughout the twentieth-century Muslims generally did not have the wherewithal to identify, plan and execute attacks in the West.[234] But by the 1990s Muslims in the West had the power to make publishers cower in fear.

Despite the book being commissioned by his publisher, once Fregosi had completed the book he had trouble getting it published.

> Mr Fregosi says that it was [the publisher] Little Brown's decision to seek an expert opinion from Dr Roger Boase, an English academic converted to Islam, that turned the publisher against his book. Dr Boase reported that he [Fregosi] had written an unbalanced account and had relied on "a fallacy that Islam was spread by the sword". Mr Fregosi said his aim had been to show that Muhammad was more of a warrior and more bloodthirsty than his image.[235]

As you know from our earlier citation of the most authoritative Muslim biography of Mohammed, the idea that Mohammed was a warlord is to be found pervading the largest part of that very detailed biography. As the past few decades of terrorist atrocities (and foiled terrorist plots) have shown, it is risible that Fregosi's publisher could commission this book then back out of publishing it based on the claim (by a Muslim) that violent jihad was not part of Islam. The mainstream and scholarly view for centuries was that Islam was a religion of war.

What could have first prompted the publisher to encourage Fregosi to write his book on jihad? Most people no longer even know that in 1993 devout Muslims set off a massive bomb in the basement of the World Trade Centre, in an attempt to destroy this symbol of Western success, an attempt to kill or maim those thousands of workers inside. Thus a few years before another group of Muslim terrorists successfully attacked America in September 2001, Muslims had tried once before to pull off that horrific crime. If academics and publishers had not been cowardly and complicit in the latter part of the twentieth century, by the end of that century informed electorates in Western democracies would have known about the true history of Islamic violence: the second terrorist attack on the World Trade Center in 2001 may never have been able to take place, and hundreds of other terrorist attacks by Muslims around the world since then may have been averted.

When future generations look back on how the literate, highly-connected liberal democracies of the West struggled to understand the threat caused by importing Islam – when the world had already undergone 1400 years of fanatical violence from devout Muslims and had lost untold millions of men, women and children to Islamic slavery – our descendants will see that the elite's contribution to this struggle in the twenty-first century was an alliance which aided Islamic domination. The professionals, who had the facilities and the duty to write the books and news reports and make the television shows which explained Islam to the public, did nothing but deceive us.

Islam = Islamism = Violent Islamism

"Obey Allah and obey the messenger"

Koran 5:92

It is often said that among Muslims only "Islamists" believe in no separation between personal religion and political Islam. Our Quisling leaders even distinguish between "Islamists" and "violent Islamists".[236] It seems those who make these distinctions think there is nothing wrong with transitioning to an anti-democratic state based on laws from the Dark Ages, provided the new barbaric and discriminatory theocracy is imposed upon us Kuffar by demographic change instead of terrorism. Islam would be imposed upon Christians (who would become non-citizens) and atheists and Buddhists (who would be killed), but that would not happen for decades to come, and thus the elite tell the people of the West there is nothing to worry about (since atheists out-number Christians in the UK,[237] under Islam those atheists would be offered the stark choice: become Muslims or die). What the elite never tell the electorate is that the single biggest voting bloc in the United Nations is the OIC, a grouping of Muslim countries who have rejected the principle and details of the UN's charter of universal human rights. Such international organisations of Muslim countries can openly tell the world that Islam puts slavery above human rights, and the government-supported "human rights organisations" do not say a word.

The claim we hear over and over again is that only a minority of 'Muslim extremists' are violent. However, some Muslims not being engaged in warfare is an intrinsic part of the programme of Islam. The Koran contains commands for some Muslims to hang back from the risk of being killed in battle in order to propagate the system of rules that is Islam.

> And the believers should not all go out to fight. Of every troop of them, a party only should go forth, that they (who are left behind) may gain sound knowledge in religion...[238]

The above command is among the very last commands to be uttered by Mohammed. Remember, the Koran came to be written down and collated into a single text only because the most devout Muslim followers of Mohammed were dying off in wars imposing Islam on others.[239] **Thus, not all Muslims are jihadis because already in the early days of Islam it was recognized that the doctrine of Islamic supremacism could not be perpetuated if all the devout Muslims are killed in battle at the same time. So, the number of Muslims actually going off to die to impose Islam gives us victims of Islam no indication of the number of Muslims prepared to kill and to die for Islam in any future struggle to impose Islam on the Kuffar.**

The bogus distinction between "Islam" and "Islamism" came about to try to pretend that there was a "religious Islam" and a "political Islam", with the latter supposedly being a modern Western-inspired heresy against "the religion of peace", with this supposed heresy only sometimes giving rise to Islamic terrorism. On the very rare occasions that a politician in the West has tried to grapple with the problem of politics and Islamic terrorism, this is what he said:

> Islamism is essentially a twentieth-century phenomenon. Like its sibling ideologies, fascism and communism, it offers followers a form of redemption through violence. [...] Communism, fascism and Islamism have all been responses to Enlightenment thought.[240]

Michael Gove, the British politician who wrote the above was renowned for his intellect. But this is a profoundly ahistorical understanding of Islam for someone who graduated from Oxford University. As we have been at pains to demonstrate, "redemption through violence" is precisely what Islam has offered Muslims since Mohammed was waging war in seventh-century Arabia: it is only through dying while imposing Islam on the Kuffar that Muslims are assured of an eternity in Paradise. This "right wing" politician goes on to lambast the "wilful blindness among many in the West",[241] whilst he blindly ignores the history of the rise of Islam through horrific violence (a history of violence proudly accepted by Muslims for over a thousand years). One of the only English-speaking politicians to write at any length about this civilizational threat facing the West, Gove blindly ignores the works of Western scholars writing in English, German and French from 1860 to 1960, who proved beyond doubt that the Koran culminates in commands to kill us Kuffar.

This famously intellectual politician does not seem to have even looked up the origin of the word "Islamism". Here is how the massive *Oxford English Dictionary* (1933) defines "Islamism": "the religious system of the Moslems; Mohammedism". This dictionary is famous for being the most complete and extensive dictionary of the English language in the entire world (providing examples of definitions as they first enter the English language, and examples of changes of meaning). There is absolutely no mention of Islamism being distinct from Islam. And as we saw with the famous *Encyclopaedia of Islam* (1953) there was no mention of "political Islam" being separated from "religious Islam". Thus, as far as the most highly-esteemed reference works of the twentieth century are concerned, there was no difference between Islam and Islamism, and Islam was political from year one of the Islamic calendar. Moreover, if we look at popular usage in newspaper archives, we find the word "Islamism" first being used in the early nineteenth century, and the word is used interchangeably with the word "Islam".[242]

The contemporary and novel concept of Islamism is thus not a twentieth-century phenomenon created by Muslims, but is really a twenty-first century phenomenon,[243] a unicorn conjured up by a liberal elite who dare not admit to the plebs that Islam has been a violent political ideology from year one of the its calendar. Indeed, Islam is the most enduring and most dangerous political ideology in history, because it promises its troops an eternity in Paradise if they die for the ideology: no other genocidal ideology offered its killers such a prize. And because of this enthusiasm and commitment to jihad, the Islamic State has returned, within a hundred years of it being abolished. In order not to disrupt the project of importing Muslims into the West, the liberal elite created this new word "Islamism" to describe a belief system known throughout history as "Islam". They do not want the electorate to understand that twenty-first century Islam is now as Islam has always been: a warrior religion intent on imposing its legal and social policies on the entire world.

Almost without exception, when journalists and politicians distinguish between "Islam" and "Islamism" they offer no grounds for the distinction nor cite any texts which make the distinction for them. Instead they act as if "everyone knows" that these are two very different things, as if this distinction has been known in the West throughout history, and as if this distinction is a distinction that Muslims themselves have recognized.[244] But these repetitions are simply an attempt to shore up an undefined and fake distinction, a distinction which was never articulated throughout a thousand years of interaction between Christendom and Islam, dating back to before The Crusades. It is Muslims who are going off to join ISIS, Al Shabab, etc. If asked whether they are following "Islamism" or "Islam", these terrorists will say the latter. And if the Mohammed of the authoritative biography was alive, he would be leading one of these organisations, taking the place of the Caliph of the Islamic State.

It is not in the interests of the politicians, clergy or journalists that there should be any explanation of who "Mohammed the statesman" was, because that would indicate that "political Islam" has existed since Mohammed's totalitarianism forced the multicultural Pagans to drive him out of Mecca. Even **when a "moderate Muslim" (who is one of the most distinguished professors of international politics in the West) turned his attention to writing a book-length study on the distinction between Islam and Islamism, he did so in an entirely ahistorical way, avoiding all discussion of a thousand years of Islamic doctrines and a thousand years of history of war, genocide and theocratic rule which are emblematic of the recent Islamic State in Syria.** With rare exception, this Muslim professor's 300 page book concentrates on twentieth-century comparisons between "Islamism" and Communism etc. By ignoring the events and doctrines of the previous thirteen hundred years, he convinces himself that Islamism is not Islam,[245] that Muslims who employ the most horrific violence against the Kuffar in order to bring about a theocratic state are copying Stalin and Hitler rather than emulating the behaviour of Mohammed. The Islamic State and Boko Haram do not look to Mein Kampf for the rules they must follow but instead look to the behaviour (sunnah) of Mohammed, as found in the Koran, the Hadiths, and the life of Mohammed. This distinguished professor claims that "Islamism is a political religion [...] it originated in 1928".[246] He can only make such a ridiculous claim by ignoring books like *The Origins of the Islamic State* (1916), published twelve years before this "political religion" was supposedly invented in 1928. Furthermore, the original Arabic version of *The Origins of the Islamic State* was a text published over 1000 years ago. So, within just a couple of centuries of the death of Mohammed, a Muslim author was detailing the rise of Mohammed's political religion and the conquests by his army of jihadis, more than a thousand years before Islamism was supposedly invented. Thus do the elite deceive the public about the separability of Islam (religion) and Islamism (politics). It is only with the shock of 9/11, the shock of realising that there are millions upon millions of potential Islamic terrorists in the West, that The Grand Lie was invented, and a fake distinction between Islam the religion and political Islam was created.

The elite's attempt to contain the public in an ahistorical vacuum, pretending the Islamic State is some whacky new idea invented by a bunch of Muslim lunatics in the twentieth century, when in fact the concept of the Islamic State spans the entire history of Europe from just after the fall of the Roman Empire. Throughout history the Islamic State was a concept of pivotal importance not just to Muslims but to those Kuffar who needed to understand the thinking of Muslims. Following sustained deception by Muslims, politicians, journalists, clergy and academics, we have reached the point where ex-Muslims are risking their lives to warn us about how fascistic Islam is. One of the most important of these is Hamed Abdel-Samed, an academic who for his honest, simple statement of the problem, now needs unceasing police protection (he moves home every few months, he even has police protection when he takes a flight on an airplane). This ex-Muslim is prepared to risk his life to tell the truth to you and your children:

> At one point, I insisted on drawing a clear distinction between Islamism and Islam, thinking it would shield ordinary Muslims from generalized suspicion. Over time, though, it became clear to me that doing so only played into Islamists' hands, much as the concepts of Islamophobia and moderate Islamism do. Calling Islam a religion of peace while criticizing Islamists as if in a vacuum suggests that political Islam's ideas are sound and only require the proper implementation...[247]

That Islam is a politics and religion of war is explained in one simple fact, requiring no knowledge of the texts of Islam. Unlike the Christian calendar, the Islamic calendar does *not* start with the birth of the founder of the doctrine, it does *not even* start with the date of Mohammed's first "revelation" (the way the Buddhist calendar dates from when Buddha achieved enlightenment). The Islamic calendar starts from when Mohammed became a political and military leader in Medina: as the West's scholars of Islam were saying more than sixty years ago, the Islamic calendar "marked the date when the Prophet began to assume sovereign power".[248] From the very first day of the Islamic calendar, Islam was political and warfare was essential to Islam.[249] The calendar also marks that each successive year of that calendar is just one more year in the unending war between Islam and all other belief systems.[250] The fact that the Islamic calendar starts from some point halfway through the "revelations" of the Koran shows how an understanding of the chronology is of vital importance in understanding Islam. To signify this, our chronological Koran is split into two halves: one half is the violent Koran from when Mohammed was a politician, the other, (earlier) half is from when Mohammed was just a preacher. **The latter (violent) Koran is the only part of the Koran which has a date within the Islamic calendar. When exceptional Muslim scholars advocate abandoning the later part of the Koran, they are killed for apostasy.[251] This proves that there is no hope of reforming Islam.**

"But Not All Muslims Are Violent"

*"Those of the believers who sit still [avoiding jihad], other than those
who have a (disabling) hurt, are not on an equality with those
[Muslims] who strive in the way of Allah [perform jihad] with their
wealth and lives. Allah hath conferred on those who strive with their
wealth and lives a rank above the sedentary [Muslims who pay for
Jihad or die performing Jihad are superior to those Muslim slackers
who are sedentary]. Unto each Allah hath promised good, but He hath
bestowed on those who strive a great reward above the sedentary"
[Jihadis are rewarded as Muslims more than slackers]*

Koran 4:95

Even the BBC's hagiography of Mohammed admits that the Islamic calendar begins with Mohammed leaving Mecca and moving to Medina:

> Muhammad's popularity was seen as threatening by the people
> in power in Mecca, and Muhammad took his followers on a
> journey from Mecca to Medina in 622. This journey is called the
> Hijrah (migration) and the event was seen as so important for
> Islam that 622 is the year in which the Islamic calendar
> begins.[252]

Yet before he moved to Medina, Mohammed was nothing but a failure as a preacher. According to the scholars of Islam, after more than a decade of non-violent preaching in Mecca, Mohammed only managed to get around 150 followers.[253] By contrast, after less than a decade of piracy, assassination and massacring Pagans and Jews around Medina, Mohammed had acquired 10,000 followers. Even Wikipedia confirms this discrepancy:

> In 630, Muhammad marched on Mecca with an enormous force,
> said to number more than ten thousand men. With minimal
> casualties, Muhammad took control of Mecca.[254]

**Of course, the Wikipedia article says nothing about just how, less than
ten years after leaving for Medina, Mohammed was able to return and
conquer Mecca with few "casualties". The Pagan Meccans, who had
tolerated his insults and abuse for so many years, surrendered when
he returned to Mecca with his army because the Pagans who had
previously tolerated him had since heard how horrific was his
treatment of those who resisted his army of jihadis (remember:
according to the accounts passed down to us by Muslim writers,
Mohammed slaughtered those who surrendered, and then sold the
wives and daughters of the slaughtered into slavery).** Despite years of
listening to Mohammed talk about Islam, the Pagan Meccans had preferred

their own flexible system of many gods, instead of Mohammed's totalizing system of one god. But when faced with the prospect of being wiped out by his army of brutal mercenaries, the Pagans surrendered and converted to Islam, offering "the religion of peace" no resistance whatsoever. These details, the most astoundingly significant details of the triumph of this religion of war, are omitted from the BBC's account of Mohammad's life.

So, since killing to impose Islam is the foundation of the Islamic calendar,[255] just how many Muslims in the West are committed to supporting Islam as a religion of war? When 99% of all terrorism is from the tiny minority of people in the West who are Muslims, normally one would expect such a vitally important question to be a routine topic of conversation in newspapers and programmes about current affairs. yet we cannot even rely on the occasional opinion poll which asks this question. Muslims in our countries have realised that having their views solicited in surveys could be the government recording which Muslims are likely to be drawn towards terrorism.[256] This means that the results of opinion polls in the West are likely to greatly understate the problem of Muslim commitment to the violent tenets of Islam. Indeed, following the public stigmatization and hounding of anyone in the West who enunciates a statement that does not accord with the politically-correct vision of the elite, even opinion polls of the general public are turning out to be unreliable.[257]

One survey shows that around 40% of UK Muslims want to live under sharia law,[258] so we can assume that *at least* that proportion of Muslims in the UK should be classed as "Islamists" i.e. that they want to live in an Islamic State, ruled by theocracy rather than democratic law-making. Marxists have long maintained that quantitative changes can bring about qualitative changes,[259] and it is a reasonable assumption that the higher the proportion of Muslims there are in a society, the stronger will be their cumulative attempts to impose Islam upon each other and upon us Kuffar. Thus, whatever the percentage of Muslims who support jihad now, as the number of Muslims in a society increases and their relative strength increases, then the percentage supporting jihad is likely to increase. As the proportion of Muslims increases, they are likely to become more and more Islamic and more and more violent, because the doctrines of Islam insist that Muslims police the behaviour of each other. Whilst the Marxist notion of a quantitative change leading to a qualitative change might be dismissed as nonsense in most fields of analysis, when it comes to Islam it appears obvious that Marxist sociologists should have anticipated what Muslim immigration to the West would mean.

When we look beyond Britain, then it does indeed appear that the proportion of Muslims whom we would describe as fundamentalist is far higher than the statistics from Britain would indicate. A pan-European survey of Muslim attitudes (in Germany, France, Belgium, Austria, Sweden and the Netherlands) showed that the proportion of Muslims in Europe who want sharia law is far higher.

According to the study [...] funded by the German government, two thirds (65%) of the Muslims interviewed say Islamic Sharia law is more important to them than the laws of the country in which they live. Three quarters (75%) of the respondents hold the opinion that there is only one legitimate interpretation of the Koran, which should apply to all Muslims, and nearly 60% of Muslims believe their community should return to "Islamic roots."[260]

One of the two authors of the above study went on to say:

> **These findings clearly contradict the often-heard claim that Islamic religious fundamentalism is a marginal phenomenon in Western Europe or that it does not differ from the extent of fundamentalism among the Christian majority. Both claims are blatantly false, as almost half of European Muslims agree that Muslims should return to the roots of Islam, that there is only one interpretation of the Koran, and that the rules laid down in it are more important than secular laws. Among native Christians, less than one in 25 can be characterized as fundamentalists in this sense.**[261]

Thus, we have good reasons for doubting any claims that "Islamists" are a minority of Muslims in the West (assuming the distinction between "Muslims" and "Islamists" has any validity). As with any group of people solely united by doctrine, it is reasonable to assume that the majority would share a uniform commitment to the ideology, with fringe interpretations being confined to minorities.

In 2016, at the height of the negative media coverage on the atrocities being carried out by the Islamic State in Syria, a survey of British Muslims found that when it came to questions about support for the Caliphate/Islamic State, 7% of the Muslims surveyed said they supported the Caliphate, whilst only 2% of a control group said they supported the Caliphate.[262] However, we can be fairly sure that the number of Muslims supporting the Caliphate is far higher, since 14% of Muslims responded to the question with "don't know", whilst no more than 1% of the control group responded that way.[263] This is a very strong indicator that Muslims in Britain have learned that it is ill-advised to tell a stranger certain opinions. It is thus likely that the number of Muslims in this group who support the Caliphate is closer to at least 20% (we cannot know how many of those who expressed opposition to the Caliphate were choosing the inverse of their real opinion i.e. saying they opposed the Caliphate when they really support it). It is far more likely that Muslims would have allegiance to the Caliphate and knowledge of its importance to Islam than would the Kuffar. There are many other indicators that Muslims in this survey were deceiving those running the survey.[264]

That surveys of political opinions are going to significantly underestimate opinion which is not considered mainstream[265] should give people in the West a great deal to worry about when it comes to understanding the scale of the threat from Islam and the demographic changes of recent decades. This problem with inaccurate survey results seems to be a general trend in Western democracies which are no longer the open societies they were just twenty or thirty years ago. **On top of this general failing in the reliability of opinion polls on political matters, one must also factor in that deception is sanctioned as a component of the religion of war. As the old saying goes, in war the truth is the first casualty. Why would this be any different when it comes to a religion whose founder used deception in order to attain his military and political ends?**

In the first decade of the twenty-first century the western media often talked-up some fatwa by an Islamic scholar which supposedly condemned terrorism (the media were far less ready to provide the public with references to fatwas which support Islamic terrorism). Sometimes the fatwa talked-up by the media might claim that Islam opposes the taking of life from innocent people (this was the language used in a fatwa from the Islamic Society of North America in 2006).[266] As a senior academic researcher on Islam noted about this fatwa:

> it does not define the "terrorism" (a concept not defined by Islamic law) that they condemn. It refers, instead, to "civilians" – a concept not recognized by the Islamic law of jihad, and brands the terrorists as "criminals", which is a category of civil [i.e. secular], not religious transgression.[267]

As this researcher quite rightly points out: it is a grievous error for us Kuffar to assume that the terms of our debate can be mapped onto the Islamic world-view. Quite often Muslims will exploit ambiguities and principles in our use of language so that Muslims can appear to be doing one thing when they are doing another. Statements by people committed to an ideology with a long history of attempts to subjugate us using lethal force should not be taken at face value. Muslims are very familiar with the discourses of the West, whilst the expertise on Islam built up in the West in the previous centuries has been concealed by our educated elite. In any debate Muslims can put forward their most-expert and best-trained deceivers, whilst our experts and best debaters are (with rare exceptions) hiding away in fear of losing their lives or at the very least their income.

The word "innocent" is one of the slippery and duplicitous terms used by Muslims. Muslims claim that the people who live in democracies are not innocent, since those who live in democratic countries believe that their governments are carrying out the will of the people,[268] i.e. since democracy claims to be the will of the people, then how are the people innocent of what their elected politicians do? It is not just that the word "innocent" has a *narrower meaning* when used in the duplicitous framework of Islam, but the word "defensive" has a *wider meaning*:

> **Islamic apologists often say that jihad can only be defensive, that it can never be directed toward civilians, and that Islam forbids the taking of innocent life. That's all very reassuring – until you realize that the terms "defensive", "civilians", and "innocent" are understood differently in Islamic and Western societies. A close reading of Islamic law books reveals that only Muslims are innocent.**[269]

After the multiple simultaneous terrorist attacks in Paris at the end of 2015, Muslim experts jumped to proclaim that Islam does not sanction violent attacks against the innocent.[270] The army of journalists who poured over every word ever uttered by Donald Trump as a presidential candidate were not remotely interested in interrogating such Muslim hand-waving, to see what kind of ambiguities are found when the followers of the religion of war claim that "Islam is opposed to violence against innocent people". Such condemnations by Muslims would prove entirely empty if subjected to scrutiny.

When we stop seeing the world from our European, Christian, humanist, universalist position, and start to see the world from within the discriminatory framework that is Islam, things look completely different. As the Koran says, the Kuffar are going to burn in Hell:

> Those who disbelieve Our revelations, We shall expose them to the Fire. As often as their skins are consumed We shall exchange them for fresh skins that they may taste the torment.[271]

Are the innocent going to be tortured by fire in Hell for the whole of eternity? Of course not. It is quite clear from the Koran that we Kuffar are never innocent. Muslims believe that we are all Muslims when we are born, hence Muslims use the term "revert" rather than "convert" to describe those who become Muslims.[272] Those who have heard of Islam but who continue to define themselves as Atheists, Buddhists, Christians, etc. instead of "reverting" to Islam, these are people whom Islam considers are determined to do evil by not becoming Muslim. Only the Muslim can be innocent (someone without guilt). And the only guaranteed way for a Muslim to become sinless is to die as a jihadi. Even most Muslims have no guarantee they will be found innocent on Judgement Day, and believers who haven't found themselves a guaranteed place in Paradise by dying fighting for Islam are facing an eternity of torment in Hell. The 'cleansing' act of dying as a martyred jihadi is such a strong guarantee that quite often Muslims might readily behave in "sinful" ways shortly before undertaking suicidal attacks.[273]

We are sure that some readers are so blinded by the deceptive world-view peddled by our political leaders and journalists that such readers are entirely accustomed to being deceived and cannot see the framework of deception. For example, earlier we discussed how the Deputy Prime Minister of Britain was not content just to "quote" Koran 5:32, but used his own edited version of Koran 5:32 to make the verse say almost the exact opposite of what it says. But when one looks at how the most famous Islamic scholars in history have explained this verse, they have made clear that the meaning is even worse than appears at first sight. Ibn Kathir, a fourteenth-century Muslim expert[274] explained in his *Tafsir* (the Arabic word for "exegesis") that Koran 5:32 is a verse that is *only* concerned with the unlawful killing of Muslims:

> (it would be as if he killed all mankind) means, "Whoever kills one soul that Allah has forbidden killing, is just like he who kills all mankind". Sa'id bin Jubayr said, "He who allows himself to shed the blood of a Muslim, is like he who allows shedding the blood of all people. **He who forbids shedding the blood of one Muslim, is like he who forbids shedding the blood of all people**".[275]

This makes it crystal clear: **according to the pre-eminent scholars of Islam, to the extent that there are any injunctions against killing in the Koran these injunctions *only apply* to the death of Muslims. Unbelievers can be killed at whim, unless they are paying protection money (Jizya) to the Islamic State to stop arbitrary acts of violence against them. Within the value framework of Islam "innocent" people never means the unbelievers. This verse of the Koran which Western politicians pretend is universally opposed to killing allows for Muslims to be killed by Muslims, provided that the Muslim who is killed is guilty of some offence within Islam. That verse offers no protection at all to the Kuffar. Which is why the betrayal by our leaders is so horrendous: our lying leaders have sided with Muslims against all non-Muslims.**

Deception Is Part Of Islamic Morality

> *"those who swear allegiance unto thee (Muhammad), swear allegiance only unto Allah. The Hand of Allah is above their hands. So whosoever breaketh his oath, breaketh it only to his soul's hurt; while whosoever keepeth his covenant with Allah, on him will He bestow immense reward."*
>
> *Koran 48:10*

The calculated deception by Muslims is an ever-present possibility and reality. Patrick Sookhdeo is an ex-Muslim with multiple research degrees from some of the most prestigious organisations in the West. In his book *Global Jihad*, **Dr. Sookhdeo has an entire chapter on the Muslim doctrine of deception (taqiyya). Quoting Iranian political scientist Hamid Enayat, Sookhdeo says that this religiously-sanctioned deception has "become the norm of public behaviour among all Muslims – both Sunni**

and Shi'a – wherever there is a conflict between faith and
expediency".[276] The hadiths claim that Mohammed permitted lying in only
three situations and one of those three was in war.[277] As we will explain in
detail below, the relationship between the world of Islam and the rest of the
world is one of permanent war. Thus, there is no reason why any Muslim
should ever tell the truth to a Kuffar. Other hadiths have Mohammed giving
people permission to lie in order to go and kill a critic of Mohammed's
religion of war.[278] Indeed, this deception even goes so far as allowing a
Muslim to (pretend to) renounce Islam, an offence which otherwise carries
the death-penalty for Muslims.[279] This act of pretending that one is not a
Muslim is actually why deception is associated with Shia Muslims (they were
so often persecuted by Sunni Muslims, that the doctrine of deception
became far more developed and explicit in Shia Islam). Dr. Sookhdeo goes on
to say that there are in fact entirely different narratives stated by Muslims,
depending on whether the audience is Muslim or Kuffar.[280] Thus there is no
reason for us Kuffar to *ever* believe what we are told by a Muslim. If we want
to know the truth about Islam, we have their texts and we have over one
thousand years of evidence of Muslims implementing the programme
detailed in these texts.

**This does not mean that over a trivial issue that one should expect a
Muslim to be untruthful (such as asking a Muslim the time of day). But
when it comes to anything which might impede Islam in its mission,
one cannot expect the truth from a Muslim.[281] The Muslim world-view
is duplicitous: everything and everyone not Islamic is outside of the
realm of truth, our very existence is the manifestation of falsity, so
there is no reason for them to tell us the truth if lies will advance Islam
further. To Muslims there is no truth other than Islam: outside of Islam
there is no truth. Thus when a Muslim is deceiving a Kuffar, it is not a
sin to the Muslim, because the Kuffar is someone who lives outside of
truth. This is what it means for an ideology to be totalitarian: it is a
hermetic system, immune to any correction from outside the system.
No matter how rational the Kuffar's critique of Islam might be, to a
Muslim the Kuffar's opinion has no more importance than the barking
of a dog.**

An example of such deception is when Muslims are in debate with non-
Muslims, and the latter refers to something in the hadiths. The Muslim may
dismiss what is said by saying "only the Koran is authentic; that hadith is a
fabrication". By saying this the Muslim will hope that those listening will
assume "fabrication" means "fiction" or "false". But in reality, all the Muslim
is saying is that the hadiths are stories told by Muslims (humans) about
Mohammed, while the Koran is thought (by Muslims) to be a flawless
repetition of the words of Allah (hence authentic as in "coming directly from
the author, the creator"). The trusting victim of Islam (the Kuffar) might take
from this that some hadith which makes Islam look bad was something that
all Muslims would dismiss as fake, when in fact that hadith was instead
crucial to the way Muslims practice Islam. But "fabricated" here just means

that the hadith has come from the voice of man rather than having been supposedly repeated verbatim by Mohammed from Allah. This is the kind of underhand tactic a Muslim would use if there were other Muslims who might object to a flat-out lie (in making a bold lie the debating Muslim might be construed as an apostate by Muslims who heard this lie). In a situation where there was a tremendous benefit to be gained for the Ummah from a Muslim pretending not to be a Muslim, this too would be permitted (for example, if the Muslim had the opportunity of becoming President of a country which had a very small Muslim population, Muslims would not object to him claiming to be a Christian). Power over us Kuffar is the primary directive of Islam.

There are many other forms of deception in use, for example, Muslims citing Koran 2:256 "There is no compulsion in religion", when the Muslim is aware of the many verses which contradict this and aware of the fact that the verse has been cancelled (see our chronological Koran). Only those verses which allow the Muslim to win a debate would be cited (those verses which would be an impediment to furthering Islam being treated as if they did not exist). Another example is Islamic texts which are translated out of Arabic and into a language where most speakers are Kuffar. The translation would omit those things which might make the Kuffar say Islam is evil or objectionable. This is demonstrable with those texts where there are parallel translations, for example, the manual of sharia law named *Reliance of the Traveller: A Classic Manual of Islamic Sacred Law*. When it comes to the eternal Islamic laws governing slavery, these laws are omitted in the English translation but are to be found in the parallel Arabic text.[282] Thus do Muslims make Islam look less objectionable to a Kuffar audience, an audience who will only find out that slavery is legal in Islam when the unbelievers have converted to Islam (or when the unbelievers find themselves enslaved). This kind of deception is practised when Muslims do not feel they are strong enough to simply use violence to force conversions to Islam.

It is hardly worth even raising the point that Muslims will bend the truth and will even brazenly lie to us Kuffar, since the Kuffar are people whom Muslims deem to be essentially inferior to Muslims, not just for now, but inferior for all time.[283] The Koran says that those who do not believe in Islam "are the worst of created beings" (98:6). In Islam, unbelievers are even worse than animals (because unlike animals, unbelievers are refusing to believe Islam, the only truth as far as Muslims are concerned)! Do people worry about not telling the truth to animals? As we have seen, Winston Churchill was not the only Prime Minister of Britain who compared Islam to Nazism. During World War II, did Britain and America expect National Socialists to honestly explain their war plans to us? Of course not. And during World War II a huge effort was undertaken to break the encryption used by the Germans, so that the Allies would be able to see what the true plans of the Germans were. Would any army offer its battle plans up to those they intend to dominate and for whom they have contempt? Since Muslims do not want the victims of Islam to be forewarned, why would Muslims want to put the Koran in a sensible order, an order which would enable the Kuffar to understand what plan Islam has in store for the Kuffar? In the nineteenth century our own Western experts decrypted the Koran. But their work has been concealed, crowded out and ignored by the dozens of translations of the Koran in the traditional order.

No sooner had the West started to recover from fighting off National Socialism and Soviet Bolshevism than the political elite started to ensure that the people of the West became ignorant about Islam, in order to facilitate the immigration of millions upon millions of Muslims into the West. By the mid-1960s, even the Second Vatican Council[284] **deceived the world's one billion Catholics about the existential threat that Islam has been to Christianity from shortly after Mohammed's death.**[285] The deception of the Kuffar by Muslims is hardly surprising, but what will incense future generations is that our own highly-educated politicians and journalists actually magnified the deception inherent in Islam. It's not the first time in history that an elite has betrayed their nation and imported Muslims: this was precisely how Muslims gained entry to Spain at the start of the eighth century.[286] It took the people of Spain seven hundred years to remove the Muslims who became the vicious masters of the Kuffar in that peninsula. **It is no wonder that the Islamisation of Spain has been turned into another deceit, the supposedly savage Europeans being civilised by the culture of the warrior tribes who spread out from the uncivilised Arabian desert just a few decades before! Our elite cannot let the people of the West know that it took centuries and the help of armies from around Europe to remove Islam from the Iberian peninsula, with an eleventh-century Pope promoting a defensive Christian jihad to save Christendom from the genocidal assault by Muslims. The myth of the Golden Age of tolerance in Spain is just one more lie of the many lies our elite tell us to make us quiescent.**[287] **This elite prefer to lie to us about a period in history that was horribly violent and discriminatory and tell us that it was instead a time of multicultural harmony.**

When Muslims and their Quisling allies hear of the book you are reading, one of the principal deceits they will adopt will be to question the translation of the Koran we use. Indeed, they may even question the very possibility of any translation of the Koran,[288] or say that only an Arab can comment on the content of the Koran. They might even go so far as to say that the Arabic commentator *must also* be a Muslim as well as a speaker of Arabic. Let us dismiss these arguments with the brevity they deserve: we would never accept a Nazi telling us that only a German speaker, and an actual paid-up member of the National Socialist Party, could comment on Hitler's *Mein Kampf*. Universal hostility towards National Socialism and *Mein Kampf* is expected from all of us, even if we have never read the book and cannot speak German. **If we are supposed to be able to form an independent view of an ideology and its founding texts, then we can have an opinion on the Koran just as easily as an opinion on** *Mein*

***Kampf*, an opinion on Islam just as validly as an opinion on Nazism. And to have an opinion on *Mein Kampf* we do not need to read it in German; reading it in translation is sufficient.** In fact, the near-universal hostility there is towards National Socialism comes from people who have never even read *Mein Kampf*. No-one objects that it is "Naziphobic" to oppose National Socialism out of ignorance. So, no time should be given to this specious objection to reading the Koran in translation.

Muslims sometimes object to the Koran being translated out of Arabic, saying that the Koran cannot be translated. This is a ridiculous notion both theoretically and practically. In practical terms it is nonsense since most of the world's Muslims read the Koran in languages other than Arabic.

> The majority of Muslims have to read the Koran in translation in order to understand it. Contrary to what one might think, there have been translations of the Koran into, for instance, Persian, since [as long ago as] the tenth or eleventh century, and there are translations into Turkish and Urdu. The Koran has now been translated into over a hundred languages, many of them by Muslims themselves, despite some sort of disapproval from the religious authorities.[289]

So, ignore those Quislings who might say that this book is dealing with a translation rather than the original Arabic Koran. The translation we use is one of the most widely-accepted translations of the Koran into English. You might find the kind of English used in this translation reminds you of studying Shakespeare in school and that might seem old-fashioned, but that is a matter of style, not proof of the impossibility of translation. **Suffice to say, the Koran we are using was translated into English by a scholar of Arabic, a man who also was a convert to Islam. The allies of Islam would be hard-pressed to find a more suitable candidate to present the Koran in the most favourable light to the Kuffar readership. If anything, we Kuffar should be more worried that his translation is likely to make Islam sound less violent and less discriminatory than Islam really is.**

A little history of the Koran will help explain why the chapters ("Surahs") of the Koran appear in the jumbled-up order in which they are traditionally presented, and then we will go on to discuss why this traditional ordering has no sound reasoning behind it. The Koran was not written down as a unified text in Mohammed's lifetime, but was assembled some years after his death. And whilst Muslims will claim there is only one perfect and unchanging Koran (which was supposedly passed from Allah to Mohammed via the Angel Gabriel), there were in fact multiple Korans in existence as texts. These variant Korans were all thought to be destroyed, leaving only one unified Koran.[290] This single Koran in Arabic has been the basis for all the translations which Muslims have used ever since.

Since the word "Koran" means "recitation" why was the Koran ever written down? Following Mohammed's death, a decision was made to transcribe the various fragments of the Koran into a single text. Since

Islam is a religion of war, those who knew how to recite the Koran were among the most ferocious warriors and were being killed, and it was thus feared that parts of the Koran would end up being forgotten, as all those devout Muslims who could recite it were dying in wars to impose Islam on others.[291] Whilst many early Christians were murdered simply because they held Christian beliefs, by contrast Muslims were being killed in the process of killing or enslaving unbelievers (because the jihadis believed that only this form of martyrdom guaranteed entry to Paradise). Thus, the very concept of "martyr" in Christianity and Islam are opposites: the former is killed but does not kill, the latter dies in the process of killing others. That is why it is such a travesty for our leaders to lie to us over and over again that Islam is "a religion of peace", because the Koran says that the most devoted Muslims are those who die imposing Islam on others.[292] When you turn to our chronological Koran you will be immediately struck that Mohammed spent the latter part of his life promoting genocide.

Fundamental Importance Of Abrogation

> *"Nothing of our revelation (even a single verse) do we abrogate or cause be forgotten, but we bring (in place) one better or the like thereof."*
>
> *Koran 2:106*

Any Koran the unguided reader picks up makes almost no sense, because as a book the Koran is a jumbled-up collection of chapters. Most Muslims are unguided readers, as are most of us Kuffar.[293] Are we being Eurocentric, expecting the Koran to be in some kind of rational order? For decades now, the Leftist allies of Islam have been attacking independent experts in the West, claiming these experts are "Orientalists", Westerners imposing a Eurocentric view of "the East" on quaint and colourful foreigners, people who simply do things differently from us (to the Romans the word "orient" meant "the lands east of the Mediterranean", from the Latin verb "to rise" i.e. the lands where the sun rises). There is no need for us to provide a refutation of their ridiculous Quisling notion of Orientalism[294] in order to point out that in its traditional order, the Koran is a jumbled-up mess of ideas. Why? Because Muslims have themselves needed to know the chronological order of the Koran.

Why have Muslims themselves needed to put the chapters of the Koran into chronological order? Because they are commanded to follow the Koran literally and to model their behaviour on the behaviour of Mohammed. They must follow these commands to the letter, or risk eternal damnation. **There would be no need to put the Koran in chronological order if it were not an ambiguous and contradictory text which commanded that it be taken literally. So, to resolve these contradictions and to know what one must do to be a good and literalist Muslim, the followers of these** doctrines have needed to put the Koran in chronological order. Thus, when an instruction in one part of the Koran contradicts an instruction in another part of the Koran, the later (chronological) instruction from Mohammed takes precedence. This process is called "abrogation".[295]

We are sure most of the population of the West have never encountered the word "abrogation" before, a word which means to rescind a law, most often used in a religious context. In a secular society we have laws which are open to repeal or modification and it is many centuries since religious law held sway in our societies. We have a morality and a legal system which evolves. We don't live in a nation like Pakistan which has nuclear missiles yet which also claims to conform to the legal principles laid down in seventh century Arabia. Around the world, religious groups other than Muslims might choose to live by literalist interpretations of their texts, but that is a marginal concern for us, since in the West they are but a small proportion of the population and they are not involved in terrorism at home and abroad. **If Muslims were not using terrorist violence on an almost daily basis across the world, we too might have no need to understand the role that abrogation plays in theocracy. But when our politicians and journalists tell us that "Islam is a religion of peace" we need to find some way of reconciling that claim with the frequent mass-murders carried out by devout Muslims in the name of Islam.**

We are now so accustomed to the idea of suicide bombings by Muslims we don't even recognise what a strange and unusual thing this should be. No matter if Muslims are 10% or 5% or 1% of the population of a country, 100% of those involved in terrorism in relation to Islam are Muslims. In a society where 95% of the population are not Muslims, one might reasonably expect that in response to terrorist attacks by Muslims, huge numbers of the Kuffar would fight back with terrorist attacks on Muslims. But such attacks do not exist. The terrorist attacks are all coming from "the religion of peace" not from all the other religions and belief systems which are not praised as being peaceful.

Apart from Muslims, when it comes to suicide bombing most of us might only be able to recall the Japanese Kamikaze pilots from World War II (indeed, suicide-bombing is so atypical of Western values that the French word for a Muslim suicide bomber is "Kamikaze").[296] So the only other killers who committed suicide to murder others for political advantage were from a non-Western, militaristic, imperialistic culture, which was losing a prolonged war, where surrender was not even conceivable. Their recourse to dying for Japan in this way was a tactic driven by desperation: Japan only started to use Kamikaze suicide bombers towards the end of 1944 (and for Japan, World War II began nearly a decade earlier, with their invasion of China in July 1937).[297] But in that long war the Japanese Kamikaze attacks only lasted a year or so, and only came at the end. During World War II, our politicians and journalists didn't go around telling us that the Japanese were mostly peaceful, and the Kamikaze bombers were a bunch of extremists. **In the end, the leaders in the West**

decided that the only way to get this enemy to surrender was to use a nuclear bomb to rain destruction down upon them (and even then, the culture which gave us the Kamikaze killers did not surrender until a second city was destroyed by a nuclear bomb). Since the end of World War II, the world has undergone hundreds if not thousands of Islamic Kamikaze missions. Even the man who assassinated American Senator Robert Kennedy in 1968 was a Muslim, and he demanded the death penalty (as a jihadi, he would have believed that dying for Islam would guarantee him entry to Paradise).[298] Fifty years after Robert Kennedy's assassination, and the public in the West are no closer to having the true cause of Islamic terrorism explained to them.

When we try to think of others, even in Asia, who are prepared to kill themselves for political goals, we may recall a few Buddhist monks who set fire *to themselves* in order to bring about change.[299] But these Buddhists didn't use their suicide to kill others, as do Kamikaze bombers and Muslim terrorists. We need to appreciate that the Islamic view of the world is very different from the view of the world held by atheistic, materialistic, self-obsessed Westerners. **Having a growing population of Kamikaze zealots in our society, with us unable to know which one of them will strike next or where they will strike, should be of major concern to people in the West.**

We expect by now some of the Quisling allies of Islam reading this are groaning to themselves: "they are parading Orientalist prejudices", "they are lying about Islam sanctioning murder", "they are making false claims about the order in which one needs to read the chapters of the Koran in order to understand Islam". So, let us first prove that the chronological order is a central concept *to Muslims* in understanding what is Islam. To do that, we are going to demonstrate that the concept of abrogation is mainstream for most Muslims, and for Muslims to make use pf abrogation they need to put the Koran's chapters in chronological order. **Once one puts the Koran into the chronological order assumed by scholars of Islam, then it becomes abundantly clear why Islam is a religion of war and not a religion of peace.**

Routledge is one the main academic publishers in the world, and it is unlikely they would ever consider publishing a book which sought to misrepresent Islam: if they were not obsessed with political correctness, then the fear of being targeted for assassination by Muslims would make them exceedingly careful.[300] Let us look at the Routledge book called *Islam: The Key Concepts*. The authors of this book are professors of religion who have multiple books on Islam to their names; these authors are thus highly credentialed, they teach at prestigious universities, and their book is aimed at university students. The concept of abrogation is featured in the very first pages of this book, which says:

> Abrogation... is the process through which specific revelations
> are replaced by others. Abrogation can apply to entire

revelations -- for instance, the Qur'an both corrects and perfects earlier scriptures -- or to particular sections of one revelation, where one verse or set of verses replaces another.[301]

This is not some dreary theological point. Unless one grasps the concept of abrogation, one cannot understand why the world has suffered so much slavery, terrorism, and genocide from Muslims. When one understands the concept of abrogation, then one also understands why it is that Muslims and their Quisling allies can make false claims like "there is no compulsion of religion in Islam".[302]

If we in the West had understood the role of abrogation in Islam, we would have understood the significance of the Rushdie Affair of the early 1990s. Devout Muslims all over the world vowed to kill the author of *The Satanic Verses*, bookstores around the world were bombed,[303] people died in riots,[304] and Muslims made assassination attempts (some successful) on people involved in the publication of the book.[305] **Why did Muslims all over the world come together in such a violent way about a novel which most of them had not read and which they were never going to read? Because the very title of that book draws attention to the role of abrogation in Islam.** According to Islam's own history books, when Mohammed had "revelations" about accepting other gods than Allah, Mohammed started to lose the few Muslim converts he had managed to acquire.[306] **Since Mohammed claimed that he wasn't just making up these revelations of the Koran, Mohammed had to have Allah give him a subsequent revelation which cancelled the verses accepting other gods.** But since Allah is supposedly an infallible being, it had to be "Satan" who gave Mohammed the revelations which first allowed the Muslims to be flexible in the worshipping of gods other than Allah in this multicultural environment in Mecca.[307] **Without the concept of later verses abrogating the earlier verses, the Satanic verses where Mohammed allowed Muslims to pray to other gods would still be in effect. Abrogation is the only way that Muslims can reconcile such contradictions in a book which is supposed to be the eternal and infallible word of God.**

In over a quarter of a century since The Rushdie Affair, the Quisling class have never bothered to ensure that the electorate in the West should understand why it was that Muslims did not want the Kuffar to understand that the Satanic verses of the Koran were a pivotal moment in Islam. The elite would not have had to go into too much detail but could have ensured that the electorate in different countries understood why **the concept of the Satanic verses is a fundamental issue for Islam and for Muslims. That is, once Mohammed's followers were given a choice to worship differently, to think differently, they would no longer be constrained by the totalitarian rules of Islam (this total and unchanging way of living).** Understanding why Muslims are so desperate to keep secret the significance of the Satanic verses is key to understanding the totalitarian nature of Islam.

In Islam difference and choice must not be allowed: only living as Islam prescribes is valid, the rules of Islam are the source of all authority, any dissent is to be crushed: Muslims cannot vary their lives from the strictures without ceasing to be Muslims and thus inviting murder from other Muslims. The issue behind The Rushdie Affair is key for the people in the West: Muslims are never going to stop being Muslims and are never going to worship anything other than Allah, the only god *and the only source of authority for Muslims.* **Explaining why Sunni Muslims in Britain were prepared to follow a religious edict to kill Rushdie, an edict issued by their arch-enemies the Shia Muslims in Iran, would have enabled the electorate in democracies across the West to decide: do we really want any more of this unbending ideology and its foot-soldiers in our society? Instead, the elite in the West pretended that the issue of the Satanic verses was a storm-in-a-teacup and that the death threat to Rushdie ended years ago, when in fact the threat to the author continues to the present day.**[308]

The opportunity to educate the electorate about Islam was abandoned. Instead the dogma about multiculturalism was promoted in the aftermath of the crisis, in an attempt to stop the people in the West from objecting to this alien creed which was never going to give up its founding mission: to destroy all that is not Islam. The Rushdie Affair showed that Islam and multiculturalism are mutually exclusive: **it was the tolerant multiculturalism of the Pagan Meccans which permitted Mohammed to espouse his new and hostile religion. And tolerating Islam led to tolerance being wiped out wherever Muslims hold power.** When the publication of a harmless novel proved that Islam would never be anything other than domineering in liberal democracies, rather than highlight this threat and take a stand to defend liberalism, the elite masked the threat by silencing dissent with the dogma of multiculturalism and the rules of political correctness.

As we have indicated, abrogation is not only key to understanding the significance of the Satanic verses but is also key to understanding why the Koran must be organised in the way that it is in the book you are reading. You might think that the Routledge book we cited earlier is an anomaly, and abrogation is not as important in Islam as we are claiming. Let us re-affirm the importance of abrogation by quoting from another mainstream text on Islam. Here is what the Cambridge University Press *Companion to the Qur'an* says.

> **Since qur'anic prescriptions were often mutually contradictory [...] it forced Muslim legal experts to establish the relative chronology of the 'abrogated' and the 'abrogating' verses. This required a thorough knowledge of the history of the first Muslim community in order to determine the time and circumstances... in which certain verses were revealed.**[309]

So, not only is abrogation accepted as mainstream in the study of Islam, abrogation and knowledge of the correct chronological order of the chapters of the Koran is a pre-requisite for Islamic (sharia) law. Those Muslims who say they want sharia law, are thus Muslims who are committed to the expertise of those who know the chronology of the Koran. And if significant numbers of Muslims are committed to this chronology, then significant numbers of Muslims are also committed to the Koran culminating with commands to kill the unbelievers. These commands are the first thing you will see when you turn to our Koran.

The chronological ordering of the Koran has extremely wide implications, with just a single verse of the Koran being able to cancel scores of the verses which precede it. To illustrate this, consider the following quotation from *The Cambridge Companion to the Qur'an*:

> **The abrogation theory achieved great sophistication at the hands of later legal scholars, who, for instance, argued that the famous 'Sword Verse' enjoining the believers to 'slay the idolaters wherever you find them' (Q9:5) abrogated no fewer than 124 other verses commanding 'anything less than a total offensive against the non-believers'.**[310]

These "later legal scholars" are not some twentieth-century misfits who decided to reject 1000 years of Islamic thought and practice. These legal scholars were working out the order of the Koranic verses (and the theory of abrogation) in the first few hundred years after Mohammed's death. Thus, their decisions have shaped Islam and have been followed by Muslims for over 1000 years and are still considered relevant today. We would remind you of the commentary on the Koran by Qurtubi discussed at the start of our Introduction. In 2003 moderate Muslim scholars in Britain chose to translate Qurtubi's commentary from the 1300s, a work which states that the command to fight and kill unbelievers is "an unqualified command" which abrogates any other commands which contradict it.

We Kuffar Have Lost Our Minds

"They [non-Muslims] will not fight against you in a body save in fortified villages or from behind walls. Their adversity among themselves is very great. [Diversity is weakness] Ye think of them as a whole whereas their hearts are divers. That is because they are a folk who have no sense."

Koran 59:14

We Kuffar have a vital need to understand why Muslims are doing what they are doing, a need to slash our way through the lies and deceits of the Quisling elite. Indeed, before World War II, educated English speakers knew that the Koran ended with calls to "kill the unbelievers", because English scholars translated the Koran and put the verses into chronological order.[311] The Koran in this form was in such demand that the up-market publisher J.M. Dent was reprinting its chronological Koran in the mass-market Everyman series almost every other year! For example, the 1937 copy of this Koran shows it had been previously printed in 1909, 1911, 1913, 1915, 1918, 1921, 1924, 1926, 1929, and 1933. And what is truly significant is that this most widely-read English translation of the Koran ends with the last two chapters being Chapter 9 and Chapter 5 (two of the most violent and intolerant chapters of the entire Koran). Thus, **anyone in the world reading the Koran in English from the 1860s to the 1930s could have been in no doubt: at the end of Mohammed's life he was calling for actions which we would now regard as genocide and apartheid.** And since this Rodwell translation published by Everyman was being reprinted nearly every other year, we can take this as evidence that this chronological view of the Koran was very widely known by the educated people of Britain and the United States of America (something similar to Rodwell's chronological translation also existed in German and in French). **Not only have Muslims needed scholars to know how to put the Koran into chronological order, but for the best part of eight decades prior to World War II, the principal Koran read by English-speaking people put the chapters in chronological order. This means our ancestors a century ago were less confused about Islam than we are now,** after six decades of immigration by Muslims and with Islam causing nothing but harm to our societies.[312] Our society is now almost entirely clueless about the facts of Islam.

By the 1950s, the Everyman edition of the Koran replaced the chronological Rodwell translation for the Pickthall translation we have used in this book. The Pickthall translation dates from the 1930s (although the language of this translation reads more like it was translated in the time of Shakespeare). **Thus, as Muslims were immigrating to the West in ever greater numbers, the Everyman series of books (aimed at those who are not scholars), swapped a very readable translation which showed the Koran ending with calls for war and killing, for a turgid translation by a convert to Islam (a translation which returned to encrypting the chronology of the chapters, removing the information needed by the Kuffar to make sense of the illogical ordering of the chapters of the Koran).[313]** That readable and chronological versions of the Koran should have been crowded out of the market by more turgid and encrypted translations of the Koran is highly significant.

In the latter half of the twentieth century, Muslims were exerting pressure on experts in the West to start concealing the truth about Islam. The Everyman 1991 edition of the Koran still contains Pickthall's Introduction from his 1930 translation, where even Pickthall acknowledges that in following the traditional Muslim ordering of the chapters "the arrangement is not easy to understand". Yet Everyman still chose to substitute this less readable, less coherent version of the Koran. **The English-speaking world was to be given a version of the Koran made** "authentic" by being produced by a Muslim, rather than the earlier version by a Kuffar, a version which actually helped the public understand Islam more accurately.[314] As we show below, this action by Everyman was not an isolated event, but was part of a wider movement of the educated elite submitting to Muslim demands to frame Islam in a way which suited the Islamic supremacists and which harmed us, the victims of Islam.

Even with the encrypted translation of the Koran chosen by Everyman, it is not as though the educated elite in the 1990s could have been fooled into believing Islam was a religion of peace. In the Introduction to his translation, the Muslim convert Pickthall also agreed with the earlier translator Rodwell: the Koran only came to be written down in the seventh century because the most devout Muslims, those who had memorised the entire Koran, were being killed in wars fought to force Islam on others. Thus, Pickthall says:

> in a battle which took place during the Caliphate of Abu Bakr –
> that is to say, within two years of the Prophet's death – a large
> number of those who knew the whole Koran by heart were
> killed [in battle, so] a collection of the whole Koran was made
> and put in writing.[315]

So even if politicians and journalists in the West had been reading either the chronological Rodwell translation or the later translation by Mohammed Pickthall, our elite still could not honestly have considered Mohammed's apostles to be men of peace, since the Introduction in both translations of the Koran show that the most devout early Muslims were dying off in wars imposing Islam on others. If politicians and journalists had read no more than the Introduction to either of these most popular translations of the Koran, they must have known that Islam was a religion of war.

In recent decades the world has been flooded with the publication of even more translations of the Koran, the vast majority of which conceal the chronological ordering of the chapters, thus ensuring that it is harder to find a chronological Koran. In turn this ensures that people understand less about Islam now than they did in the century leading up to World War II.[316] It has been possible to deceive the people of the West, hiding the Koran's calls for genocide and apartheid against the Kuffar behind the illogical ordering that is the traditional order of the Koran. Without this deception, it is unlikely that the people of the West would ever have allowed millions of Muslims to immigrate into our countries, bringing Islamic terrorism and violence with them. **The chronological translation by Rodwell basically disappeared from view after World War II, pushed out of the marketplace of ideas by a dozen or more obscurantist translations, which were all produced by Muslims or by apologists for Islam. It was contrary to the aim of these people (promoting Islam to us Kuffar) to have chronological Korans around.** Why would Christians be open to followers of a religion whose final message was to promote apartheid and genocide? In the wake of the totalitarian horrors of the 1930s and the 1940s, why would decent people in the West want to subscribe to an ideology which was more reminiscent of the worst excesses of Communism or National Socialism than the religion of their ancestors? But this thicket of misleading Koran translations provided the background against which the Quisling elite could deceive the public with The Grand Lie: "Islam is a religion of peace".

Politicians in the West show no readiness to stop repeating The Grand Lie. After the horrific terrorist attack by Muslims in Paris in November 2015, the woman who was to be the Democratic Party candidate for the subsequent American Presidential election said: "Let's be clear: Islam is not our adversary. Muslims are peaceful and tolerant people and have nothing to do whatsoever with terrorism".[317] This claim by Hilary Clinton about Muslims being "a peaceful and tolerant people" was sandwiched between the terrorist attack by Muslims on British tourists in Tunisia and the terrorist attack by a Muslim on a gay club in Florida (the largest single act of mass slaughter of homosexuals in recorded history).[318] So-called "progressive" politicians are clearly desperate to stop the public from noticing that it is Jews[319] and gays and Christians[320] whom Muslim terrorists are now singling out for execution in the West, in Africa and in the Middle East.

Muslims around the world must laugh at the freedom-loving, democracy-loving West, where our elected leaders can lie to us blatantly about the doctrines and history of Islam. The lies from these politicians are not contradicted by academics or religious leaders. Our so-called "free press" does nothing to hold the politicians to account for their deception. And so, the voters keep freely putting these deceitful politicians in positions of power above us. No amount of terrorist murder by Muslims in the West has seemed to affect the way we have acted as voters.[321] No doubt Muslims see our part in this cycle of deception as yet further proof that democracy is a fundamentally flawed system, and that Muslims are right to want democracy replaced by sharia law: we Kuffar keep electing leaders who work to import an ideology which throughout its entire history has been committed to the violent subjugation of the Kuffar. **Why would any Muslims in the West have respect for democracy, when they can see how corrupt it is, with an electorate who are compulsorily educated yet who cannot see for ourselves that our leaders are lying to us and, as the number of Muslims in our society continues to grow, putting us in increasing danger.**

Islam's Clear Offer: Submit Or Die

"Fight against such of those who have been given the Scripture [Jews and Christians] as believe not in Allah nor the Last Day, and [who] forbid not that which Allah hath forbidden by His messenger, and [who] follow not the Religion of Truth, until they pay the tribute [protection money] readily, being brought low."

Koran 9:29

Whilst our societies are busy discussing celebrity gossip, gay marriage and gender-neutral lavatories the Islamisation of the West continues inexorably. **With every Islamic terrorist attack since 9/11, our leaders and the media have rushed again to brainwash the public into thinking "Islam is the religion of peace".** By lying for Islam and pretending that Islam is a religion of peace, the elite are adopting the position of Dhimmi in relationship to Islam: that is, under Islam the Dhimmi is a Christian or a Jew protected from being killed by Muslims *provided* the Dhimmi exhibits nothing but respect for, and subservience to, Islam.[322] As Bat Ye'or made clear so many times in the last forty years, the refusal to criticise Islam just strengthens the position of Islam's followers.[323] **The Kuffar who conceal the doctrines of war in Islam and conceal the history of conquests and subjugation might as well be Muslims. Some Muslims will tell us Kuffar the truth about Islamic doctrine and the history of Islam, and these Muslims get branded as "extremists". But our leaders are far worse than these extremists, because unlike the extremists, our leaders are systematically lying to their own people.** Up until the time The Grand Lie was promoted in the wake of 9/11 there were mainstream experts who had the ear of government. These experts made it clear that war is so fundamental to Islam that Muslims divide the world into "the world of Islam" and "the world of War".

Professor Samuel Huntington was an acclaimed political scientist and an advisor to an American President from the Democratic Party. In a book which was the talk of the quality newspapers when published in 1996, Huntington explained: "Muslims have traditionally divided the world into Dar al-Islam and Dar al-Harb, the abode of peace and the abode of war".[324] Nowadays, in horror that these advisories from the 1990s are coming true, Huntington is portrayed as some fringe thinker, but he could hardly have been more mainstream. **In the very same year that Huntington explained this clash of civilisations, at the start of a popular chronicle of the history of Islam, a Professor in France (who had published many books on the history of Islam) offered this definition: "Dar al-Islam: lands under Muslim rule as opposed to Dar al-Harb (the lands of war). It is every Muslim's duty to help extend the Dar al-Islam by violent or peaceful means (jihad)".**[325] These are just two examples at the end of more than a century of publications in English, French and German which explained Islam in the very same terms which the Muslim "extremists" used. Thus, on both sides of the Atlantic, just a few years before The Grand Lie began, people who were highly-educated had no reason to misunderstand that Islam is an ideology that sees itself as a religion of war. But with the collapse of the World Trade Center it became clear that the West had an enormous vulnerability from Muslims within our borders. So rather than use over a century of Western insight about Islam to educate the electorate, our highly-educated elite perpetrated The Grand Lie.

In addition to the mainstream scholar Professor Huntington, the equally mainstream and highly-credentialed Islamic scholar Professor Bernard Lewis warned that since Islam acknowledges only the single god of Islam, as far as Muslims are concerned there can only be one political system on earth: Islam.[326] Indeed, as far back as the 1970s, Professor Lewis was telling the West that it was a mistake to interpret Islam from our own Christian and secular perspective.

> Christianity, during the first formative centuries of its existence, was separate from and indeed antagonistic to the state with which it only later became involved. **Islam from the lifetime of its founder was the state,** and the identity of religion and government is indelibly stamped on the memories and awareness of the faithful from their own sacred writings, history, and experience [...] Muhammad did not die on the cross. **As well as a Prophet, he was a soldier and a statesman, the head of a state and the founder of an empire**, and his followers were sustained by a belief in the manifestation of divine approval through success and victory. **Islam was associated with power from the very beginning**, from the first formative years of the Prophet and his immediate successors. [...] **It was religion which distinguished those who belonged to the group and marked them off from those outside the group.** A Muslim Iraqi would feel far closer bonds with a non-Iraqi Muslim than with a non-Muslim Iraqi.[327]

There is more accuracy and insight to be found in this single passage from the 1970s than would be found in a whole year of contemporary commentary from our highly-educated elite. This passage does not come from an obscure scholarly journal, but from a magazine on politics and culture, a magazine that was so iconic to Americans that it was often mentioned in American movies and television programmes. Thus we see, that as late as the 1970s and early 1980s, our political leaders, academics and journalists were fully aware that Islam is a religion of war and not a religion of peace: it was inextricably intertwined with political power and an empire that spread from Lisbon to Afghanistan, with a legal system that sanctioned war against unbelievers, that sanctioned enslavement or apartheid for the Kuffar. Every day the "call to prayer" from mosques enjoins Muslims to "come to success", but as the Koran shows "success" is defined as entry to Paradise,[328] something that is only guaranteed to Jihadis. Thus even the call to prayer is a call to jihad.

In one of his very readable books from the early 1980s, Professor Lewis told us that jihad is the name given to the struggle to enforce Islamic domination on the rest of the world. It took the spectacular murder of thousands of Americans in 2001 before "jihad" was a word which would become known to most people in the West. Here is what Prof. Lewis said:

> The law relating to jihad, like the greater part of the sharia, received its classical form during the first century and a half of the Islamic era, when the Arab armies were advancing on France, Byzantium [Turkey], China and India.[329]

In the decades preceding the attack on the World Trade Center in 2001, there was basically no way that an informed individual in the West could have thought that Islam was a religion of peace. If someone looked at the works of scores of Muslim and Kuffar scholars it was as plain as day that Islam was a religion of war and domination. The only actions working against the public in the West understanding Islam with clarity was the ever-increasing number of translations of the Koran in the traditional order (i.e. the crudely encrypted order), an order which Muslims could decipher by asking the experts in their own community, experts who could explain the chronological order and say which verses had been cancelled. This prevalence of obscurantist Korans allowed the allies of Islamisation to deceive the public into thinking and hoping that the terrorism from Muslims inflicted initially on the Israelis as early as the 1970s, and then subsequently on the rest of the West, was not Islamic. **After 9/11 the sales of Korans in the West shot up,[330] with the public turning to this (encrypted) core text of Islam to try to grasp what was going on. The academic experts and the Christian clergy could have stepped in to explain all the secondary literature in English enabling the public to circumvent (to some degree) the encrypted commands of the traditional Koran. But the academics and the clergy remained silent. The betrayal of the people by the elite is probably unsurpassed in the last 1000 years of history in Western Europe.**

The more jihad the West has suffered, the more our leaders have lied to us and told us that Islam is a religion of peace. The more our civilisation is attacked by an enemy at home and abroad, the more our leaders have chosen to identify with the enemy, chosen to lie to the people on whose authority those leaders claim to act. The elite are working to ensure that we do nothing to stop the growth of a fifth column. In 2002, when politician Professor Pim Fortuyn in the Netherlands was murdered by a (Kuffar) Leftist, those in the West who spoke the truth about Islam had reason to fear assassination, now not just by Muslims but also by their own people. This was the stick, but there was also the carrot: universities being induced to take an apologist attitude towards Islam, with royalty from the oil-rich Islamic states funding politically-correct departments in universities in the

West.[331] Consequently, it fell to brave writers outside of academia – Andrew Bostom, Robert Spencer, Mark Steyn, Bat Ye'or, etc. – to fill the gap left by professional academics.

The elite try to minimise the impact of these brave independent researchers by branding them "Islamophobic". For example, Robert Spencer and Pamela Geller were banned from entering the UK by a supposedly "right wing" government, despite both banned authors supporting democracy and universal human rights, and both authors being opposed to violence.[332] Following further terrorist attacks on British people, the politician behind that ban (Theresa May) went on to repeat The Grand Lie: "Islam is a religion of peace". It's quite clear why the Quisling politicians do not want to allow into Britain people brave enough and knowledgeable enough to speak publicly the truth about Islam. **Some years later, as then Prime Minister, Theresa May visited the USA in an official capacity to meet the new President Donald Trump, and she just continued the refrain: "but of course, we should always be careful to distinguish between this extreme and hateful ideology, and the peaceful religion of Islam".[333] On her return to Britain, the politician who had banned entry to writers who had reminded the West of truths about Islam our ancestors had acknowledged from the eighth century to the twentieth century, PM May proceeded to denounce President Trump for his proposed "ban" on the citizens of certain Islamic states from entering the USA.[334]** The double-standards of Theresa May are absolutely breath-taking, but from the journalists and politicians whose job it is to criticise the party in power there came nothing but silence.

Independent researchers like Spencer and Geller were not alone in being targeted in this way by the Quisling British elite. Just a couple of years after those writers were banned from entering the UK, British MPs took a vote on whether or not Donald Trump (as presidential candidate) should be banned from entering the UK.[335] British MPs spent three hours debating this ban, which is more time than they spent in the previous three decades debating the industrial entrapment and rape of English girls by gangs of Muslims in Britain.[336] And the MPs staged this virtue-signalling debate because during his campaign Trump had stated that one of his policies for his administration would be to restrict immigration by Muslims whilst America came to understand the nature of the threat the country had been fighting for over twenty years. The man who was British Prime Minister during most of Trump's campaign, the man who had compared extreme Muslims with Nazis, intervened in the American election "claiming Mr Trump was 'stupid, divisive and wrong'", whilst more minor MPs called Trump "crazy".[337] The Muslim Mayor of London said the well-travelled 70 year-old billionaire Trump was "ignorant".[338] It is against normal etiquette for British politicians to intervene in the elections in the USA. It is not as though this debate on denying Trump entry to Britain was some joke on the part of the British MPs: just a few years earlier a democratically elected politician had been denied entry to the UK. In 2009 the UK government banned Geert Wilders,

Dutch MP and MEP and leader of the PVV (The Party for Freedom), from entering the country.[339] Wilders (who has lived under the protection of armed police for more than a decade because of the threat to his life from Muslims and Leftists) had been invited by a member of the British House of Lords to show his documentary film about the connection between Islam and terrorism. British politicians, who have spent so much time insulting the future President of the United States have never shown anything but submission to Islam and its followers.

In recent decades the only other small group of people who have offered a critical view of Islam are Muslims who emigrated to the West and who have abandoned Islam. You might expect that having been Muslims themselves these critics would not be side-lined, but you would be mistaken. Often at risk to their own lives, these apostates warned the public about what is in store for the West. Over twenty years ago, in the wake of The Rushdie Affair, Ibn Warraq warned us about the nature of Islam and the place of the Kuffar in Islam:

> Mankind is divided into two groups, Muslims and non-Muslims. The Muslims are members of the Islamic community, the umma, who possess territories in the Dar al-Islam, the Land of Islam, where the edicts of Islam are fully promulgated. **The non-Muslims are the Harbi, people of the Dar al-Harb, the Land of Warfare, any country belonging to the infidels that has not been subdued by Islam but that, nonetheless, is destined to pass into Islamic jurisdiction, either by conversion or by war (Harb). All acts of war are permitted in the Dar al-Harb. Once the Dar al-Harb has been subjugated, the Harbi become prisoners of war.**[340]

At the end of the twentieth century, devout Muslims were blowing up bookshops and murdering those connected with the publication of Salman Rushdie's novel, yet at the same time here was another ex-Muslim (like Rushdie) explicitly warning the general public how the Muslim world-view does not share our concern with peace and universal human rights, but rather that Islam fundamentally divides the world in terms of war and peace, unbeliever and believer. But there is no trace that Ibn Warraq's lucid, highly-relevant and compendious explanation of Islam was even reviewed by the British newspapers.[341] The warnings could hardly have been made any clearer or with stronger evidence than is contained in books like this by Ibn Warraq. Yet the political class were not only ignoring such books, they went on to actively try to silence those who warned of such things (such as the bans on Geert Wilders, Robert Spencer, etc. preventing them entering Britain). Within Britain the government who were in power for a decade following the publication of Ibn Warraq's book, tried over and over to pass laws criminalising people who offended Muslims.[342]

When Ibn Warraq explained that Islam has always divided the world into Muslims versus non-Muslims this should have come as no surprise. If one looks to the established apologists for Islam in universities in the West (such as Professor Watt in Edinburgh), we can find that in the 1960s this Islamic division of the world was being taught.[343] However, given the lack of critical information about Islam available to those outside universities, instead of Ibn Warraq's exposition being widely discussed by the media in the aftermath of The Rushdie Affair, what the people of the West were given was deception and confusion. And a decade after Ibn Warraq's warning, thousands of people in the West were dead or injured from terrorist attacks by Muslims; in the attacks of September 11th 2001, but in the siege of a school in Beslan (2004), the attacks on the transport system of Madrid (2004) and of London (2005). In a series of books between 2004 and 2008 another ex-Muslim, Dr. Patrick Sookhdeo, also warned the West of this link between jihad and the Muslim conception of the World of War and the World of Islam:

> **Linked to the concept of jihad is the division of the world into two domains: the House of Islam (Dar al-Islam) and the House of War (Dar al-Harb). Muslims are supposed to wage jihad to change the House of War (where non-Muslims are politically dominant) into the House of Islam, politically dominated by Muslims.**[344]

But no matter how many die in terrorist attacks by jihadis, no matter what risks ex-Muslims and independent experts take to warn us, the Quisling elite ignore all the evidence and insist that Islam is a religion of peace.

It is as if the politicians, clergy, journalists and academics are wilfully blind. To show how the narrative espoused by the elite is deliberately oblivious to explanations of Islamic doctrine and history, consider the use of the word "harb" (from Dar al-Harb). If one searches *The Times'* archive for the word "harb" from the start of The Rushdie Affair (1990) until twenty years later, when Dr. Sookhdeo published the third of three books on jihad, the number of occurrences of the word "harb" can be counted on the fingers of one hand! With only three articles in twenty years by *The Times'* professional journalists, in each case the concept "Dar al-Harb" is presented as if it was the rambling of some Islamic lunatic,[345] someone holding onto a concept that only applied in the middle ages, rather than a concept which permeated all Islamic thought for over 1000 years, a concept which was being discussed by Western academic experts on Islam into the 1990s.

What this shows is that the educated elite have made a sustained effort to keep the public deceived about the nature of Islam. Whilst the West was undergoing a rapid social and ideological shift, apart from some specialist academic literature, there was a total dearth of information about even the most basic structure of the Islamic view of the world (i.e. dividing the world into war and the world of submission to Islam). There is a virtual wall between the view of Islam explained by Western scholars throughout the twentieth-century (even when this view was in popular, paperback books), and the view provided in the

twenty-first century by journalists, clergy and politicians (the people who stand between the expert view and the general public). The West has become increasingly Islamized in the decades following The Rushdie Affair; authors and artists have been terrified into not broaching any subject related to Islam;[346] there have been terrorist attacks at home and massively expensive wars fought abroad. It cannot be an accident that even *The Times*, a newspaper with one of the greatest reputations for quality journalism in the world, makes not one attempt in twenty years to seriously discuss the key ideological division the religion of war has toward Western civilisation. In *The Times* there were no reviews of *Why I Am Not A Muslim*, and the only article that came even close to a review of any of the books by the eminent Dr. Sookhdeo was a snide opinion piece.[347]

In his book *Global Jihad: the Future in the Face of Militant Islam* **Dr. Sookhdeo goes on to point out that in Islam the attitude of war towards non-Muslims is an attitude of permanent war: "unconditional jihad against all non-Muslims in Dar al-Harb is accepted as applicable today and until the end of time".**[348] Despite *The Times* presenting Dr. Sookhdeo as some kind of idiosyncratic thinker, Sookhdeo's arguments were entirely within the mainstream view among scholars of Islam in the twentieth century,[349] and even as far back as the nineteenth century.[350] Thus, whilst devout Muslims were telling journalists from *The Times* about Islam's fundamental distinction between the world of Islam and the world of war, they were being portrayed as fringe lunatics. When apostates from Islam explained this same distinction at great length in their modern and scholarly books on Islam (apostates who have put their lives at risk to warn the rest of the West), these ex-Muslims were either ignored or they were mocked. All the while journalists from one of the most prestigious newspapers in the world were ignoring the fact that the entire tradition of scholarship on Islam in the West agreed with the importance of this fundamental distinction. **How could the elite group of Quislings pull off The Grand Lie that "Islam is a religion of peace", when Islam itself fundamentally divides the world into Muslims and the world of those with whom Muslims are at war?**

Looking Over The Wall Of Fake News

"Exhort the believers to fight [...] (the disbelievers) are a folk without intelligence."

Koran 8:65

As far as Islam is concerned, in the World of War, there are no innocents: every non-Muslim is a legitimate target for death or enslavement.[351] In recent decades we in the West have had a few brave independent experts explain to us the doctrinal basis for all the terrorist attacks by Muslims. Whether the experts are atheists, ex-Muslims, Christians or Jews these brave people risk assassination by Muslims and Leftists, all because they are filling the vacuum left by professional academics. Yet instead of getting praise, these experts have been ignored by our Quisling politicians and journalists. What these independent authors say comes as shocking news to those individuals who discover their books and end up seeing proof that Islam is the opposite of a religion of peace. Any honest and educated Muslim will admit that from year one of the Islamic calendar, and in all the subsequent centuries, Islam has been at war with all that is not Islam. As we prove below Islamic texts are proud of the warrior conduct of Mohammed, so any Muslim who says this is untrue is either ignorant or is a liar.

As Muslims are authorized within Islamic doctrine to lie and to deceive non-Muslims, instead of amplifying the lies of Muslims and the Quisling politicians it was the responsibility of journalists to expose The Grand Lie. Journalists should have been disseminating the knowledge of ex-Muslims such as Ibn Warraq and Patrick Sookhdeo (particularly since the books by these apostates were in accord with the Islamic scholarly tradition *and* the Western scholarly tradition). Instead, **what the Western media have done is to only permit Muslims to speak about Islam: it as if in World War II only Nazis were permitted an opinion on Nazism.** It was not only from ex-Muslims that the elite in the West must have known of the centrality of jihad in Islam. Professor Guillaume's translation into English of Ibn Ishaq's biography of Mohammed first appeared in 1955, published by Oxford University Press. This is the most authoritative biography of Mohammed, the biography on which all other biographies of Mohammed depend. Without even getting passed the Table of Contents, one can see that part III is entitled "Muhammad's Migration to Medina, His Wars, Triumph and Death".[352] How could our politicians begin to look at core Islamic texts like these, and then go on to tell us that "Islam is a religion of peace"? How could journalists not have seen The Grand Lie for what it was, as soon as they even glanced at Ibn Ishaq's biography of Mohammed (the most authoritative Muslim biography of Mohammed)?

In his translation of this all-important biography of Mohammed, Guillaume's Introduction points out that throughout the scholarship by Muslims on Islam, this biography of Mohammed was often known as *The Book of Campaigns* (i.e. the book of military battles).[353] In 1981 another world-renowned scholar, Fred Donner, published his book *Early Islamic Conquests*, which details the wars, invasions and conquests in Arabia, Syria and Iraq by Mohammed and the first Muslims.[354] In 1999 scholar Reuven Firestone published *Jihad: The Origin of Holy War in* Islam, which shows that before 9/11 academics were openly publishing books on Jihad as holy war and how this was essential to the success of Islam.[355] But one does not need to be an academic who works through esoteric tomes: in 1996 a professor of the history of Islam published a coffee-table book of snippets about *Great Dates in Islamic History*, which by page 5 has Mohammed expelling and massacring Jewish people from their lands in Arabia (for the crime of not submitting to the rule of Islam).[356] Towards the end of this 370 page book of snippets of Islamic history, is listed the first bombing of the World Trade Center by the followers of an Egyptian Sheikh.[357] **How is Islam a religion of peace when a book dedicated to listing the "great dates" of this religion begins with genocide in Arabia, and ends fourteen-hundred years later with a Muslim bishop trying to murder thousands of Americans in New York? In between these two events are listed battle after battle, slaughter after slaughter.** Would a book on the most significant dates in the history of Buddhism list armed conflict on page after page after page? How is it that no journalists have challenged The Grand Lie, when any look through the shelves of a university library or through the pages of Amazon's website would provide evidence which contradicted the ludicrous idea that "Islam is a religion of peace"?

It is only with a significant and growing Muslim population in the West that many Muslims have begun concealing that Islam is a religion of war. Throughout the twentieth century Muslims living in other parts of the world were themselves proudly publishing details of Mohammed's wars, in titles which offered no mistaking their content. From 1939 to 1962 and beyond, Muhammad Hamidullah published (in French, Urdu, English, Arabic, Farsi and Turkish) *Battlefields of the Prophet Muhammad: A Contribution to Muslim Military History.*[358] There was even a book by a Muslim army officer the title of which could not possibly tie the Koran and war more closely. Brigadier S.K. Malik's, *The Quranic Concept of War* (1979), makes it clear that Islam is the opposite of a religion of peace.[359] In the first paragraph of the Foreword (by the President of the Islamic State of Pakistan), General Zia ul-Haq commends jihad to the Muslim civilian and the soldier alike. This Foreword is immediately preceded by a map of Mohammed's battles, entitled "Military Operations: 625-632 AD", showing that the violence of Islam is not something Muslims grafted onto Islam, but is something which they see as being the foundation of the religion. Mohammed died in 632 AD (according to the core texts of Islam, as a result of being poisoned by a woman whose own family had been massacred by Mohammed).[360] The first paragraph of the Preface to *The Quranic Concept of War* says the book attends to "special features of [sic] Holy Prophet's military campaigns". Does that sound like a religion of peace? Can you imagine a book talking about the military campaigns of Christianity, and tracing these back to the wars fought by Jesus himself?

These books by Muslims on Islamic military thought, based on the behaviour of the founder of Islam, were not just vanity projects. Malik's book on the Quranic concept of war was republished in 1992, whilst Hamidullah's book *The Battlefields of the Prophet Muhammad* was published many times in many different languages throughout the twentieth century (mostly languages where the majority of speakers are Muslims). These facts demonstrate there was a ready audience for books on this view of Islam, long before life in the West was transformed by devout Muslims murdering 3,000 Americans in September 2001. **Since throughout the twentieth-century both Muslim experts and Western scholars were openly discussing Islam as a religion of war, it took an extraordinary act of**

determination from our politicians to deceive the public with the claim "Islam is a religion of peace", as terrorist attack after terrorist attack piled the corpses of innocent members of the public onto the heap of dead victims at the start of the twenty-first century. **And at the time we are writing, there is still no sign that any member of the elite is prepared to contest The Grand Lie.** Those politicians who have been prepared to expose The Grand Lie could be numbered on the fingers of one hand. They live under the threat of execution from devout Muslims or from the fascist Left. Those brave, independent academics who speak the truth about Islam are denigrated by the elite as racists, fascists or just the vague but offensive term "far right" (even as the freedom of these courageous dissidents is curtailed by the threat of assassination by the soldiers of Allah). The dissidents are smeared as evil whilst their would-be killers are concealed in a thicket of 'moderate Muslims'. The most notable example of a dissident is Geert Wilders, the Dutch MP whom the British government banned from entering the UK, although it is hard to tell if history will even remember any of these dissidents.[361]

Since Muslims have themselves proudly written books recording that Mohammed only succeeded by becoming a warlord and slave-monger, perhaps we in the West should be able to expect our own writers of military history to tell us Kuffar the truth about the fate that Islam has in store for us?

Even Military Analysts Have Been Useless

"Allah hath given you victory on many [battle] fields"

Koran 9:25

In the immediate aftermath of the attack on the World Trade Center, the American Army War College Foundation (which trains military officers) published a book called *War, Terror and Peace in the Qu'ran and Islam*. You would be forgiven for expecting this book to be a hard-hitting critique of Islam and its doctrines of eternal war against non-Muslims. This book was written by a sociologist and ex-Marine named Timothy Schwartz-Barcott, and the Preface was written by a former Commander in Chief of the United States Central Command. The book acknowledges the input of a long list of academics and retired military officers. The author explains his education in military history and the philosophy of world religions. He explains how the attack on the World Trade Center sent him

> spending afternoons [...] leafing through the dozens of editions of Qur'ans, Qur'an commentaries, and concordances. Soon it became apparent that there were many verses in the Qur'an about war and peace that were difficult to find without a very careful and systematic reading.[362]

One might think that following the mass murder of his fellow Americans on 11th September 2001, including an attack on the Pentagon itself, that this soldier-turned-sociologist would make a major contribution to the West's understanding Islam as a religion of war. Far from it.

Schwartz-Barcott's book has an entire chapter on the verses from the Koran relating to peace and war, and this is described by the author as "the heart of this book".[363] He uses the Pickthall translation (as we do), on the basis that Pickthall was "a widely respected British scholar who converted to Islam".[364] In his discussion of these verses, the ex-Marine often offers his own moderating interpretation of the verse[365] (as if Muslims care what a Kuffar offers as an interpretation of the Koran). Schwartz-Barcott's entire project of looking for a peaceful spin on Islam is an exercise in futility, since he seems to be completely unaware of the concept of abrogation: verses which he thinks have ambiguities allowing him to find less violent interpretations are also verses which have been cancelled by abrogation.[366] That these violent verses have been cancelled does not mean that the Koran and Islam are less violent than Schwartz-Barcott realises: the verse which does the cancelling is Koran 9:5 ("the verse of Sword"), one of the most violent verses in the Koran! The verse of the sword is of such overwhelming significance that it cancels over 120 other verses in the Koran (it is the single most important abrogating verse). It is no accident that Saudi Arabia and jihadis around the world not only kill by beheading with a sword, but they also fly a flag with a sword on it. They understand the significance of the verse of the sword.

Any project that attempts to offer an understanding of the Koran without explaining abrogation and without showing which verses have been cancelled is a project that is doomed to failure.[367] When you turn to our presentation of the Koran, which begins with the last things Mohammed said, you will see that the verse of the sword is on the first page. No other Koran in history has put the Koran into reverse chronological order. Thus, our presentation of the Koran is the first Koran in history which allows the reader to see Islam from the most important perspective (the most important view for both Muslims and for the victims of Islam), seeing the Koran as it is seen by governments like Saudi Arabia and by jihadi groups like Islamic State. The part of the Koran which cancels out over 120 other parts is usually hidden away in the midst of verses which it overrides.

This ex-soldier's book contains an Appendix where he lists 214 "major" Muslim battles (his list does not even start until 633AD, the year after Mohammed died). The first ten of the battles listed were attacks initiated by "the religion of peace". Indeed, after the first ten battles following Mohammed's death, and other cultures started to fight back, from the first thirty-six battles listed, twenty-eight of them were attacks initiated by "the religion of peace". If one considers the attacks undertaken when Mohammed was alive, then we see a history with scores of battles initiated by the followers of Islam, and it was other cultures who were fighting defensive wars.

After some 350 pages rambling through hundreds of the later wars of Muslims against all manner of non-Muslims (with Muslims being the aggressors in almost all conflicts), *War, Terror and Peace in the Qu'ran and Islam* ends with an epilogue rather than a conclusion, a plea for peace and understanding. The key item of this epilogue is the idea that the Koran *could* be read in ways other than traditional literalism:

> **In the future the Qu'ran might be re-organized and recited in ways that can be very revealing, such as by the historical chronology of the suras, or by certain topics, such as instructions for making peace or for waging war".[368]**

It is as if the author had no idea that the Koran had been published in chronological order in English, French and German in the nineteenth and twentieth centuries.[369] **It seems the ex-Marine hopes that putting the Koran in chronological order might make Islam look more peaceful, when in fact the reverse is the case.** Schwartz-Barcott's book came from the press of a major military college, and its subtitle makes it clear that its intended audience was "military and government leaders". Yet it offers its intended audience nothing of any value. This is how ill-served the people of the West have been by our experts in the age of The Grand Lie.

It is hard to estimate how much damage this form of misleading presentation has caused since 2001. For example, in his Foreword Schwartz-Barcott says that people quote selectively from the Koran to find segments to legitimate their pre-existing violent aims:

> Their purpose is to use the Qur'an, and specific verses of the Qur'an, so selectively as to legitimate their own violent schemes to recruit, motivate, and instruct others according to their purpose. In all likelihood this is exactly what Osama bin Laden and the Saudi shaykh [sic] were doing at dinner when they quoted the Qur'an...[370]

To this academic it is not devout Muslims' profound understanding of the Koran which drives them to violence (we can be sure that Bin Laden and the Sheikhs were made to memorise the Koran as children).[371] No, to this soldier-turned-academic, Muslims must abuse the Koran in order to justify some pre-existing desire for violence and mass-murder (thus, he completely ignores the core texts of Islam which portray the founder of Islam as a warlord)! On this view, the Koran and Islam are innocent, the world's problems with thousands of terrorist attacks by devout Muslims are because some people are simply inexplicably evil, and it is inconceivable that their actions were the result of the most enduring violent political ideology in history. We are to believe that being immersed in the fundamentals of Islam (where the promise that to die killing unbelievers is the only guaranteed way for believers to avoid an eternity of burning torture) plays no part in prompting Muslims to kill unbelievers. All this in a book on war and peace in Islam, produced by an

American military publisher, a book supposed to serve as an intellectual guide to military and political leaders in the wake of the most shocking act of mass murder in the history of the United States! The ideology is not to blame; the cause is random bad people. An amazingly vacuous and unhelpful analysis. But then perhaps his military publisher would have refused a book that told the truth.

Given that academics and military publishers are providing this kind of misleading explanation concerning the role of war in Islam, is it any wonder that the more terrorist attacks there are by Muslims, the less impact the violence has on stopping the importation of Muslims? Serious academic works have addressed political leaders telling them that there is no connection between the doctrines of Islam and the acts of terrorist violence carried out by a variety of people; people whose only common feature was that they subscribed to the same doctrines. It seems that even after traumatic terrorist attacks in their own country, some of the toughest soldiers in our society find it inconceivable that a religion could motivate people to mass-murder. This seems to be an impossibility because people in the West are assuming Islam must be a religion like Buddhism or Christianity. This kind of assumption was precisely what Professor Bernard Lewis was warning against decades ago. Instead, when we turn to what the Muslim scholars have said about Islam throughout history and what our own historical texts show us of Islam, **what we should be doing is questioning: is Islam even a religion?**[372] **The idea of a religion of war seems like a contradiction. But what we must understand is that Islam is a set of doctrines which glorify war, genocide and apartheid.** If a highly-educated politician and subsequent Prime Minister of Great Britain can say that Muslim fundamentalists are like Nazis, should we perhaps be considering Islam to be more like a political ideology than it is like a spiritual doctrine such as Buddhism?

Islam's Relentless Hatred Of Unbelievers

> *"those who disbelieve, among the People of the Scripture [Christians and Jews] and the idolaters, will abide in fire of hell. They are the worst of created beings. (And) lo! those who believe and do good works [Muslims] are the best of created beings."*
>
> *Koran 98:6-98:7*

In the latter half of the twentieth century the West was flooded with scores of jumbled-up publications of the Koran, making the doctrines of Islam contradictory and hard to fathom. These editions of the Koran in the traditional (encrypted) order replaced the principal translation of the Koran in English, which was a chronological Koran which made it abundantly clear that Islam is a religion of war. As we discussed earlier, in the immediate aftermath of World War II, Winston Churchill compared Islam to Nazism. As we all know, National Socialism is a byword for the hatred of those who are different. But when the West's foremost historian of Islam identified the pre-eminent ideology whose believers were indoctrinated to kill those who were different, it was not Nazism to which he referred, but Islam. Thus, Professor Bernard Lewis said:

> just as the insider is defined by his acceptance of Islam, so in the same way the outsider is defined by his rejection of Islam. He is the kafir, "the unbeliever" [...] **from the time of the Prophet to the present day, the ultimate definition of the Other, the alien outsider and presumptive enemy, has been kafir, the unbeliever.**[373]

Could this world-famous expert on Islam have made any clearer the threat that the importation of Islam poses to the West? Someone who was a highly-educated adult throughout World War II, someone who lived through the Nuremberg trials, through the trial of Adolf Eichmann, a man who lived through the Cold War and the threat of nuclear annihilation: when it came to identifying the doctrine which was foremost in enshrining hatred of those who are different, he did not choose National Socialism as the paradigm case, but Islam.

Teachers, journalists, publishers, academics, clergy, politicians do not point out what the expert opinion of Islam was throughout the previous 150 years. Instead they repeat (or at least fail to challenge) The Grand Lie. They attempt to stifle any critique of Islam by bleating about multiculturalism, a doctrine which is ideologically incompatible with Islam. Not only is it incompatible in theory, it has been incompatible since Mohammed had his first "revelation": Arabia was multicultural (consisting of Pagans, Jews, Christians), and this very tolerance allowed Islam to grow and thrive, until Mohammed had a sufficiently large army that he could eradicate all that was not Islam. Even the core texts of Islam make this clear. But you and your family are not to be told this, you are to be deceived into thinking a religion of war is a religion of peace. You have been betrayed.

If you only flick through the pages of our Koran, you will see that we have highlighted the oppositions between believers and unbelievers. You do not need to take the word of Professor Lewis, as you can quickly see for yourself from our chronological Koran that on almost every single page of the Koran the unbeliever or the hypocrite is contrasted unfavourably with the believing Muslim. This contrast is frequently accompanied by descriptions of Hell (where unbelievers are destined to go), versus descriptions of the Gardens of Paradise (access to which is reserved for only the most devout and obedient Muslims). In our Koran these contrasts between believer and unbeliever have been marked out[374] to serve as a visualization of this opposition which permeates the Islamic view of the world (in around 1500 distinctions between believers and unbelievers in the Koran for every two references to Muslims, there is one reference to non-Muslims and this reference towards us Kuffar is disparaging or threatening). In fact, the single most common theme in the Koran is the opposition between the believing Muslim and the unbelieving Kuffar, something our Koran allows you to see for yourself. This theme is more pervasive in the Koran than the prayer rituals, or the nature of Halal food, or the clothing requirements. It is the underlying theme throughout the Koran. The fundamental driver of Islam is the idea that Judgement Day is coming and those who do not follow Islam will be going to Hell, yet the opposition between Muslims and non-Muslims is three times more prevalent than references to Judgement Day. In the value-system of the Koran belief is essentially connected to The Truth, whilst non-Muslims are classed as liars and traitors; believing and obeying Islam will be rewarded by an eternity in Paradise for Muslims, whilst for questioning or rejecting Islam everyone else will be punished by an eternity of torture in Hell. Leftism and multiculturalism brainwash our societies with the claim that there is no truth and everything is relative, but Islam is obsessed with the enforcement of values which Muslims see as the absolute truth. What hope is there for integration or multiculturalism when the Koran is obsessed with Muslims despising non-Muslims, when the most pivotal verse of the Koran is the Verse of the Sword which calls for Muslims to kill unbelievers in order to eradicate unbelief?[375]

This opposition to the unbeliever is found not just throughout the Koran but throughout the doctrines of Islam and the history of Islam. In this religion of war everything is divided into being either in the World of Islam or the World of War. Whilst Western values, enshrined in the Universal Declaration of Human Rights, seek to treat all of mankind as belonging to one group, Islam is riven throughout with the distinction between Muslim and non-Muslim. There is no universal concept of equality or fairness or justice in Islam. It is no accident that in 1990 the Islamic world rejected the Universal Declaration of Human Rights. As with so many things concerning Islam, our governments, our journalists and even our human rights organisations chose to keep the public ignorant of this historic event.[376]

Remember, as you start to read the following Koran, the first things you are reading are the very last commands spoken by Mohammed, commands which Muslims believe are the unchanging word of Allah, valid for all eternity and which no later Islamic leader can ever rescind. These are verses commanding war and slaughter for those unbelievers who will not convert to Islam or who will not agree to be subjugated by the rules imposed upon the unbeliever by Muslims. For decades, this view of Islam has been concealed from us by our political leaders, our journalists, our religious leaders. Yet as we have shown, this view of Islam was the standard view of Islam for more than one thousand years, up to and including the end of the twentieth century. The deception of you and your children means you are being led further and further down the road to a violent future. The deception that Islam is a religion of peace is contradicted by the example of devout jihadis who are killing your countrymen, these devout Muslims telling you they are doing this because they are following what the Koran commands them to do. The money being spent to pre-empt the terrorism from jihadis will only last so long. When this money cannot keep up with the number of Muslims imported into your country, you and your children will be living in a very dangerous world. That money could instead have been spent ensuring that the electorates in our supposed democracies knew the truth about Islam, using the voting booth to avert the violence into which our civilization will descend. When you read the Koran contained in this book you will see instantly why these jihadis are happy to kill themselves in the act of killing us Kuffar. Prepare to be shocked as the concept of "religion of peace" is turned upside-down. But the next time your child comes home from school, brainwashed by teachers into mindlessly reciting that "Islam is a religion of peace", be prepared to take this book to parent-teacher meetings and publicly expose this state-funded deception.

When David Cameron became the Prime Minister of Britain in 2010, no politician or journalist thought to expose the contradiction between the Cameron of 2005 (Islamic extremists are like Nazis) and the Cameron of 2015 (Islam is a religion of peace). No academic thought to contradict Cameron's lies by pointing to the centuries of scholarship both from Muslims and from Western scholars which flatly contradicted The Grand Lie. Pope Benedict XVI, the only religious leader in the West to point out even an iota of truth about Islam, was met with violence and political pressure; he then retired, something unheard of in the Catholic Church for nearly 1000 years.[377] **Whether Muslims admit it to the Kuffar or not, Muslims who know the Koran or who know the history of Islam have no doubt that Islam is a religion of war. Only the Kuffar are being kept in the dark, led by our own elite into a future of violence or brutal serfdom.**

If this Introduction and the Koran contained in this book fail to persuade you of the dire threat to you and your descendants as Muslims become an increasing proportion of people in the West, then Western civilisation does not stand a chance. As more and more people are killed by Muslims (who are following the rules of a religion we are told to respect), then we do not know what is required to make you open your eyes and take steps to avert the coming disaster. In this Koran not only have we made clear the scores of commands to Muslims to conduct war in order to attain entry to Paradise, but we have highlighted that the Islamic world-view is built on the division between Muslim and non-Muslim, Islam (belief) and Kuffar (unbelief). Our focus has been on the unending state of war which exists between Islam and all that is not Islam, a war that exists until Islam dominates. We have not had the space to discuss how Muslims kill other Muslims in the name of Islam (but that too is a form of jihad). For instance, the classic manual of sharia law (found in public libraries in the United Kingdom) has this to say: "When a person who has reached puberty and is sane voluntarily apostatizes from Islam, he deserves to be killed".[378] This is why there is no reform in Islam: as soon as anyone tries to reform Islam they are accused of having apostatized from Islam, and their life is in danger. This is just another manifestation of Islam's war against all that is not Islam. Muslims are publishing and buying books calling for the execution of those who leave Islam, and our governments are stocking such books in public libraries so that as many Muslims as possible can convince themselves of the need to kill those who leave Islam. And our media and politicians have nothing to say about such phenomena.

When discussing with his descendants if they should flee Britain after the Muslim terrorist attack on London in 2005, **here is what a retired British politician said he would be doing if he was still a politician**:

> **I'd be so alarmed by the situation [with Islam in Britain] I'd do everything possible to suggest it was under control. It's up to politicians to play mood music in a crisis, and up to the people to understand that there's little else governments can do. The last thing they can say is that we face a threat to which we can see no end because it's based on a fundamental clash of cultures. On the IRA we told the truth, on the Islamic problem, we lie.**[379]

Remember, a man who was a senior government Minister is saying this in a book in which he supports his descendants fleeing Britain, to move to a country where Muslims are not so far on the path to domination. It seems quite clear that this retired MP fully understands Islam and the civilizational threat faced by the West. If he understands it and admits he would be lying to the public about what he knew, we must conclude that our current politicians all understand the problem is Islam, but they would prefer to sound liberal and let *your* descendants face a far more violent and illiberal future.

In 2019 Theresa May was succeeded by Boris Johnson as the Prime Minister of the United Kingdom. **Here is what Boris Johnson (who won scholarships to study at Eton and at Oxford) had to say about Muslims and Islam** some fifteen years before he came to be chosen to be Prime Minister by MPs and the members of his party:

> **Remember what it says in the Holy Koran...** 'slay the unbelievers wherever you can find them... besiege them, and lie in ambush for them everywhere... **We will perform jihad against the Kuffar**, the unbelievers'.[380]

After Muslims committed a heinous terrorist attack in London in 2005, this future British Prime Minister described Islam as "the most viciously sectarian of all religions in its heartlessness towards unbelievers".[381] A decade after informing his readers about what motivates Islamic terrorism, Johnson turned-face and repeated The Grand Lie of President Bush, with the future Prime Minister proclaiming that "Islam is a religion of peace".[382] **Johnson went from describing Islam as "viciously sectarian" to describing it as "a religion of peace"!**

If you turn to the first page of our reverse chronological Koran you will see Koran 9:5, the very part of the Koran which matches what Johnson says in this quotation from his book: "slay the idolaters wherever ye find them, and take them (captive), and besiege them, and prepare for them each ambush". The rest of our chronological Koran is highlighted to show you how pervasive is the hatred for the Kuffar and how pervasive is the theme that Muslims are rewarded by Allah for conducting Jihad. We're not politicians, so we are not in the business of lying to you. We believe in real democracy, and we believe that in a real democracy the people must be able to make informed decisions. You cannot make these decisions if the politicians and the media are continually lying to you, and the schools are systematically lying to your children.

If you still do not believe what you have seen in this Introduction or from our presentation of this standard translation of the Koran put into chronological order, then we advise you to read the material referenced in the Notes at the end of the book. If you remain unconvinced then we do not believe there is anything other than your personal experience of violence which will convince you. You will have to discover the brute reality for yourself. You and your offspring are expendable. Every year hundreds of thousands of those who have the skills to enable them to find a new life abroad are emigrating, with this evacuation most manifest in European countries where the problem with Islam is worst.[383] Those who can are leaving for countries where the problem with Islam is not (yet) so serious. Western governments can conceal the brain drain by ensuring that immigration figures exceed emigration figures, even whilst a government claims year after year that it is committed to the opposite policy.[384]

Knowledge is power. The elite do not want you to have power, because then they will have to implement the means to protect your family. Or they must give up the riches that come with that power, and step aside for those who will do what is required. Whilst politicians and journalists trot out The Grand Lie and pretend that violent Islam is only a twentieth century phenomenon, **let these words about the Koran from William Gladstone, a great nineteenth-century British Prime Minister, ring in your ears: "So long as there is this book, there will be no peace in the world"**.[385] As you turn to look at the Koran as the experts on Islam see it, ask yourself who is giving you the better explanation concerning the readiness of Muslims to kill in the name of Islam: contemporary politicians or the ghosts of democratic leaders from the nineteenth and twentieth centuries. **Those who tell you that "Islam is a religion of peace" have aligned themselves with Islam and they are in the business of subjugating your descendants. They mean that there will be peace when there is no democracy and when your children have been subjugated by Islam.**

One last thing: if you think our book explaining why Muslims kill for Islam is a book promoting murder, then you are so deeply indoctrinated that you cannot tell the difference between the criticism of evil and the endorsement of evil.

.

CHRONOLOGICAL KORAN

**A Re-ordering of the
Pickthall Translation**

Brief Guide To The Text

This translation of the Koran was first published in 1930 by a British man. He demonstrated his conversion to Islam by changing his name to "Muhammed Pickthall". Publications of his translation normally conceal his conversion by giving his name as "Marmaduke". That the translator was a covert Muslim is reason to assume that the translation errs on the side of deceiving the reader when possible (most readers would have been non-Muslims). Unlike the illogical chapter ordering in his original translation, we have put the chapters in *reverse chronological order*, which means the first verses you see on turning the page are the last verses Mohammed "received" from Allah.[386] On that first page you will see Chapter 9 Verse 5, which is known as "The Verse of the Sword", and this verse is of huge importance, because it cancels more verses than any other.

Another change we have made to Pickthall's translation is that **the most important verses of the Koran for non-Muslims have been printed in a larger, bolder font making it easier for you to see them (for example, Islam's commands of violence in the pursuit of the subjugation of non-Muslims)**. The Koran has been split into two parts: the later part (which is the violent part of Islam), and the earlier part (the non-violent part). With the non-violent part of Islam, Mohammed attracted no more than 150 followers in thirteen years; when Mohammed turned Islam into a violent, predatory, politicized religion he acquired over 10,000 followers in less than ten years. So, for us non-Muslims, the intended victims of Islam, it is obvious that this later part of the Koran is the most important. **So, if you are only going to read part of the Koran, we urge you to read the first part, called here *The Later Koran – Mohammed's Success*.** Our aim is that you should understand the threat to non-Muslims within minutes of reading this Koran rather than you spend months trying to wade through the traditional jumbled-up (encrypted) Koran.

Remember, that any verse which says something like "strive in Allah's way" is in fact a verse of poetry which is commanding Muslims to conduct jihad.[387] Any reference to "Gardens" is a reference to the Paradise of the after-life (a place with rivers flowing with fresh milk and wine, surrounded by fruit trees, an oasis). In Islam the only guaranteed entry to Paradise is to die fighting for Islam. In the doctrines of Islam, unbelievers burn in Hell; only those Muslims who die as jihadis are guaranteed entry to Gardens of Paradise. To show how Islam is obsessed with the opposition between belief in Islam versus other beliefs (religious, secular, political, atheistic), all words referring to the opposition between Muslims (believers) versus non-Muslims (disbelievers, idolaters) have been rendered in this kind of typeface: **BELIEVERS**. [Where we summarize some highly significant or poetic part of a verse, we enclose that summary in square brackets, as we have done with this sentence.]

Towards the end of this Koran you will encounter the earlier verses, some of which have been marked as "~~cancelled~~". Verses marked in this way are cancelled (abrogated) because they are in contradiction with later verses. This is why knowing the chronological order of the Koran is crucial to understanding Islam. We follow the order used by tanzil.net (see Appendix 1).

THE LATER KORAN – MOHAMMED'S SUCCESS

Chapter 110 - Succour

110:1 When Allah's succour and the *TRIUMPH* cometh
110:2 And thou seest mankind entering *THE RELIGION OF ALLAH* in troops,
110:3 Then hymn the praises of thy Lord, and seek forgiveness of Him. Lo! He is ever ready to show mercy.

Chapter 9 - Repentance

9:1 ~~Freedom from obligation (is proclaimed) from Allah and His messenger toward those of the idolaters with whom ye made a treaty.~~ [Cancelled by verse 9:5][388]
9:2 Travel freely in the land four months, and know that *YE CANNOT ESCAPE ALLAH* and that Allah will confound the **DISBELIEVERS** (in His Guidance).
9:3 And a proclamation from Allah and His messenger to all men on the day of the Greater Pilgrimage that *ALLAH IS FREE FROM OBLIGATION TO THE IDOLATERS, AND (SO IS) HIS MESSENGER.* So, if ye repent, it will be better for you; but if ye are averse, then know that *YE CANNOT ESCAPE ALLAH*. Give tidings (O Muhammad) of *A PAINFUL DOOM TO THOSE WHO DISBELIEVE*,
9:4 *EXCEPTING* those of the **IDOLATERS** with whom ye (**MUSLIMS**) have a *TREATY*, and who have since abated nothing of your right *NOR HAVE SUPPORTED ANYONE AGAINST YOU*. (As for these), fulfil their treaty to them till their term. Lo! Allah loveth those who keep their duty (unto Him).

9:5 *THEN, WHEN* the sacred months have passed, *SLAY THE IDOLATERS [KILL THE NON-MUSLIMS] WHEREVER YE FIND THEM*, and *TAKE THEM (CAPTIVE)* [enslave them], and *BESIEGE THEM*, and prepare for them each *AMBUSH*. But if they repent and establish worship and pay the poor-due, then leave their way free. Lo! Allah is Forgiving, Merciful. [The treaty in Koran 9:4 is to be _ignored_ when the holy months have passed, even though those the unbelievers have done nothing against Muslims.]

9:6 And if anyone of the **IDOLATERS** seeketh thy protection (O Muhammad), then protect him so that he may hear the Word of Allah, and afterward convey him to his place of safety. That is because they are a folk who know not. [If an unbeliever betrays his people by expressing an interest in converting to Islam he is given the chance to convert, provided that the battle has not commenced.]
9:7 How can there be a treaty with Allah and with His messenger for the **IDOLATERS** save those with whom ye *MADE A TREATY AT THE INVIOLABLE PLACE OF WORSHIP*? So long as they are true to you, be true to them. Lo! Allah loveth those who *KEEP THEIR DUTY*. [There can be no treaty between Muslims and unbelievers other than one agreed at the Grand Mosque in Mecca.]
9:8 How (can there be any treaty for the others) when, if they have the upper hand of you, they regard not pact nor honour in respect of you? They satisfy you with their mouths the while their hearts refuse. And most of them are *WRONGDOERS*.
9:9 They have purchased with the revelations of Allah a little gain, so they debar (men) from His way. Lo! *EVIL IS THAT WHICH THEY ARE WONT TO DO*.
9:10 And they observe toward a **BELIEVER** neither pact nor honour. These are they who are *TRANSGRESSORS*.
9:11 But if they repent and establish worship and pay the poor-due, then are they your brethren in religion. We detail Our revelations for a people who have knowledge.

9:12 And if they break their pledges after their treaty (hath been made with you) and *ASSAIL YOUR RELIGION*, then *FIGHT* the heads [leaders] of disbelief - Lo! they have no binding oaths - in order that they may desist.

[Once non-Muslims have been defeated they are not to raise any criticism of Islam or else the violence from Muslims is again sanctioned.]

9:13 Will ye not _FIGHT_ a folk who broke their solemn pledges, and purposed to drive out the messenger and did attack you first? What! Fear ye them? Now _ALLAH HATH MORE RIGHT THAT YE SHOULD FEAR HIM_, if ye are _BELIEVERS_. [The most authoritative Muslim biographies of Mohammed show that it was Mohammed and his followers who were the aggressors.]

9:14 _FIGHT THEM!_ Allah will chastise them at your hands, and He will lay them low and give you _VICTORY_ over them, and He will heal the breasts of folk who are _BELIEVERS_.

9:15 And He will remove the anger of their hearts. Allah relenteth toward whom He will. Allah is Knower, Wise.

9:16 Or deemed ye that ye would be left (in peace) when Allah yet knoweth not _THOSE OF YOU WHO STRIVE [JIHAD]_, choosing for familiar none save Allah and His messenger and the _BELIEVERS_? Allah is Informed of what ye do.

9:17 It is not for the idolaters to tend Allah's sanctuaries, bearing witness against themselves of disbelief. As for such, their works are vain and _IN THE FIRE THEY WILL ABIDE._ [Even those non-Muslims who would take care of Islamic shrines are destined to an eternity of torture.]

9:18 He only shall tend Allah's sanctuaries who _BELIEVETH IN ALLAH AND THE LAST DAY_ and observeth proper worship and payeth the poor-due and feareth none save Allah. For such (only) is it possible that they can be of the rightly guided.

9:19 Count ye the slaking of a pilgrim's thirst and tendance of the Inviolable Place of Worship as (equal to the worth of) him who _BELIEVETH IN ALLAH AND THE LAST DAY_, and _STRIVETH [JIHAD] IN THE WAY OF ALLAH_? They are not equal in the sight of Allah. Allah guideth not _WRONGDOING FOLK_.

9:20 _THOSE WHO BELIEVE_, and have left their homes and _STRIVEN WITH THEIR WEALTH AND THEIR LIVES IN ALLAH'S WAY [JIHAD] ARE OF MUCH GREATER WORTH IN ALLAH'S SIGHT._ These are they who are _TRIUMPHANT_.

9:21 Their Lord giveth them good tidings of mercy from Him, and acceptance, and _GARDENS WHERE ENDURING PLEASURE WILL BE THEIRS_;

9:22 _THERE THEY WILL ABIDE FOR EVER. LO! WITH ALLAH THERE IS IMMENSE REWARD._

9:23 O _YE WHO BELIEVE_! _CHOOSE NOT YOUR FATHERS NOR YOUR BRETHREN FOR FRIENDS_ if they take pleasure in _DISBELIEF_ rather than faith. _WHOSO OF YOU TAKETH THEM FOR FRIENDS, SUCH ARE WRONG-DOERS._

9:24 Say: If your fathers, and your sons, and your brethren, and your wives, and your tribe, and the wealth ye have acquired, and merchandise for which ye fear that there will no sale, and dwellings ye desire are dearer to you than Allah and His messenger and _STRIVING [JIHAD] IN HIS WAY_: then wait till Allah bringeth His command to pass. Allah guideth not _WRONGDOING_ folk.

9:25 Allah hath given you _VICTORY ON MANY [BATTLE] FIELDS_ and on the day of Huneyn, when ye exulted in your multitude but it availed you naught, and the earth, vast as it is, was straitened for you; then ye turned back in flight;

9:26 Then Allah sent His peace of reassurance down upon His messenger and upon the _BELIEVERS_, and sent down _HOSTS [ARMIES] YE COULD NOT SEE_, and punished those who disbelieved. Such is the _REWARD_ of disbelievers.

9:27 Then afterward Allah will relent toward whom He will; for Allah is Forgiving, Merciful.

9:28 O _YE WHO BELIEVE_! The _IDOLATERS [NON-MUSLIMS] ONLY ARE UNCLEAN._ So let them not come near the Inviolable Place of Worship [Mecca] after this their year. If ye fear poverty (from the loss of their merchandise) Allah shall preserve you of His bounty if He will. Lo! Allah is Knower, Wise.

9:29 _FIGHT AGAINST SUCH OF THOSE WHO HAVE BEEN GIVEN THE SCRIPTURE_ [Jews and Christians] as _BELIEVE NOT IN ALLAH NOR THE LAST DAY_, and forbid not that which Allah hath forbidden by His messenger, and [who] follow not _THE RELIGION OF TRUTH_, until they pay the tribute [protection money] readily, being brought low [made submissive]. [Here the Koran commands Muslims to kill Jews and Christians who do not submit to Islamic rule; those who submit must pay "protection money".][389]

9:30 And the _JEWS_ say: Ezra is the son of Allah, and the _CHRISTIANS_ say: The Messiah is the son of Allah. That is their saying with their mouths. They imitate the saying of _THOSE WHO DISBELIEVED_ of old. Allah (Himself) fighteth against them. How perverse are they!

9:31 They have taken as lords beside Allah their _RABBIS_ and their _MONKS_ and the Messiah _SON OF MARY_, when they were bidden to worship only One Allah. There is no God save Him. Be He Glorified from all that _THEY ASCRIBE AS PARTNER (UNTO HIM)!_

9:32 Fain would they put out the light of Allah with their mouths, but Allah disdaineth (aught) save that He shall perfect His light, however much the _DISBELIEVERS_ are averse.

9:33 He it is Who hath sent His messenger with the guidance and **THE RELIGION OF TRUTH**, that He may cause it _TO PREVAIL OVER ALL RELIGION_, however much the _IDOLATERS_ may be averse. [Islam is to dominate all other religions, no matter how objectionable other people might find this.]

9:34 O _YE WHO BELIEVE_! Lo! many of the (_JEWISH_) _RABBIS_ and the (_CHRISTIAN_) _MONKS_ devour the wealth of mankind wantonly and debar (men) from the way of Allah. ~~They who hoard up gold and silver and spend it not in the way of Allah, unto them give tidings (O Muhammad) of a painful doom,~~ [Partial cancellation by 9:60][390]

9:35 On _THE DAY_ when it will (all) be heated in _THE FIRE OF HELL_, and their foreheads and their flanks and _THEIR BACKS WILL BE BRANDED_ therewith (and it will be said unto them): Here is that which ye hoarded for yourselves. Now taste of what ye used to hoard.

9:36 Lo! the number of the months with Allah is twelve months by Allah's ordinance in the day that He created the heavens and the earth. Four of them are sacred: that is _THE RIGHT RELIGION_. So wrong not yourselves in them. And _WAGE WAR ON ALL OF THE IDOLATERS_ [non-Muslims] as they are _WAGING WAR ON ALL OF YOU_. And know that _ALLAH IS WITH THOSE WHO KEEP THEIR DUTY (UNTO HIM)_.

9:37 Postponement (of a sacred month) is only an excess of _DISBELIEF_ whereby _THOSE WHO DISBELIEVE_ are misled; they allow it one year and forbid it (another) year, that they may make up the number of the months which Allah hath hallowed, so that they allow that which Allah hath forbidden. The _EVIL OF THEIR DEEDS_ is made fairseeming unto them. Allah guideth not _THE DISBELIEVING FOLK_.

9:38 O _YE WHO BELIEVE_! What aileth you that when it is said unto you: Go forth _IN THE WAY OF ALLAH [JIHAD]_, ye are bowed down to the ground with heaviness. _TAKE YE PLEASURE IN THE LIFE OF THE WORLD RATHER THAN IN THE_

HEREAFTER? **The comfort of the life of the world is but little in the Hereafter.**

9:39 ~~If ye go not forth He will afflict you with a painful doom, and will choose instead of you a folk other than you. Ye cannot harm Him at all. Allah is Able to do all things.~~ [Cancelled by verse 9:122 i.e. only a group of Muslims should take part in Jihad, others should stay behind to impose Islam.][391]

9:40 If ye help him not, still Allah helped him when *THOSE WHO DISBELIEVE* drove him forth, the second of two; when they two were in the cave, when he said unto his comrade: Grieve not. Lo! Allah is with us. Then Allah caused His peace of reassurance to descend upon him and supported him with *HOSTS [ARMIES]* ye cannot see, and made the word of *THOSE WHO DISBELIEVED* the nethermost, while *ALLAH'S WORD IT WAS THAT BECAME THE UPPERMOST.* Allah is Mighty, Wise.

9:41 ~~Go forth, light-armed and heavy-armed, and strive with your wealth and your lives in the way of Allah [Jihad]! That is best for you if ye but knew.~~ **[Cancelled by verse 9:122, which instructs some Muslims to stay back so that there are people to instruct others about Islam.][392]**

9:42 Had it been a near adventure and an easy journey they had followed thee, but the distance seemed too far for them. Yet will they swear by Allah (saying): If we had been able we would surely have set out with you. They destroy their souls, and Allah knoweth that they verily are *LIARS*.

9:43 Allah forgive thee (O Muhammad)! Wherefore didst thou grant them leave ere *THOSE WHO TOLD THE TRUTH WERE MANIFEST TO THEE AND THOU DIDST KNOW THE LIARS?*

9:44 *THOSE WHO BELIEVE IN ALLAH* and *THE LAST DAY* *ASK NO LEAVE* of thee lest they should *STRIVE [JIHAD]* with their *WEALTH AND THEIR LIVES.* Allah is Aware of those who keep their duty (unto Him). [Muslims who who fund Jihad or risk their lives as Jihadis have no need to ask other Muslims for permission.]

9:45 They alone ask leave of thee *WHO BELIEVE NOT* in Allah and *THE LAST DAY*, and whose hearts feel doubt, so *IN THEIR DOUBT THEY WAVER.* [Devout Muslims are imbued with certainty and do not look for excuses to avoid Jihad.]

9:46 And if they had wished to go forth they would assuredly have made ready some equipment, but Allah was averse to their being sent forth and held them back and it was said (unto them): Sit ye with the sedentary!

9:47 Had they gone forth among you they had added to you naught save trouble and had hurried to and fro among you, *SEEKING TO CAUSE SEDITION* among you; and among you there are some who would have listened to them. Allah is Aware of *EVIL-DOERS.* [Slackers who do engage in Jihad end up causing sedition. Note that Islam equates pacifism and uncertainty with sedition, and "sedition" is a concept from politics not from religion.]

9:48 Aforetime they *SOUGHT TO CAUSE SEDITION* and raised difficulties for thee till *THE TRUTH* came and the decree of Allah was made manifest, though they were loth.

9:49 Of them is he who saith: Grant me leave (to stay at home) [slackers] and tempt me not. Surely it is into temptation that they (thus) have fallen. Lo! *HELL VERILY IS ALL AROUND THE DISBELIEVERS.* [Slackers are unbelievers, to be tormented in Hell for all eternity.]

9:50 If good befalleth thee (O Muhammad) it afflicteth them, and if calamity befalleth thee, they say: We took precaution, and they turn away well pleased.

9:51 Say: Naught befalleth us save that which *ALLAH HATH DECREED* for us. He is our Protecting Friend. *IN ALLAH LET BELIEVERS PUT THEIR TRUST*!

9:52 Say: Can ye await for us aught save *ONE OF TWO GOOD THINGS (DEATH OR VICTORY IN ALLAH'S WAY [JIHAD])*? while we await for you that Allah will afflict you with a *DOOM* from Him or at our hands. Await then! Lo! We are awaiting with you. [Note: Islam defines as "good things" both killing for Islam or dying in killing for Islam.]

9:53 Say: Pay (your contribution), willingly or unwillingly, it will not be accepted from you. Lo! ye were ever froward [contrary] folk.

9:54 And naught preventeth that their contributions should be accepted from them save that they have *DISBELIEVED* in Allah and in His messenger, and *THEY COME NOT TO WORSHIP SAVE AS IDLERS [SLACKERS]*, and *PAY* not (their contribution) save *RELUCTANTLY*.

9:55 So let not their riches nor their children please thee (O Muhammad). Allah thereby intendeth but to *PUNISH THEM IN THE LIFE OF THE WORLD AND THAT THEIR SOULS SHALL PASS AWAY WHILE THEY ARE DISBELIEVERS*. [Slackers are to be punished on earth and for eternity.]

9:56 And they swear by Allah that they are in *TRUTH* of you, when they are not of you, but they are folk who are afraid [slackers afraid of Jihad].

9:57 Had they but found a refuge, or caverns, or a place to enter, they surely had resorted thither swift as runaways. [Devout Muslims do not run away from enforcing Islam with violence.]

9:58 And of them is he who defameth thee in the matter of the alms. If they are given thereof they are content, and if they are not given thereof, behold! they are enraged.

9:59 (How much more seemly) had they been content with that which Allah and His messenger had given them and had said: Allah sufficeth us. Allah will give us of His bounty, and (also) His messenger. Unto Allah we are suppliants.

9:60 The *ALMS [DONATIONS]* are only for the poor and the needy, and those who collect them, and those whose hearts are to be reconciled, and to free the captives and the debtors, *AND FOR THE CAUSE OF ALLAH [JIHAD]*, and (for) the wayfarer; a duty imposed by Allah. Allah is Knower, Wise. [One of the main purposes of "charity" in Islam is to fund Jihad.]

9:61 And of them are those who vex the Prophet and say: He is only a hearer. Say: A hearer of good for you, who *BELIEVETH* in Allah and is true to the *BELIEVERS*, and a mercy for such of you as *BELIEVE*. *THOSE WHO VEX THE MESSENGER OF ALLAH, FOR THEM THERE IS A PAINFUL DOOM*.

9:62 They swear by Allah to you (*MUSLIMS*) to please you, but Allah, with His messenger, hath more right that they should please Him if they are *BELIEVERS*.

9:63 Know they not that *WHOSO OPPOSETH ALLAH AND HIS MESSENGER, HIS VERILY IS FIRE OF HELL*, to abide therein? That is the extreme abasement.

9:64 The *HYPOCRITES* fear lest a surah should be revealed concerning them, proclaiming what is in their hearts. Say: Scoff (your fill)! Lo! Allah is disclosing what ye fear.

9:65 And if thou ask them (O Muhammad) they will say: We did but talk and jest. Say: Was it at Allah and His revelations and His messenger that ye did scoff?

9:66 Make no excuse. *YE HAVE DISBELIEVED AFTER YOUR (CONFESSION OF) BELIEF.* If We forgive a party of you, a party of you We shall *PUNISH* because they have been *GUILTY*.

9:67 The *HYPOCRITES*, both men and women, proceed one from another. They enjoin the wrong, and they forbid the right, and they *WITHHOLD THEIR HANDS (FROM SPENDING FOR THE CAUSE OF ALLAH [FUNDING JIHAD])*.

They forget Allah, so He hath forgotten them. Lo! the _HYPOCRITES, THEY_ _ARE THE TRANSGRESSORS_**. [Those Muslims who do not fund Jihad are classed as hypocrites.]**

9:68 _ALLAH PROMISETH THE HYPOCRITES_, both men and women, _AND THE DISBELIEVERS FIRE OF HELL_ for their abode. It will suffice them. _ALLAH CURSETH THEM_, and theirs is _LASTING TORMENT_.

9:69 Even as those before you who were mightier than you in strength, and more affluent than you in wealth and children. They enjoyed their lot awhile, so ye enjoy your lot awhile even as those before you did enjoy their lot awhile. And ye prate even as they prated. Such are they whose works have perished in the world and the Hereafter. _SUCH ARE THEY WHO ARE THE LOSERS_.

9:70 Hath not the fame of those before them reached them - the folk of Noah, A'ad, Thamud, the folk of Abraham, the dwellers of Midian and the disasters (which befell them)? Their messengers (from Allah) came unto them with proofs (of Allah's Sovereignty). So Allah surely wronged them not, but they did wrong themselves.

9:71 And _THE BELIEVERS, MEN AND WOMEN, ARE PROTECTING FRIENDS ONE OF ANOTHER_; they enjoin the right and forbid the wrong, and they establish worship and they pay the poor-due, and _THEY OBEY_ _ALLAH AND HIS MESSENGER_. As for these, Allah will have mercy on them. Lo! Allah is Mighty, Wise. [The spiteful Allah only has mercy for dutiful, obedient Muslims; there's no mercy for unbelievers nor for Muslim slackers, hypocrites, dissenters, etc.]

9:72 Allah _PROMISETH TO THE BELIEVERS_**, men and women,** _GARDENS_ _UNDERNEATH WHICH RIVERS FLOW_ **[Paradise], wherein they will abide - blessed dwellings in** _GARDENS OF EDEN_**. And - greater (far)! - acceptance from Allah. That is** _THE SUPREME TRIUMPH_**.**

9:73 O Prophet! _STRIVE [JIHAD] AGAINST THE DISBELIEVERS AND THE_ _HYPOCRITES! BE HARSH WITH THEM. THEIR ULTIMATE ABODE IS HELL_**, a hapless journey's end. [The Koran justifies Jihad not just against non-Muslims but also the slaughter of those Muslims who are deemed to be insufficiently devout. Both unbelievers and hypocrites are destined for an eternity of torture in Hell.]**

9:74 They swear by Allah that they said nothing (wrong), yet _THEY DID_ _SAY THE WORD OF DISBELIEF_**, and did** _DISBELIEVE_ **after their Surrender (to Allah). And they purposed that which they could not attain, and they sought revenge only that Allah by His messenger should enrich them of His bounty. If they repent it will be better for them; and if they turn away,** _ALLAH WILL AFFLICT THEM WITH A PAINFUL DOOM IN THE WORLD AND_ _THE HEREAFTER_**, and they have no protecting friend nor helper in the earth. [One word of disbelief is enough to have a Muslim classified as a hypocrite and have him marked for slaughter.]**

9:75 And of them is he who made _A COVENANT [CONTRACT] WITH ALLAH_ (saying): If He _GIVE US OF_ _HIS BOUNTY WE WILL GIVE ALMS AND BECOME OF THE RIGHTEOUS_.

9:76 Yet when He gave them of His bounty, they hoarded it and turned away, averse;

9:77 So He hath made the consequence (to be) _HYPOCRISY IN THEIR HEARTS UNTIL THE DAY WHEN THEY_ _SHALL MEET HIM_, because _THEY BROKE THEIR WORD TO ALLAH_ that they promised Him, and because they lied.

9:78 Know they not that Allah knoweth both their secret and the thought that they confide, and that Allah is the Knower of Things Hidden?

9:79 Those who point at such of _THE BELIEVERS_ **as give the alms willingly and such as can find naught to give but their endeavours, and deride them - Allah (Himself) derideth them.** _THEIRS WILL BE A PAINFUL DOOM_**. [Allah will punish those who mock Jihadis or those who fund Jihad.]**

9:80 Ask forgiveness for them (O Muhammad), or ask not forgiveness for them; though thou ask forgiveness for them seventy times *ALLAH WILL NOT FORGIVE THEM*. That is because they *DISBELIEVED* in Allah and His messenger, and Allah guideth not *WRONGDOING FOLK*. [Allah is only "merciful" to the believers and is unrelentingly harsh towards those who do not follow the rules of Islam].

9:81 Those who were left behind *[SLACKERS] REJOICED AT SITTING STILL* behind the messenger of Allah, and were *AVERSE TO STRIVING [JIHAD] WITH THEIR WEALTH AND THEIR LIVES IN ALLAH'S WAY.* And they said: Go not forth in the heat! Say: *THE FIRE OF HELL* is more intense of heat, if they but understood.

9:82 Then let them laugh a little: they will weep much, as *THE REWARD OF WHAT THEY USED TO EARN.*

9:83 *IF ALLAH BRING THEE BACK (FROM THE CAMPAIGN [THE BATTLE])* unto a party of them [the pacifist slackers] and they ask of thee leave to go out (to *FIGHT*), then say unto them: Ye shall never more go out with me nor *FIGHT* [Jihad] with me against a foe. Ye were content with sitting still the first time. So sit still, with the useless. [Whether or not some Jihadi survives a battle is up to Allah. Muslim slackers are classed as useless.]

9:84 And *NEVER (O MUHAMMAD) PRAY FOR ONE OF THEM WHO DIETH*, nor stand by his grave. Lo! they *DISBELIEVED IN ALLAH AND HIS MESSENGER, AND THEY DIED WHILE THEY WERE EVIL-DOERS.* [Muslims who die as slackers rather than Jihadis are classed as evil.]

9:85 Let not their wealth nor their children please thee! Allah purposeth only to punish them thereby in the world, and that their souls shall pass away while they are *DISBELIEVERS*. [They are to be punished even before their death.]

9:86 And when a surah is revealed (which saith): *BELIEVE IN ALLAH AND STRIVE [JIHAD] ALONG WITH HIS MESSENGER,* the men of wealth among them still ask leave of thee and say: Suffer us to be with those who sit (at home). [Mohammed was a Jihadi.]

9:87 They are *CONTENT THAT THEY SHOULD BE WITH THE USELESS [SLACKERS]* and their hearts are sealed, so that they apprehend not.

9:88 But *THE MESSENGER AND THOSE WHO BELIEVE WITH HIM STRIVE [JIHAD] WITH THEIR WEALTH AND THEIR LIVES*. Such are they for whom are the good things. *SUCH ARE THEY WHO ARE THE SUCCESSFUL.*

9:89 Allah hath made ready for them *GARDENS UNDERNEATH* which rivers flow [Paradise], wherein they will abide. That is *THE SUPREME TRIUMPH.*

9:90 And those among the wandering Arabs who had an excuse came in order that permission might be granted them. And *THOSE WHO LIED* to Allah and His messenger *SAT AT HOME [SLACKERS]*. *A PAINFUL DOOM WILL FALL ON THOSE OF THEM WHO DISBELIEVE.*

9:91 Not unto the weak nor unto the sick nor unto those who can find naught to spend is any fault (to be imputed though they stay at home) if they are true to Allah and His messenger. Not unto the good is there any road (of blame). Allah is Forgiving, Merciful. [Those who are slackers through ill-health or poverty are regarded as blameless; those who are able and have money are expected to become Jihadis.]

9:92 Nor unto those whom, when they came to thee (asking) that thou shouldst mount them, thou didst tell: I cannot find whereon to mount you. They turned back with eyes flowing with tears, for sorrow that they could not find the means to spend.

9:93 *THE ROAD (OF BLAME)* is only against those who ask for leave of thee (to stay at home) *WHEN THEY ARE RICH*. They are *CONTENT TO BE WITH THE USELESS*. Allah hath sealed their hearts so that they know not. [Muslims

with the financial means to be Jihadis but who avoid Jihad are classed as "useless" to the cause of Allah.]

9:94 They will make excuse to you (Muslims) when ye return unto them. Say: Make no excuse, for we shall not believe you. Allah hath told us tidings of you. Allah and His messenger will see your conduct, and then ye will be brought back unto Him Who knoweth the Invisible as well as the Visible, and He will tell you what ye used to do.

9:95 They will swear by Allah unto you, when ye return unto them, that ye may let them be. Let them be, for lo! *THEY [SLACKERS] ARE UNCLEAN,* **and** *THEIR ABODE IS HELL* **as** *THE REWARD FOR WHAT THEY USED TO EARN.* **[Slackers are designated as "unclean", the same category of disgust into which non-Muslims are placed.]**

9:96 They swear unto you, that ye may accept them. Though ye accept them. Allah verily accepteth not wrongdoing folk.

9:97 ~~The wandering Arabs are more hard in~~ *DISBELIEF* ~~and hypocrisy, and more likely to be ignorant of the limits which Allah hath revealed unto His messenger. And Allah is Knower, Wise.~~ [Cancelled by verse 9:99][393]

9:98 ~~And of the wandering Arabs there is he who taketh that which he expendeth (for the cause of Allah) as a loss, and awaiteth (evil) turns of fortune for you (that he may be rid of it). The evil turn of fortune will be theirs. Allah is Hearer, Knower.~~ [Cancelled by verse 9:99][394]

9:99 And of the wandering Arabs there is *HE WHO BELIEVETH IN ALLAH AND THE LAST DAY,* and taketh that which he expendeth and also the prayers of the messenger as acceptable offerings in the sight of Allah. Lo! verily it is an acceptable offering for them. Allah will bring them into His mercy. Lo! Allah is Forgiving, Merciful.

9:100 And the first to lead the way, of the Muhajirin [Immigrants] and the Ansar [Helpers], and those who followed them in goodness - Allah is well pleased with them and they are well pleased with Him, and He hath made ready for them *GARDENS UNDERNEATH* **which rivers flow [Paradise], wherein they will abide for ever. That is** *THE SUPREME TRIUMPH.*

9:101 And among those around you of the wandering Arabs there are *HYPOCRITES,* and among the townspeople of Al-Madinah (there are some who) persist in *HYPOCRISY* whom thou (O Muhammad) knowest not. We, We know them, and We shall chastise them twice; then they will be *RELEGATED TO A PAINFUL DOOM.*

9:102 And (there are) others who have acknowledged their faults. They mixed a righteous action with another that was bad. It may be that Allah will relent toward them. Lo! Allah is Forgiving, Merciful.

9:103 Take alms of their wealth, wherewith thou mayst purify them and mayst make them grow, and pray for them. Lo! thy prayer is an assuagement for them. Allah is Hearer, Knower.

9:104 Know they not that Allah is He Who accepteth repentance from His *BONDMEN* and taketh the alms, and that Allah is He Who is the Relenting, the Merciful.

9:105 And say (unto them): *ACT! ALLAH WILL BEHOLD YOUR ACTIONS, AND (SO WILL) HIS MESSENGER AND THE BELIEVERS,* and ye will be brought back to the Knower of the Invisible and the Visible, and He will tell you what ye used to do.

9:106 And (there are) others who await Allah's decree, whether He will punish them or will forgive them. Allah is Knower, Wise.

9:107 And as for those who chose a place of worship out of *OPPOSITION AND DISBELIEF,* and in order to *CAUSE DISSENT AMONG THE BELIEVERS,* and as an outpost for those who warred against Allah and His messenger aforetime, they will surely swear: We purposed naught save good. Allah beareth witness that they verily *ARE LIARS.* [Those Muslims who seek to reform Islam are classed as "liars".]

9:108 Never stand (to pray) there. A place of worship which was found upon duty (to Allah) from the first day is more worthy that thou shouldst stand (to pray) therein, wherein are men who love to purify themselves. Allah loveth *THE PURIFIERS.*

9:109 Is he who founded his building upon *DUTY TO ALLAH* and His good pleasure better; or he who founded his building on the brink of a crumbling, overhanging precipice so that it toppled with him into *THE FIRE OF HELL?* Allah guideth not *WRONGDOING FOLK.*

9:110 The building which they built will never cease to be a misgiving in their hearts unless their hearts be torn to pieces. Allah is Knower, Wise.

9:111 Lo! *ALLAH HATH BOUGHT FROM THE BELIEVERS THEIR LIVES* **and their wealth because** *THE GARDEN [PARADISE] WILL BE THEIRS*: *THEY SHALL FIGHT [JIHAD] IN THE WAY OF ALLAH AND SHALL SLAY AND BE SLAIN [KILL AND BE KILLED]*. **It is** *A PROMISE WHICH IS BINDING* **on Him in the Torah and the Gospel and the Qur'an. Who fulfilleth His** *COVENANT* **[contract] better than Allah?** *REJOICE THEN IN YOUR BARGAIN THAT YE HAVE MADE, FOR THAT IS THE SUPREME TRIUMPH.* **[Muslims are contractually bound to fulfil the commands of Islam, Allah has bought their earthly lives in exchange for an eternity in Paradise should the Muslims fulfil their duty to Allah.]**

9:112 *(TRIUMPHANT) ARE* those who turn repentant (to Allah), *THOSE WHO SERVE (HIM)*, those who praise (Him), those who fast, those who bow down, those who fall prostrate (in worship), those who enjoin the right and who forbid the wrong and those who keep the limits (ordained) of Allah - And give glad tidings to *BELIEVERS*!

9:113 *IT IS NOT FOR THE PROPHET, AND THOSE WHO BELIEVE, TO PRAY FOR THE FORGIVENESS OF IDOLATERS EVEN THOUGH THEY MAY BE NEAR OF KIN (TO THEM) AFTER IT HATH BECOME CLEAR THAT THEY ARE PEOPLE OF HELL-FIRE.*

9:114 The prayer of Abraham for the forgiveness of his father was only because of a promise he had promised him, but when it had become clear unto him that he (his father) was an enemy to Allah he (Abraham) disowned him. Lo! Abraham was soft of heart, long-suffering.

9:115 It was never Allah's (part) that He should send a folk astray after He had guided them until He had made clear unto them what they should avoid. Lo! Allah is Aware of all things.

9:116 Lo! Allah! Unto Him belongeth the Sovereignty of the heavens and the earth. He quickeneth and He giveth death. And ye have, instead of Allah, no protecting friend nor helper.

9:117 Allah hath turned in mercy to the Prophet, and to the Muhajirin [Immigrants] and the Ansar [Helpers] who followed him in the hour of hardship. After the hearts of a party [group] of them had almost swerved aside, then turned He unto them in mercy. Lo! He is Full of Pity, Merciful for them.

9:118 And to the three also (did He turn in mercy) who were left behind, when the earth, vast as it is, was straitened for them, and their own souls were straitened for them till they bethought them that *THERE IS NO REFUGE FROM ALLAH* save toward Him. Then turned He unto them in mercy that they (too) might turn (repentant unto Him). Lo! Allah! He is the Relenting, the Merciful.

9:119 O *YE WHO BELIEVE*! Be careful of *YOUR DUTY TO ALLAH*, and be with *THE TRUTHFUL.*

9:120 It is not for the townsfolk of Al-Madinah and for those around them of the wandering Arabs [slackers] to stay behind the messenger of Allah and *PREFER THEIR LIVES TO HIS LIFE*. **That is because neither thirst nor toil nor hunger afflicteth them in the way of Allah, nor step they any step that angereth the** *DISBELIEVERS*, **nor gain they from** *THE ENEMY* **a gain, but a good deed is recorded for them therefor. Lo! Allah loseth not** *THE WAGES OF THE GOOD.* **[Jihadis are repaid with an eternity in Paradise. The slackers try to avoid conflict with unbelievers (the enemy), but this passivity will not result in any reward for the slackers.]**

9:121 Nor spend they any spending, small or great, nor do they cross a valley, but it is recorded for them, that *ALLAH MAY REPAY THEM THE BEST OF WHAT THEY USED TO DO.*

9:122 And *THE BELIEVERS SHOULD NOT ALL GO OUT TO FIGHT*. **Of every troop of them, a party only should go forth, that they (who are left behind) may gain sound knowledge in religion, and that they may warn their folk when they return to them, so that they may beware. [Only a group of Muslims should take part in Jihad, others should stay behind to impose Islam.]**

9:123 O *YE WHO BELIEVE!* *FIGHT THOSE OF THE DISBELIEVERS WHO ARE NEAR TO YOU, AND LET THEM FIND HARSHNESS* in you, and know that *ALLAH IS WITH THOSE WHO KEEP THEIR DUTY* (unto Him) [Jihad].

9:124 And whenever a surah is revealed there are some of them who say: Which one of you hath thus increased in faith? As for *THOSE WHO BELIEVE,* it hath increased them in faith and they rejoice (therefor).

9:125 But as for those in whose hearts is disease, it only addeth wickedness to their wickedness, and *THEY DIE WHILE THEY ARE DISBELIEVERS,*

9:126 See they not that *THEY ARE TESTED ONCE OR TWICE IN EVERY YEAR? STILL THEY TURN NOT IN REPENTANCE,* neither pay they heed. [Unbelievers are to receive punishment at least once a year, but still they do not convert to Islam.]

9:127 And whenever a surah is revealed, they look one at another (as who should say): Doth anybody see you? Then they turn away. Allah turneth away their hearts because *THEY ARE A FOLK WHO UNDERSTAND NOT.*

9:128 There hath come unto you a messenger, (one) of yourselves, unto whom aught that ye are overburdened is grievous, full of concern for you, for *THE BELIEVERS* full of pity, merciful.

9:129 Now, if they turn away (O Muhammad) say: Allah sufficeth me. There is no God save Him. In Him have I put my trust, and He is Lord of the Tremendous Throne.

Chapter 5 - The Table Spread

5:1 O *YE WHO BELIEVE*! Fulfil your indentures. The beast of cattle is made lawful unto you (for food) except that which is announced unto you (herein), game being unlawful when ye are on the pilgrimage. Lo! Allah ordaineth that which pleaseth Him.

5:2 ~~O ye who *BELIEVE!* Profane not Allah's monuments nor the Sacred Month nor the offerings nor the garlands, nor those repairing to the Sacred House, seeking the grace and pleasure of their Lord~~. But when ye have left the sacred territory, then go hunting (if ye will). And let not your hatred of a folk who (once) stopped your going to the inviolable place of worship seduce you to transgress; but *HELP YE ONE ANOTHER UNTO RIGHTEOUSNESS AND PIOUS DUTY.* Help not one another unto sin and transgression, but *KEEP YOUR DUTY TO ALLAH.* Lo! *ALLAH IS SEVERE IN PUNISHMENT.* [Partial Cancellation by 9:5][395]

5:3 *FORBIDDEN UNTO YOU (FOR FOOD)* are carrion and blood and *SWINE FLESH,* and that which hath been dedicated unto any other than Allah, and the strangled, and the dead through beating, and the dead through falling from a height, and that which hath been killed by (the goring of) horns, and the devoured of wild beass, saving that which ye make lawful (by the death-stroke), and that which hath been immolated unto idols. And (forbidden is it) that ye swear by the divining arrows. This is an abomination. *THIS DAY ARE THOSE WHO DISBELIEVE IN DESPAIR OF (EVER HARMING) YOUR RELIGION;* so fear them not, *FEAR ME*! This day have *I PERFECTED YOUR RELIGION FOR YOU* and completed My favour unto you, and have chosen for you as religion al-Islam. *WHOSO IS FORCED BY HUNGER, NOT BY WILL, TO SIN: (FOR HIM) LO! ALLAH IS FORGIVING, MERCIFUL.* [Hungry Muslims can eat pork.]

5:4 They ask thee (O Muhammad) what is made lawful for them. Say: (all) good things are made lawful for you. And those beasts and birds of prey which ye have trained as hounds are trained, ye teach them that which Allah taught you; so eat of that which they catch for you and mention Allah's name upon it, and *OBSERVE YOUR DUTY TO ALLAH.* Lo! Allah is swift to take account.

5:5 This day are (all) good things made lawful for you. The food of those who have received the Scripture is lawful for you, and your food is lawful for them. And so are the virtuous women of the *BELIEVERS* and the virtuous women of those who received the Scripture before you (lawful for you) when ye give them their marriage portions and live with them in honour, not in fornication, nor taking them as secret concubines. *WHOSO DENIETH THE FAITH, HIS WORK IS VAIN AND HE WILL BE AMONG THE LOSERS IN THE HEREAFTER.*

5:6 O *YE WHO BELIEVE*! When ye rise up for prayer, wash you faces, and your hands up to the elbows, and lightly rub your heads and (wash) your feet up to the ankles. And if ye are unclean, purify yourselves. And if ye are sick or on a journey, or one of you cometh from the closet, or ye have had contact with women, and ye find not water, then go to clean, high ground and rub your faces and your hands with some of it. Allah would not place a burden on you, but He would purify you and would perfect His grace upon you, that ye may give thanks.

5:7 Remember Allah's grace upon you and *HIS COVENANT BY WHICH HE BOUND YOU* when *YE SAID: WE HEAR AND WE OBEY*; And *KEEP YOUR DUTY TO ALLAH*. Lo! He knoweth what is in the breasts (of men).

5:8 O *YE WHO BELIEVE*! Be steadfast witnesses for Allah in equity, and *LET NOT HATRED OF ANY PEOPLE SEDUCE YOU THAT YE DEAL NOT JUSTLY*. Deal justly, that is nearer to your duty. *OBSERVE YOUR DUTY TO ALLAH*. Lo! Allah is Informed of what ye do. [Commands to be equitable and just refer to Muslims only imposing the punishments prescribed by sharia, the plain road. Muslims are not allowed to veer from the path and remain Muslims.]

5:9 *ALLAH HATH PROMISED THOSE WHO BELIEVE AND DO GOOD WORKS: THEIRS WILL BE FORGIVENESS AND IMMENSE REWARD.* ["Good works" includes the killing done as Jihadis which guarantees entry to Paradise.]

5:10 And *THEY WHO DISBELIEVE AND DENY OUR REVELATIONS, SUCH ARE RIGHTFUL OWNERS OF HELL.*

5:11 O *YE WHO BELIEVE*! Remember Allah's favour unto you, how a people were minded to stretch out their hands against you but He withheld their hands from you; and *KEEP YOUR DUTY TO ALLAH. IN ALLAH LET BELIEVERS PUT THEIR TRUST.* [The Koran is considered by Muslims to be the only record of the literal word of Allah, so Muslims are to obey and trust what is said in the Koran.]

5:12 Allah made a *COVENANT* of old with *THE CHILDREN OF ISRAEL* and We raised among them twelve chieftains, and Allah said: Lo! I am with you. If ye establish worship and pay the poor-due, and *BELIEVE* in My messengers and support them, and *LEND UNTO ALLAH A KINDLY LOAN*, surely I shall remit your sins, and surely I shall *BRING YOU INTO GARDENS UNDERNEATH* which rivers flow. Whoso among you *DISBELIEVETH* after this will go astray from *A PLAIN ROAD.*

5:13 And because of their breaking their *COVENANT*, We have *CURSED THEM* and made hard their hearts. *THEY CHANGE WORDS FROM THEIR CONTEXT* and forget a part of that whereof they were admonished. Thou wilt not cease to *DISCOVER TREACHERY* from all save a few of them. ~~But bear with them and pardon them. Lo! Allah loveth the kindly.~~ [Partial Cancellation by Koran 9:29 i.e. Muslims are not to be kind, not to pardon unbelievers, but are instead to inflict the slaughter commanded by 9.29][396]

5:14 And with those who say: "Lo! we are *CHRISTIANS*," We made a *COVENANT*, but they forgot a part of that whereof they were admonished. Therefore *WE HAVE STIRRED UP ENMITY AND HATRED AMONG THEM TILL THE DAY OF RESURRECTION*, when Allah will inform them of their handiwork. [The Koran claims Allah created dissent among Christians.]

5:15 O *PEOPLE OF THE SCRIPTURE*! Now hath Our messenger come unto you, expounding unto you much of that which ye used to hide in the Scripture, and forgiving much. Now hath come unto you light from Allah and plain Scripture.

5:16 Whereby Allah guideth him who seeketh His good pleasure unto paths of peace. He bringeth them out of darkness unto light by His decree, and guideth them unto *A STRAIGHT PATH*. [The straight path is Sharia law.] [397]

5:17 *THEY INDEED HAVE DISBELIEVED WHO SAY: LO! ALLAH IS THE MESSIAH, SON OF MARY*. Say: Who then can do aught against Allah, if He had willed to destroy the Messiah *SON OF MARY*, and his mother and everyone on earth? Allah's is the Sovereignty of the heavens and the earth and all that is between them. He createth what He will. And Allah is Able to do all things. [Christians are unbelievers.]

5:18 The *JEWS* and *CHRISTIANS* say: We are sons of Allah and His loved ones. Say: Why then doth He chastise you for your sins? Nay, ye are but mortals of His creating. He *FORGIVETH WHOM HE WILL*, and chastiseth whom He will. Allah's is the Sovereignty of the heavens and the earth and all that is between them, and unto Him is the journeying.

5:19 O *PEOPLE OF THE SCRIPTURE*! Now hath Our messenger come unto you to make things plain unto you after an interval (of cessation) of the messengers, lest ye should say: There came not unto us a messenger of cheer nor any warner. Now hath a messenger of cheer and a warner come unto you. Allah is Able to do all things.

5:20 And (remember) when Moses said unto his people: O my people! Remember Allah's favour unto you, how He placed among you prophets, and He made you kings, and gave you that (which) He gave not to any (other) of (His) creatures.

5:21 O my people! Go into the holy land which Allah hath ordained for you. Turn not in flight, for surely ye turn back as losers:

5:22 They said: O Moses! Lo! a giant people (dwell) therein and lo! we go not in till they go forth from thence. When they go forth from thence, then we will enter (not till then).

5:23 Then out spake two of those who feared (their Lord, men) unto whom Allah had been gracious: Enter in upon them by the gate, for if ye enter by it, lo! *YE WILL BE VICTORIOUS*. So *PUT YOUR TRUST (IN ALLAH) IF YE ARE INDEED BELIEVERS.*

5:24 They said: O Moses! We will never enter (the land) while they are in it. So go thou and thy Lord and fight! We will sit here.

5:25 He said: My Lord! I have control of none but myself and my brother, so distinguish between us and the *WRONG-DOING FOLK.*

5:26 (Their Lord) said: For this the land will surely be forbidden them for forty years that they will wander in the earth, bewildered. So grieve not over the wrongdoing folk.

5:27 But recite unto them with truth the tale of the two sons of Adam, how they offered each a sacrifice, and it was accepted from the one of them and it was not accepted from the other. (The one) said: I will surely kill thee. (The other) answered: Allah accepteth only from those who ward off (*EVIL*).

5:28 Even if thou stretch out thy hand against me to kill me, I *SHALL NOT STRETCH OUT MY HAND AGAINST THEE TO KILL THEE*, lo! I fear Allah, the Lord of the Worlds. [This is NOT a command to Muslims, but is instead part of the summary of the story of Cain and Abel, and applies to Jews not Muslims – see the surrounding context in Koran 5:27 to 5:32]

5:29 Lo! I would rather thou shouldst bear the punishment of the sin against me and thine own sin and become one of the *OWNERS OF THE FIRE. THAT IS THE REWARD OF EVIL-DOERS.*

5:30 But (the other's) mind imposed on him the killing of his brother, so he slew him and became one of the losers.

5:31 Then Allah sent a raven scratching up the ground, to show him how to hide his brother's naked corpse. He said: Woe unto me! Am I not able to be as this raven and so hide my brother's naked corpse? And he became repentant.

5:32 For that cause *WE DECREED FOR THE CHILDREN OF ISRAEL* that *WHOSOEVER KILLETH A HUMAN BEING FOR OTHER THAN MANSLAUGHTER OR CORRUPTION IN THE EARTH, IT SHALL BE AS IF HE HAD KILLED ALL MANKIND*, and *WHOSO SAVETH THE LIFE OF ONE, IT SHALL BE AS IF HE HAD SAVED THE LIFE OF ALL MANKIND*. Our messengers came unto them of old with *CLEAR PROOFS* (of Allah's Sovereignty), but afterwards lo! many of them became prodigals in the earth. [The only verse of the Koran that supposedly rejects all violence is in fact a statement which applies to Jews not to Muslims.]

5:33 The only *REWARD* of *THOSE WHO MAKE WAR UPON ALLAH AND HIS MESSENGER* [Mohammed] and strive after *CORRUPTION IN THE LAND* will be that *THEY WILL BE KILLED* or crucified, or have their hands and feet on alternate sides cut off, or will be expelled out of the land. Such will be their degradation in the world, and *IN THE HEREAFTER THEIRS WILL BE AN AWFUL DOOM*; [Those who object to Islam are to be killed or mutilated...]

5:34 *SAVE THOSE WHO REPENT BEFORE YE OVERPOWER THEM*. For know that Allah is Forgiving, Merciful. [...unless they convert to Islam before they know their slaughter is imminent.]

5:35 O *YE WHO BELIEVE*! Be mindful of *YOUR DUTY TO ALLAH*, and seek the way of approach unto Him, and *STRIVE [JIHAD] IN HIS WAY* in order that ye may *SUCCEED*.

5:36 As for *THOSE WHO DISBELIEVE*, lo! if all that is in the earth were theirs, and as much again therewith, to ransom them from the doom on *THE DAY OF RESURRECTION*, it would not be accepted from them. Theirs will be *A PAINFUL DOOM.*

5:37 They will wish to come forth from *THE FIRE*, but they will not come forth from it. *THEIRS WILL BE A LASTING DOOM.*

5:38 As for the thief, both male and female, *CUT OFF THEIR HANDS*. It is the *REWARD OF THEIR OWN DEEDS*, an *EXEMPLARY PUNISHMENT* from Allah. Allah is Mighty, Wise. [In Islam those who are punished are getting their reward.]

5:39 But whoso repenteth after his wrongdoing and amendeth, lo! Allah will relent toward him. Lo! Allah is Forgiving, Merciful.

5:40 Knowest thou not that unto Allah belongeth the Sovereignty of the heavens and the earth? *HE PUNISHETH WHOM HE WILL, AND FORGIVETH WHOM HE WILL.* Allah is Able to do all things.

5:41 O Messenger! Let not them grieve thee who vie one with another in the race to *DISBELIEF*, of such as say with their mouths: "We *BELIEVE*," but their hearts *BELIEVE* not, and of the *JEWS*: listeners for the sake of *FALSEHOOD*, listeners on behalf of other folk who come not unto thee, *CHANGING WORDS FROM THEIR CONTEXT* and saying: If this be given unto you, receive it, but if this be not given unto you, then beware! He whom Allah doometh unto sin, thou (by thine efforts) wilt avail him naught against Allah. Those are they for whom the Will of Allah is that He cleanse not their hearts. Theirs in the world will be ignominy, and in the Hereafter *AN AWFUL DOOM*; [The Islamic texts must be taken literally, the words cannot be changed from their context. Those who try to change the meaning of the texts are condemned to an eternity of torture.]

5:42 Listeners for the sake of falsehood! Greedy for illicit gain! ~~If then they have recourse unto thee (Muhammad) judge between them or disclaim jurisdiction.~~ If thou disclaimest jurisdiction, then they cannot harm thee at all. But if thou judgest, judge between them with equity. Lo! Allah loveth the equitable. [Partial Cancellation by 5:49][398]

5:43 How come they unto thee for judgment when they have the Torah, wherein Allah hath delivered judgment (for them)? Yet even after that they turn away. Such (folk) are not *BELIEVERS*.

5:44 Lo! We did reveal the Torah, wherein is guidance and a light, by which the prophets who surrendered (unto Allah) judged the *JEWS*, and the *RABBIS* and the *PRIESTS* (judged) by such of Allah's Scripture as they were bidden to observe, and thereunto were they witnesses. So *FEAR NOT MANKIND, BUT FEAR ME.* And My revelations for a little gain. *WHOSO JUDGETH NOT BY THAT WHICH ALLAH HATH REVEALED: SUCH ARE DISBELIEVERS.*

5:45 And We prescribed for them therein: The life for the life, and the *EYE FOR THE EYE*, and the nose for the nose, and the ear for the ear, and the tooth for the tooth, and for wounds retaliation. But whoso forgoeth it (in the way of charity) it shall be expiation for him. *WHOSO JUDGETH NOT BY THAT WHICH ALLAH HATH REVEALED: SUCH ARE WRONG-DOERS.*

5:46 And We caused *JESUS, SON OF MARY*, to follow in their footsteps, confirming that which was (revealed) before him in the Torah, and We bestowed on him the Gospel wherein is guidance and a light, confirming that which was (revealed) before it in the Torah - a guidance and an admonition unto those who ward off (*EVIL*).

5:47 Let the *PEOPLE OF THE GOSPEL* judge by that which Allah hath revealed therein. *WHOSO JUDGETH NOT BY THAT WHICH ALLAH HATH REVEALED: SUCH ARE EVIL-LIVERS. [ANYONE WHO DOES NOT BEHAVE IN ACCORDANCE WITH ISLAM IS CLASSED AS "EVIL".]*

5:48 And unto thee have We revealed THE SCRIPTURE WITH THE TRUTH, confirming whatever Scripture was before it, and a watcher over it. So judge between them by that which Allah hath revealed, and follow not their desires away from *THE TRUTH* which hath come unto thee. For each We have appointed a divine law and a traced-out way. Had Allah willed He could have made you one community. But that He may try you by that which He hath given you (He hath made you as ye are). So vie one with another in good works. Unto Allah ye will all return, and He will then inform you of that wherein ye differ.

5:49 So judge between them by that which Allah hath revealed, and follow not their desires, but *BEWARE OF THEM* lest they seduce thee from some part of that which Allah hath revealed unto thee.

And if they turn away, then know that *ALLAH'S WILL IS TO SMITE THEM* for some sin of theirs. Lo! *MANY OF MANKIND ARE EVIL-LIVERS*. [Allah's will is that the People of the Gospel be physically hurt.]
5:50 Is it a judgment of the time of (pagan) ignorance that they are seeking? Who is better than Allah for judgment to *A PEOPLE WHO HAVE CERTAINTY (IN THEIR BELIEF)*?

5:51 *O ye who believe! Take not the Jews and the Christians for friends.* **They are friends one to another.** *He among you who taketh them for friends is (one) of them.* **Lo! Allah guideth not wrongdoing folk. [Any Muslim who befriends Jews/Christians is no longer a Muslim.]**

5:52 And thou seest those in whose heart is a disease race toward them, saying: We fear lest a change of fortune befall us. And it may happen that Allah will vouchsafe (unto thee) the *VICTORY*, or a commandment from His presence. Then will they repent them of their secret thoughts.
5:53 Then will *THE BELIEVERS* say (unto the *PEOPLE OF THE SCRIPTURE*): are these they who swore by Allah their most binding oaths that they were surely with you? Their works have failed, and they have become the *LOSERS*.

5:54 O *ye who believe*! **Whoso of you becometh a** *RENEGADE FROM HIS RELIGION*, **(know that in his stead) Allah will bring a people whom He loveth and who love Him,** *HUMBLE TOWARD BELIEVERS, STERN TOWARD DISBELIEVERS, STRIVING IN THE WAY OF ALLAH* **[Jihad], and fearing not the blame of any blamer. Such is the grace of Allah which He giveth unto whom He will. Allah is All-Embracing, All-Knowing. [Koran says that Jihadis should have no concern about criticism from non-Jihadis.]**

5:55 *YOUR GUARDIAN CAN BE ONLY ALLAH; AND HIS MESSENGER AND THOSE WHO BELIEVE*, who establish worship and pay the poordue, and bow down (in prayer).
5:56 And whoso taketh Allah and His messenger and those who *BELIEVE* for guardian (will know that), lo! the party of Allah, *THEY ARE THE VICTORIOUS*.
5:57 O *YE WHO BELIEVE*! Choose not for guardians such of those who received the Scripture before you, and of the *DISBELIEVERS*, as make a jest and sport of your religion. But *KEEP YOUR DUTY TO ALLAH* if ye are *TRUE BELIEVERS*.
5:58 And when ye call to prayer they take it for a jest and sport. That is because they are a folk who understand not.
5:59 Say: O *PEOPLE OF THE SCRIPTURE*! Do ye blame us for aught else than that we *BELIEVE* in Allah and that which is revealed unto us and that which was revealed aforetime, and because *MOST OF YOU ARE EVIL-LIVERS*?
5:60 Shall I tell thee of a worse (case) than theirs for retribution with Allah? (Worse is the case of him) *WHOM ALLAH HATH CURSED*, him on whom His wrath hath fallen and of whose sort Allah hath *TURNED SOME TO APES AND SWINE, AND WHO SERVETH IDOLS*. Such are in worse plight and further astray from *THE PLAIN ROAD*.
5:61 When they come unto you (*MUSLIMS*), they say: We *BELIEVE*; but they came in *UNBELIEF* and they went out in the same; and Allah knoweth best what they were hiding.
5:62 And thou seest many of them vying one with another in sin and transgression and their devouring of illicit gain. Verily *EVIL IS WHAT THEY DO*.

5:63 Why do not the *RABBIS* **and the** *PRIESTS* **forbid their** *EVIL-SPEAKING* **and their devouring of illicit gain? Verily** *EVIL* **is their handiwork.**

5:64 The *JEWS* say: Allah's hand is fettered. Their hands are fettered and they are accursed for saying so. Nay, but both His hands are spread out wide in bounty. He bestoweth as He will. That which hath been revealed unto thee from thy Lord is certain to increase the contumacy and *DISBELIEF OF MANY OF THEM*, and We have *CAST AMONG THEM ENMITY* and hatred till *THE DAY OF RESURRECTION*. As often as they light a fire for war, Allah extinguisheth it. *THEIR EFFORT IS FOR* corruption *IN THE LAND*, and Allah loveth not corrupters. [Islam claims Allah is responsible for division and hostility which exists between non-Muslims.]

5:65 *IF ONLY THE PEOPLE OF THE SCRIPTURE WOULD BELIEVE AND WARD OFF (EVIL)*, surely We should remit their sins from them and surely We should *BRING THEM INTO GARDENS OF DELIGHT*. [If Jews/Christians believed in Islam and became Jihadis, they would go to Paradise after death.]

5:66 If they had observed the Torah and the Gospel and that which was revealed unto them from their Lord, they would surely have been nourished from above them and from beneath their feet. Among them *THERE ARE PEOPLE WHO ARE MODERATE, BUT MANY OF THEM ARE OF EVIL CONDUCT.* [Many Jews and Christians are evil.]

5:67 O Messenger! Make known that which hath been revealed unto thee from thy Lord, for if thou do it not, thou wilt not have conveyed His message. Allah will protect thee from mankind. Lo! Allah guideth not the *DISBELIEVING* folk.

5:68 Say O *PEOPLE OF THE SCRIPTURE*! Ye have naught (of guidance) till ye observe the Torah and the Gospel and that which was revealed unto you from your Lord. That which is revealed unto thee (Muhammad) from thy Lord is certain to increase the contumacy and *DISBELIEF OF MANY OF THEM*. But *GRIEVE NOT FOR THE DISBELIEVING FOLK*.

5:69 Lo! *THOSE WHO BELIEVE*, and those who are *JEWS*, and Sabaeans, and *CHRISTIANS* - Whosoever *BELIEVETH IN ALLAH AND THE LAST DAY AND DOETH RIGHT* - there shall no fear come upon them neither shall they grieve. [Jews and Christians are considered to be Muslims if they believe Allah is the only god, believe that Judgement Day is coming, and behave in accordance with the sharia.]

5:70 We made a *COVENANT* of old with *THE CHILDREN OF ISRAEL* and We sent unto them messengers. As often as a messenger came unto them with that which their souls desired not (they became rebellious). Some (of them) they denied and some they slew.

5:71 They thought no harm would come of it, so *THEY WERE WILFULLY BLIND AND DEAF*. And afterward Allah turned (in mercy) toward them. Now (even after that) are many of them wilfully blind and deaf. Allah is Seer of what they do.

5:72 *THEY SURELY DISBELIEVE* who say: Lo! Allah is the Messiah, *SON OF MARY* [Christians are unbelievers]. The Messiah (himself) said: O *CHILDREN OF ISRAEL*, worship Allah, my Lord and your Lord. Lo! whoso *ASCRIBETH PARTNERS* unto Allah, for him Allah hath forbidden paradise. His abode is *THE FIRE. FOR EVIL-DOERS* there will be no helpers. [Christians are unbelievers and are going to Hell.]

5:73 They surely *DISBELIEVE* who say: Lo! Allah is the third of three; when there is no God save the One Allah. If they desist not from so saying *A PAINFUL DOOM* will fall on those of them who *DISBELIEVE*.

5:74 Will they not rather turn unto Allah and seek forgiveness of Him? For Allah is Forgiving, Merciful.

5:75 The Messiah, *SON OF MARY, WAS NO OTHER THAN A MESSENGER*, messengers (the like of whom) had passed away before him. And his mother was a saintly woman. And they both used to eat (earthly) food. See how We make the revelations clear for them, and see how they are turned away! [Denies the Christian belief that Jesus was the son of God, which is blasphemy to Christians.]

5:76 Say: Serve ye in place of Allah that which possesseth for you neither hurt nor use? Allah it is Who is the Hearer, the Knower.

5:77 Say: O *PEOPLE OF THE SCRIPTURE*! Stress not in your religion other than *THE TRUTH*, and follow not the vain desires of folk who erred of old and led many astray, and erred from *A PLAIN ROAD*.

5:78 Those of the *CHILDREN OF ISRAEL* who went astray were cursed by the tongue of David, and of *JESUS, SON OF MARY*. That was because they rebelled and used to transgress.

5:79 They restrained not one another from the wickedness they did. Verily evil was that they used to do!

5:80 Thou seest many of them *MAKING FRIENDS WITH THOSE WHO DISBELIEVE*. Surely ill for them is that which they themselves send on before them: that Allah will be wroth with them and in the doom they will abide.

5:81 *IF THEY BELIEVED IN ALLAH* and the Prophet and that which is revealed unto him, they would *NOT CHOOSE THEM FOR THEIR FRIENDS. BUT MANY OF THEM ARE OF EVIL CONDUCT.* [Muslims who befriend Christians are evil.]

5:82 Thou wilt find *THE MOST VEHEMENT OF MANKIND IN HOSTILITY TO THOSE WHO BELIEVE (TO BE) THE JEWS AND THE IDOLATERS.* And thou wilt find the *NEAREST OF THEM IN AFFECTION TO THOSE WHO BELIEVE* (to be) those who say: Lo! We are *CHRISTIANS.* That is because there are among them *PRIESTS* and *MONKS,* and because they are not proud.

5:83 When they listen to that which hath been revealed unto the messengers, thou seest their eyes overflow with tears because of *THEIR RECOGNITION OF THE TRUTH. THEY SAY: OUR LORD, WE BELIEVE.* Inscribe us as among the witnesses.

5:84 How should we not *BELIEVE* in Allah and that which hath come unto us of *THE TRUTH.* And (how should we not) hope that our Lord will bring us in along with righteous folk?

5:85 Allah hath rewarded them for that their saying - *GARDENS UNDERNEATH* which rivers flow [Paradise], wherein they will abide for ever. That is *THE REWARD OF THE GOOD.*

5:86 But *THOSE WHO DISBELIEVE AND DENY OUR REVELATIONS, THEY ARE OWNERS OF HELL-FIRE.*

5:87 O *YE WHO BELIEVE*! Forbid not the good things which Allah hath made lawful for you, and transgress not, Lo! Allah loveth not transgressors.

5:88 Eat of that which Allah hath bestowed on you as food lawful and good, and *KEEP YOUR DUTY TO ALLAH IN WHOM YE ARE BELIEVERS.*

5:89 Allah will not take you to task for that which is unintentional in your oaths, but He will take you to task for the oaths which ye swear in earnest. The expiation thereof is the feeding of ten of the needy with the average of that wherewith ye feed your own folk, or the clothing of them, or the liberation of a slave, and for him who findeth not (the wherewithal to do so) then a three days' fast. This is the expiation of your oaths when ye have sworn; and keep your oaths. Thus Allah expoundeth unto you His revelations in order that ye may give thanks.

5:90 O *YE WHO BELIEVE*! *STRONG DRINK* and games of chance and idols and divining arrows are only an infamy of Satan's handiwork. *LEAVE IT ASIDE IN ORDER THAT YE MAY SUCCEED.* [Avoidance of alcohol is a tactical measure NOT a moral prohibition, i.e. it is avoided in order for Muslims to succeed in their subjugation of non-Muslims. In the Islamic system of values once they die as Jihadis and granted entry to Paradise, they are rewarded in Paradise with unlimited alcohol.]

5:91 Satan seeketh only to cast among you enmity and hatred by means of strong drink and games of chance, and to turn you from remembrance of Allah and from (His) worship. Will ye then have done?

5:92 *OBEY ALLAH AND OBEY THE MESSENGER,* and beware! But if ye turn away, then know that the duty of Our messenger is only plain conveyance (of the message).

5:93 There shall be no sin (imputed) unto *THOSE WHO BELIEVE AND DO GOOD WORKS* for what they may have eaten (in the past). So *BE MINDFUL OF YOUR DUTY (TO ALLAH),* and *BELIEVE,* and do good works; and again: *BE MINDFUL OF YOUR DUTY,* and *BELIEVE*; and once again: *BE MINDFUL OF YOUR DUTY,* and do right. Allah loveth the good.

5:94 O *YE WHO BELIEVE*! Allah will surely try you somewhat (in the matter) of the game which ye take with your hands and your spears, that Allah may know him who feareth Him in secret. Whoso transgresseth after this, for him there is *A PAINFUL DOOM.*

5:95 O *YE WHO BELIEVE*! Kill no wild game while ye are on the pilgrimage. Whoso of you killeth it of set purpose he shall pay its forfeit in the equivalent of that which he hath killed, of domestic animals, the judge to be two men among you known for justice, (the forfeit) to be brought as an offering to the Ka'bah; or, for expiation, he shall feed poor persons, or the equivalent thereof in fasting, that he may taste the *EVIL* consequences of his deed. Allah forgiveth whatever (of this kind) may have happened in the past, but whoso relapseth, Allah will take retribution from him. Allah is Mighty, Able to Requite (the wrong). [Islamic charity is only extended to Muslims or in attempting to win converts to Islam.]

5:96 To hunt and to eat the fish of the sea is made lawful for you, a provision for you and for seafarers; but to hunt on land is forbidden you so long as ye are on the pilgrimage. *BE MINDFUL OF YOUR DUTY TO ALLAH,* unto Whom ye will be gathered.

5:97 Allah hath appointed the Ka'bah, the Sacred House, a standard for mankind, and the Sacred Month and the offerings and the garlands. That is so that ye may know that Allah knoweth whatsoever is in the heavens and whatsoever is in the earth, and that Allah is Knower of all things.

5:98 Know that Allah is severe in punishment, but that Allah (also) is Forgiving, Merciful.

5:99 ~~The duty of the messenger is only to convey (the message). Allah knoweth what ye proclaim and what ye hide.~~ [Cancelled by verse 9:5][399]

5:100 Say: The *EVIL* and the good are not alike even *THOUGH THE PLENTY OF THE EVIL ATTRACT THEE*. So *BE MINDFUL OF YOUR DUTY TO ALLAH*, O men of understanding, *THAT YE MAY SUCCEED*.

5:101 O *YE WHO BELIEVE*! Ask not of things which, if they were made unto you, would trouble you; but if ye ask of them when the Qur'an is being revealed, they will be made known unto you. Allah pardoneth this, for Allah is Forgiving, Clement.

5:102 A folk before you asked (for such disclosures) *AND THEN DISBELIEVED* therein.

5:103 Allah hath not appointed anything in the nature of a Bahirah or a Sa'ibah or a Wasilah or a Hami, but *THOSE WHO DISBELIEVE INVENT A LIE AGAINST ALLAH*. Most of them have no sense.

5:104 And when it is said unto them: Come unto that which Allah hath revealed and unto the messenger, they say: Enough for us is that wherein we found our fathers. What! Even though *THEIR FATHERS HAD NO KNOWLEDGE WHATSOEVER, AND NO GUIDANCE?*

5:105 O *YE WHO BELIEVE*! Ye have charge of your own souls. He who erreth cannot injure you if ye are rightly guided. Unto Allah ye will all return; and then He will inform you of what ye used to do.

5:106 O *YE WHO BELIEVE*! Let there be witnesses between you when death draweth nigh unto one of you, at the time of bequest - two witnesses, just men from among you, or two others from another tribe, in case ye are campaigning in the land and the calamity of death befall you. Ye shall empanel them both after the prayer, and, if ye doubt, they shall be made to swear by Allah (saying): We will not take a bribe, even though it were (on behalf of) a near kinsman nor will we hide the testimony of Allah, for then indeed we should be of the sinful.

5:107 But then, if it is afterwards ascertained that both of them merit (the suspicion of) sin, let two others take their place of those nearly concerned, and let them swear by Allah, (saying): Verily our testimony is truer than their testimony and we have not transgressed (the bounds of duty), for them indeed we should be of the *EVIL-DOERS*.

5:108 Thus it is more likely that they will bear true witness or fear that after their oaths the oaths (of others) will be taken. So *BE MINDFUL OF YOUR DUTY (TO ALLAH)* and hearken. Allah guideth not the froward [contrary] folk.

5:109 In the day when Allah gathereth together the messengers, and saith: What was your response (from mankind)? they say: We have no knowledge. Lo! Thou, only Thou art the Knower of Things Hidden,

5:110 When Allah saith: O *JESUS, SON OF MARY*! Remember My favour unto thee and unto thy mother; how I strengthened thee with the holy Spirit, so that thou spakest unto mankind in the cradle as in maturity; and how I taught thee the Scripture and Wisdom and the Torah and the Gospel; and how thou didst shape of clay as it were the likeness of a bird by My permission, and didst blow upon it and it was a bird by My permission, and thou didst heal him who was born blind and the leper by My permission; and how thou didst raise the dead by My permission; and how I restrained *THE CHILDREN OF ISRAEL* from (harming) thee when thou camest unto them with *CLEAR PROOFS*, and those of them who *DISBELIEVED* exclaimed: This is naught else than mere magic; [Koran admits Jesus performed miracles; no mention of Mohammed performing miracles.]

5:111 And when I inspired the disciples, (saying): *BELIEVE* in Me and in My messenger, they said: We *BELIEVE*. Bear witness that we have surrendered (unto Thee) "we are *MUSLIMS*". [The Pickthall translation goes as far as claiming the Disciples of Jesus were Muslims.]

5:112 When the disciples said: O *JESUS, SON OF MARY*! Is thy Lord able to send down for us a table spread with food from heaven? He said: Observe *YOUR DUTY TO ALLAH*, if ye are true *BELIEVERS*.

5:113 (They said:) We wish to eat thereof, that we may satisfy our hearts and know that thou hast spoken truth to us, and that thereof we may be witnesses.

5:114 *JESUS, SON OF MARY*, said: O Allah, Lord of us! Send down for us a table spread with food from heaven, that it may be a feast for us, for the first of us and for the last of us, and a sign from Thee. Give us sustenance, for Thou art the Best of Sustainers.

5:115 Allah said: Lo! I send it down for you. And *WHOSO DISBELIEVETH OF YOU AFTERWARD, HIM SURELY WILL I PUNISH WITH A PUNISHMENT WHEREWITH I HAVE NOT PUNISHED ANY OF (MY) CREATURES.* [Allah reserves his worst punishment for those who leave Islam.]

5:116 And when Allah saith: O *JESUS, SON OF MARY*! Didst thou say unto mankind: Take me and my mother for two gods beside Allah? he saith: Be glorified! It was not mine to utter that to which I had no right. If I used to say it, then Thou knewest it. Thou knowest what is in my mind, and I know not what is in Thy Mind. Lo! Thou, only Thou, art the Knower of Things Hidden?

5:117 I spake unto them only that which Thou commandedst me, (saying): Worship Allah, my Lord and your Lord. I was a witness of them while I dwelt among them, and when Thou tookest me Thou wast the Watcher over them. Thou art Witness over all things.

5:118 *IF THOU PUNISH THEM, LO! THEY ARE THY SLAVES, AND IF THOU FORGIVE THEM (LO! THEY ARE THY SLAVES)*. Lo! Thou, only Thou, art the Mighty, the Wise.

5:119 Allah saith: *THIS IS A DAY* in which their *TRUTHFULNESS PROFITETH THE TRUTHFUL, FOR THEIRS ARE GARDENS UNDERNEATH WHICH RIVERS FLOW, WHEREIN THEY ARE SECURE FOR EVER*, Allah taking pleasure in them and they in Him. That is the great *TRIUMPH*. [According to the Koran only Muslims are truthful and only devout Muslims are going to Paradise.]

5:120 Unto Allah belongeth the Sovereignty of the heavens and the earth and whatsoever is therein, and He is Able to do all things.

Chapter 48 - Victory

48:1 Lo! We have given thee (O Muhammad) *A SIGNAL VICTORY*,

48:2 That *ALLAH MAY FORGIVE THEE OF THY SIN* that which is past and that which is to come, and may perfect His favour unto thee, and may guide thee on *A RIGHT PATH*,

48:3 And that Allah may help thee with strong help -

48:4 He it is Who sent down peace of reassurance into the hearts of the *BELIEVERS* that they might add faith unto their faith. *ALLAH'S ARE THE HOSTS [ARMIES] OF THE HEAVENS AND THE EARTH*, and Allah is ever Knower, Wise -

48:5 That He may bring *THE BELIEVING MEN* and the *BELIEVING* women into *GARDENS UNDERNEATH* which rivers flow [Paradise], wherein they will abide, and may remit from them their *EVIL* deeds - That, in the sight of Allah, is the *SUPREME TRIUMPH* -

48:6 And may *PUNISH THE HYPOCRITICAL MEN* and the *HYPOCRITICAL* women, and the *IDOLATROUS* men and the *IDOLATROUS* women, *WHO THINK AN EVIL THOUGHT CONCERNING ALLAH*. For them is the *EVIL* turn of fortune, and *ALLAH IS WROTH* [angry] against them and *HATH CURSED THEM, AND HATH MADE READY FOR THEM HELL*, a hapless journey's end.

48:7 *ALLAH'S ARE THE HOSTS [ARMIES] OF THE HEAVENS AND THE EARTH*, and Allah is ever Mighty, Wise.

48:8 Lo! We have sent thee (O Muhammad) as a witness and a bearer of good tidings and a warner,

48:9 That *YE (MANKIND) MAY BELIEVE IN ALLAH AND HIS MESSENGER,* and may honour Him, and may revere Him, and may glorify Him at early dawn and at the close of day.

48:10 Lo! *THOSE WHO SWEAR ALLEGIANCE UNTO THEE (MUHAMMAD), SWEAR ALLEGIANCE ONLY UNTO ALLAH*. The Hand of Allah is above their hands. So whosoever breaketh his oath, breaketh it only to his soul's hurt; while *WHOSOEVER KEEPETH HIS COVENANT WITH ALLAH, ON HIM WILL HE BESTOW IMMENSE REWARD.*

48:11 Those of the wandering Arabs who were left behind will tell thee: Our possessions and our households occupied us, so ask forgiveness for us! They speak with their tongues that which is not in their hearts. Say: *WHO CAN AVAIL YOU AUGHT AGAINST ALLAH, IF HE INTEND YOU HURT OR INTEND YOU PROFIT?* Nay, but Allah is ever Aware of what ye do.

48:12 Nay, but _YE DEEMED THAT THE MESSENGER AND THE BELIEVERS WOULD NEVER RETURN TO THEIR_ _OWN FOLK_, and that was made fairseeming in your hearts, and _YE DID THINK AN EVIL THOUGHT_, and _YE_ _WERE WORTHLESS FOLK._

48:13 And so for _HIM WHO BELIEVETH NOT IN ALLAH AND HIS MESSENGER_ - Lo! _WE HAVE PREPARED A_ _FLAME FOR DISBELIEVERS._

48:14 And Allah's is the Sovereignty of the heavens and the earth. He _FORGIVETH WHOM HE WILL_, and punisheth whom He will. And Allah is ever Forgiving, Merciful.

48:15 Those who were left behind will say, when ye _SET FORTH TO CAPTURE_ _BOOTY [SLAVES AND LOOT]_: Let us go with you. They fain would change the verdict of Allah. Say (unto them, O Muhammad): Ye shall not go with us. Thus hath Allah said beforehand. Then they will say: Ye are envious of us. Nay, but they understand not, save a little.

48:16 Say unto those of the wandering Arabs who were left behind: Ye will be called against a folk of mighty prowess, to _FIGHT THEM UNTIL THEY_ _SURRENDER_; and _IF YE OBEY, ALLAH WILL GIVE YOU A FAIR REWARD_; but _IF YE_ _TURN AWAY AS YE DID TURN AWAY BEFORE, HE WILL PUNISH YOU_ with _A PAINFUL_ _DOOM._

48:17 There is _NO BLAME FOR THE BLIND_, nor is there blame for the lame, _NOR IS THERE BLAME FOR THE SICK (THAT THEY GO NOT FORTH TO WAR)_. And whoso obeyeth Allah and His messenger, He will make him enter _GARDENS UNDERNEATH_ which rivers flow; and whoso turneth back, him will He punish with _A PAINFUL DOOM_. [Jihadis will go to Paradise, slackers will go to Hell.]

48:18 Allah was well pleased with _THE BELIEVERS_ when they _SWORE_ _ALLEGIANCE_ unto thee beneath the tree, and He knew what was in their hearts, and He sent down peace of reassurance on them, and hath rewarded them with a near _VICTORY_;

48:19 And _MUCH BOOTY [SLAVES AND LOOT] THAT THEY WILL CAPTURE_. Allah is ever Mighty, Wise.

48:20 _ALLAH PROMISETH YOU MUCH BOOTY [SLAVES AND LOOT] THAT YE WILL_ _CAPTURE_, and hath given you this in advance, and hath withheld men's hands from you, that it may be a token for _THE BELIEVERS_, and that He may guide you on _A RIGHT PATH_.

48:21 And other (gain), which ye have not been able to achieve, Allah will compass it, Allah is Able to do all things.

48:22 And _IF THOSE WHO DISBELIEVE JOIN BATTLE WITH YOU_ they will take to _FLIGHT_, and afterward _THEY WILL FIND NO PROTECTING FRIEND NOR HELPER_.

48:23 It is the law of Allah which hath taken course aforetime. Thou wilt not find for the law of Allah aught of power to change.

48:24 And He it is Who hath withheld men's hands from you, and hath withheld your hands from them, in the valley of Mecca, after He had _MADE YOU VICTORS OVER THEM_. Allah is Seer of what ye do.

48:25 These it was who _DISBELIEVED_ and debarred you from the Inviolable Place of Worship, and debarred the offering from reaching its goal. And if it had not been for _BELIEVING_ men and _BELIEVING_ women, whom ye know not - lest ye should tread them under foot and thus incur guilt for them unknowingly; that Allah might bring into His mercy whom He will - If (the *BELIEVERS* and the *DISBELIEVERS*) had been clearly separated We verily had *PUNISHED THOSE OF THEM WHO DISBELIEVED WITH PAINFUL PUNISHMENT.*

48:26 When *THOSE WHO DISBELIEVE* had set up in their hearts zealotry, *THE ZEALOTRY OF THE AGE OF IGNORANCE,* then Allah sent down His peace of reassurance upon His messenger and upon the *BELIEVERS* and imposed on them the word of self-restraint, for they were worthy of it and meet for it. And Allah is Aware of all things.

48:27 Allah hath fulfilled the vision for His messenger in very *TRUTH.* Ye shall indeed enter the Inviolable Place of Worship, if Allah will, secure, (having your hair) shaven and cut, not fearing. But He knoweth that which ye know not, and hath given you a near *VICTORY* beforehand.

48:28 He it is Who hath sent His messenger with the guidance and *THE RELIGION OF TRUTH,* that He may cause it *TO PREVAIL OVER ALL RELIGION.* And Allah sufficeth as a Witness. [All other religions are lies and are to be subjugated to Islam. So much for inter-faith dialogue.]

48:29 *MUHAMMAD IS THE MESSENGER OF ALLAH. AND THOSE WITH HIM ARE HARD AGAINST THE DISBELIEVERS* and merciful among themselves. Thou (O Muhammad) seest them bowing and falling prostrate (in worship), seeking bounty from Allah and (His) acceptance. The mark of them is on their foreheads from the traces of prostration. Such is their likeness in the Torah and their likeness in the Gospel - like as sown corn that sendeth forth its shoot and strengtheneth it and riseth firm upon its stalk, delighting the sowers - that He may *ENRAGE THE DISBELIEVERS* with (the sight of) them. *ALLAH HATH PROMISED, UNTO SUCH OF THEM AS BELIEVE AND DO GOOD WORKS, FORGIVENESS AND IMMENSE REWARD.* [Since believers are hard against unbelievers, clearly "good works" and "forgiveness" are only applicable in relations between believers.]

Chapter 62 - The Congregation

62:1 All that is in the heavens and all that is in the earth glorifieth Allah, the Sovereign Lord, the Holy One, the Mighty, the Wise.

62:2 He it is Who hath sent among the unlettered ones a messenger of their own, to recite unto them His revelations and to make them grow, and to teach them the Scripture and wisdom, though heretofore they were indeed in error manifest,

62:3 Along with others of them who have not yet joined them. He is the Mighty, the Wise.

62:4 That is the bounty of Allah; which He giveth unto whom He will. Allah is of Infinite Bounty.

62:5 The likeness of those who are entrusted with the Law of Moses, yet apply it not, is as the likeness of the ass carrying books. Wretched is the likeness of folk who deny the revelations of Allah. And Allah guideth not wrongdoing folk.

62:6 Say (O Muhammad): O *YE WHO ARE JEWS! IF YE CLAIM THAT YE ARE FAVOURED OF ALLAH APART FROM (ALL) MANKIND, THEN LONG FOR DEATH IF YE ARE TRUTHFUL.*

62:7 But they will never long for it because of all that their own hands have sent before, and *ALLAH IS AWARE OF EVIL-DOERS.*

62:8 Say (unto them, O Muhammad): Lo! the death from which ye shrink will surely meet you, and afterward ye will be returned unto the Knower of the Invisible and the Visible, and He will tell you what ye used to do.

62:9 O *YE WHO BELIEVE*! When the call is heard for the prayer of the day of congregation, haste unto remembrance of Allah and leave your trading. That is better for you if ye did but know.

62:10 And when the prayer is ended, then disperse in the land and seek of Allah's bounty, and remember Allah much, *THAT YE MAY BE SUCCESSFUL.*

62:11 But when they spy some merchandise or pastime they break away to it and leave thee standing. Say: That which Allah hath is better than pastime and than merchandise, and *ALLAH IS THE BEST OF PROVIDERS.*

Chapter 61 - The Ranks

61:1 All that is in the heavens and all that is in the earth glorifieth Allah, and He is the Mighty, the Wise.

61:2 O *YE WHO BELIEVE*! Why say ye that which ye do not?

61:3 *IT IS MOST HATEFUL IN THE SIGHT OF ALLAH THAT YE SAY THAT WHICH YE DO NOT.* [Allah hates Muslims who do not act on the words from the Koran which they recite.]

61:4 Lo! *ALLAH LOVETH THEM WHO BATTLE FOR HIS CAUSE IN RANKS [AN ARMY OF JIHADIS]*, **as if they were a solid structure.**

61:5 And (remember) when Moses said unto his people: O my people! Why persecute ye me, when ye well know that I am Allah's messenger unto you? So when they went astray Allah sent their hearts astray. And *ALLAH GUIDETH NOT THE EVIL-LIVING FOLK*.

61:6 And when *JESUS SON OF MARY* said: O *CHILDREN OF ISRAEL*! Lo! I am the messenger of Allah unto you, confirming that which was (revealed) before me in the Torah, and bringing good tidings of a messenger who cometh after me, whose name is the Praised One. Yet when he hath come unto them with *CLEAR PROOFS*, they say: This is mere magic.

61:7 And who doeth greater wrong than *HE WHO INVENTETH A LIE AGAINST ALLAH* when he is summoned unto Al-Islam? And Allah guideth not *WRONGDOING FOLK*.

61:8 Fain would they put out the light of Allah with their mouths, but Allah will perfect His light however much the *DISBELIEVERS* are averse.

61:9 He it is Who hath sent His messenger with the guidance and the *RELIGION OF TRUTH*, **that He may** *MAKE IT CONQUEROR OF ALL RELIGION HOWEVER MUCH IDOLATERS MAY BE AVERSE*. **[Islam is to subjugate all other beliefs and followers, regardless of how much non-Muslims might hate this.]**

61:10 O *YE WHO BELIEVE*! **Shall I show you** *A COMMERCE THAT WILL SAVE YOU* **from** *A PAINFUL DOOM*?

61:11 *YE SHOULD BELIEVE* **in Allah and His messenger, and should** *STRIVE [JIHAD] FOR THE CAUSE OF ALLAH WITH YOUR WEALTH AND YOUR LIVES*. **That is better for you, if ye did but know.**

61:12 *HE WILL FORGIVE YOU YOUR SINS AND BRING YOU INTO GARDENS UNDERNEATH* **which rivers flow [Paradise], and pleasant dwellings in** *GARDENS OF EDEN*. *THAT IS THE SUPREME TRIUMPH*. **[Allah is clear that Jihadis** will be forgiven **their sins.]**

61:13 And (He will give you) another (blessing) which ye love: help from Allah and present *VICTORY*. **Give good tidings (O Muhammad) to** *BELIEVERS*.

61:14 O *YE WHO BELIEVE*! Be Allah's helpers, even as *JESUS SON OF MARY* said unto the disciples: Who are my helpers for Allah? They said: We are Allah's helpers. And *A PARTY OF THE CHILDREN OF ISRAEL BELIEVED*, while *A PARTY DISBELIEVED*. Then We *STRENGTHENED THOSE WHO BELIEVED* against their foe, and *THEY BECAME THE UPPERMOST*. [Islam has a strategy of divide and conquer, whilst demanding absolute unity from Muslims.]

Chapter 64 - Mutual Dissillusion

64:1 All that is in the heavens and all that is in the earth glorifieth Allah; unto Him belongeth Sovereignty and unto Him belongeth praise, and He is Able to do all things.

64:2 He it is Who created you, but *ONE OF YOU IS A DISBELIEVER AND ONE OF YOU IS A BELIEVER*, and Allah is Seer of what ye do.

64:3 He created the heavens and the earth with truth, and He shaped you and made good your shapes, and unto Him is the journeying.

64:4 He knoweth all that is in the heavens and the earth, and He knoweth what ye conceal and what ye publish. And Allah is Aware of what is in the breasts (of men).

64:5 Hath not the story reached you of *THOSE WHO DISBELIEVED* of old and so did taste the ill-effects of their conduct, and *THEIRS WILL BE A PAINFUL DOOM.*

64:6 That was because their messengers (from Allah) kept coming unto them with *CLEAR PROOFS* (of Allah's Sovereignty), but they said: Shall mere mortals guide us? So *THEY DISBELIEVED AND TURNED AWAY*, and Allah was independent (of them). Allah is Absolute, Owner of Praise.

64:7 *THOSE WHO DISBELIEVE ASSERT THAT THEY WILL NOT BE RAISED AGAIN.* Say (unto them, O Muhammad): Yea, verily, by my Lord! ye will be raised again and then ye will be informed of what ye did; and that is easy for Allah.

64:8 So *BELIEVE* in Allah and His messenger and the light which We have revealed. And Allah is Informed of what ye do.

64:9 The day when He shall gather you unto the *DAY OF ASSEMBLING*, that will be a day of mutual disillusion. And *WHOSO BELIEVETH IN ALLAH AND DOETH RIGHT, HE WILL REMIT FROM HIM HIS EVIL DEEDS AND WILL BRING HIM UNTO GARDENS UNDERNEATH* which rivers flow [Paradise], therein to abide for ever. That is the *SUPREME TRIUMPH*. [The evil deeds of a Muslim are forgiven provided he has done the right things, i.e. conducted Jihad.]

64:10 But those who *DISBELIEVE* and deny Our revelations, such are *OWNERS OF THE FIRE*; they will abide therein - a hapless journey's end!

64:11 No calamity befalleth save by Allah's leave. And whosoever *BELIEVETH* in Allah, He guideth his heart. And Allah is Knower of all things.

64:12 *OBEY ALLAH AND OBEY HIS MESSENGER*; but if ye turn away, then the duty of Our messenger is only to convey (the message) plainly.

64:13 Allah! There is no God save Him. In Allah, therefore, let *BELIEVERS* put their trust.

64:14 O *YE WHO BELIEVE!* Lo! *AMONG YOUR WIVES AND YOUR CHILDREN THERE ARE ENEMIES FOR YOU*, therefore beware of them. And if ye efface and overlook and forgive, then lo! Allah is Forgiving, Merciful. [Muslims cannot trust their own family.]

64:15 *YOUR WEALTH AND YOUR CHILDREN ARE ONLY A TEMPTATION*, whereas Allah! *WITH HIM IS AN IMMENSE REWARD*.

64:16 So *KEEP YOUR DUTY TO ALLAH* as best ye can, and *LISTEN, AND OBEY, AND SPEND*; that is better for your souls. And whoso is saved from his own greed, *SUCH ARE THE SUCCESSFUL*.

64:17 If ye *LEND UNTO ALLAH A GOODLY LOAN, HE WILL DOUBLE IT FOR YOU* and will forgive you, for Allah is Responsive, Clement,

64:18 Knower of the Invisible and the Visible, the Mighty, the Wise.

Chapter 66 - Banning

66:1 O Prophet! Why bannest thou that which Allah hath made lawful for thee, seeking to please thy wives? And Allah is Forgiving, Merciful.

66:2 *ALLAH HATH MADE LAWFUL FOR YOU (MUSLIMS) ABSOLUTION FROM YOUR OATHS* (of such a kind), and Allah is your Protector. He is the Knower, the Wise. [Muslims are forgiven for breaking promises to their wives.]

66:3 When the Prophet confided a fact unto one of his wives and when she afterward divulged it and Allah apprised him thereof, he made known (to her) part thereof and passed over part. And when he told it her she said: Who hath told thee? He said: The Knower, the Aware hath told me.

66:4 If ye twain turn unto Allah repentant, (ye have cause to do so) for your hearts desired (the ban); and if ye aid one another against him (Muhammad) then lo! Allah, even He, is his Protecting Friend, and Gabriel and the righteous among the *BELIEVERS*; and furthermore the angels are his helpers.

66:5 It may happen that his Lord, if he divorce you, will give him in your stead wives better than you, submissive (to Allah), *BELIEVING*, pious, penitent, devout, inclined to fasting, widows and maids.

66:6 O *YE WHO BELIEVE*! Ward off from yourselves and your families *A FIRE WHEREOF THE FUEL IS MEN* and stones, over which are set angels strong, severe, who resist not Allah in that which He commandeth them, but do that which they are commanded.

66:7 (Then it will be said): O *YE WHO DISBELIEVE*! Make no excuses for yourselves this day. Ye are *ONLY BEING PAID FOR WHAT YE USED TO DO.*

66:8 O _YE WHO BELIEVE_! Turn unto Allah in sincere repentance! It _MAY BE THAT YOUR LORD WILL REMIT FROM YOU YOUR EVIL DEEDS AND BRING YOU INTO GARDENS UNDERNEATH_ which rivers flow [Paradise], on the day when Allah will not abase the Prophet and _THOSE WHO BELIEVE_ with him. Their light will run before them and on their right hands; they will say: Our Lord! Perfect our light for us, and forgive us! Lo! Thou art Able to do all things. [Jihadis are promised Paradise. Other Muslims are told that Allah "may" remit their sins.]

66:9 O Prophet! _STRIVE [JIHAD] AGAINST THE DISBELIEVERS_ and the _HYPOCRITES_, and _BE STERN WITH THEM. HELL WILL BE THEIR HOME_, a hapless journey's end. [Jihad is to be targeted not just at non-Muslims but also at Muslims who are judged not sufficiently devout.]

66:10 Allah citeth an example for *THOSE WHO DISBELIEVE*: the wife of Noah and the wife of Lot, who were under two of Our righteous *SLAVES* yet betrayed them so that they (the husbands) availed them naught against Allah and it was said (unto them): Enter *THE FIRE* along with those who enter.

66:11 And Allah citeth an example for those who *BELIEVE*: the wife of Pharaoh when she said: My Lord! Build for me a home with thee in the Garden, and deliver me from Pharaoh and his work, and deliver me from evil-doing folk;

66:12 And Mary, daughter of 'Imran, whose body was chaste, therefor We breathed therein something of Our Spirit. And she put faith in the words of her Lord and His scriptures, and was of the obedient.

Chapter 49 - The Private Apartments

49:1 *O YE WHO BELIEVE*! Be not forward in the presence of Allah and His messenger, and *KEEP YOUR DUTY TO ALLAH*. Lo! Allah is Hearer, Knower.

49:2 *O YE WHO BELIEVE*! Lift not up your voices above the voice of the Prophet, nor shout when speaking to him as ye shout one to another, lest your works be rendered vain while ye perceive not.

49:3 Lo! they who subdue their voices in the presence of the messenger of Allah, those are they whose hearts Allah hath proven unto righteousness. Theirs will be forgiveness and immense reward.

49:4 Lo! those who call thee from behind the private apartments, most of them have no sense.

49:5 And if they had had patience till thou camest forth unto them, it had been better for them. And Allah is Forgiving, Merciful.

49:6 O *YE WHO BELIEVE*! **If an evil-liver bring you tidings, verify it,** *LEST YE SMITE SOME FOLK IN IGNORANCE* **and afterward repent of what ye did. [Muslims are to regard unbelievers and slackers as liars.]**

49:7 And know that the messenger of Allah is among you. If he were to obey you in much of the government, ye would surely be in trouble; but Allah hath endeared the faith to you and hath beautified it in your hearts, and hath *MADE DISBELIEF AND LEWDNESS AND REBELLION HATEFUL UNTO YOU.* Such are they who are the rightly guided.

49:8 (It is) a bounty and a grace from Allah; and Allah is Knower, Wise.

49:9 And *IF TWO PARTIES OF BELIEVERS FALL TO FIGHTING, THEN MAKE PEACE BETWEEN THEM*. And if one party of them doeth wrong to the other, fight ye that which doeth wrong till it return unto the ordinance of Allah; then, if it return, make peace between them justly, and act equitably. Lo! Allah loveth the equitable.

49:10 *THE BELIEVERS ARE NAUGHT ELSE THAN BROTHERS.* **Therefore make peace between your brethren and** *OBSERVE YOUR DUTY TO ALLAH THAT HAPLY YE MAY OBTAIN MERCY.*

49:11 O *YE WHO BELIEVE*! Let not a folk deride a folk who may be better than they (are), not let women (deride) women who may be better than they are; neither defame one another, nor insult one another by nicknames. Bad is the name of lewdness after faith. And whoso turneth not in repentance, *SUCH ARE EVIL-DOERS.*

49:12 O *YE WHO BELIEVE!* Shun much suspicion; for lo! some suspicion is a crime. And *SPY NOT, NEITHER BACKBITE ONE ANOTHER.* Would one of you love to eat the flesh of his dead brother? Ye abhor that (so abhor the other)! And *KEEP YOUR DUTY (TO ALLAH)*. Lo! Allah is Relenting, Merciful.

49:13 O mankind! Lo! We have created you male and female, and have made you nations and tribes that ye may know one another. Lo! the noblest of you, in the sight of Allah, is the best in conduct. Lo! Allah is Knower, Aware.

49:14 The *WANDERING ARABS SAY: WE BELIEVE*. Say (unto them, O Muhammad): *YE BELIEVE NOT,* but *RATHER SAY "WE SUBMIT,"* for the faith hath not yet entered into your hearts. Yet, if ye *OBEY ALLAH AND HIS MESSENGER,* He will not withhold from you aught of *(THE REWARD OF) YOUR DEEDS*. Lo! Allah is Forgiving, Merciful.

49:15 *THE (TRUE) BELIEVERS ARE THOSE ONLY WHO BELIEVE IN ALLAH AND HIS MESSENGER AND AFTERWARD DOUBT NOT, BUT STRIVE [JIHAD] WITH THEIR WEALTH AND THEIR LIVES FOR THE CAUSE OF ALLAH.* **Such are the sincere.**

49:16 Say (unto them, O Muhammad): Would ye teach Allah your religion, when Allah knoweth all that is in the heavens and all that is in the earth, and Allah is Aware of all things?

49:17 They make it a favour unto thee (Muhammad) that they have surrendered (unto Him). Say: Deem not your Surrender a favour unto me; but Allah doth confer a favour on you, inasmuch as He hath led you to the Faith, if ye are earnest.

49:18 Lo! Allah knoweth the Unseen of the heavens and the earth. And Allah is Seer of what ye do.

Chapter 58 - She That Disputeth

58:1 Allah hath heard the saying of her that disputeth with thee (Muhammad) concerning her husband, and complaineth unto Allah. And Allah heareth your colloquy. Lo! Allah is Hearer, Knower.

58:2 Such of you as put away your wives (by saying they are as their mothers) - They are not their mothers; none are their mothers except those who gave them birth - they indeed utter an ill word and a lie. And lo! Allah is Forgiving, Merciful.

58:3 Those who put away their wives (by saying they are as their mothers) and afterward would go back on that which they have said, *(THE PENALTY) IN THAT CASE (IS) THE FREEING OF A SLAVE* before they touch one another. Unto this ye are exhorted; and Allah is Informed of what ye do.

58:4 And he who findeth not (the wherewithal), let him fast for two successive months before they touch one another; and for him who is unable to do so (the penance is) the feeding of sixty needy ones. This, that ye may put trust in Allah and His Messenger. Such are the limits (imposed by Allah); and *FOR DISBELIEVERS IS A PAINFUL DOOM.*

58:5 Lo! *THOSE WHO OPPOSE ALLAH AND HIS MESSENGER WILL BE ABASED* even as those before them were abased; and We *HAVE SENT DOWN CLEAR TOKENS,* and *FOR DISBELIEVERS IS A SHAMEFUL DOOM*

58:6 On the day when Allah will raise them all together and inform them of what they did. *ALLAH HATH KEPT ACCOUNT* of it while they forgot it. And Allah is Witness over all things.

58:7 Hast thou not seen that Allah knoweth all that is in the heavens and all that is in the earth? There is no secret conference of three but He is their fourth, nor of five but He is their sixth, nor of less than that or more but He is with them wheresoever they may be; and afterward, on *THE DAY OF RESURRECTION,* He will inform them of what they did. Lo! Allah is Knower of all things.

58:8 Hast thou not observed *THOSE WHO WERE FORBIDDEN CONSPIRACY* and afterward returned to that which they had been forbidden, and (now) conspire together for crime and wrongdoing and *DISOBEDIENCE TOWARD THE MESSENGER*? And when they come unto thee they greet thee with a greeting wherewith Allah greeteth thee not, and say within themselves: Why should Allah punish us for what we say? Hell will suffice them; *THEY WILL FEEL THE HEAT* thereof - a hapless journey's end!

58:9 O *YE WHO BELIEVE*! When ye conspire together, conspire not together for crime and wrongdoing and disobedience toward the messenger, but *CONSPIRE TOGETHER FOR RIGHTEOUSNESS AND PIETY, AND KEEP YOUR DUTY TOWARD ALLAH,* unto whom ye will be gathered. [Under Islam devout Muslims are allowed to conspire in secret, whilst all others are punished for conspiracy.]

58:10 Lo! Conspiracy is only of the devil, that he may vex those who *BELIEVE*; but he can harm them not at all unless by Allah's leave. In Allah let *BELIEVERS* put their trust.

58:11 O *YE WHO BELIEVE*! when it is said unto you: Make room! in assemblies, then make room; Allah will make way for you (hereafter). And when it is said: Come up higher! go up higher; Allah will *EXALT THOSE WHO BELIEVE AMONG YOU, AND THOSE WHO HAVE KNOWLEDGE,* to high ranks. Allah is informed of what ye do.

58:12 O *YE WHO BELIEVE*! When ye hold conference with the messenger, offer an alms before your conference. That is better and purer for you. But if ye cannot find (the wherewithal) then lo! Allah is Forgiving, Merciful.

58:13 Fear ye to offer alms before your conference? Then, when ye do it not and Allah hath forgiven you, establish worship and pay the poor-due and *OBEY ALLAH AND HIS MESSENGER.* And Allah is Aware of what ye do.

58:14 Hast thou not seen *THOSE WHO TAKE FOR FRIENDS* a folk with whom Allah is wroth? *THEY ARE NEITHER OF YOU NOR OF THEM,* and they swear a false oath knowingly.

58:15 *ALLAH HATH PREPARED FOR THEM A DREADFUL DOOM.* Evil indeed is that which they are wont to do.

58:16 They make a shelter of their oaths and turn (men) from the way of Allah; so theirs will be a shameful doom.

58:17 Their wealth and their children will avail them naught against Allah. Such are *RIGHTFUL OWNERS OF THE FIRE*; they will abide therein.

58:18 On the day when Allah will raise them all together, then will they swear unto Him as they (now) swear unto you, and they will fancy that they have some standing. Lo! *IS IT NOT THEY WHO ARE THE LIARS?*

58:19 The devil hath engrossed them and so hath caused them to forget remembrance of Allah. They are the devil's party. Lo! is it not the devil's party who will be the *LOSERS*?

58:20 Lo! *THOSE WHO OPPOSE ALLAH* and His messenger, they will be among the lowest.

58:21 *ALLAH HATH DECREED: LO! I VERILY SHALL CONQUER,* I and My messengers. Lo! Allah is Strong, Almighty.

58:22 Thou wilt *NOT FIND FOLK WHO BELIEVE IN ALLAH AND THE LAST DAY LOVING THOSE WHO OPPOSE ALLAH AND HIS MESSENGER, EVEN THOUGH THEY BE THEIR FATHERS OR THEIR SONS OR THEIR BRETHREN OR THEIR CLAN.* [Muslim converts cannot love their real family if the family are critical of Islam.] As for such, He hath written faith upon their hearts and hath strengthened them with a Spirit from Him, and He will bring them into

GARDENS UNDERNEATH **which rivers flow, wherein they will abide. Allah is well pleased with them, and they are well pleased with Him. They are Allah's party. Lo! is it not Allah's party** *WHO ARE THE SUCCESSFUL***?**

Chapter 63 - The Hypocrites

63:1 When *THE HYPOCRITES* come unto thee (O Muhammad), they say: We bear witness that thou art indeed Allah's messenger. And Allah knoweth that thou art indeed His messenger, and Allah beareth witness that *THE HYPOCRITES INDEED ARE SPEAKING FALSELY.*

63:2 They make their faith a pretext so that they may turn (men) from the way of Allah. Verily *EVIL* is that which they are wont to do,

63:3 That is *BECAUSE THEY BELIEVED, THEN DISBELIEVED,* therefore their hearts are sealed so that they understand not.

63:4 And when thou seest them their figures please thee; and if they speak thou givest ear unto their speech. (They are) as though they were blocks of wood in striped cloaks. They deem every shout to be against them. *THEY ARE THE ENEMY, SO BEWARE OF THEM.* Allah confound them! How *THEY ARE PERVERTED!*

63:5 And when it is said unto them: Come! The messenger of Allah will ask forgiveness for you! they avert their faces and thou seest them turning away, disdainful.

63:6 *WHETHER THOU ASK FORGIVENESS FOR THEM OR ASK NOT FORGIVENESS FOR THEM IS ALL ONE FOR THEM; ALLAH WILL NOT FORGIVE THEM.* Lo! Allah guideth not *THE EVIL-LIVING FOLK.*

63:7 They it is who say: Spend not on behalf of those (who dwell) with Allah's messenger that they may disperse (and go away from you); when Allah's are the treasures of the heavens and the earth; but the *HYPOCRITES* comprehend not.

63:8 They say: Surely, if we return to Al-Madinah *THE MIGHTIER WILL SOON DRIVE OUT THE WEAKER*; when *MIGHT BELONGETH TO ALLAH* and to His messenger and to *THE BELIEVERS*; but *THE HYPOCRITES* know not. [In Islam, might is right.]

63:9 O *YE WHO BELIEVE*! *LET NOT YOUR WEALTH NOR YOUR CHILDREN DISTRACT YOU* from remembrance of Allah. Those who do so, they are the *LOSERS.*

63:10 And *SPEND OF THAT WHEREWITH WE HAVE PROVIDED YOU* before death cometh unto one of you and he saith: My Lord! If only thou wouldst reprieve me for a little while, then I would give alms and be among the righteous.

63:11 But Allah reprieveth no soul when its term cometh, and Allah is Informed of what ye do.

Chapter 22 - The Pilgrimage

22:1 O mankind! Fear your Lord. Lo! the earthquake of *THE HOUR (OF DOOM)* is a tremendous thing.

22:2 On the day when ye behold it, every nursing mother will forget her nursling and every pregnant one will be delivered of her burden, and thou (Muhammad) wilt see mankind as drunken, yet they will not be drunken, but *THE DOOM OF ALLAH* will be strong (upon them).

22:3 Among mankind is *HE WHO DISPUTETH CONCERNING ALLAH* without knowledge, and followeth each froward [contrary] devil;

22:4 For him it is decreed that *WHOSO TAKETH HIM FOR FRIEND***, he verily will mislead him and will guide him to the** *PUNISHMENT OF THE FLAME***. [There is to be no dissent, no free thought among Muslims; they must not take dissenters as friends or Muslim are also promised eternal punishment.]**

22:5 O mankind! if ye are in doubt concerning *THE RESURRECTION,* then lo! We have created you from dust, then from a drop of seed, then from a clot, then from a little lump of flesh shapely and shapeless, that We may make (it) clear for you. And We cause what We will to remain in the wombs for an appointed time, and afterward We bring you forth as infants, then (give you growth) that ye attain your full strength. And among you there is he who dieth (young), and among you there is he who is brought back to the most abject time of life, so that, after knowledge, he knoweth naught. And thou (Muhammad) seest the earth barren, but when We send down water thereon, it doth thrill and swell and put forth every lovely kind (of growth).

22:6 That is because *ALLAH, HE IS THE TRUTH* and because He quickeneth the dead, and because He is Able to do all things;

22:7 And because the Hour will come, there is no doubt thereof; and because Allah will raise those who are in the graves.

22:8 And among mankind is *HE WHO DISPUTETH CONCERNING ALLAH* without knowledge or guidance or a scripture giving light,

22:9 Turning away in pride to beguile (men) from the way of Allah. For him in this world is ignominy, and on *THE DAY OF RESURRECTION* We make him *TASTE THE DOOM OF BURNING.*

22:10 (And unto him it will be said): This is for that which thy two hands have sent before, and because *ALLAH IS NO OPPRESSOR OF HIS SLAVES.*

22:11 And among mankind is he who worshippeth Allah upon a narrow marge so that if good befalleth him he is content therewith, but if a trial befalleth him, he falleth away utterly. He loseth both the world and the Hereafter. That is the sheer loss.

22:12 He calleth, beside Allah, unto that which hurteth him not nor benefiteth him. That is the far error.

22:13 He calleth unto him whose harm is nearer than his benefit; verily an *EVIL* patron and verily an *EVIL* friend!

22:14 Lo! Allah causeth *THOSE WHO BELIEVE AND DO GOOD WORKS TO ENTER GARDENS UNDERNEATH* which rivers flow. Lo! Allah doth what He intendeth. [Jihadis go to Paradise. Funding Jihad is one of the main forms of "charity" in Islam.]

22:15 Whoso is wont to think (through envy) that Allah will not give him (Muhammad) *VICTORY IN THE WORLD AND THE HEREAFTER* (and is enraged at the thought of his *VICTORY*), let him stretch a rope up to the roof (of his dwelling), and *LET HIM HANG HIMSELF.* Then let him see whether his strategy dispelleth that whereat he rageth!

22:16 Thus We reveal it as *PLAIN REVELATIONS,* and verily *ALLAH GUIDETH WHOM HE WILL.*

22:17 Lo! *THOSE WHO BELIEVE* (this revelation), and those who are *JEWS,* and the Sabaeans and the *CHRISTIANS* and the Magians and the *IDOLATERS* - Lo! Allah will decide between them on *THE DAY OF RESURRECTION.* Lo! Allah is Witness over all things.

22:18 Hast thou not seen that unto Allah payeth adoration whosoever is in the heavens and whosoever is in the earth, and the sun, and the moon, and the stars, and the hills, and the trees, and the beasts, and many of mankind, while there are many unto whom the doom is justly due. He whom Allah scorneth, there is none to give him honour. Lo! Allah doeth what He will.

22:19 These twain *(THE BELIEVERS AND THE DISBELIEVERS) ARE TWO OPPONENTS* who contend concerning their Lord. But as *FOR THOSE WHO DISBELIEVE,* garments of fire will be cut out for them; *BOILING FLUID WILL BE POURED DOWN ON THEIR HEADS,* [Unbelievers to be tortured in Hell]

22:20 Whereby that which is in their bellies, and *THEIR SKINS TOO, WILL BE MELTED*;

22:21 And for them are *HOOKED RODS OF IRON.*

22:22 Whenever, in their anguish, they would go forth from thence they are driven back therein and (it is said unto them): *TASTE THE DOOM OF BURNING.*

22:23 Lo! *ALLAH WILL CAUSE THOSE WHO BELIEVE AND DO GOOD WORKS TO ENTER GARDENS UNDERNEATH* which rivers flow, wherein they will be

allowed *ARMLETS OF GOLD, AND PEARLS, AND THEIR RAIMENT THEREIN WILL BE SILK*. **[The luxuries of Paradise contrasted with the horrors of Hell.]**

22:24 They are guided unto gentle speech; they are guided unto the path of the Glorious One.

22:25 Lo! *THOSE WHO DISBELIEVE* and bar (men) from the way of Allah and from the Inviolable Place of Worship, which We have appointed for mankind together, the dweller therein and the nomad: whosoever seeketh wrongful partiality therein, him *WE SHALL CAUSE TO TASTE A PAINFUL DOOM.*

22:26 And (remember) when We prepared for Abraham the place of the (holy) House, saying: Ascribe thou no thing as partner unto Me, and purify My House for those who make the round (thereof) and those who stand and those who bow and make prostration.

22:27 And proclaim unto mankind the pilgrimage. They will come unto thee on foot and on every lean camel; they will come from every deep ravine,

22:28 That they may witness things that are of benefit to them, and mention the name of Allah on appointed days over the beast of cattle that He hath bestowed upon them. Then eat thereof and feed therewith the poor unfortunate.

22:29 Then let them make an end of their unkemptness and pay their vows and go around the ancient House.

22:30 That (is the command). And whoso magnifieth the sacred things of Allah, it will be well for him in the sight of his Lord. The cattle are lawful unto you save that which hath been told you. So *SHUN THE FILTH OF IDOLS, AND SHUN LYING SPEECH*, [Note: total lack of respect for any other religion. Islam is "the religion of truth" whilst all other religions are lies. So much for inter-faith dialogue.]

22:31 Turning unto Allah (only), not ascribing partners unto Him; for *WHOSO ASCRIBETH PARTNERS UNTO ALLAH*, it is as if he had fallen from the sky and the birds had snatched him or the wind had blown him to a far-off place.

22:32 That (is the command). And whoso magnifieth the offerings consecrated to Allah, it surely is from devotion of the hearts,

22:33 Therein are benefits for you for an appointed term; and afterward they are brought for sacrifice unto the ancient House.

22:34 And for every nation have We appointed a ritual, that they may mention the name of Allah over the beast of cattle that He hath given them for food; and your Allah is One Allah, therefor surrender unto Him. And give good tidings (O Muhammad) to the humble,

22:35 Whose hearts fear when Allah is mentioned, and the patient of whatever may befall them, and those who establish worship and who spend of that We have bestowed on them.

22:36 And the camels! We have appointed them among the ceremonies of Allah. Therein ye have much good. So mention the name of Allah over them when they are drawn up in lines. Then when their flanks fall (dead), eat thereof and feed the beggar and the suppliant. Thus have We made them subject unto you, that haply ye may give thanks.

22:37 Their flesh and their food reach not Allah, but the devotion from you reacheth Him. Thus have We made them subject unto you that ye may magnify Allah that He hath guided you. And give good tidings (O Muhammad) to the good.

22:38 Lo! *ALLAH DEFENDETH THOSE WHO ARE TRUE*. Lo! Allah loveth not each *TREACHEROUS* ingrate.

22:39 *SANCTION IS GIVEN UNTO THOSE WHO FIGHT [JIHAD] BECAUSE THEY HAVE BEEN WRONGED*; and Allah is indeed Able to give them *VICTORY*;

22:40 *THOSE WHO HAVE BEEN DRIVEN FROM THEIR HOMES UNJUSTLY* only because they said: Our Lord is Allah - For had it not been for Allah's repelling some men by means of others, cloisters and churches and oratories and mosques, wherein the name of Allah is oft mentioned, would assuredly have been pulled down. Verily Allah helpeth one who helpeth Him. Lo! Allah is Strong, Almighty -

22:41 Those who, if We give them power in the land, establish worship and pay the poor-due and enjoin kindness and forbid iniquity. And Allah's is the sequel of events.

22:42 If they deny thee (Muhammad), even so the folk of Noah, and (the tribes of) A'ad and Thamud, before thee, denied (Our messengers);

22:43 And the folk of Abraham and the folk of Lot;

22:44 (And) the dwellers in Midian. And Moses was denied; but I indulged the *DISBELIEVERS* a long while, then I seized them, and how (terrible) was My abhorrence!

22:45 *HOW MANY A TOWNSHIP HAVE WE DESTROYED* while it was sinful, so that it lieth (to this day) in ruins, and (how many) a deserted well and lofty tower!

22:46 Have they not travelled in the land, and have they hearts wherewith to feel and ears wherewith to hear? For indeed it is not the eyes that grow blind, but it is the hearts, which are within the bosoms, that grow blind.

22:47 And they will bid thee hasten on the Doom, and Allah faileth not His promise, but lo! *A DAY WITH ALLAH IS AS A THOUSAND YEARS* of what ye reckon.

22:48 And how many a township did I suffer long though it was sinful! Then I grasped it. Unto Me is the return.

22:49 ~~Say: O mankind! I am only a plain warner unto you.~~ [Cancelled by verse 9:5][400]

22:50 *THOSE WHO BELIEVE AND DO GOOD WORKS, FOR THEM IS PARDON AND A RICH PROVISION;*

22:51 While *THOSE WHO STRIVE TO THWART OUR REVELATIONS,* such *ARE RIGHTFUL OWNERS OF THE FIRE.*

22:52 Never sent We a messenger or a prophet before thee but when He recited (the message) Satan proposed (opposition) in respect of that which he recited thereof. But Allah abolisheth that which Satan proposeth. Then Allah establisheth His revelations. Allah is Knower, Wise;

22:53 That He may make that which the devil proposeth a temptation for those in whose hearts is a disease, and those whose hearts are hardened - Lo! *THE EVIL-DOERS ARE IN OPEN SCHISM* – [Islam commands uniformity from Muslims, because Islam recognizes that diversity is weakness.]

22:54 And that those who have been given knowledge may know that *IT IS THE TRUTH FROM THY LORD,* so that *THEY MAY BELIEVE* therein and their hearts may submit humbly unto Him. Lo! Allah verily is guiding *THOSE WHO BELIEVE* unto *A RIGHT PATH*.

22:55 And *THOSE WHO DISBELIEVE* will not cease to be in doubt thereof until the Hour come upon them unawares, or there come unto them the doom of a disastrous day.

22:56 ~~The Sovereignty on that day will be Allah's, He will judge between them.~~ Then *THOSE WHO BELIEVED AND DID GOOD WORKS WILL BE IN GARDENS OF DELIGHT,* [Part Cancelled by verse 9:5][401]

22:57 While *THOSE WHO DISBELIEVED AND DENIED OUR REVELATIONS,* for them will be a shameful doom.

22:58 Those who fled their homes *FOR THE CAUSE OF ALLAH [JIHAD] AND THEN WERE SLAIN OR DIED, ALLAH VERILY WILL PROVIDE FOR THEM A GOOD PROVISION.* Lo! Allah, He verily is Best of all who make provision. [Jihadi "martyrs" go to Paradise]

22:59 Assuredly *HE WILL CAUSE THEM TO ENTER BY AN ENTRY THAT THEY WILL LOVE.* Lo! Allah verily is Knower, Indulgent.

22:60 That (is so). And whoso hath retaliated with the like of that which he was made to suffer and then hath (again) been wronged, Allah will succour him. Lo! Allah verily is Mild, Forgiving.

22:61 That is because Allah maketh the night to pass into the day and maketh the day to pass into the night, and because Allah is Hearer, Seer.

22:62 That is because Allah, *HE IS THE TRUE,* and that whereon they call instead of Him, it is the false, and because Allah, He is the High, the Great.

22:63 Seest thou not how Allah sendeth down water from the sky and then the earth becometh green upon the morrow? Lo! Allah is Subtile, Aware.

22:64 Unto Him belongeth all that is in the heavens and all that is in the earth. Lo! Allah, He verily is the Absolute, the Owner of Praise.

22:65 Hast thou not seen how Allah hath made all that is in the earth subservient unto you? And the ship runneth upon the sea by His command, and He holdeth back the heaven from falling on the earth unless by His leave. Lo! Allah is, for mankind, Full of Pity, Merciful.

22:66 And He it is Who gave you life, then He will cause you to die, and then will give you life (again). Lo! man is verily an ingrate.

22:67 Unto each nation have We given sacred rites which they are to perform; so let them not dispute with thee of the matter, but summon thou unto thy Lord. Lo! thou indeed followest right guidance.

22:68 ~~And if they wrangle with thee, say: Allah is Best Aware of what ye do.~~ [Cancelled by verse 9:5][402]

22:69 *ALLAH WILL JUDGE BETWEEN YOU ON THE DAY OF RESURRECTION* concerning that wherein ye used to differ.

22:70 Hast thou not known that Allah knoweth all that is in the heaven and the earth? Lo! it is in a record. Lo! that is easy for Allah.

22:71 And they worship instead of Allah that for which He hath sent down no warrant, and that whereof they have no knowledge. For *EVIL-DOERS* there is no helper.

22:72 And when Our revelations are recited unto them, thou knowest the denial in the faces of *THOSE WHO DISBELIEVE; THEY ALL BUT ATTACK THOSE WHO RECITE OUR REVELATIONS* unto them. Say: Shall I proclaim unto you worse than that? *THE FIRE! ALLAH HATH PROMISED IT FOR THOSE WHO DISBELIEVE*. A hapless journey's end! [Muslims denounce non-Muslims and are then surprised when non-Muslims criticise these denunciations.]

22:73 O mankind! A similitude is coined, so pay ye heed to it: Lo! those on whom ye call beside Allah will never create a fly though they combine together for the purpose. And if the fly took something from them, they could not rescue it from it. So weak are (both) the seeker and the sought!

22:74 They measure not Allah His rightful measure. Lo! Allah is Strong, Almighty.

22:75 Allah chooseth from the angels messengers, and (also) from mankind. Lo! Allah is Hearer, Seer.

22:76 He knoweth all that is before them and all that is behind them, and unto Allah all things are returned.

22:77 O *YE WHO BELIEVE*! Bow down and prostrate yourselves, and *WORSHIP YOUR LORD, AND DO GOOD,* that haply *YE MAY PROSPER*.

22:78 ~~And strive [Jihad] for Allah with the endeavour which is His right. He hath chosen you and hath not laid upon you in religion any hardship;~~ the faith of your father Abraham (is yours). He hath named you *MUSLIMS* of old time and in this (Scripture), that the messenger may be a witness against you, and that ye may be witnesses against mankind. So establish worship, pay the poor-due, and hold fast to Allah. He is your Protecting friend. A blessed Patron and a blessed Helper! [Part cancelled by verse 64:16 i.e. abrogation means Muslims are to endure hardship in undertaking Jihad.][403]

Chapter 24 - Light

24:1 (Here is) a surah which We have revealed and enjoined, and wherein *WE HAVE REVEALED PLAIN TOKENS*, that haply ye may take heed.

24:2 *THE ADULTERER AND THE ADULTERESS, SCOURGE YE EACH ONE OF THEM* (with) a hundred stripes. And *LET NOT PITY FOR THE TWAIN WITHHOLD YOU* from *OBEDIENCE* to Allah, if *YE BELIEVE IN ALLAH AND THE LAST DAY*. And let a *PARTY OF BELIEVERS WITNESS THEIR PUNISHMENT*. [Adulterers are to be whipped in public, and Muslims are to feel no pity for them.]

24:3 ~~The adulterer shall not marry save an adulteress or an idolatress, and the adulteress none shall marry save an adulterer or an IDOLATER. All that is forbidden unto BELIEVERS.~~ [Cancelled by verse 24:32][404]

24:4 ~~And those who accuse honourable women but bring not four witnesses, scourge them (with) eighty stripes and never (afterward) accept their testimony - They indeed are EVIL-DOERS~~ [Cancelled by verse 24:5][405]

24:5 Save those who afterward repent and make amends. (For such) lo! Allah is Forgiving, Merciful.

24:6 As for those who accuse their wives but have no witnesses except themselves; let the testimony of one of them be four testimonies, (swearing) by Allah that he is of those who speak the truth;

24:7 And yet a fifth, invoking the curse of Allah on him if he is of those who lie.

24:8 And it shall avert the punishment from her if she bear witness before Allah four times that the thing he saith is indeed false,

24:9 And a fifth (time) that the wrath of Allah be upon her if he speaketh truth.

24:10 And had it not been for the grace of Allah and His mercy unto you, and that Allah is Clement, Wise, (ye had been undone).

24:11 Lo! they who spread the *SLANDER* are a gang among you. Deem it not a bad thing for you; nay, it is good for you. Unto every man of them (will be paid) that which he hath earned of the sin; and as for him among them who had the greater share therein, *HIS WILL BE AN AWFUL DOOM*. [Speaking ill of other Muslims is punished by an eternity of torture in Hell.]

24:12 *WHY DID NOT THE BELIEVERS, MEN AND WOMEN, WHEN YE HEARD IT, THINK GOOD OF THEIR OWN FOLK, AND SAY: IT IS A MANIFEST UNTRUTH?*
[Muslims are to be biased towards other Muslims.]

24:13 Why did they not produce four witnesses? Since they produce not witnesses, they verily are liars in the sight of Allah.

24:14 Had it not been for the grace of Allah and His mercy unto you in the world and the Hereafter an awful doom had overtaken you for that whereof ye murmured.

24:15 When ye welcomed it with your tongues, and uttered with your mouths that whereof ye had no knowledge, ye counted it a trifle. In the sight of Allah it is very great.

24:16 Wherefor, when ye heard it, said ye not: It is not for us to speak of this. Glory be to Thee (O Allah)! This is awful calumny.

24:17 Allah admonisheth you that ye repeat not the like thereof ever, if ye are (in truth) *BELIEVERS*.

24:18 And He expoundeth unto you the revelations. Allah is Knower, Wise.

24:19 Lo! those who love *THAT SLANDER SHOULD BE SPREAD CONCERNING THOSE WHO BELIEVE*, theirs will be a *PAINFUL PUNISHMENT IN THE WORLD AND THE HEREAFTER*. Allah knoweth. Ye know not. [Note Muslims are free to slander non-Muslims.]

24:20 Had it not been for the grace of Allah and His mercy unto you, and that Allah is Clement, Merciful, (ye had been undone).

24:21 O *YE WHO BELIEVE*! Follow not the footsteps of the devil. Unto whomsoever followeth the footsteps of the devil, lo! he commandeth filthiness and wrong. Had it not been for the grace of Allah and His mercy unto you, not one of you would ever have grown pure. But Allah causeth whom He will to grow. And Allah is Hearer, Knower.

24:22 And let not those who possess dignity and ease among you swear not to *GIVE TO THE NEAR OF KIN AND TO THE NEEDY, AND TO FUGITIVES FOR THE CAUSE OF ALLAH.* Let them forgive and show indulgence. Yearn ye not that Allah may forgive you? Allah is Forgiving, Merciful. [Islamic charity funds Jihad.]

24:23 Lo! as for those who traduce virtuous, *BELIEVING* women (who are) careless, *CURSED ARE THEY IN THE WORLD AND THE HEREAFTER. THEIRS WILL BE AN AWFUL DOOM.*

24:24 *ON THE DAY* when their tongues and their hands and their feet testify against them as to what they used to do,

24:25 *ON THAT DAY ALLAH WILL PAY THEM THEIR JUST DUE*, and they will know that *ALLAH, HE IS THE MANIFEST TRUTH.*

24:26 Vile women are for vile men, and vile men for vile women. Good women are for good men, and good men for good women; such are innocent of that which people say: For them is pardon and a bountiful provision.

24:27 ~~O ye who *BELIEVE*! Enter not houses other than your own without first announcing your presence and invoking peace upon the folk thereof. That is better for you, that ye may be heedful.~~ [Cancelled by verse 24:29][406]

24:28 And if ye find no-one therein, still enter not until permission hath been given. And if it be said unto you: Go away again, then go away, for it is purer for you. Allah knoweth what ye do.

24:29 (It is) no sin for you to enter uninhabited houses wherein is comfort for you. Allah knoweth what ye proclaim and what ye hide.

24:30 Tell *THE BELIEVING MEN* to lower their gaze and be modest. That is purer for them. Lo! Allah is aware of what they do.

24:31 ~~And tell the *BELIEVING* women to lower their gaze and be modest, and to display of their adornment only that which is apparent, and to draw their veils over their bosoms, and not to reveal their adornment save to their own husbands or fathers or husbands' fathers, or their sons or their husbands' sons, or their brothers or their brothers' sons or sisters' sons, or their women, or their slaves, or male attendants who lack vigour, or children who know naught of women's nakedness. And let them not stamp their feet so as to reveal what they hide of their adornment. And turn unto Allah together, O *BELIEVERS*, in order that ye may succeed.~~ [Cancelled by verse 24:60][407]

24:32 And marry such of you as are solitary and *THE PIOUS OF YOUR SLAVES* and maid-servants. If they be poor, Allah will enrich them of His bounty. Allah is of ample means, Aware.

24:33 And let those who cannot find a match keep chaste till Allah give them independence by His grace. *AND SUCH OF YOUR SLAVES* as seek a writing (of emancipation), write it for them if ye are aware of aught of good in them, and bestow upon them of the wealth of Allah which He hath bestowed upon you. Force not your slave-girls to whoredom that ye may seek enjoyment of the life of the world, if they would preserve their chastity. And if one force them, then (unto them), after their compulsion, lo! Allah will be Forgiving, Merciful.

24:34 And verily We have sent down for you *REVELATIONS THAT MAKE PLAIN*, and the example of those who passed away before you. An admonition unto those who ward off (*EVIL*).

24:35 Allah is the Light of the heavens and the earth. The similitude of His light is as a niche wherein is a lamp. The lamp is in a glass. The glass is as it were a shining star. (This lamp is) kindled from a blessed tree, an olive neither of the East nor of the West, whose oil would almost glow forth (of itself) though no fire touched it. Light upon light. Allah guideth unto His light whom He will. And Allah speaketh to mankind in allegories, for Allah is Knower of all things.

24:36 (This lamp is found) in houses which Allah hath allowed to be exalted and that His name shall be remembered therein. Therein do offer praise to Him at morn and evening.

24:37 Men whom neither merchandise nor sale beguileth from remembrance of Allah and constancy in prayer and paying to the poor their due; who fear a day when hearts and eyeballs will be overturned;

24:38 That *ALLAH MAY REWARD THEM WITH THE BEST OF WHAT THEY DID*, and *INCREASE REWARD FOR THEM OF HIS BOUNTY*. Allah giveth blessings without stint *TO WHOM HE WILL*.

24:39 As for *THOSE WHO DISBELIEVE*, their deeds are as a mirage in a desert. The thirsty one supposeth it to be water till he cometh unto it and findeth it naught, and findeth, in the place thereof, *ALLAH WHO PAYETH HIM HIS DUE*; and Allah is swift at reckoning.

24:40 Or as darkness on a vast, abysmal sea. There covereth him a wave, above which is a wave, above which is a cloud. Layer upon layer of darkness. When he holdeth out his hand he scarce can see it. And he for whom Allah hath not appointed light, for him there is no light.

24:41 Hast thou not seen that Allah, He it is Whom all who are in the heavens and the earth praise, and the birds in their flight? Of each He knoweth verily the worship and the praise; and Allah is Aware of what they do.

24:42 And unto Allah belongeth the Sovereignty of the heavens and the earth, and unto Allah is the journeying.

24:43 Hast thou not seen how Allah wafteth the clouds, then gathereth them, then maketh them layers, and thou seest the rain come forth from between them; He sendeth down from the heaven mountains wherein is hail, and smiteth therewith whom He will, and averteth it from whom He will. The flashing of His lightning all but snatcheth away the sight.

24:44 Allah causeth the revolution of the day and the night. Lo! herein is indeed a lesson for those who see.

24:45 Allah hath created every animal of water. Of them is (a kind) that goeth upon its belly and (a kind) that goeth upon two legs and (a kind) that goeth upon four. Allah createth what He will. Lo! Allah is Able to do all things.

24:46 Verily We have sent down revelations and explained them. *ALLAH GUIDETH WHOM HE WILL UNTO A STRAIGHT PATH.*

24:47 And they say: *WE BELIEVE* in Allah and the messenger, and *WE OBEY*; then after that *A FACTION OF THEM TURN AWAY. SUCH ARE NOT BELIEVERS.*

24:48 And when they appeal unto Allah and His messenger to judge between them, lo! a faction of them are averse;

24:49 But if right had been with them they would have come unto him willingly.

24:50 Is there in their hearts a disease, or have they doubts, or fear they lest Allah and His messenger should wrong them in judgment? Nay, but *SUCH ARE EVIL-DOERS.*

24:51 *THE SAYING OF (ALL TRUE) BELIEVERS* when they appeal unto Allah and His messenger to judge between them is only that they say: *WE HEAR AND WE OBEY*. And *SUCH ARE THE SUCCESSFUL*. [There is no room in Islam for conscience or free thinking; Islam commands nothing but unquestioning obedience.]

24:52 He who obeyeth Allah and His messenger, and feareth Allah, and keepeth duty (unto Him): *SUCH INDEED ARE THE VICTORIOUS.*

24:53 They [slackers] swear by Allah solemnly that, if thou *ORDER THEM, THEY WILL GO FORTH [JIHAD]. SAY: SWEAR NOT; KNOWN OBEDIENCE (IS BETTER).* **Lo! Allah is Informed of what ye do. [The Koran says that when it comes to Jihad it is action which counts more than words.]**

24:54 Say: *OBEY ALLAH AND OBEY THE MESSENGER*. But if ye turn away, then (it is) for him (to do) only that wherewith he hath been charged, and for you (to do) only that wherewith ye have been charged. If ye obey him, ye will go aright. But the messenger hath no other charge than to convey (the message) plainly. [Part Cancelled by verse 9:5][408]

24:55 Allah hath promised *SUCH OF YOU AS BELIEVE AND DO GOOD WORK THAT HE WILL SURELY MAKE THEM TO SUCCEED* (the present rulers) in the earth even as He caused those who were before them to succeed (others); and that He will surely *ESTABLISH FOR THEM THEIR RELIGION* which He hath approved for them, and will give them in exchange safety after their fear. They serve Me. They *ASCRIBE NO THING AS PARTNER UNTO ME. THOSE WHO DISBELIEVE HENCEFORTH, THEY ARE THE MISCREANTS.*

24:56 Establish worship and pay the poor-due and *OBEY THE MESSENGER*, that haply ye may find mercy.

24:57 *THINK NOT THAT THE DISBELIEVERS CAN ESCAPE IN THE LAND. FIRE WILL BE THEIR HOME* - a hapless journey's end!

24:58 O *YE WHO BELIEVE! LET YOUR SLAVES,* and those of you who have not come to puberty, ask leave of you at three times (before they come into your presence): Before the prayer of dawn, and when ye lay aside your raiment for the heat of noon, and after the prayer of night. Three times of privacy for you. It is no sin for them or for you at other times, when some of you go round attendant upon others (if they come into your presence without leave). Thus Allah maketh clear the revelations for you. Allah is Knower, Wise.

24:59 And when the children among you come to puberty then let them ask leave even as those before them used to ask it. Thus Allah maketh clear His revelations for you. Allah is Knower, Wise.

24:60 As for women past child-bearing, who have no hope of marriage, it is no sin for them if they discard their (outer) clothing in such a way as not to show adornment. But to refrain is better for them. Allah is Hearer, Knower.

24:61 No blame is there upon the blind nor any blame upon the lame nor any blame upon the sick nor on yourselves if ye eat from your houses, or the houses of your fathers, or the houses of your mothers, or the houses of your brothers, or the houses of your sisters, or the houses of your fathers' brothers, or the houses of your fathers' sisters, or the houses of your mothers' brothers, or the houses of your mothers' sisters, or (from that) whereof ye hold the keys, or (from the house) of a friend. No sin shall it be for you whether ye eat together or apart. But when ye enter houses, salute one another with a greeting from Allah, blessed and sweet. Thus Allah maketh clear His revelations for you, that haply ye may understand.

24:62 *THEY ONLY ARE THE TRUE BELIEVERS* who *BELIEVE IN ALLAH* and His messenger and, when they are with him on some common errand, go not away until they have asked leave of him. Lo! those who ask leave of thee, those are *THEY WHO BELIEVE IN ALLAH AND HIS MESSENGER*. So, if they ask thy leave for some affair of theirs, give leave to whom thou wilt of them, and ask for them forgiveness of Allah. Lo! Allah is Forgiving, Merciful.

24:63 Make not the calling of the messenger among you as your calling one of another. Allah knoweth those of you who steal away, hiding themselves. And let those who conspire to evade orders beware lest grief or painful punishment befall them.

24:64 Lo! verily unto Allah belongeth whatsoever is in the heavens and the earth. He knoweth your condition. And (He knoweth) *THE DAY WHEN THEY ARE RETURNED UNTO HIM* so that He may inform them of what they did. Allah is Knower of all things.

Chapter 59 - Exile

59:1 All that is in the heavens and all that is in the earth glorifieth Allah, and He is the Mighty, the Wise.

59:2 He it is Who hath caused those of _THE PEOPLE OF THE SCRIPTURE_ **who** _DISBELIEVED_ **to go forth from their homes unto the first exile. Ye deemed not that they would go forth, while** _THEY DEEMED THAT THEIR STRONGHOLDS WOULD PROTECT THEM_ **from Allah. But Allah reached them from a place whereof they reckoned not, and** _CAST TERROR IN THEIR HEARTS_ **so that they ruined their houses with their own hands and** _THE HANDS OF THE BELIEVERS._ **So learn a lesson, O ye who have eyes!**

59:3 And if _ALLAH_ **had not decreed migration for them, He verily** _WOULD HAVE PUNISHED THEM IN THE WORLD_, **and theirs in the** _HEREAFTER IS THE PUNISHMENT OF THE FIRE._

59:4 That is because _THEY WERE OPPOSED TO ALLAH AND HIS MESSENGER_; **and whoso is opposed to Allah, (for him) verily** _ALLAH IS STERN IN REPRISAL._

59:5 Whatsoever palm-trees ye cut down or left standing on their roots, it was by Allah's leave, in order that He might confound _THE EVIL-LIVERS_.

59:6 And _THAT WHICH ALLAH GAVE AS SPOIL [SLAVES AND LOOT]_ **unto His messenger from them, ye urged not any horse or riding-camel for the sake thereof, but Allah giveth His messenger lordship over whom He will. Allah is Able to do all things.**

59:7 _THAT WHICH ALLAH GIVETH AS SPOIL [SLAVES AND LOOT]_ **unto His messenger** _FROM THE PEOPLE OF THE TOWNSHIPS_, **it is for Allah and His messenger and for the near of kin and the orphans and the needy and the wayfarer, that it become not a commodity between the rich among you. And whatsoever the messenger giveth you, take it. And whatsoever he forbiddeth, abstain (from it). And** _KEEP YOUR DUTY TO ALLAH_. **Lo!** _ALLAH IS STERN IN REPRISAL._

59:8 And (it is) for the poor fugitives who have been driven out from their homes and their belongings, who seek bounty from Allah and help Allah and His messenger. They are the loyal.

59:9 Those who entered the city and the faith before them love those who flee unto them for refuge, and find in their breasts no need for that which hath been given them, but prefer (the fugitives) above themselves though poverty become their lot. And whoso is saved from his own avarice - _SUCH ARE THEY WHO ARE SUCCESSFUL._

59:10 And those who came (into the faith) after them say: Our Lord! Forgive us and our brethren who were before us in the faith, and place not in our hearts any rancour toward _THOSE WHO BELIEVE_. Our Lord! Thou art Full of Pity, Merciful.

59:11 Hast thou not observed those who are _HYPOCRITES_, (how) they tell _THEIR BRETHREN WHO DISBELIEVE AMONG THE PEOPLE OF THE SCRIPTURE_: If ye are driven out, we surely will go out with you, and we will never obey anyone against you, and if ye are attacked we verily will help you. And Allah beareth witness that they verily are _LIARS_.

59:12 (For) indeed if they are driven out they go not out with them, and indeed if they are attacked they help them not, and indeed if they had helped them they would have turned and fled, and then they would not have been _VICTORIOUS_.

59:13 _YE ARE MORE AWFUL AS A FEAR IN THEIR BOSOMS THAN ALLAH_. That is because they are a folk who understand not.

59:14 _THEY [NON-MUSLIMS] WILL NOT FIGHT AGAINST YOU_ **in a body save in** _FORTIFIED VILLAGES_ **or from behind walls. [Unbelievers fight defensively; Muslims fight aggressively, it is the Muslims who are attacking the villages of the unbelievers.] Their adversity among themselves is very**

great. [Diversity is weakness] Ye think of them as a whole whereas their hearts are divers. That is because THEY ARE A FOLK WHO HAVE NO SENSE. **[Other translations say that unbelievers are people incapable of rational thought.]**

59:15 On the likeness of those (who suffered) a short time before them, they taste the ill effects of their own conduct, and theirs is painful punishment.

59:16 (And the HYPOCRITES are) on the likeness of the devil when he telleth man to DISBELIEVE, then, when he DISBELIEVETH saith: Lo! I am quit of thee. Lo! I fear Allah, the Lord of the Worlds.

59:17 And the consequence for both will be that THEY ARE IN THE FIRE, **therein abiding. Such is** THE REWARD **of** EVIL-DOERS. **[Non-Muslims and hypocritical Muslims tortured in Hell for eternity.]**

59:18 O YE WHO BELIEVE! OBSERVE YOUR DUTY TO ALLAH. And let every soul look to that which it sendeth on before for the morrow. And OBSERVE YOUR DUTY TO ALLAH. Lo! Allah is Informed of what ye do.

59:19 And be not ye as THOSE WHO FORGOT ALLAH, therefor He caused them to forget their souls. Such ARE THE EVIL-DOERS.

59:20 NOT EQUAL ARE THE OWNERS OF THE FIRE AND THE OWNERS OF THE GARDEN. **The owners of the Garden,** THEY ARE THE VICTORIOUS.

59:21 If We had caused this Qur'an to descend upon a mountain, thou (O Muhammad) verily hadst seen it humbled, rent asunder by the fear of Allah. Such similitudes coin We for mankind that haply they may reflect.

59:22 He is Allah, than Whom there is no other God, the Knower of the Invisible and the Visible. He is the Beneficent, Merciful.

59:23 He is Allah, than Whom there is no other God, the Sovereign Lord, the Holy One, Peace, the Keeper of Faith, the Guardian, the Majestic, the Compeller, the Superb. Glorified be Allah from all that they ASCRIBE AS PARTNER (unto Him).

59:24 He is Allah, the Creator, the Shaper out of naught, the Fashioner. His are the most beautiful names. All that is in the heavens and the earth glorifieth Him, and He is the Mighty, the Wise.

Chapter 98 - The Clear Proof

98:1 THOSE WHO DISBELIEVE AMONG THE PEOPLE OF THE SCRIPTURE AND THE IDOLATERS could not have left off (erring) till the CLEAR PROOF came unto them,

98:2 A messenger from Allah, reading PURIFIED pages

98:3 Containing correct scriptures.

98:4 Nor were the PEOPLE OF THE SCRIPTURE divided until after the CLEAR PROOF came unto them.

98:5 And they are ordered naught else than to serve Allah, keeping religion pure for Him, as men by nature upright, and to establish worship and to pay the poor-due. That is TRUE RELIGION.

98:6 Lo! THOSE WHO DISBELIEVE, **among the** PEOPLE OF THE SCRIPTURE **and the** IDOLATERS, **will abide in fire of** HELL. **They are** THE WORST OF CREATED BEINGS. **[Christians and Jews are the worst things to have lived, worse than rats, dogs or pigs.]**

98:7 (And) lo! THOSE WHO BELIEVE AND DO GOOD WORKS **[Jihad]** ARE THE BEST **of created beings.**

98:8 THEIR REWARD [FOR JIHAD] IS WITH THEIR LORD: GARDENS OF EDEN **[Paradise] underneath which rivers flow, wherein they dwell for ever. Allah hath pleasure in them and they have pleasure in Him. This is (in store) for him who** FEARETH HIS LORD.

Chapter 65 - Divorce

65:1 O Prophet! When ye (men) put away women, put them away for their (legal) period and reckon the period, and *KEEP YOUR DUTY TO ALLAH*, your Lord. Expel them not from their houses nor let them go forth unless they commit open immorality. Such are the limits (imposed by) Allah; and whoso transgresseth Allah's limits, he verily wrongeth his soul. Thou knowest not: it may be that Allah will afterward bring some new thing to pass.

65:2 Then, when they have reached their term, take them back in kindness or part from them in kindness, and call to witness two just men among you, and keep your testimony upright for Allah. *WHOSO BELIEVETH IN ALLAH AND THE LAST DAY* is exhorted to act thus. And whosoever *KEEPETH HIS DUTY TO ALLAH*, Allah will appoint a way out for him,

65:3 And will provide for him from (a quarter) whence he hath no expectation. And whosoever putteth his trust in Allah, He will suffice him. Lo! Allah bringeth His command to pass. Allah hath set a measure for all things.

65:4 And for such of your women as despair of menstruation, if ye doubt, *THEIR PERIOD (OF WAITING) SHALL BE THREE MONTHS, ALONG WITH THOSE WHO HAVE IT NOT.* And for those with child, their period shall be till they bring forth their burden. And whosoever keepeth his duty to Allah, He maketh his course easy for him. [In this Surah on Divorce, it is clear that pre-menstrual girls can be married and divorced before they have had their first period. This is acknowledged explicitly in manuals of sharia law.]

65:5 That is the commandment of Allah which He revealeth unto you. And *WHOSO KEEPETH HIS DUTY TO ALLAH*, He will *REMIT FROM HIM HIS EVIL* deeds and *MAGNIFY REWARD FOR HIM*.

65:6 Lodge them where ye dwell, according to your wealth, and harass them not so as to straiten life for them. And if they are with child, then spend for them till they bring forth their burden. Then, if they give suck for you, give them their due payment and consult together in kindness; but if ye make difficulties for one another, then let some other woman give suck for him (the father of the child).

65:7 Let him who hath abundance spend of his abundance, and he whose provision is measured, let him spend of that which Allah hath given him. Allah asketh naught of any soul save that which He hath given it. Allah will vouchsafe, after hardship, ease.

65:8 And how many a community revolted against the ordinance of its Lord and His messengers, and We called it to a stern account and punished it with dire punishment,

65:9 So that it tasted the ill-effects of its conduct, and the consequence of its conduct was loss.

65:10 Allah hath prepared for them stern punishment; so *KEEP YOUR DUTY TO ALLAH*, O men of understanding! *O YE WHO BELIEVE!* Now Allah hath sent down unto you a reminder,

65:11 A messenger reciting unto you the revelations of Allah made plain, that He may bring forth those who *BELIEVE* and do good works from darkness unto light. And *WHOSOEVER BELIEVETH IN ALLAH AND DOETH RIGHT, HE WILL BRING HIM INTO GARDENS UNDERNEATH* which rivers flow, therein to abide for ever. Allah hath made good provision for him.

65:12 Allah it is who hath created seven heavens, and of the earth the like thereof. The commandment cometh down among them slowly, that ye may know that Allah is Able to do all things, and that *ALLAH SURROUNDETH ALL THINGS IN KNOWLEDGE.*

Chapter 76 - Time or Man

76:1 Hath there come upon man (ever) any period of time in which he was a thing unremembered?

76:2 Lo! We create man from a drop of thickened fluid to test him; so We make him hearing, knowing.

76:3 Lo! We have shown him the way, whether he be grateful or *DISBELIEVING*.

76:4 Lo! We have prepared for *DISBELIEVERS* manacles and carcans and a raging fire.

76:5 Lo! the righteous shall drink of a cup whereof the mixture is of Kafur,

76:6 A spring wherefrom *THE SLAVES OF ALLAH* drink, making it gush forth abundantly,

76:7 (Because) they perform the vow and fear a day whereof the *EVIL* is wide-spreading,

76:8 ~~And feed with food the needy wretch, the orphan and the prisoner, for love of Him,~~ [Cancelled by verse 9:5][409]

76:9 (Saying): We feed you, for the sake of Allah only. We wish for no _REWARD_ nor thanks from you;

76:10 Lo! we fear from our Lord a day of frowning and of fate.

76:11 Therefor Allah hath warded off from them the _EVIL_ of that day, and hath made them find brightness and joy;

76:12 And hath _AWARDED THEM FOR ALL THAT THEY ENDURED, A GARDEN AND SILK ATTIRE;_

76:13 Reclining therein upon couches, they will find there neither (heat of) a sun nor bitter cold.

76:14 The shade thereof is close upon them and the clustered fruits thereof bow down.

76:15 _GOBLETS OF SILVER_ are brought round for them, and beakers (as) of glass

76:16 (Bright as) glass but (made) of silver, which they (themselves) have measured to the measure (of their deeds).

76:17 There are they watered with a cup whereof the mixture is of Zanjabil,

76:18 (The water of) a spring therein, named Salsabil.

76:19 _THERE WAIT ON THEM IMMORTAL YOUTHS_, whom, when thou seest, thou wouldst take for _SCATTERED PEARLS._

76:20 When thou seest, thou wilt see there bliss and high estate.

76:21 Their raiment will be fine _GREEN SILK AND GOLD EMBROIDERY_. Bracelets of silver will they wear. Their Lord will slake their thirst with a pure drink.

76:22 (And it will be said unto them): Lo! _THIS IS A REWARD FOR YOU. YOUR ENDEAVOUR (UPON EARTH)_ hath found acceptance. [Eternity in Paradise for those Muslims who implemented Islam on earth.]

76:23 Lo! We, even We, have revealed unto thee the Qur'an, a revelation;

76:24 ~~So submit patiently to thy Lord's command, and obey not of them any guilty one or DISBELIEVER.~~ [Cancelled by verse 9:5 i.e. command to be patient replaced by command to be violent][410]

76:25 Remember the name of thy Lord at morn and evening.

76:26 And worship Him (a portion) of the night. And glorify Him through the livelong night.

76:27 Lo! these love fleeting life, and put behind them (the remembrance of) a grievous day.

76:28 We, even We, created them, and strengthened their frame. And when We will, We can replace them, bringing others like them in their stead.

76:29 ~~Lo! this is an Admonishment, that whosoever will may choose a way unto his Lord.~~ [Cancelled by verse 9:5 i.e. command to kill abrogates command to tolerance or indifference][411]

76:30 Yet ye will not, unless Allah willeth. Lo! Allah is Knower, Wise.

76:31 He maketh whom He will to enter His mercy, _AND FOR EVIL-DOERS HATH PREPARED A PAINFUL DOOM._

Chapter 55 - The Beneficent

55:1 The Beneficent

55:2 Hath made known the Qur'an.

55:3 He hath created man.

55:4 He hath taught him utterance.

55:5 The sun and the moon are made punctual.

55:6 The stars and the trees prostrate.

55:7 And the sky He hath uplifted; and He hath set the measure,

55:8 That ye exceed not the measure,

55:9 But observe the measure strictly, nor fall short thereof.

55:10 And the earth hath He appointed for (His) creatures,

55:11 Wherein are fruit and sheathed palm-trees,

55:12 Husked grain and scented herb.

55:13 Which is it, of the favours of your Lord, that ye deny?

55:14 He created man of clay like the potter's,

55:15 And the jinn did He create of smokeless fire.

55:16 Which is it, of the favours of your Lord, that ye deny?
55:17 Lord of the two Easts, and Lord of the two Wests!
55:18 Which is it, of the favours of your Lord, that ye deny?
55:19 He hath loosed the two seas. They meet.
55:20 There is a barrier between them. They encroach not (one upon the other).
55:21 Which is it, of the favours of your Lord, that ye deny?
55:22 There cometh forth from both of them the pearl and coral-stone.
55:23 Which is it, of the favours of your Lord, that ye deny?
55:24 His are the ships displayed upon the sea, like banners.
55:25 Which is it, of the favours of your Lord, that ye deny?
55:26 Everyone that is thereon will pass away;
55:27 There remaineth but the Countenance of thy Lord of Might and Glory.
55:28 Which is it, of the favours of your Lord, that ye deny?
55:29 All that are in the heavens and the earth entreat Him. *EVERY DAY HE EXERCISETH (UNIVERSAL) POWER.*
55:30 Which is it, of the favours of your Lord, that ye deny?
55:31 We shall dispose of you, O ye two dependents (man and jinn).
55:32 Which is it, of the favours of your Lord, that ye deny?
55:33 O company of jinn and men, if ye have power to penetrate (all) regions of the heavens and the earth, then penetrate (them)! Ye will never penetrate them save with (Our) sanction.
55:34 Which is it, of the favours of your Lord, that ye deny?
55:35 There will be sent, against you both, heat of fire and flash of brass, and ye will not escape.
55:36 Which is it, of the favours of your Lord, that ye deny?
55:37 And when the heaven splitteth asunder and becometh rosy like red hide-
55:38 Which is it, of the favours of your Lord, that ye deny? -
55:39 On that day neither man nor jinni will be questioned of his sin.
55:40 Which is it, of the favours of your Lord, that ye deny?
55:41 The guilty will be known by their marks, and will be taken by the forelocks and the feet.
55:42 Which is it, of the favours of your Lord, that ye deny?
55:43 This is *HELL WHICH THE GUILTY DENY.*
55:44 *THEY GO CIRCLING ROUND BETWEEN IT AND FIERCE, BOILING WATER.*
55:45 Which is it, of the favours of your Lord, that ye deny?
55:46 But for him who feareth the standing before his Lord there are two gardens.
55:47 Which is it, of the favours of your Lord, that ye deny?
55:48 Of spreading branches.
55:49 Which is it, of the favours of your Lord, that ye deny?
55:50 Wherein are two fountains flowing.
55:51 Which is it, of the favours of your Lord, that ye deny?
55:52 Wherein is every kind of fruit in pairs.
55:53 Which is it, of the favours of your Lord, that ye deny?
55:54 Reclining upon couches lined with silk brocade, the fruit of both the gardens near to hand.
55:55 Which is it, of the favours of your Lord, that ye deny?
55:56 Therein are *THOSE OF MODEST GAZE, WHOM NEITHER MAN NOR JINN WILL HAVE TOUCHED BEFORE THEM*.
55:57 Which is it, of the favours of your Lord, that ye deny?
55:58 (In beauty) like the jacynth and the coral-stone.
55:59 Which is it, of the favours of your Lord, that ye deny?
55:60 Is the *REWARD* of goodness aught save goodness?
55:61 Which is it, of the favours of your Lord, that ye deny?
55:62 And beside them are two other gardens,
55:63 Which is it, of the favours of your Lord, that ye deny?
55:64 Dark green with foliage.
55:65 Which is it, of the favours of your Lord, that ye deny?
55:66 Wherein are two abundant springs.
55:67 Which is it, of the favours of your Lord, that ye deny?
55:68 Wherein is fruit, the date-palm and pomegranate.
55:69 Which is it, of the favours of your Lord, that ye deny?
55:70 *WHEREIN (ARE FOUND) THE GOOD AND BEAUTIFUL COMPANIONS-*
55:71 Which is it, of the favours of your Lord, that ye deny? -

55:72 Fair ones, close-guarded in pavilions -
55:73 Which is it, of the favours of your Lord, that ye deny? -
55:74 Whom *NEITHER MAN NOR JINN WILL HAVE TOUCHED BEFORE THEM -*
55:75 Which is it, of the favours of your Lord, that ye deny?
55:76 *RECLINING ON GREEN CUSHIONS AND FAIR CARPETS.*
55:77 Which is it, of the favours of your Lord, that ye deny?
55:78 Blessed be the name of thy Lord, Mighty and glorious!

Chapter 13 - The Thunder

13:1 Alif. Lam. Mim. Ra. These are verses of the Scripture. That which is revealed unto thee from *THY LORD IS THE TRUTH*, but *MOST OF MANKIND BELIEVE NOT.*

13:2 Allah it is Who raised up the heavens without visible supports, then mounted the Throne, and compelled the sun and the moon to be of service, each runneth unto an appointed term; He ordereth the course; He detaileth the revelations, that haply ye may be certain of the meeting with your Lord.

13:3 And He it is Who spread out the earth and placed therein firm hills and flowing streams, and of all fruits He placed therein two spouses (male and female). He covereth the night with the day. Lo! herein verily are portents for people who take thought.

13:4 And in the Earth are neighbouring tracts, vineyards and ploughed lands, and date-palms, like and unlike, which are watered with one water. And we have made some of them to excel others in fruit. Lo! herein verily are portents for people who have sense.

13:5 And if thou wonderest, then wondrous is their saying: When we are dust, are we then forsooth (to be raised) in a new creation? Such are *THEY WHO DISBELIEVE* in their Lord; such have carcans on their necks; such are rightful *OWNERS OF THE FIRE*, they will abide therein.

13:6 And *THEY BID THEE HASTEN ON THE EVIL RATHER THAN THE GOOD*, when *EXEMPLARY PUNISHMENTS* have indeed occurred before them. But lo! thy Lord is rich in pardon for mankind despite their wrong, and lo! thy Lord is strong in punishment.

13:7 *THOSE WHO DISBELIEVE* say: If only some portent were sent down upon him from his Lord! Thou art a warner only, and for every folk a guide.

13:8 Allah knoweth that which every female beareth and that which the wombs absorb and that which they grow. And everything with Him is measured.

13:9 He is the Knower of the Invisible and the Visible, the Great, the High Exalted.

13:10 Alike of you is he who hideth the saying and he who noiseth it abroad, he who lurketh in the night and he who goeth freely in the daytime.

13:11 For him are angels ranged before him and behind him, who guard him by Allah's command. Lo! Allah changeth not the condition of a folk until they (first) change that which is in their hearts; and if Allah willeth misfortune for a folk there is none that can repel it, nor have they a defender beside Him.

13:12 He it is Who showeth you the lightning, a fear and a hope, and raiseth the heavy clouds.

13:13 The thunder hymneth His praise and (so do) the angels for awe of Him. He launcheth the thunderbolts and smiteth with them whom He will while they dispute (in doubt) concerning Allah, and He is mighty in wrath.

13:14 Unto Him is the real prayer. Those unto whom they pray beside Allah respond to them not at all, save as (is the response to) one who stretcheth forth his hands toward water (asking) that it may come unto his mouth, and it will never reach it. The *PRAYER OF DISBELIEVERS GOETH (FAR) ASTRAY. [IN ITS INTOLERANCE ISLAM DOES NOT ACCEPT OTHER RELIGIONS OR OTHER DEITIES ARE ANYTHING BUT A WASTE OF TIME.]*

13:15 And unto Allah falleth prostrate whosoever is in the heavens and the earth, willingly or unwillingly, as do their shadows in the morning and the evening hours.

13:16 Say (O Muhammad): Who is Lord of the heavens and the earth? Say: Allah. Say: Take ye then (others) beside Him for protectors, which, even for themselves, have neither benefit nor hurt? Say: Is the blind man equal to the seer, or is darkness equal to light? Or *ASSIGN THEY UNTO ALLAH PARTNERS* who created the like of His creation so that the creation (which they made and His creation) seemed alike to them? Say: Allah is the Creator of all things, and He is the One, the Almighty.

13:17 He sendeth down water from the sky, so that valleys flow according to their measure, and the flood beareth (on its surface) swelling foam - from that which they smelt in the fire in order to make ornaments and tools riseth a foam like unto it - thus Allah coineth (the similitude of) the true and the false. Then, as for the foam, it passeth away as scum upon the banks, while, as for that which is of use to mankind, it remaineth in the earth. Thus Allah coineth the similitudes.

13:18 *FOR THOSE WHO ANSWERED ALLAH'S CALL IS BLISS*; **and for those who answered not His call, if they had all that is in the earth, and therewith the like thereof, they would proffer it as ransom. Such will have a woeful** *RECKONING*, **and** *THEIR HABITATION WILL BE HELL*, **a dire abode. [Those who answer Allah's call receive eternal pleasure; those who do not answer it receive eternal torture.]**

13:19 Is he who knoweth that what is revealed unto thee from *THY LORD IS THE TRUTH* like him who is blind? But only men of understanding heed;

13:20 Such as keep the pact of Allah, and *BREAK NOT THE COVENANT;*

13:21 Such as unite that which Allah hath commandeth should be joined, and fear their Lord, and dread a woeful *RECKONING*;

13:22 Such as persevere in seeking their Lord's Countenance and are regular in prayer and *SPEND OF THAT WHICH WE BESTOW UPON THEM SECRETLY AND OPENLY*, and overcome *EVIL* with good. Theirs will be the sequel of the (heavenly) Home,

13:23 *GARDENS OF EDEN* **which they enter,** *ALONG WITH ALL WHO DO RIGHT OF THEIR FATHERS AND THEIR HELPMEETS AND THEIR SEED*. **The angels enter unto them from every gate, [The relatives of Jihadis are also granted eternal pleasure.]**

13:24 (Saying): Peace be unto you because ye persevered. Ah, passing sweet will be the sequel of the (heavenly) Home.

13:25 And those who break the *COVENANT* of Allah after ratifying it, and sever that which Allah hath commanded should be joined, and *MAKE MISCHIEF IN THE EARTH*: theirs is the curse and theirs the ill abode.

13:26 Allah enlargeth livelihood for whom He will, and straiteneth (it for whom He will); and they rejoice in the life of the world, whereas *THE LIFE OF THE WORLD IS BUT BRIEF COMFORT AS COMPARED WITH THE HEREAFTER.*

13:27 *THOSE WHO DISBELIEVE* say: If only a portent were sent down upon him from his Lord! Say: Lo! Allah sendeth whom He will astray, and guideth unto Himself all who turn (unto Him),

13:28 *WHO HAVE BELIEVED* and whose hearts have rest in the remembrance of Allah. Verily in the remembrance of Allah do hearts find rest!

13:29 *THOSE WHO BELIEVE* and do right: Joy is for them, and bliss (their) journey's end.

13:30 Thus We send thee (O Muhammad) unto a nation, before whom other nations have passed away, that thou mayst recite unto them that which We have inspired in thee, while *THEY ARE DISBELIEVERS* in the Beneficent. Say: He is my Lord; there is no God save Him. In Him do I put my trust and unto Him is my recourse.

13:31 Had it been possible for a Lecture to cause the mountains to move, or the earth to be torn asunder, or the dead to speak, (this Qur'an would have done so). Nay, but Allah's is the whole command. Do not *THOSE WHO BELIEVE* know that, *HAD ALLAH WILLED, HE COULD HAVE GUIDED ALL MANKIND*? As for *THOSE WHO DISBELIEVE*, disaster ceaseth not to strike them because of what they do, or it dwelleth near their home until the threat of Allah come to pass. Lo! Allah faileth not to keep the tryst.

13:32 And verily messengers (of Allah) were mocked before thee, but long I bore with *THOSE WHO DISBELIEVED*. At length I seized them, and *HOW (AWFUL) WAS MY PUNISHMENT!*

13:33 Is He Who is aware of the deserts of every soul (as he who is aware of nothing)? Yet they ascribe unto Allah partners. Say: Name them. Is it that ye would inform Him of something which He knoweth not in the earth? Or is it but a way of speaking? Nay but their contrivance is made seeming fair for *THOSE WHO DISBELIEVE* and they are kept from the right road. He whom *ALLAH SENDETH ASTRAY*, for him there is no guide.

13:34 For them is *TORMENT IN THE LIFE OF THE WORLD, AND VERILY THE DOOM OF THE HEREAFTER IS MORE PAINFUL*, and they have no defender from Allah.

13:35 A similitude of _THE_ _GARDEN_ _WHICH_ _IS_ _PROMISED_ _UNTO_ _THOSE_ _WHO_ _KEEP THEIR DUTY (TO ALLAH) [JIHAD]_**: Underneath it rivers flow; its food is everlasting, and its shade; this is** _THE REWARD OF THOSE WHO KEEP THEIR_ _DUTY_**, while** _THE REWARD OF DISBELIEVERS IS THE FIRE_**. [Obedient Muslims get an eternity in Paradise; non-Muslims get an eternity of torture in Hell.]**

13:36 Those unto whom We gave the Scripture rejoice in that which is revealed unto thee. And of the clans there are who deny some of it. Say: I am commanded only that I serve Allah and _ASCRIBE UNTO_ _HIM NO PARTNER_. Unto Him I cry, and unto Him is my return.

13:37 Thus have _WE REVEALED IT, A DECISIVE UTTERANCE IN ARABIC_; and if thou shouldst follow their desires after that which hath come unto thee of knowledge, then truly wouldst thou have from Allah no protecting friend nor defender.

13:38 And verily We sent messengers (to mankind) before thee, and We appointed for them wives and offspring, and it was not (given) to any messenger that he should bring a portent save by Allah's leave. For everything there is a time prescribed.

13:39 Allah effaceth what He will, and establisheth (what He will), and with Him is the source of ordinance.

13:40 Whether We let thee see something of that which We have promised them, or make thee die (before its happening), ~~thine is but conveyance (of the message). Ours the reckoning.~~ [Part Cancelled by verse 9:5 i.e. Muslims commanded to take violent action, not just convey a message from Allah][412]

13:41 See they not how we aim to the land, reducing it of its outlying parts? (When) Allah doometh there is none that can postpone His doom, and He is swift at reckoning.

13:42 _THOSE WHO WERE BEFORE THEM PLOTTED; BUT ALL PLOTTING IS ALLAH'S_. He knoweth that which each soul earneth. The _DISBELIEVERS_ will come to know for whom will be the sequel of the (heavenly) Home.

13:43 _THEY WHO DISBELIEVE_ say: Thou art no messenger (of Allah). Say: Allah, and whosoever hath knowledge of the Scripture, is sufficient witness between me and you.

Chapter 47 - Muhammad

47:1 _THOSE WHO DISBELIEVE_ and turn (men) from the way of Allah, He rendereth their actions vain.

47:2 And _THOSE WHO BELIEVE AND DO GOOD WORKS_ and _BELIEVE_ in that which is revealed unto Muhammad - and it is _THE TRUTH_ from their Lord - He riddeth them of their ill-deeds and improveth their state.

47:3 That is because _THOSE WHO DISBELIEVE FOLLOW FALSEHOOD_ and because _THOSE WHO BELIEVE_ _FOLLOW THE TRUTH_ from their Lord. Thus Allah coineth their similitudes for mankind.

47:4 Now _WHEN YE MEET IN BATTLE THOSE WHO DISBELIEVE_**, then it is** _SMITING OF THE NECKS_ **[throat cutting, beheading] until, when ye have routed [defeated] them, then** _MAKING FAST OF BONDS [ENSLAVE THOSE NOT_ _KILLED]_**;** ~~and afterward either grace or ransom till the war lay down its burdens.~~ **That (is the ordinance). And if Allah willed He could have punished them (without you) but (thus it is ordained) that He may try some of you by means of others. And** _THOSE WHO ARE SLAIN IN THE WAY OF_ _ALLAH [DYING DURING JIHAD], HE RENDERETH NOT THEIR ACTIONS VAIN_ **[Part Cancelled by verse 9:5. Muslims who are killed during this Jihad will go to Paradise – see 47:6 below.][413]**

47:5 He will guide them and improve their state,

47:6 And _BRING THEM IN UNTO THE GARDEN_ **which He hath made known to them. [Those who obey the Koran rewarded by an eternity in Paradise]**

47:7 O _YE WHO BELIEVE_! If ye help Allah, He will help you and will make your foothold firm.

47:8 And *THOSE WHO DISBELIEVE*, perdition is for them, and He will make their actions vain.

47:9 That is because they are averse to that which Allah hath revealed, therefor maketh He their actions fruitless.

47:10 Have they not travelled in the land to see the nature of the consequence for those who were before them? *ALLAH WIPED THEM OUT. AND FOR THE DISBELIEVERS THERE WILL BE THE LIKE* thereof.

47:11 That is because Allah is patron of *THOSE WHO BELIEVE*, and because the *DISBELIEVERS* have no patron.

47:12 Lo! Allah will cause *THOSE WHO BELIEVE AND DO GOOD WORKS TO ENTER GARDENS UNDERNEATH* **which rivers flow; while** *THOSE WHO DISBELIEVE TAKE THEIR COMFORT IN THIS LIFE AND EAT EVEN AS THE CATTLE EAT*, **and** *THE FIRE* **is their habitation.**

47:13 And *HOW MANY A TOWNSHIP* stronger than thy township (O Muhammad) which hath cast thee out, *HAVE WE DESTROYED*, and they had no helper!

47:14 Is he who relieve on a *CLEAR PROOF* from his Lord like those for whom the *EVIL* that they do is beautified while they follow their own lusts?

47:15 A similitude of *THE GARDEN WHICH THOSE WHO KEEP THEIR DUTY (TO ALLAH) ARE PROMISED*: **Therein are rivers of water unpolluted, and rivers of milk whereof the flavour changeth not, and** *RIVERS OF WINE DELICIOUS TO THE DRINKERS*, **and rivers of clear-run honey; therein for them is every kind of fruit, with pardon from their Lord. (Are those who enjoy all this) like** *THOSE WHO ARE IMMORTAL IN THE FIRE AND ARE GIVEN BOILING WATER TO DRINK* **so that it teareth their bowels?**

47:16 Among them are some who give ear unto thee (Muhammad) till, when they go forth from thy presence they say unto those who have been given knowledge: What was that he said just now? Those are they whose hearts Allah hath sealed, and they follow their own lusts.

47:17 While as for those who walk aright, He addeth to their guidance, and giveth them their protection (against *EVIL*).

47:18 Await they aught save *THE HOUR*, that it should come upon them unawares? And the beginnings thereof have already come. But how, when it hath come upon them, can they take their warning?

47:19 So know (O Muhammad) that *THERE IS NO GOD SAVE ALLAH*, and ask forgiveness for thy sin and for *BELIEVING* men and *BELIEVING* women. Allah knoweth (both) your place of turmoil and your place of rest.

47:20 And *THOSE WHO BELIEVE* **say: If only a surah were revealed! But** *WHEN A DECISIVE SURAH IS REVEALED AND WAR IS MENTIONED THEREIN, THOU SEEST THOSE IN WHOSE HEARTS IS A DISEASE* **looking at thee with the look of men fainting unto death [slackers]. Therefor woe unto them! [Koran acknowledges that the uncommitted Muslims are scared of the commands to go to war.]**

47:21 Obedience and a civil word. Then, when the matter is determined, if they are loyal to Allah it will be well for them.

47:22 Would ye then, if ye were given the command, work *CORRUPTION IN THE LAND* and *SEVER YOUR TIES OF KINSHIP*?

47:23 Such are they *WHOM ALLAH CURSETH SO THAT HE DEAFENETH THEM AND MAKETH BLIND THEIR EYES.*

47:24 Will they then not meditate on the Qur'an, or are there locks on the hearts?

47:25 Lo! those who turn back after the guidance hath been manifested unto them, Satan hath seduced them, and He giveth them the rein.

47:26 That is because *THEY SAY UNTO THOSE WHO HATE WHAT ALLAH HATH REVEALED: WE WILL OBEY YOU IN SOME MATTERS*; and Allah knoweth their secret talk. [Muslims cannot have loyalty to systems other than Islam.]

47:27 Then how (will it be with them) when the angels gather them, *SMITING THEIR FACES AND THEIR BACKS!*

47:28 That will be because they followed that which angereth Allah, and hated that which pleaseth Him. Therefor He hath made their actions vain.

47:29 Or do those in whose hearts is a disease deem that Allah will not bring to light their (secret) hates?

47:30 And if We would, We could show them unto thee (Muhammad) so that thou shouldst know them surely by their marks. And thou shalt know them by the burden of their talk. And Allah knoweth your deeds.

47:31 And verily *WE SHALL TRY YOU TILL WE KNOW THOSE OF YOU WHO STRIVE [JIHAD] HARD (FOR THE CAUSE OF ALLAH)* and the steadfast, and till We test your record. [Jihad is a test which distinguishes between devout Muslims and slackers.]

47:32 Lo! *THOSE WHO DISBELIEVE AND TURN FROM THE WAY OF ALLAH* and oppose the messenger after the guidance hath been manifested unto them, they hurt Allah not a jot, and He will make their actions fruitless.

47:33 O *YE WHO BELIEVE*! *OBEY ALLAH AND OBEY THE MESSENGER*, and render not your actions vain.

47:34 Lo! *THOSE WHO DISBELIEVE AND TURN FROM THE WAY OF ALLA*h and then die *DISBELIEVERS*, Allah surely will not pardon them.

47:35 So *DO NOT FALTER AND CRY OUT FOR PEACE WHEN YE (WILL BE) THE UPPERMOST*, and Allah is with you, and He will not grudge *(THE REWARD OF) YOUR ACTIONS*. [Muslims are commanded not to seek peace if they can be those who subjugate non-Muslims, and Muslims will be paid for their striving as Jihadis.]

47:36 The life of the world is but a sport and a pastime. And *IF YE BELIEVE AND WARD OFF (EVIL), HE WILL GIVE YOU YOUR WAGES*, and will not ask of you your wordly wealth. [Part Cancelled by verse 47:38][414]

47:37 If He should ask it of you and importune you, ye would hoard it, and He would bring to light your (secret) hates. [Cancelled by verse 47:38][415]

47:38 Lo! ye are those who are called to *SPEND IN THE WAY OF ALLAH*, yet among you there are some who hoard. And as for him who hoardeth, he hoardeth only from his soul. And Allah is the Rich, and ye are the poor. And if ye turn away He will exchange you for some other folk, and they will not be the likes of you.

Chapter 57 - Iron

57:1 All that is in the heavens and the earth glorifieth Allah; and He is the Mighty, the Wise.

57:2 His is the Sovereignty of the heavens and the earth; He quickeneth and He giveth death; and He is Able to do all things.

57:3 He is the First and the Last, and the Outward and the Inward; and He is Knower of all things.

57:4 He it is Who created the heavens and the earth in six Days; then He mounted the Throne. He knoweth all that entereth the earth and all that emergeth therefrom and all that cometh down from the sky and all that ascendeth therein; and He is with you wheresoever ye may be. And Allah is Seer of what ye do.

57:5 His is the Sovereignty of the heavens and the earth, and unto Allah (all) things are brought back.

57:6 He causeth the night to pass into the day, and He causeth the day to pass into the night, and He is knower of all that is in the breasts.

57:7 *BELIEVE IN ALLAH AND HIS MESSENGER, AND SPEND* of that whereof He hath made you trustees; and such of you as *BELIEVE* and spend (aright), *THEIRS WILL BE A GREAT REWARD.*

57:8 What aileth you that ye *BELIEVE* not in Allah, when the messenger calleth you to *BELIEVE* in your Lord, and He hath already *MADE A COVENANT WITH YOU, IF YE ARE BELIEVERS*?

57:9 He it is Who sendeth down _CLEAR REVELATIONS_ **unto His slave, that He may bring you forth from darkness unto light; and lo! for you, Allah is Full of Pity, Merciful. [Koran claims it is clear and that it provides illumination]**

57:10 And what aileth you that _YE SPEND NOT IN THE WAY OF ALLAH [JIHAD]_ **when unto Allah belongeth the inheritance of the heavens and the earth?** _THOSE WHO SPENT AND FOUGHT [JIHAD]_ **before the** _VICTORY_ **are** _NOT UPON A LEVEL (WITH THE REST OF YOU)_. **Such are** _GREATER IN RANK THAN THOSE WHO SPENT AND FOUGHT AFTERWARDS._ **Unto each hath Allah promised good. And Allah is Informed of what ye do. [Those Muslims who are in the forefront of Jihad are considered to be better Muslims.]**

57:11 Who is he that will _LEND UNTO ALLAH A GOODLY LOAN_, that He may double it for him and his may be a rich _REWARD_?

57:12 On _THE DAY WHEN THOU (MUHAMMAD) WILT SEE THE BELIEVERS_, **men and women, their light shining forth before them and on their right hands, (and wilt hear it said unto them): Glad news for you this day:** _GARDENS UNDERNEATH WHICH RIVERS FLOW, WHEREIN YE ARE IMMORTAL._ **That is** _THE SUPREME TRIUMPH._

57:13 _ON THE DAY WHEN THE HYPOCRITICAL_ men and the hypocritical women will say unto _THOSE WHO BELIEVE_: Look on us that we may borrow from your light! it will be said: Go back and seek for light! Then there will separate them a wall wherein is a gate, the inner side whereof containeth mercy, while the outer side thereof is toward the doom.

57:14 They will cry unto them (saying): Were we not with you? They will say: Yea, verily; but ye tempted one another, and hesitated, and doubted, and vain desires beguiled you till the ordinance of Allah came to pass; and the deceiver deceived you concerning Allah;

57:15 So _THIS DAY_ **no ransom can be taken from you nor from** _THOSE WHO DISBELIEVED. YOUR HOME IS THE FIRE_; **that is your patron, and a hapless journey's end.**

57:16 Is not the time ripe for the hearts of _THOSE WHO BELIEVE TO SUBMIT_ to Allah's reminder and to _THE TRUTH WHICH IS REVEALED_, that they become _NOT AS THOSE WHO RECEIVED THE SCRIPTURE OF OLD_ but the term was prolonged for them and so their hearts were hardened, and many of them are _EVIL-LIVERS_.

57:17 Know that Allah quickeneth the earth after its death. We have _MADE CLEAR OUR REVELATIONS_ for you, that haply ye may understand.

57:18 Lo! those who give alms, both men and women, and _LEND UNTO ALLAH A GOODLY LOAN, IT WILL BE DOUBLED_ for them, and theirs will be _A RICH REWARD_.

57:19 And _THOSE WHO BELIEVE_ **in Allah and His messengers,** _THEY ARE THE LOYAL, AND THE MARTYRS ARE WITH THEIR LORD; THEY HAVE THEIR REWARD_ **and their light; while as for** _THOSE WHO DISBELIEVE AND DENY OUR REVELATIONS, THEY ARE OWNERS OF HELL-FIRE._

57:20 Know that _THE LIFE OF THE WORLD IS ONLY PLAY_, and idle talk, and pageantry, and boasting among you, and rivalry in respect of wealth and children; as the likeness of vegetation after rain, whereof the growth is pleasing to the husbandman, but afterward it drieth up and thou seest it turning yellow, then it becometh straw. And _IN THE HEREAFTER THERE IS GRIEVOUS PUNISHMENT_, and (also) forgiveness from Allah and His good pleasure, whereas the life of the world is but matter of illusion.

57:21 Race one with another for forgiveness from your Lord and a _GARDEN_ whereof the breadth is as the breadth of the heavens and the earth, _WHICH IS IN STORE FOR THOSE WHO BELIEVE IN ALLAH_ and His messengers. Such is the bounty of Allah, which He bestoweth upon whom He will, and Allah is of Infinite Bounty.

57:22 Naught of disaster befalleth in the earth or in yourselves but it is in a Book before we bring it into being - Lo! that is easy for Allah -

57:23 That ye grieve not for the sake of that which hath escaped you, nor yet exult because of that which hath been given. Allah loveth not all prideful boasters,

57:24 Who hoard and who enjoin upon the people avarice. And whosoever turneth away, still Allah is the Absolute, the Owner of Praise.

57:25 We verily sent Our messengers with *CLEAR PROOFS*, and revealed with them the Scripture and the Balance, that mankind may observe right measure; and He revealed iron, wherein is mighty power and (many) uses for mankind, and that Allah may know him who helpeth Him and His messengers, though unseen. Lo! Allah is Strong, Almighty.

57:26 And We verily sent Noah and Abraham and placed the Prophethood and the Scripture among their seed, and among them there is he who goeth right, but many of them are *EVIL-LIVERS*.

57:27 Then We caused Our messengers to follow in their footsteps; and We caused *JESUS, SON OF MARY*, to follow, and gave him the Gospel, and placed compassion and mercy in the hearts of those who followed him. But *MONASTICISM THEY INVENTED - WE ORDAINED IT NOT FOR THEM* - only seeking Allah's pleasure, and they observed it not with right observance. So *WE GIVE THOSE OF THEM WHO BELIEVE THEIR REWARD,* but *MANY OF THEM ARE EVIL-LIVERS.*

57:28 O *YE WHO BELIEVE! BE MINDFUL OF YOUR DUTY TO ALLAH AND PUT FAITH IN HIS MESSENGER.* He will give you twofold of His mercy and will appoint for you a light wherein ye shall walk, and will forgive you. Allah is Forgiving, Merciful;

57:29 That *THE PEOPLE OF THE SCRIPTURE* may know that they control naught of the bounty of Allah, but that the bounty is in Allah's hand to give to whom He will. And Allah is of Infinite Bounty.

Chapter 99 - The Earthquake

99:1 When Earth is shaken with her (final) earthquake

99:2 And Earth yieldeth up her burdens,

99:3 And man saith: What aileth her?

99:4 That day she will relate her chronicles,

99:5 Because thy Lord inspireth her.

99:6 *THAT DAY MANKIND WILL ISSUE FORTH IN SCATTERED GROUPS TO BE SHOWN THEIR DEEDS.*

99:7 And whoso doeth good an atom's weight will see it then,

99:8 And whoso doeth ill an atom's weight will see it then.

Chapter 4 - Women

4:1 O mankind! Be careful of *YOUR DUTY TO YOUR LORD* Who created you from a single soul and from it created its mate and from them twain hath spread abroad a multitude of men and women. Be careful of *YOUR DUTY TOWARD ALLAH* in Whom ye claim (your rights) of one another, and toward the wombs (that bare you). Lo! Allah hath been a watcher over you.

4:2 Give unto orphans their wealth. Exchange not the good for the bad (in your management thereof) nor absorb their wealth into your own wealth. Lo! that would be a great sin.

4:3 And if ye fear that ye will not deal fairly by the orphans, marry of the women, who seem good to you, two or three or four; and if ye fear that ye cannot do justice (to so many) then one (only) or (the captives) that *YOUR RIGHT HANDS POSSESS* [slaves]. Thus it is more likely that ye will not do injustice.

4:4 And give unto the women (whom ye marry) free gift of their marriage portions; but if they of their own accord remit unto you a part thereof, then ye are welcome to absorb it (in your wealth).

4:5 Give not unto the foolish (what is in) your (keeping of their) wealth, which Allah hath given you to maintain; but feed and clothe them from it, and speak kindly unto them.

4:6 Prove orphans till they reach the marriageable age; then, if ye find them of sound judgment, deliver over unto them their fortune; and devour it not by squandering and in haste lest they should grow up Whoso (of the guardians) is rich, let him abstain generously (from taking of the property of orphans); and whoso is poor let him take thereof in reason (for his guardianship). And when ye deliver up their fortune unto orphans, have (the transaction) witnessed in their presence. Allah sufficeth as a Reckoner.

4:7 Unto the men (of a family) belongeth a share of that which parents and near kindred leave, and unto the women a share of that which parents and near kindred leave, whether it be little or much - a legal share.

4:8 And when kinsfolk and orphans and the needy are present at the division (of the heritage), bestow on them therefrom and speak kindly unto them.

4:9 And let those fear (in their behaviour toward orphans) who if they left behind them weak offspring would be afraid for them. So let them mind their duty to Allah, and speak justly.

4:10 Lo! Those who devour the wealth of orphans wrongfully, they do but *SWALLOW FIRE INTO THEIR BELLIES*, and they will be *EXPOSED TO BURNING FLAME*.

4:11 Allah chargeth you concerning (the provision for) your children: to the male the equivalent of the portion of two females, and if there be women more than two, then theirs is two-thirds of the inheritance, and if there be one (only) then the half. And to each of his parents a sixth of the inheritance, if he have a son; and if he have no son and his parents are his heirs, then to his mother appertaineth the third; and if he have brethren, then to his mother appertaineth the sixth, after any legacy he may have bequeathed, or debt (hath been paid). Your parents and your children: Ye know not which of them is nearer unto you in usefulness. It is an injunction from Allah. Lo! Allah is Knower, Wise.

4:12 And unto you belongeth a half of that which your wives leave, if they have no child; but if they have a child then unto you the fourth of that which they leave, after any legacy they may have bequeathed, or debt (they may have contracted, hath been paid). And unto them belongeth the fourth of that which ye leave if ye have no child, but if ye have a child then the eighth of that which ye leave, after any legacy ye may have bequeathed, or debt (ye may have contracted, hath been paid). And if a man or a woman have a distant heir (having left neither parent nor child), and he (or she) have a brother or a sister (only on the mother's side) then to each of them twain (the brother and the sister) the sixth, and if they be more than two, then they shall be sharers in the third, after any legacy that may have been bequeathed or debt (contracted) not injuring (the heirs by willing away more than a third of the heritage) hath been paid. A commandment from Allah. Allah is Knower, Indulgent.

4:13 These are the limits (imposed by) Allah. Whoso *OBEYETH ALLAH AND HIS MESSENGER*, He will make him *ENTER GARDENS UNDERNEATH WHICH RIVERS FLOW, WHERE SUCH WILL DWELL FOR EVER.* That will be the *GREAT SUCCESS.*

4:14 And *WHOSO DISOBEYETH ALLAH AND HIS MESSENGER* and transgresseth His limits, He will make him *ENTER FIRE, WHERE HE WILL DWELL FOR EVER; HIS WILL BE A SHAMEFUL DOOM.*

4:15 As for those of your women who are guilty of lewdness, call to witness four of you against them. And if they testify (to the truth of the allegation) then confine them to the houses until death take them or (until) Allah appoint for them a way (through new legislation).

4:16 And as for the two of you who are guilty thereof, punish them both. And if they repent and improve, then let them be. Lo! Allah is ever relenting, Merciful.

4:17 Forgiveness is only incumbent on Allah toward those who do *EVIL* in ignorance (and) then turn quickly (in repentance) to Allah. These are they toward whom Allah relenteth. Allah is ever Knower, Wise.

4:18 The forgiveness is not for those who do ill-deeds until, when death attendeth upon one of them, he saith: Lo! I repent now; nor yet *FOR THOSE WHO DIE WHILE THEY ARE DISBELIEVERS. FOR SUCH WE HAVE PREPARED A PAINFUL DOOM.*

4:19 O *YE WHO BELIEVE!* It is not lawful for you forcibly to inherit the women (of your deceased kinsmen), nor (that) ye should put constraint upon them that ye may take away a part of that which ye have given them, unless they be guilty of flagrant lewdness. But consort with them in kindness, for if ye hate them *IT MAY HAPPEN THAT YE HATE A THING WHEREIN ALLAH HATH PLACED MUCH GOOD.*

4:20 And if ye wish to exchange one wife for another and ye have given unto one of them a sum of money (however great), take nothing from it. Would ye take it by the way of calumny and open wrong?

4:21 How can ye take it (back) after one of you hath gone in unto the other, and they have taken a strong pledge from you?

4:22 And marry not those women whom your fathers married, except what hath already happened (of that nature) in the past. Lo! it was ever lewdness and abomination, and an evil way.

4:23 Forbidden unto you are your mothers, and your daughters, and your sisters, and your father's sisters, and your mother's sisters, and your brother's daughters and your sister's daughters, and your foster-mothers, and your foster-sisters, and your mothers-in-law, and your step-daughters who are under your protection (born) of your women unto whom ye have gone in - but if ye have not gone in unto them, then it is no sin for you (to marry their daughters) - and the wives of your sons who (spring) from your own loins. And (it is forbidden unto you) that ye should have two sisters together, except what hath already happened (of that nature) in the past. Lo! Allah is ever Forgiving, Merciful.

4:24 And *ALL MARRIED WOMEN (ARE FORBIDDEN UNTO YOU) SAVE THOSE (CAPTIVES) WHOM YOUR RIGHT HANDS POSSESS [SLAVES]*. It is a decree of Allah for you. Lawful unto you are all beyond those mentioned, so that ye seek them with your wealth in honest wedlock, not debauchery. And those of whom ye seek content (by marrying them), give unto them their portions as a duty. And there is no sin for you in what ye do by mutual agreement after the duty (hath been done). Lo! Allah is ever Knower, Wise.

4:25 And *WHOSO IS NOT ABLE TO AFFORD TO MARRY FREE, BELIEVING WOMEN, LET THEM MARRY FROM THE BELIEVING MAIDS WHOM YOUR RIGHT HANDS POSSESS [SLAVES]*. Allah knoweth best (concerning) your faith. Ye (proceed) one from another; so wed them by permission of their folk, and give unto them their portions in kindness, they being honest, not debauched nor of loose conduct. And if when they are honourably married they commit lewdness they shall incur the half of the punishment (prescribed) for free women (in that case). This is for him among you who feareth to commit sin. But to have patience would be better for you. Allah is Forgiving, Merciful.

4:26 Allah would explain to you and guide you by the examples of those who were before you, and would turn to you in mercy. Allah is Knower, Wise.

4:27 And Allah would turn to you in mercy; but those who follow vain desires would have you go tremendously astray.

4:28 Allah would make the burden light for you, for man was created weak.

4:29 O *YE WHO BELIEVE*! Squander not your wealth among yourselves in vanity, except it be a trade by mutual consent, and *KILL NOT ONE ANOTHER*. Lo! Allah is ever Merciful unto you. [This command only applies to the killing of Muslims, unless the Muslim is classed as behaving as an unbeliever or an apostate in which case his life is in danger.]

4:30 *WHOSO DOETH THAT THROUGH* aggression and *INJUSTICE, WE SHALL CAST HIM INTO FIRE*, and that is ever easy for Allah. [Muslims can kill Muslims who break sharia laws which carry the death penalty.]

4:31 If ye avoid the great (things) which ye are forbidden, We will *REMIT FROM YOU YOUR EVIL DEEDS AND MAKE YOU ENTER AT A NOBLE GATE.*

4:32 And covet not the thing in which Allah hath made some of you excel others. Unto men a fortune from that which they have earned, and unto women a fortune from that which they have earned. (Envy not one another) but ask Allah of His bounty. Lo! Allah is ever Knower of all things.

4:33 And unto each We have appointed heirs of that which parents and near kindred leave; and as for those with whom *YOUR RIGHT HANDS* have made a *COVENANT*, give them their due. Lo! Allah is ever Witness over all things.

4:34 *MEN ARE IN CHARGE OF WOMEN*, because Allah hath made the one of them to excel the other, and because they spend of their property (for the support of women). So *GOOD WOMEN ARE THE OBEDIENT*, guarding in secret that which Allah hath guarded. As for those from whom ye fear rebellion, admonish them and banish them to beds apart, and *SCOURGE THEM*. Then *IF THEY OBEY YOU*, seek not a way against them. Lo! Allah is ever High, Exalted, Great.

4:35 And if ye fear a breach between them twain (the man and wife), appoint an arbiter from his folk and an arbiter from her folk. If they desire amendment Allah will make them of one mind. Lo! Allah is ever Knower, Aware.

4:36 And *SERVE ALLAH. ASCRIBE NO THING AS PARTNER UNTO HIM.* (Show) kindness unto parents, and unto near kindred, and orphans, and the needy, and unto the neighbour who is of kin (unto you) and the neighbour who is not of kin, and the fellow-traveller and the wayfarer and *(THE SLAVES) WHOM YOUR RIGHT HANDS POSSESS*. Lo! Allah loveth not such as are proud and boastful,

4:37 Who hoard their wealth and enjoin avarice on others, and hide that which Allah hath bestowed upon them of His bounty. *FOR DISBELIEVERS WE PREPARE A SHAMEFUL DOOM;*

4:38 And (also) those who spend their wealth in order to be seen of men, and *BELIEVE NOT IN ALLAH NOR THE LAST DAY.* Whoso taketh Satan for a comrade, a bad comrade hath he.

4:39 What have they (to fear) if they *BELIEVE IN ALLAH AND THE LAST DAY AND SPEND (ARIGHT) OF THAT WHICH ALLAH HATH BESTOWED UPON THEM*, when Allah is ever Aware of them (and all they do)?

4:40 Lo! Allah wrongeth not even of the weight of an ant; and if there is a good deed, He will double it and will give (the doer) from His presence an immense *REWARD*.

4:41 But how (will it be with them) when We bring of every people a witness, and We bring thee (O Muhammad) a witness against these?

4:42 *ON THAT DAY THOSE WHO DISBELIEVED* and *DISOBEYED THE MESSENGER* will wish that they were level with the ground, and they can hide no fact from Allah.

4:43 O *YE WHO BELIEVE*! *DRAW NOT NEAR UNTO PRAYER WHEN YE ARE DRUNKEN*, till ye know that which ye utter, nor when ye are polluted, save when journeying upon the road, till ye have bathed. And if ye be ill, or on a journey, or one of you cometh from the closet, or ye have touched women, and ye find not water, then go to high clean soil and rub your faces and your hands (therewith). Lo! Allah is Benign, Forgiving.

4:44 Seest thou not those unto whom a portion of the Scripture hath been given, how they purchase error, and seek to make you (*MUSLIMS*) err from the right way?

4:45 *ALLAH KNOWETH BEST (WHO ARE) YOUR ENEMIES.* Allah is sufficient as a Guardian, and Allah is sufficient as a Supporter.

4:46 Some of those who are *JEWS CHANGE WORDS* from their context and say: "We hear and disobey; hear thou as one who heareth not" and "Listen to us!" distorting with their tongues and slandering religion. If they had said: "We hear and we obey: hear thou, and look at us" it had been better for them, and more upright. But *ALLAH HATH CURSED THEM* for their *DISBELIEF*, so *THEY BELIEVE NOT, SAVE A FEW.*

4:47 O *YE UNTO WHOM THE SCRIPTURE HATH BEEN GIVEN! BELIEVE* in what We have revealed confirming that which ye possess, before We destroy countenances so as to confound them, or curse them as We cursed the Sabbath-breakers (of old time). *THE COMMANDMENT OF ALLAH IS ALWAYS EXECUTED.*

4:48 Lo! *ALLAH FORGIVETH NOT THAT A PARTNER SHOULD BE ASCRIBED UNTO HIM*. He forgiveth (all) save that to whom He will. Whoso ascribeth partners to Allah, he hath indeed invented a *TREMENDOUS SIN.*

4:49 Hast thou not seen those who praise themselves for purity? Nay, Allah purifieth whom He will, and they will not be wronged even the hair upon a date-stone.

4:50 See, how they invent lies about Allah! That of itself is flagrant sin.

4:51 Hast thou not seen those unto whom a portion of the Scripture hath been given, how they *BELIEVE* in idols and false deities, and how they say of those (*IDOLATERS*) who *DISBELIEVE*: "These are more *RIGHTLY GUIDED* than those who *BELIEVE*" ?

4:52 Those are *THEY WHOM ALLAH HATH CURSED*, and he whom Allah hath cursed, thou (O Muhammad) wilt find for him no helper.

4:53 Or have they even a share in the Sovereignty? Then in that case, they would not give mankind even the speck on a date-stone.

4:54 Or are they jealous of mankind because of that which Allah of His bounty hath bestowed upon them? For We bestowed upon the house of Abraham (of old) the Scripture and wisdom, and We bestowed on them a mighty kingdom.

4:55 And of them were *(SOME) WHO BELIEVED* therein and of them were *(SOME) WHO TURNED AWAY* from it. *HELL IS SUFFICIENT FOR (THEIR) BURNING.*

4:56 Lo! *THOSE WHO DISBELIEVE OUR REVELATIONS, WE SHALL EXPOSE THEM TO THE FIRE.* As often as their skins are consumed We shall *EXCHANGE THEM FOR FRESH SKINS THAT THEY MAY TASTE THE TORMENT.* Lo! Allah is ever Mighty, Wise. [Unbelievers to be tortured in Hell for eternity.]

4:57 And as for *THOSE WHO BELIEVE AND DO GOOD WORKS*, We shall make them *ENTER GARDENS UNDERNEATH WHICH RIVERS FLOW* - to dwell therein for ever; there *FOR THEM ARE PURE COMPANIONS* - and We shall make them enter plenteous shade. [This is why Jihadis claim they will be rewarded with virgins in Paradise.]

4:58 Lo! Allah commandeth you that ye restore deposits to their owners, and, if ye judge between mankind, that ye judge justly. Lo! comely is this which Allah admonisheth you. Lo! Allah is ever Hearer, Seer.

4:59 O *YE WHO BELIEVE*! ***OBEY ALLAH, AND OBEY THE MESSENGER*** and those of you who are in authority; and if ye have a dispute concerning any matter, refer it to Allah and the messenger if ye are (in truth) *BELIEVERS IN ALLAH AND THE LAST DAY*. That is better and more seemly in the end.

4:60 Hast thou not seen *THOSE WHO PRETEND THAT THEY BELIEVE* in that which is revealed unto thee and that which was revealed before thee, how they would go for judgment (in their disputes) to false deities when they have been ordered to abjure them? Satan would mislead them far astray.

4:61 And when it is said unto them: Come unto that which Allah hath revealed and unto the messenger, thou seest the *HYPOCRITES* turn from thee with aversion.

4:62 How would it be if a misfortune smote them because of that which their own hands have sent before (them)? Then would they come unto thee, swearing by Allah that they were seeking naught but harmony and kindness.

4:63 ~~Those are they, the secrets of whose hearts Allah knoweth. So oppose them and admonish them, and address them in plain terms about their souls.~~ [Cancelled by 9:5, i.e. violence replaces speech][416]

4:64 ~~We sent no messenger save that he should be obeyed by Allah's leave. And if, when they had wronged themselves, they had but come unto thee and asked forgiveness of Allah, and asked forgiveness of the messenger, they would have found Allah Forgiving, Merciful.~~ [Cancelled by verse 9:80 & 63:6 i.e. Muslims are not to be forgiving to unbelievers][417]

4:65 But nay, by thy Lord, *THEY WILL NOT BELIEVE* (in truth) until they make thee judge of what is in dispute between them and find within themselves no dislike of that which thou decidest, and *SUBMIT WITH FULL SUBMISSION*. [Muslims cannot dispute or dislike anything decided by the Messenger of Allah; Muslim means 'one who submits'. Islam does not mean 'Peace', it means 'submission'.]

4:66 And *IF WE HAD DECREED FOR THEM: LAY DOWN YOUR LIVES OR GO FORTH FROM YOUR DWELLINGS, BUT FEW OF THEM WOULD HAVE DONE IT*; though if they did what they are exhorted to do it would be better for them, and more strengthening;

4:67 *AND THEN WE SHOULD BESTOW UPON THEM FROM OUR PRESENCE AN IMMENSE REWARD,*
4:68 And should guide them unto *A STRAIGHT PATH.*

4:69 *WHOSO OBEYETH ALLAH AND THE MESSENGER, THEY ARE WITH THOSE UNTO WHOM ALLAH HATH SHOWN FAVOUR*, of the prophets and the saints and the martyrs and the righteous. The best of company are they!

4:70 That is bounty from Allah, and Allah sufficeth as Knower.

4:71 ~~O ye who believe! Take your precautions, then advance the proven ones, or advance all together.~~ [verse 9:122, some to refrain from jihad][418]

4:72 Lo! among you there is he who loitereth; and if disaster overtook you, he would say: Allah hath been gracious unto me since I was not present with them.

4:73 And if a *BOUNTY [SLAVES AND LOOT] FROM ALLAH* befell you, he would surely cry, as if there had been no love between you and him: Oh, would that I had been with them, then should I have achieved a great *SUCCESS*! [See Koran 4:66 and 4:74 to see that this success in acquiring bounty comes from Jihad.]

4:74 Let *THOSE FIGHT IN THE WAY OF ALLAH [JIHADIS] WHO SELL THE LIFE OF THIS WORLD FOR THE OTHER. WHOSO FIGHTETH IN THE WAY OF ALLAH, BE HE SLAIN OR BE HE VICTORIOUS, ON HIM WE SHALL BESTOW A VAST REWARD.* [Those who die imposing Islam get the greatest reward from Allah.]

4:75 How should ye not *FIGHT FOR THE CAUSE OF ALLAH [JIHAD]* and of the feeble among men and of the women and the children who are crying: Our Lord! Bring us forth from out this town of which the people are oppressors! Oh, give us from thy presence some protecting friend! Oh, give us from Thy presence some defender!

4:76 *THOSE WHO BELIEVE DO BATTLE FOR THE CAUSE OF ALLAH* [Jihad]; and *THOSE WHO DISBELIEVE DO BATTLE FOR THE CAUSE OF IDOLS*. So *FIGHT THE MINIONS OF THE DEVIL*. Lo! the devil's strategy is ever weak. [Non-Muslims are working for the devil.]

4:77 Hast thou not seen those unto whom it was said: Withhold your hands, establish worship and pay the poor due, but when *FIGHTING [JIHAD] WAS PRESCRIBED FOR THEM* behold! a party [group] of them fear mankind even as their fear of Allah or with greater fear, and say: Our Lord! *WHY HAST THOU ORDAINED FIGHTING FOR US?* If only Thou wouldst give us respite yet a while! [slackers] Say (unto them, O Muhammad): *THE COMFORT OF THIS WORLD IS SCANT; THE HEREAFTER [MARTYRDOM] WILL BE BETTER FOR HIM WHO WARDETH OFF (EVIL);* and ye will not be wronged the down upon a date-stone.

4:78 Wheresoever ye may be, death will overtake you, even though ye were in lofty towers. Yet if a happy thing befalleth them they say: This is from Allah; and if an *EVIL* thing befalleth them they say: This is of thy doing (O Muhammad). Say (unto them): All is from Allah. What is amiss with these people that they come not nigh to understand a happening?

4:79 Whatever of good befalleth thee (O man) it is from Allah, and whatever of ill befalleth thee it is from thyself. We have sent thee (Muhammad) as a messenger unto mankind and Allah is sufficient as Witness.

4:80 Whoso *OBEYETH THE MESSENGER HATH OBEYED ALLAH*, ~~and whoso turneth away: We have not sent thee as a warder over them.~~ [Part cancelled by verse 9:5, i.e. violence replaces indifference][419]

4:81 And they say: (It is) obedience; but when they have gone forth from thee a party of them spend the night in planning other than what thou sayest. ~~Allah recordeth what they plan by night.~~ So oppose them and put thy trust in Allah. Allah is sufficient as Trustee. [Part cancelled by verse 9:5][420]

4:82 Will they not then ponder on the Qur'an? If it had been from other than Allah they would have found therein much incongruity.

4:83 And if any tidings, whether of safety or fear, come unto them, they noise it abroad, whereas if they had referred it to the messenger and to such of them as are in authority, those among them who are able to think out the matter would have known it. If it had not been for the grace of Allah upon you and His mercy ye would have followed Satan, save a few (of you).

4:84 ~~So fight (O Muhammad) in the way of Allah Thou art not taxed (with the responsibility for anyone) except thyself -- and~~ *URGE ON THE BELIEVERS*. Peradventure *ALLAH WILL RESTRAIN THE MIGHT OF THOSE WHO DISBELIEVE*. Allah is stronger in might and stronger in *INFLICTING PUNISHMENT*. [Cancelled by verse 9:5, violence replaces indifference][421]

4:85 Whoso interveneth in a good cause will have the *REWARD* thereof, and whoso interveneth in an *EVIL* cause will bear the consequence thereof. Allah overseeth all things.

4:86 When ye are greeted with a greeting, greet ye with a better than it or return it. Lo! Allah taketh count of all things.

4:87 Allah! There is no God save Him. He gathereth you all unto *A DAY OF RESURRECTION WHEREOF THERE IS NO DOUBT. WHO IS MORE TRUE IN STATEMENT THAN ALLAH?*

4:88 ~~What aileth you that ye are become two parties regarding the hypocrites, when Allah cast them back (to disbelief) because of what they earned? Seek ye to guide him whom Allah hath sent astray?~~

~~He whom Allah sendeth astray, for him thou (O Muhammad) canst not find a road.~~ [Cancelled by verse 9:5, i.e. violence replaces indifference][422]

4:89 *THEY [NON-MUSLIMS] LONG THAT YE SHOULD DISBELIEVE* **even as they disbelieve, that ye may be upon a level (with them).** *SO CHOOSE NOT FRIENDS FROM THEM TILL THEY FORSAKE THEIR HOMES IN THE WAY OF ALLAH;* **if they turn back (to enmity) then** *TAKE THEM AND KILL THEM WHEREVER YE FIND THEM,* **and choose no friend nor helper from among them,**

4:90 ~~Except those who seek refuge with a people between whom and you there is a covenant,~~ **or (those who) come unto you because** *THEIR HEARTS FORBID THEM TO MAKE WAR ON YOU OR MAKE WAR ON THEIR OWN FOLK.* **Had Allah willed He could have given them power over you so that assuredly they would have fought you. So,** *IF THEY HOLD ALOOF FROM YOU AND WAGE NOT WAR AGAINST YOU AND OFFER YOU PEACE,* **Allah alloweth you no way against them. [Part cancelled by verse 9:5, no treaty is to be honoured. Those who are passive in the face of Islamic Jihad are to be left alone, because they will not resist subjugation by Muslims.][423]**

4:91 ~~Ye will find others who desire that they should have security from you, and security from their own folk.~~ **So often as they are returned to** *HOSTILITY* **they are plunged therein. If they keep not aloof from you nor offer you peace nor hold their hands, then** *TAKE THEM AND KILL THEM WHEREVER YE FIND THEM.* **Against such We have given you clear warrant. [Partial Cancellation by 9:1][424]**

4:92 *IT IS NOT FOR A BELIEVER TO KILL A BELIEVER* **unless (it be) by mistake. He who hath killed a** *BELIEVER* **by mistake must set free a** *BELIEVING SLAVE,* **and pay the blood-money to the family of the slain, unless they remit it as a charity.** ~~If he (the victim) be of a people hostile unto you, and he is a~~ *BELIEVER,* ~~then (the penance is) to set free a~~ *BELIEVING* ~~slave.~~ **And if he cometh of a folk between whom and you there is a** *COVENANT,* **then the blood-money must be paid unto his folk and (also) a** *BELIEVING SLAVE* **must be set free. And whoso hath not the wherewithal must fast two consecutive months. A penance from Allah. Allah is Knower, Wise. [Part cancelled by verse 9:5. Note that the killing of unbelievers who will not submit to Islam carries no penalty i.e. such killing is sanctioned.][425]**

4:93 ~~Whoso slayeth [kills] a *BELIEVER* of set purpose, his reward is hell for ever. Allah is wroth against him and He hath cursed him and prepared for him an awful doom.~~ [Cancelled by verse 4:116 & by verse 4:48. This is why Muslims kill those Muslims who engage in shirk (i.e. the worship of anything other than Allah is considered to diminish Allah's authority.)][426]

4:94 O *YE WHO BELIEVE!* **When ye** *GO FORTH (TO FIGHT) IN THE WAY OF ALLAH [JIHAD],* **be careful to discriminate, and say not unto one who offereth you peace:** *"THOU ART NOT A BELIEVER,"* **seeking the chance profits of this life (so that ye may despoil him).** *WITH ALLAH ARE PLENTEOUS SPOILS [SLAVES AND LOOT].* **Even thus (as he now is) were ye before; but Allah hath since then been gracious unto you. Therefore take care to discriminate. Allah is ever Informed of what ye do.**

4:95 *THOSE OF THE BELIEVERS WHO SIT STILL* [slackers avoiding Jihad], **other than those who have a (disabling) hurt,** *ARE NOT ON AN EQUALITY WITH THOSE [MUSLIMS] WHO STRIVE IN THE WAY OF ALLAH [WHO PERFORM JIHAD] WITH THEIR WEALTH AND LIVES.* **Allah hath conferred on** *THOSE WHO STRIVE [JIHADIS]* **with their wealth and lives** *A RANK ABOVE THE SEDENTARY* . **Unto each Allah hath promised good, but** *HE HATH BESTOWED ON THOSE WHO STRIVE A GREAT REWARD ABOVE THE SEDENTARY*; **[Muslims who pay for Jihad or die performing Jihad are rewarded more than those Muslims who are passive slackers]**

4:96 Degrees of rank from Him, and forgiveness and mercy. Allah is ever Forgiving, Merciful.
4:97 Lo! as for those whom the angels take (in death) while they wrong themselves, (the angels) will ask: In what were ye engaged? They will say: *WE WERE OPPRESSED IN THE LAND.* (The angels) will say: Was not Allah's earth spacious that *YE COULD HAVE MIGRATED* therein? As for such, *THEIR HABITATION WILL BE HELL, AN EVIL JOURNEY'S END;*
4:98 *EXCEPT THE FEEBLE AMONG MEN, AND THE WOMEN, AND THE CHILDREN*, who are unable to devise a plan and are not shown a way.
4:99 As for such, it may be that Allah will pardon them. Allah is ever Clement, Forgiving.

4:100 Whoso *MIGRATETH FOR THE CAUSE OF ALLAH [JIHAD]* **will find much refuge and abundance in the earth, and whoso forsaketh his home, a fugitive unto Allah and His messenger, and death overtaketh him, his** *REWARD* **is then incumbent on Allah. Allah is ever Forgiving, Merciful.**

4:101 And when ye go forth in the land, it is no sin for you to *CURTAIL (YOUR) WORSHIP* **if ye fear that** *THOSE WHO DISBELIEVE* **may** *ATTACK* **you. In** *TRUTH* **the disbelievers** *ARE AN OPEN ENEMY TO YOU*. **[Non-Muslims are the eternal enemy of Muslims, therefore Muslims can deceive non-Muslims]**

4:102 And when thou (O Muhammad) art among them and arrangest *(THEIR) WORSHIP* **for them, let only a party of them stand with thee (to worship) and** *LET THEM TAKE THEIR ARMS [WEAPONS]*. **Then when they have performed their prostrations let them fall to the rear and let another party come that hath not worshipped and let them worship with thee, and let them take their precaution and their arms [weapons]. Those who** *DISBELIEVE LONG FOR YOU TO NEGLECT YOUR ARMS [WEAPONS]* **and your baggage that they may attack you once for all. It is no sin for you to lay aside your arms [weapons], if rain impedeth you or ye are sick. But take your precaution. Lo! Allah prepareth** *FOR THE DISBELIEVERS SHAMEFUL PUNISHMENT*. **[All the major translations agree that this verse is about praying alongside weaponry. Note: the Quislings lie to you that Islam is a religion of peace.]**[427]

4:103 When ye have performed the act of worship, remember Allah, standing, sitting and reclining. And when ye are in safety, observe proper worship. Worship at fixed times hath been enjoined on the *BELIEVERS*.

4:104 *RELENT NOT IN PURSUIT OF THE ENEMY.* **If ye are suffering, lo!** *THEY SUFFER EVEN AS YE SUFFER* **and ye hope from Allah that for which they cannot hope. Allah is ever Knower, Wise.**

4:105 Lo! We reveal unto thee *THE SCRIPTURE WITH THE TRUTH*, that thou mayst judge between mankind by that which Allah showeth thee. And be not thou a pleader for the treacherous;

4:106 And seek forgiveness of Allah. Lo! Allah is ever Forgiving, Merciful.

4:107 And plead not on behalf of (people) who deceive themselves. Lo! Allah loveth not one who is treacherous and sinful.

4:108 They seek to hide from men and seek not to hide from Allah. He is with them when by night they hold discourse displeasing unto Him. Allah ever surroundeth what they do.

4:109 Ho! ye are they who pleaded for them in the life of the world. But who will plead with Allah for them on *THE DAY OF RESURRECTION,* or who will then be their defender?

4:110 Yet whoso doeth *EVIL* or wrongeth his own soul, then seeketh pardon of Allah, will find Allah Forgiving, Merciful.

4:111 Whoso committeth sin committeth it only against himself. Allah is ever Knower, Wise.

4:112 And whoso committeth a delinquency or crime, then throweth (the blame) thereof upon the innocent, hath burdened himself with falsehood and a flagrant crime.

4:113 But for the grace of Allah upon thee (Muhammad), and His mercy, a party of them had *RESOLVED TO MISLEAD THEE*, but they will mislead only themselves and they will hurt thee not at all. Allah revealeth unto thee the Scripture and wisdom, and teacheth thee that which thou knewest not. The grace of Allah toward thee hath been infinite.

4:114 There is no good in much of their secret conferences save (in) him who enjoineth almsgiving and kindness and peace-making among the people. Whoso doeth that, seeking the good pleasure of Allah, *WE SHALL BESTOW ON HIM A VAST REWARD.*

4:115 And *WHOSO OPPOSETH THE MESSENGER AFTER THE GUIDANCE* (of Allah) hath been manifested unto him, and *FOLLOWETH OTHER THAN THE BELIEVER'S WAY*, We appoint for him that unto which he himself *HATH TURNED, AND EXPOSE HIM UNTO HELL* - a hapless journey's end!

4:116 Lo! *ALLAH PARDONETH NOT THAT PARTNERS SHOULD BE ASCRIBED UNTO HIM*. He pardoneth all save that to whom He will. *WHOSO ASCRIBETH PARTNERS UNTO ALLAH HATH WANDERED FAR ASTRAY.* [The Islamic concept of "shirk" is that of not accepting that Allah as the ultimate authority. This is the most unforgivable sin a Muslim can commit.][428]

4:117 They invoke in His stead only females; they pray to none else than Satan, a rebel.

4:118 *WHOM ALLAH CURSED*, and he said: Surely I will take of Thy *BONDMEN* an appointed portion,

4:119 And surely I will lead them astray, and surely I will arouse desires in them, and surely I will command them and they will cut the cattle' ears, and surely I will command them and they will change Allah's creation. Whoso chooseth Satan for a patron instead of Allah is verily a loser and his loss is manifest.

4:120 He promiseth them and stirreth up desires in them, and Satan promiseth them only to beguile.

4:121 For such, their habitation will be *HELL,* and they will find no refuge therefrom.

4:122 But as for *THOSE WHO BELIEVE AND DO GOOD WORKS WE SHALL BRING THEM INTO GARDENS UNDERNEATH WHICH RIVERS FLOW*, wherein they will abide for ever. It is a promise from Allah in truth; and who can be more truthful than Allah in utterance?

4:123 It will not be in accordance with your desires, nor the desires of the *PEOPLE OF THE SCRIPTURE*. He who doeth wrong will have the recompense thereof, and will not find against Allah any protecting friend or helper.

4:124 And *WHOSO DOETH GOOD WORKS*, whether of male or female, and he (or she) *IS A BELIEVER, SUCH WILL ENTER PARADISE* and they will not be wronged the dint in a date-stone. [Since funding Jihad is one of the principal goals of Islamic "charity" there can be no doubt that "doing good" in Islam includes Jihad.][429]

4:125 *WHO IS BETTER IN RELIGION THAN HE WHO SURRENDERETH HIS PURPOSE TO ALLAH WHILE DOING GOOD* (to men) and followeth the tradition of Abraham, the upright? Allah (Himself) chose Abraham for friend. [The Jihadis surrender this life for their belief in an eternity in Paradise.]

4:126 Unto Allah belongeth whatsoever is in the heavens and whatsoever is in the earth. Allah ever surroundeth all things.

4:127 They consult thee concerning women. Say: Allah giveth you decree concerning them, and the Scripture which hath been recited unto you (giveth decree), concerning female orphans and those unto whom ye give not that which is ordained for them though ye desire to marry them, and (concerning) the weak among children, and that ye should deal justly with orphans. Whatever good ye do, lo! Allah is ever Aware of it.

4:128 If a woman feareth ill treatment from her husband, or desertion, it is no sin for them twain if they make terms of peace between themselves. Peace is better. But greed hath been made present in the minds (of men). If ye *DO GOOD AND KEEP FROM EVIL*, lo! Allah is ever Informed of what ye do.

4:129 Ye will not be able to deal equally between (your) wives, however much ye wish (to do so). But turn not altogether away (from one), leaving her as in suspense. If ye *DO GOOD AND KEEP FROM EVIL*, lo! Allah is ever Forgiving, Merciful. [Remember: Jihad is considered good.]

4:130 But if they separate, Allah will compensate each out of His abundance. Allah is ever All-Embracing, All-Knowing.

4:131 Unto Allah belongeth whatsoever is in the heavens and whatsoever is in the earth. And We charged those who received the Scripture before you, and (We charge) you, that ye *KEEP YOUR DUTY TOWARD ALLAH*. And if ye *DISBELIEVE*, lo! unto Allah belongeth whatsoever is in the heavens and whatsoever is in the earth, and Allah is ever Absolute, Owner of Praise.

4:132 Unto Allah belongeth whatsoever is in the heavens and whatsoever is in the earth. And Allah is sufficient as Defender.

4:133 If He will, He can remove you, O people, and produce others (in your stead). Allah is Able to do that.

4:134 Whoso desireth the reward of the world, (let him know that) with Allah is *THE REWARD OF THE WORLD AND THE HEREAFTER*. Allah is ever Hearer, Seer. [

4:135 O *YE WHO BELIEVE*! Be ye staunch in justice, witnesses for Allah, even though it be against yourselves or (your) parents or (your) kindred, whether (the case be of) a rich man or a poor man, for Allah is nearer unto both (them ye are). So follow not passion lest ye lapse (from truth) and if ye lapse or fall away, then lo! Allah is ever Informed of what ye do.

4:136 O *YE WHO BELIEVE*! *BELIEVE* in Allah and His messenger and the Scripture which He hath revealed unto His messenger, and the Scripture which He revealed aforetime. Whoso *DISBELIEVETH* in Allah and His angels and His scriptures and His messengers and *THE LAST DAY*, he verily hath wandered far astray.

4:137 Lo! *THOSE WHO BELIEVE, THEN DISBELIEVE* and then (again) *BELIEVE*, then *DISBELIEVE*, and then increase in *DISBELIEF, ALLAH WILL NEVER PARDON THEM*, nor will He guide them unto a way.

4:138 Bear unto the *HYPOCRITES* the tidings that *FOR THEM THERE IS A PAINFUL DOOM;*

4:139 *THOSE WHO CHOSE DISBELIEVERS FOR THEIR FRIENDS* instead of *BELIEVERS*! Do they look for power at their hands? Lo! all power appertaineth to Allah.

4:140 He hath already revealed unto you in the Scripture that, *WHEN YE HEAR THE REVELATIONS OF ALLAH REJECTED AND DERIDED, (YE) SIT NOT WITH THEM (WHO DISBELIEVE* and mock) until they engage in some other conversation. Lo! in that case (if ye stayed) ye would be like unto them. Lo! Allah will *GATHER HYPOCRITES* and *DISBELIEVERS*, all together, into *HELL*; [Muslims most not even associate with anyone who is anything other than respectful towards the genocidal doctrines of Islam. Even if those criticising Islam are or were believers before (see 4.137). Thus there is no tolerance for the criticism of Islam even by current or former Muslims.]

4:141 Those who wait upon occasion in regard to you and, if a *VICTORY* cometh unto you from Allah, say: Are we not with you? and if the *DISBELIEVERS* meet with a success say: Had we not the mastery of you, and did we not protect you from the *BELIEVERS*? - Allah will judge between you at *THE DAY OF RESURRECTION*, and *ALLAH WILL NOT GIVE THE DISBELIEVERS ANY WAY (OF SUCCESS) AGAINST THE BELIEVERS*.

4:142 Lo! the *HYPOCRITES* seek to beguile Allah, but it is He Who beguileth them. When they stand up to worship they perform it languidly and to be seen of men, and are mindful of Allah but little;

4:143 Swaying between this (and that), (belonging) neither to these nor to those. He whom Allah causeth to go astray, thou (O Muhammad) wilt not find a way for him:

4:144 O *YE WHO BELIEVE! CHOOSE NOT DISBELIEVERS FOR (YOUR) FRIENDS IN PLACE OF BELIEVERS.* **Would ye give Allah a clear warrant against you? [Muslims are always to side with Muslims against non-Muslims. To take the side of a non-Muslim would mean the Muslim has abandoned Islam.]**

4:145 ~~Lo! the *HYPOCRITES* (will be) in the lowest deep of the Fire, and thou wilt find no helper for them;~~ [Abrogated by 4:146][430]

4:146 Save those who repent and amend and hold fast to Allah and make their religion pure for Allah (only). Those are with the *BELIEVERS*. And *ALLAH WILL BESTOW ON THE BELIEVERS AN IMMENSE REWARD*.

4:147 What concern hath Allah for your punishment if ye are thankful (for His mercies) and *BELIEVE* (in Him)? Allah was ever Responsive, Aware.

4:148 Allah loveth not the utterance of harsh speech save by one who hath been wronged. Allah is ever Hearer, Knower.

4:149 If ye do good openly or keep it secret, or forgive *EVIL*, lo! Allah is ever Forgiving, Powerful.

4:150 Lo! *THOSE WHO DISBELIEVE* **in Allah and His messengers, and** *SEEK TO MAKE DISTINCTION BETWEEN ALLAH AND HIS MESSENGERS*, **and say: We** *BELIEVE* **in some and** *DISBELIEVE* **in others, and** *SEEK TO CHOOSE A WAY* **in between; [There is no moderating Islam. It must be accepted in its entirety. Not accepting it entirely makes someone a disbeliever, to be tortured in Hell for eternity.]**

4:151 *SUCH ARE DISBELIEVERS IN TRUTH; AND FOR DISBELIEVERS WE PREPARE A SHAMEFUL DOOM*.

4:152 But *THOSE WHO BELIEVE* in Allah and His messengers and make no distinction between any of them, unto them *ALLAH WILL GIVE THEIR WAGES*; and Allah was ever Forgiving, Merciful.

4:153 The *PEOPLE OF THE SCRIPTURE* ask of thee that thou shouldst cause an (actual) Book to descend upon them from heaven. They asked a greater thing of Moses aforetime, for they said: Show us Allah plainly. The storm of lightning seized them for their wickedness. Then (even after that) they chose the calf (for worship)after *CLEAR PROOFS (OF ALLAH'S SOVEREIGNTY)* had come unto them. And We forgave them that! And We bestowed on Moses evident authority.

4:154 And We caused the Mount to tower above them at (the taking of) their *COVENANT*: and We bade them: Enter the gate, prostrate! and We bode them: Transgress not the Sabbath! and We took from them a firm *COVENANT*.

4:155 Then because of their breaking of their *COVENANT*, and their *DISBELIEVING IN THE REVELATIONS OF ALLAH*, and their slaying [killing] of the prophets wrongfully, and their saying: Our hearts are hardened - Nay, but Allah set a seal upon them for their *DISBELIEF*, so that they *BELIEVE* not save a few -

4:156 And *BECAUSE OF THEIR DISBELIEF* and of their speaking against Mary a tremendous calumny;

4:157 And because of their saying: We slew the Messiah, *JESUS SON OF MARY*, Allah's messenger - *THEY SLEW HIM NOT NOR CRUCIFIED HIM*, but it appeared so unto them; and lo! those who disagree concerning it are in doubt thereof; they have no knowledge thereof save pursuit of a conjecture; they *SLEW HIM NOT FOR CERTAIN*.

4:158 But Allah took him up unto Himself. Allah was ever Mighty, Wise.

4:159 There is *NOT ONE OF THE PEOPLE OF THE SCRIPTURE BUT WILL BELIEVE* in him before his death, and on *THE DAY OF RESURRECTION* he will be a witness against them -

4:160 Because of the wrongdoing of the *JEWS* We forbade them good things which were (before) made lawful unto them, and because of their much hindering from Allah's way,

4:161 And of their taking usury when they were forbidden it, and of their devouring people's wealth by false pretences, *WE HAVE PREPARED FOR THOSE OF THEM WHO DISBELIEVE A PAINFUL DOOM.*

4:162 But those of them who are firm in knowledge and *THE BELIEVERS BELIEVE* in that which is revealed unto thee, and that which was revealed before thee, especially the diligent in prayer and those who pay the poor-due, *THE BELIEVERS IN ALLAH AND THE LAST DAY. UPON THESE WE SHALL BESTOW IMMENSE REWARD.*

4:163 Lo! We inspire thee as We inspired Noah and the prophets after him, as We inspired Abraham and Ishmael and Isaac and Jacob and the tribes, and *JESUS* and Job and Jonah and Aaron and Solomon, and as We imparted unto David the Psalms;

4:164 And messengers We have mentioned unto thee before and messengers We have not mentioned unto thee; and Allah spake directly unto Moses;

4:165 Messengers of good cheer and of warning, in order that mankind might have no argument against Allah after the messengers. Allah was ever Mighty, Wise.

4:166 But Allah (Himself) testifieth concerning that which He hath revealeth unto thee; in His knowledge hath He revealed it; and the angels also testify. And Allah is sufficient Witness.

4:167 Lo! *THOSE WHO DISBELIEVE* and hinder (others) from the way of Allah, they verily have wandered far astray.

4:168 Lo! *THOSE WHO DISBELIEVE* and deal in wrong, *ALLAH WILL NEVER FORGIVE THEM*, neither will He guide them unto a road,

4:169 Except *THE ROAD OF HELL, WHEREIN THEY WILL ABIDE FOR EVER.* And that is ever easy for Allah.

4:170 O mankind! The messenger hath come unto you with *THE TRUTH* from your Lord. Therefor *BELIEVE*; (it is) better for you. But if ye *DISBELIEVE*, still, lo! unto Allah belongeth whatsoever is in the heavens and the earth. Allah is ever Knower, Wise.

4:171 O *PEOPLE OF THE SCRIPTURE*! Do not exaggerate in your religion nor utter aught concerning Allah save *THE TRUTH*. The Messiah, *JESUS SON OF MARY, WAS ONLY A MESSENGER* of Allah, and His word which He conveyed unto Mary, and a spirit from Him. *SO BELIEVE IN ALLAH AND HIS MESSENGERS, AND SAY NOT "THREE"* - Cease! (it is) better for you! - *ALLAH IS ONLY ONE ALLAH. FAR IS IT REMOVED FROM HIS TRANSCENDENT MAJESTY THAT HE SHOULD HAVE A SON*. His is all that is in the heavens and all that is in the earth. And Allah is sufficient as Defender. [Islam explicitly denies the foundations of Christianity. Those Christians who promote and support Islam have submitted to Islam.]

4:172 The Messiah will never scorn to be a slave unto Allah, nor will the favoured angels. Whoso scorneth His service and is proud, all such will He assemble unto Him;

4:173 Then, as for *THOSE WHO BELIEVED AND DID GOOD WORKS*, unto *THEM WILL HE PAY THEIR WAGES IN FULL*, adding unto them of His bounty; and as for *THOSE WHO WERE SCORNFUL* and proud, them will *HE PUNISH WITH A PAINFUL DOOM*. And they will not find for them, against Allah, any protecting friend or helper. [Jihadis rewarded with eternity in Paradise.]

4:174 O mankind! Now hath a proof from your Lord come unto you, and We have sent down unto you a clear light;

4:175 As for those who *BELIEVE* in Allah, and hold fast unto Him, them He will cause to enter into His mercy and grace, and will guide them unto Him by a straight road.

4:176 They ask thee for a pronouncement. Say: Allah hath pronounced for you concerning distant kindred. If a man die childless and he have a sister, hers is half the heritage, and he would have inherited from her had she died childless. And if there be two sisters, then theirs are two-thirds of the heritage, and if they be brethren, men and women, unto the male is the equivalent of the share of two females. Allah expoundeth unto you, so that ye err not. Allah is Knower of all things.

Chapter 60 - She That Is To Be Examined

60:1 O *YE WHO BELIEVE*! *CHOOSE NOT MY ENEMY AND YOUR ENEMY FOR ALLIES.* Do ye give them friendship when *THEY DISBELIEVE IN THAT TRUTH* which hath come unto you, driving out the messenger and you because ye *BELIEVE* in Allah, your Lord? If ye have come forth to *STRIVE IN MY WAY [JIHAD] AND SEEKING MY GOOD PLEASURE*, (show them not friendship). Do ye show friendship unto them in secret, when I am Best Aware of what ye hide and what ye proclaim? And *WHOSOEVER DOETH IT AMONG YOU, HE VERILY HATH STRAYED FROM THE RIGHT WAY.* [Muslims who treat non-Muslims as the enemy are sharia-compliant. Those Muslims who truly befriend unbelievers are destined for an eternity of torture in Hell. Allah is pleased by Jihad.]

60:2 If they have the upper hand of you, they will be your foes, and will stretch out their hands and their tongues toward you with *EVIL* (intent), and *THEY LONG FOR YOU TO DISBELIEVE*.

60:3 Your ties of kindred and your children will avail you naught upon *THE DAY OF RESURRECTION.* He will part you. Allah is Seer of what ye do.

60:4 There is *A GOODLY PATTERN* for you in Abraham and those with him, when they told their folk: Lo! we are guiltless of you and all that ye worship beside Allah. We have done with you. And there hath arisen between us and you hostility and hate for ever *UNTIL YE BELIEVE IN ALLAH ONLY* - save that which Abraham promised his father (when he said): I will ask forgiveness for thee, though I own nothing for thee from Allah - Our Lord! In Thee we put our trust, and unto Thee we turn repentant, and unto Thee is the journeying.

60:5 Our Lord! Make us not a prey for *THOSE WHO DISBELIEVE*, and forgive us, our Lord! Lo! Thou, only Thou, are the Mighty, the Wise.

60:6 Verily ye have in them a goodly *PATTERN FOR EVERYONE WHO LOOKETH TO ALLAH AND THE LAST DAY*. And whosoever may turn away, lo! still Allah, He is the Absolute, the Owner of Praise.

60:7 It may be that Allah will ordain love between you and those of them with whom ye are at enmity. Allah is Mighty, and Allah is Forgiving, Merciful.

60:8 ~~Allah forbiddeth you not those who warred not against you on account of religion and drove you not out from your homes, that ye should show them kindness and deal justly with them. Lo! Allah loveth the just dealers.~~[Cancelled by 60:9][431]

60:9 Allah forbiddeth you only those who *WARRED AGAINST YOU ON ACCOUNT OF RELIGION* and have driven you out from your homes and helped to drive you out, that ye make friends of them. *WHOSOEVER MAKETH FRIENDS OF THEM - (ALL) SUCH ARE WRONG-DOERS.*

60:10 *O YE WHO BELIEVE*! When *BELIEVING* women come unto you as fugitives, examine them. Allah is Best Aware of their faith. Then, if ye know them for *TRUE BELIEVERS*, send them not back unto the *DISBELIEVERS*. They are not lawful for them (*THE DISBELIEVERS*), nor are they (*THE DISBELIEVERS*) lawful for them. And give them (*THE DISBELIEVERS*) that which they have spent (upon them). And it is *NO SIN FOR YOU TO MARRY SUCH WOMEN* when ye have given them their dues. And hold not to the ties of *DISBELIEVING* women; and ask for (the return of) that which ye have spent; and let them (the *DISBELIEVERS*) ask for that which they have spent. *THAT IS THE JUDGMENT OF ALLAH. HE JUDGETH BETWEEN YOU*. Allah is Knower, Wise. [Muslim men can marry non-Muslim women, in order to sire more Muslims. Muslim women cannot marry non-Muslim men.]

60:11 ~~And if any of your wives have gone from you unto the *DISBELIEVERS* and afterward ye have your turn (of triumph), then give unto those whose wives have gone the like of that which they have spent, and keep your duty to Allah in Whom ye are *BELIEVERS*.~~ [Cancelled by verse 9:5][432]

60:12 O Prophet! If *BELIEVING* women come unto thee, taking oath of allegiance unto thee that they will *ASCRIBE NO THING AS PARTNER UNTO ALLAH*, and will neither steal nor commit adultery nor kill their children, nor produce any lie that they have devised between their hands and feet, nor disobey thee in what is right, then accept their allegiance and ask Allah to forgive them. Lo! Allah is Forgiving, Merciful.

60:13 O *YE WHO BELIEVE! BE NOT FRIENDLY WITH A FOLK WITH WHOM ALLAH IS WROTH [ANGRY]*, (a folk) who have despaired of the Hereafter as the disbelievers despair of those who are in the graves. [Muslims are not to take non-Muslims as friends.]

Chapter 33 - The Clans

33:1 O Prophet! *KEEP THY DUTY TO ALLAH AND OBEY NOT THE DISBELIEVERS AND THE HYPOCRITES*. Lo! Allah is Knower, Wise.

33:2 And follow that which is inspired in thee from thy Lord. Lo! Allah is Aware of what ye do.

33:3 And put thy trust in Allah, for Allah is sufficient as Trustee.

33:4 Allah hath not assigned unto any man two hearts within his body, nor hath He made your wives whom ye declare (to be your mothers) your mothers, nor hath He made those whom ye claim (to be your sons) your sons. This is but a saying of your mouths. But *ALLAH SAITH THE TRUTH AND HE SHOWETH THE WAY*.

33:5 Proclaim their real parentage. That will be more equitable in the sight of Allah. And if ye know not their fathers, then (they are) your brethren in the faith, and your clients. And there is no sin for you in the mistakes that ye make unintentionally, but what your hearts purpose (that will be a sin for you). Allah is ever Forgiving, Merciful.

33:6 *THE PROPHET IS CLOSER TO THE BELIEVERS THAN THEIR SELVES*, **and his wives are (as) their mothers. And the owners of kinship are closer one to another in the ordinance of Allah than (other)** *BELIEVERS* **and the fugitives (who fled from Mecca), except that** *YE SHOULD DO KINDNESS TO YOUR FRIENDS*. **This is written in the Book (of nature). [Note: Islam bans Muslims from being friends with non-Muslims. The "owners of kinship" means that blood relatives are closer than Muslims to each other, however this only refers to blood relatives who are Muslims – see Koran 58:22.]**[433]

33:7 And when We exacted a *COVENANT* from the prophets, and from thee (O Muhammad) and from Noah and Abraham and Moses and *JESUS SON OF MARY*. We took from them a solemn *COVENANT*;
33:8 That He may *ASK THE LOYAL OF THEIR LOYALTY. AND HE HATH PREPARED A PAINFUL DOOM FOR THE UNFAITHFUL.*
33:9 O *YE WHO BELIEVE*! Remember Allah's favour unto you *WHEN THERE CAME AGAINST YOU HOSTS [ARMIES], AND WE SENT AGAINST THEM A GREAT WIND AND HOSTS [ARMIES] YE COULD NOT SEE.* And Allah is ever Seer of what ye do.
33:10 When they came upon you from above you and from below you, and when eyes grew wild and hearts reached to the throats, and ye were imagining vain thoughts concerning Allah.
33:11 There were the *BELIEVERS* sorely tried, and shaken with a mighty shock.

33:12 And when the *HYPOCRITES*, **and those in whose hearts is a disease, were saying: Allah and His messenger promised us naught but delusion.**

33:13 And when a party of them said: O folk of Yathrib! [Medina] There is no stand (possible) for you, therefor turn back. And certain of them (even) sought permission of the Prophet, saying: Our homes lie open (to *THE ENEMY*). And they lay not open. *THEY BUT WISHED TO FLEE.*
33:14 If *THE ENEMY* had entered from all sides and they had been exhorted to *TREACHERY*, they would have committed it, and would have hesitated thereupon but little.

33:15 And verily *THEY HAD ALREADY SWORN UNTO ALLAH THAT THEY WOULD NOT TURN THEIR BACKS (TO THE FOE)*. **An** *OATH TO ALLAH MUST BE ANSWERED* **for.**

33:16 Say: Flight will not avail you *IF YE FLEE FROM DEATH OR KILLING*, **and then ye dwell in comfort but a little while. [Muslims who run away from killing or being killed are destined to go to Hell.]**

33:17 Say: Who is he who can preserve you from Allah if He intendeth harm for you, or intendeth mercy for you. They will not find that they have any friend or helper other than Allah.
33:18 Allah already knoweth those of you who hinder, and those who say unto their brethren: "Come ye hither unto us!" and they come not to *THE STRESS OF BATTLE* save a little,
33:19 Being sparing of their help to you (*BELIEVERS*). But when the fear cometh, then thou (Muhammad) seest them regarding thee with rolling eyes like one who fainteth unto death. Then, when the fear departeth, they scald you with sharp tongues in *THEIR GREED FOR WEALTH (FROM THE SPOIL [SLAVES AND LOOT]). SUCH HAVE NOT BELIEVED.* Therefor Allah maketh their deeds fruitless. And that is easy for Allah.

33:20 They hold that the clans have not retired (for good); and if the clans should advance (again), they would fain be in the desert with the wandering Arabs, asking for the news of you; and if they were among you, *THEY WOULD NOT GIVE BATTLE, SAVE A LITTLE*.

33:21 Verily *IN THE MESSENGER OF ALLAH YE HAVE A GOOD EXAMPLE* **for him who looketh unto** *ALLAH AND THE LAST DAY*, **and remembereth Allah**

much. [The behaviour of Mohammed is the example which Muslims are to follow.]

33:22 And when the *TRUE BELIEVERS* saw the clans, they said: This is that which Allah and His messenger promised us. Allah and His messenger are true. It did but confirm them in their faith and resignation.

33:23 Of the *BELIEVERS* are *MEN WHO ARE TRUE TO THAT WHICH THEY COVENANTED WITH ALLAH. SOME OF THEM HAVE PAID THEIR VOW BY DEATH (IN BATTLE)*, and some of them still are waiting; and they have not altered in the least; [The promise between Allah and Muslims is that the latter will go to Paradise if they die as Jihadis.]

33:24 That Allah may *REWARD THE TRUE MEN FOR THEIR TRUTH*, and *PUNISH THE HYPOCRITES* if He will, or relent toward them (if He will). Lo! Allah is Forgiving, Merciful.

33:25 And Allah repulsed the *DISBELIEVERS* in their wrath; they gained no good. *ALLAH AVERTED THEIR ATTACK FROM THE BELIEVERS. ALLAH IS EVER STRONG, MIGHTY.*

33:26 And He brought those of the *PEOPLE OF THE SCRIPTURE* [Jews] who supported them *DOWN FROM THEIR STRONGHOLDS, AND CAST PANIC INTO THEIR HEARTS [TERRORISED THEM]. SOME YE SLEW [KILLED], AND YE MADE CAPTIVE [ENSLAVED] SOME.* [After they surrendered the Jewish men and boys were slaughtered; the women and girls were taken as slaves. If these victims were inside their fortresses, then they were fighting defensively and it was the Muslim army who were the aggressors.]

33:27 And He caused *YOU TO INHERIT THEIR LAND AND THEIR HOUSES AND THEIR WEALTH*, and land ye have not trodden. Allah is ever Able to do all things.

33:28 O Prophet! Say unto thy wives: If ye desire the world's life and its adornment, come! I will content you and will release you with a fair release.
33:29 But *IF YE DESIRE ALLAH AND HIS MESSENGER AND THE ABODE OF THE HEREAFTER, THEN LO! ALLAH HATH PREPARED FOR THE GOOD AMONG YOU AN IMMENSE REWARD.*

33:30 O ye wives of the Prophet! Whosoever of you committeth manifest lewdness, the punishment for her will be doubled, and that is easy for Allah. [The rules for punishing Muslim wives are twice as bad if the woman is married to Mohammed. So much for the rule of law and Islam being all about equity and justice.]

33:31 And whosoever of you is submissive unto Allah and His messenger and doeth right, We shall give her *REWARD* twice over, and We have prepared for her a rich provision.
33:32 O ye wives of the Prophet! Ye are not like any other women. If ye *KEEP YOUR DUTY (TO ALLAH)*, then be not soft of speech, lest he in whose heart is a disease aspire (to you), but utter customary speech.
33:33 And stay in your houses. Bedizen not yourselves with the bedizenment of *THE TIME OF IGNORANCE*. Be regular in prayer, and pay the poor-due, and *OBEY ALLAH AND HIS MESSENGER*. Allah's wish is but to remove uncleanness far from you, O Folk of the Household, and cleanse you with a thorough cleansing.
33:34 And bear in mind that which is recited in your houses of the revelations of Allah and wisdom. Lo! Allah is Subtile, Aware.

33:35 Lo! *MEN WHO SURRENDER UNTO ALLAH*, and women who surrender, and *MEN WHO BELIEVE AND WOMEN WHO BELIEVE*, and *MEN WHO OBEY AND WOMEN WHO OBEY, AND MEN WHO SPEAK THE TRUTH AND WOMEN WHO SPEAK THE TRUTH*, and men who persevere (in righteousness) and women who persevere, and men who are humble and women who are humble, and men who give alms and women who give alms, and men who fast and women who fast, and men who guard their modesty and women who guard (their modesty), and men who remember Allah much and women who remember - *ALLAH HATH PREPARED FOR THEM FORGIVENESS AND A VAST REWARD.*

33:36 And it becometh not a *BELIEVING* man or a *BELIEVING* woman, when Allah and His messenger have decided an affair (for them), that they should (after that) claim any say in their affair; and *WHOSO IS REBELLIOUS TO ALLAH AND HIS MESSENGER, HE VERILY GOETH ASTRAY IN ERROR MANIFEST.* [No Muslim can disagree with the commands or decisions of Allah and Mohammed contained in the Koran or the Hadiths.]

33:37 And when thou saidst unto him on whom Allah hath conferred favour and thou hast conferred favour: Keep thy wife to thyself, and fear Allah. And thou didst hide in thy mind that which Allah was to bring to light, and thou didst fear mankind whereas Allah hath a better right that thou shouldst fear Him. So when Zeyd had performed that necessary formality (of divorce) from her, We gave her unto thee in marriage, so that (henceforth) there may be no sin for *BELIEVERS* in respect of wives of their adopted sons, when the latter have performed the necessary formality (of release) from them. *THE COMMANDMENT OF ALLAH MUST BE FULFILLED.*

33:38 There is no reproach for the Prophet in that which Allah maketh his due. That was Allah's way with those who passed away of old - and *THE COMMANDMENT OF ALLAH IS CERTAIN DESTINY* -

33:39 Who delivered the messages of Allah and feared Him, and *FEARED NONE SAVE ALLAH*. Allah keepeth good account.

33:40 Muhammad is not the father of any man among you, but he is the messenger of Allah and the Seal of the Prophets; and Allah is ever Aware of all things.

33:41 O *YE WHO BELIEVE*! Remember Allah with much remembrance.

33:42 And glorify Him early and late.

33:43 He it is Who blesseth you, and His angels (bless you), that He may bring you forth from darkness unto light; and He is ever Merciful to the *BELIEVERS*.

33:44 Their salutation *ON THE DAY WHEN THEY SHALL MEET HIM* will be: Peace. And *HE HATH PREPARED FOR THEM A GOODLY RECOMPENSE.*

33:45 O Prophet! Lo! We have sent thee as a witness and a bringer of good tidings and a warner.

33:46 And as a summoner unto Allah by His permission, and as a lamp that giveth light.

33:47 And announce unto the *BELIEVERS* the good tidings that they *WILL HAVE GREAT BOUNTY FROM ALLAH.*

33:48 ~~And incline not to the *DISBELIEVERS* and the *HYPOCRITES*. Disregard their noxious talk, and put thy trust in Allah. Allah is sufficient as Trustee.~~ [Indifference abrogated by the violence of verse 9:5][434]

33:49 O *YE WHO BELIEVE*! If ye wed *BELIEVING* women and divorce them before ye have touched them, then there is no period that ye should reckon. But content them and release them handsomely.

33:50 O Prophet! Lo! *WE HAVE MADE LAWFUL UNTO THEE THY WIVES UNTO WHOM THOU HAST PAID THEIR DOWRIES, AND THOSE WHOM THY RIGHT HAND POSSESSETH [SLAVES] OF THOSE WHOM ALLAH HATH GIVEN THEE AS SPOILS OF WAR [SLAVES AND LOOT],* and the daughters of thine uncle on the father's side and the daughters of thine aunts on the father's side, and the daughters of thine uncle on the mother's side and the daughters of thine aunts on the mother's side who emigrated with thee, *AND A BELIEVING WOMAN IF SHE GIVE HERSELF UNTO THE PROPHET AND THE PROPHET DESIRE TO ASK HER IN MARRIAGE - A PRIVILEGE FOR THEE ONLY, NOT FOR THE (REST OF) BELIEVERS* - We are Aware of that which We enjoined upon them concerning their wives and those whom their right hands possess [slaves]

- that thou mayst be free from blame, for Allah is ever Forgiving, Merciful. [Mohammed is exempt from the sexual rules which apply to all other Muslim men.]

33:51 Thou canst defer whom thou wilt of them and receive unto thee whom thou wilt, and whomsoever thou desirest of those whom thou hast set aside (temporarily), it is no sin for thee (to receive her again); that is better; that they may be comforted and not grieve, and may all be pleased with what thou givest them. Allah knoweth what is in your hearts (O men), and Allah is ever Forgiving, Clement.

33:52 It is not allowed thee to take (other) women henceforth, nor that thou shouldst change them for other wives even though their beauty pleased thee, *SAVE THOSE WHOM THY RIGHT HAND POSSESSETH [SLAVES]*. And Allah is ever Watcher over all things.

33:53 O *YE WHO BELIEVE*! Enter not the dwellings of the Prophet for a meal without waiting for the proper time, unless permission be granted you. But if ye are invited, enter, and, when your meal is ended, then disperse. Linger not for conversation. Lo! that would cause annoyance to the Prophet, and he would be shy of (asking) you (to go); but Allah is not shy of the truth. And when ye ask of them (the wives of the Prophet) anything, ask it of them from behind a curtain. That is purer for your hearts and for their hearts. And it is not for you to cause annoyance to the messenger of Allah, nor that ye should ever marry his wives after him. Lo! that in Allah's sight would be an enormity.
33:54 Whether ye divulge a thing or keep it hidden, lo! Allah is ever Knower of all things.

33:55 *IT IS NO SIN FOR THEM (THY WIVES) (TO CONVERSE FREELY) WITH THEIR FATHERS, OR THEIR SONS, OR THEIR BROTHERS*, or their brothers' sons, or the sons of their sisters or of their own women, *OR THEIR SLAVES.* O women! KEEP YOUR DUTY TO ALLAH. Lo! Allah is ever Witness over all things.

33:56 Lo! Allah and His angels shower blessings on the Prophet. O *YE WHO BELIEVE*! Ask blessings on him and salute him with a worthy salutation.
33:57 Lo! *THOSE WHO MALIGN ALLAH AND HIS MESSENGER, ALLAH HATH CURSED THEM IN THE WORLD AND THE HEREAFTER, AND HATH PREPARED FOR THEM THE DOOM OF THE DISDAINED.*
33:58 And *THOSE WHO MALIGN BELIEVING MEN AND BELIEVING WOMEN UNDESERVEDLY*, they bear the guilt of slander and manifest sin.

33:59 O Prophet! Tell thy wives and thy daughters and the *WOMEN OF THE BELIEVERS TO DRAW THEIR CLOAKS CLOSE ROUND THEM* (when they go abroad). That will be better, so that they may be recognised and *NOT ANNOYED.* Allah is ever Forgiving, Merciful. [The foundation for the hijab, burka, etc. - to prevent Muslims women from being molested by Muslim men – Pickthall inserts the idea of this being "abroad".]

33:60 If the *HYPOCRITES*, and those in whose hearts is a disease, and the alarmists in the city do not cease, We verily shall urge thee on against them, then they will be your neighbours in it but a little while.

33:61 Accursed, they will be *SEIZED WHEREVER FOUND* and *SLAIN* with a (FIERCE) SLAUGHTER.

33:62 That was *THE WAY OF ALLAH* in the case of those who passed away of old; thou wilt not find for the way of Allah aught of power to change.
33:63 *MEN ASK THEE OF THE HOUR.* Say: The knowledge of it is with Allah only. What can convey (the knowledge) unto thee? It may be that *THE HOUR IS NIGH.* [1400 years later, and still the imminent Day of Judgment has not arrived.]
33:64 Lo! *ALLAH HATH CURSED THE DISBELIEVERS*, and hath *PREPARED FOR THEM A FLAMING FIRE,*
33:65 Wherein they will abide for ever. They will find (then) no protecting friend nor helper.
33:66 On the day when *THEIR FACES ARE TURNED OVER IN THE FIRE*, they say: Oh, would that we had *OBEYED ALLAH AND HAD OBEYED HIS MESSENGER*!

33:67 And they say: Our Lord! Lo! we *OBEYED OUR PRINCES AND GREAT MEN*, and they misled us from *THE WAY.*

33:68 Our Lord! Oh, *GIVE THEM DOUBLE TORMENT AND CURSE THEM WITH A MIGHTY CURSE.*

33:69 O *YE WHO BELIEVE*! Be not as those who slandered Moses, but Allah proved his innocence of that which they alleged, and he was well esteemed in Allah's sight.

33:70 O *YE WHO BELIEVE*! Guard *YOUR DUTY TO ALLAH*, and speak words straight to the point;

33:71 He will adjust your works for you and will forgive you your sins. Whosoever *OBEYETH ALLAH AND HIS MESSENGER*, he verily hath gained *A SIGNAL VICTORY.*

33:72 Lo! We offered the trust unto the heavens and the earth and the hills, but they shrank from bearing it and were afraid of it. And man assumed it. Lo! he hath proved a tyrant and a fool.

33:73 So *ALLAH PUNISHETH HYPOCRITICAL MEN AND HYPOCRITICAL WOMEN*, and *IDOLATROUS MEN AND IDOLATROUS WOMEN*. But *ALLAH PARDONETH BELIEVING MEN AND BELIEVING WOMEN*, and Allah is ever Forgiving, Merciful.

Chapter 3 - The Family of Imran

3:1 Alim. Lam. Mim.

3:2 *ALLAH! THERE IS NO GOD SAVE HIM*, the Alive, the Eternal.

3:3 He hath revealed unto thee (Muhammad) *THE SCRIPTURE WITH TRUTH,* confirming that which was (revealed) before it, even as He revealed the Torah and the Gospel.

3:4 Aforetime, for a guidance to mankind; and hath revealed the Criterion (of right and wrong). Lo! *THOSE WHO DISBELIEVE THE REVELATIONS OF ALLAH, THEIRS WILL BE A HEAVY DOOM*. Allah is Mighty, Able to Requite (the wrong).

3:5 Lo! nothing in the earth or in the heavens is hidden from Allah.

3:6 He it is Who fashioneth you in the wombs as pleaseth Him. There is no Allah save Him, the Almighty, the Wise.

3:7 He it is Who hath revealed unto thee (Muhammad) *THE SCRIPTURE WHEREIN ARE CLEAR REVELATIONS* **- they are the substance of the Book - and others (which are) allegorical. But those in whose hearts is doubt pursue, forsooth, that which is allegorical seeking (to cause) dissension by seeking to explain it. None knoweth its explanation save Allah. And those who are of sound instruction say:** *WE BELIEVE THEREIN; THE WHOLE IS FROM OUR LORD; BUT ONLY MEN OF UNDERSTANDING REALLY HEED.* *[MUSLIMS MUST BELIEVE THE ENTIRETY OF THE KORAN AND MUST NOT DISSENT BECAUSE OF THE AMBIGUITIES IT CONTAINS.]*

3:8 Our Lord! Cause not our hearts to stray after Thou hast guided us, and bestow upon us mercy from Thy Presence. Lo! Thou, only Thou, art the Bestower.

3:9 Our Lord! Lo! it is Thou Who gatherest mankind together to *A DAY OF WHICH THERE IS NO DOUBT.* Lo! Allah faileth not to keep the tryst.

3:10 (On *THAT DAY*) neither the riches nor the progeny of *THOSE WHO DISBELIEVE* will aught avail them with Allah. They will be *FUEL FOR FIRE*.

3:11 Like Pharaoh's folk and those who were before them, they *DISBELIEVED* Our revelations and so Allah seized them for their sins. And *ALLAH IS SEVERE IN PUNISHMENT.*

3:12 Say (O Muhammad) unto *THOSE WHO DISBELIEVE*: Ye shall be *OVERCOME AND GATHERED UNTO HELL, AN EVIL RESTING-PLACE.*

3:13 There was a token for you in *TWO HOSTS [ARMIES] WHICH MET: ONE ARMY FIGHTING IN THE WAY OF ALLAH, AND ANOTHER DISBELIEVING*, **whom they saw as twice their number, clearly, with their very eyes. Thus** *ALLAH STRENGTHENETH WITH HIS SUCCOUR WHOM HE WILL*. **Lo! herein verily is a lesson for those who have eyes.**

3:14 Beautified for mankind is love of the joys (that come) from women and offspring; and stored-up *HEAPS OF GOLD AND SILVER,* and horses branded (with their mark), and cattle and land. *THAT IS COMFORT OF THE LIFE OF THE WORLD.* Allah! With Him is a more excellent abode.

3:15 Say: Shall I inform you of something better than that? For *THOSE WHO KEEP FROM EVIL,* **with their Lord, are** *GARDENS UNDERNEATH WHICH RIVERS FLOW WHEREIN THEY WILL ABIDE, AND PURE COMPANIONS,* **and contentment from Allah. Allah is Seer of His** *BONDMEN,*

3:16 Those who say: Our Lord! Lo! *WE BELIEVE.* So forgive us our sins and *GUARD US FROM THE PUNISHMENT OF FIRE;*

3:17 The *STEADFAST, AND THE TRUTHFUL, AND THE OBEDIENT, THOSE WHO SPEND* (and hoard not), those who pray for pardon in the watches of the night.

3:18 Allah (Himself) is Witness that there is no God save Him. And the angels and the men of learning (too are witness). Maintaining His creation in justice, there is no God save Him the Almighty, the Wise.

3:19 Lo! religion with Allah (is) the Surrender (to His Will and Guidance). Those who (formerly) received the Scripture differed only after knowledge came unto them, through transgression among themselves. *WHOSO DISBELIEVETH THE REVELATIONS OF ALLAH* (will find that) lo! *ALLAH IS SWIFT AT RECKONING.*

3:20 And if they argue with thee, (O Muhammad), say: I have surrendered my purpose to Allah and (so have) those who follow me. And say unto those who have received the Scripture and those who read not: Have ye (too) surrendered? ~~If they surrender, then truly they are rightly guided, and if they turn away, then it is thy duty only to convey the message (unto them).~~ Allah is Seer of (His) *BONDMEN.* [Abrogated by verse 9:5, even if the Kuffar surrender, the violence does not stop][435]

3:21 Lo! *THOSE WHO DISBELIEVE* **the revelations of Allah, and slay [kill] the prophets wrongfully, and slay those of mankind who enjoin equity:** *PROMISE THEM A PAINFUL DOOM.* **[Other translations use "justice" for "equity". Since the Day of Judgement is when Allah hands out just desserts, those who enjoin justice refers to the followers of Mohammed.]**

3:22 Those are they whose works have failed in the world and the Hereafter; and they have no helpers.

3:23 Hast thou not seen how those who have received a portion of the Scripture invoke the Scripture of Allah (in their disputes) that it may judge between them; then a faction of them turn away, being opposed (to it)?

3:24 That is because *THEY SAY: THE FIRE WILL NOT TOUCH US SAVE FOR A CERTAIN NUMBER OF DAYS. THAT WHICH THEY USED TO INVENT HATH DECEIVED THEM REGARDING THEIR RELIGION.*

3:25 How (will it be with them) when We have brought them all together to a Day of which there is no doubt, when every soul will be paid in full what it hath earned, and they will not be wronged.

3:26 Say: O *ALLAH! OWNER OF SOVEREIGNTY! THOU GIVEST SOVEREIGNTY UNTO WHOM THOU WILT, AND THOU WITHDRAWEST SOVEREIGNTY FROM WHOM THOU WILT.* Thou exaltest whom Thou wilt, and Thou abasest whom Thou wilt. In Thy hand is the good. Lo! Thou art Able to do all things.

3:27 Thou causest the night to pass into the day, and Thou causest the day to pass into the night. And Thou bringest forth the living from the dead, and Thou bringest forth the dead from the living. And Thou givest sustenance to whom Thou choosest, without stint.

3:28 *LET NOT THE BELIEVERS TAKE DISBELIEVERS FOR THEIR FRIENDS IN PREFERENCE TO BELIEVERS.* **Whoso doeth that hath no connection with Allah** ~~unless (it be) that ye but guard yourselves against them, taking (as it were) security.~~ **Allah biddeth you beware (only) of Himself. Unto Allah is the journeying. [Part cancelled by verse 9:5 i.e. final commands of Koran are total war, not any pretence at friendship][436]**

3:29 Say, (O Muhammad): Whether ye hide that which is in your breasts or reveal it, Allah knoweth it. He knoweth that which is in the heavens and that which is in the earth, and Allah is Able to do all things.

3:30 On *THE DAY WHEN EVERY SOUL WILL FIND ITSELF CONFRONTED* with all that it hath done of good and all that it hath done of *EVIL* (every soul) will long that there might be a mighty space of distance between it and that (*EVIL*). Allah biddeth you beware of Him. And Allah is Full of Pity for (His) *BONDMEN*.

3:31 Say, (O Muhammad, to mankind): If ye love Allah, follow me; Allah will love you and forgive you your sins. Allah is Forgiving, Merciful.

3:32 Say: *OBEY ALLAH AND THE MESSENGER*. But if they turn away, lo! Allah loveth not the *DISBELIEVERS* (in His guidance).

3:33 Lo! Allah preferred Adam and Noah and the Family of Abraham and the Family of 'Imran above (all His) creatures.

3:34 They were descendants one of another. Allah is Hearer, Knower.

3:35 (Remember) when the wife of 'Imran said: My Lord! I have vowed unto Thee that which is in my belly as a consecrated (offering). Accept it from me. Lo! Thou, only Thou, art the Hearer, the Knower!

3:36 And when she was delivered she said: My Lord! Lo! I am delivered of a female - Allah knew best of what she was delivered - the male is not as the female; and lo! I have named her Mary, and lo! I crave Thy protection for her and for her offspring from Satan the outcast.

3:37 And her Lord accepted her with full acceptance and vouchsafed to her a goodly growth; and made Zachariah her guardian. Whenever Zachariah went into the sanctuary where she was, he found that she had food. He said: O Mary! Whence cometh unto thee this (food)? She answered: It is from Allah. Allah giveth without stint to whom He will.

3:38 Then Zachariah prayed unto his Lord and said: My Lord! Bestow upon me of Thy bounty goodly offspring. Lo! Thou art the Hearer of Prayer.

3:39 And the angels called to him as he stood praying in the sanctuary: Allah giveth thee glad tidings of (a son whose name is) John, (who cometh) to confirm a word from Allah lordly, chaste, a prophet of the righteous.

3:40 He said: My Lord! How can I have a son when age hath overtaken me already and my wife is barren? (The angel) answered: So (it will be). Allah doeth what He will.

3:41 He said: My Lord! Appoint a token for me. (The angel) said: The token unto thee (shall be) that thou shalt not speak unto mankind three days except by signs. Remember thy Lord much, and praise (Him) in the early hours of night and morning.

3:42 And when the angels said: O Mary! Lo! Allah hath chosen thee and made thee pure, and hath preferred thee above (all) the women of creation.

3:43 O Mary! Be obedient to thy Lord, prostrate thyself and bow with those who bow (in worship).

3:44 This is of the tidings of things hidden. We reveal it unto thee (Muhammad). Thou wast not present with them when they threw their pens (to know) which of them should be the guardian of Mary, nor wast thou present with them when they quarrelled (thereupon).

3:45 (And remember) when the angels said: O Mary! Lo! Allah giveth thee glad tidings of a word from him, whose name is the Messiah, *JESUS, SON OF MARY*, illustrious in the world and the Hereafter, and one of those brought near (unto Allah).

3:46 He will speak unto mankind in his cradle and in his manhood, and he is of the righteous.

3:47 She said: My Lord! How can I have a child when no mortal hath touched me? He said: So (it will be). Allah createth what He will. If He decreeth a thing, He saith unto it only: Be! and it is. [The Koran acknowledges the birth of *JESUS* as a miracle, yet lists no comparable miracles in relation to Mohammed.]

3:48 And He will teach him the Scripture and wisdom, and the Torah and the Gospel,

3:49 And will make him a messenger unto *THE CHILDREN OF ISRAEL*, (saying): Lo! I come unto you with a sign from your Lord. Lo! I fashion for you out of clay the likeness of a bird, and I breathe into it and it is a bird, by Allah's leave. I heal him who was born blind, and the leper, and I raise the dead, by Allah's leave. And I announce unto you what ye eat and what ye store up in your houses. Lo! herein verily is a portent for you, if ye are to be *BELIEVERS*.

3:50 And (I come) confirming that which was before me of the Torah, and to make lawful some of that which was forbidden unto you. I come unto you with a sign from your Lord, so *KEEP YOUR DUTY TO ALLAH AND OBEY ME*.

3:51 Lo! Allah is my Lord and your Lord, so worship Him. *THAT IS A STRAIGHT PATH.*

3:52 But when *JESUS* became conscious of their *DISBELIEF*, he cried: Who will be my helpers in the cause of Allah? The disciples said: We will be Allah's helpers. We *BELIEVE* in Allah, and bear thou witness that we have surrendered (unto Him).

3:53 Our Lord! We *BELIEVE* in that which Thou hast revealed and we follow him whom Thou hast sent. Enroll us among *THOSE WHO WITNESS (TO THE TRUTH)*.

3:54 And *THEY (THE DISBELIEVERS) SCHEMED, AND ALLAH SCHEMED (AGAINST THEM); AND ALLAH IS THE BEST OF SCHEMERS.*

3:55 (And remember) when Allah said: O *JESUS*! Lo! I am gathering thee and causing thee to ascend unto Me, and am cleansing thee of *THOSE WHO DISBELIEVE* and am setting those who follow thee above *THOSE WHO DISBELIEVE UNTIL THE DAY OF RESURRECTION*. Then unto Me ye will (all) return, and I shall *JUDGE BETWEEN YOU* as to that wherein ye used to differ.

3:56 *AS FOR THOSE WHO DISBELIEVE I SHALL CHASTISE THEM WITH A HEAVY CHASTISEMENT IN THE WORLD AND THE HEREAFTER*; and they will have no helpers. [The foundation of the system of apartheid under Islamic rule, where unbelievers are sub-humans.]

3:57 And as *FOR THOSE WHO BELIEVE AND DO GOOD WORKS, HE WILL PAY THEM THEIR WAGES IN FULL*. Allah loveth not wrong-doers.

3:58 This (which) We recite unto thee is a revelation and a wise reminder.

3:59 Lo! the likeness of *JESUS* with Allah is as the likeness of Adam. He created him of dust, then He said unto him: Be! and he is.

3:60 (This is) *THE TRUTH* from thy Lord (O Muhammad), so be not thou of *THOSE WHO WAVER*.

3:61 And whoso disputeth with thee concerning him, after the knowledge which hath come unto thee, say (unto him): Come! We will summon our sons and your sons, and our women and your women, and ourselves and yourselves, then we will pray humbly (to our Lord) and (solemnly) invoke the curse of Allah upon those who lie.

3:62 Lo! *THIS VERILY IS THE TRUE NARRATIVE. THERE IS NO GOD SAVE ALLAH*, and lo! Allah, He verily is, is the Mighty, the Wise.

3:63 And if they turn away, then lo! Allah is Aware of (who are) the corrupters.

3:64 Say: O *PEOPLE OF THE SCRIPTURE! COME TO AN AGREEMENT BETWEEN US AND YOU: THAT WE SHALL WORSHIP NONE BUT ALLAH, AND THAT WE SHALL ASCRIBE NO PARTNER UNTO HIM*, and that none of us shall take others for lords beside Allah. And if they turn away, then say: Bear witness that *WE ARE THEY WHO HAVE SURRENDERED* (unto Him). [Islam has no respect for Christianity as a system of belief, and demands that Christians renounce the foundation of their religion.]

3:65 O *PEOPLE OF THE SCRIPTURE*! Why will ye argue about Abraham, when the Torah and the Gospel were not revealed till after him? Have ye then no sense?

3:66 Lo! ye are those who argue about that whereof ye have some knowledge: Why then argue ye concerning that whereof ye have no knowledge? Allah knoweth. Ye know not.

3:67 *ABRAHAM WAS NOT A JEW*, nor yet a *CHRISTIAN*; but he was an upright man who had surrendered (to Allah), and he was not of the *IDOLATERS*.

3:68 Lo! those of mankind who have the best claim to Abraham are those who followed him, and this Prophet and those who *BELIEVE* (with him); and Allah is the Protecting Guardian of the *BELIEVERS*.

3:69 A party of the *PEOPLE OF THE SCRIPTURE LONG TO MAKE YOU GO ASTRAY*; and they make none to go astray except themselves, but they perceive not.

3:70 O *PEOPLE OF THE SCRIPTURE*! Why *DISBELIEVE* ye in the revelations of Allah, when ye (yourselves) bear witness (to their truth)?

3:71 O *PEOPLE OF THE SCRIPTURE*! *WHY CONFOUND YE TRUTH WITH FALSEHOOD AND KNOWINGLY CONCEAL THE TRUTH?*

3:72 And a party of the *PEOPLE OF THE SCRIPTURE* say: *BELIEVE* in that which hath been revealed unto those who *BELIEVE* at the opening of the day, and *DISBELIEVE* at the end thereof, in order that they may return;

3:73 And *BELIEVE NOT SAVE IN ONE WHO FOLLOWETH YOUR RELIGION* - Say (O Muhammad): Lo! the guidance is Allah's Guidance - that anyone is given the like of that which was given unto you or that they may argue with you in the presence of their Lord. Say (O Muhammad): Lo! the bounty is in Allah's hand. He bestoweth it on whom He will. Allah is All-Embracing, All-Knowing.

3:74 He selecteth for His mercy whom He will. Allah is of Infinite Bounty.

3:75 Among *THE PEOPLE OF THE SCRIPTURE* there is he who, if thou trust him with a weight of treasure, will return it to thee. And among them there is he who, if thou trust him with a piece of gold, will not return it to thee unless thou keep standing over him. That is because they say: We have no duty to the Gentiles. They speak a lie concerning Allah knowingly.

3:76 Nay, but (the chosen of Allah is) he who fulfilleth his pledge and wardeth off (*EVIL*); for lo! Allah loveth those who ward off (*EVIL*).

3:77 Lo! those who purchase a small gain at the cost of Allah's *COVENANT* and their oaths, they have no portion in the Hereafter. Allah will neither speak to them nor look upon them on *THE DAY OF RESURRECTION*, nor will He make them grow. *THEIRS WILL BE A PAINFUL DOOM.*

3:78 And lo! *THERE IS A PARTY OF THEM WHO DISTORT THE SCRIPTURE* with their tongues, that ye may think that what they say is from the Scripture, when it is not from the Scripture. And they say: It is from Allah, when it is not from Allah; and *THEY SPEAK A LIE CONCERNING ALLAH* knowingly.

3:79 It is not (possible) for any human being unto whom Allah had given the Scripture and wisdom and the prophethood that he should afterwards have said unto mankind: Be slaves of me instead of Allah; but (what he said was): Be ye faithful servants of the Lord by virtue of your *CONSTANT TEACHING OF THE SCRIPTURE AND OF YOUR CONSTANT STUDY THEREOF.*

3:80 And he commanded you not that ye should take the angels and the prophets for lords. Would he command you to *DISBELIEVE* after ye had surrendered (to Allah)?

3:81 When Allah made (His) *COVENANT* with the prophets, (He said): Behold that which I have given you of the Scripture and knowledge. And afterward *THERE WILL COME UNTO YOU A MESSENGER,* confirming that which ye possess. *YE SHALL BELIEVE IN HIM AND YE SHALL HELP HIM.* He said: Do ye agree, and will ye take up My burden (which I lay upon you) in this (matter)? They answered: We agree. He said: Then bear ye witness. I will be a witness with you.

3:82 Then whosoever after this shall turn away: they will be miscreants.

3:83 *SEEK THEY OTHER THAN THE RELIGION OF ALLAH*, when unto Him submitteth whosoever is in the heavens and the earth, willingly or unwillingly, and unto Him they will be returned.

3:84 Say (O Muhammad): We *BELIEVE* in Allah and that which is revealed unto us and that which was revealed unto Abraham and Ishmael and Isaac and Jacob and the tribes, and that which was vouchsafed unto Moses and *JESUS* and the prophets from their Lord. We make no distinction between any of them, and unto Him *WE HAVE SURRENDERED.*

3:85 And whoso seeketh as *RELIGION OTHER THAN THE SURRENDER (TO ALLAH)* it will not be accepted from him, and he will be *A LOSER IN THE HEREAFTER.* [Islam has no respect for any belief other than Islam.]

3:86 How shall Allah guide *A PEOPLE WHO DISBELIEVED AFTER THEIR BELIEF* and (after) they bore witness that *THE MESSENGER IS TRUE* and after *CLEAR PROOFS* (of Allah's Sovereignty) had come unto them. And Allah guideth not *WRONGDOING FOLK.*

3:87 As for such, their guerdon [*REWARD*] is that on them rests *THE CURSE OF ALLAH* and of angels and of men combined.

3:88 They will abide therein. *THEIR DOOM WILL NOT BE LIGHTENED*, neither will they be reprieved;

3:89 Save those who afterward repent and do right. Lo! Allah is Forgiving, Merciful.

3:90 Lo! *THOSE WHO DISBELIEVE* after their (profession of) *BELIEF,* and afterward grow violent in *DISBELIEF:* their repentance will not be accepted. And such are those who are astray.

3:91 Lo! *THOSE WHO DISBELIEVE, AND DIE IN DISBELIEF,* the (whole) earth full of gold would not be accepted from such an one if it were offered as a ransom (for his soul). *THEIRS WILL BE A PAINFUL DOOM* and they will have no helpers.

3:92 *YE WILL NOT ATTAIN UNTO PIETY UNTIL YE SPEND OF THAT WHICH YE LOVE. AND WHATSOEVER YE SPEND, ALLAH IS AWARE THEREOF.*

3:93 All food was lawful unto *THE CHILDREN OF ISRAEL*, save that which Israel forbade himself, (in days) before the Torah was revealed. Say: Produce the Torah and read it (unto us) if ye are *TRUTHFUL*.

3:94 And *WHOEVER SHALL INVENT A FALSEHOOD AFTER THAT CONCERNING ALLAH, SUCH WILL BE WRONG-DOERS.*

3:95 Say: *ALLAH SPEAKETH TRUTH*. So follow the religion of Abraham, the upright. He was not of the *IDOLATERS*.

3:96 Lo! the first Sanctuary appointed for mankind was that at Becca, a blessed place, a guidance to the peoples;

3:97 Wherein are plain memorials (of Allah's guidance); the place where Abraham stood up to pray; and whosoever entereth it is safe. And pilgrimage to the House is a duty unto Allah for mankind, for him who can find a way thither. *AS FOR HIM WHO DISBELIEVETH*, (let him know that) lo! Allah is Independent of (all) creatures.

3:98 Say: O *PEOPLE OF THE SCRIPTURE!* Why *DISBELIEVE* ye in the revelations of Allah, when Allah (Himself) is Witness of what ye do?

3:99 Say: O *PEOPLE OF THE SCRIPTURE!* Why drive ye back *BELIEVERS* from the way of Allah, seeking to make it crooked, when ye are witnesses (to Allah's guidance)? Allah is not unaware of what ye do.

3:100 O *YE WHO BELIEVE*! If ye *OBEY* a party of those who have received the Scripture *THEY WILL MAKE YOU DISBELIEVERS AFTER YOUR BELIEF.* [Muslims who allow Jews or Christians to have superiority over them are Muslims on the way to becoming unbelievers.]

3:101 How can ye *DISBELIEVE*, when it is ye unto whom Allah's revelations are recited, and His messenger is in your midst? He who holdeth fast to Allah, he indeed is *GUIDED UNTO A RIGHT PATH.*

3:102 *O YE WHO BELIEVE! OBSERVE YOUR DUTY TO ALLAH* with right observance, and die not save as those who have surrendered (unto Him)

3:103 And *HOLD FAST, ALL OF YOU TOGETHER, TO THE CABLE OF ALLAH, AND DO NOT SEPARATE.* And remember Allah's favour unto you: How ye were enemies and He made friendship between your hearts so that *YE BECAME AS BROTHERS* by His grace; and (how) ye were upon the brink of an abyss of fire, and He did save you from it. Thus Allah maketh clear His revelations unto you, that haply ye may be guided, [Muslims are commanded to stick together, as if they were brothers.]

3:104 And there may spring from you a nation who invite to goodness, and enjoin right conduct and forbid indecency. *SUCH ARE THEY WHO ARE SUCCESSFUL.*

3:105 And be ye not as those who separated and disputed after the *CLEAR PROOFS* had come unto them. For such there is an awful doom,

3:106 On *THE DAY* when (some) faces will be whitened and (some) faces will be blackened; and as for those whose faces have been blackened, it will be said unto them: *DISBELIEVED YE AFTER YOUR (PROFESSION OF) BELIEF*? Then *TASTE THE PUNISHMENT FOR THAT YE DISBELIEVED.*

3:107 And as for those whose faces have been whitened, in the mercy of Allah they dwell for ever.

3:108 These are revelations of Allah. We recite them unto thee in truth. Allah willeth no injustice to (His) creatures.

3:109 Unto Allah belongeth whatsoever is in the heavens and whatsoever is in the earth; and unto Allah all things are returned.

3:110 *YE ARE THE BEST COMMUNITY THAT HATH BEEN RAISED UP FOR MANKIND.* Ye enjoin right conduct and forbid indecency; and ye *BELIEVE* in Allah. And if the *PEOPLE OF THE SCRIPTURE* had *BELIEVED* it had been better for them. Some of them are *BELIEVERS*; but most of them are *EVIL-LIVERS*.

3:111 ~~They will not harm you save a trifling hurt,~~ and *IF THEY FIGHT AGAINST YOU THEY WILL TURN AND FLEE. AND AFTERWARD THEY WILL NOT BE HELPED.* [Part cancelled by verse 9:29][437]

3:112 Ignominy shall be their portion wheresoever they are found save (where they grasp) a rope from Allah and a rope from men. They have incurred anger from their Lord, and wretchedness is laid upon them. That is because *THEY USED TO DISBELIEVE THE REVELATIONS OF ALLAH, AND SLEW THE PROPHETS WRONGFULLY.* That is because they were rebellious and used to transgress.

3:113 They are not all alike. *OF THE PEOPLE OF THE SCRIPTURE THERE IS A STAUNCH COMMUNITY* who recite the revelations of Allah in the night season, falling prostrate (before Him). [Some Jews and Christians are actually Muslims.]

3:114 *THEY BELIEVE IN ALLAH AND THE LAST DAY*, **and enjoin right conduct and forbid indecency, and vie one with another in good works. These are of the righteous.**

3:115 And whatever good they do, they will not be denied the meed thereof. Allah is Aware of those who ward off (*EVIL*).

3:116 Lo! the riches and the progeny of *THOSE WHO DISBELIEVE* will not avail them aught against Allah; and such are *RIGHTFUL OWNERS OF THE FIRE*. They will abide therein.

3:117 The likeness of that which they spend in this life of the world is as the likeness of a biting, icy wind which smiteth the harvest of a people who have wronged themselves, and devastateth it. Allah wronged them not, but they do wrong themselves.

3:118 *O YE WHO BELIEVE! TAKE NOT FOR INTIMATES OTHERS THAN YOUR OWN FOLK*, **who would spare no pains to ruin you; they love to hamper you.** *HATRED IS REVEALED BY (THE UTTERANCE OF) THEIR MOUTHS, BUT THAT WHICH THEIR BREASTS HIDE IS GREATER.* **We have made plain for you the revelations if ye will understand. [Believers are not to trust unbelievers, because whatever criticisms unbelievers voice, their unspoken criticisms of Islam are far worse.]**

3:119 Lo! ye are those who love them though they love you not, and ye *BELIEVE* in all the Scripture. When they fall in with you they say: We *BELIEVE*; but when they go apart they bite their finger-tips at you, for rage. Say: Perish in your rage! Lo! Allah is Aware of what is hidden in (your) breasts.

3:120 *IF A LUCKY CHANCE BEFALL YOU, IT IS EVIL UNTO THEM, AND IF DISASTER STRIKE YOU THEY REJOICE THEREAT.* But if ye persevere and keep from evil their guile will never harm you. Lo! Allah is Surrounding what they do.

3:121 And when thou settedst forth at daybreak from thy housefolk to *ASSIGN TO THE BELIEVERS THEIR POSITIONS FOR THE BATTLE*, **Allah was Hearer, Knower.**

3:122 When two parties of you almost fell away [two groups of Jihadis were about to lose courage], and Allah was their Protecting Friend. *IN ALLAH LET BELIEVERS PUT THEIR TRUST.*

3:123 Allah had already *GIVEN YOU THE VICTORY AT BADR*, **when ye were contemptible. So** *OBSERVE YOUR DUTY TO ALLAH* **in order that ye may be** *THANKFUL*. **[The Muslims who obey the commands of Islam will be thankful as they will be those who spend eternity in Paradise.]**

3:124 When thou didst say unto the *BELIEVERS*: Is it not sufficient for you that your Lord should support you with three thousand angels sent down (to your help)?

3:125 Nay, but *IF YE PERSEVERE, AND KEEP FROM EVIL, AND (THE ENEMY) ATTACK YOU SUDDENLY*, **your Lord will help you with five thousand angels sweeping on.**

3:126 Allah ordained this only as a message of good cheer for you, and that thereby your hearts might be at rest - *VICTORY* cometh only from Allah, the Mighty, the Wise -

3:127 That *HE MAY CUT OFF A PART OF THOSE WHO DISBELIEVE*, **or overwhelm them so that they retire, frustrated. [Allah provides Muslims with assistance in their warfare.]**

3:128 *IT IS NO CONCERN AT ALL OF THEE (MUHAMMAD) WHETHER HE RELENT TOWARD THEM OR PUNISH THEM; FOR THEY ARE EVIL-DOERS.*

3:129 Unto Allah belongeth whatsoever is in the heavens and whatsoever is in the earth. *HE FORGIVETH WHOM HE WILL, AND PUNISHETH WHOM HE WILL. ALLAH IS FORGIVING, MERCIFUL.*

3:130 O *ye who believe*! Devour not usury, doubling and quadrupling (the sum lent). *Observe your duty to Allah, that ye may be successful.*

3:131 And ward off (from yourselves) *the Fire prepared for disbelievers*.

3:132 And *obey Allah and the Messenger*, that ye may find mercy.

3:133 And vie one with another for forgiveness from your Lord, and for *a paradise as wide as are the heavens and the earth, prepared for those who ward off (evil);* [Warding off evil means promoting Islam and destroying unbelief.]

3:134 Those who spend (of that which Allah hath given them) in ease and in adversity, those who control their wrath and are forgiving toward mankind; Allah loveth the good;

3:135 And those who, when they do an *evil* thing or wrong themselves, remember Allah and implore forgiveness for their sins - Who forgiveth sins save Allah only? - and will not knowingly repeat (the wrong) they did.

3:136 *The reward* of such will be forgiveness from their Lord, and *Gardens underneath which rivers flow, wherein they will abide for ever* - a bountiful reward for workers!

3:137 *Systems have passed away before you.* Do but travel in the land and see the nature of the consequence for those who did deny (the messengers).

3:138 *This is a declaration for mankind,* a guidance *and* an admonition unto those who ward off (evil)

3:139 Faint not nor grieve, for *ye will overcome them* if ye are (indeed) *believers*.

3:140 *If ye have received a blow, the (disbelieving) people have received a blow* the like thereof. These are (only) the vicissitudes which We cause to follow one another for mankind, *to the end that Allah may know those who believe and may choose* witnesses *from among you*; and *Allah loveth not wrong-doers*. [Jihad is a test of belief in Judgement Day and the path to Paradise.]

3:141 And that Allah may prove *those who believe*, and may blight the *disbelievers*.

3:142 Or *deemed ye that ye would enter paradise while yet Allah knoweth not those of you who really strive [Jihad], nor knoweth those (of you) who are steadfast?* [Only the devout Jihadi is guaranteed entry to Paradise.]

3:143 And verily *ye used to wish for death before ye met it (in the field) [battlefield]. Now ye have seen it with your eyes!*

3:144 Muhammad is but a messenger, messengers (the like of whom) have passed away before him. *Will it be that, when he dieth or is slain, ye will turn back on your heels?* He who turneth back on his heels doth no hurt to Allah, and *Allah will reward* the thankful. [Mohammed is a Jihadi too and risks dying imposing Islam.]

3:145 No soul can ever die except by Allah's leave and at a term appointed. Whoso desireth the *reward* of the world, We bestow on him thereof; and *whoso desireth the reward of the hereafter*, We bestow on him thereof. We shall *reward* the thankful.

3:146 And with *how many a prophet have there been a number of devoted men who fought (beside him).* They quailed not for aught that befell them in the way of Allah, *nor did they weaken*, nor were they brought low. *Allah loveth the steadfast.* [The disciples of Mohammed fought alongside him and never weakened, never complained. Jihad is

rewarded with Paradise as it proves (tests) which Muslims have the most devout belief in Islam.]

3:147 Their cry was only that they said: Our Lord! forgive us for our sins and wasted efforts, make our foothold sure, and *GIVE US VICTORY OVER THE DISBELIEVING FOLK.*

3:148 So *ALLAH GAVE THEM THE REWARD* of the world and *THE GOOD REWARD OF THE HEREAFTER.* Allah loveth *THOSE WHOSE DEEDS ARE GOOD.* [Jihad is considered a moral virtue in Islam.]

3:149 O *YE WHO BELIEVE! IF YE OBEY THOSE WHO DISBELIEVE, THEY WILL MAKE YOU TURN BACK* on your heels, and ye turn back as *LOSERS*. [Muslims who wish to avoid Hell are not to listen to the disapproval of Jihad from the unbelievers.]

3:150 But Allah is your Protector, and He is the Best of Helpers.

3:151 *WE SHALL CAST TERROR INTO THE HEARTS OF THOSE WHO DISBELIEVE* because *THEY ASCRIBE UNTO ALLAH PARTNERS* [Pagans & Christians, who diversify the authority of a unitary god], for which no warrant hath been revealed. *THEIR HABITATION IS THE FIRE*, and hapless the abode of the *WRONG-DOERS.*

3:152 Allah verily *MADE GOOD HIS PROMISE* unto you *WHEN YE ROUTED [UTTERLY DEFEATED UNBELIEVERS IN BATTLE]* them by His leave, until (the moment) *WHEN YOUR COURAGE FAILED YOU, AND YE DISAGREED ABOUT THE ORDER AND YE DISOBEYED*, after He had shown you that for which ye long. Some of you desired the world, and *SOME OF YOU DESIRED THE HEREAFTER.* Therefore *HE MADE YOU FLEE FROM THEM*, that He might try you. Yet now He hath forgiven you. Allah is a Lord of Kindness to *BELIEVERS*. [Koran says that for Jihads to succeed they are to be united in their love of death over their love of life.]

3:153 When ye climbed (the hill) and paid no heed to anyone, while *THE MESSENGER, IN YOUR REAR, WAS CALLING YOU (TO FIGHT)* [Mohammed was a Jihadi]. Therefor He rewarded you grief for (his) grief, that (He might teach) you not to sorrow either for that which ye missed or for that which befell you. Allah is Informed of what ye do. [Other translations than Pickthall emphasise that "which ye missed" refers to the loot and slaves that the Muslim armies failed to acquire.][438]

3:154 Then, after grief, He sent down security for you. As slumber did it overcome a party of you, while *(THE OTHER) PARTY [FACTION], WHO WERE ANXIOUS ON THEIR OWN ACCOUNT, THOUGHT WRONGLY OF ALLAH, THE THOUGHT OF IGNORANCE.* They said: Have we any part in the cause? Say (O Muhammad): *THE CAUSE BELONGETH WHOLLY TO ALLAH.* They hide within themselves (a thought) which they reveal not unto thee, saying: Had we had any part *IN THE CAUSE WE SHOULD NOT HAVE BEEN SLAIN HERE. SAY: EVEN THOUGH YE HAD BEEN IN YOUR HOUSES, THOSE APPOINTED TO BE SLAIN WOULD HAVE GONE FORTH TO THE PLACES WHERE THEY WERE TO LIE.* (All this hath been) in order that Allah *MIGHT TRY WHAT IS IN YOUR BREASTS AND*

PROVE WHAT IS IN YOUR HEARTS. **Allah is Aware of what is hidden in the breasts (of men). [Pointless lamenting those Jihadis who die, the determinism of Islam says Allah would have killed those he allowed to die even if they had remained at home. Jihad is Allah probing Muslims to see how devout is their belief.]**

3:155 Lo! *THOSE OF YOU WHO TURNED BACK ON THE DAY WHEN THE TWO HOSTS [ARMIES] MET,* **Satan alone it was who caused them to backslide, because of some of that which they have earned. Now Allah hath forgiven them. Lo! Allah is Forgiving, Clement. [Since Allah is supposedly all-powerful, how is it that Satan can force Muslims to backslide?]**

3:156 O *YE WHO BELIEVE*! **Be not as** *THOSE WHO DISBELIEVED* **and said of their brethren who went abroad in the land or** *WERE FIGHTING IN THE [BATTLE] FIELD*: **If they had been (here) with us they would not have died or been killed: that Allah may make it anguish in their hearts.** *ALLAH GIVETH LIFE AND CAUSETH DEATH*; **and Allah is Seer of what ye do. [Muslims are not allowed to wish that Jihadis had not to regret those who went off to kill.]**

3:157 *AND WHAT THOUGH YE BE SLAIN IN ALLAH'S WAY OR DIE THEREIN [THOSE WHO DIE DURING JIHAD]? SURELY PARDON FROM ALLAH AND MERCY ARE BETTER THAN ALL THAT THEY AMASS.* **[Allah forgives Jihadi martyrs all their sins – ensuring they spend an eternity in Paradise.]**

3:158 *WHAT THOUGH YE BE SLAIN OR DIE, WHEN UNTO ALLAH YE ARE GATHERED?* **[Allah forgives Jihadi martyrs all their sins – ensuring they spend an eternity in Paradise.]**

3:159 It was by the mercy of Allah that thou wast lenient with them (O Muhammad), for if thou hadst been stern and fierce of heart they would have dispersed from round about thee. So pardon them and ask forgiveness for them and consult with them upon the conduct of affairs. And when thou art resolved, then put thy trust in Allah. Lo! Allah loveth those who put their trust (in Him).

3:160 If Allah is your helper none can overcome you, and if He withdraw His help from you, who is there who can help you after Him? *IN ALLAH LET BELIEVERS PUT THEIR TRUST*.

3:161 *IT IS NOT FOR ANY PROPHET TO EMBEZZLE.* Whoso embezzleth will bring what he embezzled with him on *THE DAY OF RESURRECTION*. Then *EVERY SOUL WILL BE PAID IN FULL WHAT IT HATH EARNED*; and they will not be wronged. [Can you imagine the New Testament warning Jesus not to embezzle?]

3:162 Is one who followeth the pleasure of Allah as one who hath earned condemnation from Allah, *WHOSE HABITATION IS THE FIRE*, a hapless journey's end?

3:163 There are degrees (of grace and reprobation) with Allah, and Allah is Seer of what they do.

3:164 Allah verily hath shown grace to the *BELIEVERS* by sending unto them a messenger of their own who reciteth unto them His revelations, and causeth them to grow, and teacheth them the Scripture and wisdom; although before (he came to them) they were in flagrant error.

3:165 And was it so, when a disaster smote you, though ye had smitten (them with a disaster) twice (as great), that ye said: How is this? Say (unto them, O Muhammad): It is from yourselves. Lo! Allah is Able to do all things.

3:166 That which befell you, *ON THE DAY WHEN THE TWO ARMIES MET*, **was by permission of Allah;** *THAT HE MIGHT KNOW THE TRUE BELIEVERS;* **[Jihad is seen by the Koran as a test of faith.]**

3:167 And that He might know the _HYPOCRITES_, unto whom it was said: _COME, FIGHT IN THE WAY OF ALLAH, [JIHAD] OR DEFEND YOURSELVES_. They answered: If we knew aught of _FIGHTING_ we would follow you. _ON THAT DAY THEY WERE NEARER DISBELIEF THAN FAITH._ They utter with their mouths a thing which is not in their hearts. Allah is Best Aware of what they hide. [Note the difference here between fighting and defense. Also offering an excuse of not being a soldier is akin to becoming an unbeliever.]

3:168 Those who, while they sat at home, said of their brethren (who _WERE FIGHTING FOR THE CAUSE OF ALLAH): IF THEY HAD BEEN GUIDED BY US THEY WOULD NOT HAVE BEEN SLAIN_. Say (unto them, O Muhammad): Then avert death from yourselves if ye are truthful. [The slackers say that if the Jihadis had not gone forth to war they would still be alive. Note how the Koran tries to refute the claims of the slackers in order to promote Jihad amont Muslims.]

3:169 _THINK NOT OF THOSE, WHO ARE SLAIN IN THE WAY OF ALLAH [JIHADIS], AS DEAD. NAY, THEY ARE LIVING. WITH THEIR LORD THEY HAVE PROVISION._ [Allah forgives Jihadi martyrs all their sins – ensuring they spend an eternity in Paradise.]

3:170 _JUBILANT (ARE THEY) BECAUSE OF THAT WHICH ALLAH HATH BESTOWED UPON THEM OF HIS BOUNTY, REJOICING FOR THE SAKE OF THOSE WHO HAVE NOT JOINED THEM BUT ARE LEFT BEHIND:_ That there shall no fear come upon them _NEITHER SHALL THEY GRIEVE._ [The Koran says that Muslims are not to grieve about the dead Jihadis who are in Paradise for eternity. This is why it is an empty gesture when Muslims say they will not offer prayers for dead Jihadis; Muslims know they are to be proud of Jihadis and are not to pray nor grieve for dead Jihadis.]

3:171 They rejoice because of favour from Allah and kindness, and that _ALLAH WASTETH NOT THE WAGE OF THE BELIEVERS._ [Believers are repaid by Allah for their part in extending the control of Islam.]

3:172 As for _THOSE WHO HEARD THE CALL OF ALLAH AND HIS MESSENGER_ after the harm befell them (in the fight); for such of them as do right and ward off (evil), _THERE IS GREAT REWARD_.

3:173 Those unto whom men said: Lo! the people have gathered against you, therefor fear them. _(THE THREAT OF DANGER) BUT INCREASED THE FAITH OF THEM_ and they cried: Allah is Sufficient for us! Most Excellent is He in Whom we trust!

3:174 So they returned with grace and favour from Allah, and no harm touched them. They followed the good pleasure of Allah, and Allah is of Infinite Bounty.

3:175 It is only the devil who would make (men) fear his partisans. Fear them not; _FEAR ME, IF YE ARE TRUE BELIEVERS_.

3:176 Let not their conduct grieve thee, who run easily to _DISBELIEF_, for lo! they injure Allah not at all. It is Allah's Will to assign them no portion in the Hereafter, and _THEIRS WILL BE AN AWFUL DOOM._

3:177 _THOSE WHO PURCHASE DISBELIEF AT THE PRICE OF FAITH HARM ALLAH NOT AT ALL, BUT THEIRS WILL BE A PAINFUL DOOM._

3:178 And let not _THOSE WHO DISBELIEVE_ imagine that the rein We give them bodeth good unto their souls. We only give them rein that they may grow in sinfulness. And _THEIRS WILL BE A SHAMEFUL DOOM._

3:179 It is not (the purpose) of Allah to leave you in your present state till He shall separate the wicked from the good. And it is not (the purpose of) Allah to let you know the Unseen. But Allah chooseth of His messengers whom He will, (to receive knowledge thereof). So *BELIEVE* in Allah and His messengers. *IF YE BELIEVE AND WARD OFF (EVIL), YOURS WILL BE A VAST REWARD.*

3:180 And let not those who hoard up that which Allah hath bestowed upon them of His bounty think that it is better for them. Nay, it is worse for them. That which they hoard will be their collar on *THE DAY OF RESURRECTION.* Allah's is the heritage of the heavens and the earth, and Allah is Informed of what ye do.

3:181 Verily Allah heard the saying of those who said, (when asked for contributions to the war): "Allah, forsooth, is poor, and we are rich!" We shall record their saying with their *SLAYING OF THE PROPHETS WRONGFULLY* and We shall say: Taste ye *THE PUNISHMENT OF BURNING!* [In Islam some prophets can be rightfully murdered.]

3:182 This is *ON ACCOUNT OF THAT WHICH YOUR OWN HANDS HAVE SENT BEFORE (YOU TO THE JUDGMENT).* Allah is no oppressor of (His) *BONDMEN.*

3:183 (The same are) those who say: Lo! Allah hath charged us that we *BELIEVE* not in any messenger until he bring us an offering which fire (from heaven) shall devour. Say (unto them, O Muhammad): Messengers came unto you before me with miracles, and with that (very miracle) which ye describe. Why then did ye slay them? (Answer that) if ye are *TRUTHFUL!*

3:184 And if they deny thee, even so did they deny messengers who were before thee, who came with miracles and with the Psalms and with the Scripture giving light.

3:185 *EVERY SOUL WILL TASTE OF DEATH. AND YE WILL BE PAID ON THE DAY OF RESURRECTION* only that which ye have fairly earned. *WHOSO IS REMOVED FROM THE FIRE AND IS MADE TO ENTER PARADISE, HE INDEED IS TRIUMPHANT. THE LIFE OF THIS WORLD IS BUT COMFORT OF ILLUSION.*

3:186 ~~Assuredly ye will be tried in your property and in your persons, and ye will hear much wrong from those who were given the Scripture before you, and from the idolaters. But if ye persevere and ward off (evil), then that is of the steadfast heart of things.~~ [Cancelled by verse 9:28][439]

3:187 And (remember) when *ALLAH LAID A CHARGE ON THOSE WHO HAD RECEIVED THE SCRIPTURE (HE SAID): YE ARE TO EXPOUND IT TO MANKIND AND NOT TO HIDE IT.* But they flung it behind their backs and bought thereby a little gain. Verily evil is that which they have gained thereby.

3:188 Think not that those who exult in what they have given, and love to be praised for what they have not done - Think not, they are in safety from the doom. *A PAINFUL DOOM IS THEIRS.*

3:189 Unto Allah belongeth the Sovereignty of the heavens and the earth. Allah is Able to do all things.

3:190 Lo! In the creation of the heavens and the earth and (in) the difference of night and day are tokens (of His Sovereignty) for *MEN OF UNDERSTANDING,*

3:191 Such as remember Allah, standing, sitting, and reclining, and consider the creation of the heavens and the earth, (and say): Our Lord! Thou createdst not this in vain. Glory be to Thee! *PRESERVE US FROM THE DOOM OF FIRE.*

3:192 Our Lord! Whom Thou *CAUSEST TO ENTER THE FIRE*: him indeed Thou hast confounded. For *EVIL-DOERS* there will be no helpers.

3:193 Our Lord! Lo! we have heard a crier calling unto Faith: "*BELIEVE* ye in your Lord!" So we *BELIEVED*. Our Lord! Therefor forgive us our sins, and remit from us our *EVIL* deeds, and make us die the death of the righteous.

3:194 Our Lord! And give us that which Thou hast promised to us by Thy messengers. Confound us not upon *THE DAY OF RESURRECTION*. Lo! *THOU BREAKEST NOT THE TRYST [PROMISE].*

3:195 And their Lord hath heard them (and He saith): Lo! I suffer not the work of any worker, male or female, to be lost. Ye proceed one from another. So *THOSE WHO FLED* and were driven forth from their homes and *SUFFERED DAMAGE FOR MY CAUSE*, and *FOUGHT AND WERE SLAIN*, verily I shall remit their *EVIL* deeds from them and verily *I SHALL BRING THEM INTO GARDENS UNDERNEATH WHICH RIVERS FLOW - A REWARD FROM ALLAH*. And with Allah is the fairest of rewards. [Allah forgives Jihadi martyrs all their sins – ensuring they spend an eternity in Paradise. Most translations distinguish between those who fled and those who fought and were killed. Koran 8.15 and 8.16 make it clear that those who do not stand and fight are going to Hell.][440]

3:196 Let not the vicissitude (of the success) of *THOSE WHO DISBELIEVE, IN THE LAND, DECEIVE THEE* (O Muhammad).

3:197 It is but a brief comfort. And afterward *THEIR HABITATION WILL BE HELL*, an ill abode.

3:198 But *THOSE WHO KEEP THEIR DUTY* to their Lord, for them are *GARDENS UNDERNEATH WHICH RIVERS FLOW, WHEREIN THEY WILL BE SAFE FOR EVER.* A gift of welcome from their Lord. That which Allah hath in store is better for the righteous.

3:199 And lo! *OF THE PEOPLE OF THE SCRIPTURE THERE ARE SOME WHO BELIEVE IN ALLAH* and that which is revealed unto you and that which was revealed unto them, humbling themselves before

Allah. They purchase not a trifling gain at the price of the revelations of Allah. Verily *THEIR REWARD IS WITH THEIR LORD.* Lo! Allah is swift to take account. [Some Jews and Christians are secretly Muslims, and they will be rewarded in Paradise.]

3:200 O *YE WHO BELIEVE! ENDURE, OUTDO ALL OTHERS IN ENDURANCE, BE READY, AND OBSERVE YOUR DUTY TO ALLAH, IN ORDER THAT YE MAY SUCCEED.*

Chapter 8 - The Spoils of War

8:1 ~~They ask thee (O Muhammad) of the spoils of war [slaves and loot]. Say: The spoils of war belong to Allah and the messenger, so keep your duty to Allah, and adjust the matter of your difference, and obey Allah and His messenger, if ye are (true)~~ *BELIEVERS.* [Cancelled by verse 8:41][441]

8:2 *THEY ONLY ARE THE (TRUE) BELIEVERS WHOSE HEARTS FEEL FEAR WHEN ALLAH IS MENTIONED*, and when His revelations are recited unto them they increase their faith, and who trust in their Lord;

8:3 Who establish worship and *SPEND OF THAT WE HAVE BESTOWED ON THEM.*

8:4 *THOSE ARE THEY WHO ARE IN TRUTH BELIEVERS.* For them are *GRADES (OF HONOUR) WITH THEIR LORD, AND PARDON*, and a bountiful provision.

8:5 *EVEN AS THY LORD CAUSED THEE (MUHAMMAD) TO GO FORTH FROM THY HOME WITH THE TRUTH, AND LO! A PARTY OF THE BELIEVERS WERE AVERSE (TO IT).* **[Note from the name of this entire Surah it is about acquiring loot and slaves from Islamic warfare.]**

8:6 *DISPUTING WITH THEE OF THE TRUTH AFTER IT HAD BEEN MADE MANIFEST*, as if they were being driven to death visible.

8:7 And when Allah promised you one of the two bands (of the enemy) that it should be yours, and ye longed that other than the *ARMED* one might be yours. And Allah willed that He should *CAUSE THE TRUTH TO TRIUMPH* by His words, and *CUT THE ROOT OF THE DISBELIEVERS;*

8:8 That He might *CAUSE THE TRUTH TO TRIUMPH* and bring vanity to naught, *HOWEVER MUCH THE GUILTY MIGHT OPPOSE;*

8:9 When ye sought help of your Lord and He answered you (saying): I will help you with a thousand of the angels, rank on rank.

8:10 Allah appointed it only as good tidings, and that your hearts thereby might be at rest. *VICTORY COMETH ONLY BY THE HELP OF ALLAH*. Lo! Allah is Mighty, Wise.

8:11 When He made the slumber fall upon you as a reassurance from him and sent down water from the sky upon you, that thereby He might purify you, and remove from you the fear of Satan, and make strong your hearts and firm (your) feet thereby.

8:12 When thy Lord inspired the angels, (saying): I am with you. So *MAKE THOSE WHO BELIEVE STAND FIRM.* **I will throw fear into the hearts of** *THOSE WHO DISBELIEVE. THEN SMITE THE NECKS* **[cut their throats, behead them] and smite of them each finger. [This is why Jihadis behead those who are not Islamic.]**

8:13 That is *BECAUSE THEY OPPOSED ALLAH AND HIS MESSENGER.* Whoso opposeth Allah and His messenger, (for him) lo! *ALLAH IS SEVERE IN PUNISHMENT.*

8:14 That (is the award), so taste it, and (know) that *FOR DISBELIEVERS IS THE TORMENT OF THE FIRE.*

8:15 O *YE WHO BELIEVE!* **When ye** *MEET THOSE WHO DISBELIEVE IN BATTLE, TURN NOT YOUR BACKS TO THEM.*

8:16 *WHOSO ON THAT DAY TURNETH HIS BACK TO THEM*, **unless** *MANEUVERING FOR BATTLE* **or intent to join a company, he truly hath incurred wrath from Allah, and** *HIS HABITATION WILL BE HELL*, **a hapless journey's end. [Muslims who retreat in battle are destined for an eternity of torture.]**

8:17 *YE (MUSLIMS) SLEW THEM NOT, BUT ALLAH SLEW THEM.* **[Muslims who kill according to Islam are absolved of any guilt.] And thou**

(Muhammad) threwest not when thou didst throw, but Allah threw, _THAT_ _HE MIGHT TEST THE BELIEVERS_ by a fair test from Him. Lo! Allah is Hearer, Knower.

8:18 That (is the case); and (know) that Allah (it is) Who maketh weak _THE PLAN OF DISBELIEVERS_.

8:19 (O Qureysh!) If ye sought a judgment, now hath the judgment come unto you. And if ye cease (from persecuting the _BELIEVERS_) it will be better for you, but if ye return (to the attack) We also shall return. And your host will avail you naught, however numerous it be, and (know) that Allah is with the _BELIEVERS_ (in His Guidance). [Pickthall inserts "(from persecuting the Believers)", whilst other translations just say "(if you desist from disobedience)". Most translators insert a reference to some refusal to submit to Islam as an act of aggression by non-Muslims, in order to create a casus bellus which is not to be found in 8:19 itself.   In addition, Pickthall is out of step in inserting the (historically bound) reference to the Qureysh tribe, thus predenting that these violent verses only pertain to a single past incident, when the Koran claims to be universal and eternal.]

8:20 O _YE WHO BELIEVE_! _OBEY ALLAH AND HIS MESSENGER_, and turn not away from him when ye hear (him speak).

8:21 _BE NOT AS THOSE WHO SAY, WE HEAR, AND THEY HEAR NOT._

8:22 Lo! _THE WORST OF BEASTS IN ALLAH'S SIGHT_ are the deaf, the dumb, who _HAVE NO SENSE_. [In Islam non-Muslims are the lowest form of life, ignorant and senseless.]

8:23 Had Allah known of any good in them He would have made them hear, but had He made them hear they would have turned away, averse.

8:24 O _YE WHO BELIEVE_! _OBEY ALLAH, AND THE MESSENGER_ when He calleth you to that which quickeneth you, and know that Allah cometh in between the man and his own heart, and that He it is unto Whom ye will be gathered.

8:25 And _GUARD YOURSELVES_ against a chastisement which cannot fall exclusively on those of you who _ARE WRONG-DOERS, AND KNOW THAT ALLAH IS SEVERE IN PUNISHMENT._

8:26 And remember, when ye were few and reckoned feeble in the land, and were in fear lest men should extirpate you, how He gave you refuge, and strengthened you with His help, and made provision of good things for you, that haply ye might be thankful.

8:27 O _YE WHO BELIEVE_! Betray not Allah and His messenger, nor knowingly betray your trusts.

8:28 And know that _YOUR POSSESSIONS AND YOUR CHILDREN ARE A TEST_, and that with Allah is _IMMENSE_ _REWARD._

8:29 O _YE WHO BELIEVE_! If ye _KEEP YOUR DUTY TO ALLAH_, He will give you discrimination (between right and wrong) and will rid you of _YOUR EVIL THOUGHTS AND DEEDS,_ and _WILL FORGIVE YOU_. Allah is of Infinite Bounty.

8:30 And when _THOSE WHO DISBELIEVE_ plot against thee (O Muhammad) to wound thee fatally, or to kill thee or to drive thee forth; _THEY PLOT, BUT ALLAH (ALSO) PLOTTETH; AND ALLAH IS THE BEST OF_ _PLOTTERS._

8:31 And when Our revelations are recited unto them _THEY SAY:_ We have heard. If we wish we can speak the like of this. Lo! _THIS IS NAUGHT BUT FABLES OF THE MEN OF OLD._ [Contemporaries of Mohammed heard what he had to say about Islam and were not persuaded to join him, saying either he said nothing new or that he was insane.]

8:32 And when they said: O Allah! If this be indeed the truth from Thee, then rain down stones on us or bring on us some painful doom!

8:33 But Allah would not punish them while thou wast with them, nor will _HE PUNISH THEM WHILE_ _THEY SEEK FORGIVENESS._

8:34 What (plea) have they that Allah should not punish them, when they debar (His servants) from the Inviolable Place of Worship, though they are not its fitting guardians. Its fitting guardians are those only who _KEEP THEIR DUTY TO ALLAH_. But most of them know not.

8:35 And their worship at the (holy) House is naught but whistling and hand-clapping. Therefore (it is said unto them): Taste of the doom because ye disbelieve.

8:36 Lo! _THOSE WHO DISBELIEVE_ spend their wealth in order that they may debar (men) from the way of Allah. They will spend it, then it will become an anguish for them, then _THEY WILL BE CONQUERED._ And _THOSE WHO DISBELIEVE WILL BE GATHERED UNTO HELL,_

8:37 That Allah may separate the wicked from the good, _THE WICKED WILL HE_ place piece upon piece, and heap them all together, and _CONSIGN THEM UNTO HELL. SUCH VERILY ARE THE LOSERS._

8:38 Tell *THOSE WHO DISBELIEVE* that if they cease (from persecution of *BELIEVERS*) that which is past will be forgiven them; but if they return (thereto) then the example of the men of old hath already gone (before them, for a warning). [Unlike other translators Pickthall inserts "(from persecution of Believers)". Perhaps we are to assume that Pickthall considers us being non-Muslims is a form of persecution towards Muslims.][442]

8:39 And *FIGHT THEM UNTIL PERSECUTION IS NO MORE, AND RELIGION IS ALL FOR ALLAH.* But if they cease, then lo! Allah is Seer of what they do. [Jihad until there is no belief system other than Islam.]

8:40 And if they turn away, then know that Allah is your Befriender - a Transcendent Patron, a Transcendent Helper!

8:41 And know that whatever ye *TAKE AS SPOILS OF WAR [SLAVES AND LOOT],* lo! *A FIFTH THEREOF IS FOR ALLAH, AND FOR THE MESSENGER* and for the kinsman (who hath need) and orphans and the needy and the wayfarer, if ye *BELIEVE IN ALLAH* and that which We revealed unto Our slave on *THE DAY OF DISCRIMINATION*, the day *WHEN THE TWO ARMIES MET.* And Allah is Able to do all things.

8:42 When ye were on the near bank (of the valley) and they were on the yonder bank, and the caravan was below you (on the coast plain). And had ye trysted to meet one another ye surely would have failed to keep the tryst, but (it happened, as it did, without the forethought of either of you) that Allah might conclude a thing that must be done; that he who perished (on that day) might perish by a *CLEAR PROOF* (of His Sovereignty) and he who survived might survive by a *CLEAR PROOF* (of His Sovereignty). Lo! Allah in truth is Hearer, Knower.

8:43 When Allah showed them unto thee (O Muhammad) in thy dream as few in number, and if He had shown them to thee as many, ye (Muslims) would have faltered and would have quarreled over the affair. But Allah saved (you). Lo! He knoweth what is in the breasts (of men).

8:44 And when He made you (Muslims), when ye met (them), see them with your eyes as few, and lessened you in their eyes, (it was) that Allah might conclude a thing that must be done. Unto Allah all things are brought back.

8:45 O *YE WHO BELIEVE*! When *YE MEET AN ARMY, HOLD FIRM AND THINK OF ALLAH* much, *THAT YE MAY BE SUCCESSFUL.*

8:46 And *OBEY ALLAH AND HIS MESSENGER, AND DISPUTE NOT ONE WITH ANOTHER* lest ye falter and your strength depart from you; but be steadfast! Lo! Allah is with the steadfast.

8:47 Be not as those who came forth from their dwellings boastfully and to be seen of men, and debar (men) from the way of Allah, while Allah is surrounding all they do.

8:48 And when Satan made their deeds seem fair to them and said: No one of mankind can conquer you this day, for I am your protector. But *WHEN THE ARMIES CAME IN SIGHT OF ONE ANOTHER,* he took flight, saying: Lo! I am guiltless of you. Lo! I see that which ye see not. Lo! I fear Allah. And *ALLAH IS SEVERE IN PUNISHMENT.*

8:49 When the *HYPOCRITES* and those in whose hearts is a disease said: Their religion hath deluded these. Whoso putteth his trust in Allah (will find that) lo! Allah is Mighty, Wise.

8:50 If thou couldst see how the *ANGELS* receive *THOSE WHO DISBELIEVE*, smiting faces and their backs and (saying): *TASTE THE PUNISHMENT OF BURNING!*

8:51 This is for that which your own hands have sent before (to the Judgment), and (know) that Allah is not a tyrant to His slaves.

8:52 (Their way is) as the way of Pharaoh's folk and those before them; they *DISBELIEVED* the revelations of Allah, and Allah took them in their sins. Lo! *ALLAH IS STRONG, SEVERE IN PUNISHMENT.*

8:53 That is because Allah never changeth the grace He hath bestowed on any people until they first change that which is in their hearts, and (that is) because Allah is Hearer, Knower.

8:54 (Their way is) as the way of Pharaoh's folk and those before them; they denied the revelations of their Lord, so *WE DESTROYED THEM IN THEIR SINS*. And We drowned the folk of Pharaoh. All were *EVIL-DOERS*.

8:55 Lo! *THE WORST OF BEASTS IN ALLAH'S SIGHT ARE THE UNGRATEFUL WHO WILL NOT BELIEVE.* [This "religion" says that unbelievers are worse than all dirty or voracious wild animals.]

8:56 Those of them with whom thou madest a treaty, and then at every opportunity they break their treaty, and they keep not duty (to Allah).

8:57 If thou comest on them *IN THE WAR, DEAL WITH THEM SO AS TO STRIKE FEAR IN THOSE WHO ARE BEHIND THEM*, **that haply they may remember.**

8:58 And if thou *FEAREST TREACHERY FROM ANY FOLK, THEN THROW BACK TO THEM (THEIR TREATY)* **fairly. Lo! Allah loveth not the treacherous. [Islam sanctions Muslims renaging on promises on the slightest excuse.]**

8:59 And let not *THOSE WHO DISBELIEVE* **suppose that they can outstrip (Allah's Purpose). Lo! they cannot escape.**

8:60 Make ready for them *ALL THOU CANST OF (ARMED) FORCE* **and of horses tethered, that thereby** *YE MAY DISMAY THE ENEMY OF ALLAH AND YOUR ENEMY*, **and others beside them whom ye know not. Allah knoweth them.** *WHATSOEVER YE SPEND IN THE WAY OF ALLAH IT WILL BE REPAID TO YOU IN FULL,* **and ye will not be wronged. [Dying imposing Islam on those who reject it will be rewarded with an eternity in Paradise.]**

8:61 ~~And if they incline to peace, incline thou also to it, and trust in Allah. Lo! He, even He, is the Hearer, the Knower.~~ [Cancelled by verse 9:29 i.e. unbelievers seeking peace are to be ignored][443]

8:62 And if they would deceive thee, then lo! Allah is Sufficient for thee. He it is Who supporteth thee with His help and with the *BELIEVERS*,

8:63 And (as for the *BELIEVERS*) hath attuned their hearts. If thou hadst spent all that is in the earth thou couldst not have attuned their hearts, but Allah hath attuned them. Lo! He is Mighty, Wise.

8:64 O Prophet! Allah is Sufficient for thee and those who follow thee of the *BELIEVERS*.

8:65 O Prophet! *EXHORT THE BELIEVERS TO FIGHT.* **If there be of you twenty steadfast they shall overcome two hundred, and if there be of you a hundred (steadfast) they shall overcome a thousand of** *THOSE WHO DISBELIEVE*, **because they** (*THE DISBELIEVERS*) *ARE A FOLK WITHOUT INTELLIGENCE.*

8:66 Now hath Allah lightened your burden, for He knoweth that there is weakness in you. So if there be of you a steadfast hundred they shall overcome two hundred, and if there be of you a thousand (steadfast) they shall overcome two thousand by permission of Allah. Allah is with the steadfast.

8:67 *IT IS NOT FOR ANY PROPHET TO HAVE CAPTIVES [SLAVES] UNTIL HE HATH MADE SLAUGHTER IN THE LAND.* **Ye desire the lure of this world and Allah desireth (for you) the Hereafter, and Allah is Mighty, Wise.**

8:68 Had it not been for an ordinance of Allah which had gone before, an awful doom had come upon you on account of what ye took.

8:69 Now enjoy what ye have won, as lawful and good, and *KEEP YOUR DUTY TO ALLAH*. Lo! Allah is Forgiving, Merciful.

8:70 O Prophet! Say unto those captives who are in your hands: If Allah knoweth any good in your hearts He will give you better than that which hath been taken from you, and will forgive you. Lo! Allah is Forgiving, Merciful.

8:71 And if they would betray thee, they betrayed Allah before, and He gave (thee) power over them. Allah is Knower, Wise.

8:72 Lo! *THOSE WHO BELIEVED AND LEFT THEIR HOMES AND STROVE [JIHAD] WITH THEIR WEALTH AND THEIR LIVES FOR THE CAUSE OF ALLAH*, **and those who took them in and helped them: these are protecting friends one of another. And** *THOSE WHO BELIEVED BUT DID NOT LEAVE THEIR HOMES, YE HAVE NO DUTY TO PROTECT THEM TILL THEY LEAVE THEIR HOMES;* ~~but if they seek help from you in the matter of religion then it is your duty to help (them) except against a folk between whom and you there is a treaty.~~ **Allah is Seer of what ye do. [Part cancelled by verse 9:5, i.e. no treaty is to be honoured. Note that Jihadis are not to defend those Muslims who do not engage in Jihad.]**[444]

8:73 And *THOSE WHO DISBELIEVE ARE PROTECTORS ONE OF ANOTHER* ~~If ye do not so [protect one another as non-Muslims do], there will be confusion in the land, and great corruption.~~ **[Abrogated by 9:5; absolves Muslims of the responsibility to protect all other Muslims.]**[445]

8:74 *THOSE WHO BELIEVED* **and left their homes and** *STROVE FOR THE CAUSE OF ALLAH [JIHAD]*, **and** *THOSE WHO TOOK THEM IN AND HELPED THEM - THESE ARE THE BELIEVERS IN TRUTH. FOR THEM IS PARDON, AND BOUNTIFUL PROVISION.*

8:75 And those who afterwards believed and left their homes and strove along with you, they are of you; and those who are akin are nearer one to another in the ordinance of Allah. Lo! Allah is Knower of all things.

Chapter 2 - The Cow

2:1 Alif. Lam. Mim.

2:2 This is *THE SCRIPTURE WHEREOF THERE IS NO DOUBT*, a guidance unto those who ward off (*EVIL*).

2:3 Who *BELIEVE* in the Unseen, and establish worship, and spend of that We have bestowed upon them;

2:4 And who *BELIEVE* in that which is revealed unto thee (Muhammad) and that which was revealed before thee, and are certain of the Hereafter.

2:5 These depend on guidance from their Lord. *THESE ARE THE SUCCESSFUL.*

2:6 As for the *DISBELIEVERS*, Whether thou warn them or thou warn them not it is all one for them; they *BELIEVE* not.

2:7 Allah hath sealed their hearing and their hearts, and on their eyes there is a covering. Theirs will be an awful doom.

2:8 And of mankind are some who say: *WE BELIEVE IN ALLAH AND THE LAST DAY*, when they *BELIEVE* not.

2:9 They think to beguile Allah and *THOSE WHO BELIEVE*, and they beguile none save themselves; but they perceive not.

2:10 *IN THEIR HEARTS IS A DISEASE*, and *ALLAH INCREASETH THEIR DISEASE. A PAINFUL DOOM IS THEIRS* because *THEY LIE.*

2:11 And when it is said unto them: *MAKE NOT MISCHIEF IN THE EARTH*, they say: We are peacemakers only.

2:12 Are not they indeed *THE MISCHIEF-MAKERS*? But they perceive not.

2:13 And when it is said unto them: *BELIEVE* as the people *BELIEVE*, they say: shall we *BELIEVE* as the foolish *BELIEVE*? are not they indeed the foolish? But they know not.

2:14 And when they fall in with those who *BELIEVE*, they say: We *BELIEVE*; but when they go apart to their devils they declare: Lo! we are with you; verily *WE DID BUT MOCK.*

2:15 Allah (Himself) doth mock them, leaving them to wander blindly on in their contumacy.

2:16 These are they who purchase error at the price of guidance, so their commerce doth not prosper, neither are they guided.

2:17 Their likeness is as the likeness of one who kindleth fire, and when it sheddeth its light around him Allah taketh away their light and leaveth them in darkness, where they cannot see,

2:18 Deaf, dumb and blind; and they return not.

2:19 Or like a rainstorm from the sky, wherein is darkness, thunder and the flash of lightning. They thrust their fingers in their ears by reason of the thunder-claps, for fear of death, Allah encompasseth the *DISBELIEVERS* (in His guidance, His omniscience and His omnipotence).

2:20 The lightning almost snatcheth away their sight from them. As often as it flasheth forth for them they walk therein, and when it darkeneth against them they stand still. If Allah willed, He could destroy their hearing and their sight. Lo! Allah is able to do all things.

2:21 O mankind! worship your Lord, Who hath created you and those before you, so that ye may ward off (*EVIL*).

2:22 Who hath appointed the earth a resting-place for you, and the sky a canopy; and causeth water to pour down from the sky, thereby producing fruits as food for you. And do not set up rivals to Allah when ye know (better).

2:23 And if ye are *IN DOUBT CONCERNING THAT WHICH WE REVEAL UNTO OUR SLAVE (MUHAMMAD), THEN PRODUCE A SURAH OF THE LIKE THEREOF,* and call your witness beside Allah if ye are truthful.

2:24 And if ye do it not- and ye can never do it - then *GUARD YOURSELVES* against *THE FIRE PREPARED FOR DISBELIEVERS,* whose fuel is of men and stones.

2:25 And give glad tidings (O Muhammad) unto *THOSE WHO BELIEVE AND DO GOOD WORKS*; that theirs are *GARDENS UNDERNEATH WHICH RIVERS FLOW*; as often as they are regaled with food of the fruit thereof, they say: this is what was given us aforetime; and it is given to them in resemblance. *THERE FOR THEM ARE PURE COMPANIONS; THERE FOREVER THEY ABIDE.*

2:26 Lo! Allah disdaineth not to coin the similitude even of a gnat. *THOSE WHO BELIEVE KNOW THAT IT IS THE TRUTH* from their Lord; but *THOSE WHO DISBELIEVE* say: What doth Allah wish (to teach) by such a similitude? He misleadeth many thereby, and He guideth many thereby; and He misleadeth thereby only miscreants;

2:27 Those who break the *COVENANT* of Allah after ratifying it, and sever that which Allah ordered to be joined, and (who) *MAKE MISCHIEF IN THE EARTH; THOSE ARE THEY WHO ARE THE LOSERS.*

2:28 How *DISBELIEVE* ye in Allah when ye were dead and He gave life to you! Then He will give you death, then life again, and then unto Him ye will return.

2:29 He it is Who created for you all that is in the earth. Then turned He to the heaven, and fashioned it as seven heavens. And He is knower of all things.

2:30 And when thy Lord said unto the angels: Lo! I am about to place a viceroy in the earth, they said: Wilt thou place therein one who will do harm therein and will shed blood, while we, we hymn Thy praise and sanctify Thee? He said: Surely I know that which ye know not.

2:31 And He taught Adam all the names, then showed them to the angels, saying: Inform Me of the names of these, if ye are truthful.

2:32 They said: Be glorified! We have no knowledge saving that which Thou hast taught us. Lo! Thou, only Thou, art the Knower, the Wise.

2:33 He said: O Adam! Inform them of their names, and when he had informed them of their names, He said: Did I not tell you that I know the secret of the heavens and the earth? And I know that which ye disclose and which ye hide.

2:34 And when We said unto the angels: Prostrate yourselves before Adam, they fell prostrate, all save Iblis. He demurred through pride, and so *BECAME A DISBELIEVER*.

2:35 And We said: O Adam! Dwell thou and thy wife in the Garden, and eat ye freely (of the fruits) thereof where ye will; but come not nigh this tree lest ye become wrong-doers.

2:36 But Satan caused them to deflect therefrom and expelled them from the (happy) state in which they were; and We said: Fall down, one of you a foe unto the other! There shall be for you on earth a habitation and provision for a time.

2:37 Then Adam received from his Lord words (of revelation), and He relented toward him. Lo! He is the relenting, the Merciful.

2:38 We said: Go down, all of you, from hence; but verily there cometh unto you from Me a guidance; and whoso followeth My guidance, there shall no fear come upon them neither shall they grieve.

2:39 But *THEY WHO DISBELIEVE, AND DENY OUR REVELATIONS, SUCH ARE RIGHTFUL PEOPLES OF THE FIRE*. They will abide therein.

2:40 O *CHILDREN OF ISRAEL*! Remember My favour wherewith I favoured you, and fulfil your (part of the) *COVENANT*, I shall fulfil My (part of the) *COVENANT*, and *FEAR ME*.

2:41 And *BELIEVE IN THAT WHICH I REVEAL*, confirming that which ye possess already (of the Scripture), and be not first to *DISBELIEVE* therein, and part not with My revelations for a trifling price, *AND KEEP YOUR DUTY UNTO ME*.

2:42 *CONFOUND NOT TRUTH WITH FALSEHOOD, NOR KNOWINGLY CONCEAL THE TRUTH.*

2:43 Establish worship, pay the poor-due, and bow your heads with those who bow (in worship).

2:44 Enjoin ye righteousness upon mankind while ye yourselves forget (to practise it)? And ye are readers of the Scripture! Have ye then no sense?

2:45 Seek help in patience and prayer; and truly it is hard save for the humble-minded,

2:46 Who know that they will have to meet their Lord, and that unto Him they are returning.

2:47 O *CHILDREN OF ISRAEL*! Remember My favour wherewith I favoured you and how I preferred you to (all) creatures.

2:48 And *GUARD YOURSELVES AGAINST A DAY* when no soul will in aught avail another, nor will intercession be accepted from it, nor will compensation be received from it, nor will they be helped.

2:49 And (remember) when We did deliver you from Pharaoh's folk, who were afflicting you with dreadful torment, slaying your sons and sparing your women: that was a tremendous trial from your Lord.

2:50 And when We brought you through the sea and rescued you, and drowned the folk of Pharaoh in your sight.

2:51 And when We did appoint for Moses forty nights (of solitude), and then ye chose the calf, when he had gone from you, and were wrong-doers.

2:52 Then, even after that, We pardoned you in order that ye might give thanks.

2:53 And when We gave unto Moses the Scripture and the criterion (of right and wrong), that ye might be led aright.

2:54 And when Moses said unto his people: O my people! Ye have wronged yourselves by your choosing of the calf (for worship) so turn in penitence to your Creator, and kill (the guilty) yourselves. That will be best for you with your Creator and He will relent toward you. Lo! He is the Relenting, the Merciful.

2:55 And when ye said: O Moses! We will not *BELIEVE* in thee till we see Allah plainly; and even while ye gazed the lightning seized you.

2:56 Then We revived you after your extinction, that ye might give thanks.

2:57 And We caused the white cloud to overshadow you and sent down on you the manna and the quails, (saying): Eat of the good things wherewith We have provided you- they wronged Us not, but they did wrong themselves.

2:58 And when We said: Go into this township and eat freely of that which is therein, and enter the gate prostrate, and say: "Repentance." We will forgive you your sins and will increase (*REWARD*) for the right-doers.

2:59 But *THOSE WHO DID WRONG CHANGED THE WORD WHICH HAD BEEN TOLD THEM FOR ANOTHER SAYING, AND WE SENT DOWN UPON THE EVIL-DOERS WRATH FROM HEAVEN FOR THEIR EVIL-DOING.*

2:60 And when Moses asked for water for his people, We said: Smite with thy staff the rock. And there gushed out therefrom twelve springs (so that) each tribe knew their drinking-place. Eat and drink of that which Allah hath provided, and *DO NOT ACT CORRUPTLY*, making mischief in the earth.

2:61 And when ye said: O Moses! We are weary of one kind of food; so call upon thy Lord for us that He bring forth for us of that which the earth groweth - of its herbs and its cucumbers and its corn and its lentils and its onions. He said: Would ye exchange that which is higher for that which is lower? Go down to settled country, thus ye shall get that which ye demand. And *HUMILIATION AND WRETCHEDNESS WERE STAMPED UPON THEM AND THEY WERE VISITED WITH WRATH FROM ALLAH. THAT WAS BECAUSE THEY DISBELIEVED IN ALLAH'S REVELATIONS AND SLEW THE PROPHETS WRONGFULLY.* That was for their disobedience and transgression. [Each translation agrees that there are good reasons for killing Prophets.]

2:62 ~~Lo! Those who believe (in that which is revealed unto thee, Muhammad), and those who are Jews, and Christians, and Sabaeans -- whoever believeth in Allah and the Last Day and doeth right - surely their reward is with their Lord, and there shall no fear come upon them neither shall they grieve.~~ [Cancelled by verse 3:85 i.e. Allah is not the God of Christians and Jews.][446]

2:63 And (remember, *O CHILDREN OF ISRAEL*) when We made a *COVENANT* with you and caused the mount to tower above you, (saying): Hold fast that which We have given you, and remember that which is therein, that ye may ward off (*EVIL*).

2:64 Then, even after that, ye turned away, and if it had not been for the grace of Allah and His mercy ye had been among the losers.

2:65 And ye know of those of you who broke the Sabbath, how We said unto them: Be ye apes, despised and hated!

2:66 And We made it an example to their own and to succeeding generations, and an admonition to the Allah-fearing.

2:67 And when Moses said unto his people: Lo! Allah commandeth you that ye sacrifice a cow, they said: Dost thou make game of us? He answered: Allah forbid that I should be among the foolish!

2:68 They said: Pray for us unto thy Lord that He make clear to us what (cow) she is. (Moses) answered: Lo! He saith, Verily she is a cow neither with calf nor immature; (she is) between the two conditions; so do that which ye are commanded.

2:69 They said: Pray for us unto thy Lord that He make clear to us of what colour she is. (Moses) answered: Lo! He saith: Verily she is a yellow cow. Bright is her colour, gladdening beholders.

2:70 They said: Pray for us unto thy Lord that He make clear to us what (cow) she is. Lo! cows are much alike to us; and Lo! if Allah wills, we may be led aright.

2:71 (Moses) answered: Lo! He saith: Verily she is a cow unyoked; she plougheth not the soil nor watereth the tilth; whole and without mark. They said: Now thou bringest *THE TRUTH*. So they sacrificed her, though almost they did not.

2:72 And (remember) when ye slew a man and disagreed concerning it and Allah brought forth that which ye were hiding.

2:73 And We said: Smite him with some of it. Thus Allah bringeth the dead to life and showeth you His portents so that ye may understand.

2:74 Then, even after that, your hearts were hardened and became as rocks, or worse than rocks, for hardness. For indeed there are rocks from out which rivers gush, and indeed there are rocks which split asunder so that water floweth from them. And indeed there are rocks which fall down for the fear of Allah. Allah is not unaware of what ye do.

2:75 Have ye any hope that they will be true to you when *A PARTY OF THEM USED TO LISTEN TO THE WORD OF ALLAH, THEN USED TO CHANGE IT*, after they had understood it, knowingly?

2:76 And when they fall in with those who *BELIEVE*, they say: We *BELIEVE*. But when they go apart one with another they say: Prate ye to them of that which Allah hath disclosed to you that they may contend with you before your Lord concerning it? Have ye then no sense?

2:77 Are they then unaware that Allah knoweth that which they keep hidden and that which they proclaim?

2:78 Among them are unlettered folk who know the Scripture not except from hearsay. They but guess.

2:79 Therefore *WOE BE UNTO THOSE WHO WRITE THE SCRIPTURE WITH THEIR HANDS AND THEN SAY, "THIS IS FROM ALLAH,"* that they may purchase a small gain therewith. Woe unto them for that their hands have written, and woe unto them for that they earn thereby.

2:80 *AND THEY SAY: THE FIRE (OF PUNISHMENT) WILL NOT TOUCH US* save for a certain number of days. Say: Have ye received a *COVENANT* from Allah - truly Allah will not break His *COVENANT* - or tell ye concerning Allah that which ye know not?

2:81 Nay, but whosoever hath done *EVIL* and his sin surroundeth him; such are rightful *OWNERS OF THE FIRE*; they will abide therein.

2:82 And *THOSE WHO BELIEVE AND DO GOOD WORKS; SUCH ARE RIGHTFUL OWNERS OF THE GARDEN*. They will abide therein.

2:83 And (remember) when We made a *COVENANT* with the *CHILDREN OF ISRAEL*, (saying): Worship none save Allah (only), and be good to parents and to kindred and to orphans and the needy, and speak kindly to mankind; and establish worship and pay the poor-due. Then, after that, ye slid back, save a few of you, being averse.[Part cancelled by verse 9:5][447]

2:84 And when We made with you a *COVENANT* (saying): Shed not the blood of *YOUR PEOPLE* nor turn (a party of) your people out of your dwellings. Then ye ratified (Our *COVENANT*) and ye were witnesses (thereto).

2:85 Yet ye it is who slay each other and drive out a party of *YOUR PEOPLE* from their homes, supporting one another against them by sin and transgression? - and if they came to you as captives ye would ransom them, whereas their expulsion was itself unlawful for you - *BELIEVE YE IN PART OF THE SCRIPTURE AND DISBELIEVE YE IN PART THEREOF*? And what is the *REWARD* of those who do so save ignominy in the life of the world, and on *THE DAY OF RESURRECTION* they will be consigned to the *MOST GRIEVOUS DOOM*. For Allah is not unaware of what ye do.

2:86 Such are those who buy the life of the world at the price of the Hereafter. Their punishment will not be lightened, neither will they have support.

2:87 And verily We gave unto Moses the Scripture and We caused a train of messengers to follow after him, and We gave unto *JESUS, SON OF MARY*, *CLEAR PROOFS* (of Allah's sovereignty), and We supported him with the Holy spirit. Is it ever so, that, when there cometh unto you a messenger (from Allah) with that which ye yourselves desire not, ye grow arrogant, and some ye *DISBELIEVE* and some ye slay?

2:88 And they say: Our hearts are hardened. Nay, but *ALLAH HATH CURSED THEM FOR THEIR UNBELIEF. LITTLE IS THAT WHICH THEY BELIEVE*.

2:89 And when there cometh unto them a scripture from Allah, confirming that in their possession - though before that they were asking for *A SIGNAL TRIUMPH OVER THOSE WHO DISBELIEVED* - and when there cometh unto them that which they know (to be *THE TRUTH*) they *DISBELIEVE* therein. *THE CURSE OF ALLAH IS ON DISBELIEVERS*.

2:90 *EVIL IS THAT FOR WHICH THEY SELL THEIR SOULS*: that they should *DISBELIEVE* in that which Allah hath revealed, grudging that Allah should reveal of His bounty unto *WHOM HE WILL OF HIS SLAVES*. They have incurred anger upon anger. *FOR DISBELIEVERS IS A SHAMEFUL DOOM*.

2:91 And when it is said unto them: *BELIEVE* in that which Allah hath revealed, they say: We *BELIEVE* in that which was revealed unto us. And they *DISBELIEVE* in that which cometh after it, though *IT IS THE TRUTH* confirming that which they possess. Say (unto them, O Muhammad): Why then slew ye the prophets of Allah aforetime, if ye are (indeed) *BELIEVERS*?

2:92 And Moses came unto you with *CLEAR PROOFS* (of Allah's Sovereignty), yet, while he was away, ye chose the calf (for worship) and ye were wrong-doers.

2:93 And when We made with you a *COVENANT* and caused the Mount to tower above you, (saying): Hold fast by that which We have given you, and hear (Our Word), they said: We hear and we rebel. And (worship of) the calf was made to sink into their hearts because of their rejection (of the *COVENANT*). Say (unto them): *EVIL* is that which your *BELIEF* enjoineth on you, if ye are *BELIEVERS*.

2:94 Say (unto them): If the abode of the Hereafter in the providence of Allah is indeed for you alone and not for others of mankind (as ye pretend), *THEN LONG FOR DEATH* (for ye must long for death) if ye are truthful. [This sentiment is the basis for the Jihadi threat "we love death as you love life". Note that Pickthall inserts the idea that those who believe in Islam "long for death".]

2:95 But they will never long for it, because of that which their own hands have sent before them. *ALLAH IS AWARE OF EVIL-DOERS*.

2:96 And thou wilt find them *GREEDIEST OF MANKIND FOR LIFE AND (GREEDIER) THAN THE IDOLATERS. (EACH) ONE OF THEM WOULD LIKE TO BE ALLOWED TO LIVE A THOUSAND YEARS*. And to live (a thousand years) would be no means remove him from the doom. Allah is Seer of what they do. [Again, believers hold earthly life in scant regard, seeing that a concern to preserve life as a characteristic of people other than Muslims.]

2:97 Say (O Muhammad, to mankind): Who is an enemy to Gabriel! For he it is who hath revealed (this Scripture) to thy heart by Allah's leave, confirming that which was (revealed) before it, and a guidance and glad tidings to *BELIEVERS*;

2:98 Who is an enemy to Allah, and His angels and His messengers, and Gabriel and Michael! Then, lo! *ALLAH (HIMSELF) IS AN ENEMY TO THE DISBELIEVERS*.

2:99 Verily We have revealed unto thee clear tokens, and *ONLY MISCREANTS WILL DISBELIEVE* in them.

2:100 Is it ever so that when they make a *COVENANT* a party of them set it aside? *THE TRUTH IS, MOST OF THEM BELIEVE NOT.*

2:101 And when there cometh unto them a messenger from Allah, confirming that which they possess, a party of those who have received the Scripture fling the Scripture of Allah behind their backs as if they knew not,

2:102 And follow that which the devils falsely related against the kingdom of Solomon. Solomon *DISBELIEVED* not; but the devils *DISBELIEVED*, teaching mankind magic and that which was revealed to the two angels in Babel, Harut and Marut. Nor did they (the two angels) teach it to anyone till they had said: We are only a temptation, therefore *DISBELIEVE* not (in the guidance of Allah). And from these two (angles) people learn that by which they cause division between man and wife; but they injure thereby no-one save by Allah's leave. And they learn that which harmeth them and profiteth them not. And surely they do know that he who trafficketh therein will have no (happy) portion in the Hereafter; and surely *EVIL IS THE PRICE FOR WHICH THEY SELL THEIR SOULS*, if they but knew.

2:103 And *IF THEY HAD BELIEVED AND KEPT FROM EVIL*, a *RECOMPENSE FROM ALLAH* would be better, if they only knew.

2:104 O *YE WHO BELIEVE*, say not (unto the Prophet): "Listen to us" but say "Look upon us," and be ye listeners. *FOR DISBELIEVERS IS A PAINFUL DOOM.*

2:105 Neither *THOSE WHO DISBELIEVE AMONG THE PEOPLE OF THE SCRIPTURE* nor the *IDOLATERS* love that there should be sent down unto you any good thing from your Lord. But *ALLAH CHOOSETH FOR HIS MERCY WHOM HE WILL*, and Allah is of Infinite Bounty.

2:106 Nothing of our revelation (even a single verse) do we *ABROGATE* or cause be forgotten, but we bring (in place) one better or the like thereof. Knowest thou not that Allah is Able to do all things?

2:107 Knowest thou not that it is Allah unto Whom belongeth the Sovereignty of the heavens and the earth; and ye have not, beside Allah, any guardian or helper?

2:108 Or would ye question your messenger as Moses was questioned aforetime? He *WHO CHOOSETH DISBELIEF INSTEAD OF FAITH*, verily he *HATH GONE ASTRAY FROM A PLAIN ROAD.*

2:109 ~~Many of the people of the Scripture long to make you disbelievers after your belief, through envy on their own account, after the truth hath become manifest unto them. Forgive and be indulgent (toward them) until Allah give command. Lo! Allah is Able to do all things.~~ [Cancelled by verse 9:29, i.e. there is to be no tolerance of those who reject Islam.][448]

2:110 Establish worship, and pay the poor-due; and whatever of good ye send before (you) for your souls, ye will find it with Allah. Lo! Allah is Seer of what ye do.

2:111 And they say: None entereth paradise unless he be a *JEW* or a *CHRISTIAN*. These are their own desires. Say: Bring your proof (of what ye state) if ye are truthful.

2:112 Nay, but whosoever surrendereth his purpose to Allah while doing good, his *REWARD* is with his Lord; and there shall no fear come upon them neither shall they grieve.

2:113 And *THE JEWS SAY THE CHRISTIANS FOLLOW NOTHING (TRUE), AND THE CHRISTIANS SAY THE JEWS FOLLOW NOTHING (TRUE);* yet both are readers of the Scripture. Even thus speak *THOSE WHO KNOW NOT.* Allah will judge between them on *THE DAY OF RESURRECTION* concerning that wherein they differ.

2:114 And who doth greater wrong than he who forbiddeth the approach to the sanctuaries of Allah lest His name should be mentioned therein, and striveth for their ruin. As for such, it was never meant that they should enter them except in fear. *THEIRS IN THE WORLD IS IGNOMINY AND THEIRS IN THE HEREAFTER IS AN AWFUL DOOM.*

2:115 ~~Unto Allah belong the East and the West, and whithersoever ye turn, there is Allah's Countenance. Lo! Allah is All-Embracing, All-Knowing.~~ [Cancelled by verse 2:144][449]

2:116 *AND THEY SAY: ALLAH HATH TAKEN UNTO HIMSELF A SON.* Be He glorified! Nay, but whatsoever is in the heavens and the earth is His. All are subservient unto Him.

2:117 The Originator of the heavens and the earth! When He decreeth a thing, He saith unto it only: Be! and it is.

2:118 *AND THOSE WHO HAVE NO KNOWLEDGE SAY: WHY DOTH NOT ALLAH SPEAK UNTO US, OR SOME SIGN COME UNTO US? EVEN THUS, AS THEY NOW SPEAK, SPAKE THOSE (WHO WERE) BEFORE THEM. THEIR HEARTS ARE ALL ALIKE. WE HAVE MADE CLEAR THE REVELATIONS FOR PEOPLE WHO ARE SURE.* [Those who ask for evidence for the veracity of Islam are unbelievers. Believers are judged believers on the grounds that they are completely unquestioning. Islam is thus purely dogmatic.]

2:119 Lo! We have sent thee (O Muhammad) with *THE TRUTH,* a bringer of glad tidings and a warner. And thou wilt not be asked about the *OWNERS OF HELL-FIRE*.

2:120 And *THE JEWS WILL NOT BE PLEASED WITH THEE, NOR WILL THE CHRISTIANS, TILL THOU FOLLOW THEIR CREED.* Say: Lo! the guidance of Allah (Himself) is Guidance. And if thou shouldst follow their desires after the knowledge which hath come unto thee, then wouldst thou have from Allah no protecting guardian nor helper.

2:121 Those unto whom We have given the Scripture, who read it with the right reading, those *BELIEVE* in it. And *WHOSO DISBELIEVETH IN IT, THOSE ARE THEY WHO ARE THE LOSERS.*

2:122 O *CHILDREN OF ISRAEL*! Remember My favour wherewith I favoured you and how I preferred you to (all) creatures.

2:123 And *GUARD (YOURSELVES) AGAINST A DAY* when no soul will in aught avail another, nor will compensation be accepted from it, nor will intercession be of use to it; nor will they be helped.

2:124 And (remember) when his Lord tried Abraham with (His) commands, and he fulfilled them, He said: Lo! I have appointed thee a leader for mankind. (Abraham) said: And of my offspring (will there be leaders)? He said: *MY COVENANT INCLUDETH NOT WRONG-DOERS.*

2:125 And when We made the House (at Makka) a resort for mankind and sanctuary, (saying): Take as your place of worship the place where Abraham stood (to pray). And We imposed a duty upon Abraham and Ishmael, (saying): Purify My house for those who go around and those who meditate therein and those who bow down and prostrate themselves (in worship).

2:126 And when Abraham prayed: My Lord! Make this a region of security and bestow upon its people fruits, *SUCH OF THEM AS BELIEVE IN ALLAH AND THE LAST DAY,* He answered: As for him who *DISBELIEVETH,* I shall leave him in contentment for a while, then I shall *COMPEL HIM TO THE DOOM OF FIRE* - a hapless journey's end!

2:127 And when Abraham and Ishmael were raising the foundations of the House, (Abraham prayed): Our Lord! Accept from us (this duty). Lo! Thou, only Thou, art the Hearer, the Knower.

2:128 Our Lord! And make us submissive unto Thee and of our seed a nation submissive unto Thee, and show us our ways of worship, and relent toward us. Lo! Thou, only Thou, art the Relenting, the Merciful.

2:129 Our Lord! And raise up in their midst a messenger from among them who shall recite unto them Thy revelations, and shall instruct them in the Scripture and in wisdom and shall make them grow. Lo! Thou, only Thou, art the Mighty, Wise.

2:130 And who forsaketh the religion of Abraham save him who befooleth himself? Verily We chose him in the world, and lo! in the Hereafter he is among the righteous.

2:131 When his Lord said unto him: Surrender! he said: I have surrendered to the Lord of the Worlds.

2:132 The same did Abraham enjoin upon his sons, and also Jacob, (saying): O my sons! Lo! Allah hath chosen for you the (true) religion; therefore die not save as men who have surrendered (unto Him).

2:133 Or were ye present when death came to Jacob, when he said unto his sons: What will ye worship after me? They said: We shall worship thy god, the god of thy fathers, Abraham and Ishmael and Isaac, One Allah, and unto Him we have surrendered.

2:134 Those are a people who have passed away. Theirs is that which they earned, and yours is that which ye earn. And ye will not be asked of what they used to do.

2:135 And they say: Be *JEWS* or *CHRISTIANS*, then ye will be rightly guided. Say (unto them, O Muhammad): Nay, but (we follow) the religion of Abraham, the upright, and he was not of the *IDOLATERS*.

2:136 Say (O *MUSLIMS*): We *BELIEVE* in Allah and that which is revealed unto us and that which was revealed unto Abraham, and Ishmael, and Isaac, and Jacob, and the tribes, and that which Moses and *JESUS* received, and that which the prophets received from their Lord. We make no distinction between any of them, and unto Him *WE HAVE SURRENDERED.*

2:137 And *IF THEY BELIEVE IN THE LIKE OF THAT WHICH YE BELIEVE, THEN ARE THEY RIGHTLY GUIDED. BUT IF THEY TURN AWAY, THEN ARE THEY IN SCHISM,* and Allah will suffice thee (for defence) against them. He is the Hearer, the Knower.

2:138 (We take our) colour from Allah, and who is better than Allah at colouring. We are His worshippers.

2:139 ~~Say (unto the People of the Scripture): Dispute ye with us concerning Allah when He is our Lord and your Lord? Ours are our works and yours your works. We look to Him alone.~~ [Cancelled by verse 9:5, i.e. commands to tolerance replaced by commands to violence][450]

2:140 Or say ye that Abraham, and Ishmael, and Isaac, and Jacob, and the tribes were *JEWS* or *CHRISTIANS*? Say: Do ye know best, or doth Allah? And who is more unjust than he who hideth a testimony which he hath received from Allah? Allah is not unaware of what ye do.

2:141 Those are a people who have passed away; theirs is that which they earned and yours that which ye earn. And ye will not be asked of what they used to do.

2:142 The foolish of the people will say: What hath turned them from the qiblah which they formerly observed? Say: Unto Allah belong the East and the West. He guideth whom He will unto *A STRAIGHT PATH*.

2:143 Thus We have appointed you a middle nation, that ye may be witnesses against mankind, and that the messenger may be a witness against you. And We appointed the qiblah which ye formerly observed only that We might know him who followeth the messenger, from him who turneth on his heels. In truth it was a hard (test) save for those whom Allah guided. But it was not Allah's purpose that your faith should be in vain, for Allah is Full of Pity, Merciful toward mankind.

2:144 We have seen the turning of thy face to heaven (for guidance, O Muhammad). And now verily We shall make thee turn (in prayer) toward a qiblah which is dear to thee. So turn thy face toward the Inviolable Place of Worship, and ye (O *MUSLIMS*), wheresoever ye may be, turn your faces (when ye pray) toward it. Lo! Those who have received the Scripture know that *(THIS REVELATION) IS THE TRUTH* from their Lord. And Allah is not unaware of what they do.

2:145 And even if thou broughtest unto those who have received the Scripture all kinds of portents, they would not follow thy qiblah, nor canst thou be a follower of their qiblah; nor are some of them followers of the qiblah of others. And if thou shouldst follow their desires after the knowledge which hath come unto thee, then surely wert thou of the *EVIL-DOERS*.

2:146 Those unto whom We gave the Scripture recognise (this revelation) as they recognise their sons. But lo! *A PARTY OF THEM KNOWINGLY CONCEAL THE TRUTH*.

2:147 *IT IS THE TRUTH FROM THY LORD (O MUHAMMAD), SO BE NOT THOU OF THOSE WHO WAVER.*

2:148 And each one hath a goal toward which he turneth; so vie with one another in good works. Wheresoever ye may be, Allah will bring you all together. Lo! Allah is Able to do all things.

2:149 And whencesoever thou comest forth (for prayer, O Muhammad) turn thy face toward the Inviolable Place of Worship. Lo! *IT IS THE TRUTH FROM THY LORD*. Allah is not unaware of what ye do.

2:150 Whencesoever thou comest forth turn thy face toward the Inviolable Place of Worship; and wheresoever ye may be (O *MUSLIMS*) turn your faces toward it (when ye pray) so that men may have no argument against you, save such of them as do injustice - Fear them not, but *FEAR ME*! - and so that I may complete My grace upon you, and that ye may be guided.

2:151 Even as We have sent unto you a messenger from among you, who reciteth unto you Our revelations and causeth you to grow, and teacheth you the Scripture and wisdom, and teacheth you that which ye knew not.

2:152 Therefore remember Me, I will remember you. Give thanks to Me, and reject not Me.

2:153 O *YE WHO BELIEVE*! Seek help in steadfastness and prayer. Lo! Allah is with the steadfast.

2:154 And *CALL NOT THOSE [JIHADIS] WHO ARE SLAIN IN THE WAY OF ALLAH "DEAD"*. Nay, they are living, only ye perceive not. [Jihadi martyrs are alive in Paradise for eternity]

2:155 And surely We shall try you with something of fear and hunger, and loss of wealth and lives and crops; but give glad tidings to the steadfast,

2:156 Who say, when a misfortune striketh them: Lo! we are Allah's and lo! unto Him we are returning.

2:157 Such are they on whom are blessings from their Lord, and mercy. Such are the rightly guided.

2:158 Lo! (the mountains) As-Safa and Al-Marwah are among the indications of Allah. It is therefore no sin for him who is on pilgrimage to the House (of Allah) or visiteth it, to go around them (as the pagan custom is). And he who doeth good of his own accord, (for him) lo! Allah is Responsive, Aware.

2:159 ~~Lo! Those who hide the proofs and the guidance which We revealed, after We had made it clear to mankind in the Scripture: such are accursed of Allah and accursed of those who have the power to curse.~~ [Cancelled by verse 2:160][451]

2:160 Except those who repent and amend and make manifest (*THE TRUTH*). These it is toward whom I relent. I am the Relenting, the Merciful.

2:161 Lo! *THOSE WHO DISBELIEVE, AND DIE WHILE THEY ARE DISBELIEVERS; ON THEM IS THE CURSE OF ALLAH* and of angels and of men combined.

2:162 They ever dwell therein. *THE DOOM WILL NOT BE LIGHTENED FOR THEM*, neither will they be reprieved.

2:163 Your Allah is One Allah; there is no God save Him, the Beneficent, the Merciful.

2:164 Lo! In the creation of the heavens and the earth, and the difference of night and day, and the ships which run upon the sea with that which is of use to men, and the water which Allah sendeth down from the sky, thereby reviving the earth after its death, and dispersing all kinds of beasts therein, and (in) the ordinance of the winds, and the clouds obedient between heaven and earth: are signs (of Allah's Sovereignty) for people who have sense.

2:165 Yet of mankind are some who take unto themselves (objects of worship which they set as) rivals to Allah, loving them with a love like (that which is the due) of Allah (only) - *THOSE WHO BELIEVE ARE STAUNCHER IN THEIR LOVE FOR ALLAH* - Oh, that *THOSE WHO DO EVIL* had but known, (on the day) when they behold the doom, that power belongeth wholly to Allah, and that *ALLAH IS SEVERE IN PUNISHMENT!*

2:166 *(ON THE DAY) WHEN THOSE WHO WERE FOLLOWED DISOWN THOSE WHO FOLLOWED (THEM), AND THEY BEHOLD THE DOOM*, and all their aims collapse with them.

2:167 And those who were but followers will say: If a return were possible for us, we would disown them even as they have disowned us. Thus will Allah show them their own deeds as anguish for them, and *THEY WILL NOT EMERGE FROM THE FIRE*.

2:168 O mankind! Eat of that which is lawful and wholesome in the earth, and follow not the footsteps of the devil. Lo! he is an open enemy for you.

2:169 He enjoineth upon you only the *EVIL* and the foul, and that ye should tell concerning Allah that which ye know not.

2:170 And when it is said unto them: Follow that which Allah hath revealed, they say: *WE FOLLOW THAT WHEREIN WE FOUND OUR FATHERS. WHAT! EVEN THOUGH THEIR FATHERS WERE WHOLLY UNINTELLIGENT AND HAD NO GUIDANCE?* [Islam has no respect for *OTHER* belief systems.]

2:171 The likeness of *THOSE WHO DISBELIEVE* (in relation to the messenger) is as the likeness of one who calleth unto that which heareth naught except a shout and cry. *DEAF, DUMB, BLIND, THEREFORE THEY HAVE NO SENSE.*

2:172 O *YE WHO BELIEVE*! Eat of the good things wherewith We have provided you, and render thanks to Allah if it is (indeed) He Whom ye worship.

2:173 He hath forbidden you only carrion, and blood, and swineflesh, and that which hath been immolated to (the name of) any other than Allah. *BUT HE WHO IS DRIVEN BY NECESSITY, NEITHER CRAVING NOR TRANSGRESSING, IT IS NO SIN FOR HIM.* Lo! Allah is Forgiving, Merciful. [Again, "forbidden" foods can be eaten, including pork, provided such foods are eaten out of hunger and not out of desire.]

2:174 Lo! those who hide aught of the Scripture which Allah hath revealed and purchase a small gain therewith, *THEY EAT INTO THEIR BELLIES NOTHING ELSE THAN FIRE*. Allah will not speak to them on *THE DAY OF RESURRECTION*, nor will He make them grow. Theirs will be *A PAINFUL DOOM*.

2:175 Those are they who purchase error at the price of guidance, and torment at the price of pardon. *HOW CONSTANT ARE THEY IN THEIR STRIFE TO REACH THE FIRE*!

2:176 That is because Allah hath revealed *THE SCRIPTURE WITH THE TRUTH*. Lo! *THOSE WHO FIND (A CAUSE OF) DISAGREEMENT IN THE SCRIPTURE ARE IN OPEN SCHISM*.

2:177 It is not righteousness that ye turn your faces to the East and the West; but *RIGHTEOUS IS HE WHO BELIEVETH IN ALLAH AND THE LAST DAY* and the angels and the Scripture and the prophets; and giveth wealth, for love of Him, to kinsfolk and to orphans and the needy and the wayfarer and to those who ask, and to set slaves free; and observeth proper worship and payeth the poor-due. And those who keep their treaty when they make one, and the patient in tribulation and adversity and time of stress. Such are they who are sincere. Such are the Allah-fearing.

2:178 O *YE WHO BELIEVE*! *RETALIATION IS PRESCRIBED FOR YOU IN THE MATTER OF THE MURDERED*; the freeman for the freeman, and the slave for the slave, and the female for the female. And for him who is forgiven somewhat by his (injured) brother, prosecution according to usage and payment unto him in kindness. This is an alleviation and a mercy from your Lord. He who transgresseth after this will have *A PAINFUL DOOM*.

2:179 And there is life for you in retaliation, O men of understanding, that ye may ward off (evil).

2:180 ~~It is prescribed for you, when death approacheth one of you, if he leave wealth, that he bequeath unto parents and near relatives in kindness. (This is) a duty for all those who ward off (evil).~~ [Cancelled by verse 4:11][452]

2:181 And whoso changeth (the will) after he hath heard it - the sin thereof is only upon those who change it. Lo! Allah is Hearer, Knower.

2:182 But he who feareth from a testator some unjust or sinful clause, and maketh peace between the parties, (it shall be) no sin for him. Lo! Allah is Forgiving, Merciful.

2:183 ~~O ye who believe! Fasting is prescribed for you, even as it was prescribed for those before you, that ye may ward off (evil);~~ [Cancelled by verse 2:187][453]

2:184 ~~(Fast) a certain number of days; and (for) him who is sick among you, or on a journey, (the same) number of other days; and for those who can afford it there is a ransom: the feeding of a man in need - but whoso doeth good of his own accord, it is better for him: and that ye fast is better for you if ye did but know -~~ [Cancelled by verse 2:185][454]

2:185 The month of Ramadan in which was revealed the Qur'an, a guidance for mankind, and *CLEAR PROOFS* of the guidance, and the Criterion (of right and wrong). And whosoever of you is present, let him fast the month, and whosoever of you is sick or on a journey, (let him fast the same) number of other days. Allah desireth for you ease; He desireth not hardship for you; and (He desireth) that ye should complete the period, and that ye should magnify Allah for having guided you, and that peradventure ye may be thankful.

2:186 And when My servants question thee concerning Me, then surely I am nigh. I answer the prayer of the suppliant when he crieth unto Me. So let them hear My call and let them trust in Me, in order that they may be led aright.

2:187 It is made lawful for you to go in unto your wives on the night of the fast. They are raiment for you and ye are raiment for them. Allah is Aware that ye were deceiving yourselves in this respect and He hath turned in mercy toward you and relieved you. So hold intercourse with them and seek that which Allah hath ordained for you, and *EAT AND DRINK UNTIL THE WHITE THREAD BECOMETH DISTINCT TO YOU FROM THE BLACK THREAD OF THE DAWN*. Then strictly observe the fast till nightfall and touch them not, but be at your devotions in the mosques. These are the limits imposed by Allah, so approach them not. Thus Allah expoundeth His revelation to mankind that they may ward off (*EVIL*).

2:188 And eat not up your property among yourselves in vanity, nor seek by it to gain the hearing of the judges that ye may knowingly devour a portion of the property of others wrongfully.

2:189 They ask thee, (O Muhammad), of new moons, say: They are fixed seasons for mankind and for the pilgrimage. It is not righteousness that ye go to houses by the backs thereof (as do the *IDOLATERS* at certain seasons), but the righteous man is he who wardeth off (*EVIL*). So go to houses by the gates thereof, and *OBSERVE YOUR DUTY TO ALLAH, THAT YE MAY BE SUCCESSFUL*.

2:190 ~~Fight in the way of Allah against those who fight against you, but begin not hostilities. Lo! Allah loveth not aggressors.~~ [Cancelled by verse 9:36, i.e. Jihad is not just a response to violence initiated by others.][455]

2:191 ~~And slay [kill] them wherever ye find them, and drive them out of the places whence they drove you out, for persecution is worse than slaughter. And fight not with them at the Inviolable Place of Worship until they first attack you there, but if they attack you (there) then slay [kill] them. Such is the reward of disbelievers.~~ [Cancelled by verse 9:5 i.e. the Verse of the Sword permits aggression instead of defence.][456]

2:192 ~~But if they desist, then lo! Allah is Forgiving, Merciful.~~ [Cancelled by verse 9:5, i.e. defensive jihad cancelled by permanent jihad][457]

2:193 And *FIGHT THEM UNTIL PERSECUTION IS NO MORE, AND RELIGION IS FOR ALLAH.* But if they desist, then let there be no hostility except against wrong-doers. [When the opponents submit, violence is only to be used against those who have been subjugated yet break the rules of Islam. Note that any freedom from Islam is seen as persecution of Muslims.]

2:194 The forbidden month for the forbidden month, and forbidden things in *RETALIATION*. And *ONE WHO ATTACKETH YOU, ATTACK HIM IN LIKE MANNER AS HE ATTACKED YOU. OBSERVE YOUR DUTY TO ALLAH*, and know that Allah is with those who ward off (*EVIL*).

2:195 *SPEND YOUR WEALTH FOR THE CAUSE OF ALLAH [JIHAD]*, and be not cast by your own hands to ruin; and do good. Lo! Allah loveth the beneficent.

2:196 Perform the pilgrimage and the visit (to Makka) for Allah. And if ye are prevented, then send such gifts as can be obtained with ease, and shave not your heads until the gifts have reached their destination. And whoever among you is sick or hath an ailment of the head must pay a ransom of fasting or almsgiving or offering. And if ye are in safety, then whosoever contenteth himself with the visit for the pilgrimage (shall give) such gifts as can be had with ease. And whosoever cannot find (such gifts), then a fast of three days while on the pilgrimage, and of seven when ye have returned; that is, ten in all. That is for him whoso folk are not present at the Inviolable Place of Worship. *OBSERVE YOUR DUTY TO ALLAH, AND KNOW THAT ALLAH IS SEVERE IN PUNISHMENT.*

2:197 The pilgrimage is (in) the well-known months, and whoever is minded to perform the pilgrimage therein (let him remember that) there is (to be) no lewdness nor abuse nor angry conversation on the pilgrimage. And whatsoever good ye do Allah knoweth it. So make provision for yourselves (hereafter); for the best provision is to ward off *EVIL*. Therefore *KEEP YOUR DUTY* unto Me, O *MEN OF UNDERSTANDING*.

2:198 It is no sin for you that ye seek the bounty of your Lord (by trading). But, when ye press on in the multitude from 'Arafat, remember Allah by the sacred monument. Remember Him as He hath guided you, although before ye were of those astray.

2:199 Then hasten onward from the place whence the multitude hasteneth onward, and ask forgiveness of Allah. Lo! Allah is Forgiving, Merciful.

2:200 And when ye have completed your devotions, then remember Allah as ye remember your fathers or with a more lively remembrance. But of mankind is he who saith: "Our Lord! Give unto us in the world," and he hath no portion in the Hereafter.

2:201 And of them (also) is he who saith: "Our Lord! Give unto us in the world that which is good and in the Hereafter that which is good, and *GUARD US FROM THE DOOM OF FIRE*."

2:202 For them *THERE IS IN STORE A GOODLY PORTION OUT OF THAT WHICH THEY HAVE EARNED. ALLAH IS SWIFT AT RECKONING.*

2:203 Remember Allah through the appointed days. Then whoso hasteneth (his departure) by two days, it is no sin for him, and whoso delayeth, it is no sin for him; that is for him who wardeth off (*EVIL*). *BE CAREFUL OF YOUR DUTY TO ALLAH*, and know that unto Him ye will be gathered.

2:204 And of mankind there is he whoso conversation on the life of this world pleaseth thee (Muhammad), and he calleth Allah to witness as to that which is in his heart; yet he is the most rigid of opponents.

2:205 And when he *TURNETH AWAY (FROM THEE) HIS EFFORT IN THE LAND IS TO MAKE MISCHIEF* therein and to destroy the crops and the cattle; and *ALLAH LOVETH NOT MISCHIEF.*

2:206 And when it is said unto him: *BE CAREFUL OF THY DUTY TO ALLAH*, pride taketh him to sin. *HELL WILL SETTLE HIS ACCOUNT, AN EVIL RESTING-PLACE.*

2:207 And of mankind is he who would sell himself, seeking the pleasure of Allah; and Allah hath compassion on (His) *BONDMEN*.

2:208 O *YE WHO BELIEVE*! Come, all of you, into submission (unto Him); and follow not the footsteps of the devil. Lo! he is an open enemy for you.

2:209 And *IF YE SLIDE BACK AFTER THE CLEAR PROOFS* have come unto you, then know that Allah is Mighty, Wise.

2:210 Wait they for naught else than that Allah should come unto them in the shadows of the clouds with the angels? Then the case would be already judged. *ALL CASES GO BACK TO ALLAH (FOR JUDGMENT).*

2:211 Ask of *THE CHILDREN OF ISRAEL* how many a clear revelation We gave them! He who altereth the grace of Allah after it hath come unto him (for him), lo! Allah is severe in punishment.

2:212 Beautified is the life of the world for *THOSE WHO DISBELIEVE*; they make a *JEST* of the *BELIEVERS*. But *THOSE WHO KEEP THEIR DUTY TO ALLAH WILL BE ABOVE THEM ON THE DAY OF RESURRECTION*. Allah giveth without stint to whom He will.

2:213 Mankind were one community, and Allah sent (unto them) prophets as bearers of good tidings and as warners, and revealed therewith the *SCRIPTURE WITH THE TRUTH* that it might judge between mankind concerning that wherein they differed. And only those unto whom (the Scripture) was given differed concerning it, after *CLEAR PROOFS* had come unto them, through hatred one of another. And Allah by His Will *GUIDED THOSE WHO BELIEVE UNTO THE TRUTH* of that concerning which they differed. *ALLAH GUIDETH WHOM HE WILL* unto *A STRAIGHT PATH*.

2:214 Or *THINK YE THAT YE WILL ENTER PARADISE* while yet there hath not come unto you the like of (that which came to) those who passed away before you? Affliction and adversity befell them, they were shaken as with earthquake, till the messenger (of Allah) and *THOSE WHO BELIEVED* along with him said: When cometh Allah's help? Now surely Allah's help is nigh.

2:215 ~~They ask thee, (O Muhammad), what they shall spend. Say: that which ye spend for good (must go) to parents and near kindred and orphans and the needy and the wayfarer. And whatsoever good ye do, lo! Allah is Aware of it.~~ [Cancelled by verse 9:60, which commands funding of jihad][458]

2:216 *WARFARE IS ORDAINED FOR YOU, THOUGH IT IS HATEFUL UNTO YOU*; but it may happen that *YE HATE A THING WHICH IS GOOD FOR YOU*, and it may happen that ye love a thing which is bad for you. Allah knoweth, ye know not.

2:217 ~~They question thee (O Muhammad) with regard to warfare in the sacred month.~~ Say: Warfare therein is a great (transgression), but to turn (men) from the way of Allah, and *TO DISBELIEVE IN HIM* and in the Inviolable Place of Worship, and to expel His people thence, *IS A GREATER SIN* with Allah; for persecution is worse than killing. And *THEY WILL NOT CEASE FROM FIGHTING AGAINST YOU TILL THEY HAVE MADE YOU RENEGADES FROM YOUR RELIGION*, if they can. And *WHOSO BECOMETH A RENEGADE AND DIETH IN HIS DISBELIEF; SUCH ARE THEY WHOSE WORKS HAVE FALLEN BOTH IN THE WORLD AND THE HEREAFTER. SUCH ARE RIGHTFUL OWNERS OF THE FIRE*: they will abide therein. [Note that disbelief is considered a worse sin than slaughtering disbelievers in warfare. Part cancelled by verse 9:5.][459]

2:218 Lo! *THOSE WHO BELIEVE*, and *THOSE WHO EMIGRATE* (to escape the persecution) *AND STRIVE [JIHAD] IN THE WAY OF ALLAH, THESE HAVE HOPE OF ALLAH'S MERCY*. Allah is Forgiving, Merciful. [Note that Pickthall inserts "to escape the persecution"; most other translations do not include this insertion, i.e. Muslims emigrate as part of expansionist Jihad, not to escape persecution. Also, the only Muslims with any hope of mercy from Allah on Judgement Day are those who spread Islam through Jihad or by emigrating to a non-Muslim land to colonise it.]

2:219 They question thee about strong drink and games of chance. Say: In both is great sin, and (some) utility for men; but the sin of them is greater than their usefulness. And they ask thee what they ought to spend. Say: that which is superfluous. Thus Allah maketh plain to you (His) revelations, that haply ye may reflect.

2:220 Upon the world and the Hereafter. And they question thee concerning orphans. Say: To improve their lot is best. And if ye mingle your affairs with theirs, then (they are) your brothers. Allah knoweth him who spoileth from him who improveth. Had Allah willed He could have overburdened you. Allah is Mighty, Wise.

2:221 ~~Wed not idolatresses till they believe; for lo!~~ *A BELIEVING BONDWOMAN [SLAVE] IS BETTER THAN AN IDOLATRESS THOUGH SHE PLEASE YOU;* and give not your daughters in marriage to *IDOLATERS* till they believe, for lo! a *BELIEVING* slave is better than an idolater though he please you. These invite unto *THE FIRE*, and Allah inviteth unto the Garden, and unto forgiveness by His grace, and expoundeth His revelations to mankind that haply they may remember. [Part cancelled by verse 5:5. Pickthall tries to conceal that he is talking about sex-slaves when he refers to "bondwoman".][460]

2:222 They question thee (O Muhammad) concerning menstruation. Say: It is an illness, so let women alone at such times and go not in unto them till they are cleansed. And when they have purified themselves, then go in unto them as Allah hath enjoined upon you. Truly Allah loveth those who turn unto Him, and loveth those who have a care for cleanness.

2:223 Your women are a tilth for you (to cultivate) so go to your tilth as ye will, and send (good deeds) before you for your souls, and fear Allah, and know that ye will (one day) meet Him. Give glad tidings to *BELIEVERS*, (O Muhammad).

2:224 And make not Allah, by your oaths, a hindrance to your being righteous and observing your duty unto Him and making peace among mankind. Allah is Hearer, Knower.

2:225 Allah will not take you to task for that which is unintentional in your oaths. But He will take you to task for that which your hearts have garnered. Allah is Forgiving, Clement.

2:226 Those who forswear their wives must wait four months; then, if they change their mind, lo! Allah is Forgiving, Merciful.

2:227 And if they decide upon divorce (let them remember that) Allah is Hearer, Knower.

2:228 ~~Women who are divorced shall wait, keeping themselves apart, three (monthly) courses. And it is not lawful for them that they should conceal that which Allah hath created in their wombs if they are believers in Allah and the Last Day. And their husbands would do better to take them back in that case if they desire a reconciliation. And they (women) have rights similar to those (of men) over them in kindness, and men are a degree above them. Allah is Mighty, Wise.~~ [Cancelled by verse 2:229 and by verse 2:230][461]

2:229 Divorce must be pronounced twice and then (a woman) must be retained in honour or released in kindness. ~~And it is not lawful for you that ye take from women aught of that which ye have given them~~; except (in the case) when both fear that they may not be able to keep within the limits (imposed by) Allah. And if ye fear that they may not be able to keep the limits of Allah, in that case it is no sin for either of them if the woman ransom herself. These are the limits (imposed by) Allah. Transgress them not. For whoso transgresseth Allah's limits: such are wrong-doers. [Part cancelled by the subsequent "except" clause of by verse 2:229][462]

2:230 And if he hath divorced her (the third time), then she is not lawful unto him thereafter until she hath wedded another husband. Then if he (the other husband) divorce her it is no sin for both of them that they come together again if they consider that they are able to observe the limits of Allah. These are the limits of Allah. He manifesteth them for people who have knowledge.

2:231 When ye have divorced women, and they have reached their term, then retain them in kindness or release them in kindness. Retain them not to their hurt so that ye transgress (the limits). He who doeth that hath wronged his soul. *MAKE NOT THE REVELATIONS OF ALLAH A LAUGHING-STOCK* (by your behaviour), but remember Allah's grace upon you and that which He hath revealed unto you of the Scripture and of wisdom, whereby He doth exhort you. *OBSERVE YOUR DUTY TO ALLAH* and know that Allah is Aware of all things.

2:232 And when ye have divorced women and they reach their term, place not difficulties in the way of their marrying their husbands if it is agreed between them in kindness. This is an admonition for him among *YOU WHO BELIEVETH IN ALLAH AND THE LAST DAY*. That is more virtuous for you, and cleaner. Allah knoweth; ye know not.

2:233 Mothers shall suckle their children for two whole years; (that is) for those who wish to complete the suckling. The duty of feeding and clothing nursing mothers in a seemly manner is upon the father of the child. No-one should be charged beyond his capacity. A mother should not be made to suffer because of her child, nor should he to whom the child is born (be made to suffer) because of his child. And on the (father's) heir is incumbent the like of that (which was incumbent on the father). If they desire to wean the child by mutual consent and (after) consultation, it is no sin for them; and if ye wish to give your children out to nurse, it is no sin for you, provide that ye pay what is due from you in kindness. *OBSERVE YOUR DUTY TO ALLAH*, and know that Allah is Seer of what ye do.

2:234 Such of you as die and leave behind them wives, they (the wives) shall wait, keeping themselves apart, four months and ten days. And when they reach the term (prescribed for them) then there is no sin for you in aught that they may do with themselves in decency. Allah is informed of what ye do.

2:235 There is no sin for you in that which ye proclaim or hide in your minds concerning your troth with women. Allah knoweth that ye will remember them. But plight not your troth with women except by uttering a recognised form of words. And do not consummate the marriage until (the term) prescribed is run. Know that Allah knoweth what is in your minds, so beware of Him; and know that Allah is Forgiving, Clement.

2:236 It is no sin for you if ye divorce women while yet ye have not touched them, nor appointed unto them a portion. Provide for them, the rich according to his means, and the straitened according to his means, a fair provision. (This is) a bounden duty for those who do good.

2:237 If ye divorce them before ye have touched them and ye have appointed unto them a portion, then (pay the) half of that which ye appointed, unless they (the women) agree to forgo it, or he agreeth to forgo it in whose hand is the marriage tie. To forgo is nearer to piety. And forget not kindness among yourselves. Allah is Seer of what ye do.

2:238 Be guardians of your prayers, and of the midmost prayer, and stand up with devotion to Allah.

2:239 And if ye go in fear, then (pray) standing or on horseback. And when ye are again in safety, remember Allah, as He hath taught you that which (heretofore) ye knew not.

2:240 (In the case of) those of you who are about to die and leave behind them wives, they should bequeath unto their wives a provision for the year without turning them out, but if they go out (of their own accord) there is no sin for you in that which they do of themselves within their rights. Allah is Mighty, Wise.

2:241 For divorced women a provision in kindness: a duty for those who ward off (*EVIL*).

2:242 Thus Allah expoundeth unto you His revelations so that ye may understand.

2:243 Bethink thee (O Muhammad) of those of old, who went forth from their habitations in their thousands, fearing death, and Allah said unto them: Die; and then He brought them back to life. Lo! Allah is a Lord of Kindness to mankind, but most of mankind give not thanks.

2:244 *FIGHT IN THE WAY OF ALLAH*, and know that Allah is Hearer, Knower.

2:245 *WHO IS IT THAT WILL LEND UNTO ALLAH A GOODLY LOAN, SO THAT HE MAY GIVE IT INCREASE MANIFOLD?* Allah straiteneth and enlargeth. Unto Him ye will return.

2:246 Bethink thee of the leaders of *THE CHILDREN OF ISRAEL* after Moses, how they said unto a prophet whom they had: Set up for us a king and *WE WILL FIGHT IN ALLAH'S WAY*. He said: *WOULD YE THEN REFRAIN FROM FIGHTING IF FIGHTING WERE PRESCRIBED FOR YOU?* They said: Why should we not fight in Allah's way when we have been driven from our dwellings with our children? Yet, *WHEN FIGHTING WAS PRESCRIBED FOR THEM, THEY TURNED AWAY, ALL SAVE A FEW OF THEM,* Allah is aware of *EVIL-DOERS.* [Those Muslims who will not fight when the conditions are right are considered evil in the value-system of Islam.]

2:247 Their Prophet said unto them: Lo! Allah hath raised up Saul to be a king for you. They said: How can he have kingdom over us when we are more deserving of the kingdom than he is, since he hath not been given wealth enough? He said: Lo! Allah hath chosen him above you, and hath increased him abundantly in wisdom and stature. Allah bestoweth His Sovereignty on whom He will. Allah is All-Embracing, All-Knowing.

2:248 And their Prophet said unto them: Lo! the token of his kingdom is that there shall come unto you the ark wherein is peace of reassurance from your Lord, and a remnant of that which the house of Moses and the house of Aaron left behind, the angels bearing it. Lo! herein shall be a token for you if (in truth) ye are *BELIEVERS*.

2:249 And when Saul set out with the army, he said: Lo! Allah will try you by (the ordeal of) a river. Whosoever therefore drinketh thereof he is not of me, and whosoever tasteth it not he is of me, save him who taketh (thereof) in the hollow of his hand. But they drank thereof, all save a few of them. And after he had crossed (the river), he and *THOSE WHO BELIEVED* with him, they said: We have no power this day against Goliath and his hosts [armies]. But those who knew that they would meet Allah exclaimed: How many a little company hath overcome a mighty host by Allah's leave! Allah is with the steadfast.

2:250 And when they went into the field against Goliath and his *HOSTS [ARMIES]* they said: Our Lord! Bestow on us endurance, make our foothold sure, and give us help against the *DISBELIEVING* folk.

2:251 So they routed them by Allah's leave and David slew Goliath; and Allah gave him the kingdom and wisdom, and taught him of that which He willeth. And if Allah had not repelled some men by others the earth would have been corrupted. But Allah is a Lord of Kindness to (His) creatures.

2:252 These are the portents of Allah which We recite unto thee (Muhammad) with truth, and lo! thou art of the number of (Our) messengers;

2:253 Of those messengers, some of whom We have caused to excel others, and of whom there are some unto whom Allah spake, while some of them He exalted (above others) in degree; and We gave *JESUS, SON OF MARY, CLEAR PROOFS* (of Allah's Sovereignty) and We supported him with the holy Spirit. And if Allah had so wiled it, those who followed after them would not have fought one with another after the *CLEAR PROOFS* had come unto them. But they differed, some of them *BELIEVING* and some *DISBELIEVING*. And if Allah had so willed it, they would not have fought one with another; but Allah doeth what He will.

2:254 O *YE WHO BELIEVE*! Spend of that wherewith We have provided you ere a day come when there will be no trafficking, nor friendship, nor intercession. *THE DISBELIEVERS, THEY ARE THE WRONG-DOERS.*

2:255 Allah! There is no deity save Him, the Alive, the Eternal. Neither slumber nor sleep overtaketh Him. Unto Him belongeth whatsoever is in the heavens and whatsoever is in the earth. Who is he that intercedeth with Him save by His leave? He knoweth that which is in front of them and that which is behind them, while they encompass nothing of His knowledge save what He will. His throne includeth the heavens and the earth, and He is never weary of preserving them. He is the Sublime, the Tremendous.

2:256 ~~There is no compulsion in religion. The right direction is henceforth distinct from error.~~ And he who rejecteth false deities and *BELIEVETH* in Allah hath grasped a firm handhold which will never break. Allah is Hearer, Knower. [Part cancelled by verse 9:5][463]

2:257 Allah is the Protecting Guardian of those who *BELIEVE*. He bringeth them out of darkness into light. As *FOR THOSE WHO DISBELIEVE, THEIR PATRONS ARE FALSE DEITIES*. They bring them out of light into darkness. *SUCH ARE RIGHTFUL OWNERS OF THE FIRE. THEY WILL ABIDE THEREIN.*

2:258 Bethink thee of him who had an argument with Abraham about his Lord, because Allah had given him the kingdom; how, when Abraham said: My Lord is He Who giveth life and causeth death, he answered: I give life and cause death. Abraham said: Lo! Allah causeth the sun to rise in the East, so do thou cause it to come up from the West. Thus was the *DISBELIEVER* abashed. And Allah guideth not wrongdoing folk.

2:259 Or (bethink thee of) the like of him who, passing by a township which had fallen into utter ruin, exclaimed: How shall Allah give this township life after its death? And Allah made him die a hundred years, then brought him back to life. He said: How long hast thou tarried? (The man) said: I have tarried a day or part of a day. (He said): Nay, but thou hast tarried for a hundred years. Just look at thy food and drink which have not rotted! Look at thine ass! And, that We may make thee a token unto mankind, look at the bones, how We adjust them and then cover them with flesh! And when (the matter) became clear unto him, he said: I know now that Allah is Able to do all things.

2:260 And when Abraham said (unto his Lord): My Lord! Show me how Thou givest life to the dead, He said: Dost thou not *BELIEVE*? Abraham said: Yea, but (I ask) in order that my heart may be at ease. (His Lord) said: Take four of the birds and cause them to incline unto thee, then place a part of them on each hill, then call them, they will come to thee in haste, and know that Allah is Mighty, Wise.

2:261 The likeness of *THOSE WHO SPEND THEIR WEALTH IN ALLAH'S WAY* [Jihad] is as the likeness of a grain which groweth seven ears, in every ear a hundred grains. Allah giveth increase manifold to whom He will. Allah is All-Embracing, All-Knowing.

2:262 *THOSE WHO SPEND THEIR WEALTH FOR THE CAUSE OF ALLAH [JIHAD]* and afterward make not reproach and injury to follow that which they have spent; *THEIR REWARD IS WITH THEIR LORD*, and there shall no fear come upon them, *NEITHER SHALL THEY GRIEVE*.

2:263 A kind word with forgiveness is better than almsgiving followed by injury. Allah is Absolute, Clement.

2:264 O *YE WHO BELIEVE*! Render not vain your almsgiving by reproach and injury, like him who spendeth his wealth only to be seen of men and *BELIEVETH* not in *ALLAH AND THE LAST DAY*. His likeness is as the likeness of a rock whereon is dust of earth; a rainstorm smiteth it, leaving it smooth and bare. They have no control of aught of that which they have gained. Allah guideth not the *DISBELIEVING* folk.

2:265 And the likeness of those who spend their wealth in search of Allah's pleasure, and for the strengthening of their souls, is as the likeness of a garden on a height. The rainstorm smiteth it and it bringeth forth its fruit twofold. And if the rainstorm smite it not, then the shower. Allah is Seer of what ye do.

2:266 Would any of you like to have a garden of palm-trees and vines, with rivers flowing underneath it, with all kinds of fruit for him therein; and old age hath stricken him and he hath feeble offspring; and a fiery whirlwind striketh it and it is (all) consumed by fire. Thus Allah maketh plain His revelations unto you, in order that ye may give thought.

2:267 O *YE WHO BELIEVE*! Spend of the good things which ye have earned, and of that which We bring forth from the earth for you, and seek not the bad (with intent) to spend thereof (in charity) when ye would not take it for yourselves save with disdain; and know that Allah is Absolute, Owner of Praise.

2:268 The devil promiseth you destitution and enjoineth on you lewdness. But Allah promiseth you forgiveness from Himself with bounty. Allah is All-Embracing, All-Knowing.

2:269 *HE GIVETH WISDOM UNTO WHOM HE WILL*, and he unto whom wisdom is given, he truly hath received abundant good. But none remember except men of understanding.

2:270 Whatever alms ye spend or vow ye vow, lo! Allah knoweth it. Wrong-doers have no helpers.

2:271 If ye publish your almsgiving, it is well, but if ye hide it and give it to the poor, it will be better for you, and will atone for some of your ill-deeds. Allah is Informed of what ye do.

2:272 The guiding of them is not thy duty (O Muhammad), but *ALLAH GUIDETH WHOM HE WILL*. And whatsoever good thing ye spend, it is for yourselves, when ye spend not save in search of Allah's Countenance; and whatsoever good thing ye spend, it will be repaid to you in full, and ye will not be wronged.

2:273 (Alms are) for the poor who are straitened for the cause of Allah, who cannot travel in the land (for trade). The unthinking man accounteth them wealthy because of their restraint. Thou shalt know them by their mark: They do not beg of men with importunity. And whatsoever good thing ye spend, lo! Allah knoweth it.

2:274 *THOSE WHO SPEND THEIR WEALTH* by night and day, *BY STEALTH AND OPENLY*, verily *THEIR REWARD IS WITH THEIR LORD*, and their shall no fear come upon them neither shall they grieve.

2:275 *THOSE WHO SWALLOW USURY* cannot rise up save as he ariseth whom the devil hath prostrated by (his) touch. That is because they say: Trade is just like usury; whereas Allah permitteth trading and forbiddeth usury. He unto whom an admonition from his Lord cometh, and (he) refraineth (in obedience thereto), he shall keep (the profits of) that which is past, and his affair (henceforth) is with Allah. As for him who returneth (to usury) - Such are *RIGHTFUL OWNERS OF THE FIRE*. They will abide therein.

2:276 Allah hath blighted usury and made almsgiving fruitful. Allah loveth not the impious and guilty.

2:277 Lo! *THOSE WHO BELIEVE AND DO GOOD WORKS AND ESTABLISH WORSHIP* and pay the poor-due, their *REWARD IS WITH THEIR LORD* and there shall no fear come upon them neither shall they grieve. [The "poor due" is a deceitful way of translating "Zakat" - and Zakat includes the funding of Jihad.]

2:278 *O YE WHO BELIEVE! OBSERVE YOUR DUTY TO ALLAH, AND GIVE UP WHAT REMAINETH (DUE TO YOU) FROM USURY, IF YE ARE (IN TRUTH) BELIEVERS*.

2:279 *AND IF YE DO NOT, THEN BE WARNED OF WAR (AGAINST YOU) FROM ALLAH AND HIS MESSENGER.* And if ye repent, then ye have your principal (without interest). Wrong not, and ye shall not be wronged.

2:280 And if the debtor is in straitened circumstances, then (let there be) postponement to (the time of) ease; and that ye remit the debt as almsgiving would be better for you if ye did but know.

2:281 And guard yourselves against *A DAY IN WHICH YE WILL BE BROUGHT BACK TO ALLAH*. Then every soul *WILL BE PAID IN FULL THAT WHICH IT HATH EARNED*, and they will not be wronged.

2:282 O *YE WHO BELIEVE*! When ye contract a debt for a fixed term, record it in writing. Let a scribe record it in writing between you in (terms of) equity. No scribe should refuse to write as Allah hath taught him, so let him write, and let him who incurreth the debt dictate, and let him observe his duty to Allah his Lord, and diminish naught thereof. But if he who oweth the debt is of low understanding, or weak, or unable himself to dictate, then let the guardian of his interests dictate in (terms of) equity. And call to witness, from among your men, two witnesses. And if two men be not (at hand) then a man and two women, of such as ye approve as witnesses, so that if the one erreth (through forgetfulness) the other will remember. And the witnesses must not refuse when they are summoned. Be not averse to writing down (the contract) whether it be small or great, with (record of) the term thereof. That is more equitable in the sight of Allah and more sure for testimony, and the best way of avoiding doubt between you; save only in the case when it is actual merchandise which ye transfer among yourselves from hand to hand. In that case it is no sin for you if ye write it not. And have witnesses when ye sell one to another, and let no harm be done to scribe or witness. If ye do (harm to them) lo! it is a sin in you. *OBSERVE YOUR DUTY TO ALLAH*. Allah is teaching you. And Allah is knower of all things.

2:283 If ye be on a journey and cannot find a scribe, then a pledge in hand (shall suffice). And if one of you entrusteth to another let him who is trusted deliver up that which is entrusted to him (according to the pact between them) and let him observe his duty to Allah his Lord. Hide not testimony. He who hideth it, verily his heart is sinful. Allah is Aware of what ye do.

2:284 Unto Allah (belongeth) whatsoever is in the heavens and whatsoever is in the earth; and whether ye make known what is in your minds or hide it, Allah will bring you to account for it. He will forgive whom He will and *HE WILL PUNISH WHOM HE WILL.* Allah is Able to do all things.

2:285 The messenger believeth in that which hath been revealed unto him from his Lord and (so do) BELIEVERS. Each one believeth in Allah and His angels and His scriptures and His messengers - We make no distinction between any of His messengers - and they say: *WE HEAR, AND WE OBEY.* (Grant us) Thy forgiveness, our Lord. Unto Thee is the journeying.

2:286 *ALLAH TASKETH NOT A SOUL BEYOND ITS SCOPE*. For it (is only) that which it hath earned, and against it (only) that which it hath deserved. Our Lord! Condemn us not if we forget, or miss the mark! Our Lord! Lay not on us such a burden as thou didst lay on those before us! Our Lord! Impose not on us that which we have not the strength to bear! Pardon us, absolve us and have mercy on us, Thou, our Protector, and *GIVE US VICTORY OVER THE DISBELIEVING FOLK*. [When Allah demands Jihad of some Muslim, that Muslim has no excuse unless he is crippled and poverty-stricken.]

THE EARLY KORAN – MOHAMMED'S FAILURE

Chapter 83 - Defrauding

83:1 Woe unto the defrauders:

83:2 Those who when they take the measure from mankind demand it full,

83:3 But if they measure unto them or weight for them, they cause them loss.

83:4 Do such (men) not consider that they will be raised again

83:5 Unto *AN AWFUL DAY,*

83:6 *THE DAY WHEN (ALL) MANKIND STAND BEFORE THE LORD* of the Worlds?

83:7 Nay, but the record of the vile is in Sijjin -

83:8 Ah! what will convey unto thee what Sijjin is! -

83:9 A written record.

83:10 *WOE UNTO THE REPUDIATORS ON THAT DAY!*

83:11 *THOSE WHO DENY THE DAY OF JUDGMENT*

83:12 Which *NONE DENIETH SAVE EACH CRIMINAL TRANSGRESSOR,* [Pickthall says rejecting Islam is a crime.]

83:13 Who, *WHEN THOU READEST UNTO HIM OUR REVELATIONS, SAITH: (MERE) FABLES OF THE MEN OF OLD.*

83:14 Nay, but that which they have earned is rust upon their hearts.

83:15 Nay, but surely on that day they will be covered from (the mercy of) their Lord.

83:16 Then lo! *THEY VERILY WILL BURN IN HELL,*

83:17 *AND IT WILL BE SAID (UNTO THEM): THIS IS THAT WHICH YE USED TO DENY.*

83:18 Nay, but the record of the righteous is in 'Illiyin -

83:19 Ah, what will convey unto thee what 'Illiyin is! -

83:20 A written record,

83:21 Attested by those who are brought near (unto their Lord).

83:22 Lo! *THE RIGHTEOUS VERILY ARE IN DELIGHT,*

83:23 *ON COUCHES, GAZING,*

83:24 Thou wilt know in their faces the radiance of delight.

83:25 *THEY ARE GIVEN TO DRINK OF A PURE WINE, SEALED,*

83:26 Whose seal is musk - for this let (all) those strive who strive for bliss -

83:27 And mixed with water of Tasnim,

83:28 A spring whence those brought near (to Allah) drink.

83:29 Lo! *THE GUILTY USED TO LAUGH AT THOSE WHO BELIEVED,*

83:30 And wink one to another when they passed them;

83:31 *AND WHEN THEY RETURNED TO THEIR OWN FOLK, THEY RETURNED JESTING;*

83:32 And when they saw them said: Lo! these have gone astray.

83:33 Yet they were not sent as guardians over them.

83:34 *THIS DAY IT IS THOSE WHO BELIEVE WHO HAVE THE LAUGH OF DISBELIEVERS,*

83:35 On high couches, gazing.

83:36 *ARE NOT THE DISBELIEVERS PAID FOR WHAT THEY USED TO DO?*

Chapter 29 - The Spider

29:1 Alif. Lam. Mim.

29:2 Do men imagine that they will be left (at ease) because they say, We *BELIEVE,* and will not be tested with affliction?

29:3 Lo! We tested those who were before you. Thus *ALLAH KNOWETH THOSE WHO ARE SINCERE, AND KNOWETH THOSE WHO FEIGN.*

29:4 Or do those who do ill-deeds imagine that they can outstrip Us? *EVIL* (for them) is that which they decide.

29:5 Whoso looketh forward to the meeting with Allah (let him know that) *ALLAH'S RECKONING IS SURELY NIGH*, and He is the Hearer, the Knower.

29:6 And *WHOSOEVER STRIVETH [JIHAD], STRIVETH ONLY FOR HIMSELF*, for lo! Allah is altogether Independent of (His) creatures. [Jihad is an autonomous choice made by the individual in order for the Believer to be guaranteed eternity into Paradise.]

29:7 And as for *THOSE WHO BELIEVE* and *DO GOOD WORKS*, We shall remit from them their *EVIL* deeds and *SHALL REPAY THEM* the best that they did. [Killing for Islam is seen as a good deed, resulting in reward in Paradise.]

29:8 We have enjoined on man kindness to parents; but if they *STRIVE* to make thee join with Me that of which thou hast no knowledge, then *OBEY* them not. Unto Me is your return and I shall tell you what you used to do.

29:9 And as for *THOSE WHO BELIEVE AND DO GOOD WORKS*, We verily shall make them enter in among the righteous.

29:10 Of mankind is he who saith: We *BELIEVE* in Allah, but, if he be made to suffer for the sake of Allah, he mistaketh the persecution of mankind for Allah's punishment; and then, if *VICTORY* cometh from thy Lord, will say: Lo! we were with you (all the while). Is not Allah Best Aware of what is in the bosoms of (His) creatures?

29:11 Verily Allah knoweth those who *BELIEVE*, and verily He knoweth the *HYPOCRITES*.

29:12 *THOSE WHO DISBELIEVE* say unto *THOSE WHO BELIEVE*: Follow our way (of religion) and we verily will bear your sins (for you). They cannot bear aught of their sins. Lo! *THEY VERILY ARE LIARS.*

29:13 But they verily will bear their own loads and other loads beside their own, and they verily will be *QUESTIONED ON THE DAY OF RESURRECTION CONCERNING THAT WHICH THEY INVENTED.*

29:14 And verily we sent Noah (as Our messenger) unto his folk, and he continued with them for a thousand years save fifty years; and the flood engulfed them, for they were wrong-doers.

29:15 And We rescued him and those with him in the ship, and made of it a portent for the peoples.

29:16 And Abraham! (Remember) when he said unto his folk: Serve Allah, and *KEEP YOUR DUTY UNTO HIM*; that is better for you if ye did but know.

29:17 *YE SERVE INSTEAD OF ALLAH ONLY IDOLS, AND YE ONLY INVENT A LIE*. Lo! those whom ye serve instead of Allah own no provision for you. So seek your provision from Allah, and serve Him, and give thanks unto Him, (for) unto Him ye will be brought back.

29:18 But if ye deny, then nations have denied before you. The messenger is only to convey (the message) plainly.

29:19 See they not how Allah produceth creation, then reproduceth it? Lo! for Allah that is easy.

29:20 Say (O Muhammad): Travel in the land and see how He originated creation, then Allah bringeth forth the later growth. Lo! Allah is Able to do all things.

29:21 He punisheth whom He will and showeth mercy unto whom He will, and unto Him ye will be turned.

29:22 Ye cannot escape (from Him) in the earth or in the sky, and beside Allah there is for you no friend or helper.

29:23 *THOSE WHO DISBELIEVE* in the revelations of Allah and in (their) Meeting with Him, such have no hope of My mercy. *FOR SUCH THERE IS A PAINFUL DOOM.*

29:24 But the answer of his folk was only that they said: "Kill him" or "Burn him." Then Allah saved him from *THE FIRE*. Lo! herein verily are portents for folk who *BELIEVE*.

29:25 He said: Ye have chosen only idols instead of Allah. The love between you is only in the life of the world. Then on *THE DAY OF RESURRECTION* ye will deny each other and curse each other, and your *ABODE WILL BE THE FIRE*, and ye will have no helpers.

29:26 *AND LOT BELIEVED HIM*, and said: Lo! I am a fugitive unto my Lord. Lo! He, only He, is the Mighty, the Wise.

29:27 And We bestowed on him Isaac and Jacob, and We established the prophethood and the Scripture among his seed, and We *GAVE HIM HIS REWARD IN THE WORLD, AND LO! IN THE HEREAFTER HE VERILY IS AMONG THE RIGHTEOUS.*

29:28 And Lot! (Remember) when he said unto his folk: Lo! ye commit lewdness such as no creature did before you.

29:29 For come ye not in unto males, and cut ye not the road (for travellers), and commit ye not abomination in your meetings? But the answer of his folk was only that they said: Bring Allah's doom upon us if thou art a truthteller!

29:30 He said: My Lord! Give me *VICTORY* over folk who work *CORRUPTION*.

29:31 And when Our messengers brought Abraham the good news, they said: Lo! we are about to *DESTROY THE PEOPLE OF THAT TOWNSHIP, FOR ITS PEOPLE ARE WRONG-DOERS,*

29:32 He said: Lo! Lot is there. They said: We are best aware of who is there. We are to deliver him and his household, all save his wife, who is of those who stay behind.

29:33 And when Our messengers came unto Lot, he was troubled upon their account, for he could not protect them; but they said: Fear not, nor grieve! Lo! we are to deliver thee and thy household, (all) save thy wife, who is of those who stay behind.

29:34 Lo! We are about to *BRING DOWN UPON THE FOLK OF THIS TOWNSHIP A FURY* from the sky because they are *EVIL-LIVERS*.

29:35 And verily of that We have left a clear sign for people who have sense.

29:36 And unto Midian We sent Shu'eyb, their brother. He said: O my people! Serve Allah, and look forward to *THE LAST DAY*, and do not *EVIL, MAKING MISCHIEF, IN THE EARTH*.

29:37 But *THEY DENIED HIM*, and the dreadful earthquake took them, and morning found them prostrate in their dwelling place.

29:38 And (the tribes of) A'ad and Thamud! (Their fate) is manifest unto you from their (ruined and deserted) dwellings. Satan made their deeds seem fair unto them and so debarred them from the Way, though they were keen observers.

29:39 And Korah, Pharaoh and Haman! Moses came unto them with *CLEAR PROOFS* (of Allah's Sovereignty), but they were boastful in the land. And they were not winners (in the race).

29:40 So We took each one in his sin; of them was he on whom We sent a hurricane, and of them was he who was overtaken by the (Awful) Cry, and of them was he whom We caused the earth to swallow, and of them was he whom We drowned. It was not for Allah to wrong them, but they wronged themselves.

29:41 The likeness of *THOSE WHO CHOOSE OTHER PATRONS THAN ALLAH* is as the likeness of the spider when she taketh unto herself a house, and lo! the frailest of all houses is the spider's house, if they but knew.

29:42 Lo! Allah knoweth what thing they invoke instead of Him. He is the Mighty, the Wise.

29:43 As for these similitudes, We coin them for mankind, but none will grasp their meaning save the wise.

29:44 Allah created the heavens and the earth with truth. Lo! therein is indeed a portent for *BELIEVERS*.

29:45 Recite that which hath been inspired in thee of the Scripture, and establish worship. Lo! worship preserveth from lewdness and iniquity, but verily remembrance of Allah is more important. And Allah knoweth what ye do.

29:46 And argue not with the People of the Scripture unless it be in (a way) that is better, save with such of them as do wrong; and say: We *BELIEVE* in that which hath been revealed unto us and revealed unto you; our Allah and your Allah is One, and unto Him we surrender. [Part cancelled by verse 9:29 i.e. command to violent subjugation of unbelievers replaces command to indifference][464]

29:47 In like manner We have revealed unto thee the Scripture, and those unto whom We gave the Scripture aforetime will *BELIEVE* therein; and of these (also) there are some who *BELIEVE* therein. And none deny Our revelations save the *DISBELIEVERS*.

29:48 And thou (O Muhammad) wast not a reader of any scripture before it, nor didst thou write it with thy right hand, for then might those have doubted, who follow falsehood.

29:49 But it is clear revelations in the hearts of *THOSE WHO HAVE BEEN GIVEN KNOWLEDGE, AND NONE DENY OUR REVELATIONS SAVE WRONG-DOERS.*

29:50 And they say: Why are not portents sent down upon him from his Lord? Say: Portents are with Allah only, and I am but a plain warner. [Cancelled by verse 9:5, i.e. violence replaces speech][465]

29:51 Is it not enough for them that We have sent down unto thee the Scripture which is read unto them? Lo! herein verily is mercy, and a reminder *FOR FOLK WHO BELIEVE*.

29:52 Say (unto them, O Muhammad): Allah sufficeth for witness between me and you. He knoweth whatsoever is in the heavens and the earth. And *THOSE WHO BELIEVE IN VANITY AND DISBELIEVE IN ALLAH, THEY IT IS WHO ARE THE LOSERS*.

29:53 They bid thee hasten on the doom (of Allah). And if a term had not been appointed, the doom would assuredly have come unto them (ere now). And verily it will come upon them suddenly when they perceive not.

29:54 They bid thee hasten on the doom, when lo! *HELL VERILY WILL ENCOMPASS THE DISBELIEVERS.*

29:55 On *THE DAY WHEN THE DOOM WILL OVERWHELM THEM* from above them and from underneath their feet, and He will say: Taste what ye used to do!

29:56 O my *BONDMEN* who *BELIEVE*! Lo! My earth is spacious. Therefor *SERVE ME ONLY.*

29:57 Every soul will taste of death. Then unto Us ye will be returned.

29:58 *THOSE WHO BELIEVE AND DO GOOD WORKS,* them verily We shall house in lofty dwellings of the *GARDEN UNDERNEATH WHICH RIVERS FLOW.* There they will dwell secure. How sweet the guerdon of the toilers,

29:59 Who persevere, and put their trust in their Lord!

29:60 And how many an animal there is that beareth not its own provision! Allah provideth for it and for you. He is the Hearer, the Knower.

29:61 And if thou wert to ask them: Who created the heavens and the earth, and constrained the sun and the moon (to their appointed work)? they would say: Allah. How then are they turned away?

29:62 Allah maketh the provision wide for whom He will of His *BONDMEN*, and straiteneth it for whom (He will). Lo! Allah is Aware of all things.

29:63 And if thou wert to ask them: Who causeth water to come down from the sky, and therewith reviveth the earth after its death? they verily would say: Allah. Say: Praise be to Allah! But most of them have no sense.

29:64 This life of the world is but a pastime and a game. Lo! the home of the Hereafter - that is Life, if they but knew.

29:65 And when they mount upon the ships they pray to Allah, making their faith pure for Him only, but when He bringeth them safe to land, behold! they ascribe partners (unto Him),

29:66 *THAT THEY MAY DISBELIEVE* in that which We have given them, and that they may take their ease. *BUT THEY WILL COME TO KNOW.*

29:67 Have they not seen that We have appointed a sanctuary immune (from violence), while mankind are ravaged all around them? *DO THEY THEN BELIEVE IN FALSEHOOD AND DISBELIEVE IN THE BOUNTY OF ALLAH?*

29:68 Who doeth greater wrong than he who inventeth a lie concerning Allah, or denieth *THE TRUTH* when it cometh unto him? *IS NOT THERE A HOME IN HELL FOR DISBELIEVERS?*

29:69 *AS FOR THOSE WHO STRIVE* [Jihad] in Us, We surely guide them to *OUR PATHS*, and lo! Allah is with the good. [Jihad is rewarded.]

Chapter 30 - The Romans

30:1 Alif. Lam. Mim.

30:2 The Romans have been defeated,

30:3 In the nearer land, and they, after their defeat *WILL BE VICTORIOUS,*

30:4 Within ten years - Allah's is the command in the former case and in the latter - and in that day *BELIEVERS* will rejoice,

30:5 In Allah's help to *VICTORY. HE HELPETH TO VICTORY WHOM HE WILL*. He is the Mighty, the Merciful.

30:6 It is a promise of Allah. Allah faileth not His promise, but most of mankind know not.

30:7 They know only some appearance of the life of the world, and are heedless of the Hereafter.

30:8 Have they not pondered upon themselves? Allah created not the heavens and the earth, and that which is between them, save with truth and for a destined end. But truly many of mankind are *DISBELIEVERS* in the meeting with their Lord.

30:9 Have they not travelled in the land and seen the nature of the consequence for those who were before them? They were stronger than these in power, and they dug the earth and built upon it more than these have built. Messengers of their own came unto them with *CLEAR PROOFS* (of Allah's Sovereignty). Surely Allah wronged them not, but they did wrong themselves.

30:10 Then *EVIL WAS THE CONSEQUENCE TO THOSE WHO DEALT IN EVIL, BECAUSE THEY DENIED THE REVELATIONS OF ALLAH AND MADE A MOCK OF THEM.* [Islam cannot withstand mockery.]

30:11 Allah produceth creation, then He reproduceth it, then unto Him ye will be returned.

30:12 And in the day when the Hour riseth the unrighteous will despair.

30:13 There will be none to intercede for them of those whom they made equal with Allah. And *THEY WILL REJECT THEIR PARTNERS (WHOM THEY ASCRIBED UNTO HIM).*

30:14 *IN THE DAY WHEN THE HOUR COMETH*, in that day they will be sundered.

30:15 As for *THOSE WHO BELIEVED AND DID GOOD WORKS*, they *WILL BE MADE HAPPY IN A GARDEN*. [Eternal pleasure for Jihadis.]

30:16 But as for *THOSE WHO DISBELIEVED AND DENIED OUR REVELATIONS*, and *DENIED THE MEETING OF THE HEREAFTER*, such will be brought to doom. [No matter how good a non-Muslim is, he's destined for eternal torture simply for refusing to believe in eternal torture.]

30:17 So glory be to Allah when ye enter the night and when ye enter the morning -

30:18 Unto Him be praise in the heavens and the earth! - and at the sun's decline and in the noonday.

30:19 He bringeth forth the living from the dead, and He bringeth forth the dead from the living, and He reviveth the earth after her death. And even so will ye be brought forth.

30:20 And of His signs is this: He created you of dust, and behold you human beings, ranging widely!

30:21 And of His signs is this: He created for you helpmeets from yourselves that ye might find rest in them, and He ordained between you love and mercy. Lo! herein indeed are portents for folk who reflect.

30:22 And of His signs is the creation of the heavens and the earth, and the difference of your languages and colours. Lo! herein indeed are portents for *MEN OF KNOWLEDGE.*

30:23 And of His signs is your slumber by night and by day, and your seeking of His bounty. Lo! herein indeed are portents for folk who heed.

30:24 And of His signs is this: He showeth you the lightning for a fear and for a hope, and sendeth down water from the sky, and thereby quickeneth the earth after her death. Lo! herein indeed are portents for folk who understand.

30:25 And of His signs is this: The heavens and the earth stand fast by His command, and afterward, when He calleth you, lo! from the earth ye will emerge.

30:26 Unto Him belongeth whosoever is in the heavens and the earth. All are *OBEDIENT* unto Him.

30:27 He it is Who produceth creation, then reproduceth it, and it is easier for Him. His is the Sublime Similitude in the heavens and the earth. He is the Mighty, the Wise.

30:28 He coineth for you a similitude of yourselves. Have ye, *FROM AMONG THOSE WHOM YOUR RIGHT HANDS POSSESS [SLAVES]*, partners in the wealth We have bestowed upon you, equal with you in respect thereof, so that ye fear them as ye fear each other (that ye ascribe unto Us partners out of that which We created)? Thus *WE DISPLAY THE REVELATIONS FOR PEOPLE WHO HAVE SENSE.*

30:29 Nay, but *THOSE WHO DO WRONG* follow their own lusts without knowledge. *WHO IS ABLE TO GUIDE HIM WHOM ALLAH HATH SENT ASTRAY?* For such there are no helpers.

30:30 So set thy purpose (O Muhammad) for religion as a man by nature upright - the nature (framed) of Allah, in which He hath created man. There is no altering (the laws of) Allah's creation. *THAT IS THE RIGHT RELIGION, BUT MOST MEN KNOW NOT -*

30:31 Turning unto Him (only); and *BE CAREFUL OF YOUR DUTY UNTO HIM* and establish worship, and be not of those who ascribe partners (unto Him);

30:32 Of those who split up their religion and became schismatics, each sect exulting in its tenets.

30:33 And when harm toucheth men they cry unto their Lord, turning to Him in repentance; then, when they have tasted of His mercy, behold! some of them attribute partners to their Lord.

30:34 So as to *DISBELIEVE* in that which We have given them. (Unto such it is said): Enjoy yourselves awhile, but ye will come to know.

30:35 Or have We revealed unto them any warrant which speaketh of that which they associate with Him?

30:36 And when We cause mankind to taste of mercy they rejoice therein; but if an *EVIL* thing befall them as the consequence of their own deeds, lo! they are in despair!

30:37 See they not that Allah enlargeth the provision for whom He will, and straiteneth (it for whom He will). Lo! herein indeed are *PORTENTS FOR FOLK WHO BELIEVE.*

30:38 So give to the kinsman his due, and to the needy, and to the wayfarer. That is best for those who seek Allah's Countenance. And *SUCH ARE THEY WHO ARE SUCCESSFUL.*

30:39 That which ye give in usury in order that it may increase on (other) people's property hath no increase with Allah; but that which ye give in charity, seeking Allah's Countenance, hath increase manifold.

30:40 Allah is He Who created you and then sustained you, then causeth you to die, then giveth life to you again. Is there any of your (so-called) partners (of Allah) that doeth aught of that? Praised and Exalted be He above what they associate (with Him)!

30:41 *CORRUPTION* doth appear on land and sea because of (the *EVIL*) which men's hands have done, that He may make them taste a part of that which they have done, in order that they may return.

30:42 Say (O Muhammad, to the *DISBELIEVERS*): Travel in the land, and see the nature of the consequence for those who were before you! *MOST OF THEM WERE IDOLATERS.*

30:43 So set thy purpose resolutely for *THE RIGHT RELIGION*, before the inevitable day cometh from Allah. *ON THAT DAY* mankind will be sundered-

30:44 Whoso *DISBELIEVETH* must (then) *BEAR THE CONSEQUENCES OF HIS DISBELIEF*, while those who do right make provision for themselves -

30:45 That He may *REWARD* out of His bounty *THOSE WHO BELIEVE AND DO GOOD WORKS.* Lo! He loveth not the *DISBELIEVERS* (in His guidance).

30:46 And of His signs is this: He sendeth herald winds to make you taste His mercy, and that the ships may sail at His command, and that ye may seek his favour, and that haply ye may be thankful.

30:47 Verily We sent before thee (Muhammad) messengers to their own folk. Then we took vengeance upon those who were guilty (in regard to them). To *HELP BELIEVERS* is ever incumbent upon Us.

30:48 Allah is He Who sendeth the winds so that they raise clouds, and spreadeth them along the sky as pleaseth Him, and causeth them to break and thou seest the rain downpouring from within them. And when He maketh it to fall on whom He will of His *BONDMEN*, lo! they rejoice;

30:49 Though before that, even before it was sent down upon them, they were in despair.

30:50 Look, therefore, at the prints of Allah's mercy (in creation): how He quickeneth the earth after her death. Lo! He verily is the Quickener of the Dead, and He is Able to do all things.

30:51 And if We sent a wind and they beheld it yellow, they verily would still continue in their *DISBELIEF.*

30:52 For verily thou (Muhammad) canst not make the dead to hear, nor canst thou make the deaf to hear the call when they have turned to flee.

30:53 *NOR CANST THOU GUIDE THE BLIND OUT OF THEIR ERROR. THOU CANST MAKE NONE TO HEAR SAVE THOSE WHO BELIEVE IN OUR REVELATIONS SO THAT THEY SURRENDER (UNTO HIM).*

30:54 Allah is He Who shaped you out of weakness, then appointed after weakness strength, then, after strength, appointed weakness and grey hair. He createth what He will. He is the Knower, the Mighty.

30:55 And *ON THE DAY WHEN THE HOUR RISETH THE GUILTY WILL VOW* that they did tarry but an hour - thus were they ever deceived.

30:56 But those to whom knowledge and faith are given will say: The truth is, ye have tarried, by Allah's decree, until *THE DAY OF RESURRECTION*. This is *THE DAY OF RESURRECTION*, but ye used not to know.

30:57 In that day their excuses will not profit those who did injustice, nor will they be allowed to make amends.

30:58 Verily We have coined for mankind in this Qur'an all kinds of similitudes; and indeed if thou camest unto them with a miracle, *THOSE WHO DISBELIEVE* would verily exclaim: Ye are but tricksters!

30:59 Thus doth Allah seal the hearts of those who know not.

30:60 So have patience (O Muhammad)! Allah's promise is the very truth, and let not those who have no certainty make thee impatient. [Cancelled by verse 9:5, i.e. violence replaces patience][466]

Chapter 84 - The Sundering

84:1 When the heaven is split asunder

84:2 And attentive to her Lord in fear,

84:3 And when the earth is spread out

84:4 And hath cast out all that was in her, and is empty

84:5 And attentive to her Lord in fear!

84:6 Thou, verily, O man, art working toward thy Lord a work which thou wilt meet (in His presence).

84:7 Then *WHOSO IS GIVEN HIS ACCOUNT IN HIS RIGHT HAND* (other translators render "account" as "book" or "record").

84:8 He truly *WILL RECEIVE AN EASY RECKONING*
84:9 And will return unto his folk in joy.
84:10 But *WHOSO IS GIVEN HIS ACCOUNT BEHIND HIS BACK,*
84:11 He surely *WILL INVOKE DESTRUCTION*
84:12 And *BE THROWN TO SCORCHING FIRE.*
84:13 He verily lived joyous with his folk.
84:14 He verily deemed that he would never return (unto Allah).
84:15 Nay, but lo! his Lord is ever looking on him!
84:16 Oh, I swear by the afterglow of sunset,
84:17 And by the night and all that it enshroudeth,
84:18 And by the moon when she is at the full,
84:19 That ye shall journey on from plane to plane.
84:20 What aileth them, then, *THAT THEY BELIEVE NOT*
84:21 And, when the Qur'an is recited unto them, worship not (Allah)?
84:22 Nay, but *THOSE WHO DISBELIEVE WILL DENY;*
84:23 And *ALLAH KNOWETH BEST WHAT THEY ARE HIDING.*
84:24 So give them tidings of *A PAINFUL DOOM,*
84:25 Save *THOSE WHO BELIEVE AND DO GOOD WORKS, FOR THEIRS IS A REWARD UNFAILING.*

Chapter 82 - The Cleaving

82:1 When the heaven is cleft asunder,
82:2 When the planets are dispersed,
82:3 When the seas are poured forth,
82:4 And the sepulchres are overturned,
82:5 A soul will know what it hath sent before (it) and what left behind.
82:6 O man! What hath made thee careless concerning thy Lord, the Bountiful,
82:7 Who created thee, then fashioned, then proportioned thee?
82:8 Into whatsoever form He will, He casteth thee.
82:9 Nay, but *YE DENY THE JUDGMENT.*
82:10 Lo! there are above you guardians,
82:11 Generous and recording,
82:12 Who know (all) that ye do.
82:13 Lo! the righteous verily will be in delight.
82:14 And lo! *THE WICKED VERILY WILL BE IN HELL*;
82:15 *THEY WILL BURN THEREIN ON THE DAY OF JUDGMENT,*
82:16 And will not be absent thence.
82:17 Ah, what will convey unto thee what the Day of Judgment is!
82:18 Again, what will convey unto thee what the Day of Judgment is!
82:19 A day on which no soul hath power at all for any (other) soul. The (absolute) command on that day is Allah's.

Chapter 79 - Those who Drag Forth

79:1 By those who drag forth to destruction,
79:2 By the meteors rushing,
79:3 By the lone stars floating,
79:4 By the angels hastening,
79:5 And those who govern the event,
79:6 *ON THE DAY* when the first trump resoundeth.
79:7 And the second followeth it,
79:8 *ON THAT DAY* hearts beat painfully
79:9 While eyes are downcast
79:10 (Now) they are saying: Shall we really be restored to our first state
79:11 Even after we are crumbled bones?
79:12 They say: Then that would be a vain proceeding.

79:13 Surely it will need but one shout,
79:14 And lo! they will be awakened.
79:15 Hath there come unto thee the history of Moses?
79:16 How his Lord called him in the holy vale of Tuwa,
79:17 (Saying:) Go thou unto Pharaoh - Lo! he hath rebelled -
79:18 And say (unto him): Hast thou (will) to grow (in grace)?
79:19 Then I will guide thee to thy Lord and thou shalt fear (Him).
79:20 And he showed him the tremendous token.
79:21 But he denied and disobeyed,
79:22 Then turned he away in haste,
79:23 Then gathered he and summoned
79:24 And proclaimed: "I (Pharaoh) am your Lord the Highest."
79:25 So Allah seized him (and made him) an example for the after (life) and for the former.
79:26 Lo! herein is indeed a lesson for him who feareth.
79:27 Are ye the harder to create, or is the heaven that He built?
79:28 He raised the height thereof and ordered it;
79:29 And He made dark the night thereof, and He brought forth the morn thereof.
79:30 And after that He spread the earth,
79:31 And produced therefrom the water thereof and the pasture thereof,
79:32 And He made fast the hills,
79:33 A provision for you and for your cattle.
79:34 But when the great disaster cometh,
79:35 *THE DAY* when man will call to mind his (whole) endeavour,
79:36 And *HELL* will stand forth visible to him who seeth,
79:37 Then, *AS FOR HIM WHO REBELLED*
79:38 *AND CHOSE THE LIFE OF THE WORLD,*
79:39 Lo! *HELL WILL BE HIS HOME,*
79:40 But as *FOR HIM WHO FEARED* to stand before his Lord and restrained his soul from lust,
79:41 Lo! *THE GARDEN WILL BE HIS HOME.*
79:42 *THEY ASK THEE OF THE HOUR: WHEN WILL IT COME* to port?
79:43 Why (ask they)? What hast thou to tell thereof?
79:44 Unto thy Lord belongeth (knowledge of) the term thereof.
79:45 Thou art but a warner unto him who feareth it.
79:46 On the day when they behold it, it will be as if they had but tarried for an evening or the morn thereof.

Chapter 78 - The Tidings

78:1 Whereof do they question one another?
78:2 (It is) of the awful tidings,
78:3 Concerning which they are in disagreement.
78:4 Nay, but they will come to know!
78:5 Nay, again, but they will come to know!
78:6 Have We not made the earth an expanse,
78:7 And the high hills bulwarks?
78:8 And We have created you in pairs,
78:9 And have appointed your sleep for repose,
78:10 And have appointed the night as a cloak,
78:11 And have appointed the day for livelihood.
78:12 And We have built above you seven strong (heavens),
78:13 And have appointed a dazzling lamp,
78:14 And have sent down from the rainy clouds abundant water,
78:15 Thereby to produce grain and plant,
78:16 And gardens of thick foliage.
78:17 Lo! *THE DAY OF DECISION IS A FIXED TIME,*
78:18 *A DAY WHEN THE TRUMPET IS BLOWN* and ye come in multitudes,
78:19 And the heaven is opened and becometh as gates,

78:20 And the hills are set in motion and become as a mirage.
78:21 Lo! *HELL LURKETH IN AMBUSH,*
78:22 *A HOME FOR THE REBELLIOUS.*
78:23 They will abide therein for ages.
78:24 Therein taste they neither coolness nor (any) drink
78:25 Save *BOILING WATER AND A PARALYSING COLD*:
78:26 *REWARD PROPORTIONED (TO THEIR EVIL DEEDS).*
78:27 For lo! they looked not for a reckoning;
78:28 *THEY CALLED OUR REVELATIONS FALSE WITH STRONG DENIAL.*
78:29 Everything have We recorded in a Book.
78:30 So taste (of that which ye have earned). No increase do We give you save of *TORMENT.*
78:31 Lo! *FOR THE DUTEOUS IS ACHIEVEMENT -*
78:32 *GARDENS ENCLOSED AND VINEYARDS,*
78:33 *AND VOLUPTUOUS WOMEN OF EQUAL AGE;*
78:34 And a full cup.
78:35 There hear they never vain discourse, nor lying -
78:36 Requital from thy Lord - *A GIFT IN PAYMENT* – [most translations use "payment" or "recompense" for this verse].
78:37 Lord of the heavens and the earth, and (all) that is between them, the Beneficent; with Whom none can converse.
78:38 On *THE DAY WHEN THE ANGELS AND THE SPIRIT STAND ARRAYED*, they speak not, saving him whom the Beneficent alloweth and who speaketh right.
78:39 *THAT IS THE TRUE DAY.* So whoso will should seek recourse unto his Lord.
78:40 Lo! We warn you of a doom at hand, a day whereon a man will look on that which his own hands have sent before, and the *DISBELIEVER* will cry: "Would that I were dust!"

Chapter 70 - The Ascending Stairways

70:1 A questioner questioned concerning the doom about to fall
70:2 Upon the *DISBELIEVERS*, which none can repel,
70:3 From Allah, Lord of the Ascending Stairways
70:4 (Whereby) the angels and the Spirit ascend unto Him in a Day whereof the span is fifty thousand years.
70:5 ~~But be patient (O Muhammad) with a patience fair to see.~~ [Cancelled by verse 9:5][467]
70:6 Lo! they behold it afar off
70:7 While we behold it nigh:
70:8 *THE DAY* when the sky will become as molten copper,
70:9 And the hills become as flakes of wool,
70:10 And no familiar friend will ask a question of his friend
70:11 Though they will be given sight of them. The guilty man will long to be able to ransom himself from *THE PUNISHMENT OF THAT DAY* at the price of his children
70:12 And his spouse and his brother
70:13 And his kin that harboured him
70:14 And all that are in the earth, if then it might deliver him.
70:15 But nay! for lo! *IT IS THE FIRE OF HELL*
70:16 Eager to roast;
70:17 *IT CALLETH HIM WHO TURNED AND FLED (FROM TRUTH),*
70:18 And hoarded (wealth) and withheld it.
70:19 Lo! man was created anxious,
70:20 Fretful when evil befalleth him
70:21 And, when good befalleth him, grudging;
70:22 *SAVE WORSHIPPERS.*
70:23 *WHO ARE CONSTANT AT THEIR WORSHIP*
70:24 And in whose wealth there is a right acknowledged
70:25 For the beggar and the destitute;
70:26 And *THOSE WHO BELIEVE IN THE DAY OF JUDGMENT.*
70:27 And those who are fearful of their Lord's doom -

70:28 Lo! *THE DOOM OF THEIR LORD IS THAT BEFORE WHICH NONE CAN FEEL SECURE-*
70:29 And those who preserve their chastity
70:30 Save with their wives and *THOSE WHOM THEIR RIGHT HANDS POSSESS [SLAVES]*, for thus they are not blameworthy;
70:31 But whoso seeketh more than that, those are *THEY WHO ARE TRANSGRESSORS;*
70:32 And *THOSE WHO KEEP THEIR PLEDGES AND THEIR COVENANT,*
70:33 And those who stand by their testimony
70:34 And those who are attentive at their worship.
70:35 *THESE WILL DWELL IN GARDENS, HONOURED.*
70:36 What aileth *THOSE WHO DISBELIEVE*, that they keep staring toward thee (O Muhammad), open-eyed,
70:37 On the right and on the left, in groups?
70:38 Doth every man among them hope to enter *THE GARDEN OF DELIGHT*?
70:39 Nay, verily. Lo! We created them from what they know.
70:40 But nay! I swear by the Lord of the rising-places and the setting-places (of the planets) that We verily are Able
70:41 To replace them by (others) better than them. And we are not to be outrun.
70:42 ~~So let them chat and play until they meet their Day which they are promised,~~ [Cancelled by verse 9:5, i.e. command to violence replaces command to indifference and patience][468]
70:43 The day when they come forth from the graves in haste, as racing to a goal,
70:44 With eyes aghast, abasement stupefying them: Such is *THE DAY WHICH THEY ARE PROMISED.*

Chapter 69 - The Reality

69:1 The Reality!
69:2 What is the Reality?
69:3 Ah, what will convey unto thee what the reality is!
69:4 (The tribes of) Thamud and A'ad *DISBELIEVED IN THE JUDGMENT TO COME*.
69:5 As for Thamud, they were destroyed by the lightning.
69:6 And as for A'ad, they were destroyed by a fierce roaring wind,
69:7 Which He imposed on them for seven long nights and eight long days so that thou mightest have seen men lying overthrown, as they were hollow trunks of palm-trees.
69:8 Canst thou (O Muhammad) see any remnant of them?
69:9 And Pharaoh and those before him, and the communities that were destroyed, brought error,
69:10 And *THEY DISOBEYED THE MESSENGER OF THEIR LORD*, therefor did He grip them with a tightening grip.
69:11 Lo! when the waters rose, We carried you upon the ship
69:12 That We might make it a memorial for you, and that remembering ears (that heard the story) might remember.
69:13 And when *THE TRUMPET SHALL SOUND* one blast
69:14 And the earth with the mountains shall be lifted up and crushed with one crash,
69:15 Then, on that day will the Event befall.
69:16 And the heaven will split asunder, for that day it will be frail.
69:17 And the angels will be on the sides thereof, and eight will uphold the Throne of thy Lord that day, above them.
69:18 *ON THAT DAY YE WILL BE EXPOSED*; not a secret of you will be hidden.
69:19 Then, as for him *WHO IS GIVEN HIS RECORD IN HIS RIGHT HAND*, he will say: Take, read my book!
69:20 Surely I knew that I should have to *MEET MY RECKONING*.
69:21 *THEN HE WILL BE IN BLISSFUL STATE*
69:22 *IN A HIGH GARDEN*
69:23 Whereof the clusters are in easy reach.
69:24 (And it will be said unto those therein): Eat and drink at ease for that which ye sent on before you in past days.
69:25 But as for *HIM WHO IS GIVEN HIS RECORD IN HIS LEFT HAND*, he will say: Oh, would that I had not been given my book
69:26 And *KNEW NOT WHAT MY RECKONING*!
69:27 Oh, would that it had been death!

69:28 My wealth hath not availed me,

69:29 My power hath gone from me.

69:30 (It will be said): Take him and fetter him

69:31 And then *EXPOSE HIM TO HELL-FIRE*

69:32 And then insert him in a chain whereof the length is seventy cubits.

69:33 Lo! *HE USED NOT TO BELIEVE IN ALLAH* the Tremendous,

69:34 And urged not on the feeding of the wretched.

69:35 Therefor *HATH HE NO LOVER HERE THIS DAY,*

69:36 *NOR ANY FOOD SAVE FILTH*

69:37 Which none but sinners eat.

69:38 But nay! I swear by all that ye see

69:39 And all that ye see not

69:40 That it is indeed the speech of an illustrious messenger.

69:41 It is not poet's speech - little is it that ye *BELIEVE*!

69:42 Nor diviner's speech - little is it that ye remember!

69:43 It is a revelation from the Lord of the Worlds.

69:44 And if he had invented false sayings concerning Us,

69:45 We assuredly had taken him by the right hand

69:46 And then severed his life-artery,

69:47 And not one of you could have held Us off from him.

69:48 And lo! it is a warrant unto those who ward off (*EVIL*).

69:49 And lo! We know that some among you will deny (it).

69:50 And lo! it is indeed an *ANGUISH FOR THE DISBELIEVERS*.

69:51 And lo! *IT IS ABSOLUTE TRUTH*.

69:52 So glorify the name of thy Tremendous Lord.

Chapter 67 - The Sovereignty

67:1 Blessed is He in Whose hand is the Sovereignty, and, He is Able to do all things.

67:2 Who hath created life and death that He may try you which of you is best in conduct; and He is the Mighty, the Forgiving,

67:3 Who hath created seven heavens in harmony. Thou (Muhammad) canst see no fault in the Beneficent One's creation; then look again: Canst thou see any rifts?

67:4 Then look again and yet again, thy sight will return unto thee weakened and made dim.

67:5 And verily We have beautified the world's heaven with lamps, and We have made them missiles for the devils, and for them *WE HAVE PREPARED THE DOOM OF FLAME*.

67:6 And for *THOSE WHO DISBELIEVE* in their Lord there is *THE DOOM OF HELL*, a hapless journey's end!

67:7 When they are flung therein they hear its roaring as it boileth up,

67:8 As it would burst with rage. Whenever a (fresh) host is flung therein the wardens thereof ask them: Came there unto you no warner?

67:9 They say: Yea, verily, a warner came unto us; but we denied and said: Allah hath naught revealed; ye are in naught but a great error.

67:10 And they say: Had we been wont to listen or have sense, we had not been among *THE DWELLERS IN THE FLAMES.*

67:11 So they acknowledge their sins; but far removed (from mercy) are the dwellers in the flames.

67:12 Lo! those who fear their Lord in secret, theirs will be forgiveness and a great *REWARD*.

67:13 And keep your opinion secret or proclaim it, lo! He is Knower of all that is in the breasts (of men).

67:14 Should He not know what He created? And He is the Subtle, the Aware.

67:15 He it is Who hath made the earth subservient unto you, so Walk in the paths thereof and eat of His providence. And unto Him will be *THE RESURRECTION* (of the dead).

67:16 Have ye taken security from Him Who is in the heaven that He will not cause the earth to swallow you when lo! it is convulsed?

67:17 Or have ye taken security from Him Who is in the heaven that He will not let loose on you a hurricane? But ye shall know the manner of My warning.

67:18 And verily those before them denied, then (see) the manner of My wrath (with them)!

67:19 Have they not seen the birds above them spreading out their wings and closing them? Naught upholdeth them save the Beneficent. Lo! He is Seer of all things.

67:20 Or who is he that will be an army unto you to help you instead of the Beneficent? The *DISBELIEVERS ARE IN NAUGHT BUT ILLUSION.*

67:21 Or who is he that will provide for you if He should withhold His providence? Nay, but they are set in pride and frowardness.

67:22 Is he who goeth groping on his face more rightly guided, or he who walketh upright on a straight road?

67:23 Say (unto them, O Muhammad): He it is who gave you being, and hath assigned unto you ears and eyes and hearts. Small thanks give ye!

67:24 Say: He it is Who multiplieth you in the earth, and unto Whom ye will be gathered.

67:25 And they say: *WHEN (WILL) THIS PROMISE (BE FULFILLED), IF YE ARE TRUTHFUL?* [A reasonable question for his contemporaries to ask. Mohammed's predicted Day of Judgement is yet to arrive, 1400 years later.]

67:26 Say: The knowledge is with Allah only, and *I AM BUT A PLAIN WARNER;*

67:27 But when they see it nigh, the faces of *THOSE WHO DISBELIEVE* will be awry, and it will be said (unto them): This is that for which ye used to call.

67:28 Say (O Muhammad): Have ye thought: Whether Allah causeth me (Muhammad) and those with me to perish or hath mercy on us, still, *WHO WILL PROTECT THE DISBELIEVERS FROM A PAINFUL DOOM?*

67:29 Say: He is the Beneficent. In Him we *BELIEVE* and in Him we put our trust. And ye will soon know who it is that is in error manifest.

67:30 Say: Have ye thought: If (all) your water were to disappear into the earth, who then could bring you gushing water?

Chapter 52 - The Mount

52:1 By the Mount,

52:2 And a Scripture inscribed

52:3 On fine parchment unrolled,

52:4 And the House frequented,

52:5 And the roof exalted,

52:6 And the sea kept filled,

52:7 Lo! the doom of thy Lord will surely come to pass;

52:8 There is none that can ward it off.

52:9 On the day when the heaven will heave with (awful) heaving,

52:10 And the mountains move away with (awful) movement,

52:11 Then woe that day unto the deniers

52:12 Who play in talk of grave matters;

52:13 *THE DAY WHEN THEY ARE THRUST WITH A (DISDAINFUL) THRUST, INTO THE FIRE OF HELL.*

52:14 (And it is said unto them): This is *THE FIRE* which ye were wont to deny.

52:15 Is this magic, or do ye not see?

52:16 Endure the heat thereof, and whether ye are patient of it or impatient of it is all one for you. *YE ARE ONLY BEING PAID FOR WHAT YE USED TO DO.* [Other translations render this verse as "payment" or "recompense".]

52:17 Lo! *THOSE WHO KEPT THEIR DUTY DWELL IN GARDENS AND DELIGHT,*

52:18 Happy because of what their Lord hath given them, and (because) their Lord hath warded off *FROM THEM THE TORMENT OF HELL-FIRE.*

52:19 (And it is said unto them): *EAT AND DRINK IN HEALTH (AS A REWARD) FOR WHAT YE USED TO DO,*

52:20 Reclining on ranged couches. And *WE WED THEM UNTO FAIR ONES WITH WIDE, LOVELY EYES.*

52:21 And *THEY WHO BELIEVE AND WHOSE SEED FOLLOW THEM IN FAITH, WE CAUSE THEIR SEED TO JOIN THEM* (there), and We deprive them of nought of their (life's) work. Every man is a pledge for *THAT WHICH HE HATH EARNED.* [Those Muslims who get to Paradise can bring their relatives too.]

52:22 And We provide them with fruit and meat such as they desire.

52:23 There *THEY PASS FROM HAND TO HAND A CUP WHEREIN IS NEITHER VANITY NOR CAUSE OF SIN.*

52:24 And *THERE GO ROUND, WAITING ON THEM MENSERVANTS OF THEIR OWN, AS THEY WERE HIDDEN PEARLS.*

52:25 And some of them draw near unto others, questioning,

52:26 Saying: Lo! of old, when we were with our families, we were ever anxious;

52:27 But Allah hath been gracious unto us and hath preserved us from the torment of the breath of Fire.

52:28 Lo! we used to pray unto Him of old. Lo! He is the Benign, the Merciful.

52:29 Therefor *warn (men, O Muhammad). By the grace of Allah thou art neither soothsayer nor madman.* [Contemporaries of Mohammed said he was insane or a fantasist.]

52:30 Or say they: (he is) a poet, (one) for whom we may expect the accident of time?

52:31 ~~Say (unto them): Except (your fill)! Lo! I am with you among the expectant.~~ [Cancelled by verse 9:5][469]

52:32 Do their minds command them to do this, or are they an outrageous folk?

52:33 *Or say they: He hath invented it? Nay, but they will not believe*!

52:34 Then *let them produce speech the like thereof*, if they are truthful. [The literary quality of the Koran is supposed to be unsurpassed, that is the supposed guarantee of the truth of Islam.]

52:35 Or were they created out of naught? Or are they the creators?

52:36 Or did they create the heavens and the earth? Nay, but they are sure of nothing!

52:37 Or do they own the treasures of thy Lord? Or have they been given charge (thereof)?

52:38 Or have they any stairway (unto heaven) by means of which they overhear (decrees). Then let their listener produce some warrant manifest!

52:39 Or hath He daughters whereas ye have sons?

52:40 Or askest thou (Muhammad) a fee from them so that they are plunged in debt?

52:41 Or possess they the Unseen so that they can write (it) down?

52:42 Or seek they to ensnare (the messenger)? But *those who disbelieve, they are the ensnared*!

52:43 Or have they any god beside Allah? Glorified be Allah from all that they *ascribe as partner* (unto Him)!

52:44 And if they were to see a fragment of the heaven falling, they would say: A heap of clouds.

52:45 ~~Then let them be (O Muhammad), till they meet their day, in which they will be thunder-stricken,~~ [Cancelled by verse 9:5, command to violence replaces command to indifference][470]

52:46 *A day* in which their guile will naught avail them, nor will they be helped.

52:47 And verily, *for those who do wrong, there is a punishment beyond that*. But most of them know not.

52:48 ~~So wait patiently (O Muhammad) for thy Lord's decree, for surely thou art in Our sight;~~ and hymn the praise of thy Lord when thou uprisest, [patience abrogated by violence with verse 9:5]

52:49 And in the night-time also hymn His praise, and at the setting of the stars.

Chapter 32 - The Prostration

32:1 Alif. Lam. Mim

32:2 The revelation of *the Scripture whereof there is no doubt* is from the Lord of the Worlds.

32:3 Or say they: He hath invented it? Nay, but it is *the Truth* from thy Lord, that thou mayst warn a folk to whom no warner came before thee, that haply they may walk aright.

32:4 Allah it is Who created the heavens and the earth, and that which is between them, in six Days. Then He mounted the Throne. Ye have not, beside Him, a protecting friend or mediator. Will ye not then remember?

32:5 He directeth the ordinance from the heaven unto the earth; then it *ascendeth unto Him in a Day*, whereof the measure is a thousand years of that ye reckon.

32:6 Such is the Knower of the Invisible and the Visible, the Mighty, the Merciful,

32:7 Who made all things good which He created, and He began the creation of man from clay;

32:8 Then He made his seed from a draught of despised fluid;

32:9 Then He fashioned him and breathed into him of His Spirit; and appointed for you hearing and sight and hearts. Small thanks give ye!

32:10 And they say: When we are lost in the earth, how can we then be re-created? Nay but they are *disbelievers* in the meeting with their Lord.

32:11 Say: The angel of death, who hath charge concerning you, will gather you, and afterward unto your Lord ye will be returned.

32:12 Couldst thou but see when the guilty hang their heads before their Lord, (and say): Our Lord! We have now seen and heard, so send us back; we will do right, now we are sure.

32:13 And if We had so willed, We could have given every soul its guidance, but the word from Me concerning evildoers took effect: that *I WILL FILL HELL WITH THE JINN AND MANKIND TOGETHER.*

32:14 So *TASTE (THE EVIL OF YOUR DEEDS)*. Forasmuch as ye forgot *THE MEETING OF THIS YOUR DAY*, lo! We forget you. *TASTE THE DOOM OF IMMORTALITY* because of what ye used to do.

32:15 Only *THOSE BELIEVE* in Our revelations who, when they are reminded of them, fall down prostrate and hymn the praise of their Lord, and they are not scornful,

32:16 Who forsake their beds to cry unto their Lord in fear and hope, and spend of that We have bestowed on them.

32:17 No soul knoweth what is kept hid for them of joy, *AS A REWARD FOR WHAT THEY USED TO DO.*

32:18 *IS HE WHO IS A BELIEVER LIKE UNTO HIM WHO IS AN EVIL-LIVER*? They are not alike.

32:19 But as *FOR THOSE WHO BELIEVE AND DO GOOD WORKS, FOR THEM ARE THE GARDENS OF RETREAT* - a welcome (*IN REWARD*) *FOR WHAT THEY USED TO DO.*

32:20 And as *FOR THOSE WHO DO EVIL, THEIR RETREAT IS THE FIRE*. Whenever they desire to issue forth from thence, they are brought back thither. Unto them it is said: *TASTE THE TORMENT OF THE FIRE WHICH YE USED TO DENY.*

32:21 And verily We make them taste the lower punishment before the greater, that haply they may return.

32:22 And who doth greater wrong than he who is reminded of the revelations of his Lord, then turneth from them. Lo! *WE SHALL REQUITE THE GUILTY.*

32:23 We verily gave Moses the Scripture; so be not ye in doubt of his receiving it; and We appointed it a guidance for *THE CHILDREN OF ISRAEL*.

32:24 And when they became steadfast and *BELIEVED* firmly in Our revelations, *WE APPOINTED FROM AMONG THEM LEADERS WHO GUIDED BY OUR COMMAND.*

32:25 Lo! thy Lord will *JUDGE BETWEEN THEM* on *THE DAY OF RESURRECTION* concerning that wherein they used to differ.

32:26 Is it not a guidance for them (to observe) *HOW MANY GENERATIONS WE DESTROYED BEFORE THEM,* amid whose dwelling places they do walk? Lo! therein verily are portents! Will they not then heed?

32:27 Have they not seen how We lead the water to the barren land and therewith bring forth crops whereof their cattle eat, and they themselves? Will they not then see?

32:28 And they say: When cometh this *VICTORY* (of yours) if ye are *TRUTHFUL*?

32:29 Say (unto them): *ON THE DAY OF THE VICTORY* the faith of *THOSE WHO DISBELIEVE* (and who then will *BELIEVE*) will not avail them, neither will they be reprieved.

32:30 ~~So withdraw from them (O Muhammad), and await (the event). Lo! they (also) are awaiting (it).~~ [Cancelled by verse 9:5, i.e. command to violence replaces command to patience][471]

Chapter 23 - The Believers

23:1 *SUCCESSFUL INDEED ARE THE BELIEVERS*

23:2 Who are humble in their prayers,

23:3 And who shun vain conversation,

23:4 And who are payers of the poor-due;

23:5 And who guard their modesty -

23:6 Save from their wives or the *(SLAVES) THAT THEIR RIGHT HANDS POSSESS*, for then they are not blameworthy,

23:7 But whoso craveth beyond that, such are transgressors -

23:8 And who are shepherds of their pledge and their *COVENANT*,

23:9 And who pay heed to their prayers.

23:10 These are the heirs

23:11 *WHO WILL INHERIT PARADISE. THERE THEY WILL ABIDE.*

23:12 Verily We created man from a product of wet earth;

23:13 Then placed him as a drop (of seed) in a safe lodging;

23:14 Then fashioned We the drop a clot, then fashioned We the clot a little lump, then fashioned We the little lump bones, then clothed the bones with flesh, and then produced it as another creation. So blessed be Allah, the Best of creators!

23:15 Then lo! after that ye surely die.

23:16 Then lo! on *THE DAY OF RESURRECTION* ye are raised (again).

23:17 And We have created above you seven paths, and We are never unmindful of creation.

23:18 And we send down from the sky water in measure, and We give it lodging in the earth, and lo! We are Able to withdraw it.

23:19 Then We produce for you therewith gardens of date-palms and grapes, wherein is much fruit for you and whereof ye eat;

23:20 And a tree that springeth forth from Mount Sinai that groweth oil and relish for the eaters.

23:21 And lo! in the cattle there is verily a lesson for you. We give you to drink of that which is in their bellies, and many uses have ye in them, and of them do ye eat;

23:22 And on them and on the ship ye are carried.

23:23 And We verily sent Noah unto his folk, and he said: O my people! Serve Allah. Ye have no other Allah save Him. Will ye not ward off (*EVIL*)?

23:24 But the chieftains of his folk, *WHO DISBELIEVED, SAID: THIS IS ONLY A MORTAL LIKE YOU WHO WOULD MAKE HIMSELF SUPERIOR TO YOU.* Had Allah willed, He surely could have sent down angels. We heard not of this in the case of our fathers of old.

23:25 *HE IS ONLY A MAN IN WHOM IS A MADNESS*, so watch him for a while.

23:26 He said: My Lord! Help me because they deny me.

23:27 Then We inspired in him, saying: Make the ship under Our eyes and Our inspiration. Then, when Our command cometh and the oven gusheth water, introduce therein of every (kind) two spouses, and thy household save him thereof against whom the Word hath already gone forth. And plead not with Me on behalf of those who have done wrong. Lo! they will be drowned.

23:28 And when thou art on board the ship, thou and whoso is with thee, then say: Praise be to Allah Who hath saved us from the wrongdoing folk!

23:29 And say: My Lord! Cause me to land at a blessed landing-place, for Thou art Best of all who bring to land.

23:30 Lo! herein verily are portents, for lo! We are ever putting (mankind) to the test.

23:31 Then, after them, We brought forth another generation;

23:32 And we sent among them a messenger of their own, saying: Serve Allah, Ye have no other Allah save Him. Will ye not ward off (*EVIL*)?

23:33 And the chieftains of his folk, *WHO DISBELIEVED AND DENIED THE MEETING OF THE HEREAFTER*, and whom We had made soft in the life of the world, said: This is only a mortal like you, who eateth of that whereof ye eat and drinketh of that ye drink.

23:34 *IF YE WERE TO OBEY A MORTAL LIKE YOURSELVES, THEN, LO! YE SURELY WOULD BE LOSERS.* [Islam merges religion and politics, those who do not put Islam above all other beliefs are unbelievers to be tortured for eternity.]

23:35 Doth he promise you that you, when ye are dead and have become dust and bones, will (again) be brought forth?

23:36 Begone, begone, with that which ye are promised!

23:37 There is naught but our life of the world; we die and we live, and we shall not be raised (again).

23:38 *HE IS ONLY A MAN WHO HATH INVENTED A LIE ABOUT ALLAH. WE ARE NOT GOING TO PUT FAITH IN HIM.*

23:39 He said: My Lord! Help me because they deny me.

23:40 He said: In a little while they surely will become repentant.

23:41 So the (Awful) Cry overtook them rightfully, and We made them like as wreckage (that a torrent hurleth). A far removal for wrongdoing folk!

23:42 Then after them We brought forth other generations.

23:43 No nation can outstrip its term, nor yet postpone it.

23:44 Then We sent our messengers one after another. Whenever its messenger came unto a nation they denied him; so We caused them to follow one another (to disaster) and We made them bywords. A far removal for *FOLK WHO BELIEVE NOT!*

23:45 Then We sent Moses and his brother Aaron with Our tokens and a clear warrant,

23:46 Unto Pharaoh and his chiefs, but they scorned (them) and they were despotic folk.

23:47 And they said: Shall we put faith in two mortals like ourselves, and whose folk are servile unto us?

23:48 So *THEY DENIED THEM, AND BECAME OF THOSE WHO WERE DESTROYED.*

23:49 And We verily gave Moses the Scripture, that haply they might go aright.

23:50 And We made *THE SON OF MARY* and his mother a portent, and We gave them refuge on a height, a place of flocks and watersprings.

23:51 O ye messengers! Eat of the good things, and do right. Lo! I am Aware of what ye do.

23:52 And lo! this your religion is one religion and I am your Lord, so *KEEP YOUR DUTY UNTO ME.*

23:53 But they (mankind) *HAVE BROKEN THEIR RELIGION AMONG THEM INTO SECTS*, each group rejoicing in its tenets. [Islam permits for no diversity in belief or behaviour.]

23:54 ~~So leave them in their error till a time.~~ [Cancelled by verse 9:5][472]

23:55 Think they that in the wealth and sons wherewith We provide them

23:56 We hasten unto them with good things? Nay, but they perceive not.

23:57 Lo! those who go in awe for fear of their Lord.

23:58 And *THOSE WHO BELIEVE IN THE REVELATIONS* of their Lord,

23:59 And *THOSE WHO ASCRIBE NOT PARTNERS UNTO THEIR LORD,*

23:60 And those who give that which they give with hearts afraid because they are about to return unto their Lord,

23:61 These race for the good things, and they shall win them in the race.

23:62 And *WE TASK NOT ANY SOUL BEYOND ITS SCOPE, AND WITH US IS A RECORD WHICH SPEAKETH THE TRUTH, AND THEY WILL NOT BE WRONGED,*

23:63 Nay, but their hearts are in ignorance of this (Qur'an), and they have other works, besides, which they are doing;

23:64 Till when We *GRASP THEIR LUXURIOUS ONES WITH THE PUNISHMENT*, behold! they supplicate.

23:65 *SUPPLICATE NOT THIS DAY! ASSUREDLY YE WILL NOT BE HELPED BY US*.

23:66 My revelations were recited unto you, but ye used to turn back on your heels,

23:67 In scorn thereof. Nightly did ye rave together.

23:68 Have they not pondered the Word, or hath that come unto them which came not unto their fathers of old?

23:69 Or know they not their messenger, and so reject him?

23:70 Or *SAY THEY: THERE IS A MADNESS IN HIM*? Nay, but he bringeth them *THE TRUTH*; and most of them are *HATERS OF THE TRUTH*. [Non-Muslims said Mohammed was insane.]

23:71 And if *THE TRUTH* had followed their desires, verily the heavens and the earth and whosoever is therein had been corrupted. Nay, We have brought them their Reminder, but from their Reminder they now turn away.

23:72 Or dost thou ask of them (O Muhammad) any tribute? But the bounty of thy Lord is better, for He is Best of all who make provision.

23:73 And lo! thou summonest them indeed unto *A STRAIGHT PATH*.

23:74 And lo! *THOSE WHO BELIEVE NOT IN THE HEREAFTER ARE INDEED ASTRAY FROM THE PATH,*

23:75 Though We had mercy on them and relieved them of the harm afflicting them, they still would wander blindly on in their contumacy.

23:76 Already have We grasped them with punishment, but they humble not themselves unto their Lord, nor do they pray,

23:77 Until, when *WE OPEN FOR THEM THE GATE OF EXTREME PUNISHMENT*, behold! they are aghast thereat.

23:78 He it is Who hath created for you ears and eyes and hearts. Small thanks give ye!

23:79 And He it is Who hath sown you broadcast in the earth, and unto Him ye will be gathered.

23:80 And He it is Who giveth life and causeth death, and His is the difference of night and day. Have ye then no sense?

23:81 Nay, but they say the like of that which said the men of old;

23:82 They say: When we are dead and have become (mere) dust and bones, shall we then, forsooth, be raised again?

23:83 We were already promised this, we and our forefathers. Lo! *THIS IS NAUGHT BUT FABLES OF THE MEN OF OLD.* [Contemporaries said Mohammed said nothing new.]

23:84 Say: Unto Whom (belongeth) the earth and whosoever is therein, if ye have knowledge?

23:85 They will say: Unto Allah. Say: Will ye not then remember?

23:86 Say: Who is Lord of the seven heavens, and Lord of the Tremendous Throne?

23:87 They will say: Unto Allah (all that belongeth). Say: Will ye not then keep duty (unto Him)?

23:88 Say: In Whose hand is the dominion over all things and He protecteth, while against Him there is no protection, if ye have knowledge?

23:89 They will say: Unto Allah (all that belongeth). Say: How then are ye bewitched?

23:90 Nay, but *WE HAVE BROUGHT THEM THE TRUTH, AND LO! THEY ARE LIARS.*

23:91 Allah hath not chosen any son, nor is there any god along with Him; else would each god have assuredly championed that which he created, and some of them would assuredly have overcome others. Glorified be Allah above all that they allege.

23:92 Knower of the invisible and the visible! and exalted be He over all that *THEY ASCRIBE AS PARTNERS (UNTO HIM)!*

23:93 Say: My Lord! If Thou shouldst show me that which they are promised.

23:94 My Lord! then set me not among *THE WRONGDOING FOLK.*

23:95 And verily We are Able to show thee that which We have promised them.

23:96 ~~Repel evil with that which is better. We are Best Aware of that which they allege.~~ [Cancelled by verse 9:5, i.e. command to violence replaces command to demonstrate good behaviour][473]

23:97 And say: My Lord! *I SEEK REFUGE IN THEE FROM SUGGESTIONS OF THE EVIL ONES,*

23:98 And I seek refuge in Thee, my Lord, lest they be present with me,

23:99 Until, when death cometh unto one of them, he saith: My Lord! Send me back,

23:100 That I may do right in that which I have left behind! But nay! It is but a word that he speaketh; and behind them is a barrier until *THE DAY WHEN THEY ARE RAISED.*

23:101 And *WHEN THE TRUMPET IS BLOWN THERE WILL BE NO KINSHIP AMONG THEM THAT DAY,* nor will they ask of one another.

23:102 Then those whose scales are heavy, *THEY ARE THE SUCCESSFUL.*

23:103 And those whose scales are light are those who lose their souls, *IN HELL ABIDING.*

23:104 *THE FIRE BURNETH THEIR FACES,* and they are glum therein.

23:105 (It will be said): Were not My revelations recited unto you, and then ye used to deny them?

23:106 They will say: Our Lord! Our evil fortune conquered us, and we were erring folk.

23:107 Our Lord! Oh, bring us forth from hence! If we return (to evil) then indeed *WE SHALL BE WRONG-DOERS.*

23:108 He saith: Begone therein, and speak not unto Me.

23:109 Lo! there was *A PARTY OF MY SLAVES* who said: Our Lord! We *BELIEVE,* therefor forgive us and have mercy on us for Thou art Best of all who show mercy;

23:110 But *YE CHOSE THEM FOR A LAUGHING-STOCK UNTIL THEY CAUSED YOU TO FORGET REMEMBRANCE OF ME, WHILE YE LAUGHED AT THEM.*

23:111 Lo! I have rewarded them this day forasmuch as they were steadfast; and *THEY SURELY ARE THE TRIUMPHANT.*

23:112 He will say: How long tarried ye in the earth, counting by years?

23:113 They will say: We tarried by a day or part of a day. Ask of those who keep count!

23:114 He will say: Ye tarried but a little if ye only knew.

23:115 Deemed ye then that We had created you for naught, and that ye would not be returned unto Us?

23:116 Now Allah be Exalted, the True King! There is no God save Him, the Lord of the Throne of Grace.

23:117 He who crieth unto any other god along with Allah hath no proof thereof. His reckoning is only with his Lord. Lo! *DISBELIEVERS WILL NOT BE SUCCESSFUL.*

23:118 And (O Muhammad) say: My Lord! Forgive and have mercy, for Thou art best of all who show mercy.

Chapter 21 - The Prophets

21:1 Their reckoning draweth nigh for mankind, while they turn away in heedlessness.

21:2 Never cometh there unto them a new reminder from their Lord but they listen to it while they play,

21:3 With hearts preoccupied. And they confer in secret. The wrong-doers say: Is this other than a mortal like you? Will ye then succumb to magic when ye see (it)?

21:4 He saith: My Lord knoweth what is spoken in the heaven and the earth. He is the Hearer, the Knower.

21:5 Nay, say they, (these are but) muddled dreams; nay, he hath but invented it; nay, he is but a poet. Let him bring us a portent even as those of old (who were Allah's messengers) were sent (with portents).

21:6 *NOT A TOWNSHIP BELIEVED OF THOSE WHICH WE DESTROYED* before them (though We sent them portents): would they then *BELIEVE*?

21:7 And We sent not (as Our messengers) before thee other than men, whom We inspired. Ask the followers of the Reminder if ye know not?

21:8 We gave them not bodies that would not eat food, nor were they immortals.

21:9 Then we fulfilled the promise unto them. So we delivered them and whom We would, and We destroyed the prodigals.

21:10 Now We have revealed unto you a Scripture wherein is your Reminder. Have ye then no sense?

21:11 How many a community that dealt unjustly have We shattered, and raised up after them another folk!

21:12 And, when they felt Our might, behold them fleeing from it!

21:13 (But it was said unto them): Flee not, but return to that (existence) which emasculated you and to your dwellings, that ye may be questioned.

21:14 They cried: Alas for us! we were *WRONG-DOERS*.

21:15 And this their crying ceased not till We made them as reaped corn, extinct.

21:16 We created not the heaven and the earth and all that is between them in play.

21:17 If We had wished to find a pastime, We could have found it in Our presence - if We ever did.

21:18 Nay, but We hurl the true against the false, and it doth break its head and lo! it vanisheth. And yours will be woe for that which ye ascribe (unto Him).

21:19 Unto Him belongeth whosoever is in the heavens and the earth. And those who dwell in His presence are not too proud to worship Him, nor do they weary;

21:20 They glorify (Him) night and day; they flag not.

21:21 Or have they chosen gods from the earth who raise the dead?

21:22 If there were therein gods beside Allah, then verily both (the heavens and the earth) had been disordered. Glorified be Allah, the Lord of the Throne, from all that they ascribe (unto Him).

21:23 He will not be questioned as to that which He doeth, but they will be questioned.

21:24 Or have they chosen other gods beside Him? say: Bring your proof (of their godhead). This is the Reminder of those with me and those before me, but most of them know not *THE TRUTH* and so they are averse.

21:25 And We sent no messenger before thee but We inspired him, (saying): There is no God save Me (Allah), so worship Me.

21:26 And they say: The Beneficent hath taken unto Himself a son. Be He Glorified! Nay, but (those whom they call sons) are honoured slaves;

21:27 They speak not until He hath spoken, and they act by His command.

21:28 He knoweth what is before them and what is behind them, and they cannot intercede except for him whom He accepteth, and they quake for awe of Him.

21:29 And one of them who should say: Lo! I am a god beside Him, that one We should *REPAY WITH HELL*. Thus *WE REPAY WRONG-DOERS*.

21:30 Have not *THOSE WHO DISBELIEVE* known that the heavens and the earth were of one piece, then We parted them, and we made every living thing of water? Will they not then *BELIEVE*?

21:31 And We have placed in the earth firm hills lest it quake with them, and We have placed therein ravines as roads that haply they may find their way.

21:32 And we have made the sky a roof withheld (from them). Yet they turn away from its portents.

21:33 And He it is Who created the night and the day, and the sun and the moon. They float, each in an orbit.

21:34 We appointed immortality for no mortal before thee. What! if thou diest, can they be immortal!

21:35 Every soul must taste of death, and *WE TRY YOU WITH EVIL AND WITH GOOD*, for ordeal. And unto Us ye will be returned.

21:36 And when *THOSE WHO DISBELIEVE* behold thee, they but choose thee out for mockery, (saying): Is this he who maketh mention of your gods? And they would deny all mention of the Beneficent.

21:37 Man is made of haste. I shall show you My portents, but ask Me not to hasten.

21:38 And they say: *WHEN WILL THIS PROMISE (BE FULFILLED)*, if ye are truthful?

21:39 If *THOSE WHO DISBELIEVED* but knew the time when they will not be able to drive off *THE FIRE* from their faces and from their backs, and they will not be helped!

21:40 Nay, but it will come upon them unawares so that it will stupefy them, and they will be unable to repel it, neither will they be reprieved.

21:41 Messengers before thee, indeed, were mocked, but that whereat they mocked surrounded those who scoffed at them.

21:42 Say: Who guardeth you in the night or in the day from the Beneficent? Nay, but they turn away from mention of their Lord!

21:43 Or have they gods who can shield them from Us? They cannot help themselves nor can they be defended from Us.

21:44 Nay, but We gave these and their fathers ease until life grew long for them. See they not how we aim to the land, reducing it of its outlying parts? Can they then be the victors?

21:45 Say (O Muhammad, unto mankind): I warn you only by the Inspiration. But the deaf hear not the call when they are warned.

21:46 And if a breath of thy Lord's punishment were to touch them, they assuredly would say: Alas for us! Lo! we were wrong-doers.

21:47 And We set a just balance for *THE DAY OF RESURRECTION* so that no soul is wronged in aught. Though it be of the weight of a grain of mustard seed, We bring it. And We suffice for reckoners.

21:48 And We verily gave Moses and Aaron the Criterion (of right and wrong) and a light and a Reminder for those who keep from *EVIL*,

21:49 Those who fear their Lord in secret and who *DREAD THE HOUR (OF DOOM),*

21:50 This is a blessed Reminder that we have revealed: Will ye then reject it?

21:51 And We verily gave Abraham of old his proper course, and We were Aware of him,

21:52 When he said unto his father and his folk: What are these images unto which ye pay devotion?

21:53 They said: We found our fathers worshippers of them.

21:54 He said: Verily ye and your fathers were in plain error.

21:55 They said: Bringest thou unto us *THE TRUTH*, or art thou some jester?

21:56 He said: Nay, but your Lord is the Lord of the heavens and the earth, Who created them; and I am of those who testify unto that.

21:57 And, by Allah, I shall circumvent your idols after ye have gone away and turned your backs.

21:58 Then he reduced them to fragments, all save the chief of them, that haply they might have recourse to it.

21:59 They said: Who hath done this to our gods? Surely it must be *SOME EVIL-DOER.*

21:60 They said: We heard a youth make mention of them, who is called Abraham.

21:61 They said: Then bring him (hither) before the people's eyes that they may testify.

21:62 They said: Is it thou who hast done this to our gods, O Abraham?

21:63 He said: But this, their chief hath done it. So question them, if they can speak.

21:64 Then gathered they apart and said: Lo! ye yourselves are the wrong-doers.

21:65 And they were utterly confounded, and they said: Well thou knowest that these speak not.

21:66 He said: Worship ye then instead of Allah that which cannot profit you at all, nor harm you?

21:67 Fie on you and all that ye worship instead of Allah! Have ye then no sense?

21:68 They cried: Burn him and stand by your gods, if ye will be doing.

21:69 We said: O fire, be coolness and peace for Abraham,

21:70 And they wished to set a snare for him, but We made them the greater losers.

21:71 And We rescued him and Lot (and brought them) to the land which We have blessed for (all) peoples.

21:72 And We bestowed upon him Isaac, and Jacob as a grandson. Each of them We made righteous.

21:73 And We made them chiefs who guide by Our command, and We inspired in them the doing of good deeds and the right establishment of worship and the giving of alms, and they were worshippers of Us (alone).

21:74 And *UNTO LOT WE GAVE JUDGMENT AND KNOWLEDGE, AND WE DELIVERED HIM FROM THE COMMUNITY THAT DID ABOMINATIONS. LO! THEY WERE FOLK OF EVIL, LEWD.*

21:75 And We brought him in unto Our mercy. Lo! he was of the righteous.

21:76 And Noah, when he cried of old, We heard his prayer and saved him and his household from the great affliction.

21:77 And delivered him from the people who denied Our revelations. Lo! *THEY WERE FOLK OF EVIL*, therefor did We drown them all.

21:78 And David and Solomon, when they gave judgment concerning the field, when people's sheep had strayed and browsed therein by night; and We were witnesses to their judgment.

21:79 And We made Solomon to understand (the case); and unto each of them We gave judgment and knowledge. And we subdued the hills and the birds to hymn (His) praise along with David. We were the doers (thereof).

21:80 And We taught him the art of making garments (of mail) to protect you in your daring. Are ye then thankful?

21:81 And unto Solomon (We subdued) the wind in its raging. It set by his command toward the land which We had blessed. And of everything We are Aware.

21:82 And of *THE EVIL ONES* (subdued We unto him) some who dived (for pearls) for him and did other work, and We were warders unto them.

21:83 And Job, when he cried unto his Lord, (saying): Lo! adversity afflicteth me, and Thou art Most Merciful of all who show mercy.

21:84 Then We heard his prayer and removed that adversity from which he suffered, and We gave him his household (that he had lost) and the like thereof along with them, a mercy from Our store, and a remembrance for the worshippers;

21:85 And (mention) Ishmael, and Idris, and Dhu'l-Kifl. All were of the steadfast.

21:86 And We brought them in unto Our mercy. Lo! they are among the righteous.

21:87 And (mention) Dhu'n-Nun, when he went off in anger and deemed that We had no power over him, but he cried out in the darkness, saying: There is no God save Thee. Be Thou Glorified! Lo! I have been a wrong-doer.

21:88 Then we heard his prayer and saved him from the anguish. Thus we save *BELIEVERS*.

21:89 And Zachariah, when he cried unto his Lord: My Lord! Leave me not childless, though Thou art the Best of inheritors.

21:90 Then We heard his prayer, and bestowed upon him John, and adjusted his wife (to bear a child) for him. Lo! they used to vie one with the other in good deeds, and they cried unto Us in longing and in fear, and were submissive unto Us.

21:91 And she who was chaste, therefor We breathed into her (something) of Our Spirit and made her and her son a token for (all) peoples.

21:92 Lo! this, your religion, is one religion, and I am your Lord, so worship Me.

21:93 And they have broken their religion (into fragments) among them, (yet) all are returning unto Us.

21:94 Then whoso doeth some good works and is a *BELIEVER*, there will be no rejection of his effort. Lo! We record (it) for him.

21:95 And *THERE IS A BAN UPON ANY COMMUNITY WHICH WE HAVE DESTROYED: THAT THEY SHALL NOT RETURN.*

21:96 Until, when Gog and Magog are let loose, and they hasten out of every mound,

21:97 And *THE TRUE PROMISE DRAWETH NIGH; THEN BEHOLD THEM, STARING WIDE (IN TERROR), THE EYES OF THOSE WHO DISBELIEVE*! (They say): Alas for us! We (lived) in forgetfulness of this. Ah, but *WE WERE WRONG-DOERS!*

21:98 ~~Lo! ye (idolaters) and that which ye worship beside Allah are fuel of hell. Thereunto ye will come.~~ [Cancelled by verse 21:101][474]

21:99 ~~If these had been gods they would not have come thither, but all will abide therein.~~ [Cancelled by verse 21:102][475]

21:100 ~~Therein wailing is their portion, and therein they hear not.~~ [Cancelled by verse 21:103][476]

21:101 Lo! those unto whom kindness hath gone forth before from Us, they will be far removed from thence.

21:102 They will not hear the slightest sound thereof, while they abide in that which their souls desire.

21:103 The Supreme Horror will not grieve them, and the angels will welcome them, (saying): This is *YOUR DAY WHICH YE WERE PROMISED;*

21:104 The Day when We shall roll up the heavens as a recorder rolleth up a written scroll. As We began the first creation, We shall repeat it. (It is) a promise (binding) upon Us. Lo! We are to perform it.

21:105 And verily we have written in the Scripture, after the Reminder: *MY RIGHTEOUS SLAVES* will inherit the earth:

21:106 Lo! *THERE IS A PLAIN STATEMENT FOR FOLK WHO ARE DEVOUT.*

21:107 We sent thee not save as a mercy for the peoples.

21:108 Say: It is only inspired in me that your Allah is One Allah. Will ye then surrender (unto Him)?

21:109 But if they are averse, then say: I have warned you all alike, although I know not whether nigh or far is that which ye are promised.

21:110 Lo! He knoweth that which is said openly, and that which ye conceal.

21:111 And I know not but that this may be a trial for you, and enjoyment for a while.

21:112 He saith: My Lord! Judge Thou with truth. Our Lord is the Beneficent, Whose help is to be implored against that which ye ascribe (unto Him).

Chapter 14 - Abraham

14:1 Alif. Lam. Ra. (This is) a Scripture which We have revealed unto thee (Muhammad) that thereby thou mayst bring forth mankind from darkness unto light, by the permission of their Lord, unto the path of the Mighty, the Owner of Praise,

14:2 Allah, unto Whom belongeth whatsoever is in the heavens and whatsoever is in the earth. And woe unto the *DISBELIEVERS* from an awful doom;

14:3 *THOSE WHO LOVE THE LIFE OF THE WORLD MORE THAN THE HEREAFTER,* and debar (men) from the way of Allah and would have it crooked: such *ARE FAR ASTRAY.* [The basis on which Jihadis claim "we love death as much as you love life".]

14:4 And We never sent a messenger save with the language of his folk, that he might make (the message) clear for them. Then Allah sendeth whom He will astray, and guideth whom He will. He is the Mighty, the Wise.

14:5 We verily sent Moses with Our revelations, saying: Bring thy people forth from darkness unto light. And remind them of the days of Allah. Lo! therein are revelations for each steadfast, thankful (heart).

14:6 And (remind them) how Moses said unto his people: Remember Allah's favour unto you when He delivered you from Pharaoh's folk who were afflicting you with dreadful torment, and were slaying your sons and sparing your women; that was a tremendous trial from your Lord.

14:7 And when your Lord proclaimed: If ye give thanks, I will give you more; but if ye are thankless, lo! My punishment is dire.

14:8 And Moses said: Though ye and all who are in the earth prove thankless, lo! Allah verily is Absolute, Owner of Praise.

14:9 Hath not the history of those before you reached you: the folk of Noah, and (the tribes of) A'ad and Thamud, and those after them? None save Allah knoweth them. Their messengers came unto them with *CLEAR PROOFS,* but they thrust their hands into their mouths, and said: Lo! we *DISBELIEVE* in that wherewith ye have been sent, and lo! we are in grave doubt concerning that to which ye call us.

14:10 Their messengers said: Can there be doubt concerning Allah, the Creator of the heavens and the earth? He calleth you that He may forgive you your sins and reprieve you unto an appointed term. They said: Ye are but mortals like us, who would fain turn us away from what our fathers used to worship. Then bring some clear warrant.

14:11 Their messengers said unto them: We are but mortals like you, but Allah giveth grace unto whom He will of His *SLAVES.* It is not ours to bring you a warrant unless by the permission of Allah. *IN ALLAH LET BELIEVERS PUT THEIR TRUST!*

14:12 How should we not put our trust in Allah when He hath shown us our ways? We surely will endure the hurt ye do us. In Allah let the trusting put their trust.

14:13 And *THOSE WHO DISBELIEVED* said unto their messengers: Verily we will drive you out from our land, unless ye return to our religion. Then their Lord inspired them, (saying): Verily we shall destroy the wrong-doers,

14:14 And verily We shall make you to dwell in the land after them. This is for him who feareth My Majesty and feareth My threats.

14:15 And they sought help (from their Lord) and every froward potentate was bought to naught;

14:16 *HELL IS BEFORE HIM, AND HE IS MADE TO DRINK A FESTERING WATER,*

14:17 Which he sippeth but can hardly swallow, and death cometh unto him from every side while yet he cannot die, and before him is a harsh doom.

14:18 A similitude of *THOSE WHO DISBELIEVE* in their Lord: Their works are as ashes which the wind bloweth hard upon a stormy day. They have no control of aught that they have earned. That is the extreme failure.

14:19 Hast thou not seen that Allah hath created the heavens and the earth with *TRUTH*? If He will, He can remove you and bring (in) some new creation;

14:20 And that is no great matter for Allah.

14:21 They all come forth unto their Lord. Then those who were despised say unto those who were scornful: We were unto you a following, can ye then avert from us aught of Allah's doom? They say: Had Allah guided us, we should have guided you. Whether we rage or patiently endure is (now) all one for us; we have no place of refuge.

14:22 And Satan saith, when the matter hath been decided: Lo! *ALLAH PROMISED YOU A PROMISE OF TRUTH*; and I promised you, then failed you. And I had no power over you save that I called unto you and ye obeyed me. So blame not, but blame yourselves. I cannot help you, nor can ye help me, Lo! I *DISBELIEVED* in that which ye before ascribed to me. Lo! *FOR WRONG-DOERS IS A PAINFUL DOOM.*

14:23 And *THOSE WHO BELIEVED* and did good works are made to enter *GARDENS UNDERNEATH WHICH RIVERS FLOW*, therein abiding by permission of their Lord, their greeting therein: Peace!

14:24 Seest thou not how Allah coineth a similitude: A goodly saying, as a goodly tree, its root set firm, its branches reaching into heaven,

14:25 Giving its fruit at every season by permission of its Lord? Allah coineth the similitudes for mankind in order that they may reflect.

14:26 And the similitude of a bad saying is as a bad tree, uprooted from upon the earth, possessing no stability.

14:27 Allah confirmeth those who *BELIEVE* by a firm saying in the life of the world and in the Hereafter, and Allah sendeth **WRONG-DOERS** astray. And *ALLAH DOETH WHAT HE WILL*.

14:28 Hast thou not seen those who gave the grace of Allah in exchange for thanklessness and led their people down to the Abode of Loss,

14:29 (Even to) hell? They are exposed thereto. A hapless end!

14:30 And *THEY SET UP RIVALS TO ALLAH THAT THEY MAY MISLEAD (MEN) FROM HIS WAY. SAY: ENJOY LIFE (WHILE YE MAY) FOR LO! YOUR JOURNEY'S END WILL BE THE FIRE.*

14:31 Tell My *BONDMEN* who *BELIEVE* to establish worship and *SPEND OF THAT WHICH WE HAVE GIVEN THEM, SECRETLY AND PUBLICLY*, before *A DAY COMETH* wherein there will be neither bargaining nor befriending.

14:32 Allah is He Who created the heavens and the earth, and causeth water to descend from the sky, thereby producing fruits as food for you, and maketh the ships to be of service unto you, that they may run upon the sea at His command, and hath made of service unto you the rivers;

14:33 And maketh the sun and the moon, constant in their courses, to be of service unto you, and hath made of service unto you the night and the day.

14:34 And He giveth you of all ye ask of Him, and if ye would count the bounty of Allah ye cannot reckon it. Lo! man is verily a wrong-doer, an ingrate.

14:35 And when Abraham said: My Lord! Make safe this territory, and preserve me and my sons from serving idols.

14:36 My Lord! Lo! they have led many of mankind astray. But whoso followeth me, he verily is of me. And whoso disobeyeth me - Still Thou art Forgiving, Merciful.

14:37 Our Lord! Lo! I have settled some of my posterity in an uncultivable valley near unto Thy holy House, our Lord! that they may establish proper worship; so incline some hearts of men that they may yearn toward them, and provide Thou them with fruits in order that they may be thankful.

14:38 Our Lord! Lo! Thou knowest that which we hide and that which we proclaim. Nothing in the earth or in the heaven is hidden from Allah.

14:39 Praise be to Allah Who hath given me, in my old age, Ishmael and Isaac! Lo! my Lord is indeed the Hearer of Prayer.

14:40 My Lord! Make me to establish proper worship, and some of my posterity (also); our Lord! and accept my prayer.

14:41 Our Lord! Forgive me and my parents and *BELIEVERS* on *THE DAY WHEN THE ACCOUNT IS CAST.*

14:42 Deem not that Allah is unaware of what the wicked do. He but giveth them a respite till a day when eyes will stare (in terror),

14:43 As they come hurrying on in fear, their heads upraised, their gaze returning not to them, and their hearts as air.

14:44 And warn mankind of *A DAY WHEN THE DOOM WILL COME UPON THEM*, and those who did wrong will say: Our Lord! Reprieve us for a little while. *WE WILL OBEY* Thy call and will follow the messengers. (It will be answered): Did ye not swear before that there would be no end for you?

14:45 And (have ye not) dwelt in the dwellings of those who wronged themselves (of old) and (hath it not) become plain to you how We dealt with them and made examples for you?

14:46 Verily they have plotted their plot, and their plot is with Allah, though their plot were one whereby the mountains should be moved.

14:47 So think not that Allah will fail to keep His promise to His messengers. Lo! Allah is Mighty, Able to Requite (the wrong).

14:48 *ON THE DAY* when the earth will be changed to other than the earth, and the heavens (also will be changed) and they will come forth unto Allah, the One, the Almighty,

14:49 Thou wilt *SEE THE GUILTY ON THAT DAY LINKED TOGETHER IN CHAINS,*

14:50 Their raiment of pitch, and *THE FIRE COVERING THEIR FACES,*

14:51 That Allah may repay each soul what it hath earned. Lo! *ALLAH IS SWIFT AT RECKONING.*

14:52 This is a clear message for mankind in order that they may be warned thereby, and that they may know that He is only One Allah, and that men of understanding may take heed.

Chapter 71 - Noah

71:1 Lo! We sent Noah unto his people (saying): Warn thy people ere the painful doom come unto them.

71:2 He said: O my people! Lo! I am a plain warner unto you

71:3 (Bidding you): *SERVE ALLAH AND KEEP YOUR DUTY* unto Him and *OBEY ME,*

71:4 That He may forgive you somewhat of your sins and respite you to an appointed term. Lo! the term of Allah, when it cometh, cannot be delayed, if ye but knew.

71:5 He said: My Lord! Lo! I have called unto my people night and day

71:6 But all my calling doth but add to their repugnance;

71:7 And lo! whenever I call unto them that Thou mayst pardon them they thrust their fingers in their ears and cover themselves with their garments and persist (in their refusal) and magnify themselves in pride.

71:8 And lo! I have called unto them aloud,

71:9 And lo! I have made public proclamation unto them, and I have appealed to them in private.

71:10 And I have said: Seek pardon of your Lord. Lo! He was ever Forgiving.

71:11 He will let loose the sky for you in plenteous rain,

71:12 And will help you with wealth and sons, and will assign unto you Gardens and will assign unto you rivers.

71:13 What aileth you that ye hope not toward Allah for dignity

71:14 When He created you by (divers) stages?

71:15 See ye not how Allah hath created seven heavens in harmony,

71:16 And hath made the moon a light therein, and made the sun a lamp?

71:17 And Allah hath caused you to grow as a growth from the earth,

71:18 And afterward He maketh you return thereto, and He will bring you forth again, a (new) forthbringing.

71:19 And Allah hath made the earth a wide expanse for you

71:20 That ye may thread the valley-ways thereof.

71:21 Noah said: My Lord! Lo! they have disobeyed me and followed one whose wealth and children increase him in naught save ruin;

71:22 And they have plotted a mighty plot,

71:23 And they have said: Forsake not your gods. Forsake not Wadd, nor Suwa', nor Yaghuth and Ya'uq and Nasr.

71:24 And they have led many astray, and Thou increasest the wrong-doers in naught save error.

71:25 Because of their sins they were drowned, then made to enter a Fire. And they found they had no helpers in place of Allah.

71:26 And Noah said: My Lord! *LEAVE NOT ONE OF THE DISBELIEVERS IN THE LAND.*

71:27 *IF THOU SHOULDST LEAVE THEM, THEY WILL MISLEAD THY SLAVES AND WILL BEGET NONE SAVE LEWD INGRATES.*

71:28 My Lord! Forgive me and my parents and him who entereth my house *BELIEVING*, and *BELIEVING* men and *BELIEVING* women, and increase not the wrong-doers in aught save ruin.

Chapter 16 - The Bee

16:1 *THE COMMANDMENT OF ALLAH WILL COME TO PASS*, so seek not ye to hasten it. Glorified and Exalted be He above all that they associate (with Him).

16:2 He sendeth down the angels with the Spirit of His command unto whom He will of His *BONDMEN*, (saying): Warn mankind that there is no God save Me, so *KEEP YOUR DUTY UNTO ME.*

16:3 He hath created the heavens and the earth with truth. High be He Exalted above all that they associate (with Him).

16:4 He hath created man from a drop of fluid, yet behold! he is an open opponent.

16:5 And the cattle hath He created, whence ye have warm clothing and uses, and whereof ye eat;

16:6 And wherein is beauty for you, when ye bring them home, and when ye take them out to pasture.

16:7 And they bear your loads for you unto a land ye could not reach save with great trouble to yourselves. Lo! your Lord is Full of Pity, Merciful.

16:8 And horses and mules and asses (hath He created) that ye may ride them, and for ornament. And He createth that which ye know not.

16:9 And Allah's is the direction of the way, and some (roads) go not straight. And had He willed He would have led you all aright.

16:10 He it is Who sendeth down water from the sky, whence ye have drink, and whence are trees on which ye send your beasts to pasture.

16:11 Therewith He causeth crops to grow for you, and the olive and the date-palm and grapes and all kinds of fruit. Lo! herein is indeed a portent for people who reflect.

16:12 And He hath constrained the night and the day and the sun and the moon to be of service unto you, and the stars are made subservient by His command. Lo! herein indeed are portents for people who have sense.

16:13 And whatsoever He hath created for you in the earth of divers hues, lo! therein is indeed a portent for people who take heed.

16:14 And He it is Who hath constrained the sea to be of service that ye eat fresh meat from thence, and bring forth from thence ornaments which ye wear. And thou seest the ships ploughing it that ye (mankind) may seek of His bounty and that haply ye may give thanks.

16:15 And He hath cast into the earth firm hills that it quake not with you, and streams and roads that ye may find a way.

16:16 And landmarks (too), and by the star they find a way.

16:17 Is He then Who createth as him who createth not? Will ye not then remember?

16:18 And if ye would count the favour of Allah ye cannot reckon it. Lo! Allah is indeed Forgiving, Merciful.

16:19 And Allah knoweth that which ye keep hidden and that which ye proclaim.

16:20 Those unto whom they cry beside Allah created naught, but are themselves created.

16:21 (They are) dead, not living. And they know not when they will be raised.

16:22 Your Allah is One Allah. But as for *THOSE WHO BELIEVE NOT IN THE HEREAFTER THEIR HEARTS REFUSE TO KNOW, FOR THEY ARE PROUD.*

16:23 Assuredly Allah knoweth that which they keep hidden and that which they proclaim. Lo! He loveth not the proud.

16:24 And when it is said unto them: *WHAT HATH YOUR LORD REVEALED? THEY SAY: (MERE) FABLES OF THE MEN OF OLD,*

16:25 That they may bear their burdens undiminished on *THE DAY OF RESURRECTION*, with somewhat of the burdens of those whom they mislead without knowledge. Ah! *EVIL* is that which they bear!

16:26 Those before them plotted, so Allah struck at the foundations of their building, and then the roof fell down upon them from above them, and the doom came on them whence they knew not;

16:27 Then on *THE DAY OF RESURRECTION* He will disgrace them and will say: Where are My partners, for whose sake ye opposed (My guidance)? Those who have been given knowledge will say: Disgrace this day and *EVIL* are upon the *DISBELIEVERS*,

16:28 Whom the angels cause to die while they are wronging themselves. Then will they make full submission (saying): We used not to do any wrong. Nay! Surely Allah is Knower of what ye used to do.

16:29 *SO ENTER THE GATES OF HELL, TO DWELL THEREIN FOR EVER.* Woeful indeed will be the lodging of the arrogant.

16:30 And it is said unto those who ward off (*EVIL*): What hath your Lord revealed? They say: Good. *FOR THOSE WHO DO GOOD IN THIS WORLD THERE IS A GOOD (REWARD) AND THE HOME OF THE HEREAFTER* will be better. Pleasant indeed will be the home of those who ward off (*EVIL*) -

16:31 *GARDENS OF EDEN WHICH THEY ENTER, UNDERNEATH WHICH RIVERS FLOW, WHEREIN THEY HAVE WHAT THEY WILL.* Thus *ALLAH REPAYETH* those who ward off (*EVIL*),

16:32 Those whom the angels cause to die (when they are) good. They say: Peace be unto you! Enter the Garden because of what ye used to do.

16:33 Await they aught say that the angels should come unto them or thy Lord's command should come to pass? Even so did those before them. Allah wronged them not, but they did wrong themselves,

16:34 So that the evils of what they did smote them, and that which they used to mock surrounded them.

16:35 And the *IDOLATERS* say: Had Allah willed, we had not worshipped aught beside Him, we and our fathers, nor had we forbidden aught without (command from) Him. Even so did those before them. Are the messengers charged with aught save plain conveyance (of the message)?

16:36 And verily We have raised in every nation a messenger, (proclaiming): Serve Allah and shun false gods. Then some of them (there were) whom Allah guided, and some of them (there were) upon whom error had just hold. Do but travel in the land and see the nature of the consequence for the deniers!

16:37 Even if thou (O Muhammad) desirest their right guidance, still Allah assuredly will not guide him who misleadeth. Such have no helpers.

16:38 And they swear by Allah their most binding oaths (that) Allah will not raise up him who dieth. Nay, but it is a promise (binding) upon Him in truth, but most of mankind know not,

16:39 That He may explain unto them that wherein they differ, and that *THOSE WHO DISBELIEVED MAY KNOW THAT THEY WERE LIARS*.

16:40 And Our word unto a thing, when We intend it, is only that We say unto it: Be! and it is.

16:41 And *THOSE WHO BECAME FUGITIVES FOR THE CAUSE OF ALLAH AFTER THEY HAD BEEN OPPRESSED, WE VERILY SHALL GIVE THEM GOODLY LODGING IN THE WORLD, AND SURELY THE REWARD OF THE HEREAFTER IS GREATER,* if they but knew;

16:42 Such as are steadfast and put their trust in Allah.

16:43 And We sent not (as Our messengers) before thee other than men whom We inspired - Ask the followers of the Remembrance if ye know not! -

16:44 With *CLEAR PROOFS* and writings; and We have revealed unto thee the Remembrance that thou mayst explain to mankind that which hath been revealed for them, and that haply they may reflect.

16:45 Are they who plan ill-deeds then secure that Allah will not cause the earth to swallow them, or that the doom will not come on them whence they know not?

16:46 Or that He will not seize them in their going to and fro so that there be no escape for them?

16:47 Or that He will not seize them with a gradual wasting? Lo! thy Lord is indeed Full of Pity, Merciful.

16:48 Have they not observed all things that Allah hath created, how their shadows incline to the right and to the left, making prostration unto Allah, and they are lowly?

16:49 And unto Allah maketh prostration whatsoever is in the heavens and whatsoever is in the earth of living creatures, and the angels (also) and they are not proud.

16:50 They *FEAR THEIR LORD* above them, and *DO WHAT THEY ARE BIDDEN*.

16:51 *ALLAH HATH SAID: CHOOSE NOT TWO GODS. THERE IS ONLY ONE ALLAH. SO OF ME, ME ONLY, BE IN AWE.*

16:52 Unto Him belongeth whatsoever is in the heavens and the earth, and religion is His for ever. Will ye then fear any other than Allah?

16:53 And whatever of comfort ye enjoy, it is from Allah. Then, when misfortune reacheth you, unto Him ye cry for help.

16:54 And afterward, when He hath rid you of the misfortune, behold! *A SET OF YOU ATTRIBUTE PARTNERS TO THEIR LORD,*

16:55 So as to deny that which We have given them. Then enjoy life (while ye may), for ye will come to know.

16:56 And they assign a portion of that which We have given them unto what they know not. By Allah! but ye will indeed be asked concerning (all) that ye used to invent.

16:57 And they assign unto Allah daughters - Be He Glorified! - and unto themselves what they desire;

16:58 When if one of them receiveth tidings of the birth of a female, his face remaineth darkened, and he is wroth inwardly.

16:59 He hideth himself from the folk because of the *EVIL* of that whereof he hath had tidings, (asking himself): Shall he keep it in contempt, or bury it beneath the dust. Verily *EVIL* is their judgment.

16:60 For *THOSE WHO BELIEVE NOT IN THE HEREAFTER* is an *EVIL* similitude, and Allah's is the Sublime Similitude. He is the Mighty, the Wise.

16:61 If Allah were to take mankind to task for their *WRONG-DOING*, he would not leave hereon a living creature, but He reprieveth them to an appointed term, and when their term cometh they cannot put (it) off an hour nor (yet) advance (it).

16:62 And they assign unto Allah that which they (themselves) dislike, and *THEIR TONGUES EXPOUND THE LIE THAT THE BETTER PORTION WILL BE THEIRS. ASSUREDLY THEIRS WILL BE THE FIRE*, and they will be abandoned.

16:63 By Allah, We verily sent messengers unto the nations before thee, but the devil made their deeds fairseeming unto them. So *HE IS THEIR PATRON THIS DAY, AND THEIRS WILL BE A PAINFUL DOOM*.

16:64 And We have revealed the Scripture unto thee only that thou mayst explain unto them that wherein they differ, and (as) a guidance and a mercy for a people who *BELIEVE*.

16:65 Allah sendeth down water from the sky and therewith reviveth the earth after her death. Lo! herein is indeed a portent for a folk who hear.

16:66 And lo! in the cattle there is a lesson for you. We give you to drink of that which is in their bellies, from betwixt the refuse and the blood, pure milk palatable to the drinkers.

16:67 ~~And of the fruits of the date-palm, and grapes, whence ye derive strong drink and (also) good nourishment. Lo! therein is indeed a portent for people who have sense.~~ [Cancelled by verse 5:90 and by verse 5:91 i.e. conformance to this abrogation is the reason Muslims avoid alcohol.][477]

16:68 And thy Lord inspired the bee, saying: Choose thou habitations in the hills and in the trees and in that which they thatch;

16:69 Then eat of all fruits, and follow the ways of thy Lord, made smooth (for thee). There cometh forth from their bellies a drink divers of hues, wherein is healing for mankind. Lo! herein is indeed a portent for people who reflect.

16:70 And Allah createth you, then causeth you to die, and among you is he who is brought back to the most abject stage of life, so that he knoweth nothing after (having had) knowledge. Lo! Allah is Knower, Powerful.

16:71 And Allah hath favoured some of you above others in provision. Now those who are more favoured will by no means hand over their provision to those *(SLAVES) WHOM THEIR RIGHT HANDS POSSESS*, so that they may be equal with them in respect thereof. Is it then the grace of Allah that they deny? [Note slavery is not forbidden]

16:72 And Allah hath given you wives of your own kind, and hath given you, from your wives, sons and grandsons, and hath made provision of good things for you. Is it then in vanity that they *BELIEVE* and in the grace of Allah that they *DISBELIEVE*?

16:73 And they worship beside Allah that which owneth no provision whatsoever for them from the heavens or the earth, nor have they (whom they worship) any power.

16:74 So coin not similitudes for Allah. Lo! Allah knoweth; ye know not.

16:75 Allah coineth a similitude: (on the one hand) a (mere) chattel slave, who hath control of nothing, and (on the other hand) one on whom we have bestowed a fair provision from Us, and he spendeth thereof secretly and openly. Are they equal? Praise be to Allah! But most of them know not.

16:76 And Allah coineth a similitude: Two men, one of them dumb, having control of nothing, and he is a burden on his owner; whithersoever he directeth him to go, he bringeth no good. Is he equal with one who enjoineth justice and followeth *A STRAIGHT PATH (OF CONDUCT)*?

16:77 And unto Allah belongeth the Unseen of the heavens and the earth, and the matter of *THE HOUR* (of Doom) is but as a twinkling of the eye, or it is nearer still. Lo! Allah is Able to do all things.

16:78 And Allah brought you forth from the wombs of your mothers knowing nothing, and gave you hearing and sight and hearts that haply ye might give thanks.

16:79 Have they not seen the birds obedient in mid-air? None holdeth them save Allah. Lo! herein, verily, are portents for a people who *BELIEVE*.

16:80 And Allah hath given you in your houses an abode, and hath given you (also), of the hides of cattle, houses which ye find light (to carry) on the day of migration and on the day of pitching camp; and of their wool and their fur and their hair, caparison and comfort for a while.

16:81 And Allah hath given you, of that which He hath created, shelter from the sun; and hath given you places of refuge in the mountains, and hath given you coats to ward off the heat from you, and coats (of armour) to save you from your own foolhardiness. Thus doth He perfect His favour unto you, in order that ye may surrender (unto Him).

16:82 ~~Then, if they turn away, thy duty (O Muhammad) is but plain conveyance (of the message).~~ [Cancelled by verse 9:5, i.e. jihadi violence cancels out commands to convey a message][478]

16:83 They know the favour of Allah and then deny it. Most of them are ingrates.

16:84 And (bethink you of) *THE DAY* when we raise up of every nation a witness, then there is no leave for *DISBELIEVERS*, nor are they allowed to make amends.

16:85 And when those who did wrong behold the doom, it will not be made light for them, nor will they be reprieved.

16:86 And when *THOSE WHO ASCRIBED PARTNERS TO ALLAH* behold those partners of theirs, they will say: Our Lord! these are our partners unto whom we used to cry instead of Thee. But they will fling to them the saying: Lo! ye verily are *LIARS*!

16:87 And *THEY PROFFER UNTO ALLAH SUBMISSION ON THAT DAY, AND ALL THAT THEY USED TO INVENT HATH FAILED THEM.*

16:88 For *THOSE WHO DISBELIEVE AND DEBAR (MEN) FROM THE WAY OF ALLAH*, We add doom to doom because they *WROUGHT CORRUPTION*, [See Koran 5:32, where being killed is sanctioned for "corruption".]

16:89 And (bethink you of) *THE DAY* when We raise in every nation a witness against them of their own folk, and We bring thee (Muhammad) as a witness against these. And *WE REVEAL THE SCRIPTURE UNTO THEE AS AN EXPOSITION OF ALL THINGS*, and a guidance and a mercy and good tidings for *THOSE WHO HAVE SURRENDERED* (to Allah).

16:90 Lo! Allah enjoineth justice and kindness, and giving to kinsfolk, and forbiddeth lewdness and abomination and wickedness. He exhorteth you in order that ye may take heed.

16:91 *FULFIL THE COVENANT OF ALLAH* when ye have covenanted, and break not your oaths after the asseveration of them, and after ye have made Allah surety over you. Lo! Allah knoweth what ye do.

16:92 And be not like unto her who unravelleth the thread, after she hath made it strong, to thin filaments, making your oaths a deceit between you because of a nation being more numerous than (another) nation. Allah only trieth you thereby, and He verily will explain to you on *THE DAY OF RESURRECTION* that wherein ye differed.

16:93 Had Allah willed He could have made you (all) one nation, but He *SENDETH WHOM HE WILL ASTRAY AND GUIDETH WHOM HE WILL*, and ye will indeed be asked of what ye used to do. [In the system of Islam Allah is an arbitrary and all-powerful tyrant who makes some people believers and makes others be disbelievers, thus believers are Allah's "chosen people".]

16:94 Make not your oaths a deceit between you, lest a foot should slip after being firmly planted and ye should taste *EVIL* forasmuch as ye debarred (men) from the way of Allah, and yours should be an awful doom.

16:95 And purchase not a small gain at *THE PRICE OF ALLAH'S COVENANT*. Lo! that which Allah hath is better for you, if ye did but know. [Many translators discuss the price of the contract with Allah.]

16:96 That which ye have wasteth away, and that which Allah hath remaineth. And verily *WE SHALL PAY THOSE WHO ARE STEADFAST A RECOMPENSE IN PROPORTION TO THE BEST OF WHAT THEY USED TO DO.*

16:97 *WHOSOEVER DOETH RIGHT, WHETHER MALE OR FEMALE, AND IS A BELIEVER, HIM VERILY WE SHALL QUICKEN WITH GOOD LIFE, AND WE SHALL PAY THEM A RECOMPENSE IN PROPORTION TO THE BEST OF WHAT THEY USED TO DO. [IT IS STANDARD FOR TRANSLATIONS TO REFER TO PAYMENT/RECOMPENSE HERE.]*

16:98 And when thou recitest the Qur'an, seek refuge in Allah from Satan the outcast.

16:99 Lo! he hath no power over those who *BELIEVE* and put trust in their Lord.

16:100 His power is only over those who make a friend of him, and those who ascribe partners unto Him (Allah).

16:101 And when We put a revelation in place of (another) revelation, - and Allah knoweth best what He revealeth - they say: Lo! thou art but inventing. Most of them know not.

16:102 Say: The holy Spirit hath delivered it from thy Lord with truth, that it may confirm (the faith of) those who *BELIEVE*, and as guidance and good tidings for those who have surrendered (to Allah).

16:103 And We know well that they say: Only a man teacheth him. The speech of him at whom they falsely hint is outlandish, and this is clear Arabic speech.

16:104 Lo! *THOSE WHO DISBELIEVE* the revelations of Allah, Allah guideth them not and *THEIRS WILL BE A PAINFUL DOOM*.

16:105 *ONLY THEY INVENT FALSEHOOD WHO BELIEVE NOT ALLAH'S REVELATIONS, AND (ONLY) THEY ARE THE LIARS*.

16:106 Whoso *DISBELIEVETH* in Allah after his *BELIEF* - save him who is forced thereto and *WHOSE HEART IS STILL CONTENT WITH THE FAITH* - but whoso findeth *EASE IN DISBELIEF*: On them is wrath from Allah. *THEIRS WILL BE AN*

AWFUL DOOM. [The Koran permits Muslims to pretend they are not Muslims; the foundation of Islam's doctrines of deception.]

16:107 That is because they *HAVE CHOSEN THE LIFE OF THE WORLD RATHER THAN THE HEREAFTER*, and because *ALLAH GUIDETH NOT THE DISBELIEVING FOLK.*

16:108 Such are they whose hearts and ears and eyes Allah hath sealed. And such are the heedless.

16:109 Assuredly in the Hereafter they are the losers.

16:110 Then lo! thy Lord - for those who became fugitives after they had been persecuted, and then *FOUGHT AND WERE STEADFAST* - lo! thy Lord afterward is (for them) indeed Forgiving, Merciful.

16:111 On *THE DAY WHEN EVERY SOUL WILL COME PLEADING* for itself, and *EVERY SOUL WILL BE REPAID WHAT IT DID*, and they will not be wronged.

16:112 Allah coineth a similitude: *A TOWNSHIP THAT DWELT SECURE AND WELL CONTENT*, its provision coming to it in abundance from every side, but it *DISBELIEVED* in Allah's favours, so *ALLAH MADE IT EXPERIENCE THE GARB OF DEARTH AND FEAR* because of what they used to do.

16:113 And verily there had come unto them a messenger from among them, but they had denied him, and so the torment seized them while they were wrong-doers.

16:114 So eat of the lawful and good food which Allah hath provided for you, and thank the bounty of your Lord if it is Him ye serve.

16:115 He hath forbidden for you only carrion and blood and swineflesh and that which hath been immolated in the name of any other than Allah; but *HE WHO IS DRIVEN THERETO, NEITHER CRAVING NOR TRANSGRESSING*, lo! then Allah is Forgiving, Merciful. [Muslims can eat pork, provided they do not desire to eat it.]

16:116 And speak not, concerning that which your own tongues qualify (as clean or unclean), the falsehood: "This is lawful, and this is forbidden," so that ye invent *A LIE AGAINST ALLAH*. Lo! *THOSE WHO INVENT A LIE AGAINST ALLAH WILL NOT SUCCEED.*

16:117 A brief enjoyment (will be theirs); and theirs *A PAINFUL DOOM.*

16:118 And unto those who are *JEWS* We have forbidden that which We have already related unto thee. And We wronged them not, but they were wont to wrong themselves.

16:119 Then lo! thy Lord - for those who do *EVIL* in ignorance and afterward repent and amend - lo! (for them) thy Lord is afterward indeed Forgiving, Merciful.

16:120 Lo! Abraham was a nation obedient to Allah, by nature upright, and he was not of the *IDOLATERS*;

16:121 Thankful for His bounties; He chose him and He guided him unto *A STRAIGHT PATH.*

16:122 And We gave him good in the world, and in the Hereafter he is among the righteous.

16:123 And afterward We inspired thee (Muhammad, saying): Follow the religion of Abraham, as one by nature upright. He was not of the *IDOLATERS*.

16:124 The Sabbath was appointed only for those who differed concerning it, and lo! thy Lord will *JUDGE BETWEEN THEM ON THE DAY OF RESURRECTION CONCERNING THAT WHEREIN THEY USED TO DIFFER.*

16:125 ~~Call unto the way of thy Lord with wisdom and fair exhortation, and reason with them in the better way. Lo! thy Lord is Best Aware of him who strayeth from His way, and He is Best Aware of those who go aright.~~ [Cancelled by verse 9:5, command to violence replaces command to persuade][479]

16:126 If ye punish, then punish with the like of that wherewith ye were afflicted. But if ye endure patiently, verily it is better for the patient.

16:127 ~~Endure thou patiently (O Muhammad). Thine endurance is only by (the help of) Allah. Grieve not for them, and be not in distress because of that which they devise.~~ [Cancelled by verse 9:5][480]

16:128 Lo! *ALLAH IS WITH THOSE WHO KEEP THEIR DUTY UNTO HIM* and *THOSE WHO ARE DOERS OF GOOD.*

Chapter 18 - The Cave

18:1 Praise be to Allah Who hath revealed the Scripture unto His slave, and hath not placed therein any crookedness,

18:2 (But hath made it) straight, to give warning of stern punishment from Him, and to bring unto the *BELIEVERS WHO DO GOOD WORKS* the news that *THEIRS WILL BE A FAIR REWARD,*

18:3 Wherein they will abide for ever;

18:4 And to warn those who say: Allah hath chosen a son,

18:5 (A thing) whereof they have no knowledge, nor (had) their fathers, Dreadful is the word that cometh out of their mouths. They speak naught but a lie.

18:6 Yet it may be, if they *BELIEVE* not in this statement, that thou (Muhammad) wilt torment thy soul with grief over their footsteps.

18:7 Lo! We have placed all that is on the earth as an ornament thereof that We may try them: which of them is best in conduct.

18:8 And lo! We shall make all that is thereon a barren mound.

18:9 Or deemest thou that the People of the Cave and the Inscription are a wonder among Our portents?

18:10 When the young men fled for refuge to the Cave and said: Our Lord! Give us mercy from Thy presence, and shape for us right conduct in our plight.

18:11 Then We sealed up their hearing in the Cave for a number of years.

18:12 And afterward We raised them up that We might know which of the two parties would best calculate the time that they had tarried.

18:13 We narrate unto thee their story with truth. Lo! they were young men who *BELIEVED* in their Lord, and We increased them in guidance.

18:14 And We made firm their hearts when they stood forth and said: Our Lord is the Lord of the heavens and the earth. We cry unto no God beside Him, for then should we utter an enormity.

18:15 These, our people, have chosen (other) gods beside Him though they bring no clear warrant (vouchsafed) to them. And who doth greater wrong than *HE WHO INVENTETH A LIE CONCERNING ALLAH?*

18:16 And when ye withdraw from them and that which they worship except Allah, then seek refuge in the Cave; your Lord will spread for you of His mercy and will prepare for you a pillow in your plight.

18:17 And thou mightest have seen the sun when it rose move away from their cave to the right, and when it set go past them on the left, and they were in the cleft thereof. That was (one) of the portents of Allah. He whom Allah guideth, he indeed is led aright, and he whom He sendeth astray, for him thou wilt not find a guiding friend.

18:18 And thou wouldst have deemed them waking though they were asleep, and We caused them to turn over to the right and the left, and their dog stretching out his paws on the threshold. If thou hadst observed them closely thou hadst assuredly turned away from them in flight, and hadst been filled with awe of them.

18:19 And in like manner We awakened them that they might question one another. A speaker from among them said: How long have ye tarried? They said: We have tarried a day or some part of a day, (Others) said: Your Lord best knoweth what ye have tarried. Now send one of you with this your silver coin unto the city, and let him see what food is purest there and bring you a supply thereof. Let him be courteous and let no man know of you.

18:20 For they, if they should come to know of you, will stone you or turn you back to their religion; then ye will never prosper.

18:21 And in like manner We disclosed them (to the people of the city) that they might know that *THE PROMISE OF ALLAH IS TRUE, AND THAT, AS FOR THE HOUR, THERE IS NO DOUBT CONCERNING IT.* When (the people of the city) disputed of their case among themselves, they said: Build over them a building; their Lord knoweth best concerning them. Those who won their point said: We verily shall build a place of worship over them.

18:22 (Some) will say: They were three, their dog the fourth, and (some) say: Five, their dog the sixth, guessing at random; and (some) say: Seven, and their dog the eighth. Say (O Muhammad): My Lord is Best Aware of their number. None knoweth them save a few. So contend not concerning them except with an outward contending, and ask not any of them to pronounce concerning them.

18:23 And say not of anything: Lo! I shall do that tomorrow,

18:24 Except if Allah will. And remember thy Lord when thou forgettest, and say: It may be that my Lord guideth me unto a nearer way of truth than this.

18:25 And (it is said) they tarried in their Cave three hundred years and add nine.

18:26 Say: Allah is Best Aware how long they tarried. His is the Invisible of the heavens and the earth. How clear of sight is He and keen of hearing! They have no protecting friend beside Him, and He maketh none to share in His government.

18:27 And recite that which hath been revealed unto thee of *THE SCRIPTURE OF THY LORD. THERE IS NONE WHO CAN CHANGE HIS WORDS*, and thou wilt find no refuge beside Him.

18:28 Restrain thyself along with those who cry unto their Lord at morn and evening, seeking His Countenance; and let not thine eyes overlook them, desiring the pomp of the life of the world; and *OBEY* not him whose heart We have made heedless of Our remembrance, who followeth his own lust and whose case hath been abandoned.

18:29 Say: (It is) *THE TRUTH FROM THE LORD* of you (all). Then whosoever will, let him *BELIEVE*, and whosoever will, let him *DISBELIEVE*. Lo! *WE HAVE PREPARED FOR DISBELIEVERS FIRE*. Its tent encloseth them. If they ask for showers, *THEY WILL BE SHOWERED WITH WATER LIKE TO MOLTEN LEAD WHICH BURNETH THE FACES*. Calamitous the drink and ill the resting-place!

18:30 Lo! as for *THOSE WHO BELIEVE AND DO GOOD WORKS* - Lo! We suffer not *THE REWARD OF ONE WHOSE WORK IS GOODLY* to be lost.

18:31 As for such, *THEIRS WILL BE GARDENS OF EDEN, WHEREIN RIVERS FLOW BENEATH THEM; THEREIN THEY WILL BE GIVEN ARMLETS OF GOLD* and will wear green *ROBES OF FINEST SILK AND GOLD EMBROIDERY*, reclining upon throne therein. Blest the *REWARD*, and fair the resting-place!

18:32 Coin for them a similitude: Two men, unto one of whom We had assigned two gardens of grapes, and We had surrounded both with date-palms and had put between them tillage.

18:33 Each of the gardens gave its fruit and withheld naught thereof. And We caused a river to gush forth therein.

18:34 And he had fruit. And he said unto his comrade, when he spake with him: I am more than thee in wealth, and stronger in respect of men.

18:35 And he went into his garden, while he (thus) wronged himself. He said: I think not that all this will ever perish.

18:36 I think not that *THE HOUR* will ever come, and if indeed I am brought back unto my Lord I surely shall find better than this as a resort.

18:37 His comrade, when he (thus) spake with him, exclaimed: Disbelievest thou in Him Who created thee of dust, then of a drop (of seed), and then fashioned thee a man?

18:38 But He is Allah, my Lord, and I ascribe unto my Lord no partner.

18:39 If only, when thou enteredst thy garden, thou hadst said: That which Allah willeth (will come to pass)! There is no strength save in Allah! Though thou seest me as less than thee in wealth and children,

18:40 Yet it may be that my Lord will give me better than thy garden, and will send on it a bolt from heaven, and some morning it will be a smooth hillside,

18:41 Or some morning the water thereof will be lost in the earth so that thou canst not make search for it.

18:42 And his fruit was beset (with destruction). Then began he to wring his hands for all that he had spent upon it, when (now) it was all ruined on its trellises, and to say: Would that I had ascribed no partner to my Lord!

18:43 And he had no troop of men to help him as against Allah, nor could he save himself.

18:44 In this case is protection only from Allah, the True, He is Best for *REWARD*, and best for consequence.

18:45 And coin for them the similitude of the life of the world as water which We send down from the sky, and the vegetation of the earth mingleth with it and then becometh dry twigs that the winds scatter. Allah is able to do all things.

18:46 Wealth and children are an ornament of the life of the world. But the good deeds which endure are better in thy Lord's sight for *REWARD*, and better in respect of hope.

18:47 And (bethink you of) *THE DAY* when we remove the hills and ye see the earth emerging, and We gather them together so as to leave not one of them behind.

18:48 And they are set before thy Lord in ranks (and it is said unto them): Now verily have ye come unto Us as We created you at the first. But ye thought that We had set no tryst for you.

18:49 And *THE BOOK IS PLACED, AND THOU SEEST THE GUILTY FEARFUL OF THAT WHICH IS THEREIN*, and they say: What kind of a Book is this that leaveth not a small thing nor a great thing but hath counted it! And they find all that they did confronting them, and thy Lord wrongeth no-one.

18:50 And (remember) when We said unto the angels: Fall prostrate before Adam, and they fell prostrate, all save Iblis. He was of the jinn, so he rebelled against his Lord's command. Will ye choose him and his seed for your protecting friends instead of Me, when they are an enemy unto you? Calamitous is the exchange for *EVIL-DOERS*.

18:51 I made them not to witness the creation of the heavens and the earth, nor their own creation; nor choose I misleaders for (My) helpers.

18:52 And *(BE MINDFUL OF) THE DAY* when He will say: Call those partners of Mine whom ye pretended. Then they will cry unto them, but they will not hear their prayer, and We shall set a gulf of doom between them.

18:53 *AND THE GUILTY BEHOLD THE FIRE* and know that they are about to fall therein, and they find no way of escape thence.

18:54 And verily We have displayed for mankind in this Qur'an all manner of similitudes, but man is more than anything contentious.

18:55 And *NAUGHT HINDERETH MANKIND FROM BELIEVING WHEN THE GUIDANCE COMETH UNTO THEM*, and from asking forgiveness of their Lord unless (it be that they wish) that the judgment of the men of old should come upon them or (that) they should be confronted with the Doom.

18:56 We send not the messengers save as bearers of good news and warners. *THOSE WHO DISBELIEVE CONTEND WITH FALSEHOOD IN ORDER TO REFUTE THE TRUTH* thereby. And they take Our revelations and that wherewith they are threatened as a jest.

18:57 And who doth greater wrong than he who hath been reminded of the revelations of his Lord, yet turneth away from them and forgetteth what his hands send forward (to the Judgment)? Lo! on their hearts We have placed coverings so that they understand not, and in their ears a deafness. And though thou call them to the guidance, in that case they can never be led aright.

18:58 Thy Lord is the Forgiver, Full of Mercy. If He took them to task (now) for what they earn, He would hasten on the doom for them; but theirs is an appointed term from which they will find no escape.

18:59 *AND (ALL) THOSE TOWNSHIPS! WE DESTROYED THEM WHEN THEY DID WRONG, AND WE APPOINTED A FIXED TIME FOR THEIR DESTRUCTION.*

18:60 And when Moses said unto his servant: I will not give up until I reach the point where the two rivers meet, though I march on for ages.

18:61 And when they reached the point where the two met, they forgot their fish, and it took its way into the waters, being free.

18:62 And when they had gone further, he said unto his servant: Bring us our breakfast. Verily we have found fatigue in this our journey.

18:63 He said: Didst thou see, when we took refuge on the rock, and I forgot the fish - and none but Satan caused me to forget to mention it - it took its way into the waters by a marvel.

18:64 He said: This is that which we have been seeking. So they retraced their steps again.

18:65 Then found they one of Our slaves, unto whom We had given mercy from Us, and had taught him knowledge from Our presence.

18:66 Moses said unto him: May I follow thee, to the end that thou mayst teach me right conduct of that which thou hast been taught?

18:67 He said: Lo! thou canst not bear with me.

18:68 How canst thou bear with that whereof thou canst not compass any knowledge?

18:69 He said: Allah willing, thou shalt find me patient and I shall not in aught gainsay thee.

18:70 He said: Well, if thou go with me, ask me not concerning aught till I myself make mention of it unto thee.

18:71 So they twain set out till, when they were in the ship, he made a hole therein. (Moses) said: Hast thou made a hole therein to drown the folk thereof? Thou verily hast done a dreadful thing.

18:72 He said: Did I not tell thee that thou couldst not bear with me?

18:73 (Moses) said: Be not wroth with me that I forgot, and be not hard upon me for my fault.

18:74 So they twain journeyed on till, when they met a lad, he slew him. (Moses) said: What! Hast thou slain an innocent soul who hath slain no man? Verily thou hast done a horrid thing.

18:75 He said: Did I not tell thee that thou couldst not bear with me?

18:76 (Moses) said: If I ask thee after this concerning aught, keep not company with me. Thou hast received an excuse from me.

18:77 So they twain journeyed on till, when they came unto the folk of a certain township, they asked its folk for food, but they refused to make them guests. And they found therein a wall upon the point of falling into ruin, and he repaired it. (Moses) said: If thou hadst wished, thou couldst have taken payment for it.

18:78 He said: This is the parting between thee and me! I will announce unto thee the interpretation of that thou couldst not bear with patience.

18:79 As for the ship, it belonged to poor people working on the river, and I wished to mar it, for there was a king behind them who is taking every ship by force.

18:80 And as for the lad, *HIS PARENTS WERE BELIEVERS AND WE FEARED LEST HE SHOULD OPPRESS THEM BY REBELLION AND DISBELIEF.*

18:81 And we intended that their Lord should change him for them for one better in purity and nearer to mercy.

18:82 And as for the wall, it belonged to two orphan boys in the city, and there was beneath it a treasure belonging to them, and their father had been righteous, and thy Lord intended that they should come to their full strength and should bring forth their treasure as a mercy from their Lord; and I did it not upon my own command. Such is the interpretation of that wherewith thou couldst not bear.

18:83 They will ask thee of Dhu'l-Qarneyn. Say: I shall recite unto you a remembrance of him.

18:84 Lo! We made him strong in the land and gave him unto every thing a road.

18:85 And he followed a road

18:86 Till, when he reached the setting-place of the sun, he found it setting in a muddy spring, and found a people thereabout. We said: O Dhu'l-Qarneyn! Either punish or show them kindness.

18:87 He said: As for him who doeth wrong, we shall punish him, and then he will be brought back unto his Lord, Who will punish him with awful punishment!

18:88 But as for *HIM WHO BELIEVETH AND DOETH RIGHT*, good will be his *REWARD*, and We shall speak unto him a mild command.

18:89 Then he followed a road

18:90 Till, when he reached the rising-place of the sun, he found it rising on a people for whom We had appointed no shelter therefrom.

18:91 So (it was). And We knew all concerning him.

18:92 Then he followed a road

18:93 Till, when he came between the two mountains, he found upon their hither side a folk that scarce could understand a saying.

18:94 They said: O Dhu'l-Qarneyn! Lo! Gog and Magog are spoiling the land. So may we pay thee tribute on condition that thou set a barrier between us and them?

18:95 He said: That wherein my Lord hath established me is better (than your tribute). Do but help me with strength (of men), I will set between you and them a bank.

18:96 Give me pieces of iron - till, when he had levelled up (the gap) between the cliffs, he said: Blow! - till, when he had made it a fire, he said: Bring me molten copper to pour thereon.

18:97 And (Gog and Magog) were not able to surmount, nor could they pierce (it).

18:98 He said: This is a mercy from my Lord; but when the promise of my Lord cometh to pass, He will lay it low, for the promise of my Lord is true.

18:99 And on that day we shall let some of them surge against others, and *THE TRUMPET WILL BE BLOWN.* Then We shall gather them together in one gathering.

18:100 On that day *WE SHALL PRESENT HELL TO THE DISBELIEVERS*, plain to view,

18:101 Those whose eyes were hoodwinked from My reminder, and who could not bear to hear.

18:102 *DO THE DISBELIEVERS RECKON THAT THEY CAN CHOOSE MY BONDMEN AS PROTECTING FRIENDS BESIDE ME? LO! WE HAVE PREPARED HELL AS A WELCOME FOR THE DISBELIEVERS.*

18:103 Say: Shall We inform you who will be the greatest losers by their works?

18:104 Those whose effort goeth astray in the life of the world, and yet they reckon that they do good work.

18:105 Those are *THEY WHO DISBELIEVE IN THE REVELATIONS OF THEIR LORD AND IN THE MEETING WITH HIM*. Therefor their works are vain, and on *THE DAY OF RESURRECTION* We assign no weight to them.

18:106 *THAT IS THEIR REWARD: HELL, BECAUSE THEY DISBELIEVED, AND MADE A JEST OF OUR REVELATIONS* and Our messengers.

18:107 Lo! *THOSE WHO BELIEVE AND DO GOOD WORKS* [Jihad], theirs are the *GARDENS OF PARADISE* for welcome,

18:108 Wherein they will abide, with no desire to be removed from thence.
18:109 Say: Though the sea became ink for the Words of my Lord, verily the sea would be used up before the words of my Lord were exhausted, even though We brought the like thereof to help.
18:110 Say: I am only a mortal like you. My Lord inspireth in me that your Allah is only One Allah. And whoever hopeth for the meeting with his Lord, let him do righteous work, and make none sharer of the worship due unto his Lord.

Chapter 88 - The Overwhelming

88:1 Hath there come unto thee tidings of the Overwhelming?
88:2 *ON THAT DAY (MANY) FACES WILL BE DOWNCAST,*
88:3 Toiling, weary,
88:4 *SCORCHED BY BURNING FIRE,*
88:5 *DRINKING FROM A BOILING SPRING,*
88:6 No food for them save bitter thorn-fruit
88:7 Which doth not nourish nor release from hunger.
88:8 *IN THAT DAY OTHER FACES WILL BE CALM,*
88:9 Glad for their effort past,
88:10 *IN A HIGH GARDEN*
88:11 Where they hear no idle speech,
88:12 Wherein is a gushing spring,
88:13 Wherein are couches raised
88:14 And *GOBLETS SET AT HAND*
88:15 And cushions ranged
88:16 And *SILKEN CARPETS SPREAD.*
88:17 Will they not regard the camels, how they are created?
88:18 And the heaven, how it is raised?
88:19 And the hills, how they are set up?
88:20 And the earth, how it is spread?
88:21 ~~Remind them, for thou art but an admonisher,~~ [Cancelled by verse 9:5][481]
88:22 ~~Thou art not at all a warder over them.~~ [Cancelled by verse 9:5 i.e. violence commanded][482]
88:23 ~~But whoso is averse and *DISBELIEVETH,*~~ [Cancelled by verse 9:5][483]
88:24 Allah will punish him with direst punishment.
88:25 Lo! unto Us is their return
88:26 And Ours their reckoning.

Chapter 51 - The Winnowing Winds

51:1 By those that winnow with a winnowing
51:2 And those that bear the burden (of the rain)
51:3 And those that glide with ease (upon the sea)
51:4 And those who distribute (blessings) by command,
51:5 Lo! *THAT WHEREWITH YE ARE THREATENED IS INDEED TRUE,*
51:6 And lo! the judgment will indeed befall.
51:7 By the heaven full of paths,
51:8 Lo! ye, forsooth, are of various opinion (concerning *THE TRUTH*).
51:9 He is made to turn away from it who is (himself) averse.
51:10 Accursed be the conjecturers
51:11 Who are careless in an abyss!
51:12 They ask: *WHEN IS THE DAY OF JUDGMENT?*
51:13 *(IT IS) THE DAY WHEN THEY WILL BE TORMENTED AT THE FIRE,*
51:14 (And it will be said unto them): Taste your torment (which ye inflicted). This is what ye sought to hasten.
51:15 Lo! *THOSE WHO KEEP FROM EVIL WILL DWELL AMID GARDENS AND WATERSPRINGS,*
51:16 Taking that which their Lord giveth them; for lo! aforetime they were doers of good;
51:17 They used to sleep but little of the night,

51:18 And ere the dawning of each day would seek forgiveness,

51:19 And in their wealth the beggar and the outcast had due share.

51:20 And in the earth are portents for those whose faith is sure.

51:21 And (also) in yourselves. Can ye then not see?

51:22 And in the heaven is your providence and that which ye are promised;

51:23 And by the Lord of the heavens and the earth, it is *THE TRUTH*, even as (it is true) that ye speak.

51:24 Hath the story of Abraham's honoured guests reached thee (O Muhammad)?

51:25 When they came in unto him and said: Peace! he answered, Peace! (and thought): Folk unknown (to me).

51:26 Then he went apart unto his housefolk so that they brought a fatted calf;

51:27 And he set it before them, saying: Will ye not eat?

51:28 Then he conceived a fear of them. They said: Fear not! and gave him tidings of (the birth of) a wise son.

51:29 Then his wife came forward, making moan, and smote her face, and cried: A barren old woman!

51:30 They said: Even so saith thy Lord. Lo! He is the Wise, the Knower.

51:31 (Abraham) said: And (afterward) what is your errand, O ye sent (from Allah)?

51:32 They said: Lo! we are sent unto a guilty folk,

51:33 That we may send upon them stones of clay,

51:34 Marked by thy Lord for (the destruction of) the wanton.

51:35 Then We brought forth such *BELIEVERS* as were there.

51:36 But We found there but one house of those surrendered (to Allah).

51:37 And We left behind therein a portent for *THOSE WHO FEAR A PAINFUL DOOM.*

51:38 And in Moses (too, there is a portent) when We sent him unto Pharaoh with clear warrant,

51:39 But he withdrew (confiding) in his might, and said: A wizard or *A MADMAN*.

51:40 So We seized him and his *HOSTS [ARMIES]* and flung them in the sea, for he was reprobate.

51:41 And in (the tribe of) A'ad (there is a portent) when we sent the fatal wind against them.

51:42 It spared naught that it reached, but made it (all) as dust.

51:43 And in (the tribe of) Thamud (there is a portent) when it was told them: Take your ease awhile.

51:44 But they rebelled against their Lord's decree, and so the thunderbolt overtook them even while they gazed;

51:45 And they were unable to rise up, nor could they help themselves.

51:46 And the folk of Noah aforetime. Lo! they were licentious folk.

51:47 We have built the heaven with might, and We it is Who make the vast extent (thereof).

51:48 And the earth have We laid out, how gracious is the Spreader (thereof)!

51:49 And all things We have created by pairs, that haply ye may reflect.

51:50 Therefor flee unto Allah; lo! I am a plain warner unto you from him.

51:51 And set not any other god along with Allah; lo! I am a plain warner unto you from Him.

51:52 Even so there came no messenger unto those before them but *THEY SAID: A WIZARD OR A MADMAN!*

51:53 Have they handed down (the saying) as an heirloom one unto another? Nay, but *THEY ARE FROWARD [CONTRARY] FOLK.*

51:54 So withdraw from them (O Muhammad), for thou art in no wise blameworthy,

51:55 And warn, for warning profiteth *BELIEVERS*.

51:56 I created the jinn and humankind only that they might worship Me.

51:57 I seek no livelihood from them, nor do I ask that they should feed Me.

51:58 Lo! Allah! He it is that giveth livelihood, the Lord of unbreakable might.

51:59 And lo! *FOR THOSE WHO (NOW) DO WRONG THERE IS AN EVIL DAY* like unto the evil day (which came for) their likes (of old); so let them not ask Me to hasten on (that day).

51:60 And woe unto *THOSE WHO DISBELIEVE*, from (that) *THEIR DAY WHICH THEY ARE PROMISED.*

Chapter 46 - The Wind-Curved Sandhills

46:1 Ha. Mim.

46:2 The revelation of the Scripture is from Allah the Mighty, the Wise.

46:3 We created not the heavens and the earth and all that is between them save with truth, and for a term appointed. But *THOSE WHO DISBELIEVE* turn away from that whereof they are warned.

46:4 Say (unto them, O Muhammad): Have ye thought on all that ye invoke beside Allah? Show me what they have created of the earth. Or have they any portion in the heavens? Bring me a scripture before this (Scripture), or some vestige of knowledge (in support of what ye say), if ye are truthful.

46:5 And who is further astray than those who, instead of Allah, pray unto such as hear not their prayer until *THE DAY OF RESURRECTION,* and are unconscious of their prayer,

46:6 And when mankind are gathered (to the Judgment) will become enemies for them, and will become deniers of having been worshipped.

46:7 And when Our clear revelations are recited unto them, *THOSE WHO DISBELIEVE SAY OF THE TRUTH WHEN IT REACHETH THEM: THIS IS MERE MAGIC.*

46:8 *OR SAY THEY: HE HATH INVENTED IT?* Say (O Muhammad): If I have invented it, still ye have no power to support me against Allah. He is Best Aware of what ye say among yourselves concerning it. He sufficeth for a witness between me and you. And He is the Forgiving, the Merciful.

46:9 ~~Say: I am no new thing among the messengers (of Allah), nor know I what will be done with me or with you. I do but follow that which is inspired in me, and I am but a plain warner.~~ [Cancelled by verses 48:1 to 48:6, persuasion is replaced by commands to violent jihad][484]

46:10 Bethink you: If it is from Allah and ye *DISBELIEVE* therein, and a witness of *THE CHILDREN OF ISRAEL* hath already testified to the like thereof and *HATH BELIEVED*, and ye are too proud (what plight is yours)? Lo! Allah guideth not *WRONG-DOING FOLK.*

46:11 And *THOSE WHO DISBELIEVE SAY OF THOSE WHO BELIEVE*: If it had been (any) good, they would not have been before us in attaining it. And since they will not be guided by it, they say: *THIS IS AN ANCIENT LIE;*

46:12 When before it there was the Scripture of Moses, an example and a mercy; and this is a confirming *SCRIPTURE IN THE ARABIC LANGUAGE*, that it may warn those who do wrong and bring good tidings for the righteous.

46:13 Lo! those who say: Our Lord is Allah, and thereafter walk aright, there shall no fear come upon them neither shall they grieve.

46:14 *SUCH ARE RIGHTFUL OWNERS OF THE GARDEN, IMMORTAL THEREIN, AS A REWARD FOR WHAT THEY USED TO DO.*

46:15 And We have commended unto man kindness toward parents. His mother beareth him with reluctance, and bringeth him forth with reluctance, and the bearing of him and the weaning of him is thirty months, till, when he attaineth full strength and reacheth forty years, he saith: My Lord! Arouse me that I may give thanks for the favour wherewith Thou hast favoured me and my parents, and that I may do right acceptable unto Thee. And be gracious unto me in the matter of my seed. Lo! I have turned unto Thee repentant, and lo! I am of those who surrender (unto Thee).

46:16 Those are they from whom We accept the best of what they do, and *OVERLOOK THEIR EVIL DEEDS.* (They are) among the *OWNERS OF THE GARDEN*. This is the true promise *WHICH THEY WERE PROMISED* (in the world).

46:17 And whoso saith unto his parents: Fie upon you both! Do ye threaten me that I shall be brought forth (again) when generations before me have passed away? And they twain cry unto Allah for help (and say): Woe unto thee! *BELIEVE*! Lo! *THE PROMISE OF ALLAH IS TRUE*. But he saith: This is naught save fables of the men of old:

46:18 Such are those on whom the Word concerning nations of the jinn and mankind which have passed away before them hath effect. Lo! they are the losers.

46:19 And for all there will be ranks from what they do, that He may *PAY THEM FOR THEIR DEEDS*; and they will not be wronged.

46:20 And on *THE DAY WHEN THOSE WHO DISBELIEVE ARE EXPOSED TO THE FIRE* (it will be said): Ye squandered your good things in the life of the world and sought comfort therein. Now *THIS DAY YE ARE REWARDED WITH THE DOOM OF IGNOMINY BECAUSE YE WERE DISDAINFUL* in the land without a right, and because ye used to transgress.

46:21 And make mention (O Muhammad) of the brother of A'ad when he warned his folk among the wind-curved sandhills - and verily warners came and went before and after him - saying: Serve none but Allah. Lo! *I FEAR FOR YOU THE DOOM OF A TREMENDOUS DAY.*

46:22 They said: Hast come to turn us away from our gods? Then bring upon us that wherewith thou threatenest us, if thou art of the *TRUTHFUL.*

46:23 He said: *THE KNOWLEDGE IS WITH ALLAH ONLY.* I convey unto you that wherewith I have been sent, but I see you are a folk that know not.

46:24 Then, when they beheld it as a dense cloud coming toward their valleys, they said: Here is a cloud bringing us rain. Nay, but it is that which ye did seek to hasten, a wind wherein is painful torment,

46:25 Destroying all things by commandment of its Lord. And morning found them so that naught could be seen save their dwellings. *THUS DO WE REWARD THE GUILTY FOLK.*

46:26 And verily We had empowered them with that wherewith We have not empowered you, and had assigned them ears and eyes and hearts; but their ears and eyes and hearts availed them naught since *THEY DENIED THE REVELATIONS OF ALLAH;* and *WHAT THEY USED TO MOCK BEFELL THEM.*

46:27 And verily We have destroyed townships round about you, and displayed (for them) Our revelation, that haply they might return.

46:28 Then why did those whom they had chosen for gods as a way of approach (unto Allah) not help them? Nay, but they did fail them utterly. And (all) *THAT WAS THEIR LIE, AND WHAT THEY USED TO INVENT.*

46:29 And when We inclined toward thee (Muhammad) certain of the jinn, who wished to hear the Qur'an and, when they were in its presence, said: Give ear! and, when it was finished, turned back to their people, warning.

46:30 They said: O *OUR PEOPLE*! Lo! we have heard a Scripture which hath been revealed after Moses, confirming that which was before it, guiding unto *THE TRUTH* and *A RIGHT ROAD.*

46:31 O *OUR PEOPLE*! respond to Allah's summoner and *BELIEVE* in Him. He will forgive you some of your sins and guard you from *A PAINFUL DOOM.*

46:32 And whoso respondeth not to Allah's summoner he can nowise escape in the earth, and he hath *NO PROTECTING FRIENDS* instead of Him. Such are in error manifest.

46:33 Have they not seen that Allah, Who created the heavens and the earth and was not wearied by their creation, is Able to give life to the dead? Aye, He verily is Able to do all things.

46:34 And on *THE DAY WHEN THOSE WHO DISBELIEVE ARE EXPOSED TO THE FIRE* (they will be asked): Is not this real? They will say: Yea, by our Lord. He will say: Then taste the doom for that ye *DISBELIEVED*.

46:35 ~~Then have patience (O Muhammad) even as the stout of heart among the messengers (of old) had patience, and seek not to hasten on (the doom) for them.~~ On the day when they see that which they are promised (it will seem to them) as though they had tarried but an hour of daylight. A clear message. *SHALL ANY BE DESTROYED SAVE EVIL-LIVING FOLK?* [The violence of verse 9:5 replaces patience][485]

Chapter 45 - Crouching

45:1 Ha. Mim.

45:2 The revelation of the Scripture is from Allah, the Mighty, the Wise.

45:3 Lo! in the heavens and the earth are portents for *BELIEVERS*.

45:4 And in your creation, and all the beasts that He scattereth in the earth, are portents for *A FOLK WHOSE FAITH IS SURE.*

45:5 And the difference of night and day and the provision that Allah sendeth down from the sky and thereby quickeneth the earth after her death, and the ordering of the winds, are portents for a people who have sense.

45:6 These are the portents of Allah which We recite unto thee (Muhammad) with truth. Then in what fact, after Allah and His portents, will they *BELIEVE*?

45:7 Woe unto each sinful liar,

45:8 Who heareth the revelations of Allah recited unto him, and then continueth in pride as though he heard them not. Give him tidings of *A PAINFUL DOOM.*

45:9 And *WHEN HE KNOWETH AUGHT OF OUR REVELATIONS HE MAKETH IT A JEST. FOR SUCH THERE IS A SHAMEFUL DOOM.* [Those who laugh at Islam.]

45:10 Beyond them there is *HELL,* and *THAT WHICH THEY HAVE EARNED* will naught avail them, nor those whom they have *CHOSEN FOR PROTECTING FRIENDS BESIDE ALLAH. THEIRS WILL BE AN AWFUL DOOM.*

45:11 This is guidance. And *THOSE WHO DISBELIEVE THE REVELATIONS OF THEIR LORD, FOR THEM THERE IS A PAINFUL DOOM OF WRATH.*

45:12 Allah it is Who hath made the sea of service unto you that the ships may run thereon by His command, and that ye may seek of His bounty, and that haply ye may be thankful;

45:13 And hath made of service unto you whatsoever is in the heavens and whatsoever is in the earth; it is all from Him. Lo! herein verily are portents for a people who reflect.

45:14 ~~Tell those who believe to forgive those who hope not for the days of Allah; in order that He may requite folk what they used to earn.~~ [Cancelled by verse 9:5 i.e. violence commanded][486]

45:15 Whoso doeth right, it is for his soul, and whoso doeth wrong, it is against it. And afterward unto your Lord ye will be brought back.

45:16 And verily we gave *THE CHILDREN OF ISRAEL* the Scripture and the Command and the Prophethood, and provided them with good things and favoured them above (all) peoples;

45:17 And gave them plain commandments. And they differed not until after the knowledge came unto them, through rivalry among themselves. Lo! thy Lord will judge between them on *THE DAY OF RESURRECTION CONCERNING THAT WHEREIN THEY USED TO DIFFER.*

45:18 And now have We set thee (O Muhammad) on a clear road of (Our) commandment; so follow it, and follow not the whims of those who know not.

45:19 Lo! they can avail thee naught against Allah. And lo! as for *THE WRONG-DOERS*, some of them are friends of others; and Allah is the Friend of those who ward off (*EVIL*).

45:20 This is clear indication for mankind, and a guidance and a *MERCY FOR A FOLK WHOSE FAITH IS SURE.*

45:21 Or do those who commit ill-deeds suppose that We shall make them as those who *BELIEVE* and do good works, the same in life and death? Bad is their judgment!

45:22 And Allah hath created the heavens and the earth with truth, and that every soul may be repaid what it hath earned. And they will not be wronged.

45:23 Hast thou seen him who maketh his desire his god, and Allah sendeth him astray purposely, and sealeth up his hearing and his heart, and setteth on his sight a covering? Then who will lead him after Allah (hath condemned him)? Will ye not then heed?

45:24 And they say: There is naught but our life of the world; we die and we live, and naught destroyeth us save time; when they have no knowledge whatsoever of (all) that; they do but guess.

45:25 And when *OUR CLEAR REVELATIONS ARE RECITED UNTO THEM THEIR ONLY ARGUMENT IS THAT THEY SAY: BRING (BACK) OUR FATHERS THEN, IF YE ARE TRUTHFUL.* [Islam exists to conquer all other beliefs, it is the very opposite of tolerance and multiculturalism.]

45:26 Say (unto them, O Muhammad): Allah giveth life to you, then causeth you to die, then gathereth you unto *THE DAY OF RESURRECTION* whereof there is no doubt. But most of mankind know not.

45:27 And unto *ALLAH BELONGETH THE SOVEREIGNTY OF THE HEAVENS AND THE EARTH*; and on the day when the Hour riseth, *ON THAT DAY THOSE WHO FOLLOW FALSEHOOD WILL BE LOST.*

45:28 And thou wilt see each nation crouching, each nation summoned to its record. (And it will be said unto them): This day ye are requited what ye used to do.

45:29 *THIS OUR BOOK PRONOUNCETH AGAINST YOU WITH TRUTH.* Lo! We have caused (all) that ye did to be recorded.

45:30 Then, as for *THOSE WHO BELIEVED* and did good works, their Lord will bring them in unto His mercy. That is the evident triumph.

45:31 And as for *THOSE WHO DISBELIEVED* (it will be said unto them): Were not Our revelations recited unto you? But ye were scornful and became a guilty folk.

45:32 And when it was said: Lo! *ALLAH'S PROMISE IS THE TRUTH*, and there is *NO DOUBT OF THE HOUR'S COMING*, ye said: We know not what the Hour is. We deem it naught but a conjecture, and we are by no means convinced.

45:33 And the evils of what they did will appear unto them, and that which they used to deride will befall them.

45:34 And it will be said: This day We forget you, even as ye forgot the meeting of this your day; and *YOUR HABITATION IS THE FIRE*, and there is none to help you.

45:35 This, forasmuch as *YE MADE THE REVELATIONS OF ALLAH A JEST*, and the life of the world beguiled you. Therefor this day they come not forth from thence, nor can they make amends.

45:36 Then praise be to Allah, Lord of the heavens and Lord of the earth, the Lord of the Worlds.

45:37 And unto Him (alone) belongeth Majesty in the heavens and the earth, and He is the Mighty, the Wise.

Chapter 44 - Smoke

44:1 Ha. Mim.

44:2 By *THE SCRIPTURE THAT MAKETH PLAIN*

44:3 Lo! We revealed it on a blessed night - Lo! We are ever warning -

44:4 Whereon *EVERY WISE COMMAND IS MADE CLEAR*

44:5 As a command from Our presence - Lo! We are ever sending -

44:6 A mercy from thy Lord. Lo! He, even He is the Hearer, the Knower,

44:7 Lord of the heavens and the earth and all that is between them, if ye would be sure.

44:8 There is no God save Him. He quickeneth and giveth death; your Lord and Lord of your forefathers.

44:9 Nay, but they play in doubt.

44:10 But watch thou (O Muhammad) for *THE DAY* when the sky will produce visible smoke

44:11 That will envelop the people. *THIS WILL BE A PAINFUL TORMENT.*

44:12 (Then they will say): Our Lord relieve us of the torment. Lo! we are *BELIEVERS*.

44:13 How can there be remembrance for them, when a messenger *MAKING PLAIN (THE TRUTH)* had already come unto them,

44:14 And *THEY HAD TURNED AWAY FROM HIM AND SAID: ONE TAUGHT (BY OTHERS), A MADMAN?* [Mohammed's contemporaries thought he was mad.]

44:15 Lo! We withdraw the torment a little. Lo! ye return (to *DISBELIEF*).

44:16 On the day when We shall seize them with the greater seizure, (then) in truth *WE SHALL PUNISH*.

44:17 And verily We tried before them Pharaoh's folk, when there came unto them a noble messenger,

44:18 Saying: Give up to me *THE SLAVES OF ALLAH*. Lo! I am a faithful messenger unto you.

44:19 And saying: Be not proud against Allah. Lo! I bring you a clear warrant.

44:20 And lo! I have sought refuge in my Lord and your Lord lest ye stone me to death.

44:21 And if ye put no faith in me, then let me go.

44:22 And he cried unto his Lord, (saying): These are guilty folk.

44:23 Then (his Lord commanded): Take away My *SLAVES* by night. Lo! ye will be followed,

44:24 And leave the sea behind at rest, for lo! they are a drowned host.

44:25 How many were the gardens and the watersprings that they left behind,

44:26 And the cornlands and the goodly sites

44:27 And pleasant things wherein they took delight!

44:28 Even so (it was), and We made it an inheritance for other folk;

44:29 And the heaven and the earth wept not for them, nor were they reprieved.

44:30 And We delivered *THE CHILDREN OF ISRAEL* from the shameful doom;

44:31 (We delivered them) from Pharaoh. Lo! he was a tyrant of the wanton ones.

44:32 And We chose them, purposely, above (all) creatures.

44:33 And We gave them portents wherein was a clear trial.

44:34 Lo! these, forsooth, are saying:

44:35 There is naught but our first death, and we shall not be raised again.

44:36 Bring back our fathers, if ye speak the truth!

44:37 Are they better, or the folk of Tubb'a and those before them? We destroyed them, for surely they were guilty.

44:38 And We created not the heavens and the earth, and all that is between them, in play.

44:39 We created them not save with truth; but most of them know not.

44:40 Assuredly *THE DAY OF DECISION* is the term for all of them,

44:41 A day when friend can in naught avail friend, nor can they be helped,

44:42 *SAVE HIM ON WHOM ALLAH HATH MERCY.* Lo! He is the Mighty, the Merciful. [All powerful Allah will only have mercy on the most dutiful Believers; everyone else is to be tortured by Allah.]

44:43 Lo! the tree of Zaqqum,

44:44 The food of the sinner! [Not following Islam is a sin.]

44:45 Like *MOLTEN BRASS*, it seetheth *IN THEIR BELLIES*

44:46 As the seething of boiling water. [Eternity of torture.]

44:47 (And it will be said): Take him and *DRAG HIM TO THE MIDST OF HELL*,

44:48 Then *POUR UPON HIS HEAD THE TORMENT OF BOILING WATER.*

44:49 (Saying): Taste! Lo! thou wast forsooth the mighty, the noble!

44:50 Lo! *THIS IS THAT WHEREOF YE USED TO DOUBT.*

44:51 Lo! *THOSE WHO KEPT THEIR DUTY* will be in a place secured.

44:52 Amid *GARDENS* and watersprings, [Eternity living in Paradise]

44:53 *ATTIRED IN SILK* and silk embroidery, facing one another.

44:54 Even so (it will be). And We shall *WED THEM UNTO FAIR ONES* with wide, lovely eyes.

44:55 They call therein for every fruit in safety.

44:56 They taste not death therein, save the first death. And He *HATH SAVED THEM FROM THE DOOM OF HELL,*

44:57 A bounty from thy Lord. *THAT IS THE SUPREME TRIUMPH.*

44:58 And We have made (this Scripture) easy in thy language only that they may heed.
44:59 ~~Wait then (O Muhammad). Lo! they (too) are waiting.~~ [replaced by the violence of verse 9:5][487]

Chapter 43 - Ornaments of Gold

43:1 Ha. Mim.
43:2 By *THE SCRIPTURE WHICH MAKETH PLAIN,*
43:3 Lo! We have appointed it a Lecture, in Arabic that haply ye may understand.
43:4 And Lo! in the Source of Decrees, which We possess, it is indeed sublime, decisive.
43:5 Shall We utterly ignore you because ye are a wanton folk?
43:6 How many a prophet did We send among the men of old!
43:7 And never came there unto them *A PROPHET BUT THEY USED TO MOCK HIM.*
43:8 Then We destroyed men mightier than these in prowess; and the example of the men of old hath gone (before them).
43:9 And if thou (Muhammad) ask them: Who created the heavens and the earth, they will surely answer: The Mighty, the Knower created them;
43:10 Who made the earth a resting-place for you, and placed roads for you therein, that haply ye may find your way;
43:11 And Who sendeth down water from the sky in (due) measure, and We revive a dead land therewith. Even so will ye be brought forth;
43:12 He Who created all the pairs, and appointed for you ships and cattle whereupon ye ride.
43:13 That ye may mount upon their backs, and may remember your Lord's favour when ye mount thereon, and may say: Glorified be He Who hath subdued these unto us, and we were not capable (of subduing them);
43:14 And lo! unto our Lord we surely are returning.
43:15 And they allot to Him a portion of His *BONDMEN*! Lo! man is verily a mere ingrate.
43:16 Or chooseth He daughters of all that He hath created, and honoureth He you with sons?
43:17 And if one of them hath tidings of that which he likeneth to the Beneficent One, his countenance becometh black and he is full of inward rage.
43:18 (Liken they then to Allah) that which is bred up in outward show, and in dispute cannot make itself plain?
43:19 And they make the angels, who are the slaves of the Beneficent, females. Did they witness their creation? Their testimony will be recorded and they will be questioned.
43:20 And they say: If the Beneficent One had (so) willed, we should not have worshipped them. They have no knowledge whatsoever of that. They do but guess.
43:21 Or have We given them any scripture before (this Qur'an) so that they are holding fast thereto?
43:22 Nay, for they say only: Lo! we found our fathers following a religion, and we are guided by their footprints.
43:23 And even so We sent not a warner before thee (Muhammad) into any township but its luxurious ones said: Lo! we found our fathers following a religion, and we are following their footprints.
43:24 (And the warner) said: What! Even though I bring you better guidance than that ye found your fathers following? They answered: Lo! in what ye bring we are *DISBELIEVERS*.
43:25 So We requited them. Then see the nature of the consequence for the rejecters!

43:26 And when Abraham said unto his father and his folk: Lo! I am innocent of what ye worship

43:27 Save Him Who did create me, for He will surely guide me.

43:28 And he made it a word enduring among his seed, that haply they might return.

43:29 Nay, but I let these and their fathers enjoy life (only) till there should come unto them *THE TRUTH* and a messenger making plain.

43:30 And now that *THE TRUTH* hath come unto them they say: This is mere magic, and lo! we are *DISBELIEVERS* therein.

43:31 And they say: If only this Qur'an had been revealed to some great man of the two towns?

43:32 Is it they who apportion thy Lord's mercy? We have apportioned among them their livelihood in the life of the world, and raised some of them above others in rank that some of them may take labour from others; and the mercy of thy Lord is better than (the wealth) that they amass.

43:33 And were it not that mankind would have become one community, We might well have appointed, for *THOSE WHO DISBELIEVE* in the Beneficent, roofs of silver for their houses and stairs (of silver) whereby to mount,

43:34 And for their houses doors (of silver) and couches of silver whereon to recline,

43:35 And ornaments of gold. Yet all that would have been but a provision of the life of the world. And the Hereafter with your Lord would have been for *THOSE WHO KEEP FROM EVIL.*

43:36 And he whose sight is dim to the remembrance of the Beneficent, We assign unto him a devil who becometh his comrade;

43:37 And lo! *THEY SURELY TURN THEM FROM THE WAY OF ALLAH, AND YET THEY DEEM THAT THEY ARE RIGHTLY GUIDED;*

43:38 Till, when he cometh unto Us, he saith (unto his comrade): Ah, would that between me and thee there were the distance of the two horizons - *AN EVIL COMRADE!*

43:39 And it profiteth you not *THIS DAY, BECAUSE YE DID WRONG, THAT YE WILL BE SHARERS IN THE DOOM.*

43:40 Canst thou (Muhammad) make the deaf to hear, or canst thou guide the blind or him who is in error manifest?

43:41 And if We take thee away, *WE SURELY SHALL TAKE VENGEANCE ON THEM,*

43:42 Or (if) We show thee that wherewith We threaten them; for lo! We have complete command of them.

43:43 So hold thou fast to that which is inspired in thee. Lo! thou art on *A RIGHT PATH.*

43:44 And lo! it is in truth a Reminder for thee and for thy folk; and ye will be questioned.

43:45 And ask those of Our messengers whom We sent before thee: Did We ever appoint gods to be worshipped beside the Beneficent?

43:46 And verily We sent Moses with Our revelations unto Pharaoh and his chiefs, and he said: I am a messenger of the Lord of the Worlds.

43:47 But when he brought them Our tokens, behold! they laughed at them.

43:48 And every token that We showed them was greater than its sister (token), and We grasped them with the torment, that haply they might turn again.

43:49 And they said: O wizard! Entreat thy Lord for us by the pact that He hath made with thee. Lo! we verily will walk aright.

43:50 But when We eased them of the torment, behold! they broke their word.

43:51 And Pharaoh caused a proclamation to be made among his people saying: O my people! Is not mine the sovereignty of Egypt and these rivers flowing under me? Can ye not then discern?

43:52 I am surely better than this fellow, who is despicable and can hardly make (his meaning) plain!

43:53 Why, then, have armlets of gold not been set upon him, or angels sent along with him?

43:54 Thus he persuaded his people to make light (of Moses), and they obeyed him. Lo! they were a wanton folk.

43:55 So, when they angered Us, We punished them and drowned them every one.

43:56 And We made them a thing past, and an example for those after (them).

43:57 And when the *SON OF MARY* is quoted as an example, behold! the folk laugh out,

43:58 And say: Are our gods better, or is he? They raise not the objection save for argument. Nay! but they are a contentious folk.

43:59 He is nothing but a slave on whom We bestowed favour, and We made him a pattern for *THE CHILDREN OF ISRAEL.*

43:60 And had We willed We could have set among you angels to be viceroys in the earth.

43:61 And lo! verily there is knowledge of *THE HOUR.* So doubt ye not concerning it, but *FOLLOW ME. THIS IS THE RIGHT PATH.*

43:62 And let not Satan turn you aside. Lo! he is an open enemy for you.

43:63 When *JESUS* came with *CLEAR PROOFS* (of Allah's Sovereignty), he said: I have come unto you with wisdom, and to make plain some of that concerning which ye differ. So *KEEP YOUR DUTY TO ALLAH*, and *OBEY ME*.

43:64 Lo! Allah, He is my Lord and your Lord. So worship Him. This is *A RIGHT PATH*.

43:65 But the factions among them differed. Then woe unto *THOSE WHO DO WRONG* from *THE DOOM OF A PAINFUL DAY*.

43:66 Await they aught save *THE HOUR*, that it shall come upon them suddenly, when they know not?

43:67 *FRIENDS ON THAT DAY WILL BE FOES ONE TO ANOTHER*, save those who kept their duty (to Allah).

43:68 O My slaves! For you there is no fear this day, nor is it ye who grieve;

43:69 (Ye) who *BELIEVED OUR REVELATIONS AND WERE SELF-SURRENDERED*,

43:70 *ENTER THE GARDEN, YE AND YOUR WIVES*, to be made glad.

43:71 Therein are brought round for them *TRAYS OF GOLD* and goblets, and therein is all that souls desire and eyes find sweet. And *YE ARE IMMORTAL THEREIN*.

43:72 This is the Garden which ye are made to inherit because of what ye used to do.

43:73 Therein for you is fruit in plenty whence to eat.

43:74 Lo! *THE GUILTY ARE IMMORTAL IN HELL'S TORMENT*.

43:75 It is not relaxed for them, and they despair therein.

43:76 We wronged them not, but they it was who did the wrong.

43:77 And they cry: O master! Let thy Lord make an end of us. He saith: Lo! here ye must remain.

43:78 *WE VERILY BROUGHT THE TRUTH UNTO YOU, BUT YE WERE, MOST OF YOU, AVERSE TO THE TRUTH*.

43:79 Or do they determine any thing (against the Prophet)? Lo! We (also) are determining.

43:80 Or deem they that We cannot hear their secret thoughts and private confidences? Nay, but Our envoys, present with them, do record.

43:81 Say (O Muhammad): If the Beneficent One hath a son, then, I shall be first among the worshippers. (But there is no son).

43:82 Glorified be the Lord of the heavens and the earth, the Lord of the Throne, from that which they ascribe (unto Him)!

43:83 ~~So let them flounder (in their talk) and play until they meet the Day which they are promised.~~ [Cancelled by verse 9:5 i.e. violence was commanded instead of indifference][488]

43:84 And He it is Who in the heaven is Allah, and in the earth Allah. He is the Wise, the Knower.

43:85 And blessed be He unto Whom belongeth the Sovereignty of the heavens and the earth and all that is between them, and with Whom is knowledge of *THE HOUR*, and *UNTO WHOM YE WILL BE RETURNED*.

43:86 And those unto whom they cry instead of Him possess no power of intercession, saving him who beareth witness unto *THE TRUTH* knowingly.

43:87 And if thou ask them who created them, they will surely say: Allah. How then are they turned away?

43:88 And he saith: O my Lord! Lo! these are *A FOLK WHO BELIEVE NOT*.

43:89 ~~Then bear with them (O Muhammad) and say: Peace. But they will come to know.~~ [Cancelled by verse 9:5 i.e. replaced by commands for Jihad][489]

Chapter 42 - Counsel

42:1 Ha. Mim.

42:2 A'in. Sin. Qaf.

42:3 Thus Allah the Mighty, the Knower inspireth thee (Muhammad) as (He inspired) those before thee.

42:4 Unto Him belongeth all that is in the heavens and all that is in the earth, and He is the Sublime, the Tremendous.

42:5 Almost might the heavens above be rent asunder while the angels hymn the praise of their Lord and ask forgiveness for those on the earth. Lo! Allah, He is the Forgiver, the Merciful.

42:6 And as for those who choose protecting friends beside Him~~, Allah is Warden over them, and thou art in no wise a guardian over them.~~ [Part Cancelled by verse 9:5][490]

42:7 And thus We have inspired in thee *A LECTURE IN ARABIC*, that thou mayst warn the mother-town and those around it, and mayst warn of *A*

DAY OF ASSEMBLING WHEREOF THERE IS NO DOUBT. **A host [group] will be** *IN THE GARDEN,* **and a host [group] of them** *IN THE FLAME.*

42:8 Had Allah willed, He could have made them one community, but Allah bringeth whom He will into His mercy. And the wrong-doers have no friend nor helper.

42:9 Or have they chosen protecting friends besides Him? But Allah, He (alone) is the Protecting Friend. He quickeneth the dead, and He is Able to do all things.

42:10 And in whatsoever ye differ, the verdict therein belongeth to Allah. Such is my Lord, in Whom I put my trust, and unto Whom I turn.

42:11 The Creator of the heavens and the earth. He hath made for you pairs of yourselves, and of the cattle also pairs, whereby He multiplieth you. Naught is as His likeness; and He is the Hearer, the Seer.

42:12 His are the keys of the heavens and the earth. He enlargeth providence for whom He will and straiteneth (it for whom He will). Lo! He is Knower of all things.

42:13 He hath ordained for you that religion which He commended unto Noah, and that which We inspire in thee (Muhammad), and that which We commended unto Abraham and Moses and *JESUS,* saying: Establish the religion, and be not divided therein. Dreadful for the *IDOLATERS* is that unto which thou callest them. *ALLAH CHOOSETH FOR HIMSELF WHOM HE WILL,* and guideth unto Himself him who turneth (toward Him).

42:14 And they were not divided until after the knowledge came unto them, through rivalry among themselves; and had it not been for a Word that had already gone forth from thy Lord for an appointed term, it surely had been judged between them. And those who were made to inherit the Scripture after them are verily in hopeless doubt concerning it.

42:15 ~~Unto this, then, summon (O Muhammad). And be thou upright as thou art commanded, and follow not their lusts, but say: I believe in whatever scripture Allah hath sent down, and I am commanded to be just among you. Allah is our Lord and your Lord. Unto us our works and unto you your works; no argument between us and you. Allah will bring us together, and unto Him is the journeying.~~ [Cancelled by verse 9:5 and verse 9:29 i.e. violence commanded instead][491]

42:16 And those who argue concerning Allah after He hath been acknowledged, their argument hath no weight with their Lord, and wrath is upon them and theirs will be an awful doom.

42:17 Allah it is Who hath revealed *THE SCRIPTURE WITH TRUTH,* and the Balance. How canst thou know? It may be that the Hour is nigh.

42:18 Those who *BELIEVE* not therein seek to hasten it, while those who *BELIEVE* are fearful of it and *KNOW THAT IT IS THE TRUTH.* Are not they who dispute, in doubt concerning the Hour, far astray?

42:19 *ALLAH IS GRACIOUS UNTO HIS SLAVES.* He provideth for whom He will. And He is the Strong, the Mighty.

42:20 Whoso desireth the harvest of the Hereafter, We give him increase in its harvest. And whoso desireth the harvest of the world, We give him thereof, and he hath no portion in the Hereafter.

42:21 Or *HAVE THEY PARTNERS (OF ALLAH)* who have made lawful for them in religion that which Allah allowed not? And but for a decisive word (gone forth already), it would have been judged between them. Lo! *FOR WRONG-DOERS IS A PAINFUL DOOM.*

42:22 Thou seest the wrong-doers fearful of that which they have earned, and it will surely befall them, while *THOSE WHO BELIEVE AND DO GOOD WORKS (WILL BE) IN FLOWERING MEADOWS OF THE GARDENS, HAVING WHAT THEY WISH FROM THEIR LORD.* This is the great preferment.

42:23 This it is which Allah announceth unto His *BONDMEN [SLAVES] WHO BELIEVE AND DO GOOD WORKS.* Say (O Muhammad, unto mankind): I ask of you no fee therefor, save loving kindness among kinsfolk. And whoso scoreth a good deed We add unto its good for him. Lo! Allah is Forgiving, Responsive.

42:24 Or say they: He hath invented a lie concerning Allah? If Allah willed, He could have sealed thy heart (against them). And *ALLAH WILL WIPE OUT THE LIE AND WILL VINDICATE THE TRUTH BY HIS WORDS.* Lo! He is Aware of what is hidden in the breasts (of men).

42:25 And He it is Who accepteth repentance from His *BONDMEN,* and *PARDONETH THE EVIL DEEDS,* and knoweth what ye do,

42:26 And accepteth those who do good works, and giveth increase unto them of His bounty. And as *FOR DISBELIEVERS, THEIRS WILL BE AN AWFUL DOOM.*

42:27 And if Allah were to enlarge the provision for His *SLAVES* they would surely rebel in the earth, but He sendeth down by measure as He willeth. Lo! He is Informed, a Seer of His *BONDMEN.*

42:28 And He it is Who sendeth down the saving rain after they have despaired, and spreadeth out His mercy. He is the Protecting Friend, the Praiseworthy.

42:29 And of His portents is the creation of the heaven and the earth, and of whatever beasts He hath dispersed therein. And He is Able to gather them when He will.

42:30 Whatever of misfortune striketh you, it is what your right hands have earned. And He forgiveth much.

42:31 Ye cannot escape in the earth, for beside Allah ye have no protecting friend nor any helper.

42:32 And of His portents are the ships, like banners on the sea;

42:33 If He will He calmeth the wind so that they keep still upon its surface - Lo! herein verily are signs for every steadfast grateful (heart)-

42:34 Or He causeth them to perish on account of that which they have earned - And He forgiveth much -

42:35 And that *THOSE WHO ARGUE CONCERNING OUR REVELATIONS MAY KNOW THEY HAVE NO REFUGE.*

42:36 Now whatever ye have been given is but a passing comfort for the life of the world, and that which Allah hath is better and more lasting for *THOSE WHO BELIEVE* and put their trust in their Lord,

42:37 And those who shun the worst of sins and indecencies and, when they are wroth, forgive,

42:38 And *THOSE WHO ANSWER THE CALL OF THEIR LORD AND ESTABLISH WORSHIP,* and whose affairs are a matter of counsel, and *WHO SPEND OF WHAT WE HAVE BESTOWED ON THEM,*

42:39 And *THOSE WHO, WHEN GREAT WRONG IS DONE TO THEM, DEFEND THEMSELVES,*

42:40 The guerdon of an ill-deed is an ill the like thereof. But whosoever pardoneth and amendeth, his wage is the affair of Allah. Lo! He loveth not wrong-doers.

42:41 And *WHOSO DEFENDETH HIMSELF AFTER HE HATH SUFFERED WRONG - FOR SUCH, THERE IS NO WAY (OF BLAME) AGAINST THEM.*

42:42 The way (of blame) is only against those who oppress mankind, and *WRONGFULLY REBEL IN THE EARTH. For such THERE IS A PAINFUL DOOM.*

42:43 And verily whoso is patient and forgiveth - lo! that, verily, is (of) the steadfast heart of things.

42:44 He whom Allah sendeth astray, for him there is no protecting friend after Him. And thou (Muhammad) wilt see *THE EVIL-DOERS WHEN THEY SEE THE DOOM,* (how) they say: Is there any way of return?

42:45 And thou wilt *SEE THEM EXPOSED TO (THE FIRE), MADE HUMBLE BY DISGRACE,* and looking with veiled eyes. And those who *BELIEVE* will say: Lo! the (eternal) losers are they who lose themselves and their housefolk *ON THE DAY OF RESURRECTION. LO! ARE NOT THE WRONG-DOERS IN PERPETUAL TORMENT?*

42:46 And *THEY WILL HAVE NO PROTECTING FRIENDS* to help them instead of Allah. *HE WHOM ALLAH SENDETH ASTRAY, FOR HIM THERE IS NO ROAD.*

42:47 Answer the call of your Lord before there cometh unto you from Allah a Day which there is no averting. *YE HAVE NO REFUGE ON THAT DAY, NOR HAVE YE ANY (POWER OF) REFUSAL.*

42:48 But if they are averse, We have not sent thee as a warder over them. Thine is only to convey (the message). And lo! when We cause man to taste of mercy from Us he exulteth therefor. And if some evil striketh them because of that which their own hands have sent before, then lo! man is an ingrate. [Part cancelled by verse 9:5 i.e. violence, not speech, was later the later command][492]

42:49 Unto Allah belongeth the *SOVEREIGNTY OF THE HEAVENS AND THE EARTH.* He createth what He will. He bestoweth female (offspring) upon whom He will, and bestoweth male (offspring) upon whom He will;

42:50 Or He mingleth them, males and females, and *HE MAKETH BARREN WHOM HE WILL.* Lo! He is Knower, Powerful.

42:51 And it was not (vouchsafed) to any mortal that Allah should speak to him unless (it be) by revelation or from behind a veil, or (that) He sendeth a messenger to reveal what He will by His leave. Lo! He is Exalted, Wise.

42:52 And thus have We inspired in thee (Muhammad) a Spirit of Our command. Thou knewest not what the Scripture was, nor what the Faith. But We have made it a light whereby We guide whom We will of Our *BONDMEN.* And lo! thou verily dost *GUIDE UNTO A RIGHT PATH,*

42:53 The path of Allah, unto Whom belongeth whatsoever is in the heavens and whatsoever is in the earth. Do not all things reach Allah at last?

Chapter 41 – Fusilat

41:1 Ha. Mim.

41:2 A revelation from the Beneficent, the Merciful,

41:3 A Scripture whereof the verses are expounded, a Lecture in Arabic for *PEOPLE WHO HAVE KNOWLEDGE*, [Koran claims that its details have been explained, that it is in Arabic and is for the Arabs is often repeated]

41:4 Good tidings and a warning. But *MOST OF THEM TURN AWAY SO THAT THEY HEAR NOT.*

41:5 And they say: Our hearts are protected from that unto which thou (O Muhammad) callest us, and in our ears there is a deafness, and between us and thee there is a veil. Act, then. Lo! we also shall be acting.

41:6 Say (unto them O Muhammad): I am only a mortal like you. It is inspired in me that your Allah is One Allah, therefor take the straight path unto Him and seek forgiveness of Him. And *WOE UNTO THE IDOLATERS,*

41:7 Who give not the poor-due, and who are *DISBELIEVERS* in the Hereafter.

41:8 Lo! as *FOR THOSE WHO BELIEVE AND DO GOOD WORKS, FOR THEM IS A REWARD ENDURING.*

41:9 Say (O Muhammad, unto the *IDOLATERS*): *DISBELIEVE* ye verily in Him Who created the earth in two Days, and ascribe ye unto Him rivals? He (and none else) is the Lord of the Worlds.

41:10 He placed therein firm hills rising above it, and blessed it and measured therein its sustenance in four Days, alike for (all) who ask;

41:11 Then turned He to the heaven when it was smoke, and said unto it and unto the earth: Come both of you, willingly or loth. They said: We come, obedient.

41:12 Then He ordained them seven heavens in two Days and inspired in each heaven its mandate; and We decked the nether heaven with lamps, and rendered it inviolable. That is the measuring of the Mighty, the Knower.

41:13 But if they turn away, then say: I warn you of a thunderbolt like the thunderbolt (which fell of old upon the tribes) of A'ad and Thamud;

41:14 When their messengers came unto them from before them and behind them, saying: Worship none but Allah! they said: If our Lord had willed, He surely would have sent down angels (unto us), so lo! we are *DISBELIEVERS* in that wherewith ye have been sent.

41:15 As for A'ad, they were arrogant in the land without right, and they said: Who is mightier than us in power? Could they not see that Allah Who created them, He was mightier than them in power? And they denied Our revelations.

41:16 Therefor We let loose on them a raging wind in evil days, that We might make them taste the torment of disgrace in the life of the world. And verily the doom of the Hereafter will be more shameful, and they will not be helped.

41:17 And as for Thamud, We gave them guidance, but they preferred blindness to the guidance, so the bolt of the doom of humiliation overtook them because of what they used to earn.

41:18 And *WE DELIVERED THOSE WHO BELIEVED AND USED TO KEEP THEIR DUTY TO ALLAH.*

41:19 And (make mention of) *THE DAY WHEN THE ENEMIES OF ALLAH ARE GATHERED UNTO THE FIRE,* they are driven on

41:20 Till, when they reach it, *THEIR EARS AND THEIR EYES AND THEIR SKINS TESTIFY AGAINST THEM AS TO WHAT THEY USED TO DO.*

41:21 And they say unto their skins: Why testify ye against us? They say: Allah hath given us speech Who giveth speech to all things, and Who created you at the first, and unto Whom ye are returned.

41:22 Ye did not hide yourselves lest your ears and your eyes and your skins should testify against you, but ye deemed that Allah knew not much of what ye did.

41:23 That, *YOUR THOUGHT* which ye did think about your Lord, *HATH RUINED YOU*; and *YE FIND YOURSELVES (THIS DAY) AMONG THE LOST.*

41:24 *AND THOUGH THEY ARE RESIGNED, YET THE FIRE IS STILL THEIR HOME; AND IF THEY ASK FOR FAVOUR, YET THEY ARE NOT OF THOSE UNTO WHOM FAVOUR CAN BE SHOWN.*

41:25 And We assigned them comrades (in the world), who made their present and their past fairseeming unto them. And the Word concerning nations of the jinn and humankind who passed away before them hath effect for them. Lo! they were ever losers.

41:26 *THOSE WHO DISBELIEVE* say: Heed not this Qur'an, and drown the hearing of it; haply ye may conquer.

41:27 But verily *WE SHALL CAUSE THOSE WHO DISBELIEVE TO TASTE AN AWFUL DOOM*, and verily We shall requite them the worst of what they used to do.

41:28 *THAT IS THE REWARD OF ALLAH'S ENEMIES: THE FIRE. THEREIN IS THEIR IMMORTAL HOME, PAYMENT FORASMUCH AS THEY DENIED OUR REVELATIONS.* [The translators are in agreement in using Payment/Recompense as the translation for this verse].

41:29 And *THOSE WHO DISBELIEVE* will say: Our Lord! Show us those who beguiled us of the jinn and humankind. We will place them underneath our feet that they may be among the nethermost.

41:30 Lo! those who say: Our Lord is Allah, and afterward are upright, the angels descend upon them, saying: Fear not nor grieve, but hear good tidings of the paradise which ye are promised.

41:31 *WE ARE YOUR PROTECTING FRIENDS IN THE LIFE OF THE WORLD AND IN THE HEREAFTER. THERE YE WILL HAVE (ALL) THAT YOUR SOULS DESIRE*, and there ye will have (all) for which ye pray.

41:32 A gift of welcome from One Forgiving, Merciful.

41:33 And who is better in speech than him who prayeth unto his Lord and doeth right, and saith: Lo! I am of those who are *MUSLIMS* (surrender unto Him).

41:34 ~~The good deed and the evil deed are not alike. Repel the evil deed with one which is better, then lo! he, between whom and thee there was enmity (will become) as though he was a bosom friend.~~ [Cancelled by verse 9:5 i.e. the later command was violence, not kindness][493]

41:35 But none is granted it save those who are steadfast, and none is granted it save the owner of great happiness.

41:36 And if a whisper from the devil reach thee (O Muhammad) then seek refuge in Allah. Lo! He is the Hearer, the Knower.

41:37 And of His portents are the night and the day and the sun and the moon. Do not prostrate to the sun or the moon; but prostrate to Allah Who created them, if it is in truth Him Whom ye worship.

41:38 But if they are too proud - still those who are with thy Lord glorify Him night and day, and tire not.

41:39 And of His portents (is this): that thou seest the earth lowly, but when We send down water thereon it thrilleth and groweth. Lo! He Who quickeneth it is verily the Quickener of the Dead. Lo! He is Able to do all things.

41:40 Lo! those who distort Our revelations are not hid from Us. Is he who *IS HURLED INTO THE FIRE* better, or he who cometh secure on *THE DAY OF RESURRECTION*? Do what ye will. Lo! He is Seer of what ye do.

41:41 Lo! *THOSE WHO DISBELIEVE IN THE REMINDER WHEN IT COMETH UNTO THEM (ARE GUILTY)*, for lo! it is an unassailable Scripture.

41:42 Falsehood cannot come at it from before it or from behind it. (It is) a revelation from the Wise, the Owner of Praise.

41:43 Naught is said unto thee (Muhammad) save what was said unto the messengers before thee. Lo! thy Lord is owner of forgiveness, and owner (also) of dire punishment.

41:44 And if We had appointed it a Lecture in a foreign tongue they would assuredly have said: If only its verses were expounded (so that we might understand)? What! *A FOREIGN TONGUE AND AN ARAB?* - Say unto them (O Muhammad): For those who *BELIEVE* it is a guidance and a healing; and as for *THOSE WHO DISBELIEVE, THERE IS A DEAFNESS IN THEIR EARS, AND IT IS BLINDNESS FOR THEM*. Such are called to from afar.

41:45 And We verily gave Moses the Scripture, but there hath been dispute concerning it; and but for a Word that had already gone forth from thy Lord, it would ere now have been judged between them; but lo! they are in hopeless doubt concerning it.

41:46 Whoso doeth right it is for his soul, and whoso doeth wrong it is against it. And thy Lord is not at all a tyrant to *HIS SLAVES*.

41:47 Unto Him is referred (all) knowledge of the Hour. And no fruits burst forth from their sheaths, and no female carrieth or bringeth forth but with His knowledge. And on *THE DAY WHEN HE CALLETH UNTO THEM: WHERE ARE NOW MY PARTNERS?* they will say: We confess unto Thee, not one of us is a witness (for them).

41:48 And those to whom they used to cry of old have failed them, and they perceive they have no place of refuge.

41:49 Man tireth not of praying for good, and if ill toucheth him, then he is disheartened, desperate.

41:50 And verily, if We cause him to taste mercy after some hurt that hath touched him, he will say: This is my own; and I deem not that the Hour will ever rise, and if I am brought back to my Lord, I surely shall be better off with Him - But We verily shall tell *THOSE WHO DISBELIEVE* (all) that they did, and We verily shall make them *TASTE HARD PUNISHMENT*.

41:51 When We show favour unto man, he withdraweth and turneth aside, but when ill toucheth him then he aboundeth in prayer.

41:52 Bethink you: If it is from Allah and ye reject it - Who is further astray than one who is at open feud (with Allah)?

41:53 We shall show them Our portents on the horizons and within themselves until it will be manifest unto them *THAT IT IS THE TRUTH*. Doth not thy Lord suffice, since He is Witness over all things?

41:54 How! Are they still in doubt about the meeting with their Lord? Lo! Is not He surrounding all things?

Chapter 40 – The Believer

40:1 Ha. Mim.

40:2 The revelation of the Scripture is from Allah, the Mighty, the Knower,

40:3 The Forgiver of sin, the Accepter of repentance, the Stern in punishment, the Bountiful. There is no God save Him. Unto Him is the journeying.

40:4 None argue concerning the revelations of Allah save *THOSE WHO DISBELIEVE*, so let not their turn of fortune in the land deceive thee (O Muhammad).

40:5 The folk of Noah and the factions after them denied (their messengers) before these, and every nation purposed to seize their messenger and *ARGUED FALSELY, (THINKING) THEREBY TO REFUTE THE TRUTH. THEN I SEIZED THEM, AND HOW (AWFUL) WAS MY PUNISHMENT.*

40:6 Thus was the word of thy Lord concerning *THOSE WHO DISBELIEVE* **fulfilled: That they** *ARE OWNERS OF THE FIRE.*

40:7 Those who bear the Throne, and all who are round about it, hymn the praises of their Lord and *BELIEVE* in Him and ask forgiveness *FOR THOSE WHO BELIEVE* (saying): Our Lord! Thou comprehendest all things in mercy and knowledge, therefor forgive those who repent and follow Thy way. Ward off from them *THE PUNISHMENT OF HELL.*

40:8 Our Lord! And *MAKE THEM ENTER THE GARDENS OF EDEN WHICH THOU HAST PROMISED THEM*, **with such of their fathers and their wives and their descendants as do right. Lo! Thou, only Thou, art the Mighty, the Wise. [Jihadis not only enter the Gardens of Eden, but can also bring along ancestors and descendants.]**

40:9 And ward off from them ill-deeds; and he from whom Thou wardest off ill-deeds that day, him verily hast Thou taken into mercy. That is *THE SUPREME TRIUMPH.*

40:10 Lo! *(ON THAT DAY) THOSE WHO DISBELIEVE ARE INFORMED BY PROCLAMATION: VERILY ALLAH'S ABHORRENCE IS MORE TERRIBLE THAN YOUR ABHORRENCE ONE OF ANOTHER, WHEN YE WERE CALLED UNTO THE FAITH BUT DID REFUSE.*

40:11 They say: Our Lord! Twice hast Thou made us die, and twice hast Thou made us live. Now we confess our sins. Is there any way to go out?

40:12 (It is said unto them): This is (your plight) because, when Allah only was invoked, ye *DISBELIEVED*, but when some partner was ascribed to Him ye were *BELIEVING*. ~~But the command belongeth only to Allah, the Sublime, the Majestic.~~ [Part cancelled by verse 9:5][494]

40:13 He it is Who showeth you His portents, and sendeth down for you provision from the sky. None payeth heed save him who turneth (unto Him) repentant.

40:14 Therefor (O *BELIEVERS*) pray unto Allah, making religion pure for Him (only), however much the *DISBELIEVERS* be averse -

40:15 The Exalter of Ranks, the Lord of the Throne. He causeth the Spirit of His command upon *WHOM HE WILL OF HIS SLAVES*, that He may warn of *THE DAY OF MEETING,*

40:16 The day when they come forth, nothing of them being hidden from Allah. Whose is the Sovereignty this day? It is Allah's, the One, the Almighty.

40:17 This day is each soul requited that which it hath earned; no wrong (is done) this day. Lo! Allah is swift at reckoning.

40:18 Warn them (O Muhammad) of *THE DAY OF THE APPROACHING (DOOM)*, when the hearts will be choking the throats, (when) there will be no friend for the wrong-doers, nor any intercessor who will be heard.

40:19 He knoweth the traitor of the eyes, and that which the bosoms hide.

40:20 *ALLAH JUDGETH WITH TRUTH*, while those to whom they cry instead of Him judge not at all. Lo! Allah, He is the Hearer, the Seer.

40:21 Have they not travelled in the land to see the nature of the consequence for *THOSE WHO DISBELIEVED* before them? They were mightier than these in power and (in the) traces (which they left behind them) in the earth. Yet Allah seized them for their sins, and they had no protector from Allah.

40:22 That was because their messengers kept bringing them *CLEAR PROOFS* (of Allah's Sovereignty) but they *DISBELIEVED*; so Allah seized them. Lo! He is Strong, *SEVERE IN PUNISHMENT.*

40:23 And verily We sent Moses with Our revelations and a clear warrant

40:24 Unto Pharaoh and Haman and Korah, but they said: A lying sorcerer!

40:25 And when he brought them *THE TRUTH* from Our presence, they said: Slay the sons of those who *BELIEVE* with him, and spare their women. But the plot of *DISBELIEVERS* is in naught but error.

40:26 And Pharaoh said: Suffer me to kill Moses, and let him cry unto his Lord. Lo! I fear that he will alter your religion or that he will cause confusion in the land.

40:27 Moses said: Lo! I seek refuge in my Lord and your Lord from every scorner who *BELIEVETH* not in a *DAY OF RECKONING.*

40:28 And a *BELIEVING* man of Pharaoh's family, who hid his faith, said: Would ye kill a man because he saith: My Lord is Allah, and hath brought you *CLEAR PROOFS* from your Lord? If he is lying, then his lie is upon him; and if he is truthful, then some of that wherewith he threateneth you will strike you. Lo! Allah guideth not one who is a prodigal, a liar.

40:29 O my people! Yours is the kingdom to-day, ye being uppermost in the land. But who would save us from the wrath of Allah should it reach us? Pharaoh said: I do but show you what I think, and I do but guide you to wise policy.

40:30 And he who *BELIEVED* said: O my people! Lo! I fear for you a fate like that of the factions (of old);

40:31 A plight like that of Noah's folk, and A'ad and Thamud, and those after them, and Allah willeth *NO INJUSTICE FOR (HIS) SLAVES.*

40:32 And, O my people! Lo! I fear for you a *DAY OF SUMMONING,*

40:33 *A DAY WHEN YE WILL TURN TO FLEE,* having no preserver from Allah: and he whom Allah sendeth astray, for him there is no guide.

40:34 And verily Joseph brought you of old *CLEAR PROOFS,* yet ye ceased not to be in doubt concerning what he brought you till, when he died, ye said: Allah will not send any messenger after him. Thus Allah deceiveth him who is a prodigal, a doubter.

40:35 Those who wrangle concerning the revelations of Allah without any warrant that hath come unto them, it is greatly hateful in the sight of Allah and in the sight of those who *BELIEVE*. Thus doth Allah print on every arrogant, disdainful heart.

40:36 And Pharaoh said: O Haman! Build for me a tower that haply I may reach the roads,

40:37 The roads of the heavens, and may look upon the god of Moses, though verily I think him a liar. Thus was *THE EVIL THAT HE DID* made fairseeming unto Pharaoh, and he was debarred from the (right) way. The plot of Pharaoh ended but in ruin.

40:38 And he who *BELIEVED* said: O my people! Follow me. I will show you the way of right conduct.

40:39 O my people! Lo! this life of the world is but a passing comfort, and lo! the Hereafter, that is the enduring home.

40:40 *WHOSO DOETH AN ILL-DEED, HE WILL BE REPAID THE LIKE THEREOF, WHILE WHOSO DOETH RIGHT, WHETHER MALE OR FEMALE, AND IS A BELIEVER, (ALL) SUCH WILL ENTER THE GARDEN,* where they will be nourished without stint. [Note that only Muslims who do good deeds are rewarded.]

40:41 And, O my people! What aileth me that I call you unto deliverance when ye call me unto *THE FIRE*?

40:42 Ye call me to *DISBELIEVE* in Allah and ascribe unto Him as partners that whereof I have no knowledge, while I call you unto the Mighty, the Forgiver.

40:43 Assuredly that whereunto ye call me hath no claim in the world or in the Hereafter, and our return will be unto Allah, and *THE PRODIGALS WILL BE OWNERS OF THE FIRE.*

40:44 And ye will remember what I say unto you. I confide my cause unto Allah. Lo! Allah is Seer of *(HIS) SLAVES.*

40:45 So Allah warded off from him the evils which they plotted, while a dreadful doom encompassed Pharaoh's folk,

40:46 *THE FIRE; THEY ARE EXPOSED TO IT MORNING AND EVENING;* and on the day when the Hour upriseth (it is said): Cause Pharaoh's folk to enter the most awful doom.

40:47 And when they wrangle in *THE FIRE*, the weak say unto those who were proud: Lo! we were a following unto you; will ye therefor rid us of a portion of *THE FIRE*?

40:48 Those who were proud say: Lo! we are all (together) herein. Lo! *ALLAH HATH JUDGED BETWEEN (HIS) SLAVES.*

40:49 And *THOSE IN THE FIRE SAY UNTO THE GUARDS OF HELL: ENTREAT YOUR LORD THAT HE RELIEVE US OF A DAY OF THE TORMENT.*

40:50 They say: Came not your messengers unto you with *CLEAR PROOFS*? They say: Yea, verily. They say: Then do ye pray, although *THE PRAYER OF DISBELIEVERS IS IN VAIN.*

40:51 Lo! We verily do help Our messengers, and those who *BELIEVE,* in the life of the world and on the day when the witnesses arise,

40:52 *THE DAY WHEN THEIR EXCUSE AVAILETH NOT THE EVIL-DOERS, AND THEIRS IS THE CURSE, AND THEIRS THE ILL ABODE.*

40:53 And We verily gave Moses the guidance, and We caused *THE CHILDREN OF ISRAEL* to inherit the Scripture,

40:54 A guide and a reminder for men of understanding.

40:55 ~~Then have patience (O Muhammad). Lo! the promise of Allah is true. And ask forgiveness of thy sin, and hymn the praise of thy Lord at fall of night and in the early hours.~~ [Cancelled by verse 9:5 i.e. command to be patient replaced by command to kill][495]

40:56 Lo! those who wrangle concerning the revelations of Allah without a warrant having come unto them, there is naught else in their breasts save pride which they will never attain. So take thou refuge in Allah. Lo! He, only He, is the Hearer, the Seer.

40:57 Assuredly the creation of the heavens and the earth is greater than the creation of mankind; but most of mankind know not.

40:58 And the blind man and the seer are not equal, neither are *THOSE WHO BELIEVE AND DO GOOD WORKS* (equal with) the *EVIL-DOER.* Little do ye reflect!

40:59 Lo! the Hour is surely coming, there is no doubt thereof; yet *MOST OF MANKIND BELIEVE NOT.*

40:60 And your Lord hath said: Pray unto Me and I will hear your prayer. Lo! *THOSE WHO SCORN MY SERVICE, THEY WILL ENTER HELL,* disgraced.

40:61 Allah it is Who hath appointed for you night that ye may rest therein, and day for seeing. Lo! Allah is a Lord of bounty for mankind, yet most of mankind give not thanks.

40:62 Such is Allah, your Lord, the Creator of all things, There is no God save Him. How then are ye perverted?

40:63 Thus are they *PERVERTED WHO DENY THE REVELATIONS OF ALLAH.*

40:64 Allah it is Who appointed for you the earth for a dwelling-place and the sky for a canopy, and fashioned you and perfected your shapes, and hath provided you with good things. Such is Allah, your Lord. Then blessed be Allah, the Lord of the Worlds!

40:65 He is the Living One. There is no God save Him. So pray unto Him, making religion pure for Him (only). Praise be to Allah, the Lord of the Worlds!

40:66 Say (O Muhammad): I am forbidden to worship those unto whom ye cry beside Allah since there have come unto me *CLEAR PROOFS* from my Lord, and I am commanded to surrender to the Lord of the Worlds.

40:67 He it is Who created you from dust, then from a drop (of seed) then from a clot, then bringeth you forth as a child, then (ordaineth) that ye attain full strength and afterward that ye become old men - though some among you die before - and that ye reach an appointed term, that haply ye may understand.

40:68 He it is Who quickeneth and giveth death. When He ordaineth a thing, He saith unto it only: Be! and it is.

40:69 Hast thou not seen *THOSE WHO WRANGLE* [argue or dispute] concerning the revelations of Allah, how they are turned away? -

40:70 *THOSE WHO DENY THE SCRIPTURE* and that wherewith We send Our messengers. But they will come to know,

40:71 *WHEN CARCANS [SHACKLES] ARE ABOUT THEIR NECKS AND CHAINS. THEY ARE DRAGGED*

40:72 *THROUGH BOILING WATERS; THEN THEY ARE THRUST INTO THE FIRE.* [Those who question the doctrines of Islam are to be tortured for eternity, which is why Islam cannot be reformed.]

40:73 Then it is said unto them: Where are (all) that ye used to make partners (in the Sovereignty)

40:74 Beside Allah? They say: They have failed us; but we used not to pray to anything before. Thus doth Allah send astray THE DISBELIEVERS (in His guidance).

40:75 (And it is said unto them): This is because ye exulted in the earth without right, and because ye were petulant.

40:76 ENTER YE THE GATES OF HELL, TO DWELL THEREIN. EVIL IS THE HABITATION OF THE SCORNFUL.

40:77 ~~Then have patience (O Muhammad). Lo! the promise of Allah is true. And whether we let thee see a part of that which We promise them, or (whether) We cause thee to die, still unto Us they will be brought back.~~ [Cancelled by verse 9:5, i.e. command to kill replaces command to be patient.][496]

40:78 Verily We sent messengers before thee, among them those of whom We have told thee, and some of whom We have not told thee; and it was not given to any messenger that he should bring a portent save by Allah's leave, but when Allah's commandment cometh (the cause) is judged aright, and the followers of vanity will then be lost.

40:79 Allah it is Who hath appointed for you cattle, that ye may ride on some of them, and eat of some -

40:80 (Many) benefits ye have from them - and that ye may satisfy by their means a need that is in your breasts, and may be borne upon them as upon the ship.

40:81 And He showeth you His tokens. Which, then, of the tokens of Allah do ye deny?

40:82 Have they not travelled in the land to see the nature of the consequence for those before them? They were more numerous than these, and mightier in power and (in the) traces (which they left behind them) in the earth. But all that they used to earn availed them not.

40:83 And when their messengers brought them CLEAR PROOFS (of Allah's Sovereignty) they exulted in the knowledge they (themselves) possessed. And that which they were wont to mock befell them.

40:84 Then, when they saw Our doom, they said: We BELIEVE in Allah only and REJECT (ALL) THAT WE USED TO ASSOCIATE (WITH HIM).

40:85 But their faith could not avail them when they saw Our doom. This is Allah's law which hath ever taken course for His BONDMEN. And then THE DISBELIEVERS WILL BE RUINED.

Chapter 39 - The Troops

39:1 The revelation of the Scripture is from Allah, the Mighty, the Wise.

39:2 Lo! We have REVEALED THE SCRIPTURE UNTO THEE (MUHAMMAD) WITH TRUTH; SO WORSHIP ALLAH, MAKING RELIGION PURE FOR HIM (ONLY).

39:3 Surely PURE RELIGION IS FOR ALLAH ONLY. And those who choose protecting friends beside Him (say): We worship them only that they may bring us near unto Allah. Lo! ~~Allah will judge between them concerning that wherein they differ.~~ Lo! Allah guideth not him who is a liar, an ingrate. [Part cancelled by verse 9:5, i.e. believers were later commanded to be violent not patient.][497]

39:4 If Allah had willed to choose a son, He could have chosen what He would of that which He hath created. Be He Glorified! He is Allah, the One, the Absolute.

39:5 He hath created the heavens and the earth with truth. He maketh night to succeed day, and He maketh day to succeed night, and He constraineth the sun and the moon to give service, each running on for an appointed term. Is not He the Mighty, the Forgiver?

39:6 He created you from one being, then from that (being) He made its mate; and He hath provided for you of cattle eight kinds. He created you in the wombs of your mothers, creation after creation, in a threefold gloom. Such is Allah, your Lord. His is the Sovereignty. There is no God save Him. How then are ye turned away?

39:7 If ye are thankless, yet Allah is Independent of you, though He is not pleased with thanklessness for His BONDMEN; and if ye are thankful He is pleased therewith for you. No laden soul will bear another's load. Then unto your Lord is your return; and He will tell you what ye used to do. Lo! He knoweth what is in the breasts (of men).

39:8 And when some hurt toucheth man, he crieth unto his Lord, turning unto Him (repentant). Then, when He granteth him a boon from Him he forgetteth that for which he cried unto Him before, and setteth up rivals to Allah that he may beguile (men) from his way. Say (O Muhammad, unto such a one): Take pleasure in thy *DISBELIEF* a while. Lo! thou art of *THE OWNERS OF THE FIRE*.

39:9 Is he who payeth adoration in the watches of the night, prostrate and standing, bewaring of the Hereafter and hoping for the mercy of his Lord, (to be accounted equal with a *DISBELIEVER*)? Say (unto them, O Muhammad): Are those who know equal with those who know not? But only men of understanding will pay heed.

39:10 Say: *O MY BONDMEN [SLAVES] WHO BELIEVE! OBSERVE YOUR DUTY* to your Lord. For those who do good in this world there is good, and Allah's earth is spacious. Verily *THE STEADFAST WILL BE PAID THEIR WAGES* without stint.

39:11 Say (O Muhammad): Lo! I am commanded to *WORSHIP ALLAH, MAKING RELIGION PURE FOR HIM (ONLY).*

39:12 And I am commanded to be the first of those who are *MUSLIMS* (surrender unto Him).

39:13 ~~Say: Lo! if I should disobey my Lord, I fear the doom of a tremendous Day.~~ [Cancelled by verse 48:2][498]

39:14 ~~Say: Allah I worship, making my religion pure for Him (only).~~ [Cancelled by verse 9:5][499]

39:15 ~~Then worship what ye will beside Him.~~ Say: The losers will be those who lose themselves and their housefolk on *THE DAY OF RESURRECTION.* Ah, that will be the manifest loss! [Part cancelled by verse 9:5 i.e. replaced by the command to impose Islam using violence][500]

39:16 They have *AN AWNING OF FIRE ABOVE THEM AND BENEATH THEM* a dais (of fire). *WITH THIS DOTH ALLAH APPALL HIS BONDMEN. O MY BONDMEN [SLAVES], THEREFOR FEAR ME!*

39:17 And those who put away false gods lest they should worship them and turn to Allah in repentance, for them there are glad tidings. Therefore give good tidings (O Muhammad) to My *BONDMEN*

39:18 Who hear advice and follow the best thereof. Such are those whom Allah guideth, and such are men of understanding.

39:19 Is he on whom the word of doom is fulfilled (to be helped), and canst thou (O Muhammad) rescue *HIM WHO IS IN THE FIRE*?

39:20 But those who keep their duty to their Lord, for them are lofty halls with lofty halls above them, built (for them), *BENEATH WHICH RIVERS FLOW. (IT IS) A PROMISE OF ALLAH.* Allah faileth not His promise.

39:21 Hast thou not seen how Allah hath sent down water from the sky and hath caused it to penetrate the earth as watersprings, and afterward thereby produceth crops of divers hues; and afterward they wither and thou seest them turn yellow; then He maketh them chaff. Lo! herein verily is a reminder for men of understanding.

39:22 Is he whose bosom Allah hath expanded for Al-Islam, so that he followeth a light from his Lord, (as he who *DISBELIEVETH*)? Then woe unto those whose hearts are hardened against remembrance of Allah. Such are in plain error.

39:23 Allah hath (now) revealed the fairest of statements, a Scripture consistent, (wherein promises of *REWARD* are) paired (with threats of punishment), whereat *DOTH CREEP THE FLESH OF THOSE WHO FEAR THEIR LORD*, so that their flesh and their hearts soften to Allah's reminder. Such is Allah's guidance, wherewith *HE GUIDETH WHOM HE WILL. AND HIM WHOM ALLAH SENDETH ASTRAY, FOR HIM THERE IS NO GUIDE.*

39:24 Is he then, who will strike his face against the awful doom upon *THE DAY OF RESURRECTION* (as he who doeth right)? And it will be *SAID UNTO THE WRONG-DOERS: TASTE WHAT YE USED TO EARN.*

39:25 *THOSE BEFORE THEM DENIED, AND SO THE DOOM CAME ON THEM WHENCE THEY KNEW NOT.*

39:26 Thus *ALLAH MADE THEM TASTE HUMILIATION IN THE LIFE OF THE WORLD*, and verily the doom of the Hereafter will be greater if they did but know.

39:27 And verily We have coined for mankind in this Qur'an all kinds of similitudes, that haply they may reflect;

39:28 *A LECTURE IN ARABIC, CONTAINING NO CROOKEDNESS*, that haply they may ward off (*EVIL*).

39:29 Allah coineth a similitude: A man in relation to whom are several part-owners, quarrelling, and a man belonging wholly to one man. Are the two equal in similitude? Praise be to Allah! But most of them know not.

39:30 Lo! thou wilt die, and lo! they will die;

39:31 Then lo! on *THE DAY OF RESURRECTION*, before your Lord ye will dispute.

39:32 And who doth greater wrong than he who telleth a *LIE AGAINST ALLAH*, and denieth *THE TRUTH* when it reacheth him? *WILL NOT THE HOME OF DISBELIEVERS BE IN HELL?*

39:33 And whoso bringeth *THE TRUTH* and *BELIEVETH* therein - *SUCH ARE THE DUTIFUL.*
39:34 *THEY SHALL HAVE WHAT THEY WILL OF THEIR LORD'S BOUNTY. THAT IS THE REWARD OF THE GOOD:*

39:35 That *ALLAH WILL REMIT FROM THEM THE WORST OF WHAT THEY DID, AND WILL PAY THEM FOR REWARD THE BEST THEY USED TO DO*. [Dying as a Jihadi cancels out the previous sins of the Jihadi.]

39:36 Will not Allah defend His slave? Yet they would frighten thee with those beside Him. ~~He whom Allah sendeth astray, for him there is no guide.~~ [Part cancelled by verse 9:5][501]
39:37 And he whom Allah guideth, for him there can be no misleader. Is not Allah Mighty, Able to Requite (the wrong)?
39:38 And verily, if thou shouldst ask them: Who created the heavens and the earth? they will say: Allah. Say: Bethink you then of those ye worship beside Allah, if Allah willed some hurt for me, could they remove from me His hurt; or if He willed some mercy for me, could they restrain His mercy? Say: Allah is my all. In Him do (all) the trusting put their trust.
39:39 ~~Say: O my people! Act in your manner. Lo! I (too) am acting. Thus ye will come to know~~ [Cancelled by verse 9:5][502]
39:40 ~~Who it is unto whom cometh a doom that will abase him, and on whom there falleth everlasting doom.~~ [Cancelled by verse 9:5][503]
39:41 ~~Lo! We have revealed unto thee (Muhammad) the Scripture for mankind with truth. Then whosoever goeth right it is for his soul, and whosoever strayeth, strayeth only to its hurt. And thou art not a warder over them.~~ [Cancelled by verse 9:5, i.e. violence replaced indifference.][504]
39:42 Allah receiveth (men's) souls at the time of their death, and that (soul) which dieth not (yet) in its sleep. He keepeth that (soul) for which He hath ordained death and dismisseth the rest till an appointed term. Lo! herein verily are portents for people who take thought.
39:43 Or choose they intercessors other than Allah? Say: What! Even though they have power over nothing and *HAVE NO INTELLIGENCE*?
39:44 Say: Unto Allah belongeth all intercession. His is the Sovereignty of the heavens and the earth. And afterward unto Him ye will be brought back.
39:45 And *WHEN ALLAH ALONE IS MENTIONED, THE HEARTS OF THOSE WHO BELIEVE NOT IN THE HEREAFTER ARE REPELLED*, and when those (whom they worship) beside Him are mentioned, behold! they are glad.
39:46 ~~Say: O Allah! Creator of the heavens and the earth! Knower of the Invisible and the Visible! Thou wilt judge between Thy slaves concerning that wherein they used to differ.~~ [Cancelled by verse 9:5, i.e. Muslims are to punish non-Muslims because the latter will not follow Islam.][505]
39:47 And though those who do wrong possess all that is in the earth, and therewith as much again, they verily will seek to ransom themselves therewith on *THE DAY OF RESURRECTION* from the awful doom; and there will appear unto them, from their Lord, that wherewith they never reckoned.
39:48 And the evils that they earned will appear unto them, and *THAT WHEREAT THEY USED TO SCOFF WILL SURROUND THEM.*
39:49 Now when hurt toucheth a man he crieth unto Us, and afterward when We have granted him a boon from Us, he saith: Only by force of knowledge I obtained it. Nay, but it is a test. But most of them know not.
39:50 Those before them said it, yet (all) that they had earned availed them not;
39:51 But the evils that they earned smote them; and such of these as do wrong, the evils that they earn will smite them; they cannot escape.
39:52 Know they not that Allah enlargeth providence for whom He will, and straiteneth it (for whom He will). Lo! herein verily are portents *FOR PEOPLE WHO BELIEVE.*
39:53 Say: O *MY SLAVES* who have been prodigal to their own hurt! Despair not of the mercy of Allah, Who forgiveth all sins. Lo! He is the Forgiving, the Merciful.
39:54 *TURN UNTO YOUR LORD REPENTANT, AND SURRENDER UNTO HIM, BEFORE THERE COME UNTO YOU THE DOOM, WHEN YE CANNOT BE HELPED.*
39:55 And follow the better (guidance) of that which is revealed unto you from your Lord, before the doom cometh on you suddenly when ye know not,
39:56 Lest any soul should say: Alas, my grief that I was unmindful of Allah, and I was indeed *AMONG THE SCOFFERS!*
39:57 Or should say: If Allah had but guided me I should have been among the dutiful!
39:58 Or should say, when it seeth the doom: Oh, that I had but a second chance that I might be among the righteous!

39:59 (But now the answer will be): Nay, for *MY REVELATIONS CAME UNTO THEE, BUT THOU DIDST DENY THEM AND WAST SCORNFUL AND WAST AMONG THE DISBELIEVERS.*

39:60 And on *THE DAY OF RESURRECTION* thou (Muhammad) seest those who lied concerning Allah with their faces blackened. *IS NOT THE HOME OF THE SCORNERS IN HELL?*

39:61 And *ALLAH DELIVERETH THOSE WHO WARD OFF (EVIL) BECAUSE OF THEIR DESERTS. EVIL TOUCHETH THEM NOT, NOR DO THEY GRIEVE.*

39:62 Allah is Creator of all things, and He is Guardian over all things.

39:63 His are the keys of the heavens and the earth, and they who *DISBELIEVE* the revelations of Allah - *SUCH ARE THEY WHO ARE THE LOSERS.*

39:64 Say (O Muhammad, to the *DISBELIEVERS*): Do ye bid me serve other than Allah? O ye fools!

39:65 And verily it hath been revealed unto thee as unto those before thee (saying): If thou *ASCRIBE A PARTNER TO ALLAH THY WORK WILL FAIL AND THOU INDEED WILT BE AMONG THE LOSERS.*

39:66 Nay, but *ALLAH MUST THOU SERVE*, and be among the thankful!

39:67 And they esteem not Allah as He hath the right to be esteemed, when the whole earth is His handful on *THE DAY OF RESURRECTION*, and the heavens are rolled in His right hand. Glorified is He and High Exalted from *ALL THAT THEY ASCRIBE AS PARTNER* (unto Him).

39:68 And *THE TRUMPET IS BLOWN*, and all who are in the heavens and all who are in the earth swoon away, save him whom Allah willeth. Then it is blown a second time, and behold them standing waiting!

39:69 And the earth shineth with the light of her Lord, and the Book is set up, and the prophets and the witnesses are brought, and it is judged between them with truth, and they are not wronged.

39:70 And *EACH SOUL IS PAID IN FULL FOR WHAT IT DID*. And He is Best Aware of what they do.

39:71 And *THOSE WHO DISBELIEVE ARE DRIVEN UNTO HELL IN TROOPS* till, when they reach it and the gates thereof are opened, and the warders thereof say unto them: Came there not unto you messengers of your own, reciting unto you the revelations of your Lord and warning you of *THE MEETING OF THIS YOUR DAY*? they say: Yea, verily. But the word of *DOOM OF DISBELIEVERS IS FULFILLED*. [Non-Muslims are destined for an eternity in Hell]

39:72 It is said (unto them): Enter ye *THE GATES OF HELL* to dwell therein. Thus hapless is *THE JOURNEY'S END OF THE SCORNERS*.

39:73 And *THOSE WHO KEEP THEIR DUTY* to their Lord are driven unto *THE GARDEN* in troops till, when they reach it, and the gates thereof are opened, and the warders thereof say unto them: Peace be unto you! Ye are good, so enter ye (*THE GARDEN OF DELIGHT*), to dwell therein; [Obedient Muslims are destined for an eternity in Heaven.]

39:74 They say: Praise be to Allah, Who hath fulfilled His promise unto us and hath made us inherit the land, *SOJOURNING IN THE GARDEN* where we will! So bounteous is the wage of workers.

39:75 And thou (O Muhammad) seest the angels thronging round the Throne, hymning the praises of their Lord. And they are judged aright. And it is said: Praise be to Allah, the Lord of the Worlds!

Chapter 34 - Saba

34:1 Praise be to Allah, unto Whom belongeth whatsoever is in the heavens and whatsoever is in the earth. His is the praise in the Hereafter, and He is the Wise, the Aware.

34:2 He knoweth that which goeth into the earth and that which cometh forth from it, and that descendeth from the heaven and that which ascendeth into it. He is the Merciful, the Forgiving.

34:3 *THOSE WHO DISBELIEVE* say: The Hour will never come unto us. Say: Nay, by my Lord, but it is coming unto you surely. (He is) the Knower of the Unseen. Not an atom's weight, or less than that or greater, escapeth Him in the heavens or in the earth, but it is in a clear Record,

34:4 That *HE MAY REWARD THOSE WHO BELIEVE AND DO GOOD WORKS*. For them is pardon and a rich provision.

34:5 But *THOSE WHO STRIVE AGAINST OUR REVELATIONS*, challenging (Us), theirs will be *A PAINFUL DOOM OF WRATH*. [Those who critcise Islam are destined for an eternity of torture.]

34:6 *THOSE WHO HAVE BEEN GIVEN KNOWLEDGE* see that what is revealed unto thee from thy Lord is *THE TRUTH* and leadeth unto the path of the Mighty, the Owner of Praise.

34:7 *THOSE WHO DISBELIEVE* say: Shall we show you a man who will tell you (that) when ye have become dispersed in dust with most complete dispersal still, even then, ye will be created anew?

34:8 Hath he invented a lie concerning Allah, or is there in him a madness? Nay, but *THOSE WHO DISBELIEVE IN THE HEREAFTER ARE IN TORMENT AND FAR ERROR*.

34:9 Have they not observed what is before them and what is behind them of the sky and the earth? If We will, We can make the earth swallow them, or cause obliteration from the sky to fall on them. Lo! herein surely is a portent for every slave who turneth (to Allah) repentant.

34:10 And assuredly We gave David grace from Us, (saying): O ye hills and birds, echo his psalms of praise! And We made the iron supple unto him,

34:11 Saying: Make thou long coats of mail and measure the links (thereof). And do ye right. Lo! I am Seer of what ye do.

34:12 And unto Solomon (We gave) the wind, whereof the morning course was a month's journey and the evening course a month's journey, and We caused the fount of copper to gush forth for him, and (We gave him) certain of the jinn who worked before him by permission of his Lord. And such of them as deviated from Our command, them We caused to taste the punishment of flaming fire.

34:13 They made for him what he willed: synagogues and statues, basins like wells and boilers built into the ground. Give thanks, O House of David! Few of My *BONDMEN* are thankful.

34:14 And when We decreed death for him, nothing showed his death to them save a creeping creature of the earth which gnawed away his staff. And when he fell the jinn saw clearly how, if they had known the Unseen, they would not have continued in despised toil.

34:15 There was indeed a sign for Sheba in their dwelling-place: Two gardens on the right hand and the left (as who should say): Eat of the provision of your Lord and render thanks to Him. A fair land and an indulgent Lord!

34:16 But they were froward, so We sent on them the flood of 'Iram, and in exchange for their two gardens gave them two gardens bearing bitter fruit, the tamarisk and here and there a lote-tree.

34:17 This We awarded them because of their ingratitude. Punish We ever any save the ingrates?

34:18 And We set, between them and the towns which We had blessed, towns easy to be seen, and We made the stage between them easy, (saying): Travel in them safely both by night and day.

34:19 But they said: Our Lord! Make the stage between our journeys longer. And they wronged themselves, therefore We made them bywords (in the land) and scattered them abroad, a total scattering. Lo! herein verily are portents for each steadfast, grateful (heart).

34:20 And Satan indeed found his calculation true concerning them, for they follow him, all save a group of true *BELIEVERS*.

34:21 And he had no warrant whatsoever against them, save that We would know *HIM WHO BELIEVETH IN THE HEREAFTER FROM HIM WHO IS IN DOUBT THEREOF*; and thy Lord (O Muhammad) taketh note of all things.

34:22 Say (O Muhammad): Call upon those whom ye set up beside Allah! They possess not an atom's weight either in the heavens or in the earth, nor have they any share in either, nor hath He an auxiliary among them.

34:23 No intercession availeth with Him save for him whom He permitteth. Yet, when fear is banished from their hearts, they say: What was it that your Lord said? They say: *THE TRUTH*. And He is the Sublime, the Great.

34:24 Say: Who giveth you provision from the sky and the earth? Say: Allah, Lo! we or you assuredly are rightly guided or in error manifest.

34:25 ~~Say: Ye will not be asked of what we committed, nor shall we be asked of what ye do.~~ [Cancelled by verse 9:5, i.e. violence replaced indifference.]⁵⁰⁶

34:26 Say: Our Lord will bring us all together, then He *WILL JUDGE BETWEEN US WITH TRUTH*. He is the All-knowing Judge.

34:27 Say: Show me those whom ye have joined unto Him as partners. Nay (ye dare not)! For He is Allah, the Mighty, the Wise.

34:28 And We have not sent thee (O Muhammad) save as a bringer of good tidings and a warner unto all mankind; but most of mankind know not.

34:29 And they say: When is this promise (to be fulfilled) if ye are truthful?

34:30 Say (O Muhammad): Yours is *THE PROMISE OF A DAY WHICH YE CANNOT POSTPONE* nor hasten by an hour.

34:31 And *THOSE WHO DISBELIEVE* say: We *BELIEVE* not in this Qur'an nor in that which was before it; but oh, if thou couldst see, when the wrong-doers are brought up before their Lord, how they cast the blame one to another; how those who were despised (in the earth) say unto those who were proud: But for you, we should have been *BELIEVERS*.

34:32 Those who were proud say unto those who were despised: Did we drive you away from the guidance after it had come unto you? Nay, but ye were guilty.

34:33 Those who were despised say unto those who were proud: Nay but (it was your) scheming night and day, when ye commanded us to *DISBELIEVE* in Allah and set up rivals unto Him. And they are filled with remorse when they behold the doom; and We place carcans on the necks of *THOSE WHO DISBELIEVED*. Are they requited aught save what they used to do?

34:34 And We sent not unto any township a warner, but its pampered ones declared: Lo! we are *DISBELIEVERS* in that wherewith ye have been sent.

34:35 And they say: We are more (than you) in wealth and children. We are not the punished!

34:36 Say (O Muhammad): Lo! my Lord enlargeth the provision for whom He will and narroweth it (for whom He will). But most of mankind know not.

34:37 And it is not your wealth nor your children that will bring you near unto Us, but he who *BELIEVETH* and doeth good (he draweth near). As for such, *THEIRS WILL BE TWOFOLD REWARD FOR WHAT THEY DID* and they will dwell secure in lofty halls.

34:38 And as for *THOSE WHO STRIVE AGAINST OUR REVELATIONS, CHALLENGING*, they will be brought to the doom.

34:39 Say: Lo! my Lord enlargeth the provision for whom He will of His *BONDMEN*, and narroweth (it) for him. And whatsoever ye spend (for good) He replaceth it. And He is the Best of Providers.

34:40 And on *THE DAY WHEN HE WILL GATHER THEM ALL TOGETHER*, He will say unto the angels: Did these worship you?

34:41 They will say: Be Thou Glorified. Thou (alone) art our Guardian, not them! Nay, but they worshipped the jinn; most of them were *BELIEVERS* in them.

34:42 *THAT DAY* ye will possess no use nor hurt one for another. And *WE SHALL SAY UNTO THOSE WHO DID WRONG: TASTE THE DOOM OF THE FIRE WHICH YE USED TO DENY.*

34:43 And if *OUR REVELATIONS ARE RECITED UNTO THEM IN PLAIN TERMS*, they say: This is naught else than *A MAN WHO WOULD TURN YOU AWAY FROM WHAT YOUR FATHERS USED TO WORSHIP*; and they say: *THIS IS NAUGHT ELSE THAN AN INVENTED LIE. THOSE WHO DISBELIEVE* say of *THE TRUTH* when it reacheth them: This is naught else than mere magic.[Mohammed's contemporaries said he was a liar who wanted to turn them away from their religious and cultural inheritance.]

34:44 And We have given them no scriptures which they study, nor sent We unto them, before thee, any warner.

34:45 Those before them denied, and these have not attained a tithe of that which We bestowed on them (of old); yet they denied My messengers. How intense then was My abhorrence (of them)!

34:46 Say (unto them, O Muhammad): I exhort you unto one thing only: that ye awake, for Allah's sake, by twos and singly, and then reflect: *THERE IS NO MADNESS IN YOUR COMRADE.* He is naught else than a warner unto you in face of a terrific doom.

34:47 Say: Whatever *REWARD* I might have asked of you is yours. My *REWARD* is the affair of Allah only. He is Witness over all things.

34:48 Say: Lo! my Lord hurleth *THE TRUTH*. (He is) the Knower of Things Hidden.

34:49 Say: *THE TRUTH* hath come, and falsehood showeth not its face and will not return.

34:50 Say: If I err, I err only to my own loss, and if I am rightly guided it is because of that which my Lord hath revealed unto me. Lo! He is Hearer, Nigh.

34:51 Couldst thou but see when they are terrified with no escape, and are seized from near at hand,

34:52 And say: We (now) *BELIEVE* therein. But how can they reach (faith) from afar off,

34:53 When they *DISBELIEVED* in it of yore. They aim at the unseen from afar off.

34:54 And a gulf is set between them and that which they desire, as was done for people of their kind of old. Lo! they were in hopeless doubt.

Chapter 31 - Luqman

31:1 Alif. Lam. Mim.

31:2 These are revelations of the wise Scripture,

31:3 A guidance and a mercy for the good,

31:4 Those who establish worship and pay the poor-due and have sure faith in the Hereafter.

31:5 Such have guidance from their Lord. *SUCH ARE THE SUCCESSFUL.*

31:6 And of mankind is he who payeth for mere pastime of discourse, that he may mislead from Allah's way without knowledge, and maketh it the butt of mockery. For such there is a shameful doom.

31:7 And when Our revelations are recited unto him he turneth away in pride as if he heard them not, as if there were a deafness in his ears. So give him tidings of *A PAINFUL DOOM.*

31:8 Lo! *THOSE WHO BELIEVE AND DO GOOD WORKS***, for them are** *THE GARDENS OF DELIGHT***, [Islamic actions are required to enter Paradise; believing with inactivity is not enough. In the later Koran, aggressive Jihad becomes one of the good works.]**

31:9 Wherein they will abide. It is a promise of Allah in truth. He is the Mighty, the Wise.

31:10 He hath created the heavens without supports that ye can see, and hath cast into the earth firm hills, so that it quake not with you; and He hath dispersed therein all kinds of beasts. And We send down water from the sky and We cause (plants) of every goodly kind to grow therein.

31:11 This is the Creation of Allah. Now show me that which those (ye worship) beside Him have created. Nay, but the *WRONG-DOERS ARE IN ERROR* manifest!

31:12 And verily We gave Luqman wisdom, saying: Give thanks unto Allah; and whosoever giveth thanks, he giveth thanks for (the good of) his soul. And whosoever refuseth - Lo! Allah is Absolute, Owner of Praise.

31:13 And (remember) when Luqman said unto his son, when he was exhorting him: O my dear son! Ascribe no partners unto Allah. Lo! to ascribe partners (unto Him) is a tremendous wrong -

31:14 And We have enjoined upon man concerning his partners - His mother beareth him in weakness upon weakness, and his weaning is in two years - Give thanks unto Me and unto thy parents. Unto Me is the journeying.

31:15 But if they *STRIVE* with thee to make thee *ASCRIBE UNTO ME AS PARTNER* that of which thou hast no knowledge, then *OBEY THEM NOT.* Consort with them in the world kindly, and follow the path of him who repenteth unto Me. Then unto Me will be your return, and I shall tell you what ye used to do -

31:16 O my dear son! Lo! though it be but the weight of a grain of mustard-seed, and though it be in a rock, or in the heavens, or in the earth, Allah will bring it forth. Lo! Allah is Subtile, Aware.

31:17 O my dear son! Establish worship and enjoin kindness and forbid iniquity, and persevere whatever may befall thee. Lo! that is of the steadfast heart of things.

31:18 Turn not thy cheek in scorn toward folk, nor walk with pertness in the land. Lo! Allah loveth not each braggart boaster.

31:19 Be modest in thy bearing and subdue thy voice. Lo! the harshest of all voices is the voice of the ass.

31:20 See ye not how Allah hath made serviceable unto you whatsoever is in the skies and whatsoever is in the earth and hath loaded you with His favours both without and within? Yet of mankind is he who disputeth concerning Allah, without knowledge or guidance or a scripture giving light.

31:21 And if it be said unto them: Follow that which Allah hath revealed, they say: Nay, but we follow that wherein we found our fathers. What! Even though the devil were inviting them unto *THE DOOM OF FLAME?*

31:22 Whosoever *SURRENDERETH HIS PURPOSE TO ALLAH* while doing good, he verily hath grasped the firm hand-hold. Unto Allah belongeth the sequel of all things.

31:23 And whosoever *DISBELIEVETH*, let not his *DISBELIEF* afflict thee (O Muhammad). Unto Us is their return, and We shall tell them what they did. Lo! Allah is Aware of what is in the breasts (of men). [Part cancelled by verse 9:5 i.e. Muslims to be outraged by any rejection of Islam][507]

31:24 We give them comfort for a little, and then We drive them to a heavy doom.

31:25 If thou shouldst ask them: Who created the heavens and the earth? they would answer: Allah. Say: Praise be to Allah! But most of them know not.

31:26 Unto Allah belongeth whatsoever is in the heavens and the earth. Lo! Allah, He is the Absolute, the Owner of Praise.

31:27 And if all the trees in the earth were pens, and the sea, with seven more seas to help it, (were ink), the words of Allah could not be exhausted. Lo! Allah is Mighty, Wise.

31:28 Your creation and your raising (from the dead) are only as (the creation and the raising of) a single soul. Lo! Allah is Hearer, Knower.

31:29 Hast thou not seen how Allah causeth the night to pass into the day and causeth the day to pass into the night, and hath subdued the sun and the moon (to do their work), each running unto an appointed term; and that Allah is Informed of what ye do?

31:30 That (is so) because *ALLAH, HE IS THE TRUE*, and that which they invoke beside Him is the False, and because Allah, He is the Sublime, the Great.

31:31 Hast thou not seen how the ships glide on the sea by Allah's grace, that He may show you of His wonders? Lo! therein indeed are portents for every steadfast, grateful (heart).

31:32 And if a wave enshroudeth them like awnings, they cry unto Allah, making their faith pure for Him only. But when He bringeth them safe to land, some of them compromise. *NONE DENIETH OUR SIGNS SAVE EVERY TRAITOR INGRATE*.

31:33 O mankind! *KEEP YOUR DUTY TO YOUR LORD* and *FEAR A DAY WHEN THE PARENT WILL NOT BE ABLE TO AVAIL THE CHILD IN AUGHT, NOR THE CHILD TO AVAIL THE PARENT.* Lo! *ALLAH'S PROMISE IS THE VERY TRUTH*. Let not the life of the world beguile you, nor let *THE DECEIVER* beguile you, in regard to Allah.

31:34 Lo! Allah! With Him is *KNOWLEDGE OF THE HOUR*. He sendeth down the rain, and knoweth that which is in the wombs. No soul knoweth what it will earn to-morrow, and no soul knoweth in what land it will die. Lo! Allah is Knower, Aware.

Chapter 37 - Those Who Set The Ranks

37:1 By *THOSE WHO SET THE RANKS IN BATTLE ORDER*

37:2 And those who drive away (the wicked) with reproof

37:3 And those who read (the Word) for a reminder,

37:4 Lo! thy Lord is surely One;

37:5 Lord of the heavens and of the earth and all that is between them, and Lord of the sun's risings.

37:6 Lo! We have adorned the lowest heaven with an ornament, the planets;

37:7 With security from every froward devil.

37:8 They cannot listen to the Highest Chiefs for they are pelted from every side,

37:9 Outcast, and theirs is a perpetual torment;

37:10 Save him who snatcheth a fragment, and there pursueth him *A PIERCING FLAME.*

37:11 Then ask them (O Muhammad): Are they stronger as a creation, or those (others) whom we have created? Lo! We created them of plastic clay.

37:12 Nay, but *THOU DOST MARVEL WHEN THEY MOCK*

37:13 And heed not when they are reminded,

37:14 And seek to scoff when they behold a portent.

37:15 And they say: Lo! this is mere magic;

37:16 When we are dead and have become dust and bones, shall we then, forsooth, be raised (again)?

37:17 And our forefathers?

37:18 Say (O Muhammad): Ye, in truth; and ye will be brought low.

37:19 There is but one Shout, and lo! they behold,

37:20 And say: Ah, woe for us! This is *THE DAY OF JUDGMENT.*

37:21 *THIS IS THE DAY OF SEPARATION,* which ye used to deny.

37:22 (And it is said unto the angels): Assemble those who did wrong, together with their wives and what they used to worship

37:23 Instead of Allah, and *LEAD THEM TO THE PATH TO HELL;*

37:24 And stop them, for they must be questioned.

37:25 What aileth you that ye help not one another?

37:26 Nay, but this day they make full submission.

37:27 And some of them draw near unto others, mutually questioning.

37:28 They say: Lo! ye used to come unto us, imposing, (swearing that ye spoke the truth).

37:29 They answer: Nay, but ye (yourselves) were not *BELIEVERS*.

37:30 We had no power over you, but ye were wayward folk.

37:31 Now the Word of our Lord hath been fulfilled concerning us. Lo! we are about to taste (the doom).

37:32 Thus we misled you. Lo! we were (ourselves) astray.

37:33 Then lo! *THIS DAY THEY (BOTH) ARE SHARERS IN THE DOOM.*

37:34 Lo! thus deal We with the guilty.

37:35 *FOR WHEN IT WAS SAID UNTO THEM, THERE IS NO GOD SAVE ALLAH, THEY WERE SCORNFUL*

37:36 And said: Shall we forsake our gods for *A MAD POET*? [Mohammed's contemporaries thought he was insane.]

37:37 Nay, but he brought *THE TRUTH*, and he confirmed those sent (before him).

37:38 Lo! *(NOW) VERILY YE TASTE THE PAINFUL DOOM -*

37:39 Ye are requited naught save what ye did -

37:40 Save *SINGLE-MINDED SLAVES OF ALLAH*; [dutiful Muslims]

37:41 For them there is *A KNOWN PROVISION*,

37:42 Fruits. And *THEY WILL BE HONOURED*

37:43 *IN THE GARDENS OF DELIGHT*, [Paradise]

37:44 On couches facing one another;

37:45 A cup from a gushing spring is brought round for them,

37:46 White, delicious to the drinkers,

37:47 Wherein there is no headache nor are they made mad thereby.

37:48 And with them are those of modest gaze, with lovely eyes,

37:49 (Pure) as they were hidden eggs (of the ostrich).

37:50 And some of them draw near unto others, mutually questioning.

37:51 A speaker of them saith: Lo! I had a comrade

37:52 Who used to say: Art thou in truth of those who put faith (in his words)?

37:53 Can we, when we are dead and have become mere dust and bones - can we (then) verily be brought to book?

37:54 He saith: Will ye look?

37:55 Then looketh he and *SEETH HIM IN THE DEPTH OF HELL.*

37:56 He saith: By Allah, thou verily didst all but cause my ruin,

37:57 And had it not been for the favour of my Lord, I too had been of those haled forth (to doom).

37:58 Are we then not to die

37:59 Saving our former death, and are we not to be punished?

37:60 Lo! *THIS IS THE SUPREME TRIUMPH.*

37:61 For the like of this, then, let the workers work.

37:62 Is this better as a welcome, or the tree of Zaqqum?

37:63 Lo! We have appointed it *A TORMENT FOR WRONG-DOERS*.

37:64 Lo! it is a tree that springeth *IN THE HEART OF HELL.*

37:65 Its crop is as it were the heads of devils

37:66 And lo! they verily must eat thereof, and fill (their) bellies therewith.

37:67 And afterward, lo! thereupon *THEY HAVE A DRINK OF BOILING WATER*

37:68 And afterward, lo! their return is surely unto *HELL*.

37:69 They indeed found their fathers *ASTRAY,*

37:70 But they make haste (to follow) in their footsteps.

37:71 And verily most of the men of old went astray before them,

37:72 And verily We sent among them warners.

37:73 Then see the nature of the consequence for those warned,

37:74 *SAVE SINGLE-MINDED SLAVES OF ALLAH*.

37:75 And Noah verily prayed unto Us, and gracious was the Hearer of his prayer.

37:76 And We saved him and his household from the great distress,

37:77 And made his seed the survivors,

37:78 And left for him among the later folk (the salutation):

37:79 Peace be unto Noah among the peoples!

37:80 Lo! thus do *WE REWARD THE GOOD.*

37:81 Lo! he is one of Our *BELIEVING SLAVES*.

37:82 Then We did drown the others.

37:83 And lo! of his persuasion verily was Abraham

37:84 When he came unto his Lord with a whole heart;

37:85 When he said unto his father and his folk: What is it that ye worship?

37:86 Is it a falsehood - gods beside Allah - that ye desire?

37:87 What then is your opinion of the Lord of the Worlds?

37:88 And he glanced a glance at the stars

37:89 Then said: Lo! I feel sick!

37:90 And they turned their backs and went away from him.

37:91 Then turned he to their gods and said: Will ye not eat?

37:92 What aileth you that ye speak not?

37:93 Then he attacked them, striking with his right hand.

37:94 And (his people) came toward him, hastening.

37:95 He said: Worship ye that which ye yourselves do carve

37:96 When Allah hath created you and what ye make?

37:97 They said: Build for him a building and *FLING HIM IN THE RED-HOTFIRE.*

37:98 And they designed a snare for him, but We made them the undermost.

37:99 And he said: Lo! I am going unto my Lord Who will guide me.

37:100 My Lord! Vouchsafe me of the righteous.

37:101 So We gave him tidings of a gentle son.

37:102 And when (his son) was old enough to walk with him, (Abraham) said: O my dear son, I have seen in a dream that I must sacrifice thee. So look, what thinkest thou? He said: O my father! Do that which thou art commanded. Allah willing, thou shalt find me of the steadfast.

37:103 Then, when they had both *SURRENDERED (TO ALLAH)*, and he had flung him down upon his face,

37:104 We called unto him: O Abraham!

37:105 Thou hast already fulfilled the vision. Lo! *THUS DO WE REWARD THE GOOD.*

37:106 Lo! that verily was a clear test.

37:107 Then We ransomed him with a tremendous victim.

37:108 And We left for him among the later folk (the salutation):

37:109 Peace be unto ABRAHAM!

37:110 Thus do *WE REWARD THE GOOD.*

37:111 Lo! he is one of Our *BELIEVING SLAVES*.

37:112 And we gave him tidings of the birth of Isaac, a prophet of the righteous.

37:113 And We blessed him and Isaac. And of their seed are some who do good, and some who plainly wrong themselves.

37:114 And We verily gave grace unto Moses and Aaron,

37:115 And saved them and their people from the great distress,

37:116 And helped them so that they *BECAME THE VICTORS*.

37:117 And We gave them *THE CLEAR SCRIPTURE*

37:118 And showed them *THE RIGHT PATH*.

37:119 And We left for them among the later folk (the salutation):

37:120 Peace be unto Moses and Aaron!

37:121 Lo! *THUS DO WE REWARD THE GOOD.*

37:122 Lo! they are two of Our *BELIEVING SLAVES*.

37:123 And lo! Elias was of those sent (to warn),

37:124 When he said unto his folk: Will ye not ward off (*EVIL*)?

37:125 Will ye cry unto Baal and forsake the Best of creators,

37:126 Allah, your Lord and Lord of your forefathers?

37:127 But they denied him, so they surely will be haled forth (to the doom)

37:128 Save *SINGLE-MINDED SLAVES OF ALLAH*.

37:129 And we left for him among the later folk (the salutation):

37:130 Peace be unto Elias!

37:131 Lo! thus do *WE REWARD THE GOOD.*

37:132 Lo! he is one of our *BELIEVING SLAVES*.

37:133 And lo! Lot verily was of those sent (to warn).

37:134 When We saved him and his household, every one,

37:135 Save an old woman among those who stayed behind;
37:136 Then We destroyed the others.
37:137 And lo! ye verily pass by (the ruin of) them in the morning
37:138 And at night-time; have ye then no sense?
37:139 And lo! Jonah verily was of those sent (to warn)
37:140 When he fled unto the laden ship,
37:141 And then drew lots and was of those rejected;
37:142 And the fish swallowed him while he was blameworthy;
37:143 And had he not been one of those who glorify (Allah)
37:144 He would have tarried in its belly till the day when they are raised;
37:145 Then We cast him on a desert shore while he was sick;
37:146 And We caused a tree of gourd to grow above him;
37:147 And We sent him to a hundred thousand (folk) or more
37:148 And they *BELIEVED*, therefor We gave them comfort for a while.
37:149 Now ask them (O Muhammad): Hath thy Lord daughters whereas they have sons?
37:150 Or created We the angels females while they were present?
37:151 Lo! it is of their falsehood that they say:
37:152 Allah hath begotten. Allah! verily they tell a lie.
37:153 (And again of their falsehood): He hath preferred daughters to sons.
37:154 What aileth you? How judge ye?
37:155 Will ye not then reflect?
37:156 Or have ye a clear warrant?
37:157 Then produce your writ, if ye are truthful.
37:158 And they imagine kinship between him and the jinn, whereas the jinn know well that they will be brought before (Him).
37:159 Glorified be Allah from that which they attribute (unto Him),
37:160 Save *SINGLE-MINDED SLAVES OF ALLAH*.
37:161 Lo! verily, ye and that which ye worship,
37:162 Ye cannot excite (anyone) against Him.
37:163 Save *HIM WHO IS TO BURN IN HELL.*
37:164 There is not one of us but hath his known position.
37:165 Lo! we, even we are they who set the ranks,
37:166 Lo! we, even we are they who hymn His praise
37:167 And indeed they used to say:
37:168 If we had but a reminder from the men of old
37:169 We would be *SINGLE-MINDED SLAVES OF ALLAH.*
37:170 Yet (now that it is come) they *DISBELIEVE* therein; but they will come to know.
37:171 And verily Our word went forth of old unto Our *BONDMEN* sent (to warn)
37:172 That they verily would be helped,
37:173 And that Our host, they verily *WOULD BE THE VICTORS.*
37:174 ~~So withdraw from them (O Muhammad) awhile,~~ [Cancelled by verse 9:5 i.e. to attack rather than retreat.][508]
37:175 ~~And watch, for they will (soon) see.~~ [Cancelled by verse 9:5 i.e. violence replaces patience][509]
37:176 Would they hasten on Our doom?
37:177 But when it cometh home to them, then it will be a hapless morning for those who have been warned.
37:178 Withdraw from them awhile
37:179 And watch, for they will (soon) see.
37:180 Glorified be thy Lord, the Lord of Majesty, from that which they attribute (unto Him)
37:181 And peace be unto those sent (to warn).
37:182 And praise be to Allah, Lord of the Worlds!

Chapter 6 - Cattle

6:1 Praise be to Allah, Who hath created the heavens and the earth, and hath appointed darkness and light. Yet *THOSE WHO DISBELIEVE* ascribe rivals unto their Lord.

6:2 He it is Who hath created you from clay, and hath decreed a term for you. A term is fixed with Him. Yet still ye doubt!

6:3 He is Allah in the heavens and in the earth. He knoweth both your secret and your utterance, and He knoweth what ye earn.

6:4 Never came there unto them a revelation of the revelations of Allah but they did turn away from it.

6:5 And *THEY DENIED THE TRUTH* when it came unto them. But there will come unto them the tidings of that which they used to deride.

6:6 See they not how many a generation We destroyed before them, whom We had established in the earth more firmly than We have established you, and We shed on them abundant showers from the sky, and made the rivers flow beneath them. Yet we destroyed them for their sins, and created after them another generation.

6:7 Had we sent down unto thee (Muhammad) (actual) writing upon parchment, so that they could feel it with their hands, *THOSE WHO DISBELIEVE* would have said: This is naught else than mere magic.

6:8 They say: Why hath not an angel been sent down unto him? If We sent down an angel, then the matter would be judged; no further time would be allowed them (for reflection).

6:9 Had we appointed him (Our messenger) an angel, We assuredly had made him (as) a man (that he might speak to men); and (thus) obscured for them (*THE TRUTH*) they (now) obscure.

6:10 Messengers (of Allah) have been derided before thee, but that whereat they scoffed surrounded such of them as did deride.

6:11 Say (unto the *DISBELIEVERS*): Travel in the land, and see the nature of the consequence for the rejecters!

6:12 Say: Unto whom belongeth whatsoever is in the heavens and the earth? Say: Unto Allah. He hath prescribed for Himself mercy, that He may bring you all together to *THE DAY OF RESURRECTION* whereof there is no doubt. Those who ruin their souls will not *BELIEVE*.

6:13 Unto Him belongeth whatsoever resteth in the night and the day. He is the Hearer, the Knower.

6:14 Say: Shall I choose for a protecting friend other than Allah, the Originator of the heavens and the earth, Who feedeth and is never fed? Say: I am ordered to be the first to surrender (unto Him). And be not thou (O Muhammad) of the *IDOLATERS*.

6:15 Say: I fear, if I rebel against my Lord, *THE RETRIBUTION OF AN AWFUL DAY.*

6:16 He from whom (such retribution) is averted on that day, (Allah) hath in truth had mercy on him. That will be *THE SIGNAL TRIUMPH.*

6:17 If Allah touch thee with affliction, there is none that can relieve therefrom save Him, and if He touch thee with good fortune (there is none that can impair it); for He is Able to do all things.

6:18 *HE IS THE OMNIPOTENT OVER HIS SLAVES*, and He is the Wise, the Knower.

6:19 Say (O Muhammad): What thing is of most weight in testimony? Say: Allah is Witness between me and you. And this Qur'an hath been inspired in me, that I may warn therewith you and whomsoever it may reach. Do ye in sooth bear witness that there are gods beside Allah? Say: I bear no such witness. Say: He is only One Allah. Lo! I am innocent of that which ye associate (with Him).

6:20 Those unto whom We gave the Scripture recognise (this revelation) as they recognise their sons. *THOSE WHO RUIN THEIR OWN SOULS WILL NOT BELIEVE*.

6:21 *WHO DOTH GREATER WRONG THAN HE WHO INVENTETH A LIE AGAINST ALLAH OR DENIETH HIS REVELATIONS*? Lo! the *WRONGDOERS WILL NOT BE SUCCESSFUL.*

6:22 And *ON THE DAY WE GATHER THEM TOGETHER WE SHALL SAY UNTO THOSE WHO ASCRIBED PARTNERS (UNTO ALLAH): WHERE ARE (NOW) THOSE PARTNERS OF YOUR MAKE-BELIEVE*?

6:23 Then will they have no contention save that they will say: By Allah, our Lord, we never were *IDOLATERS*.

6:24 See how *THEY LIE AGAINST THEMSELVES*, and (how) the thing which they devised hath failed them!

6:25 Of them are some who listen unto thee, but We have placed upon their hearts veils, lest they should understand, and in their ears a deafness. If they saw every token they would not *BELIEVE* therein; to the point that, when they come unto thee to argue with thee, the *DISBELIEVERS SAY: THIS IS NAUGHT ELSE THAN FABLES OF THE MEN OF OLD.*

6:26 And they forbid (men) from it and avoid it, and they ruin none save themselves, though they perceive not.

6:27 If thou couldst see *WHEN THEY ARE SET BEFORE THE FIRE* and say: Oh, would that we might return! Then would we not deny the revelations of our Lord but we would be of the *BELIEVERS*!

6:28 Nay, but that hath become clear unto them which before they used to hide. And if they were sent back they would return unto that which they are forbidden. Lo! *THEY ARE LIARS.*

6:29 And they say: There is naught save our life of the world, and we shall not be raised (again).

6:30 If thou couldst see when they are set before their Lord! He will say: Is not this real? They will say: Yea, verily, by our Lord! He will say: *TASTE NOW THE RETRIBUTION FOR THAT YE USED TO DISBELIEVE*.

6:31 *THEY INDEED ARE LOSERS* who deny their meeting with Allah until, when the Hour cometh on them suddenly, they cry: Alas for us, that we neglected it! They bear upon their backs their burdens. Ah, *EVIL* is that which they bear!

6:32 *NAUGHT IS THE LIFE OF THE WORLD SAVE A PASTIME AND A SPOT. BETTER FAR IS THE ABODE OF THE HEREAFTER FOR THOSE WHO KEEP THEIR DUTY (TO ALLAH)*. Have ye then no sense?

6:33 We know well how their talk grieveth thee, though in truth they deny not thee (Muhammad) but *EVIL-DOERS* flout the revelations of Allah.

6:34 Messengers indeed have been denied before thee, and they were patient under the denial and the persecution till Our succour reached them. *THERE IS NONE TO ALTER THE DECISIONS OF ALLAH*. Already there hath reached thee (somewhat) of the tidings of the messengers (We sent before).

6:35 And if their aversion is grievous unto thee, then, if thou canst, seek a way down into the earth or a ladder unto the sky that thou mayst bring unto them a portent (to convince them all)! - *IF ALLAH WILLED, HE COULD HAVE BROUGHT THEM ALL TOGETHER TO THE GUIDANCE* - So be not thou among the foolish ones.

6:36 Only those can accept who hear. As for the dead, Allah will raise them up; then unto Him they will be returned.

6:37 They say: Why hath no portent been sent down upon him from his Lord? Say: Lo! Allah is Able to send down a portent. But most of them know not.

6:38 There is not an animal in the earth, nor a flying creature flying on two wings, but they are peoples like unto you. We have neglected nothing in the Book (of Our decrees). Then unto their Lord they will be gathered.

6:39 *THOSE WHO DENY OUR REVELATIONS ARE DEAF AND DUMB IN DARKNESS. WHOM ALLAH WILL SENDETH ASTRAY, AND WHOM HE WILL HE PLACETH ON A STRAIGHT PATH*.

6:40 Say: Can ye see yourselves, if the punishment of Allah come upon you or the Hour come upon you, (calling upon other than Allah)? Do ye then call (for help) to any other than Allah? (Answer that) if ye are truthful.

6:41 Nay, but unto Him ye call, and He removeth that because of which ye call unto Him, if He will, and ye forget whatever partners ye ascribed unto Him.

6:42 We have sent already unto peoples that were before thee, and We visited them with tribulation and adversity, in order that they might grow humble.

6:43 If only, when Our disaster came on them, they had been humble! But their hearts were hardened and the devil made all that they used to do seem fair unto them!

6:44 Then, when they forgot that whereof they had been reminded, We opened unto them the gates of all things till, even as they were rejoicing in that which they were given, We seized them unawares, and lo! they were dumbfounded.

6:45 So of the people who did wrong the last remnant was cut off. Praise be to Allah, Lord of the Worlds!

6:46 Say: Have ye imagined, if Allah should take away your hearing and your sight and seal your hearts, who is the God who could restore it to you save Allah? See how We display the revelations unto them! Yet still they turn away.

6:47 Say: Can ye see yourselves, if the punishment of Allah come upon you unawares or openly? Would any perish save wrongdoing folk?

6:48 We send not the messengers save as bearers of good news and warners. Whoso *BELIEVETH* and doeth right, there shall no fear come upon them neither shall they grieve.

6:49 But as for those who deny Our revelations, torment will afflict them for that they used to disobey.

6:50 Say (O Muhammad, to the *DISBELIEVERS*): I say not unto you (that) I possess the treasures of Allah, nor that I have knowledge of the Unseen; and I say not unto you: Lo! I am an angel. I follow only that which is inspired in me. Say: Are the blind man and the seer equal? Will ye not then take thought?

6:51 Warn hereby those who fear (because they know) that they will be gathered unto their Lord, for whom there is no protecting ally nor intercessor beside Him, that they may ward off (*EVIL*).

6:52 Repel not those who call upon their Lord at morn and evening, seeking His Countenance. Thou art not accountable for them in aught, nor are they accountable for thee in aught, that thou shouldst repel them and be of the wrong-doers.

6:53 And even so do We try some of them by others, that they say: Are these they whom Allah favoureth among us? Is not Allah best Aware of the thanksgivers?

6:54 And when those who *BELIEVE* in Our revelations come unto thee, say: Peace be unto you! Your Lord hath prescribed for Himself mercy, that whoso of you doeth *EVIL* through ignorance and repenteth afterward thereof and doeth right, (for him) lo! He is Forgiving, Merciful.

6:55 Thus do We expound the revelations that the way of the unrighteous may be manifest.

6:56 Say: I am forbidden to worship those on whom ye call instead of Allah. Say: I will not follow your desires, for then should I go astray and I should not be of the rightly guided.

6:57 Say: I am (relying) on *CLEAR PROOF* from my Lord, while ye deny Him. I have not that for which ye are impatient. The decision is for Allah only. He telleth *THE TRUTH* and He is the Best of Deciders.

6:58 Say: If I had that for which ye are impatient, then would the case (ere this) have been decided between me and you. Allah is Best Aware of *THE WRONG-DOERS*.

6:59 And with Him are the keys of the Invisible. None but He knoweth them. And He knoweth what is in the land and the sea. Not a leaf falleth but He knoweth it, not a grain amid the darkness of the earth, naught of wet or dry but (it is noted) in a clear record.

6:60 He it is Who gathereth you at night and knoweth that which ye commit by day. Then He raiseth you again to life therein, that the term appointed (for you) may be accomplished. And afterward unto Him is your return. Then He will proclaim unto you what ye used to do.

6:61 *HE IS THE OMNIPOTENT OVER HIS SLAVES*. He sendeth guardians over you until, when death cometh unto one of you, Our messengers receive him, and they neglect not.

6:62 Then are they restored unto Allah, their Lord, the Just. Surely His is the judgment. And *HE IS THE MOST SWIFT OF RECKONERS.*

6:63 Say: Who delivereth you from the darkness of the land and the sea? Ye call upon Him humbly and in secret, (saying): If we are delivered from this (fear) we truly will be of the thankful.

6:64 Say: Allah delivereth you from this and from all affliction. Yet *YE ATTRIBUTE PARTNERS UNTO HIM.*

6:65 Say: He is able to send punishment upon you from above you or from beneath your feet, or to bewilder you with dissension and make you taste the tyranny one of another. See how We display the revelations so that they may understand.

6:66 Thy people (O Muhammad) have denied it, though it is *THE TRUTH.* ~~Say: I am not put in charge of you.~~ [Part cancelled by verse 9:5, i.e. Islam is to be imposed on unbelievers][510]

6:67 For every announcement there is a term, and ye will come to know.

6:68 ~~And when thou seest those who meddle with Our revelations, withdraw from them until they meddle with another topic. And if the devil cause thee to forget, sit not, after the remembrance, with the congregation of wrong-doers.~~ [Abrogated by verse 4:140, i.e. avoid those who question Islam.][511]

6:69 ~~Those who ward off (evil) are not accountable for them in aught, but the Reminder (must be given them) that haply they (too) may ward off (evil).~~ [Abrogated by verse 4:140][512]

6:70 ~~And forsake those who take their religion for a pastime and a jest, and whom the life of the world beguileth.~~ Remind (mankind) hereby lest a soul be destroyed by what it earneth. It hath beside Allah no protecting ally nor intercessor, and though it offer every compensation it will not be accepted from it. Those are they who perish by their own deserts. *FOR THEM IS DRINK OF BOILING WATER* and *A PAINFUL DOOM*, because they *DISBELIEVED*. [Ignoring those who are half-hearted about religion is replaced by the command to subjugate in verse 9:29][513]

6:71 Say: Shall we cry, instead of unto Allah, unto that which neither profiteth us nor hurteth us, and shall we turn back after Allah hath guided us, like one bewildered whom the devils have infatuated in the earth, who hath companions who invite him to the guidance (saying): Come unto us? Say: Lo! the guidance of Allah is Guidance, and we are ordered to surrender to the Lord of the Worlds,

6:72 And to establish worship and be dutiful to Him, and He it is unto Whom ye will be gathered.

6:73 He it is Who created the heavens and the earth in truth. *IN THE DAY WHEN HE SAITH: BE! IT IS. HIS WORD IS THE TRUTH, AND HIS WILL BE THE SOVEREIGNTY* on *THE DAY WHEN THE TRUMPET IS BLOWN*. Knower of the Invisible and the Visible, He is the Wise, the Aware.

6:74 (Remember) when Abraham said unto his father Azar: Takest thou idols for gods? Lo! I see thee and thy folk in error manifest.

6:75 Thus did We show Abraham the kingdom of the heavens and the earth that he might be of those possessing certainty:

6:76 When the night grew dark upon him he beheld a star. He said: This is my Lord. But when it set, he said: I love not things that set.

6:77 And when he saw the moon uprising, he exclaimed: This is my Lord. But when it set, he said: Unless my Lord guide me, I surely shall become one of the folk who are astray.

6:78 And when he saw the sun uprising, he cried: This is my Lord! This is greater! And when it set he exclaimed: O my people! Lo! I am free from all that ye associate (with Him).

6:79 Lo! I have turned my face toward Him Who created the heavens and the earth, as one by nature upright, and I am not of the *IDOLATERS*.

6:80 His people argued with him. He said: Dispute ye with me concerning Allah when He hath guided me? I fear not at all that which ye set up beside Him unless my Lord willeth aught. My Lord includeth all things in His knowledge. Will ye not then remember?

6:81 How should I fear that which ye set up beside Him, when ye fear not to set up beside Allah that for which He hath revealed unto you no warrant? Which of the two factions hath more right to safety? (Answer me that) if ye have knowledge.

6:82 Those who *BELIEVE* and obscure not their *BELIEF* by wrongdoing, theirs is safety; and they are rightly guided.

6:83 That is Our argument. We gave it unto Abraham against his folk. We raise unto degrees of wisdom whom We will. Lo! thy Lord is Wise, Aware.

6:84 And We bestowed upon him Isaac and Jacob; each of them We guided; and Noah did We guide aforetime; and of his seed (We guided) David and Solomon and Job and Joseph and Moses and Aaron. *THUS DO WE REWARD THE GOOD.*

6:85 And Zachariah and John and *JESUS* and Elias. Each one (of them) was of the righteous.

6:86 And Ishmael and Elisha and Jonah and Lot. Each one (of them) did We prefer above (Our) creatures,

6:87 With some of their forefathers and their offspring and their brethren; and We chose them and guided them unto *A STRAIGHT PATH*.

6:88 Such is the guidance of Allah wherewith *HE GUIDETH WHOM HE WILL OF HIS BONDMEN*. But if they had set up (for worship) aught beside Him, (all) that they did would have been vain.

6:89 Those are they unto whom We gave the Scripture and command and prophethood. But if these *DISBELIEVE* therein, then indeed We shall entrust it to a people who will not be *DISBELIEVERS* therein.

6:90 Those are they whom Allah guideth, so follow their guidance. Say (O Muhammad, unto mankind): I ask of you no fee for it. Lo! it is naught but a Reminder to (His) creatures.

6:91 And they measure not the power of Allah its true measure when they say: Allah hath naught revealed unto a human being. Say (unto the *JEWS* who speak thus): Who revealed the Book which Moses brought, a light and guidance for mankind, which ye have put on parchments which ye show, but ye hide much (thereof), and (by which) ye were taught that which ye knew not yourselves nor (did) your fathers (know it)? Say: Allah. Then leave them to their play of cavilling. [Partial Cancellation by 9:5 i.e. violence replaces indifference]

6:92 And this is a blessed Scripture which We have revealed, confirming that which (was revealed) before it, that thou mayst warn the Mother of Villages and those around her. Those who *BELIEVE* in the Hereafter *BELIEVE* herein, and they are careful of their worship.

6:93 *WHO IS GUILTY OF MORE WRONG THAN HE WHO FORGETH A LIE AGAINST ALLAH*, or saith: I am inspired, when he is not inspired in aught; and who saith: I will reveal the like of that which Allah hath revealed? If thou couldst see, when the wrong-doers reach the pangs of death and the angels stretch their hands out (saying): Deliver up your souls. *THIS DAY YE ARE AWARDED DOOM OF DEGRADATION FOR THAT YE SPAKE CONCERNING ALLAH OTHER THAN THE TRUTH*, and used to scorn His portents.

6:94 Now have ye come unto Us solitary as We did create you at the first, and ye have left behind you all that We bestowed upon you, and We behold not with you those your intercessors, of whom ye claimed that they possessed a share in you. Now is the bond between you severed, and that which ye presumed hath failed you.

6:95 Lo! Allah (it is) Who splitteth the grain of corn and the date-stone (for sprouting). He bringeth forth the living from the dead, and is the bringer-forth of the dead from the living. Such is Allah. How then are ye perverted?

6:96 He is the Cleaver of the Daybreak, and He hath appointed the night for stillness, and the sun and the moon for reckoning. That is the measuring of the Mighty, the Wise.

6:97 And He it is Who hath set for you the stars that ye may guide your course by them amid the darkness of the land and the sea. We have detailed Our revelations for a people who have knowledge.

6:98 And He it is Who hath produced you from a single being, and (hath given you) a habitation and a repository. We have detailed Our revelations for a people who have understanding.

6:99 He it is Who sendeth down water from the sky, and therewith We bring forth buds of every kind; We bring forth the green blade from which We bring forth the thick-clustered grain; and from the date-palm, from the pollen thereof, spring pendant bunches; and (We bring forth) gardens of grapes, and the olive and the pomegranate, alike and unlike. Look upon the fruit thereof, when they bear fruit, and upon its ripening. Lo! herein verily are portents for *A PEOPLE WHO BELIEVE*.

6:100 Yet *THEY ASCRIBE AS PARTNERS UNTO HIM* the jinn, although He did create them, and impute falsely, without knowledge, sons and daughters unto Him. Glorified be He and High Exalted above (all) that they ascribe (unto Him).

6:101 The Originator of the heavens and the earth! How can He have a child, when there is for Him no consort, when He created all things and is Aware of all things?

6:102 Such is Allah, your Lord. There is no God save Him, the Creator of all things, so worship Him. And He taketh care of all things.

6:103 Vision comprehendeth Him not, but He comprehendeth (all) vision. He is the Subtle, the Aware.

6:104 Proofs have come unto you from your Lord, so whoso seeth, it is for his own good, and whoso is blind is blind to his own hurt. And I am not a keeper over you. [Cancelled by verse 9:5][514]

6:105 Thus do We display Our revelations that they may say (unto thee, Muhammad): "Thou hast studied," and that We may make (it) clear for people who have knowledge.

6:106 Follow that which is inspired in thee from thy Lord; there is no Allah save Him; and turn away from the idolaters. [Cancelled by verse 9:5, i.e. violence replaces indifference][515]

6:107 Had Allah willed, they had not been idolatrous. We have not set thee as a keeper over them, nor art thou responsible for them. [Cancelled by verse 9:5, i.e. violence replaces indifference][516]

6:108 Revile not those unto whom they pray beside Allah lest they wrongfully revile Allah through ignorance. Thus unto every nation have We made their deed seem fair. Then unto their Lord is their return, and He will tell them what they used to do. [Cancelled by verse 9:5][517]

6:109 And they swear a solemn oath by Allah that if there come unto them a portent they will *BELIEVE* therein. Say; Portents are with Allah and (so is) that which telleth you that if such came unto them they would not *BELIEVE*.

6:110 We confound their hearts and their eyes. As they *BELIEVED* not therein at the first, We let them wander blindly on in their contumacy.

6:111 And though We should send down the angels unto them, and the dead should speak unto them, and We should gather against them all things in array, they would not *BELIEVE* unless Allah so willed. Howbeit, most of them are ignorant.

6:112 Thus have We appointed unto every prophet an adversary - devils of humankind and jinn who inspire in one another plausible discourse through guile. If thy Lord willed, they would not do so; so leave them alone with their devising; [Part cancelled by verse 9:5 i.e. do not leave them alone.][518]

6:113 That the hearts of those who *BELIEVE* not in the Hereafter may incline thereto, and that they may take pleasure therein, and that they may earn what they are earning.

6:114 Shall I seek other than Allah for judge, when He it is Who hath revealed unto you *(THIS) SCRIPTURE, FULLY EXPLAINED*? Those unto whom We gave the Scripture (aforetime) know that it is revealed from thy Lord in truth. So be not thou (O Muhammad) of *THE WAVERERS*. [Koran claims to be fully explained.]

6:115 *PERFECTED IS THE WORD OF THY LORD* in truth and justice. *THERE IS NAUGHT THAT CAN CHANGE HIS WORDS.* He is the Hearer, the Knower. [The Koran is perfect and cannot be changed]

6:116 If thou obeyedst most of those on earth they would mislead thee far from Allah's way. They follow naught but an opinion, and they do but guess.

6:117 Lo! thy Lord, He knoweth best who erreth from His way; and He knoweth best (who are) the rightly guided.

6:118 Eat of that over which the name of Allah hath been mentioned, if ye are *BELIEVERS* in His revelations.

6:119 How should ye not eat of that over which the name of Allah hath been mentioned, when He hath explained unto you that which is forbidden unto you unless ye are compelled thereto. But lo!

many are led astray by their own lusts through ignorance. Lo! thy Lord, He is Best Aware of the transgressors.

6:120 Forsake the outwardness of sin and the inwardness thereof. Lo! those who garner sin will be awarded that which they have earned.

6:121 ~~And eat not of that whereon Allah's name hath not been mentioned, for lo! it is abomination.~~ Lo! the devils do inspire their minions to dispute with you. But if ye *OBEY* them, ye will be in truth *IDOLATERS*. [Part cancelled by verse 5:5 i.e. avoid food not rendered halal by pronouncement of "Bismillah"][519]

6:122 Is he who was dead and We have raised him unto life, and set for him a light wherein he walketh among men, as him whose similitude is in utter darkness whence he cannot emerge? Thus is their conduct made fairseeming for the *DISBELIEVERS*.

6:123 And thus have We made in every city great ones of its wicked ones, that they should plot therein. They do but plot against themselves, though they perceive not.

6:124 And when a token cometh unto them, they say: *WE WILL NOT BELIEVE* till we are given that which Allah's messengers are given. Allah knoweth best with whom to place His message. *HUMILIATION FROM ALLAH AND HEAVY PUNISHMENT WILL SMITE THE GUILTY FOR THEIR SCHEMING*.

6:125 And whomsoever it is Allah's will to guide, He expandeth his bosom unto the Surrender, and *WHOMSOEVER IT IS HIS WILL TO SEND ASTRAY*, He maketh his bosom close and narrow as if he were engaged in sheer ascent. Thus Allah layeth ignominy upon those who *BELIEVE* not.

6:126 This is the path of thy Lord, *A STRAIGHT PATH*. We have detailed Our revelations for *A PEOPLE WHO TAKE HEED*.

6:127 For them is the abode of peace with their Lord. He will be their Protecting Friend because of what they used to do.

6:128 In *THE DAY WHEN HE WILL GATHER THEM TOGETHER* (He will say): O ye assembly of the jinn! Many of humankind did ye seduce. And their adherents among humankind will say: Our Lord! We enjoyed one another, but now we have arrived at the appointed term which Thou appointedst for us. He will say: Fire is your home. Abide therein for ever, save him whom Allah willeth (to deliver). Lo! thy Lord is Wise, Aware.

6:129 Thus We let some of the *WRONG-DOERS* have power over others because of what they are wont to earn.

6:130 O ye assembly of the jinn and humankind! Came there not unto you messengers of your own who recounted unto you My tokens and warned you of the meeting of this your Day? They will say: We testify against ourselves. And the life of the world beguiled them. And they testify against themselves that they were *DISBELIEVERS*.

6:131 This is because *THY LORD DESTROYETH NOT THE TOWNSHIPS ARBITRARILY* while their people are unconscious (of the wrong they do).

6:132 For all there will be ranks from what they did. Thy Lord is not unaware of what they do.

6:133 Thy Lord is the Absolute, the Lord of Mercy. If He will, He can remove you and can cause what He will to follow after you, even as He raised you from the seed of other folk.

6:134 Lo! that which ye are promised will surely come to pass, and ye cannot escape.

6:135 ~~Say (O Muhammad): O my people! Work according to your power. Lo! I too am working. Thus ye will come to know for which of us will be the happy sequel. Lo! the wrong-doers will not be successful.~~ [Cancelled by verse 9:5][520]

6:136 They assign unto Allah, of the crops and cattle which He created, a portion, and they say: "This is Allah's" - in their make-believe - "and this is for (His) partners in regard to us." Thus that which (they assign) unto His partners in them reacheth not Allah and that which (they assign) unto Allah goeth to their (so-called) partners. *EVIL IS THEIR ORDINANCE.*

6:137 Thus have their (so-called) *PARTNERS (OF ALLAH)* made the killing of their children to seem fair unto many of the *IDOLATERS*, that they may *RUIN THEM AND MAKE THEIR FAITH OBSCURE FOR THEM.* Had Allah willed (it otherwise), they had not done so. So leave them alone with their devices. [So the Koran forbids infanticide. Note: Koran does not forbid slavery.]

6:138 And they say: Such cattle and crops are forbidden. No-one is to eat of them save whom we will - in their make-believe - cattle whose backs are forbidden, cattle over which they mention not the name of Allah. (All that is) a lie against Him. He will repay them for that which they invent.

6:139 And they say: That which is in the bellies of such cattle is reserved for our males and is forbidden to our wives; but if it be born dead, then they (all) may be partakers thereof. He will *REWARD* them for their attribution (of such ordinances unto Him). Lo, He is Wise, Aware.

6:140 They are losers who besottedly have slain their children without knowledge, and have forbidden that which Allah bestowed upon them, *INVENTING A LIE AGAINST ALLAH*. They indeed have gone astray and are not guided.

6:141 He it is Who produceth gardens trellised and untrellised, and the date-palm, and crops of divers flavour, and the olive and the pomegranate, like and unlike. Eat ye of the fruit thereof when it fruiteth, and pay the due thereof upon the harvest day, and be not prodigal. Lo! Allah loveth not the prodigals.

6:142 And of the cattle (He produceth) some for burdens, some for food. Eat of that which Allah hath bestowed upon you, and follow not the footsteps of the devil, for lo! he is an open foe to you.

6:143 Eight pairs: Of the sheep twain, and of the goats twain. Say: Hath He forbidden the two males or the two females, or that which the wombs of the two females contain? Expound to me (the case) with knowledge, if ye are truthful.

6:144 And of the camels twain and of the oxen twain. Say: Hath He forbidden the two males or the two females, or that which the wombs of the two females contain; or were ye by to witness when Allah commanded you (all) this? Then who doth greater wrong than he who deviseth a lie concerning Allah, that he may lead mankind astray without knowledge. Lo! Allah guideth not wrongdoing folk.

6:145 Say: I find not in that which is revealed unto me aught prohibited to an eater that he eat thereof, except it be carrion, or blood poured forth, or swineflesh [pork] - for that verily is foul - or the abomination which was immolated to the name of other than Allah. But whoso is compelled (thereto), *NEITHER CRAVING NOR TRANSGRESSING*, (for him) lo! thy Lord is Forgiving, Merciful. [When hungry Muslims can eat pork.]

6:146 Unto those who are *JEWS* We forbade every animal with claws. And of the oxen and the sheep forbade We unto them the fat thereof save that upon the backs or the entrails, or that which is mixed with the bone. That we awarded them for their rebellion. And lo! we verily are truthful.

6:147 So if they give the lie to thee (Muhammad), say: Your Lord is a Lord of all-embracing Mercy, and His wrath will never be withdrawn from guilty folk.

6:148 They who are *IDOLATERS* will say: Had Allah willed, we had not ascribed (unto Him) partners neither had our fathers, nor had we forbidden aught. Thus did those who were before them give the lie (to Allah's messengers) till they tasted of the fear of Us. Say: Have ye any knowledge that ye can adduce for Us? Lo! ye follow naught but an opinion, Lo! ye do but guess.

6:149 Say - For Allah's is the final argument - Had He willed He could indeed have guided all of you.

6:150 Say: Come, bring your witnesses who can bear witness that Allah forbade (all) this. And if they bear witness, do not thou bear witness with them. Follow thou not the whims of those who deny Our revelations, those who *BELIEVE* not in the Hereafter and deem (others) equal with their Lord.

6:151 Say: Come, I will recite unto you that which your Lord hath made a sacred duty for you: That ye ascribe no thing as partner unto Him and that ye do good to parents, and that ye slay not your children because of penury - We provide for you and for them - and that ye draw not nigh to lewd things whether open or concealed. And that ye slay not the life which Allah hath made sacred, save in the course of justice. This He hath command you, in order that ye may discern.

6:152 And approach not the wealth of the orphan save with that which is better, till he reach maturity. Give full measure and full weight, in justice. We task not any soul beyond its scope. And if ye give your word, do justice thereunto, even though it be (against) a kinsman; and *FULFIL THE COVENANT OF ALLAH*. This He commandeth you that haply ye may remember.

6:153 And (He commandeth you, saying): This is My straight path, so follow it. Follow not other ways, lest ye be parted from His way. This hath He ordained for you, that ye may ward off (*EVIL*).

6:154 Again, We gave the Scripture unto Moses, complete for him who would do good, an explanation of all things, a guidance and a mercy, that they might *BELIEVE* in the meeting with their Lord.

6:155 And this is a blessed Scripture which We have revealed. So follow it and ward off (*EVIL*), that ye may find mercy.

6:156 Lest ye should say: The Scripture was revealed only to two sects before us, and we in sooth were unaware of what they read;

6:157 Or lest ye should say: If the Scripture had been revealed unto us, we surely had been better guided than are they. Now hath there come unto you a *CLEAR PROOF* from your Lord, a guidance and mercy; and who doeth greater wrong than he who denieth the revelations of Allah, and turneth away from them? We award unto those who turn away from Our revelations *AN EVIL DOOM* because of their aversion.

6:158 Wait they, indeed, for nothing less than that the angels should come unto them, or thy Lord should come, or there should come one of the portents from thy Lord? In the day when one of the portents from thy Lord cometh, its *BELIEF* availeth naught a soul which theretofore *BELIEVED* not, nor in its *BELIEF* earned good (by works). ~~Say: Wait ye! Lo! We (too) are waiting.~~ [Part cancelled by verse 9:5 , i.e. commands to be violent replace commands to be patient][521]

6:159 ~~Lo! As for those who sunder their religion and become schismatics, no concern at all hast thou with them. Their case will go to Allah, Who then will tell them what they used to do.~~ [Cancelled by verse 9:5][522]

6:160 Whoso bringeth a good deed will receive tenfold the like thereof, while whoso bringeth an ill-deed will be awarded but the like thereof; and they will not be wronged.

6:161 Say: Lo! As for me, my Lord hath guided me unto *A STRAIGHT PATH, A RIGHT RELIGION*, the community of Abraham, the upright, who was no *IDOLATER*.

6:162 Say: Lo! my worship and my sacrifice and my living and my dying are for Allah, Lord of the Worlds.

6:163 HE HATH NO PARTNER. THIS AM I COMMANDED, AND I AM FIRST OF THOSE WHO SURRENDER (UNTO HIM).

6:164 Say: Shall I seek another than Allah for Lord, when He is Lord of all things? Each soul earneth only on its own account, nor doth any laden bear another's load. Then unto your Lord is your return and He will tell you that wherein ye differed.

6:165 He it is Who hath placed you as viceroys of the earth and hath exalted some of you in rank above others, that He may try you by (the test of) that which He hath given you. Lo! Thy Lord is swift in prosecution, and Lo! He verily is Forgiving, Merciful.

Chapter 15 - Al Hijr

15:1 Alif. Lam. Ra. These are verses of the Scripture and a plain Reading.

15:2 It may be that *THOSE WHO DISBELIEVE* wish ardently that they were *MUSLIMS*.

15:3 ~~Let them eat and enjoy life, and let (false) hope beguile them. They will come to know!~~ [Cancelled by verse 9:5 , i.e. violence replaces indifference][523]

15:4 And We destroyed no township but there was a known decree for it.

15:5 No nation can outstrip its term nor can they lag behind.

15:6 And they say: O thou unto whom the Reminder is revealed, lo! *THOU ART INDEED A MADMAN*!

15:7 Why bringest thou not angels unto us, if thou art of the truthful?

15:8 We send not down the angels save with the Fact, and in that case (the *DISBELIEVERS*) would not be tolerated.

15:9 Lo! We, even We, reveal the Reminder, and lo! We verily are its Guardian.

15:10 We verily sent (messengers) before thee among the factions of the men of old.

15:11 And never came there unto them a messenger but they did mock him.

15:12 Thus do We make it traverse the hearts of the guilty:

15:13 They *BELIEVE* not therein, though the example of the men of old hath gone before.

15:14 And even if We opened unto them a gate of heaven and they kept mounting through it,

15:15 They would say: Our sight is wrong - nay, but we are folk bewitched.

15:16 And verily in the heaven we have set mansions of the stars, and We have beautified it for beholders.

15:17 And We have guarded it from every outcast devil,

15:18 Save him who stealeth the hearing, and them doth a clear flame pursue.

15:19 And the earth have We spread out, and placed therein firm hills, and caused each seemly thing to grow therein.

15:20 And we have given unto you livelihoods therein, and unto those for whom ye provide not.

15:21 And there is not a thing but with Us are the stores thereof. And we send it not down save in appointed measure.

15:22 And We send the winds fertilising, and cause water to descend from the sky, and give it you to drink. It is not ye who are the holders of the store thereof.

15:23 Lo! and it is We, even We, Who quicken and give death, and We are the Inheritor.

15:24 And verily We know the eager among you and verily We know the laggards.

15:25 Lo! thy Lord will gather them together. Lo! He is Wise, Aware.

15:26 Verily We created man of potter's clay of black mud altered,

15:27 And the jinn did We create aforetime of essential fire.

15:28 And (remember) when thy Lord said unto the angels: Lo! I am creating a mortal out of potter's clay of black mud altered,

15:29 So, when I have made him and have breathed into him of My Spirit, do ye fall down, prostrating yourselves unto him.

15:30 So the angels fell prostrate, all of them together

15:31 Save Iblis. He refused to be among the prostrate.

15:32 He said: O Iblis! What aileth thee that thou art not among the prostrate?

15:33 He said: I am not one to prostrate myself unto a mortal whom Thou hast created out of potter's clay of black mud altered!

15:34 He said: Then go thou forth from hence, for lo! thou art outcast.

15:35 And lo! the curse shall be upon thee till *THE DAY OF JUDGMENT.*

15:36 He said: My Lord! Reprieve me till the day when they are raised.

15:37 He said: Then lo! thou art of those reprieved

15:38 Till the Day of appointed time.

15:39 He said: My Lord! Because Thou hast sent me astray, I verily shall adorn the path of error for them in the earth, and shall mislead them every one,

15:40 *SAVE SUCH OF THEM AS ARE THY PERFECTLY DEVOTED SLAVES.*

15:41 He said: This is a right course incumbent upon Me:

15:42 Lo! as for *MY SLAVES,* thou hast no power over any of them save such of the froward as follow thee,

15:43 And lo! for all such, *HELL WILL BE THE PROMISED PLACE,*

15:44 It hath seven gates, and each gate hath an appointed portion.

15:45 Lo! those who ward off (*EVIL*) are among gardens and watersprings.

15:46 (And it is said unto them): Enter them in peace, secure.

15:47 And We remove whatever rancour may be in their breasts. As brethren, face to face, (they rest) on couches raised.

15:48 Toil cometh not unto them there, nor will they be expelled from thence.

15:49 Announce, (O Muhammad) unto *MY SLAVES* that verily I am the Forgiving, the Merciful,

15:50 And that My doom is the dolorous doom.

15:51 And tell them of Abraham's guests,

15:52 (How) when they came in unto him, and said: Peace. He said: Lo! we are afraid of you.

15:53 They said: Be not afraid! Lo! we bring thee good tidings of a boy possessing wisdom.

15:54 He said: Bring ye me good tidings (of a son) when old age hath overtaken me? Of what then can ye bring good tidings?

15:55 They said: We bring thee good tidings in truth. So be not thou of the despairing.

15:56 He said: And who despaireth of the mercy of his Lord save those who are astray?

15:57 He said: And afterward what is your business, O ye messengers (of Allah)?

15:58 They said: We have been sent unto a guilty folk,

15:59 (All) save the family of Lot. Them we shall deliver every one,

15:60 Except his wife, of whom We had decreed that she should be of those who stay behind.

15:61 And when the messengers came unto the family of Lot,

15:62 He said: Lo! ye are folk unknown (to me).

15:63 They said: Nay, but we bring thee that concerning which they keep disputing,

15:64 And bring thee *THE TRUTH,* and lo! *WE ARE TRUTH-TELLERS.*

15:65 So travel with thy household in a portion of the night, and follow thou their backs. Let none of you turn round, but go whither ye are commanded.

15:66 And We made plain the case to him, that the root of them (who did wrong) was to be cut at early morn.

15:67 And the people of the city came, rejoicing at the news (of new arrivals).

15:68 He said: Lo! they are my guests. Affront me not!

15:69 And *KEEP YOUR DUTY TO ALLAH*, and shame me not!

15:70 They said; Have we not forbidden you from (entertaining) anyone?

15:71 He said: Here are my daughters, if ye must be doing (so).
15:72 By thy life (O Muhammad) they moved blindly in the frenzy of approaching death.
15:73 Then the (Awful) Cry overtook them at the sunrise.
15:74 And We utterly confounded them, and We rained upon them stones of heated clay.
15:75 Lo! therein verily are portents for those who read the signs.
15:76 And lo! it is upon a road still uneffaced.
15:77 Lo! therein is indeed a portent for *BELIEVERS*.
15:78 And the dwellers in the wood indeed were *EVIL-DOERS*.
15:79 So we took vengeance on them; and lo! they both are on a high-road plain to see.
15:80 And the dwellers in Al-Hijr denied (Our) messengers.
15:81 And we gave them Our revelations, but they were averse to them.
15:82 And they used to hew out dwellings from the hills, (wherein they dwelt) secure.
15:83 But the (Awful) Cry overtook them at the morning hour,
15:84 And that which they were wont to count as gain availed them not.
15:85 We created not the heavens and the earth and all that is between them save with truth, and lo! the Hour is surely coming. So forgive, (O Muhammad), with a gracious forgiveness. [Part cancelled by verse 9:5, i.e. command to violence replaces command to forgiveness][524]
15:86 Lo! Thy Lord! He is the All-Wise Creator.
15:87 We have given thee seven of the oft-repeated (verses) and the great Qur'an.
15:88 Strain not thine eyes toward that which We cause some wedded pairs among them to enjoin, and be not grieved on their account, and lower thy wing (in tenderness) for the *BELIEVERS*. [Part cancelled by verse 9:5][525]
15:89 And say: Lo! I, even I, am a plain warner, [Part cancelled by verse 9:5 i.e. violence commanded instead of warning non-Muslims.][526]
15:90 Such as We send down for those who make division,
15:91 Those who break the Qur'an into parts.
15:92 Them, by thy Lord, We shall question, every one,
15:93 Of what they used to do.
15:94 So proclaim that which thou art commanded, and withdraw from the *IDOLATERS*. [Cancelled by verse 9:5, i.e. command to violence replaces command to withdraw][527]
15:95 Lo! We defend thee from the scoffers,
15:96 Who set some other god along with Allah. But they will come to know.
15:97 Well know We that thy bosom is oppressed by what they say,
15:98 But hymn the praise of thy Lord, and be of those who make prostration (unto Him).
15:99 And serve thy Lord till the Inevitable cometh unto thee.

Chapter 12 - Joseph

12:1 Alif. Lam. Ra. These are verse of *THE SCRIPTURE THAT MAKETH PLAIN*. [Koran claims to be plain, clear]

12:2 Lo! We have revealed it, a Lecture in *ARABIC*, that ye may understand.
12:3 We narrate unto thee (Muhammad) the best of narratives in that We have inspired in thee this Qur'an, though aforetime thou wast of the heedless.
12:4 When Joseph said unto his father: O my father! Lo! I saw in a dream eleven planets and the sun and the moon, I saw them prostrating themselves unto me.
12:5 He said: O my dear son! Tell not thy brethren of thy vision, lest they plot a plot against thee. Lo! Satan is for man an open foe.
12:6 Thus thy Lord will prefer thee and will teach thee the interpretation of events, and will perfect His grace upon thee and upon the family of Jacob as He perfected it upon thy forefathers, Abraham and Isaac. Lo! thy Lord is Knower, Wise.
12:7 Verily in Joseph and his brethren are signs (of Allah's Sovereignty) for the inquiring.
12:8 When they said: Verily Joseph and his brother are dearer to our father than we are, many though we be. Lo! our father is in plain aberration.
12:9 (One said): Kill Joseph or cast him to some (other) land, so that your father's favour may be all for you, and (that) ye may afterward be righteous folk.

12:10 One among them said: Kill not Joseph but, if ye must be doing, fling him into the depth of the pit; some caravan will find him.

12:11 They said: O our father! Why wilt thou not trust us with Joseph, when lo! we are good friends to him?

12:12 Send him with us to-morrow that he may enjoy himself and play. And lo! we shall take good care of him.

12:13 He said: Lo! in truth it saddens me that ye should take him with you, and I fear less the wolf devour him while ye are heedless of him.

12:14 They said: If the wolf should devour him when we are (so strong) a band, then surely we should have already perished.

12:15 Then, when they led him off, and were of one mind that they should place him in the depth of the pit, We inspired in him: Thou wilt tell them of this deed of theirs when they know (thee) not.

12:16 And they came weeping to their father in the evening.

12:17 Saying: O our father! We went racing one with another, and left Joseph by our things, and the wolf devoured him, and thou believest not our saying even when we speak the truth.

12:18 And they came with false blood on his shirt. He said: Nay, but your minds have beguiled you into something. (My course is) comely patience. And Allah it is Whose help is to be sought in that (predicament) which ye describe.

12:19 And there came a caravan, and they sent their waterdrawer. He let down his pail (into the pit). He said: Good luck! Here is a youth. And they hid him as a treasure, and Allah was Aware of what they did.

12:20 And they sold him for a low price, a number of silver coins; and they attached no value to him.

12:21 And he of Egypt who purchased him said unto his wife: Receive him honourably. Perchance he may prove useful to us or we may adopt him as a son. Thus we established Joseph in the land that We might teach him the interpretation of events. And Allah was predominant in His career, but most of mankind know not.

12:22 And when he reached his prime We gave him wisdom and knowledge. Thus We REWARD the good.

12:23 And she, in whose house he was, asked of him an EVIL act. She bolted the doors and said: Come! He said: I seek refuge in Allah! Lo! he is my lord, who hath treated me honourably. Lo! wrong-doers never prosper.

12:24 She verily desired him, and he would have desired her if it had not been that he saw the argument of his Lord. Thus it was, that We might ward off from him evil and lewdness. Lo! he was of Our chosen slaves.

12:25 And they raced with one another to the door, and she tore his shirt from behind, and they met her lord and master at the door. She said: What shall be HIS REWARD, who wisheth EVIL to thy folk, save prison or A PAINFUL DOOM?

12:26 (Joseph) said: She it was who asked of me an EVIL act. And a witness of her own folk testified: If his shirt is torn from before, then she speaketh truth and he is of the liars.

12:27 And if his shirt is torn from behind, then she hath lied and he is of the truthful.

12:28 So when he saw his shirt torn from behind, he said: Lo! this is of the guile of you women. Lo! the guile of you is very great.

12:29 O Joseph! Turn away from this, and thou, (O woman), ask forgiveness for thy sin. Lo! thou art of the faulty.

12:30 And women in the city said: The ruler's wife is asking of her slave-boy an ill-deed. Indeed he has smitten her to the heart with love. We behold her in plain aberration.

12:31 And when she heard of their sly talk, she sent to them and prepared for them a cushioned couch (to lie on at the feast) and gave to every one of them a knife and said (to Joseph): Come out unto them! And when they saw him they exalted him and cut their hands, exclaiming: Allah Blameless! This is no a human being. This is not other than some gracious angel.

12:32 She said: This is he on whose account ye blamed me. I asked of him an EVIL act, but he proved continent, but if he do not my behest he verily shall be imprisoned, and verily shall be of those brought low.

12:33 He said: O my Lord! Prison is more dear than that unto which they urge me, and if Thou fend not off their wiles from me I shall incline unto them and become of the foolish.

12:34 So his Lord heard his prayer and fended off their wiles from him. Lo! He is Hearer, Knower.

12:35 And it seemed good to them (the men-folk) after they had seen the signs (of his innocence) to imprison him for a time.

12:36 And two young men went to prison with him. One of them said: I dreamed that I was pressing wine. The other said: I dreamed that I was carrying upon my head bread whereof the birds were eating. Announce unto us the interpretation, for we see thee of those good (at interpretation).

12:37 He said: The food which ye are given (daily) shall not come unto you but I shall tell you the interpretation ere it cometh unto you. This is of that which my Lord hath taught me. Lo! I have forsaken the religion of folk who *BELIEVE* not in Allah and are *DISBELIEVERS* in the Hereafter.

12:38 And I have followed the religion of my fathers, Abraham and Isaac and Jacob. It never was for us to attribute aught as partner to Allah. This is of the bounty of Allah unto us (the seed of Abraham) and unto mankind; but most men give not thanks.

12:39 O my fellow-prisoners! Are divers lords better, or Allah the One, Almighty?

12:40 Those whom ye worship beside Him are but names which ye have named, ye and your fathers. Allah hath revealed no sanction for them. The decision rests with Allah only, Who hath commanded you that ye worship none save Him. This is the right religion, but most men know not.

12:41 O my two fellow-prisoners! As for one of you, he will pour out wine for his lord to drink; and as for the other, he will be crucified so that the birds will eat from his head. Thus is the case judged concerning which ye did inquire.

12:42 And he said unto him of the twain who he knew would be released: Mention me in the presence of thy lord. But Satan caused him to forget to mention it to his lord, so he (Joseph) stayed in prison for some years.

12:43 And the king said: Lo! I saw in a dream seven fat kine which seven lean were eating, and seven green ears of corn and other (seven) dry. O notables! Expound for me my vision, if ye can interpret dreams.

12:44 They answered: Jumbled dreams! And we are not knowing in the interpretation of dreams.

12:45 And he of the two who was released, and (now) at length remembered, said: I am going to announce unto you the interpretation, therefore send me forth.

12:46 (And when he came to Joseph in the prison, he exclaimed): Joseph! O thou truthful one! Expound for us the seven fat kine which seven lean were eating and the seven green ears of corn and other (seven) dry, that I may return unto the people, so that they may know.

12:47 He said: Ye shall sow seven years as usual, but that which ye reap, leave it in the ear, all save a little which ye eat.

12:48 Then after that will come seven hard years which will devour all that ye have prepared for them, save a little of that which ye have stored.

12:49 Then, after that, will come a year when the people will have plenteous crops and when they will press (wine and oil).

12:50 And the king said: Bring him unto me. And when the messenger came unto him, he (Joseph) said: Return unto thy lord and ask him what was the case of the women who cut their hands. Lo! my Lord knoweth their guile.

12:51 He (the king) (then sent for those women and) said: What happened when ye asked an *EVIL* act of Joseph? They answered: Allah Blameless! We know no *EVIL* of him. Said the wife of the ruler: Now the truth is out. I asked of him an *EVIL* act, and he is surely of the truthful.

12:52 (Then Joseph said: I asked for) this, that he (my lord) may know that I betrayed him not in secret, and that surely Allah guideth not the snare of the betrayers.

12:53 I do not exculpate myself. Lo! the (human) soul enjoineth unto *EVIL*, save that whereon my Lord hath mercy. Lo! my Lord is Forgiving, Merciful.

12:54 And the king said: Bring him unto me that I may attach him to my person. And when he had talked with him he said: Lo! thou art to-day in our presence established and trusted.

12:55 He said: Set me over the storehouses of the land. Lo! I am a skilled custodian.

12:56 Thus gave We power to Joseph in the land. He was the owner of it where he pleased. We reach with Our mercy whom We will. We lose not the *REWARD* of the good.

12:57 And *THE REWARD OF THE HEREAFTER IS BETTER*, for those who *BELIEVE* and ward off (*EVIL*).

12:58 And Joseph's brethren came and presented themselves before him, and he knew them but they knew him not.

12:59 And when he provided them with their provision he said: Bring unto me a brother of yours from your father. See ye not that I fill up the measure and I am the best of hosts?

12:60 And if ye bring him not unto me, then there shall be no measure for you with me, nor shall ye draw near.

12:61 They said: We will try to win him from his father: that we will surely do.

12:62 He said unto his young men: Place their merchandise in their saddlebags, so that they may know it when they go back to their folk, and so will come again.

12:63 So when they went back to their father they said: O our father! The measure is denied us, so send with us our brother that we may obtain the measure, surely we will guard him well.

12:64 He said: Can I entrust him to you save as I entrusted his brother to you aforetime? Allah is better at guarding, and He is the Most Merciful of those who show mercy.

12:65 And when they opened their belongings they discovered that their merchandise had been returned to them. They said: O our father! What (more) can we ask? Here is our merchandise returned to us. We shall get provision for our folk and guard our brother, and we shall have the extra measure of a camel (load). This (that we bring now) is a light measure.

12:66 He said: I will not send him with you till ye give me an undertaking in the name of Allah that ye will bring him back to me, unless ye are surrounded. And when they gave him their undertaking he said: Allah is the Warden over what we say.

12:67 And he said: O my sons! Go not in by one gate; go in by different gates. I can naught avail you as against Allah. Lo! the decision rests with Allah only. In Him do I put my trust, and in Him let all the trusting put their trust.

12:68 And when they entered in the manner which their father had enjoined, it would have naught availed them as against Allah; it was but a need of Jacob's soul which he thus satisfied; and lo! he was a lord of knowledge because We had taught him; but most of mankind know not.

12:69 And when they went in before Joseph, he took his brother unto him, saying: Lo! I, even I, am thy brother, therefore sorrow not for what they did.

12:70 And when he provided them with their provision, he put the drinking-cup in his brother's saddlebag, and then a crier cried: O camel-riders! Lo! ye are surely thieves!

12:71 They cried, coming toward them: What is it ye have lost?

12:72 They said: We have lost the king's cup, and he who bringeth it shall have a camel-load, and I (said Joseph) am answerable for it.

12:73 They said: By Allah, well ye know we came not to do *EVIL* in the land, and are no thieves.

12:74 They said: And what shall be the penalty for it, if ye prove liars?

12:75 They said: The penalty for it! He in whose bag (the cup) is found, he is the penalty for it. Thus we requite wrong-doers.

12:76 Then he (Joseph) began the search with their bags before his brother's bag, then he produced it from his brother's bag. Thus did We contrive for Joseph. He could not have taken his brother according to the king's law unless Allah willed. We raise by grades (of mercy) whom We will, and over every lord of knowledge there is one more knowing.

12:77 They said: If he stealeth, a brother of his stole before. But Joseph kept it secret in his soul and revealed it not unto them. He said (within himself): Ye are in worse case, and Allah knoweth best (the truth of) that which ye allege.

12:78 They said: O ruler of the land! Lo! he hath a very aged father, so take one of us instead of him. Lo! we behold thee of those who do kindness.

12:79 He said: Allah forbid that we should seize save him with whom we found our property; then truly we should be wrong-doers.

12:80 So, When they despaired of (moving) him, they conferred together apart. The eldest of them said: Know ye not how your father took an undertaking from you in Allah's name and how ye failed in the case of Joseph aforetime? Therefore I shall not go forth from the land until my father giveth leave or Allah judgeth for me. He is the Best of Judges.

12:81 Return unto your father and say: O our father! Lo! thy son hath stolen. We testify only to that which we know; we are not guardians of the Unseen.

12:82 Ask the township where we were, and the caravan with which we travelled hither. Lo! we speak the truth.

12:83 (And when they came unto their father and had spoken thus to him) he said: Nay, but your minds have beguiled you into something. (My course is) comely patience! It may be that Allah will bring them all unto me. Lo! He, only He, is the Knower, the Wise.

12:84 And he turned away from them and said: Alas, my grief for Joseph! And his eyes were whitened with the sorrow that he was suppressing.

12:85 They said: By Allah, thou wilt never cease remembering Joseph till thy health is ruined or thou art of those who perish!

12:86 He said: I expose my distress and anguish only unto Allah, and I know from Allah that which ye know not.

12:87 Go, O my sons, and ascertain concerning Joseph and his brother, and despair not of the Spirit of Allah. Lo! none despaireth of the Spirit of Allah save *DISBELIEVING* folk.

12:88 And when they came (again) before him (Joseph) they said: O ruler! Misfortune hath touched us and our folk, and we bring but poor merchandise, so fill for us the measure and be charitable unto us. Lo! Allah will requite the charitable,

12:89 He said: Know ye what ye did unto Joseph and his brother in your ignorance?

12:90 They said: Is it indeed thou who art Joseph? He said: I am Joseph and this is my brother. Allah hath shown us favour. Lo! he who wardeth off (*EVIL*) and endureth (findeth favour); for lo! Allah loseth not the wages of the kindly.

12:91 They said: By Allah, verily Allah hath preferred thee above us, and we were indeed sinful.

12:92 He said: Have no fear this day! May Allah forgive you, and He is the Most Merciful of those who show mercy.

12:93 Go with this shirt of mine and lay it on my father's face, he will become (again) a seer; and come to me with all your folk.

12:94 When the caravan departed their father had said: Truly I am conscious of the breath of Joseph, though ye call me a dotard.

12:95 (Those around him) said: By Allah, lo! thou art in thine old aberration.

12:96 Then, when the bearer of glad tidings came, he laid it on his face and he became a seer once more. He said: Said I not unto you that I know from Allah that which ye know not?

12:97 They said: O our father! Ask forgiveness of our sins for us, for lo! we were sinful.

12:98 He said: I shall ask forgiveness for you of my Lord. Lo! He is the Forgiving, the Merciful.

12:99 And when they came in before Joseph, he took his parents unto him, and said: Come into Egypt safe, if Allah will!

12:100 And he placed his parents on the dais and they fell down before him prostrate, and he said: O my father! This is the interpretation of my dream of old. My Lord hath made it true, and He hath shown me kindness, since He took me out of the prison and hath brought you from the desert after Satan had made strife between me and my brethren. Lo! my Lord is tender unto whom He will. He is the Knower, the Wise.

12:101 O my Lord! Thou hast given me (something) of sovereignty and hast taught me (something) of the interpretation of events - Creator of the heavens and the earth! Thou art my Protecting Guardian in the world and the Hereafter. Make me to die *MUSLIM* (unto Thee), and join me to the righteous.

12:102 This is of the tidings of the Unseen which We inspire in thee (Muhammad). Thou wast not present with them when they fixed their plan and they were scheming.

12:103 And though thou try much, *MOST MEN WILL NOT BELIEVE.*

12:104 Thou askest them no fee for it. It is naught else than a reminder unto the peoples.

12:105 How many a portent is there in the heavens and the earth which they pass by with face averted!

12:106 And most of them *BELIEVE* not in Allah except that they attribute partners (unto Him).

12:107 Deem they themselves secure from the coming on them of a pall of Allah's punishment, or the coming of the Hour suddenly while they are unaware?

12:108 Say: This is my Way: I call on Allah with sure knowledge. I and whosoever followeth me - Glory be to Allah! - and I am not of the *IDOLATERS*.

12:109 We sent not before thee (any messengers) save men whom We inspired from among the folk of the townships - Have they not travelled in the land and seen the nature of the consequence for those who were before them? And verily the abode of the Hereafter, for those who ward off (*EVIL*), is best. Have ye then no sense? -

12:110 Till, when the messengers despaired and thought that they were denied, then came unto them Our help, and whom We would was saved. And Our wrath cannot be warded from the guilty.

12:111 In their history verily there is a lesson for men of understanding. It is no invented story but a confirmation of the existing (Scripture) and a detailed explanation of everything, and a guidance and a mercy for folk who *BELIEVE*.

Chapter 11 - Hud

11:1 Alif. Lam. Ra. (This is) a Scripture the revelations whereof are perfected and then expounded. (It cometh) from One Wise, Informed, [Koran claims to be perfect]

11:2 (Saying): Serve none but Allah. Lo! I am unto you from Him a warner and a bringer of good tidings.

11:3 And (bidding you): Ask pardon of your Lord and turn to Him repentant. He will cause you to enjoy a fair estate until a time appointed. He giveth His bounty unto every bountiful one. But if ye turn away, lo! (then) I fear for you *THE RETRIBUTION OF AN AWFUL DAY.*

11:4 Unto Allah is your return, and He is Able to do all things.

11:5 Lo! now they fold up their breasts that they may hide (their thoughts) from Him. At the very moment when they cover themselves with their clothing, Allah knoweth that which they keep hidden and that which they proclaim. Lo! He is Aware of what is in the breasts (of men).

11:6 And there is not a beast in the earth but the sustenance thereof dependeth on Allah. He knoweth its habitation and its repository. All is in a clear Record.

11:7 And He it is Who created the heavens and the earth in six Days - and His Throne was upon the water - that He might try you, which of you is best in conduct. Yet if thou (O Muhammad) sayest: Lo! ye will be raised again after death! t*HOSE WHO DISBELIEVE* will surely say: This is naught but mere magic.

11:8 And if *WE DELAY FOR THEM THE DOOM UNTIL A RECKONED TIME*, they will surely say: What withholdeth it? Verily on *THE DAY WHEN IT COMETH UNTO THEM*, it cannot be averted from them, and that which they derided will surround them.

11:9 And if we cause man to taste some mercy from Us and afterward withdraw it from him, lo! he is despairing, thankless.

11:10 And if We cause him to taste grace after some misfortune that had befallen him, he saith: The ills have gone from me. Lo! he is exultant, boastful;

11:11 Save *THOSE WHO PERSEVERE AND DO GOOD WORKS. THEIRS WILL BE FORGIVENESS AND A GREAT REWARD.*

11:12 A likely thing, that thou wouldst forsake aught of that which hath been revealed unto thee, and that thy breast should be straitened for it, because they say: Why hath not a treasure been sent down for him, or an angel come with him? ~~Thou art but a warner, and Allah is in charge of all things.~~ [Part cancelled by verse 9:5, i.e. violence replaces mere warning][528]

11:13 Or *THEY SAY: HE HATH INVENTED IT*. Say: Then bring ten surahs, the like thereof, invented, and call on everyone ye can beside Allah, if ye are truthful!

11:14 And if they answer not your prayer, then know that it is revealed only in the knowledge of Allah; and that there is no God save Him. Will ye then be (of) those who surrender?

11:15 Whoso desireth the life of the world and its pomp, We shall repay them their deeds herein, and therein they will not be wronged.

11:16 *THOSE ARE THEY FOR WHOM IS NAUGHT IN THE HEREAFTER SAVE THE FIRE.* (All) that they contrive here is vain and (all) that they are wont to do is fruitless.

11:17 Is he (to be counted equal with them) who relieth on a *CLEAR PROOF* from his Lord, and a witness from Him reciteth it, and before it was the Book of Moses, an example and a mercy? Such *BELIEVE* therein, and whoso *DISBELIEVETH* therein of the clans, *THE FIRE* is his appointed place. So be not thou in doubt concerning it. Lo! it is *THE TRUTH* from thy Lord; but *MOST OF MANKIND BELIEVE NOT.*

11:18 Who doeth greater wrong than he who inventeth a lie concerning Allah? Such will be brought before their Lord, and the witnesses will say: These are they who lied concerning their Lord. Now *THE CURSE OF ALLAH IS UPON WRONG-DOERS,*

11:19 Who debar (men) from the way of Allah and would have it crooked, and who are *DISBELIEVERS* in the Hereafter.

11:20 Such will not escape in the earth, nor have they any protecting friends beside Allah. For them the torment will be double. They could not bear to hear, and they used not to see.

11:21 Such are they who have lost their souls, and that which they used to invent hath failed them.

11:22 Assuredly in the Hereafter they will be the greatest losers.

11:23 Lo! *THOSE WHO BELIEVE AND DO GOOD WORKS* and humble themselves before their Lord: such are *RIGHTFUL OWNERS OF THE GARDEN*; they will abide therein.

11:24 The similitude of the two parties is as *THE BLIND AND THE DEAF AND THE SEER AND THE HEARER.* Are they equal in similitude? Will ye not then be admonished?

11:25 And We sent Noah unto his folk (and he said): Lo! I am a plain warner unto you.

11:26 That ye serve none, save Allah. Lo! I fear for you *THE RETRIBUTION OF A PAINFUL DAY.*

11:27 The chieftains of his folk, who *DISBELIEVED*, said: We see thee but a mortal like us, and we see not that any follow thee save the most abject among us, without reflection. We behold in you no merit above us - nay, *WE DEEM YOU LIARS.*

11:28 He said: O my people! Bethink you, if I rely on a *CLEAR PROOF* from my Lord and there hath come unto me a mercy from His presence, and it hath been made obscure to you, can we compel you to accept it when ye are averse thereto?

11:29 And O my people! I ask of you no wealth therefor. *MY REWARD IS THE CONCERN ONLY OF ALLAH*, and I am not going to thrust away those who *BELIEVE* - Lo! they have to meet their Lord! - but *I SEE YOU A FOLK THAT ARE IGNORANT.*

11:30 And, O my people! who would deliver me from Allah if I thrust them away? Will ye not then reflect?

11:31 I say not unto you: "I have the treasures of Allah" nor "I have knowledge of the Unseen," nor say I: "Lo! I am an angel!" Nor say I unto those whom your eyes scorn that Allah will not give them good - Allah knoweth best what is in their hearts - Lo! then indeed I should be of the wrong-doers.

11:32 They said: O Noah! Thou hast disputed with us and multiplied disputation with us; now bring upon us that wherewith thou threatenest us, if thou art of the truthful.

11:33 He said: Only Allah will bring it upon you if He will, and ye can by no means escape.

11:34 My counsel will not profit you if I were minded to advise you, if Allah's will is to keep you astray. He is your Lord and unto Him ye will be brought back.

11:35 Or *SAY THEY (AGAIN): HE HATH INVENTED IT*? Say: If I have invented it, upon me be my crimes, but I am innocent of (all) that ye commit.

11:36 And it was inspired in Noah, (saying): No-one of thy folk will *BELIEVE* save him who hath *BELIEVED* already. Be not distressed because of what they do.

11:37 Build the ship under Our eyes and by Our inspiration, and speak not unto Me on behalf of those who do wrong. Lo! they will be drowned.

11:38 And he was building the ship, and every time that chieftains of his people passed him, they made mock of him. He said: Though ye make mock of Us, yet We mock at you even as ye mock;

11:39 And ye shall know to whom a punishment that will confound him cometh, and upon whom a lasting doom will fall.

11:40 (Thus it was) till, when Our commandment came to pass and the oven gushed forth water, We said: Load therein two of every kind, a pair (the male and female), and thy household, save him against whom the word hath gone forth already, and those who *BELIEVE*. And but a few were they who *BELIEVED* with him.

11:41 And he said: Embark therein! In the name of Allah be its course and its mooring. Lo! my Lord is Forgiving, Merciful.

11:42 And it sailed with them amid waves like mountains, and Noah cried unto his son - and he was standing aloof - O my son! Come ride with us, and be not with the *DISBELIEVERS*.

11:43 He said: I shall betake me to some mountain that will save me from the water. (Noah) said: This day there is none that saveth from the commandment of Allah save him on whom He hath had mercy. And the wave came in between them, so he was among the drowned.

11:44 And it was said: O earth! Swallow thy water and, O sky! be cleared of clouds! And the water was made to subside. And the commandment was fulfilled. And it (the ship) came to rest upon (the mount) Al-Judi and it was said: A far removal for wrongdoing folk!

11:45 And Noah cried unto his Lord and said: My Lord! Lo! my son is of my household! Surely Thy promise is *THE TRUTH* and Thou are the Most Just of Judges.

11:46 He said: O Noah! Lo! he is not of thy household; lo! he is of *EVIL* conduct, so ask not of Me that whereof thou hast no knowledge. I admonish thee lest thou be among the ignorant.

11:47 He said: My Lord! Lo! in Thee do I seek refuge (from the sin) that I should ask of Thee that whereof I have no knowledge. Unless Thou forgive me and have mercy on me I shall be among the lost.

11:48 It was said (unto him): O Noah! Go thou down (from the mountain) with peace from Us and blessings upon thee and some nations (that will spring) from those with thee. (There will be other) nations unto whom We shall give enjoyment a long while and then *A PAINFUL DOOM* from Us will overtake them.

11:49 This is of the tidings of the Unseen which We inspire in thee (Muhammad). Thou thyself knewest it not, nor did thy folk (know it) before this. Then have patience. Lo! the sequel is for those who ward off (*EVIL*).

11:50 And unto (the tribe of) A'ad (We sent) their brother, Hud. He said: O my people! Serve Allah! Ye have no other Allah save Him. Lo! ye do but invent.

11:51 O my people! I ask of you no reward for it. Lo! my reward is the concern only of Him Who made me. Have ye then no sense?

11:52 And, O my people! Ask forgiveness of your Lord, then turn unto Him repentant; He will cause the sky to rain abundance on you and will add unto you strength to your strength. Turn not away, guilty!

11:53 They said: O Hud! Thou hast brought us no *CLEAR PROOF* and we are not going to forsake our gods on thy (mere) saying, and we are not *BELIEVERS* in thee.

11:54 We say naught save that one of our gods hath possessed thee in an *EVIL* way. He said: I call Allah to witness, and do ye (too) bear witness, that I am innocent of (all) that ye ascribe as partners (to Allah)

11:55 Beside Him. So (try to) circumvent me, all of you, give me no respite.

11:56 Lo! I have put my trust in Allah, my Lord and your Lord. Not an animal but He doth grasp it by the forelock! Lo! my Lord is on *A STRAIGHT PATH*.

11:57 And if ye turn away, still I have conveyed unto you that wherewith I was sent unto you, and my Lord will set in place of you a folk other than you. Ye cannot injure Him at all. Lo! my Lord is Guardian over all things.

11:58 And when Our commandment came to pass We saved Hud and *THOSE WHO BELIEVED* with him by a mercy from Us; We saved them from a harsh doom.

11:59 And such were A'ad. They denied the revelations of their Lord and flouted His messengers and followed the command of every froward potentate.

11:60 And a curse was made to follow them in the world and on *THE DAY OF RESURRECTION*. Lo! A'ad *DISBELIEVED* in their Lord. A far removal for A'ad, the folk of Hud!

11:61 And unto (the tribe of) Thamud (We sent) their brother Salih. He said: O my people! Serve Allah, Ye have no other Allah save Him. He brought you forth from the earth and hath made you husband it. So ask forgiveness of Him and turn unto Him repentant. Lo! my Lord is Nigh, Responsive.

11:62 They said: O Salih! Thou hast been among us hitherto as that wherein our hope was placed. Dost thou ask us not to worship what our fathers worshipped? Lo! we verily are in grave doubt concerning that to which thou callest us.

11:63 He said: O my people! Bethink you: if I am (acting) on *CLEAR PROOF* from my Lord and there hath come unto me a mercy from Him, who will save me from Allah if I disobey Him? Ye would add to me naught save perdition.

11:64 O my people! This is the camel of Allah, a token unto you, so suffer her to feed in Allah's earth, and touch her not with harm lest a near torment seize you.

11:65 But they hamstrung her, and then he said: Enjoy life in your dwelling-place three days! This is a threat that will not be belied.

11:66 So, when Our commandment came to pass, We saved Salih, and *THOSE WHO BELIEVED* with him, by a mercy from Us, from the ignominy of that day. Lo, thy Lord! He is the Strong, the Mighty.

11:67 And the (awful) Cry overtook those who did wrong, so that morning found them prostrate in their dwellings,

11:68 As though they had not dwelt there. Lo! Thamud *DISBELIEVED* in their Lord. A far removal for Thamud!

11:69 And Our messengers came unto Abraham with good news. They said: Peace! He answered: Peace! and delayed not to bring a roasted calf.

11:70 And when he saw their hands reached not to it, he mistrusted them and conceived a fear of them. They said: Fear not! Lo! we are sent unto the folk of Lot.

11:71 And his wife, standing by laughed when We gave her good tidings (of the birth) of Isaac, and, after Isaac, of Jacob.

11:72 She said: Oh woe is me! Shall I bear a child when I am an old woman, and this my husband is an old man? Lo! this is a strange thing!

11:73 They said: Wonderest thou at the commandment of Allah? The mercy of Allah and His blessings be upon you, O people of the house! Lo! He is Owner of Praise, Owner of Glory!

11:74 And when the awe departed from Abraham, and the glad news reached him, he pleaded with Us on behalf of the folk of Lot.

11:75 Lo! Abraham was mild, imploring, penitent.

11:76 (It was said) O Abraham! Forsake this! Lo! thy Lord's commandment hath gone forth, and lo! there cometh unto them a doom which cannot be repelled.

11:77 And when Our messengers came unto Lot, he was distressed and knew not how to protect them. He said: This is a distressful day.

11:78 And his people came unto him, running towards him - and before then they used to commit abominations - He said: O my people! Here are my daughters! They are purer for you. Beware of Allah, and degrade me not in (the person of) my guests. Is there not among you any upright man?

11:79 They said: Well thou knowest that we have no right to thy daughters, and well thou knowest what we want.

11:80 He said: Would that I had strength to resist you or had some strong support (among you)!

11:81 (The messengers) said: O Lot! Lo! we are messengers of thy Lord; they shall not reach thee. So travel with thy people in a part of the night, and let not one of you turn round - (all) save thy wife. Lo! that which smiteth them will smite her (also). Lo! their tryst is (for) the morning. Is not the morning nigh?

11:82 So when Our commandment came to pass *WE OVERTHREW (THAT TOWNSHIP) AND RAINED UPON IT STONES OF CLAY*, one after another,

11:83 Marked with fire in the providence of thy Lord (for the destruction of the wicked). And they are never far from the wrong-doers.

11:84 And unto Midian (We sent) their brother Shu'eyb. He said: O my people! Serve Allah. Ye have no other Allah save Him! And give not short measure and short weight. Lo! I see you well-to-do, and lo! I fear for you *THE DOOM OF A BESETTING DAY.*

11:85 O my people! Give full measure and full weight in justice, and wrong not people in respect of their goods. And *DO NOT EVIL IN THE EARTH, CAUSING CORRUPTION*.

11:86 That which Allah leaveth with you is better for you if ye are *BELIEVERS*; and I am not a keeper over you.

11:87 They said: O Shu'eyb! Doth thy way of prayer command thee that we should forsake that which our fathers (used to) worship, or that we (should leave off) doing what we will with our own property. Lo! thou art the mild, the guide to right behaviour.

11:88 He said: O my people! Bethink you: if I am (acting) on a *CLEAR PROOF* from my Lord and He sustaineth me with fair sustenance from Him (how can I concede aught to you)? I desire not to do behind your backs that which I ask you not to do. I desire naught save reform so far as I am able. My welfare is only in Allah. In Him I trust and unto Him I turn (repentant).

11:89 And, O my people! Let not the schism with me cause you to sin so that there befall you that which befell the folk of Noah and the folk of Hud, and the folk of Salih; and the folk of Lot are not far off from you.

11:90 Ask pardon of your Lord and then turn unto Him (repentant). Lo! my Lord is Merciful, Loving.

11:91 They said: O Shu'eyb! We understand not much of that thou tellest, and lo! we do behold thee weak among us. But for thy family, we should have stoned thee, for thou art not strong against us.

11:92 He said: O my people! Is my family more to be honoured by you than Allah? and ye put Him behind you, neglected! Lo! my Lord surroundeth what ye do.

11:93 And, O my people! Act according to your power, lo! I (too) am acting. Ye will soon know on whom there cometh a doom that will abase him, and who it is that lieth. And watch! Lo! I am a watcher with you.

11:94 And when Our commandment came to pass We saved Shu'eyb and *THOSE WHO BELIEVED* with him by a mercy from Us; and the (Awful) Cry seized those who did injustice, and morning found them prostrate in their dwellings,

11:95 As though they had not dwelt there. A far removal for Midian, even as Thamud had been removed afar!

11:96 And verily We sent Moses with Our revelations and a clear warrant

11:97 Unto Pharaoh and his chiefs, but they did follow the command of Pharaoh, and the command of Pharaoh was no right guide.

11:98 He will go before his people on *THE DAY OF RESURRECTION* and will lead them to *THE FIRE* for watering-place. Ah, hapless is the watering-place (whither they are) led.

11:99 A curse is made to follow them in the world and on *THE DAY OF RESURRECTION*. Hapless is the gift (that will be) given (them).

11:100 That is (something) of the tidings of the townships (which were destroyed of old). We relate it unto thee (Muhammad). Some of them are standing and some (already) reaped.

11:101 We wronged them not, but they did wrong themselves; and their gods on whom they call beside Allah availed them naught when came thy Lord's command; they added to them naught save ruin.

11:102 Even thus is the grasp of thy Lord when He graspeth the townships while they are doing wrong. Lo! His grasp is painful, very strong.

11:103 Lo! herein verily there is a portent for those who fear the doom of the Hereafter. That is *A DAY UNTO WHICH MANKIND WILL BE GATHERED*, and that is a day that will be witnessed.

11:104 And We defer it only to a term already reckoned.

11:105 *ON THE DAY WHEN IT COMETH* no soul will speak except by His permission; some among them will be wretched, (others) glad.

11:106 As for those who will be wretched (on that day) *THEY WILL BE IN THE FIRE*; sighing and wailing will be their portion therein,

11:107 Abiding there so long as the heavens and the earth endure save for that which thy Lord willeth. Lo! thy Lord is Doer of what He will.

11:108 And as for those who will be glad (that day) they will be in *THE GARDEN*, abiding there so long as the heavens and the earth endure save for that which thy Lord willeth: a gift unfailing.

11:109 So be not thou in doubt concerning that which these (folk) worship. They worship only as their fathers worshipped aforetime. Lo! we shall pay them their whole due unabated.

11:110 And we verily gave unto Moses the Scripture, and there was strife thereupon; and had it not been for a Word that had already gone forth from thy Lord, the case would have been judged between them, and lo! they are in grave doubt concerning it.

11:111 And lo! unto each thy Lord will verily repay his works in full. Lo! He is Informed of what they do.

11:112 So *TREAD THOU THE STRAIGHT PATH AS THOU ART COMMANDED*, and those who turn (unto Allah) with thee, and transgress not. Lo! He is Seer of what ye do.

11:113 And incline not toward those who do wrong lest *THE FIRE* touch you, and *YE HAVE NO PROTECTING FRIENDS AGAINST ALLAH*, and afterward ye would not be helped.

11:114 Establish worship at the two ends of the day and in some watches of the night. Lo! good deeds annul ill-deeds. This is reminder for the mindful.

11:115 And have patience, (O Muhammad), for lo! Allah loseth not the wages of the good.

11:116 If only there had been among the generations before you men possessing a remnant (of good sense) to warn (their people) from *CORRUPTION IN THE EARTH*, as did a few of those whom We saved from them! *THE WRONG-DOERS FOLLOWED THAT BY WHICH THEY WERE MADE SAPLESS, AND WERE GUILTY.*

11:117 In truth thy Lord destroyed not the townships tyrannously while their folk were doing right.

11:118 And if thy Lord had willed, He verily would have made mankind one nation, yet they cease not differing,

11:119 Save him on whom thy Lord hath mercy; and for that He did create them. And the Word of thy Lord hath been fulfilled: Verily *I SHALL FILL HELL* with the jinn and mankind together.

11:120 And all that We relate unto thee of the story of the messengers is in order that thereby We may make firm thy heart. And herein hath come unto thee *THE TRUTH* and an exhortation and a reminder for *BELIEVERS*.

11:121 ~~And say unto those who believe not: Act according to your power. Lo! We (too) are acting.~~ [Cancelled by verse 9:5, i.e. violence replaces patience and indifference][529]

11:122 ~~And wait! Lo! We (too) are waiting.~~ [Cancelled by verse 9:5][530]

11:123 And Allah's is the Invisible of the heavens and the earth, and unto Him the whole matter will be returned. So worship Him and put thy trust in Him. Lo! thy Lord is not unaware of what ye (mortals) do.

Chapter 10 - Jonah

10:1 Alif. Lam. Ra. These are verses of the Wise Scripture.

10:2 Is it a wonder for mankind that We have inspired a man among them, saying: Warn mankind and bring unto those who *BELIEVE* the good tidings that they have a sure footing with their Lord? The *DISBELIEVERS* say: Lo! this is a mere wizard.

10:3 Lo! your Lord is Allah Who created the heavens and the earth in six Days, then He established Himself upon the Throne, directing all things. There is no intercessor (with Him) save after His permission. That is Allah, your Lord, so worship Him. Oh, will ye not remind?

10:4 Unto Him is the return of all of you; it is a promise of Allah in truth. Lo! He produceth creation, then reproduceth it, that *HE MAY REWARD THOSE WHO BELIEVE* and do good works with equity; while, as for *THOSE WHO DISBELIEVE*, theirs will be *A BOILING DRINK* and painful doom because they *DISBELIEVED*.

10:5 He it is Who appointed the sun a splendour and the moon a light, and measured for her stages, that ye might know the number of the years, and the reckoning. Allah created not (all) that save in truth. He detaileth the revelations for people who have knowledge.

10:6 Lo! in the difference of day and night and all that Allah hath created in the heavens and the earth are portents, verily, for folk who ward off (evil).

10:7 Lo! those who expect not the meeting with Us but desire the life of the world and feel secure therein, and those who are neglectful of Our revelations,

10:8 *THEIR HOME WILL BE THE FIRE* because of what they used to *EARN*. [Most translations agree that "earn" is the appropriate word here.]

10:9 Lo! *THOSE WHO BELIEVE AND DO GOOD WORKS*, their Lord guideth them by their faith. Rivers will flow beneath them *IN THE GARDENS OF DELIGHT*,

10:10 Their prayer therein will be: Glory be to Thee, O Allah! and their greeting therein will be: Peace. And the conclusion of their prayer will be: Praise be to Allah, Lord of the Worlds!

10:11 If Allah were to hasten on for men the ill (that they have earned) as they would hasten on the good, their respite would already have expired. But We suffer those who look not for the meeting with Us to wander blindly on in their contumacy.

10:12 And if misfortune touch a man he crieth unto Us, (while reclining) on his side, or sitting or standing, but when We have relieved him of the misfortune he goeth his way as though he had not cried unto Us because of a misfortune that afflicted him. Thus is what they do made (seeming) fair unto the prodigal.

10:13 *WE DESTROYED THE GENERATIONS BEFORE YOU WHEN THEY DID WRONG*; and their messengers (from Allah) came unto them with *CLEAR PROOFS* (of His Sovereignty) but they would not *BELIEVE*. Thus do *WE REWARD THE GUILTY FOLK.*

10:14 Then We appointed you viceroys in the earth after them, that We might see how ye behave.

10:15 And when *OUR CLEAR REVELATIONS ARE RECITED UNTO THEM*, they who look not for the meeting with Us say: Bring a Lecture other than this, or change it. Say (O Muhammad): It is not for me to change it of my accord. I only follow that which is inspired in me. Lo! if I disobey my Lord I fear the *RETRIBUTION OF AN AWFUL DAY.*

10:16 Say: If Allah had so willed I should not have recited it to you nor would He have made it known to you. I dwelt among you a whole lifetime before it (came to me). Have ye then no sense?

10:17 Who doeth greater wrong than he who inventeth a lie concerning Allah and denieth His revelations? Lo! *THE GUILTY NEVER ARE SUCCESSFUL*.

10:18 They worship beside Allah that which neither hurteth them nor profiteth them, and they say: These are our intercessors with Allah. Say: Would ye inform Allah of (something) that He knoweth not in the heavens or in the earth? Praised be He and High Exalted above all that ye associate (with Him)!

10:19 Mankind were but one community; then they differed; and had it not been for a word that had already gone forth from thy Lord it had been judged between them in respect of that wherein they differ.

10:20 And they will say: If only a portent were sent down upon him from his Lord! Then say, (O Muhammad): The Unseen belongeth to Allah. So wait! Lo! I am waiting with you. [Cancelled by verse 9:5, i.e. violence replaces forebearance][531]

10:21 And when We cause mankind to taste of mercy after some adversity which had afflicted them, behold! they have some plot against Our revelations. Say: Allah is more swift in plotting. Lo! Our messengers write down that which ye plot.

10:22 He it is Who maketh you to go on the land and the sea till, when ye are in the ships and they sail with them with a fair breeze and they are glad therein, a storm-wind reacheth them and the wave cometh unto them from every side and they deem that they are overwhelmed therein; (then) they cry unto Allah, making their faith pure for Him only: If Thou deliver us from this, we truly will be of the thankful.

10:23 Yet when He hath delivered them, behold! they rebel in the earth wrongfully. O mankind! Your rebellion is only against yourselves. (Ye have) enjoyment of the life of the world; then unto Us is your return and We shall proclaim unto you what ye used to do.

10:24 The similitude of the life of the world is only as water which We send down from the sky, then the earth's growth of that which men and cattle eat mingleth with it till, when the earth hath taken on her ornaments and is embellished, and her people deem that they are masters of her, Our commandment cometh by night or by day and We make it as reaped corn as if it had not flourished yesterday. Thus do we expound the revelations for people who reflect.

10:25 And Allah summoneth to the abode of peace, and leadeth whom He will to _A STRAIGHT PATH_.

10:26 _FOR THOSE WHO DO GOOD IS THE BEST (REWARD)_ and more (thereto). Neither dust nor ignominy cometh near their faces. _SUCH ARE RIGHTFUL OWNERS OF THE GARDEN_; they will abide therein. [Those who follow sharia are rewarded with an eternity of pleasure.]

10:27 And those who earn ill-deeds, (for them) requital of each ill-deed by the like thereof; and ignominy overtaketh them - They have no protector from Allah - as if their faces had been covered with a cloak of darkest night. Such are rightful _OWNERS OF THE FIRE_; they will abide therein. [Those who do not follow sharia are punished for eternity.]

10:28 On _THE DAY WHEN WE GATHER THEM ALL TOGETHER_, then We say unto _THOSE WHO ASCRIBED PARTNERS_ (unto Us): Stand back, ye and your (pretended) partners (of Allah)! And We separate them, the one from the other, and their (pretended) partners say: It was not us ye worshipped.

10:29 Allah sufficeth as a witness between us and you, that we were unaware of your worship.

10:30 There doth every soul experience that which it did aforetime, and they are returned unto Allah, their rightful Lord, and that which they used to invent hath failed them.

10:31 Say (unto them, O Muhammad): Who provideth for you from the sky and the earth, or Who owneth hearing and sight; and Who bringeth forth the living from the dead and bringeth forth the dead from the living; and Who directeth the course? They will say: Allah. Then say: Will ye not then _KEEP YOUR DUTY_ (unto Him)?

10:32 Such then is Allah, your rightful Lord. After _THE TRUTH_ what is there saving error? How then are ye turned away!

10:33 Thus is the Word of thy Lord justified concerning those who do wrong: that _THEY BELIEVE NOT._

10:34 Say: Is there of your partners (whom ye ascribe unto Allah) one that produceth Creation and then reproduceth it? Say: Allah produceth Creation, then reproduceth it. How then, are ye misled!

10:35 Say: _IS THERE OF YOUR PARTNERS (WHOM YE ASCRIBE UNTO ALLAH) ONE THAT LEADETH TO THE TRUTH_? Say: Allah leadeth to _THE TRUTH_. Is He Who leadeth to _THE TRUTH_ more deserving that He should be followed, or he who findeth not the way unless he (himself) be guided. What aileth you? How judge ye?

10:36 Most of them follow not but conjecture. Assuredly _CONJECTURE CAN BY NO MEANS TAKE THE PLACE OF TRUTH._ Lo! Allah is Aware of what they do.

10:37 And _THIS QUR'AN IS NOT SUCH AS COULD EVER BE INVENTED_ in despite of Allah; but it is a confirmation of that which was before it and an exposition of that which is decreed for mankind - Therein is _NO DOUBT_ - from the Lord of the Worlds.

10:38 Or _SAY THEY: HE HATH INVENTED IT_? Say: Then bring a surah like unto it, and call (for help) on all ye can besides Allah, if ye are truthful. [Mohammed's contemporaries thought the Koran was fantasy.]

10:39 Nay, but they denied that, the knowledge whereof they could not compass, and whereof the interpretation (in events) hath not yet come unto them. _EVEN SO DID THOSE BEFORE THEM DENY. THEN SEE WHAT WAS THE CONSEQUENCE FOR THE WRONG-DOERS!_

10:40 And of them is he who _BELIEVETH_ therein, and of them is he who _BELIEVETH_ not therein, and thy Lord is Best Aware of the corrupters.

10:41 ~~And if they deny thee, say: Unto me my work, and unto you your work. Ye are innocent of what I do, and I am innocent of what ye do.~~ [Indifference cancelled by violence of verse 9:5][532]

10:42 And of them are some who listen unto thee. But canst thou make the deaf to hear even though they apprehend not?

10:43 And of them is he who looketh toward thee. But canst thou guide the blind even though they see not?

10:44 Lo! Allah wrongeth not mankind in aught; but mankind wrong themselves.

10:45 And on the day when He shall gather them together, (when it will seem) as though they had tarried but an hour of the day, recognising one another, those will verily have perished who denied the meeting with Allah and were not guided.

10:46 ~~Whether We let thee (O Muhammad) behold something of that which We promise them or (whether We) cause thee to die, still unto Us is their return, and Allah, moreover, is Witness over what they do.~~ [Command to patience cancelled by command to violence in verse 9:5][533]

10:47 And for every nation there is a messenger. And when their messenger cometh (on *THE DAY OF JUDGMENT*) it will be judged between them fairly, and they will not be wronged.

10:48 And they say: When will this promise be fulfilled, if ye are truthful?

10:49 Say: I have no power to hurt or benefit myself, save that which Allah willeth. For every nation there is an appointed time. When their time cometh, then they cannot put it off an hour, nor hasten (it).

10:50 Say: Have ye thought: When His doom cometh unto you as a raid by night, or in the (busy) day; what is there of it that the guilty ones desire to hasten?

10:51 Is it (only) then, when it hath befallen you, that ye will *BELIEVE*? What! (*BELIEVE*) now, when (until now) ye have been hastening it on (*THROUGH DISBELIEF*)?

10:52 Then will it be said unto those who dealt unjustly *TASTE THE TORMENT OF ETERNITY*. Are ye requited aught save what ye used to earn?

10:53 And they ask thee to inform them (saying): Is it true? Say: Yea, by my Lord, verily it is true, *AND YE CANNOT ESCAPE.*

10:54 And if *EACH SOUL THAT DOETH WRONG HAD ALL THAT IS IN THE EARTH IT WOULD SEEK TO RANSOM ITSELF THEREWITH; AND THEY WILL FEEL REMORSE WITHIN THEM, WHEN THEY SEE THE DOOM.* But it hath been judged between them fairly and they are not wronged.

10:55 Lo! verily all that is in the heavens and the earth is Allah's. Lo! verily *ALLAH'S PROMISE IS TRUE.* But most of them know not.

10:56 He quickeneth and giveth death, and unto Him ye will be returned.

10:57 O mankind! There hath come unto you an exhortation from your Lord, a balm for that which is in the breasts, a guidance and a mercy for *BELIEVERS*.

10:58 Say: In the bounty of Allah and in His mercy: therein let them rejoice. It is better than what they hoard.

10:59 Say: Have ye considered what provision Allah hath sent down for you, how ye have made of it lawful and unlawful? Hath Allah permitted you, or do ye invent a lie concerning Allah?

10:60 And what think those who invent a lie concerning Allah (will be their plight) upon *THE DAY OF RESURRECTION*? Lo! Allah truly is Bountiful toward mankind, but most of them give not thanks.

10:61 And thou (Muhammad) art not occupied with any business and thou recitest not a Lecture from this (Scripture), and ye (mankind) perform no act, but We are Witness of you when ye are engaged therein. And not an atom's weight in the earth or in the sky escapeth your Lord, nor what is less than that or greater than that, but it is (written) in a clear Book.

10:62 Lo! verily the friends of Allah are (those) on whom fear (cometh) not, nor do they grieve?

10:63 *THOSE WHO BELIEVE AND KEEP THEIR DUTY (TO ALLAH).*

10:64 Theirs are *GOOD TIDINGS IN THE LIFE OF THE WORLD AND IN THE HEREAFTER - THERE IS NO CHANGING THE WORDS OF ALLAH* - that is the *SUPREME TRIUMPH.*

10:65 And let not their speech grieve thee (O Muhammad). Lo! power belongeth wholly to Allah. He is the Hearer, the Knower.

10:66 Lo! is it not unto Allah that belongeth whosoever is in the heavens and whosoever is in the earth? Those who follow aught instead of Allah follow not (His) partners. They follow only a conjecture, and they do but guess.

10:67 He it is Who hath appointed for you the night that ye should rest therein and the day giving sight. Lo! herein verily are portents for a folk that heed.

10:68 *THEY SAY: ALLAH HATH TAKEN (UNTO HIM) A SON* - Glorified be He! He hath no needs! His is all that is in the heavens and all that is in the earth. Ye have no warrant for this. Tell ye concerning Allah that which ye know not?

10:69 Say: Verily *THOSE WHO INVENT A LIE CONCERNING ALLAH WILL NOT SUCCEED.*

10:70 This world's portion (will be theirs), then unto Us is their return. Then *WE MAKE THEM TASTE A DREADFUL DOOM BECAUSE THEY USED TO DISBELIEVE*.

10:71 Recite unto them the story of Noah, when he told his people: O my people! If my sojourn (here) and my reminding you by Allah's revelations are an offence unto you, in Allah have I put my trust, so decide upon your course of action you and your partners. Let not your course of action be in doubt for you. Then have at me, give me no respite.

10:72 But if ye are averse I have asked of you no wage. My wage is the concern of Allah only, and I am commanded to be of those who surrender (unto Him).

10:73 But they denied him, so We saved him and those with him in the ship, and made them viceroys (in the earth), while *WE DROWNED THOSE WHO DENIED OUR REVELATIONS*. See then the nature of the consequence for those who had been warned.

10:74 Then, after him, We sent messengers unto their folk, and they brought them *CLEAR PROOFS*. But they were not ready to *BELIEVE* in that which they before denied. Thus print We on the hearts of the transgressors.

10:75 Then, after them, We sent Moses and Aaron unto Pharaoh and his chiefs with Our revelations, but they were arrogant and were a guilty folk.

10:76 And when *THE TRUTH* from Our presence came unto them, they said: Lo! this is mere magic.

10:77 Moses said: Speak ye (so) of *THE TRUTH* when it hath come unto you? Is this magic? Now magicians thrive not.

10:78 They said: Hast thou come unto us to pervert us from that (faith) in which we found our fathers, and that you two may own the place of greatness in the land? We will not *BELIEVE* you two.

10:79 And Pharaoh said: Bring every cunning wizard unto me.

10:80 And when the wizards came, Moses said unto them: Cast your cast!

10:81 And when they had cast, Moses said: That which ye have brought is magic. Lo! Allah will make it vain. Lo! Allah upholdeth not the work of *MISCHIEF-MAKERS.*

10:82 And Allah will vindicate *THE TRUTH* by His words, however much the *GUILTY* be averse.

10:83 But none trusted Moses, save some scions of his people, (and they were) in fear of Pharaoh and their chiefs, that he would persecute them. Lo! Pharaoh was verily a tyrant in the land, and lo! he verily was of the wanton.

10:84 And Moses said: O my people! If ye have *BELIEVED* in Allah then put trust in Him, if ye have indeed surrendered (unto Him)!

10:85 They said: In Allah we put trust. Our Lord! Oh, make us not a lure for the wrongdoing folk;

10:86 And, of Thy mercy, save us from the folk that *DISBELIEVE*.

10:87 And We inspired Moses and his brother, (saying): Appoint houses for your people in Egypt and make your houses oratories, and establish worship. And give good news to the *BELIEVERS*.

10:88 And Moses said: Our Lord! Lo! Thou hast given Pharaoh and his chiefs splendour and riches in the life of the world, Our Lord! that they may lead men astray from Thy way. Our Lord! Destroy their riches and harden their hearts so that they *BELIEVE* not till they see the painful doom.

10:89 He said: Your prayer is heard. Do ye twain keep to the straight path, and follow not the road of those who have no knowledge.

10:90 And We brought *THE CHILDREN OF ISRAEL* across the sea, and Pharaoh with his *HOSTS [ARMIES]* pursued them in rebellion and transgression, till, when the (fate of) drowning overtook him, he exclaimed: *I BELIEVE THAT THERE IS NO GOD SAVE HIM IN WHOM THE CHILDREN OF ISRAEL BELIEVE, AND I AM OF THOSE WHO SURRENDER (UNTO HIM).*

10:91 What! Now! When hitherto thou hast rebelled and been of the wrong-doers?

10:92 But this day We save thee in thy body that thou mayst be a portent for those after thee. Lo! most of mankind are heedless of Our portents.

10:93 And We verily did allot unto *THE CHILDREN OF ISRAEL* a fixed abode, and did provide them with good things; and they differed not until the knowledge came unto them. Lo! thy Lord will judge between them *ON THE DAY OF RESURRECTION* concerning that wherein they used to differ.

10:94 And if thou (Muhammad) art in doubt concerning that which We reveal unto thee, then question those who read the Scripture (that was) before thee. Verily *THE TRUTH* from thy Lord hath come unto thee. So be not thou of *THE WAVERERS*.

10:95 And be not thou of *THOSE WHO DENY THE REVELATIONS OF ALLAH*, for then wert thou of *THE LOSERS*.

10:96 Lo! those for whom the word of thy Lord (concerning sinners) hath effect *WILL NOT BELIEVE*,

10:97 Though every token come unto them, till *THEY SEE THE PAINFUL DOOM.*

10:98 If only there had been a community (of all those that were destroyed of old) that *BELIEVED* and profited by its *BELIEF* as did the folk of Jonah! When *THEY BELIEVED* We drew off from them the torment of disgrace in the life of the world and gave them comfort for a while.

10:99 ~~And if thy Lord willed, all who are in the earth would have believed together. Wouldst thou (Muhammad) compel men until they are believers?~~ [Indifference cancelled by violence, verse 9:5][534]

10:100 It is not for any soul to *BELIEVE* save by the permission of Allah. He hath set uncleanness upon those who have no sense.

10:101 Say: Behold what is in the heavens and the earth! But revelations and warnings avail not folk who will not *BELIEVE*.

10:102 ~~What expect they save the like of the days of those who passed away before them? Say: Expect then! I am with you among the expectant.~~ [Cancelled by verse 9:5][535]

10:103 Then shall We save Our messengers and the *BELIEVERS*, in like manner (as of old). It is incumbent upon Us to save *BELIEVERS*.

10:104 Say (O Muhammad): O mankind! If ye are in doubt of my religion, then (know that) I worship not those whom ye worship instead of Allah, but I worship Allah Who causeth you to die, and I have been commanded to be of the *BELIEVERS*.

10:105 And, (O Muhammad) set thy purpose resolutely for religion, as a man by nature upright, and be not of *THOSE WHO ASCRIBE PARTNERS (TO ALLAH)*.

10:106 And cry not, beside Allah, unto that which cannot profit thee nor hurt thee, for if thou didst so then wert thou of the wrong-doers.

10:107 If Allah afflicteth thee with some hurt, there is none who can remove it save Him; and if He desireth good for thee, there is none who can repel His bounty. He striketh with it whom He will of his *BONDMEN*. He is the Forgiving, the Merciful.

10:108 ~~Say: O mankind! Now hath the Truth from your Lord come unto you. So whosoever is guided, is guided only for (the good of) his soul, and whosoever erreth erreth only against it. And I am not a warder over you.~~ [Cancelled by verse 9:5, i.e. command to impose Islam on unbelievers][536]

10:109 ~~And (O Muhammad) follow that which is inspired in thee, and forbear until Allah give judgment.~~ And He is the Best of Judges. [Forebearance cancelled by violent command in verse 9:5][537]

Chapter 17 - The Children of Israel

17:1 Glorified be He Who carried His servant by night from the Inviolable Place of Worship to the Far distant place of worship the neighbourhood whereof We have blessed, that We might show him of Our tokens! Lo! He, only He, is the Hearer, the Seer.

17:2 We gave unto Moses the Scripture, and We appointed it a guidance for *THE CHILDREN OF ISRAEL*, saying: Choose no guardian beside Me.

17:3 (They were) the seed of those whom We carried (in the ship) along with Noah. Lo! he was a grateful slave.

17:4 And We decreed for *THE CHILDREN OF ISRAEL* in the Scripture: Ye verily will *WORK CORRUPTION IN THE EARTH* twice, and ye will become great tyrants.

17:5 So when the time for the first of the two came, We roused against you *SLAVES OF OURS* of great might who ravaged (your) country, and it was a threat performed.

17:6 Then we gave you once again your turn against them, and We aided you with wealth and children and made you more in soldiery.

17:7 (Saying): If ye do good, ye do good for your own souls, and if ye do *EVIL*, it is for them (in like manner). So, when the time for the second (of the judgments) came (We roused against you others of *OUR SLAVES*) to ravage you, and to enter the Temple even as they entered it the first time, and to lay waste all that they conquered with an utter wasting.

17:8 It may be that your Lord will have mercy on you, but if ye repeat (the crime) We shall repeat (the punishment), and We have appointed *HELL A DUNGEON* for the *DISBELIEVERS*.

17:9 Lo! *THIS QUR'AN GUIDETH UNTO THAT WHICH IS STRAIGHTEST, AND GIVETH TIDINGS UNTO THE BELIEVERS WHO DO GOOD WORKS THAT THEIRS WILL BE A GREAT REWARD.*

17:10 And that *THOSE WHO BELIEVE NOT IN THE HEREAFTER, FOR THEM WE HAVE PREPARED A PAINFUL DOOM.*

17:11 Man prayeth for *EVIL* as he prayeth for good; for man was ever hasty.

17:12 And We appoint the night and the day two portents. Then We make dark the portent of the night, and We make the portent of the day sight-giving, that ye may seek bounty from your Lord, and that ye may know the computation of the years, and the reckoning; and everything have We expounded with a clear expounding.

17:13 And every man's augury have We fastened to his own neck, and We shall bring forth for him on *THE DAY OF RESURRECTION* a book which he will find wide open.

17:14 (And it will be said unto him): Read thy Book. Thy soul sufficeth as reckoner against thee this day.

17:15 Whosoever goeth right, it is only for (the good of) his own soul that he goeth right, and whosoever erreth, erreth only to its hurt. No laden soul can bear another's load, We never punish until we have sent a messenger.

17:16 And when We would *DESTROY A TOWNSHIP* We send commandment to its folk who live at ease, and afterward they commit abomination therein, and so the Word (of doom) hath effect for it, and we annihilate it with complete annihilation.

17:17 *HOW MANY GENERATIONS HAVE WE DESTROYED* since Noah! And Allah sufficeth as Knower and Beholder of *THE SINS OF HIS SLAVES*.

17:18 *WHOSO DESIRETH THAT (LIFE) WHICH HASTENETH AWAY*, We hasten for him therein what We will for whom We please. And afterward *WE HAVE APPOINTED FOR HIM HELL*; he will endure the heat thereof, condemned, rejected.

17:19 And whoso desireth the Hereafter and *STRIVETH* for it with the effort necessary, being a *BELIEVER*; for such, their effort findeth favour (with their Lord).

17:20 Each do We supply, both these and those, from the bounty of thy Lord. And the bounty of thy Lord can never be walled up.

17:21 See how We prefer one of them above another, and verily the Hereafter will be greater in degrees and greater in preferment.

17:22 Set not up with Allah any other god (O man) lest thou sit down reproved, forsaken.

17:23 ~~Thy Lord hath decreed, that ye worship none save Him, and (that ye show) kindness to parents. If one of them or both of them attain old age with thee, say not "Fie" unto them nor repulse them, but speak unto them a gracious word.~~ [Later verse 9:113 commands rejection of non-Muslim parents][538]

17:24 ~~And lower unto them the wing of submission through mercy, and say: My Lord! Have mercy on them both as they did care for me when I was little.~~ [Intolerance commanded by verse 9:113][539]

17:25 Your Lord is Best Aware of what is in your minds. If ye are righteous, then lo! He was ever Forgiving unto those who turn (unto Him).

17:26 Give the kinsman his due, and the needy, and the wayfarer, and squander not (thy wealth) in wantonness.

17:27 Lo! the squanderers were ever brothers of the devils, and the devil was ever an ingrate to his Lord.

17:28 But if thou turn away from them, seeking mercy from thy Lord, for which thou hopest, then speak unto them a reasonable word.

17:29 And let not thy hand be chained to thy neck nor open it with a complete opening, lest thou sit down rebuked, denuded.

17:30 Lo! thy Lord enlargeth the provision for whom He will, and straiteneth (it for whom He will). Lo, He was ever Knower, Seer of His *SLAVES*.

17:31 Slay not your children, fearing a fall to poverty, We shall provide for them and for you. Lo! the slaying of them is great sin.

17:32 And come not near unto adultery. Lo! it is an abomination and an *EVIL* way.

17:33 And slay not the life which Allah hath forbidden save with right. Whoso is slain wrongfully, We have given power unto his heir, but let him not commit excess in slaying. Lo! he will be helped.

17:34 Come not near the wealth of the orphan save with that which is better till he come to strength; and *KEEP THE COVENANT*. Lo! of the covenant it will be asked.

17:35 Fill the measure when ye measure, and weigh with a right balance; that is meet, and better in the end.

17:36 (O man), follow not that whereof thou hast no knowledge. Lo! the hearing and the sight and the heart - of each of these it will be asked.

17:37 And walk not in the earth exultant. Lo! thou canst not rend the earth, nor canst thou stretch to the height of the hills.

17:38 The *EVIL* of all that is hateful in the sight of thy Lord.

17:39 This is (part) of that wisdom wherewith thy Lord hath inspired thee (O Muhammad). And *SET NOT UP WITH ALLAH ANY OTHER GOD, LEST THOU BE CAST INTO HELL*, reproved, abandoned.

17:40 Hath your Lord then distinguished you (O men of Makka) by giving you sons, and hath chosen for Himself females from among the angels? Lo! verily ye speak an awful word!

17:41 We verily have displayed (Our warnings) in this Qur'an that they may take heed, but it increaseth them in naught save aversion.

17:42 Say (O Muhammad, to the *DISBELIEVERS*): If there were other gods along with Him, as they say, then had they sought a way against the Lord of the Throne.

17:43 Glorified is He, and High Exalted above what they say!

17:44 The seven heavens and the earth and all that is therein praise Him, and there is not a thing but hymneth His praise; but ye understand not their praise. Lo! He is ever Clement, Forgiving.

17:45 And when thou recitest the Qur'an we place between thee and those who *BELIEVE* not in the Hereafter a hidden barrier;

17:46 And We place upon their hearts veils lest they should understand it, and in their ears a deafness; and when thou makest mention of thy Lord alone in the Qur'an, they turn their backs in aversion.

17:47 We are Best Aware of what they wish to hear when they give ear to thee and when they take secret counsel, when the *EVIL-DOERS* say: Ye follow but a man bewitched.

17:48 See what similitudes they coin for thee, and thus are all astray, and cannot find a road!

17:49 And they say: When we are bones and fragments, shall we forsooth, be raised up as a new creation?

17:50 Say: Be ye stones or iron

17:51 Or some created thing that is yet greater in your thoughts! Then they will say: Who shall bring us back (to life). Say: He Who created you at the first. Then will they shake their heads at thee, and say: When will it be? Say: It will perhaps be soon;

17:52 *A DAY WHEN HE WILL CALL YOU* and ye will answer with His praise, and ye will think that ye have tarried but a little while.

17:53 Tell My *BONDMEN* to speak that which is kindlier. Lo! the devil soweth discord among them. Lo! the devil is for man an open foe.

17:54 ~~Your Lord is Best Aware of you. If He will, He will have mercy on you, or if He will, He will punish you. We have not sent thee (O Muhammad) as a warden over them.~~ [Cancelled by verse 9:5, i.e. Islam is to be imposed upon unbelievers using violence if necessary][540]

17:55 And thy Lord is Best Aware of all who are in the heavens and the earth. And we preferred some of the prophets above others, and unto David We gave the Psalms.

17:56 Say: Cry unto those (saints and angels) whom ye assume (to be gods) beside Him, yet they have no power to rid you of misfortune nor to change.

17:57 Those unto whom they cry seek the way of approach to their Lord, which of them shall be the nearest; they hope for His mercy and they fear His doom. Lo! the doom of thy Lord is to be shunned.

17:58 There is not a township but We shall destroy it ere *THE DAY OF RESURRECTION*, or punish it with dire punishment. That is set forth in the Book (of Our decrees).

17:59 Naught hindereth Us from sending portents save that the folk of old denied them. And We gave Thamud the she-camel - a clear portent save to warn.

17:60 And (it was a warning) when we told thee: Lo! thy Lord encompasseth mankind, and We appointed the sight which We showed thee as an ordeal for mankind, and (likewise) the Accursed Tree in the Qur'an. We warn them, but it increaseth them in naught save gross impiety.

17:61 And when We said unto the angels: Fall down prostrate before Adam and they fell prostrate all save Iblis, he said: Shall I fall prostrate before that which Thou hast created of clay?

17:62 He said: Seest Thou this (creature) whom Thou hast honoured above me, if Thou give me grace until *THE DAY OF RESURRECTION* I verily will seize his seed, save but a few.

17:63 He said: Go, and whosoever of them followeth thee - lo! *HELL WILL BE YOUR PAYMENT*, ample payment.

17:64 And excite any of them whom thou canst with thy voice, and urge thy horse and foot against them, and be a partner in their wealth and children, and promise them. Satan promiseth them only to deceive.

17:65 Lo! My (faithful) *BONDMEN* - over them thou hast no power, and thy Lord sufficeth as (their) guardian.

17:66 (O mankind), your Lord is He Who driveth for you the ship upon the sea that ye may seek of His bounty. Lo! He was ever Merciful toward you.

17:67 And when harm toucheth you upon the sea, all unto whom ye cry (for succour) fail save Him (alone), but when He bringeth you safe to land, ye turn away, for man was ever thankless.

17:68 Feel ye then secure that He will not cause a slope of the land to engulf you, or send a sand-storm upon you, and then ye will find that ye have no protector?

17:69 Or feel ye secure that He will not return you to that (plight) a second time, and send against you a hurricane of wind and drown you for your thanklessness, and then ye will not find therein that ye have any avenger against Us?

17:70 Verily we have honoured the Children of Adam. We carry them on the land and the sea, and have made provision of good things for them, and have preferred them above many of those whom We created with a marked preferment.

17:71 _ON THE DAY WHEN WE SHALL SUMMON ALL MEN_ with their record, whoso is given his book in his right hand - such will read their book and they will not be wronged a shred.

17:72 Whoso is blind here will be blind in the Hereafter, and yet further from the road.

17:73 And they indeed strove hard to beguile thee (Muhammad) away from that wherewith We have inspired thee, that thou shouldst invent other than it against Us; and then would they have accepted thee as a friend.

17:74 And if We had not made thee wholly firm thou mightest almost have inclined unto them a little.

17:75 Then had we made thee taste a double (punishment) of living and a double (punishment) of dying, then hadst thou found no helper against Us.

17:76 And they indeed wished to scare thee from the land that they might drive thee forth from thence, and then they would have stayed (there) but a little after thee.

17:77 (Such was Our) method in the case of those whom We sent before thee (to mankind), and thou wilt not find for Our method aught of power to change.

17:78 Establish worship at the going down of the sun until the dark of night, and (the recital of) the Qur'an at dawn. Lo! (the recital of) the Qur'an at dawn is ever witnessed.

17:79 And some part of the night awake for it, a largess for thee. It may be that thy Lord will raise thee to a praised estate.

17:80 And say: My Lord! Cause me to come in with a firm incoming and to go out with a firm outgoing. And give me from Thy presence a sustaining Power.

17:81 And say: Truth hath come and falsehood hath vanished away. Lo! falsehood is ever bound to vanish.

17:82 And We reveal of _THE QUR'AN_ that which is a healing and _A MERCY FOR BELIEVERS_ though it _INCREASE THE EVIL-DOERS IN NAUGHT SAVE RUIN_.

17:83 And when We make life pleasant unto man, he turneth away and is averse; and when ill toucheth him he is in despair.

17:84 Say: Each one doth according to his rule of conduct, and thy Lord is Best Aware of him whose way is right.

17:85 They are asking thee concerning the Spirit. Say: The Spirit is by command of my Lord, and of knowledge ye have been vouchsafed but little.

17:86 And if We willed We could withdraw that which We have revealed unto thee, then wouldst thou find no guardian for thee against Us in respect thereof.

17:87 (It is naught) save mercy from thy Lord. Lo! His kindness unto thee was ever great.

17:88 Say: Verily, though mankind and the jinn should assemble to produce the like of this Qur'an, they could not produce the like thereof though they were helpers one of another.

17:89 And verily We have displayed for mankind in this Qur'an all kind of similitudes, but most of mankind refuse aught save _DISBELIEF_.

17:90 And they say: We will not put faith in thee till thou cause a spring to gush forth from the earth for us;

17:91 Or thou have a garden of date-palms and grapes, and cause rivers to gush forth therein abundantly;

17:92 Or thou cause the heaven to fall upon us piecemeal, as thou hast pretended, or bring Allah and the angels as a warrant;

17:93 Or thou have a house of gold; or thou ascend up into heaven, and even then we will put no faith in thine ascension till thou bring down for us a book that we can read. Say (O Muhammad): My Lord be Glorified! Am I aught save a mortal messenger?

17:94 And naught prevented mankind from _BELIEVING_ when the guidance came unto them save that they said: Hath Allah sent a mortal as (His) messenger?

17:95 Say: If there were in the earth angels walking secure, We had sent down for them from heaven an angel as messenger.

17:96 Say: Allah sufficeth for a witness between me and you. Lo! He is Knower, Seer of His _SLAVES_.

17:97 And he whom Allah guideth, he is led aright; while, as for him whom He sendeth astray, for them thou wilt find no protecting friends beside Him, and _WE SHALL ASSEMBLE THEM ON THE DAY OF RESURRECTION ON THEIR FACES, BLIND, DUMB AND DEAF; THEIR HABITATION WILL BE HELL; WHENEVER IT ABATETH, WE INCREASE THE FLAME FOR THEM._ [Tortured for all eternity.]

17:98 That is their _REWARD_ because they _DISBELIEVED_ Our revelations and said: When we are bones and fragments shall we, forsooth, be raised up as a new creation?

17:99 Have they not seen that Allah Who created the heavens and the earth is Able to create the like of them, and hath appointed for them an end whereof there is no doubt? But the wrong-doers refuse aught save _DISBELIEF._

17:100 Say (unto them): If ye possessed the treasures of the mercy of my Lord, ye would surely hold them back for fear of spending, for man was ever grudging.

17:101 And verily We gave unto Moses nine tokens, _CLEAR PROOFS_ (of Allah's Sovereignty). Do but ask _THE CHILDREN OF ISRAEL_ how he came unto them, then Pharaoh said unto him: Lo! I deem thee one bewitched, O Moses.

17:102 He said: In truth thou knowest that none sent down these (portents) save the Lord of the heavens and the earth as proofs, and lo! (for my part) I deem thee lost, O Pharaoh.

17:103 And he wished to scare them from the land, but We drowned him and those with him, all together.

17:104 And We said unto _THE CHILDREN OF ISRAEL_ after him: Dwell in the land; but when the promise of the Hereafter cometh to pass We shall bring you as a crowd gathered out of various nations.

17:105 With _TRUTH_ have We sent it down, and with truth hath it descended. And We have sent thee as naught else save a bearer of good tidings and a warner.

17:106 And (it is) a Qur'an that We have divided, that thou mayst recite it unto mankind at intervals, and We have revealed it by (successive) revelation.

17:107 Say: _BELIEVE_ therein or _BELIEVE_ not, lo! those who were given knowledge before it, when it is read unto them, fall down prostrate on their faces, adoring,

17:108 Saying: Glory to our Lord! Verily the promise of our Lord must be fulfilled.

17:109 They fall down on their faces, weeping, and it increaseth humility in them.

17:110 Say (unto mankind): Cry unto Allah, or cry unto the Beneficent, unto whichsoever ye cry (it is the same). His are the most beautiful names. And thou (Muhammad), be not loud-voiced in thy worship nor yet silent therein, but follow a way between.

17:111 And say: Praise be to Allah, Who hath not taken unto Himself a son, and Who hath no partner in the Sovereignty, nor hath He any protecting friend through dependence. And magnify Him with all magnificence.

Chapter 28 - The Story

28:1 Ta. Sin. Mim.

28:2 _THESE ARE REVELATIONS OF THE SCRIPTURE THAT MAKETH PLAIN._

28:3 We narrate unto thee (somewhat) of the story of Moses and Pharaoh with truth, for folk who _BELIEVE._

28:4 Lo! Pharaoh exalted himself in the earth and made its people castes. A tribe among them he oppressed, killing their sons and sparing their women. Lo! _HE WAS OF THOSE WHO WORK CORRUPTION._

28:5 And We desired to show favour unto those who were oppressed in the earth, and to make them examples and to make them the inheritors,

28:6 And to establish them in the earth, and to show Pharaoh and Haman and their hosts [armies] that which they feared from them.

28:7 And We inspired the mother of Moses, saying: Suckle him and, when thou fearest for him, then cast him into the river and fear not nor grieve. Lo! We shall bring him back unto thee and shall make him (one) of Our messengers.

28:8 And the family of Pharaoh took him up, that he might become for them an enemy and a sorrow, Lo! Pharaoh and Haman and their hosts [armies] were ever sinning.

28:9 And the wife of Pharaoh said: (He will be) a consolation for me and for thee. Kill him not. Peradventure he may be of use to us, or we may choose him for a son. And they perceived not.

28:10 And the heart of the mother of Moses became void, and she would have betrayed him if We had not fortified her heart, that she might be of the *BELIEVERS*.

28:11 And she said unto his sister: Trace him. So she observed him from afar, and they perceived not.

28:12 And We had before forbidden foster-mothers for him, so she said: Shall I show you a household who will rear him for you and take care of him?

28:13 So We restored him to his mother that she might be comforted and not grieve, and that she might know that the promise of Allah is true. But most of them know not.

28:14 And when he reached his full strength and was ripe, We gave him wisdom and knowledge. *THUS DO WE REWARD THE GOOD.*

28:15 And he entered the city at a time of carelessness of its folk, and he found therein two men fighting, one of his own caste, and the other of his enemies; and he who was of his caste asked him for help against him who was of his enemies. So Moses struck him with his fist and killed him. He said: This is of the devil's doing. Lo! he is an enemy, a mere misleader.

28:16 He said: My Lord! Lo! I have wronged my soul, so forgive me. Then He forgave him. Lo! He is the Forgiving, the Merciful.

28:17 He said: My Lord! Forasmuch as Thou hast favoured me, I will nevermore be a supporter of the guilty.

28:18 And morning found him in the city, fearing, vigilant, when behold! he who had appealed to him the day before cried out to him for help. Moses said unto him: Lo! thou art indeed a mere hothead.

28:19 And when he would have fallen upon the man who was an enemy unto them both, he said: O Moses! Wouldst thou kill me as thou didst kill a person yesterday. Thou wouldst be nothing but a tyrant in the land, thou wouldst not be of the reformers.

28:20 And a man came from the uttermost part of the city, running. He said: O Moses! Lo! the chiefs take counsel against thee to slay thee; therefor escape. Lo! I am of those who give thee good advice.

28:21 So he escaped from thence, fearing, vigilant. He said: My Lord! Deliver me from the wrongdoing folk.

28:22 And when he turned his face toward Midian, he said: Peradventure my Lord will guide me in the right road.

28:23 And when he came unto the water of Midian he found there a whole tribe of men, watering. And he found apart from them two women keeping back (their flocks). He said: What aileth you? The two said: We cannot give (our flocks) to drink till the shepherds return from the water; and our father is a very old man.

28:24 So he watered (their flock) for them. Then he turned aside into the shade, and said: My Lord! I am needy of whatever good Thou sendest down for me.

28:25 Then there came unto him one of the two women, walking shyly. She said: Lo! my father biddeth thee, that he may reward thee with a payment for that thou didst water (the flock) for us. Then, when he came unto him and told him the (whole) story, he said: Fear not! Thou hast escaped from the wrongdoing folk.

28:26 One of the two women said: O my father! Hire him! For the best (man) that thou canst hire in the strong, the trustworthy.

28:27 He said: Lo! I fain would marry thee to one of these two daughters of mine on condition that thou hirest thyself to me for (the term of) eight pilgrimages. Then if thou completest ten it will be of thine own accord, for I would not make it hard for thee. Allah willing, thou wilt find me of the righteous.

28:28 He said: That (is settled) between thee and me. Whichever of the two terms I fulfil, there will be no injustice to me, and Allah is Surety over what we say.

28:29 Then, when Moses had fulfilled the term, and was travelling with his housefolk, he saw in the distance a fire and said unto his housefolk: Bide ye (here). Lo! I see in the distance a fire; peradventure I shall bring you tidings thence, or a brand from the fire that ye may warm yourselves.

28:30 And when he reached it, he was called from the right side of the valley in the blessed field, from the tree: O Moses! Lo! I, even I, am Allah, the Lord of the Worlds;

28:31 Throw down thy staff. And when he saw it writhing as it had been a demon, he turned to flee headlong, (and it was said unto him): O Moses! Draw nigh and fear not. Lo! thou art of those who are secure.

28:32 Thrust thy hand into the bosom of thy robe it will come forth white without hurt. And guard thy heart from fear. Then these shall be two proofs from your Lord unto Pharaoh and his chiefs. Lo! *THEY ARE EVIL-LIVING FOLK.*

28:33 He said: My Lord! Lo! I killed a man among them and I fear that they will kill me.

28:34 My brother Aaron is more eloquent than me in speech. Therefor send him with me as a helper to confirm me. Lo! I fear that they will give the lie to me.

28:35 He said: We will strengthen thine arm with thy brother, and We will give unto you both power so that they cannot reach you for Our portents. Ye twain, and *THOSE WHO FOLLOW YOU, WILL BE THE WINNERS.*

28:36 But when Moses came unto them with Our clear tokens, they said: This is naught but invented magic. We never heard of this among our fathers of old.

28:37 And Moses said: My Lord is Best Aware of him who bringeth guidance from His presence, and whose will be the sequel of the Home (of bliss). Lo! *WRONG-DOERS WILL NOT BE SUCCESSFUL.*

28:38 And Pharaoh said: O chiefs! I know not that ye have a god other than me, so kindle for me (a fire), O Haman, to bake the mud; and set up for me a lofty tower in order that I may survey the god of Moses; and lo! I deem him of the liars.

28:39 And he and his hosts [armies] were haughty in the land without right, and deemed that they would never be brought back to Us.

28:40 Therefor We seized him and his hosts [armies], and abandoned them unto the sea. Behold the nature of the consequence for *EVIL-DOERS*!

28:41 And We made them patterns that invite unto *THE FIRE*, and on *THE DAY OF RESURRECTION* they will not be helped.

28:42 And We made a curse to follow them in this world, and *ON THE DAY OF RESURRECTION THEY WILL BE AMONG THE HATEFUL.*

28:43 And We verily gave the Scripture unto Moses after We had destroyed the generations of old: clear testimonies for mankind, and a guidance and a mercy, that haply they might reflect.

28:44 And thou (Muhammad) wast not on the western side (of the Mount) when We expounded unto Moses the commandment, and thou wast not among those present;

28:45 But We brought forth generations, and their lives dragged on for them. And thou wast not a dweller in Midian, reciting unto them Our revelations, but We kept sending (messengers to men).

28:46 And thou was not beside the Mount when We did call; but (the knowledge of it is) a mercy from thy Lord that thou mayst warn a folk unto whom no warner came before thee, that haply they may give heed.

28:47 Otherwise, if disaster should afflict them because of that which their own hands have sent before (them), they might say: Our Lord! Why sentest Thou no messenger unto us, that we might have followed Thy revelations and been of the *BELIEVERS*?

28:48 But when there came unto them *THE TRUTH* from Our presence, they said: Why is he not given the like of what was given unto Moses? Did they not *DISBELIEVE* in that which was given unto Moses of old? They say: Two magics that support each other; and they say: Lo! in both we are *DISBELIEVERS*.

28:49 Say (unto them, O Muhammad): Then bring a scripture from the presence of Allah that giveth clearer guidance than these two (that) I may follow it, if ye are truthful.

28:50 And if they answer thee not, then know that what they follow is their lusts. And who goeth farther astray than he who followeth his lust without guidance from Allah. Lo! Allah guideth not wrongdoing folk.

28:51 And now verily We have caused the Word to reach them, that haply they may give heed.

28:52 Those unto whom We gave the Scripture before it, they *BELIEVE* in it,

28:53 And when it is recited unto them, they say: We *BELIEVE* in it. Lo! *IT IS THE TRUTH* from our Lord. Lo! even before it we were of those who surrender (unto Him).

28:54 These *WILL BE GIVEN THEIR REWARD TWICE OVER, BECAUSE THEY ARE STEADFAST* and *REPEL EVIL* with good, and spend of that wherewith We have provided them,

28:55 And when they hear vanity they withdraw from it and say: ~~Unto us our works and unto you your works. Peace be unto you! We desire not the ignorant.~~ [Part cancelled by verse 9:5][541]

28:56 Lo! thou (O Muhammad) guidest not whom thou lovest, but *ALLAH GUIDETH WHOM HE WILL*. And He is Best Aware of those who walk aright.

28:57 And they say: If we were to follow the Guidance with thee we should be torn out of our land. Have We not established for them a sure sanctuary, whereunto the produce of all things is brought (in trade), a provision from Our presence? But most of them know not.

28:58 And *HOW MANY A COMMUNITY HAVE WE DESTROYED* that was thankless for its means of livelihood! And yonder are their dwellings, which have not been inhabited after them save a little. And We, even We, were the inheritors.

28:59 And never did thy Lord *DESTROY THE TOWNSHIPS*, till He had raised up in their mother(-town) a messenger reciting unto them Our revelations. And *NEVER DID WE DESTROY THE TOWNSHIPS UNLESS THE FOLK THEREOF WERE EVIL-DOERS*.

28:60 And whatsoever ye have been given is a comfort of the life of the world and an ornament thereof; and that which Allah hath is better and more lasting. Have ye then no sense?

28:61 Is he whom We have promised a fair promise which he will find (true) like him whom We suffer to enjoy awhile the comfort of the life of the world, then on *THE DAY OF RESURRECTION* he will be of those arraigned?

28:62 *ON THE DAY WHEN HE WILL CALL UNTO THEM* and say: *WHERE ARE MY PARTNERS* whom ye imagined?

28:63 Those concerning whom the Word will have come true will say: Our Lord! These are they whom we led astray. We led them astray even as we ourselves were astray. We declare our innocence before Thee: us they never worshipped.

28:64 And it will be said: Cry unto your (so-called) partners (of Allah). And they will cry unto them, and they will give no answer unto them, and they will see the Doom. Ah, if they had but been guided!

28:65 And *ON THE DAY* when He will call unto them and say: What answer gave ye to the messengers?

28:66 *ON THAT DAY* (all) tidings will be dimmed for them, nor will they ask one of another,

28:67 But as for him who shall repent and *BELIEVE AND DO RIGHT*, he haply *MAY BE ONE OF THE SUCCESSFUL.*

28:68 Thy Lord bringeth to pass what He willeth and chooseth. They have never any choice. Glorified be Allah and Exalted above all that they associate (with Him)!

28:69 And thy Lord knoweth what their breasts conceal, and what they publish.

28:70 And *HE IS ALLAH; THERE IS NO GOD SAVE HIM*. His is all praise in the former and the latter (state), and His is the command, and unto Him ye will be brought back.

28:71 Say: Have ye thought, if Allah made night everlasting for you till *THE DAY OF RESURRECTION*, who is a god beside Allah who could bring you light? Will ye not then hear?

28:72 Say: Have ye thought, if Allah made day everlasting for you till *THE DAY OF RESURRECTION*, who is a god beside Allah who could bring you night wherein ye rest? Will ye not then see?

28:73 Of His mercy hath He appointed for you night and day, that therein ye may rest, and that ye may seek His bounty, and that haply ye may be thankful.

28:74 And *ON THE DAY* when He shall call unto them and say: *WHERE ARE MY PARTNERS WHOM YE PRETENDED?*

28:75 And We shall take out from every nation a witness and We shall say: Bring your proof. Then they will know that *ALLAH HATH THE TRUTH*, and all that they invented will have failed them.

28:76 Now Korah was of Moses' folk, but he oppressed them; and We gave him so much treasure that the stores thereof would verily have been a burden for a troop of mighty men. When his own folk said unto him: Exult not; lo! Allah loveth not the exultant;

28:77 But seek the abode of the Hereafter in that which Allah hath given thee and neglect not thy portion of the world, and be thou kind even as Allah hath been kind to thee, and seek not *CORRUPTION IN THE EARTH*; lo! Allah loveth not corrupters,

28:78 He said: I have been given it only on account of knowledge I possess. Knew he not that Allah had destroyed already of the generations before him men who were mightier than him in strength and greater in respect of following? The guilty are not questioned of their sins.

28:79 Then went he forth before his people in his pomp. Those who were desirous of the life of the world said: Ah, would that we had the like of what hath been given unto Korah! Lo! he is lord of rare good fortune.

28:80 But those who had been given knowledge said: Woe unto you! The *REWARD OF ALLAH* for him who *BELIEVETH* and doeth right is better, and *ONLY THE STEADFAST WILL OBTAIN IT.*

28:81 So We caused the earth to swallow him and his dwelling-place. Then he had no host to help him against Allah, nor was he of those who can save themselves.

28:82 And morning found those who had coveted his place but yesterday crying: Ah, welladay! Allah enlargeth the provision for whom He will of His *SLAVES* and straiteneth it (for whom He will). If Allah had not been gracious unto us He would have caused it to swallow us (also). Ah, welladay! the *DISBELIEVERS* never prosper.

28:83 As for that Abode of the Hereafter We assign it unto those who seek not oppression in the earth, nor yet *CORRUPTION*. The sequel is for those who ward off (*EVIL*).

28:84 Whoso bringeth a good deed, he will have better than the same; while as for him who bringeth an ill-deed, those who do ill-deeds will be requited only what they did.

28:85 Lo! He Who hath given thee the Qur'an for a law will surely bring thee home again. Say: My Lord is Best Aware of him who bringeth guidance and him who is in error manifest.

28:86 Thou hadst no hope that the Scripture would be inspired in thee; but it is a mercy from thy Lord, so never be a helper to the _DISBELIEVERS_.

28:87 And let them not divert thee from the revelations of Allah after they have been sent down unto thee; but call (mankind) unto thy Lord, and be not of those who ascribe partners (unto Him).

28:88 And cry not unto any other god along with Allah. There is no God save Him. Everything will perish save His countenance. His is the command, and unto Him ye will be brought back.

Chapter 27 - The Ant

27:1 Ta. Sin. These are revelations of the Qur'an and _A SCRIPTURE THAT MAKETH PLAIN_;

27:2 A guidance and good tidings for _BELIEVERS_

27:3 Who establish worship and pay the poor-due and _ARE SURE OF THE HEREAFTER._

27:4 Lo! as for those who _BELIEVE_ not in the Hereafter, We have made their works fairseeming unto them so that they are all astray.

27:5 Those are they for whom is the worst of punishment, and in the Hereafter they will be the greatest losers.

27:6 Lo! as for thee (Muhammad), thou verily receivest the Qur'an from the presence of One Wise, Aware.

27:7 (Remember) when Moses said unto his household: Lo! I spy afar off a fire; I will bring you tidings thence, or bring to you a borrowed flame that ye may warm yourselves.

27:8 But when he reached it, he was called, saying: Blessed is Whosoever is in _THE FIRE_ and Whosoever is round about it! And Glorified be Allah, the Lord of the Worlds!

27:9 O Moses! Lo! it is I, Allah, the Mighty, the Wise.

27:10 And throw down thy staff! But when he saw it writhing as it were a demon, he turned to flee headlong; (but it was said unto him): O Moses! Fear not! the emissaries fear not in My presence,

27:11 Save him who hath done wrong and afterward hath changed _EVIL_ for good. And lo! I am Forgiving, Merciful.

27:12 And put thy hand into the bosom of thy robe, it will come forth white but unhurt. (This will be one) among nine tokens unto Pharaoh and his people Lo! _THEY WERE EVER EVIL-LIVING FOLK._

27:13 But when Our tokens came unto them, plain to see, they said: This is mere magic,

27:14 And they denied them, though their souls acknowledged them, for spite and arrogance. Then see the nature of the consequence for the wrong-doers!

27:15 And We verily gave knowledge unto David and Solomon, and they said: Praise be to Allah, Who hath preferred us above many of His _BELIEVING SLAVES_!

27:16 And Solomon was David's heir. And he said: O mankind! Lo! we have been taught the language of birds, and have been given (abundance) of all things. This surely is evident favour.

27:17 And there were gathered together unto Solomon his armies of the jinn and humankind, and of the birds, and they were set in battle order;

27:18 Till, when they reached the Valley of the Ants, an ant exclaimed: O ants! Enter your dwellings lest Solomon and his armies crush you, unperceiving.

27:19 And (Solomon) smiled, laughing at her speech, and said: My Lord, arouse me to be thankful for Thy favour wherewith Thou hast favoured me and my parents, and to do good that shall be pleasing unto Thee, and include me in (the number of) Thy righteous _SLAVES_.

27:20 And he sought among the birds and said: How is it that I see not the hoopoe, or is he among the absent?

27:21 I verily will punish him with hard punishment or I verily will slay [kill] him, or he verily shall bring me a plain excuse.

27:22 But he was not long in coming, and he said: I have found out (a thing) that thou apprehendest not, and I come unto thee from Sheba with sure tidings.

27:23 Lo! I found a woman ruling over them, and she hath been given (abundance) of all things, and hers is a mighty throne.

27:24 I found her and her people worshipping the sun instead of Allah; and Satan maketh their works fairseeming unto them, and debarreth them from the way (of Truth), so that they go not aright;

27:25 So that they worship not Allah, Who bringeth forth the hidden in the heavens and the earth, and knoweth what ye hide and what ye proclaim,

27:26 Allah; there is no God save Him, the Lord of the Tremendous Throne.

27:27 (Solomon) said: We shall see whether thou speakest truth or whether thou art of the liars.

27:28 Go with this my letter and throw it down unto them; then turn away and see what (answer) they return,

27:29 (The Queen of Sheba) said (when she received the letter): O chieftains! Lo! there hath been thrown unto me a noble letter.

27:30 Lo! it is from Solomon, and lo! it is: In the name of Allah, the Beneficent, the Merciful;

27:31 Exalt not yourselves against me, but come unto me as those who surrender.

27:32 She said: O chieftains! Pronounce for me in my case. I decide no case till ye are present with me.

27:33 They said: We are lords of might and lords of great prowess, but it is for thee to command; so consider what thou wilt command.

27:34 She said: Lo! kings, when they enter a township, ruin it and make the honour of its people shame. Thus will they do.

27:35 But lo! I am going to send a present unto them, and to see with what (answer) the messengers return.

27:36 So when (the envoy) came unto Solomon, (the King) said: What! Would ye help me with wealth? But that which Allah hath given me is better than that which He hath given you. Nay it is ye (and not I) who exult in your gift.

27:37 Return unto them. We verily shall come unto them with hosts [armies] that they cannot resist, and we shall drive them out from thence with shame, and they will be abased.

27:38 He said: O chiefs! Which of you will bring me her throne before they come unto me, surrendering?

27:39 A stalwart of the jinn said: I will bring it thee before thou canst rise from thy place. Lo! I verily am strong and trusty for such work.

27:40 One with whom was knowledge of the Scripture said: I will bring it thee before thy gaze returneth unto thee. And when he saw it set in his presence, (Solomon) said: This is of the bounty of my Lord, that He may try me whether I give thanks or am ungrateful. Whosoever giveth thanks he only giveth thanks for (the good of) his own soul; and whosoever is ungrateful (is ungrateful only to his own soul's hurt). For lo! my Lord is Absolute in independence, Bountiful.

27:41 He said: Disguise her throne for her that we may see whether she will go aright or be of those not rightly guided.

27:42 So, when she came, it was said (unto her): Is thy throne like this? She said: (It is) as though it were the very one. And (Solomon said): We were given the knowledge before her and we had surrendered (to Allah).

27:43 And (all) that she was wont to worship instead of Allah hindered her, for she came of *DISBELIEVING* folk.

27:44 It was said unto her: Enter the hall. And when she saw it she deemed it a pool and bared her legs. (Solomon) said: Lo! it is a hall, made smooth, of glass. She said: My Lord! Lo! I have wronged myself, and I surrender with Solomon unto Allah, the Lord of the Worlds.

27:45 And We verily sent unto Thamud their brother Salih, saying: Worship Allah. And lo! they (then) became two parties quarrelling.

27:46 He said: O my people! Why will ye hasten on the *EVIL* rather than the good? Why will ye not ask pardon of Allah, that ye may receive mercy.

27:47 They said: We augur *EVIL* of thee and those with thee. He said: Your *EVIL* augury is with Allah. Nay, but ye are folk that are being tested.

27:48 And there were in the city nine persons who made *MISCHIEF IN THE LAND* and reformed not.

27:49 They said: Swear one to another by Allah that we verily will attack him and his household by night, and afterward we will surely say unto his friend: We witnessed not the destruction of his household. And lo! we are truthtellers.

27:50 So they plotted a plot: and We plotted a plot, while they perceived not.

27:51 Then see the nature of the consequence of their plotting, for lo! We destroyed them and their people, every one.

27:52 See, yonder are their dwellings empty and in ruins because they did wrong. Lo! herein is indeed a portent for a people who have knowledge.

27:53 And we saved *THOSE WHO BELIEVED* and used to ward off (*EVIL*).

27:54 And Lot! when he said unto his folk: Will ye commit abomination knowingly?

27:55 Must ye seek lust after men instead of women? Nay, but ye are folk who act senselessly.

27:56 But the answer of his folk was naught save that they said: Expel the household of Lot from your township, for they (forsooth) are folk who would keep clean!

27:57 Then We saved him and his household save his wife; We destined her to be of those who stayed behind.

27:58 And We rained a rain upon them. Dreadful is the rain of those who have been warned.

27:59 Say (O Muhammad): Praise be to Allah, and peace be on His slaves whom He hath chosen! Is Allah best, or (all) that ye ascribe as partners (unto Him)?

27:60 Is not He (best) Who created the heavens and the earth, and sendeth down for you water from the sky wherewith We cause to spring forth joyous orchards, whose trees it never hath been yours to cause to grow. Is there any Allah beside Allah? Nay, but they are folk who ascribe equals (unto Him)!

27:61 Is not He (best) Who made the earth a fixed abode, and placed rivers in the folds thereof, and placed firm hills therein, and hath set a barrier between the two seas? Is there any Allah beside Allah? Nay, but most of them know not!

27:62 Is not He (best) Who answereth the wronged one when he crieth unto Him and removeth the *EVIL*, and hath made you viceroys of the earth? Is there any God beside Allah? Little do they reflect!

27:63 Is not He (best) Who guideth you in the darkness of the land and the sea, He Who sendeth the winds as heralds of His mercy? Is there any God beside Allah? High Exalted be Allah from all that *THEY ASCRIBE AS PARTNER (UNTO HIM)!*

27:64 Is not He (best) Who produceth creation, then reproduceth it, and Who provideth for you from the heaven and the earth? Is there any God beside Allah? Say: Bring your proof, if ye are truthful!

27:65 Say (O Muhammad): None in the heavens and the earth knoweth the Unseen save Allah; and they know not when they will be raised (again).

27:66 Nay, but doth their knowledge reach to the Hereafter? Nay, for they are in doubt concerning it. Nay, for they cannot see it.

27:67 Yet *THOSE WHO DISBELIEVE* say: When we have become dust like our fathers, shall we verily be brought forth (again)?

27:68 We were promised this, forsooth, we and our fathers. (All) this is naught but fables of the men of old.

27:69 Say (unto them, O Muhammad): Travel in the land and see the nature of the sequel for the guilty!

27:70 And grieve thou not for them, nor be in distress because of what they plot (against thee).

27:71 And they say: *WHEN (WILL) THIS PROMISE (BE FULFILLED), IF YE ARE TRUTHFUL?*

27:72 Say: It may be that a part of that which ye would hasten on is close behind you.

27:73 Lo! thy Lord is full of bounty for mankind, but most of them do not give thanks.

27:74 Lo! thy Lord knoweth surely all that their bosoms hide, and all that they proclaim.

27:75 And there is nothing hidden in the heaven or the earth but it is in a clear Record.

27:76 Lo! this Qur'an narrateth unto *THE CHILDREN OF ISRAEL* most of that concerning which they differ.

27:77 And lo! it is a guidance and a mercy for *BELIEVERS*.

27:78 Lo! thy Lord will judge between them of His wisdom, and He is the Mighty, the Wise.

27:79 Therefor (O Muhammad) put thy trust in Allah, for thou (standest) on *THE PLAIN TRUTH.*

27:80 Lo! thou canst not make the dead to hear, nor canst thou make the deaf to hear the call when they have turned to flee;

27:81 *NOR CANST THOU LEAD THE BLIND OUT OF THEIR ERROR. THOU CANST MAKE NONE TO HEAR,* save those who *BELIEVE* Our revelations and who *HAVE SURRENDERED.*

27:82 And when the word is fulfilled concerning them, We shall bring forth a beast of the earth to speak unto them because mankind had not faith in Our revelations.

27:83 And (remind them of) *THE DAY* when We shall gather out of every nation a host of those who denied Our revelations, and they will be set in array;

27:84 Till, when they come (before their Lord), He will say: Did ye deny My revelations when ye could not compass them in knowledge, or what was it that ye did?

27:85 And the Word will be fulfilled concerning them because they have done wrong, and they will not speak.

27:86 Have they not seen how We have appointed the night that they may rest therein, and the day sight-giving? Lo! therein verily are portents for a people who *BELIEVE*.

27:87 And (remind them of) *THE DAY WHEN THE TRUMPET WILL BE BLOWN*, and all who are in the heavens and the earth will start in fear, save him whom Allah willeth. And all come unto Him, humbled.

27:88 And thou seest the hills thou deemest solid flying with the flight of clouds: the doing of Allah Who perfecteth all things. Lo! He is Informed of what ye do.

27:89 Whoso bringeth a good deed will have better than its worth; and such are safe from fear that Day.

27:90 And whoso bringeth an ill-deed, such will be flung down on their faces in *THE FIRE*. Are ye rewarded aught save what ye did?

27:91 (Say): I (Muhammad) am commanded only to serve the Lord of this land which He hath hallowed, and unto Whom all things belong. And I am commanded to be of those who surrender (unto Him),

27:92 ~~And to recite the Qur'an. And whoso goeth right, goeth right only for (the good of) his own soul; and as for him who goeth astray - (Unto him) say: Lo! I am only a warner.~~ [Cancelled by verse 9:5, i.e. Islam becomes imposed on unbelievers through violence, rather than just a warning.]⁵⁴²

27:93 And say: Praise be to Allah Who will show you His portents so that ye shall know them. And thy Lord is not unaware of what ye (mortals) do.

Chapter 26 - The Poets

26:1 Ta. Sin. Mim.

26:2 These are revelations of the Scripture that maketh plain.

26:3 It may be that thou tormentest thyself (O Muhammad) because they *BELIEVE* not.

26:4 If We will, We can send down on them from the sky a portent so that their necks would remain bowed before it.

26:5 Never cometh there unto them a fresh reminder from the Beneficent One, but they turn away from it.

26:6 Now they have denied (*THE TRUTH*); but there will come unto them tidings of that whereat they used to scoff.

26:7 Have they not seen the earth, how much of every fruitful kind We make to grow therein?

26:8 Lo! herein is indeed a portent; yet most of them are not *BELIEVERS*.

26:9 And lo! thy Lord! He is indeed the Mighty, the Merciful.

26:10 And when thy Lord called Moses, saying: Go unto the wrongdoing folk,

26:11 The folk of Pharaoh. Will they not ward off (*EVIL*)?

26:12 He said: My Lord! Lo! I fear that they will deny me,

26:13 And I shall be embarrassed, and my tongue will not speak plainly, therefor send for Aaron (to help me).

26:14 And they have a crime against me, so I fear that they will kill me.

26:15 He said: Nay, verily. So go ye twain with Our tokens. Lo! We shall be with you, Hearing.

26:16 And come together unto Pharaoh and say: Lo! we bear a message of the Lord of the Worlds,

26:17 (Saying): Let *THE CHILDREN OF ISRAEL* go with us.

26:18 (Pharaoh) said (unto Moses): Did we not rear thee among us as a child? And thou didst dwell many years of thy life among us,

26:19 And thou didst that thy deed which thou didst, and thou wast one of the ingrates.

26:20 He said: I did it then, when I was of those who are astray.

26:21 Then I fled from you when I feared you, and my Lord vouchsafed me a command and appointed me (of the number) of those sent (by Him).

26:22 And this is the past favour wherewith thou reproachest me: that thou hast enslaved *THE CHILDREN OF ISRAEL*.

26:23 Pharaoh said: And what is the Lord of the Worlds?

26:24 (Moses) said: Lord of the heavens and the earth and all that is between them, if ye had but sure *BELIEF*.

26:25 (Pharaoh) said unto those around him: Hear ye not?

26:26 He said: Your Lord and the Lord of your fathers.

26:27 (Pharaoh) said: Lo! *YOUR MESSENGER WHO HATH BEEN SENT UNTO YOU IS INDEED A MADMAN!*

26:28 He said: Lord of the East and the West and all that is between them, if ye did but understand.

26:29 (Pharaoh) said: If thou choosest a god other than me, I assuredly shall place thee among the prisoners.

26:30 He said: Even though I show thee something plain?

26:31 (Pharaoh) said: Produce it then, if thou art of the truthful!

26:32 Then he flung down his staff and it became a serpent manifest,

26:33 And he drew forth his hand and lo! it was white to the beholders.

26:34 (Pharaoh) said unto the chiefs about him: Lo! this is verily a knowing wizard,

26:35 Who would drive you out of your land by his magic. Now what counsel ye?

26:36 They said: Put him off, (him) and his brother, and send into the cities summoners,

26:37 Who shall bring unto thee every knowing wizard.

26:38 So the wizards were gathered together at a set time on a day appointed.

26:39 And it was said unto the people: Are ye (also) gathering?

26:40 (They said): Aye, so that we may follow the wizards if they are the winners.

26:41 And when the wizards came they said unto Pharaoh: Will there surely be a reward for us if we are the winners?

26:42 He said: Aye, and ye will then surely be of those brought near (to me).

26:43 Moses said unto them: Throw what ye are going to throw!

26:44 Then they threw down their cords and their staves and said: By Pharaoh's might, lo! we verily are the winners.

26:45 Then Moses threw his staff and lo! it swallowed that which they did falsely show.

26:46 And the wizards were flung prostrate,

26:47 Crying: We *BELIEVE* in the Lord of the Worlds,

26:48 The Lord of Moses and Aaron.

26:49 (Pharaoh) said: Ye put your faith in him before I give you leave. Lo! he doubtless is your chief who taught you magic! But verily ye shall come to know. Verily I will cut off your hands and your feet alternately, and verily I will crucify you every one.

26:50 They said: It is no hurt, for lo! unto our Lord we shall return.

26:51 Lo! we ardently hope that our Lord will forgive us our sins because we are the first of the *BELIEVERS*.

26:52 And We inspired Moses, saying: Take away My slaves by night, for ye will be pursued.

26:53 Then Pharaoh sent into the cities summoners,

26:54 (Who said): Lo! these indeed are but a little troop,

26:55 And lo! they are offenders against us.

26:56 And lo! we are a ready host.

26:57 Thus did We take them away from gardens and watersprings,

26:58 And treasures and a fair estate.

26:59 Thus (were those things taken from them) and We caused *THE CHILDREN OF ISRAEL* to inherit them.

26:60 And they overtook them at sunrise.

26:61 And when the two hosts [armies] saw each other, those with Moses said: Lo! we are indeed caught.

26:62 He said: Nay, verily! for lo! my Lord is with me. He will guide me.

26:63 Then We inspired Moses, saying: Smite the sea with thy staff. And it parted, and each part was as a mountain vast.

26:64 Then brought We near the others to that place.

26:65 And We saved Moses and those with him, every one;

26:66 And We drowned the others.

26:67 Lo! herein is indeed a portent, yet most of them are not *BELIEVERS*.

26:68 And lo, thy Lord! He is indeed the Mighty, the Merciful.

26:69 Recite unto them the story of Abraham:

26:70 When he said unto his father and his folk: What worship ye?

26:71 They said: We worship idols, and are ever devoted unto them.

26:72 He said: Do they hear you when ye cry?

26:73 Or do they benefit or harm you?

26:74 They said: Nay, but we found our fathers acting on this wise.

26:75 He said: See now that which ye worship,

26:76 Ye and your forefathers!

26:77 Lo! they are (all) an enemy unto me, save the Lord of the Worlds,

26:78 Who created me, and He doth guide me,

26:79 And Who feedeth me and watereth me.

26:80 And when I sicken, then He healeth me,

26:81 And Who causeth me to die, then giveth me life (again),

26:82 And Who, I ardently hope, will forgive me my sin on *THE DAY OF JUDGMENT.*

26:83 My Lord! Vouchsafe me wisdom and unite me to the righteous.

26:84 And give unto me a good report in later generations.

26:85 And place me among the inheritors of *THE GARDEN OF DELIGHT,*

26:86 And forgive my father. Lo! he is of those who err.

26:87 And abase me not on the day when they are raised,

26:88 The day when wealth and sons avail not (any man)

26:89 Save him who bringeth unto Allah a whole heart.

26:90 *AND THE GARDEN WILL BE BROUGHT NIGH FOR THOSE WHO WARD OFF (EVIL).*

26:91 *AND HELL WILL APPEAR PLAINLY TO THE ERRING.*

26:92 And it will be said unto them: Where is (all) that ye used to worship

26:93 Instead of Allah? Can they help you or help themselves?

26:94 Then will they be hurled therein, they and the seducers

26:95 And the hosts [armies] of Iblis, together.

26:96 And they will say, when they are quarrelling therein:

26:97 By Allah, of a truth we were in error manifest

26:98 When we made you equal with the Lord of the Worlds.

26:99 It was but the guilty who misled us.

26:100 Now we have no intercessors

26:101 Nor any loving friend.

26:102 Oh, that we had another turn (on earth), that we might be of the *BELIEVERS*!

26:103 Lo! herein is indeed a portent, yet most of them are not *BELIEVERS*!

26:104 And lo, thy Lord! He is indeed the Mighty, the Merciful.

26:105 Noah's folk denied the messengers (of Allah),

26:106 When their brother Noah said unto them: Will ye not ward off (*EVIL*)?

26:107 Lo! I am a faithful messenger unto you,

26:108 *SO KEEP YOUR DUTY TO ALLAH, AND OBEY ME.*

26:109 And I ask of you no wage therefor; my wage is the concern only of the Lord of the Worlds.

26:110 So *KEEP YOUR DUTY TO ALLAH*, and *OBEY ME*.

26:111 They said: Shall we put faith in thee, when the lowest (of the people) follow thee?

26:112 He said: And what knowledge have I of what they may have been doing (in the past)?

26:113 Lo! their reckoning is my Lord's concern, if ye but knew;

26:114 And I am not (here) to repulse *BELIEVERS*.

26:115 I am only a plain warner.

26:116 They said: If thou cease not, O Noah, thou wilt surely be among those stoned (to death).

26:117 He said: My Lord! Lo! my own folk deny me.

26:118 Therefor judge Thou between us, a (conclusive) judgment, and save me and those *BELIEVERS* who are with me.

26:119 And We saved him and those with him in the laden ship.

26:120 Then afterward We drowned the others.

26:121 Lo! herein is indeed a portent, yet most of them are not *BELIEVERS*.

26:122 And lo, thy Lord, He is indeed the Mighty, the Merciful.

26:123 (The tribe of) A'ad denied the messengers (of Allah).

26:124 When their brother Hud said unto them: Will ye not ward off (*EVIL*)?

26:125 Lo! I am a faithful messenger unto you,

26:126 *SO KEEP YOUR DUTY TO ALLAH AND OBEY ME.*

26:127 And I ask of you no wage therefor; my wage is the concern only of the Lord of the Worlds.

26:128 Build ye on every high place a monument for vain delight?

26:129 And seek ye out strongholds, that haply ye may last for ever?

26:130 And if ye seize by force, seize ye as tyrants?

26:131 Rather *KEEP YOUR DUTY TO ALLAH, AND OBEY ME.*

26:132 Keep your duty toward Him Who hath aided you with (the good things) that ye know,

26:133 Hath aided you with cattle and sons.

26:134 And gardens and watersprings.

26:135 Lo! I fear for you the retribution of an awful day.

26:136 They said: It is all one to us whether thou preachest or art not of those who preach;

26:137 This is but a fable of the men of old,

26:138 And we shall not be doomed.

26:139 And *THEY DENIED HIM; THEREFOR WE DESTROYED THEM.* Lo! herein is indeed a portent, yet *MOST OF THEM ARE NOT BELIEVERS*.

26:140 And lo! thy Lord, He is indeed the Mighty, the Merciful.

26:141 (The tribe of) Thamud denied the messengers (of Allah)

26:142 When their brother Salih said unto them: Will ye not ward off (*EVIL*)?

26:143 Lo! I am a faithful messenger unto you,

26:144 *SO KEEP YOUR DUTY TO ALLAH AND OBEY ME.*

26:145 And I ask of you no wage therefor; my wage is the concern only of the Lord of the Worlds.

26:146 Will ye be left secure in that which is here before us,

26:147 In gardens and watersprings.

26:148 And tilled fields and heavy-sheathed palm-trees,

26:149 Though ye hew out dwellings in the mountain, being skilful?

26:150 Therefor *KEEP YOUR DUTY TO ALLAH* and *OBEY ME,*

26:151 And obey not the command of the prodigal,

26:152 Who *SPREAD CORRUPTION IN THE EARTH*, and reform not.

26:153 They said: Thou art but one of the bewitched;

26:154 Thou art but a mortal like us. So bring some token if thou art of the truthful.

26:155 He said: (Behold) this she-camel. She hath the right to drink (at the well), and ye have the right to drink, (each) on an appointed day.

26:156 And touch her not with ill lest there come on you the retribution of an awful day.

26:157 But they hamstrung her, and then were penitent.

26:158 So the retribution came on them. Lo! herein is indeed a portent, yet most of them are not *BELIEVERS*.

26:159 And lo! thy Lord! He is indeed the Mighty, the Merciful.

26:160 The folk of Lot denied the messengers (of Allah),

26:161 When their brother Lot said unto them: Will ye not ward off (*EVIL*)?

26:162 Lo! I am a faithful messenger unto you,

26:163 So *KEEP YOUR DUTY TO ALLAH AND OBEY ME.*

26:164 And I ask of you no wage therefor; my wage is the concern only of the Lord of the Worlds.

26:165 What! Of all creatures do ye come unto the males,

26:166 And leave the wives your Lord created for you? Nay, but ye are froward folk.

26:167 They said: If thou cease not, O Lot, thou wilt soon be of the outcast.

26:168 He said: I am in truth of those who hate your conduct.

26:169 My Lord! Save me and my household from what they do.

26:170 So We saved him and his household, every one,

26:171 Save an old woman among those who stayed behind.

26:172 Then afterward We destroyed the others.

26:173 And We rained on them a rain. And dreadful is the rain of those who have been warned.

26:174 Lo! herein is indeed a portent, yet most of them are not *BELIEVERS*.

26:175 And lo! thy Lord, He is indeed the Mighty, the Merciful.

26:176 The dwellers in the wood (of Midian) denied the messengers (of Allah),

26:177 When Shu'eyb said unto them: Will ye not ward off (*EVIL*)?

26:178 Lo! I am a faithful messenger unto you,

26:179 So *KEEP YOUR DUTY TO ALLAH* and *OBEY ME,*

26:180 And I ask of you no wage for it; my wage is the concern only of the Lord of the Worlds.

26:181 Give full measure, and be not of those who give less (than the due).

26:182 And weigh with the true balance.

26:183 Wrong not mankind in their goods, and do not *EVIL, MAKING MISCHIEF, IN THE EARTH.*

26:184 And *KEEP YOUR DUTY UNTO HIM* Who created you and the generations of the men of old.

26:185 They said: Thou art but one of the bewitched;

26:186 Thou art but a mortal like us, and lo! we deem thee of the liars.

26:187 Then make fragments of the heaven fall upon us, if thou art of the truthful.

26:188 He said: My Lord is Best Aware of what ye do.

26:189 But they denied him, so there came on them *THE RETRIBUTION OF THE DAY OF GLOOM*. Lo! it was the retribution of an awful day.

26:190 Lo! herein is indeed a portent; yet *MOST OF THEM ARE NOT BELIEVERS*.

26:191 And lo! thy Lord! He is indeed the Mighty, the Merciful.

26:192 And lo! it is a revelation of the Lord of the Worlds,

26:193 Which the True Spirit hath brought down

26:194 Upon thy heart, that thou mayst be (one) of the warners,

26:195 *IN PLAIN ARABIC SPEECH.*

26:196 And lo! it is in the Scriptures of the men of old.

26:197 Is it not a token for them that the doctors of *THE CHILDREN OF ISRAEL* know it?

26:198 And if We had revealed it unto one of any other nation than the *ARABS*,

26:199 And he had read it unto them, they would not have *BELIEVED* in it.

26:200 Thus do We make it traverse the hearts of the guilty.

26:201 They will not *BELIEVE* in it till they behold the painful doom,

26:202 So that it will come upon them suddenly, when they perceive not.

26:203 Then they will say: Are we to be reprieved?

26:204 Would they (now) hasten on Our doom?

26:205 Hast thou then seen, if We content them for (long) years,

26:206 And then cometh that which they were promised,

26:207 (How) that wherewith they were contented naught availeth them?

26:208 *AND WE DESTROYED NO TOWNSHIP BUT IT HAD ITS WARNERS*

26:209 For reminder, for We never were oppressors.

26:210 The devils did not bring it down.

26:211 It is not meet for them, nor is it in their power,

26:212 Lo! verily they are banished from the hearing.

26:213 Therefor invoke not with Allah another god, lest thou be one of the doomed.

26:214 And warn thy tribe of near kindred,

26:215 And lower thy wing (in kindness) unto those *BELIEVERS* who follow thee.

26:216 And if they (thy kinsfolk) disobey thee, say: Lo! I am innocent of what they do.

26:217 And put thy trust in the Mighty, the Merciful.

26:218 Who seeth thee when thou standest up (to pray)

26:219 And (seeth) thine abasement among those who fall prostrate (in worship).

26:220 Lo! He, only He, is the Hearer, the Knower.

26:221 Shall I inform you upon whom the devils descend?

26:222 They descend on every sinful, false one.

26:223 They listen eagerly, but *MOST OF THEM ARE LIARS*.

26:224 ~~As for poets, the erring follow them.~~[Abrogated by verse 26:227 i.e. Mohammed had poets assassinated.][543]

26:225 ~~Hast thou not seen how they stray in every valley,~~ [Abrogated by verse 26:227][544]

26:226 ~~And how they say that which they do not?~~ [Abrogated by verse 26:227][545]

26:227 Save those who *BELIEVE* and do good works, and remember Allah much, and vindicate themselves after they have been wronged. Those who do wrong will come to know by what a (great) reverse they will be overturned!

Chapter 56 - The Event

56:1 When the event befalleth -

56:2 There is no denying that it will befall -

56:3 Abasing (some), exalting (others);

56:4 When the earth is shaken with a shock

56:5 And the hills are ground to powder

56:6 So that they become a scattered dust,

56:7 And ye will be three kinds:

56:8 (First) *THOSE ON THE RIGHT HAND; WHAT OF THOSE ON THE RIGHT HAND?* [The Muslims who get to Paradise.]

56:9 And (then) those on the left hand; what of those on the left hand?

56:10 And the foremost in the race, the foremost in the race:

56:11 Those are they who will be brought nigh

56:12 *IN GARDENS OF DELIGHT;*

56:13 A multitude of those of old

56:14 And a few of those of later time.

56:15 On lined couches,

56:16 Reclining therein face to face.

56:17 *THERE WAIT ON THEM IMMORTAL YOUTHS*

56:18 With bowls and ewers and a cup from a pure spring

56:19 Wherefrom they get no aching of the head nor any madness,

56:20 And fruit that they prefer

56:21 *AND FLESH OF FOWLS THAT THEY DESIRE.*

56:22 And (there are) fair ones with wide, lovely eyes,

56:23 Like unto hidden pearls,

56:24 *REWARD FOR WHAT THEY USED TO DO.*

56:25 *THERE HEAR THEY NO VAIN SPEAKING NOR RECRIMINATION*

56:26 *(NAUGHT) BUT THE SAYING: PEACE, (AND AGAIN) PEACE.*

56:27 And those on the right hand; what of those on the right hand?

56:28 Among thornless lote-trees

56:29 And clustered plantains,

56:30 And spreading shade,

56:31 And water gushing,

56:32 And fruit in plenty

56:33 Neither out of reach nor yet forbidden,

56:34 And raised couches;

56:35 *LO! WE HAVE CREATED THEM A (NEW) CREATION*

56:36 *AND MADE THEM VIRGINS,*

56:37 *LOVERS, FRIENDS,*

56:38 For *THOSE ON THE RIGHT HAND;*

56:39 A multitude of those of old

56:40 And a multitude of those of later time.

56:41 *AND THOSE ON THE LEFT HAND: WHAT OF THOSE ON THE LEFT HAND?*

56:42 *IN SCORCHING WIND AND SCALDING WATER*

56:43 And shadow of black smoke,

56:44 Neither cool nor refreshing.

56:45 Lo! heretofore they were effete with luxury

56:46 And used to persist in the awful sin.

56:47 And they used to say: When we are dead and have become dust and bones, shall we then, forsooth, be raised again,

56:48 And also our forefathers?

56:49 Say (unto them, O Muhammad): Lo! those of old and those of later time

56:50 Will all be brought together to the tryst of an appointed day.

56:51 Then lo! *YE, THE ERRING, THE DENIERS,*

56:52 Ye verily will eat of a tree called Zaqqum

56:53 And will fill your bellies therewith;

56:54 And thereon *YE WILL DRINK OF BOILING WATER,*

56:55 Drinking even as the camel drinketh.

56:56 This will be their welcome on *THE DAY OF JUDGMENT.*

56:57 We created you. Will ye then admit *THE TRUTH*?

56:58 Have ye seen that which ye emit?

56:59 Do ye create it or are We the Creator?

56:60 We mete out death among you, and We are not to be outrun,

56:61 That We may transfigure you and make you what ye know not.

56:62 And verily ye know the first creation. Why, then, do ye not reflect?

56:63 Have ye seen that which ye cultivate?

56:64 Is it ye who foster it, or are We the Fosterer?

56:65 If We willed, We verily could make it chaff, then would ye cease not to exclaim:

56:66 Lo! we are laden with debt!

56:67 Nay, but we are deprived!

56:68 Have ye observed the water which ye drink?

56:69 Is it ye who shed it from the raincloud, or are We the Shedder?

56:70 If We willed We verily could make it bitter. Why then, give ye not thanks?

56:71 Have ye observed the fire which ye strike out;

56:72 Was it ye who made the tree thereof to grow, or were We the grower?

56:73 We, even We, appointed it a memorial and a comfort for the dwellers in the wilderness.

56:74 Therefor (O Muhammad), praise the name of thy Lord, the Tremendous.

56:75 Nay, I swear by the places of the stars -

56:76 And lo! that verily is a tremendous oath, if ye but knew -

56:77 That (this) is indeed *A NOBLE QUR'AN*
56:78 In a Book kept hidden
56:79 *WHICH NONE TOUCHETH SAVE THE PURIFIED,*
56:80 A revelation from the Lord of the Worlds.
56:81 Is it this Statement that ye scorn,
56:82 And make denial thereof your livelihood?
56:83 Why, then, when (the soul) cometh up to the throat (of the dying)
56:84 And ye are at that moment looking
56:85 And We are nearer unto him than ye are, but ye see not-
56:86 Why then, if ye are not in bondage (unto Us),
56:87 Do ye not force it back, if ye are truthful?
56:88 Thus if he is of those brought nigh,
56:89 Then breath of life, and plenty, and *A GARDEN OF DELIGHT.*
56:90 And if he is of those on the right hand,
56:91 Then (the greeting) "Peace be unto thee" from *THOSE ON THE RIGHT HAND.*
56:92 But if he is of *THE REJECTERS, THE ERRING,*
56:93 Then *THE WELCOME WILL BE BOILING WATER*
56:94 And *ROASTING AT HELL-FIRE.*
56:95 Lo! this is certain truth.
56:96 Therefor (O Muhammad) praise the name of thy Lord, the Tremendous.

Chapter 20 - Ta (Ta Ha)

20:1 Ta. Ha.
20:2 We have not revealed unto thee (Muhammad) this Qur'an that thou shouldst be distressed,
20:3 But as a reminder unto him who feareth,
20:4 A revelation from Him Who created the earth and the high heavens,
20:5 The Beneficent One, Who is established on the Throne.
20:6 Unto Him belongeth whatsoever is in the heavens and whatsoever is in the earth, and whatsoever is between them, and whatsoever is beneath the sod.
20:7 And if thou speakest aloud, then lo! He knoweth the secret (thought) and (that which is yet) more hidden.
20:8 Allah! There is no God save Him. His are the most beautiful names.
20:9 Hath there come unto thee the story of Moses?
20:10 When he saw a fire and said unto his folk: Lo! Wait! I see a fire afar off. Peradventure I may bring you a brand therefrom or may find guidance at the fire.
20:11 And when he reached it, he was called by name: O Moses!
20:12 Lo! I, even I, am thy Lord. So take off thy shoes, for lo! thou art in the holy valley of Tuwa.
20:13 And I have chosen thee, so hearken unto that which is inspired.
20:14 Lo! I, even I, am Allah, There is no God save Me. So serve Me and establish worship for My remembrance.
20:15 Lo! the Hour is surely coming. But I will to keep it hidden, that every soul may be rewarded for that which it striveth (to achieve).
20:16 Therefor, let not him turn thee aside from (the thought of) it who *BELIEVETH* not therein but followeth his own desire, lest thou perish.
20:17 And what is that in thy right hand, O Moses?
20:18 He said: This is my staff whereon I lean, and wherewith I bear down branches for my sheep, and wherein I find other uses.
20:19 He said: Cast it down, O Moses!
20:20 So he cast it down, and lo! it was a serpent, gliding.
20:21 He said: Grasp it and fear not. We shall return it to its former state.
20:22 And thrust thy hand within thine armpit, it will come forth white without hurt. (That will be) another token.
20:23 That We may show thee (some) of Our greater portents,
20:24 Go thou unto Pharaoh! Lo! he hath transgressed (the bounds).
20:25 (Moses) said: My Lord! relieve my mind
20:26 And ease my task for me;

20:27 And loose a knot from my tongue,

20:28 That they may understand my saying.

20:29 Appoint for me a henchman from my folk,

20:30 Aaron, my brother.

20:31 Confirm my strength with him

20:32 And let him share my task,

20:33 That we may glorify Thee much

20:34 And much remember Thee.

20:35 Lo! Thou art ever Seeing us.

20:36 He said: Thou art granted thy request, O Moses.

20:37 And indeed, another time, already We have shown thee favour,

20:38 When we inspired in thy mother that which is inspired,

20:39 Saying: Throw him into the ark, and throw it into the river, then the river shall throw it on to the bank, and there an enemy to Me and an enemy to him shall take him. And I endued thee with love from Me that thou mightest be trained according to My will,

20:40 When thy sister went and said: Shall I show you one who will nurse him? and we restored thee to thy mother that her eyes might be refreshed and might not sorrow. And thou didst kill a man and We delivered thee from great distress, and tried thee with a heavy trial. And thou didst tarry years among the folk of Midian. Then camest thou (hither) by (My) providence, O Moses,

20:41 And I have attached thee to Myself.

20:42 Go, thou and thy brother, with My tokens, and be not faint in remembrance of Me.

20:43 Go, both of you, unto Pharaoh. Lo! he hath transgressed (the bounds).

20:44 And speak unto him a gentle word, that peradventure he may heed or fear.

20:45 They said: Our Lord! Lo! we fear that he may be beforehand with us or that he may play the tyrant.

20:46 He said: Fear not. Lo! I am with you twain, Hearing and Seeing.

20:47 So go ye unto him and say: Lo! we are two messengers of thy Lord. So let *THE CHILDREN OF ISRAEL* go with us, and torment them not. We bring thee a token from thy Lord. And peace will be for him who followeth right guidance.

20:48 Lo! it hath been revealed unto us that the doom will be for him who denieth and turneth away.

20:49 (Pharaoh) said: Who then is the Lord of you twain, O Moses?

20:50 He said: Our Lord is He Who gave unto everything its nature, then guided it aright.

20:51 He said: What then is the state of the generations of old?

20:52 He said: The knowledge thereof is with my Lord in a Record. My Lord neither erreth nor forgetteth,

20:53 Who hath appointed the earth as a bed and hath threaded roads for you therein and hath sent down water from the sky and thereby We have brought forth divers kinds of vegetation,

20:54 (Saying): Eat ye and feed your cattle. Lo! herein verily are portents for men of thought.

20:55 Thereof We created you, and thereunto We return you, and thence We bring you forth a second time.

20:56 And We verily did show him all Our tokens, but he denied them and refused.

20:57 He said: Hast come to drive us out from our land by thy magic, O Moses?

20:58 But we surely can produce for thee magic the like thereof; so appoint a tryst between us and you, which neither we nor thou shall fail to keep, at a place convenient (to us both).

20:59 (Moses) said: Your tryst shall be the day of the feast, and let the people assemble when the sun hath risen high.

20:60 Then Pharaoh went and gathered his strength, then came (to the appointed tryst).

20:61 Moses said unto them: Woe unto you! Invent not a lie against Allah, lest He extirpate you by some punishment. He who lieth faileth miserably.

20:62 Then they debated one with another what they must do, and they kept their counsel secret.

20:63 They said: Lo! these are two wizards who would drive you out from your country by their magic, and destroy your best traditions;

20:64 So arrange your plan, and *COME IN BATTLE LINE*. Whoso is uppermost this day *WILL BE INDEED SUCCESSFUL.*

20:65 They said: O Moses! Either throw first, or let us be the first to throw?

20:66 He said: Nay, do ye throw! Then lo! their cords and their staves, by their magic, appeared to him as though they ran.

20:67 And Moses conceived a fear in his mind.

20:68 We said: Fear not! Lo! thou art the higher.

20:69 Throw that which is in thy right hand! It will eat up that which they have made. Lo! that which they have made is but a wizard's artifice, and a wizard shall not be successful to whatever point (of skill) he may attain.

20:70 Then the wizards were (all) flung down prostrate, crying: We *BELIEVE* in the Lord of Aaron and Moses.

20:71 (Pharaoh) said: Ye put faith in him before I give you leave. Lo! he is your chief who taught you magic. Now surely I shall cut off your hands and your feet alternately, and I shall crucify you on the trunks of palm trees, and ye shall know for certain which of us hath sterner and more lasting punishment.

20:72 They said: We choose thee not above the *CLEAR PROOFS* that have come unto us, and above Him Who created us. So decree what thou wilt decree. Thou wilt end for us only this life of the world.

20:73 Lo! we *BELIEVE* in our Lord, that He may forgive us our sins and the magic unto which thou didst force us. Allah is better and more lasting.

20:74 Lo! whoso cometh guilty unto his Lord, verily for him is *HELL*. There he will neither die nor live.

20:75 But whoso cometh unto Him *A BELIEVER, HAVING DONE GOOD WORKS, FOR SUCH ARE THE HIGH STATIONS;*

20:76 *GARDENS OF EDEN UNDERNEATH* which rivers flow, wherein they will abide for ever [Paradise]. That is the *REWARD* of him who groweth.

20:77 And verily We inspired Moses, saying: Take away My *SLAVES* by night and strike for them a dry path in the sea, fearing not to be overtaken, neither being afraid (of the sea).

20:78 Then Pharaoh followed them with his hosts [armies] and there covered them that which did cover them of the sea.

20:79 And Pharaoh led his folk astray, he did not guide them.

20:80 O *CHILDREN OF ISRAEL*! We delivered you from your enemy, and *WE MADE A COVENANT WITH YOU* on the holy mountain's side, and sent down on you the manna and the quails,

20:81 (Saying): Eat of the good things wherewith We have provided you, and transgress not in respect thereof lest My wrath come upon you: and he on whom My wrath cometh, he is lost indeed.

20:82 And lo! verily I am Forgiving toward him who repenteth and *BELIEVETH* and doeth good, and afterward walketh aright.

20:83 And (it was said): What hath made thee hasten from thy folk, O Moses?

20:84 He said: They are close upon my track. I hastened unto Thee, my Lord, that Thou mightest be well pleased.

20:85 He said: Lo! We have tried thy folk in thine absence, and As-Samiri hath misled them.

20:86 Then Moses went back unto his folk, angry and sad. He said: O my people! Hath not your Lord promised you a fair promise? Did the time appointed then appear too long for you, or did ye wish that wrath from your Lord should come upon you, that ye broke tryst with me?

20:87 They said: We broke not tryst with thee of our own will, but we were laden with burdens of ornaments of the folk, then cast them (in *THE FIRE*), for thus As-Samiri proposed.

20:88 Then he produced for them a calf, of saffron hue, which gave forth a lowing sound. And they cried: This is your god and the god of Moses, but he hath forgotten.

20:89 See they not, then, that it returneth no saying unto them and possesseth for them neither hurt nor use?

20:90 And Aaron indeed had told them beforehand: O my people! Ye are but being seduced therewith, for lo! your Lord is the Beneficent, so follow me and obey my order.

20:91 They said: We shall by no means cease to be its votaries till Moses return unto us.

20:92 He (Moses) said: O Aaron! What held thee back when thou didst see them gone astray,

20:93 That thou followedst me not? Hast thou then disobeyed my order?

20:94 He said: O son of my mother! Clutch not my beard nor my head! I feared lest thou shouldst say: Thou hast caused division among *THE CHILDREN OF ISRAEL*, and hast not waited for my word.

20:95 (Moses) said: And what hast thou to say, O Samiri?

20:96 He said: I perceived what they perceive not, so I seized a handful from the footsteps of the messenger, and then threw it in. Thus my soul commended to me.

20:97 (Moses) said: Then go! and lo! in this life it is for thee to say: Touch me not! and lo! there is for thee a tryst thou canst not break. Now look upon thy god of which thou hast remained a votary. Verily we will burn it and will scatter its dust over the sea.

20:98 Your God is only Allah, than Whom there is no other God. He embraceth all things in His knowledge.

20:99 Thus relate We unto thee (Muhammad) some tidings of that which happened of old, and We have given thee from Our presence a reminder.

20:100 Whoso turneth away from it, he verily will bear a burden on *THE DAY OF RESURRECTION*,

20:101 Abiding under it - *AN EVIL BURDEN FOR THEM ON THE DAY OF RESURRECTION*,

20:102 The day when the Trumpet is blown. On that day we assemble the guilty white-eyed (with terror),

20:103 Murmuring among themselves: Ye have tarried but ten (days).

20:104 We are Best Aware of what they utter when their best in conduct say: Ye have tarried but a day.

20:105 They will ask thee of the mountains (on that day). Say: My Lord will break them into scattered dust.

20:106 And leave it as an empty plain,

20:107 Wherein thou seest neither curve nor ruggedness.

20:108 On that day they follow the summoner who deceiveth not, and voices are hushed for the Beneficent, and thou hearest but a faint murmur.

20:109 On that day no intercession availeth save (that of) him unto whom the Beneficent hath given leave and whose word He accepteth.

20:110 He knoweth (all) that is before them and (all) that is behind them, while they cannot compass it in knowledge.

20:111 And faces humble themselves before the Living, the Eternal. And he who beareth (a burden of) wrongdoing is indeed a failure (on that day).

20:112 And he who hath done some good works, being a *BELIEVER*, he feareth not injustice nor begrudging (of his wage).

20:113 Thus we have revealed it as *A LECTURE IN ARABIC*, and have displayed therein certain threats, that peradventure they may keep from *EVIL* or that it may cause them to take heed.

20:114 Then exalted be Allah, the True King! And hasten not (O Muhammad) with the Qur'an ere its revelation hath been perfected unto thee, and say: My Lord! Increase me in knowledge.

20:115 And verily *WE MADE A COVENANT* of old with Adam, but he forgot, and We found no constancy in him.

20:116 And when We said unto the angels: Fall prostrate before Adam, they fell prostrate (all) save Iblis; he refused.

20:117 Therefor we said: O Adam! This is an enemy unto thee and unto thy wife, so let him not drive you both out of the Garden so that thou come to toil.

20:118 It is (vouchsafed) unto thee that thou hungerest not therein nor art naked,

20:119 And that thou thirstest not therein nor art exposed to the sun's heat.

20:120 But the devil whispered to him, saying: O Adam! Shall I show thee the tree of immortality and power that wasteth not away?

20:121 Then they twain ate thereof, so that their shame became apparent unto them, and they began to hide by heaping on themselves some of the leaves of the Garden. And Adam disobeyed his Lord, so went astray.

20:122 Then his Lord chose him, and relented toward him, and guided him.

20:123 He said: Go down hence, both of you, one of you a foe unto the other. But when there come unto you from Me a guidance, then whoso followeth My guidance, he will not go astray nor come to grief.

20:124 But he who turneth away from remembrance of Me, his will be a narrow life, and I shall bring him blind to the assembly on *THE DAY OF RESURRECTION*.

20:125 He will say: My Lord! Wherefor hast Thou gathered me (hither) blind, when I was wont to see?

20:126 He will say: So (it must be). Our revelations came unto thee but thou didst forget them. In like manner thou art forgotten this Day.

20:127 Thus do We *REWARD* him who is prodigal and *BELIEVETH* not the revelations of his Lord; and verily the doom of the Hereafter will be sterner and more lasting.

20:128 Is it not a guidance for them (to know) *HOW MANY A GENERATION WE DESTROYED BEFORE THEM*, amid whose dwellings they walk? Lo! therein verily are signs for men of thought.

20:129 And but for a decree that had already gone forth from thy Lord, and a term already fixed, the judgment would have been inevitable (in this world).

20:130 ~~Therefor (O Muhammad), bear with what they say, and celebrate the praise of thy Lord ere the rising of the sun and ere the going down thereof. And glorify Him some hours of the night and at the two ends of the day, that thou mayst find acceptance.~~ [Patience is cancelled by violence of 9:5][546]

20:131 And strain not thine eyes toward that which We cause some wedded pairs among them to enjoy, the flower of the life of the world, that We may try them thereby. The provision of thy Lord is better and more lasting.

20:132 And enjoin upon thy people worship, and be constant therein. We ask not of thee a provision: We provided for thee. And the sequel is for righteousness.

20:133 And they say: If only he would bring us a miracle from his Lord! Hath there not come unto them the proof of what is in the former scriptures?

20:134 And if we had destroyed them with some punishment before it, they would assuredly have said: Our Lord! If only Thou hadst sent unto us a messenger, so that we might have followed Thy revelations before we were (thus) humbled and disgraced!

20:135 ~~Say: Each is awaiting; so await ye! Ye will come to know who are the owners of the path of equity, and who is right.~~ [Cancelled by verse 9:5, i.e. violence replaces patience][547]

Chapter 19 - Mary

19:1 Kaf. Ha. Ya. A'in. Sad.

19:2 A mention of the mercy of thy Lord unto His servant Zachariah.

19:3 When he cried unto his Lord a cry in secret,

19:4 Saying: My Lord! Lo! the bones of me wax feeble and my head is shining with grey hair, and I have never been unblest in prayer to Thee, my Lord.

19:5 Lo! I fear my kinsfolk after me, since my wife is barren. Oh, give me from Thy presence a successor,

19:6 Who shall inherit of me and inherit (also) of the house of Jacob. And make him, my Lord, acceptable (unto Thee).

19:7 (It was said unto him): O Zachariah! Lo! We bring thee tidings of a son whose name is John; we have given the same name to none before (him).

19:8 He said: My Lord! How can I have a son when my wife is barren and I have reached infirm old age?

19:9 He said: So (it will be). Thy Lord saith: It is easy for Me, even as I created thee before, when thou wast naught.

19:10 He said: My Lord! Appoint for me some token. He said: Thy token is that thou, with no bodily defect, shalt not speak unto mankind three nights.

19:11 Then he came forth unto his people from the sanctuary, and signified to them: Glorify your Lord at break of day and fall of night.

19:12 (And it was said unto his son): O John! Hold fast the Scripture. And we gave him wisdom when a child,

19:13 And compassion from Our presence, and purity; and he was devout,

19:14 And dutiful toward his parents. And he was not arrogant, rebellious.

19:15 Peace on him the day he was born, and the day he dieth and the day he shall be raised alive!

19:16 And make mention of Mary in the Scripture, when she had withdrawn from her people to a chamber looking East,

19:17 And had chosen seclusion from them. Then We sent unto her Our Spirit and it assumed for her the likeness of a perfect man.

19:18 She said: Lo! I seek refuge in the Beneficent One from thee, if thou art Allah-fearing.

19:19 He said: I am only a messenger of thy Lord, that I may bestow on thee a faultless son.

19:20 She said: How can I have a son when no mortal hath touched me, neither have I been unchaste?

19:21 He said: So (it will be). Thy Lord saith: It is easy for Me. And (it will be) that We may make of him a revelation for mankind and a mercy from Us, and it is a thing ordained.

19:22 And she conceived him, and she withdrew with him to a far place.

19:23 And the pangs of childbirth drove her unto the trunk of the palm-tree. She said: Oh, would that I had died ere this and had become a thing of naught, forgotten!

19:24 Then (one) cried unto her from below her, saying: Grieve not! Thy Lord hath placed a rivulet beneath thee,

19:25 And shake the trunk of the palm-tree toward thee, thou wilt cause ripe dates to fall upon thee.

19:26 So eat and drink and be consoled. And if thou meetest any mortal, say: Lo! I have vowed a fast unto the Beneficent, and may not speak this day to any mortal.

19:27 Then she brought him to her own folk, carrying him. They said: O Mary! Thou hast come with an amazing thing.

19:28 O sister of Aaron! Thy father was not a wicked man nor was thy mother a harlot.

19:29 Then she pointed to him. They said: How can we talk to one who is in the cradle, a young boy?

19:30 He spake: Lo! I am the slave of Allah. He hath given me the Scripture and hath appointed me a Prophet,

19:31 And hath made me blessed wheresoever I may be, and hath enjoined upon me prayer and almsgiving so long as I remain alive,

19:32 And (hath made me) dutiful toward her who bore me, and hath not made me arrogant, unblest.

19:33 Peace on me the day I was born, and the day I die, and the day I shall be raised alive!

19:34 Such was *JESUS, SON OF MARY.* (this is) a statement of *THE TRUTH* concerning which they doubt.

19:35 It *BEFITTETH NOT (THE MAJESTY OF) ALLAH THAT HE SHOULD TAKE UNTO HIMSELF A SON.* Glory be to Him! When He decreeth a thing, He saith unto it only: Be! and it is.

19:36 And lo! Allah is my Lord and your Lord. So serve Him. That is the right path.

19:37 The sects among them differ: but woe unto the *DISBELIEVERS* from *THE MEETING OF AN AWFUL DAY.*

19:38 See and hear them on the Day they come unto Us! yet the *EVIL-DOERS* are to-day in error manifest.

19:39 ~~And warn them of the Day of anguish when the case hath been decided. Now they are in a state of carelessness, and they believe not.~~ [Persuasion cancelled by violence commanded by verse 9:5][548]

19:40 Lo! We, only We, inherit the earth and all who are thereon, and unto Us they are returned.

19:41 And make mention (O Muhammad) in the Scripture of Abraham. Lo! he was a saint, a prophet.

19:42 When he said unto his father: O my father! Why worshippest thou that which heareth not nor seeth, nor can in aught avail thee?

19:43 O my father! Lo! there hath come unto me of knowledge that which came not unto thee. So follow me, and I will lead thee on *A RIGHT PATH*.

19:44 O my father! Serve not the devil. Lo! the devil is a rebel unto the Beneficent.

19:45 O my father! Lo! I fear lest a punishment from the Beneficent overtake thee so that thou become a comrade of the devil.

19:46 He said: Rejectest thou my gods, O Abraham? If thou cease not, I shall surely stone thee. Depart from me a long while!

19:47 He said: Peace be unto thee! I shall ask forgiveness of my Lord for thee. Lo! He was ever gracious unto me.

19:48 I shall withdraw from you and that unto which ye pray beside Allah, and I shall pray unto my Lord. It may be that, in prayer unto my Lord, I shall not be unblest.

19:49 So, when he had withdrawn from them and that which they were worshipping beside Allah, We gave him Isaac and Jacob. Each of them We made a prophet.

19:50 And we gave them of Our mercy, and assigned to them a high and true renown.

19:51 And make mention in the Scripture of Moses. Lo! he was chosen, and he was a messenger (of Allah), a prophet.

19:52 We called him from the right slope of the Mount, and brought him nigh in communion.

19:53 And We bestowed upon him of Our mercy his brother Aaron, a prophet (likewise).

19:54 And make mention in the Scripture of Ishmael. Lo! he was a keeper of his promise, and he was a messenger (of Allah), a prophet.

19:55 He enjoined upon his people worship and almsgiving, and was acceptable in the sight of his Lord.

19:56 And make mention in the Scripture of Idris. Lo! he was a saint, a prophet;

19:57 And We raised him to high station.

19:58 These are they unto whom Allah showed favour from among the prophets, of the seed of Adam and of those whom We carried (in the ship) with Noah, and of the seed of Abraham and Israel, and from among those whom We guided and chose. When the revelations of the Beneficent were recited unto them, they fell down, adoring and weeping.

19:59 ~~Now there hath succeeded them a later generation whom have ruined worship and have followed lusts. But they will meet deception.~~ [Cancelled by verse 19:60][549]

19:60 Save him who shall repent and *BELIEVE* and do right. *SUCH WILL ENTER THE GARDEN*, and they will not be wronged in aught -

19:61 *GARDENS OF EDEN, WHICH THE BENEFICENT HATH PROMISED TO HIS SLAVES* in the unseen. Lo! His promise is ever sure of fulfilment -

19:62 They hear therein no idle talk, but only Peace; and therein they have food for morn and evening.

19:63 *SUCH IS THE GARDEN WHICH WE CAUSE THE DEVOUT AMONG OUR BONDMEN TO INHERIT.*

19:64 We (angels) come not down save by commandment of thy Lord. Unto Him belongeth all that is before us and all that is behind us and all that is between those two, and thy Lord was never forgetful -

19:65 Lord of the heavens and the earth and all that is between them! Therefor, worship thou Him and be thou steadfast in His service. Knowest thou one that can be named along with Him?

19:66 And man saith: When I am dead, shall I forsooth be brought forth alive?

19:67 Doth not man remember that We created him before, when he was naught?

19:68 And, by thy Lord, verily We shall assemble them and the devils, then We shall bring them, crouching, around *HELL*.

19:69 Then We shall pluck out from every sect whichever of them was most stubborn in *REBELLION* to the Beneficent.

19:70 And surely We are Best Aware of *THOSE MOST WORTHY TO BE BURNED* therein.

19:71 ~~There is not one of you but shall approach it. That is a fixed ordinance of thy Lord.~~ [Cancelled by verse 19:72][550]

19:72 Then *WE SHALL RESCUE THOSE WHO KEPT FROM EVIL*, and leave the *EVIL-DOERS* crouching there.

19:73 And when Our clear revelations are recited unto them, *THOSE WHO DISBELIEVE* say unto those who *BELIEVE*: Which of the two parties (yours or ours) is better in position, and *MORE IMPOSING AS AN ARMY?*

19:74 *HOW MANY A GENERATION HAVE WE DESTROYED BEFORE* them, who were more imposing in respect of gear and outward seeming!

19:75 ~~Say: As for him who is in error, the Beneficent will verily prolong his span of life until,~~ when they behold that which they were promised, whether it be punishment (in the world), or *THE HOUR* (of doom), they will know *WHO IS WORSE IN POSITION AND WHO IS WEAKER AS AN ARMY*. [Part cancelled by verse 9:5 i.e. those whose beliefs are erroneous are not to be allowed to die of natural causes.][551]

19:76 Allah increaseth in right guidance those who walk aright, and the good deeds which endure are better in thy Lord's sight for *REWARD*, and better for resort.

19:77 Hast thou seen him who *DISBELIEVETH* in Our revelations and saith: Assuredly I shall be given wealth and children?

19:78 Hath he perused the Unseen, or hath he made a pact with the Beneficent?

19:79 Nay, but We shall record that which he saith and *PROLONG FOR HIM A SPAN OF TORMENT*. [Non-Muslims are to be tortured for eternity.]

19:80 And We shall inherit from him that whereof he spake, and he will come unto Us, alone (without his wealth and children).

19:81 And *THEY HAVE CHOSEN (OTHER) GODS BESIDE ALLAH* that they may be a power for them.

19:82 Nay, but they will deny their worship of them, and become opponents unto them.

19:83 Seest thou not that We have set the devils on the *DISBELIEVERS* to confound them with confusion?

19:84 ~~So make no haste against them (O Muhammad). We do but number unto them a sum (of days).~~ [Cancelled by verse 9:5, i.e. command to be violent replaces command to be patient][552]

19:85 On the day when We shall gather the righteous unto the Beneficent, a goodly company.

19:86 And *DRIVE THE GUILTY UNTO HELL*, a weary herd,

19:87 They will have no power of intercession, save *HIM WHO HATH MADE A COVENANT WITH HIS LORD*.

19:88 And *THEY SAY: THE BENEFICENT HATH TAKEN UNTO HIMSELF A SON.* [Christians destined for an eternity of torture.]

19:89 Assuredly ye utter a disastrous thing

19:90 Whereby almost the heavens are torn, and the earth is split asunder and the mountains fall in ruins,

19:91 That *YE ASCRIBE UNTO THE BENEFICENT A SON*,

19:92 When it is not meet for (the Majesty of) the Beneficent that He should choose a son.

19:93 There is none in the heavens and the earth but cometh unto the Beneficent as a slave.

19:94 Verily He knoweth them and numbereth them with (right) numbering.

19:95 And each one of them will come unto Him on *THE DAY OF RESURRECTION*, alone.

19:96 Lo! *THOSE WHO BELIEVE AND DO GOOD WORKS*, the Beneficent will appoint for them love.

19:97 And We make (this Scripture) easy in thy tongue, (O Muhammad) only that thou mayst bear good tidings therewith unto those who ward off (*EVIL*), and warn therewith the froward folk.

19:98 And *HOW MANY A GENERATION BEFORE THEM HAVE WE DESTROYED*! Canst thou (Muhammad) see a single man of them, or hear from them the slightest sound?

Chapter 35 - The Angels

35:1 Praise be to Allah, the Creator of the heavens and the earth, Who appointeth the angels messengers having wings two, three and four. He multiplieth in creation what He will. Lo! Allah is Able to do all things.

35:2 That which Allah openeth unto mankind of mercy none can withhold it; and that which He withholdeth none can release thereafter. He is the Mighty, the Wise.

35:3 O mankind! Remember Allah's grace toward you! Is there any creator other than Allah who provideth for you from the sky and the earth? There is no God save Him. Whither then are ye turned?

35:4 And if they deny thee, (O Muhammad), messengers (of Allah) were denied before thee. Unto Allah all things are brought back.

35:5 O mankind! Lo! the promise of Allah is true. So let not the life of the world beguile you, and let not the (avowed) beguiler beguile you with regard to Allah.

35:6 Lo! the devil is an enemy for you, so treat him as an enemy. He only summoneth his faction to be owners of the flaming Fire.

35:7 *THOSE WHO DISBELIEVE*, theirs will be *AN AWFUL DOOM*; and *THOSE WHO BELIEVE AND DO GOOD WORKS*, theirs will be *FORGIVENESS AND A GREAT REWARD.*

35:8 Is he, the *EVIL* of whose deeds is made fairseeming unto him so that he deemeth it good, (other than Satan's dupe)? Allah verily sendeth whom He will astray, and guideth whom He will; so let not thy soul expire in sighings for them. Lo! Allah is Aware of what they do!

35:9 And Allah it is Who sendeth the winds and they raise a cloud; then We lead it unto a dead land and revive therewith the earth after its death. Such is *THE RESURRECTION*.

35:10 Whoso desireth power (should know that) all power belongeth to Allah. Unto Him good words ascend, and the pious deed doth He exalt; but those who plot iniquities, theirs will be an awful doom; and the plotting of such (folk) will come to naught.

35:11 Allah created you from dust, then from a little fluid, then He made you pairs (the male and female). No female beareth or bringeth forth save with His knowledge. And no-one groweth old who groweth old, nor is aught lessened of his life, but it is recorded in a Book. Lo! that is easy for Allah.

35:12 And the two seas are not alike: this, fresh, sweet, good to drink, this (other) bitter, salt. And from them both ye eat fresh meat and derive the ornament that ye wear. And thou seest the ship cleaving them with its prow that ye may seek of His bounty, and that haply ye may give thanks.

35:13 He maketh the night to pass into the day and He maketh the day to pass into the night. He hath subdued the sun and moon to service. Each runneth unto an appointed term. Such is Allah, your Lord; His is the Sovereignty; and those unto whom ye pray instead of Him own not so much as the white spot on a date-stone.

35:14 If ye pray unto them they hear not your prayer, and if they heard they could not grant it you. *ON THE DAY OF RESURRECTION* they will disown association with you. None can inform you like Him Who is Aware.

35:15 O mankind! Ye are the poor in your relation to Allah. And Allah! He is the Absolute, the Owner of Praise.

35:16 If He will, He can be rid of you and bring (instead of you) some new creation.

35:17 That is not a hard thing for Allah.

35:18 And no burdened soul can bear another's burden, and if one heavy laden crieth for (help with) his load, naught of it will be lifted even though he (unto whom he crieth) be of kin. Thou warnest only those who fear their Lord in secret, and have established worship. He who groweth (in goodness), groweth only for himself, (he cannot by his merit redeem others). Unto Allah is the journeying.

35:19 The blind man is not equal with the seer;

35:20 Nor is darkness (tantamount to) light;

35:21 Nor is the shadow equal with the sun's full heat;

35:22 Nor are the living equal with the dead. Lo! Allah maketh whom He will to hear. Thou canst not reach those who are in the graves.

35:23 ~~Thou art but a warner.~~ [Cancelled by verse 9:5, i.e. Islam to be imposed through violence][553]
335:24 Lo! We have sent thee with *THE TRUTH*, a bearer of glad tidings and a warner; and there is not a nation but a warner hath passed among them.

35:25 And if they deny thee, those before them also denied. Their messengers came unto them with *CLEAR PROOFS* (of Allah's Sovereignty), and with the Psalms and the Scripture giving light.
35:26 Then seized I *THOSE WHO DISBELIEVED*, and how intense was My abhorrence!

35:27 Hast thou not seen that Allah causeth water to fall from the sky, and We produce therewith fruit of divers hues; and among the hills are streaks white and red, of divers hues, and (others) raven-black;
35:28 And of men and beasts and cattle, in like manner, divers hues? The erudite among His *BONDMEN* fear Allah alone. Lo! Allah is Mighty, Forgiving.
35:29 Lo! *THOSE WHO READ THE SCRIPTURE OF ALLAH*, and establish worship, *AND SPEND OF THAT WHICH WE HAVE BESTOWED ON THEM SECRETLY AND OPENLY, THEY LOOK FORWARD TO IMPERISHABLE GAIN,*
35:30 That *HE WILL PAY THEM THEIR WAGES* and increase them of His grace. Lo! He is Forgiving, Responsive.
35:31 As for that which We inspire in thee of the Scripture, it is *THE TRUTH* confirming that which was (revealed) before it. Lo! *ALLAH IS INDEED OBSERVER, SEER OF HIS SLAVES*.
35:32 Then We gave the Scripture as inheritance unto those whom We elected of Our *BONDMEN*. But of them are some who wrong themselves and of them are some who are lukewarm, and of them are some who outstrip (others) through good deeds, by Allah's leave. That is the great favour!
35:33 *GARDENS OF EDEN! THEY ENTER THEM WEARING ARMLETS OF GOLD AND PEARL AND THEIR RAIMENT THEREIN IS SILK.*
35:34 And they say: Praise be to Allah Who hath put grief away from us. Lo! Our Lord is Forgiving, Bountiful,
35:35 Who, of His grace, hath installed us in the mansion of eternity, where toil toucheth us not nor can weariness affect us.
35:36 But as *FOR THOSE WHO DISBELIEVE, FOR THEM IS FIRE OF HELL; IT TAKETH NOT COMPLETE EFFECT UPON THEM SO THAT THEY CAN DIE*, nor is its torment lightened for them. Thus We punish every ingrate. [Non-Muslims tortured to the point of death but not allowed to die.]
35:37 And they cry for help there, (saying): Our Lord! Release us; we will do right, not (the wrong) that we used to do. Did not We grant you a life long enough for him who reflected to reflect therein? And the warner came unto you. Now taste (the flavour of your deeds), for *EVIL-DOERS* have no helper.
35:38 Lo! Allah is the Knower of the Unseen of the heavens and the earth. Lo! He is Aware of the secret of (men's) breasts.
35:39 He it is Who hath made you regents in the earth; so he who *DISBELIEVETH*, his *DISBELIEF* be on his own head. Their *DISBELIEF* increaseth for the *DISBELIEVERS*, in their Lord's sight, naught save abhorrence. Their *DISBELIEF* increaseth for the *DISBELIEVERS* naught save loss.
35:40 Say: Have ye seen your partner-gods to whom ye pray beside Allah? Show me what they created of the earth! Or have they any portion in the heavens? Or have We given them a scripture so they act on *CLEAR PROOF* therefrom? Nay, the *EVIL-DOERS* promise one another only to deceive.
35:41 Lo! Allah graspeth the heavens and the earth that they deviate not, and if they were to deviate there is not one that could grasp them after Him. Lo! He is ever Clement, Forgiving.
35:42 And they swore by Allah, their most binding oath, that if a warner came unto them they would be more tractable than any of the nations; yet, when a warner came unto them it aroused in them naught save repugnance,
35:43 (Shown in their) behaving arrogantly in the land and plotting *EVIL*; and the *EVIL* plot encloseth but the men who make it. Then, can they expect aught save the treatment of the folk of old? Thou wilt not find for Allah's way of treatment any substitute, nor wilt thou find for Allah's way of treatment aught of power to change.
35:44 Have they not travelled in the land and seen the nature of the consequence for those who were before them, and they were mightier than these in power? Allah is not such that aught in the heavens or in the earth escapeth Him. Lo! He is the Wise, the Mighty.
35:45 If Allah took mankind to task by that which they deserve, He would not leave a living creature on the surface of the earth; but He reprieveth them unto an appointed term, and when their term cometh - then verily (they will know that) *ALLAH IS EVER SEER OF HIS SLAVES.*

Chapter 25 - The Criterion

25:1 Blessed is He Who hath revealed unto His slave the Criterion (of right and wrong), that he may be a warner to the peoples.

25:2 He unto Whom belongeth the Sovereignty of the heavens and the earth, *HE HATH CHOSEN NO SON NOR HATH HE ANY PARTNER IN THE SOVEREIGNTY*. He hath created everything and hath meted out for it a measure.

25:3 Yet they choose beside Him other gods who create naught but are themselves created, and possess not hurt nor profit for themselves, and possess not death nor life, nor power to raise the dead.

25:4 *THOSE WHO DISBELIEVE* say: This is naught but a lie that he hath invented, and other folk have helped him with it, so that they have produced a slander and a lie.

25:5 And they say: Fables of the men of old which he hath had written down so that they are dictated to him morn and evening.

25:6 Say (unto them, O Muhammad): He who knoweth the secret of the heavens and the earth hath revealed it. Lo! He ever is Forgiving, Merciful.

25:7 And they say: What aileth this messenger (of Allah) that he eateth food and walketh in the markets? Why is not an angel sent down unto him, to be a warner with him.

25:8 Or (why is not) treasure thrown down unto him, or why hath he not a paradise from whence to eat? And the *EVIL-DOERS* say: Ye are but following a man bewitched.

25:9 See how they coin similitudes for thee, so that they are all astray and cannot find a road!

25:10 Blessed is He Who, if He will, will assign thee better than (all) that - *GARDENS UNDERNEATH* which rivers flow - and will assign thee mansions.

25:11 Nay, but they deny (the coming of) the Hour, and *FOR THOSE WHO DENY (THE COMING OF) THE HOUR WE HAVE PREPARED A FLAME.*

25:12 When it seeth them from afar, they hear *THE CRACKLING AND THE ROAR* thereof.

25:13 And when they are flung into a narrow place thereof, *CHAINED TOGETHER, THEY PRAY FOR DESTRUCTION* there.

25:14 Pray not that day for one destruction, but pray for many destructions!

25:15 Say: Is that (doom) better or the Garden of Immortality which is promised unto those who ward off (*EVIL*)? It will be *THEIR REWARD AND JOURNEY'S END.*

25:16 Therein abiding, they have all that they desire. It is for thy Lord a promise that must be fulfilled.

25:17 And *ON THE DAY WHEN HE WILL ASSEMBLE THEM AND THAT WHICH THEY WORSHIP INSTEAD OF ALLAH AND WILL SAY: WAS IT YE WHO MISLED THESE MY SLAVES OR DID THEY (THEMSELVES) WANDER FROM THE WAY?*

25:18 They will say: Be Thou Glorified! it was not for us to choose any protecting friends beside thee; but Thou didst give them and their fathers ease till they forgot the warning and became lost folk.

25:19 Thus they will give you the lie regarding what ye say, then ye can neither avert (the doom) nor obtain help. And whoso among you doeth wrong, We shall make him taste great torment.

25:20 We never sent before thee any messengers but lo! they verily ate food and walked in the markets. And We have appointed some of you a test for others: Will ye be steadfast? And thy Lord is ever Seer.

25:21 And those who look not for a meeting with Us say: Why are angels not sent down unto us and (Why) do we not see our Lord! Assuredly they think too highly of themselves and are scornful with great pride.

25:22 On the day when they behold the angels, *ON THAT DAY THERE WILL BE NO GOOD TIDINGS FOR THE GUILTY*; and they will cry: A forbidding ban!

25:23 And We shall turn unto the work they did and make it scattered motes.

25:24 *THOSE WHO HAVE EARNED THE GARDEN ON THAT DAY* will be better in their home and happier in their place of noonday rest;

25:25 A day when the heaven with the clouds will be rent asunder and the angels will be sent down, a grand descent.

25:26 The Sovereignty on that day will be the True (Sovereignty) belonging to the Beneficent One, and it will be a hard day for *DISBELIEVERS*.

25:27 *ON THE DAY WHEN THE WRONG-DOER GNAWETH HIS HANDS*, he will say: Ah, would that I had chosen a way together with the messenger (of Allah)!

25:28 Alas for me! Ah, would that I had never taken such a one for friend!

25:29 He verily led me astray from the Reminder after it had reached me. Satan was ever man's deserter in the hour of need.

25:30 And the messenger saith: O my Lord! Lo! mine own folk make this Qur'an of no account.

25:31 Even so have We appointed unto every prophet an opponent from among the guilty; but Allah sufficeth for a Guide and Helper.

25:32 And *THOSE WHO DISBELIEVE* say: Why is the Qur'an not revealed unto him all at once? (It is revealed) thus that We may strengthen thy heart therewith; and We have arranged it in right order.

25:33 And they bring thee no similitude but We bring thee *THE TRUTH* (as against it), and better (than their similitude) as argument.

25:34 Those who will be gathered on their faces unto *HELL*: such are worse in plight and further from the right road.

25:35 We verily gave Moses the Scripture and placed with him his brother Aaron as henchman.

25:36 Then We said: Go together unto the folk who have denied Our revelations. Then We destroyed them, a complete destruction.

25:37 And Noah's folk, when they denied the messengers, We drowned them and made of them a portent for mankind. *WE HAVE PREPARED A PAINFUL DOOM* for *EVIL-DOERS*.

25:38 And (the tribes of) A'ad and Thamud, and the dwellers in Ar-Rass, and many generations in between.

25:39 Each (of them) We warned by examples, and each (of them) We brought to utter ruin.

25:40 And indeed they have passed by the township whereon was rained the fatal rain. Can it be that they have not seen it? Nay, but they hope for no resurrection.

25:41 And when they see thee (O Muhammad) they treat thee only as a jest (saying): Is this he whom Allah sendeth as a messenger?

25:42 He would have led us far away from our gods if we had not been staunch to them. They will know, when they behold the doom, who is more astray as to the road.

25:43 Hast thou seen him who chooseth for his god his own lust? Wouldst thou then be guardian over him?

25:44 Or deemest thou that most of them hear or understand? *THEY ARE BUT AS THE CATTLE* - nay, but they are farther astray?

25:45 Hast thou not seen how thy Lord hath spread the shade - And if He willed He could have made it still - then We have made the sun its pilot;

25:46 Then We withdraw it unto Us, a gradual withdrawal?

25:47 And He it is Who maketh night a covering for you, and sleep repose, and maketh day a resurrection.

25:48 And He it is Who sendeth the winds, glad tidings heralding His mercy, and We send down purifying water from the sky,

25:49 That We may give life thereby to a dead land, and We give many beasts and men that We have created to drink thereof.

25:50 And verily We have repeated it among them that they may remember, but most of mankind begrudge aught save ingratitude.

25:51 If We willed, We could raise up a warner in every village.

25:52 So *OBEY NOT THE DISBELIEVERS, BUT STRIVE AGAINST THEM* herewith with a great endeavour.

25:53 And He it is Who hath given independence to the two seas (though they meet); one palatable, sweet, and the other saltish, bitter; and hath set a bar and a forbidding ban between them.

25:54 And He it is Who hath created man from water, and hath appointed for him kindred by blood and kindred by marriage; for thy Lord is ever Powerful.

25:55 Yet they worship instead of Allah that which can neither benefit them nor hurt them. The *DISBELIEVER* was ever a partisan against his Lord.

25:56 And We have sent thee (O Muhammad) only as a bearer of good tidings and a warner.

25:57 Say: I ask of you no *REWARD* for this, save that whoso will may choose a way unto his Lord.

25:58 And trust thou in the Living One Who dieth not, and hymn His praise. He sufficeth as the Knower of His *BONDMEN'S* sins,

25:59 Who created the heavens and the earth and all that is between them in six Days, then He mounted the Throne. The Beneficent! Ask anyone informed concerning Him!

25:60 And when it is said unto them: Prostrate to the Beneficent! they say: And what is the Beneficent? Are we to prostrate to whatever thou (Muhammad) biddest us? And it increaseth aversion in them.

25:61 Blessed be He Who hath placed in the heaven mansions of the stars, and hath placed therein a great lamp and a moon giving light!

25:62 And He it is Who hath appointed night and day in succession, for him who desireth to remember, or desireth thankfulness.

25:63 The (faithful) *SLAVES* of the Beneficent are they who walk upon the earth modestly, and when the foolish ones address them answer: Peace; [Part cancelled by verse 9:5, i.e. violence not peace][554]

25:64 And who spend the night before their Lord, prostrate and standing,

25:65 And who say: Our Lord! *AVERT FROM US THE DOOM OF HELL*; lo! the doom thereof is anguish;

25:66 Lo! it is wretched as abode and station;

25:67 And those who, when they spend, are neither prodigal nor grudging; and there is ever a firm station between the two;

25:68 And those who cry not unto any other god along with Allah, nor take the life which Allah hath forbidden save in (course of) justice, nor commit adultery – and whoso doeth this shall pay the penalty; [Cancelled by verse 25:70][555]

25:69 The doom will be doubled for him on the Day of Resurrection, and he will abide therein disdained for ever; [Cancelled by verse 25:70][556]

25:70 Save him who repenteth and *BELIEVETH* and doth righteous work; as for such, *ALLAH WILL CHANGE THEIR EVIL DEEDS TO GOOD DEEDS*. Allah is ever Forgiving, Merciful.

25:71 And whosoever repenteth and doeth good, he verily repenteth toward Allah with true repentance -

25:72 And those who will not witness vanity, but when they pass near senseless play, pass by with dignity.

25:73 And those who, when they are reminded of the revelations of their Lord, fall not deaf and blind thereat.

25:74 And who say: Our Lord! Vouchsafe us comfort of our wives and of our offspring, and *MAKE US PATTERNS FOR (ALL) THOSE WHO WARD OFF (EVIL)*.

25:75 *THEY WILL BE AWARDED THE HIGH PLACE FORASMUCH AS THEY WERE STEADFAST*, and they will meet therein with welcome and the ward of peace,

25:76 Abiding there for ever. Happy is it as abode and station!

25:77 Say (O Muhammad, unto the *DISBELIEVERS*): My Lord would not concern Himself with you but for your prayer. But *NOW YE HAVE DENIED (THE TRUTH), THEREFOR THERE WILL BE JUDGMENT*.

Chapter 36 - Ya Sin

36:1 Ya Sin.

36:2 By the wise Qur'an,

36:3 Lo! thou art of those sent

36:4 On *A STRAIGHT PATH*,

36:5 A revelation of the Mighty, the Merciful,

36:6 That thou mayst warn a folk whose fathers were not warned, so they are heedless.

36:7 Already hath the judgment, (for their infidelity) proved true of most of them, for they *BELIEVE* not.

36:8 Lo! We have put on their necks carcans reaching unto the chins, so that they are made stiff-necked.

36:9 And We have set a bar before them and a bar behind them, and (thus) have covered them so that they see not.

36:10 Whether thou warn them or thou warn them not, it is alike for them, for they *BELIEVE* not.

36:11 Thou warnest only him who followeth the Reminder and feareth the Beneficent in secret. To him bear tidings of forgiveness and *A RICH REWARD*.

36:12 Lo! We it is Who bring the dead to life. We record that which they send before (them), and their footprints. And all things We have kept in a clear Register.

36:13 Coin for them a similitude: The people of the city when those sent (from Allah) came unto them;

36:14 When We sent unto them twain, and they denied them both, so We reinforced them with a third, and they said: Lo! we have been sent unto you.

36:15 They said: Ye are but mortals like unto us. The Beneficent hath naught revealed. Ye do but lie!

36:16 They answered: Our Lord knoweth that we are indeed sent unto you,

36:17 And our duty is but plain conveyance (of the message).

36:18 (The people of the city) said: We augur ill of you. If ye desist not, we shall surely stone you, and grievous torture will befall you at our hands.

36:19 They said: Your *EVIL* augury be with you! Is it because ye are reminded (of *THE TRUTH*)? Nay, but ye are froward [contrary] folk!

36:20 And there came from the uttermost part of the city a man running. He cried: O my people! Follow those who have been sent!

36:21 Follow those who ask of you no fee, and who are *RIGHTLY GUIDED.*

36:22 For what cause should I not serve Him Who hath created me, and unto Whom ye will be brought back?

36:23 Shall I take (other) gods in place of Him when, if the Beneficent should wish me any harm, their intercession will avail me naught, nor can they save?

36:24 Then truly I should be in error manifest.

36:25 Lo! I have *BELIEVED* in your Lord, so hear me!

36:26 It was said (unto him): Enter paradise. He said: Would that my people knew,

36:27 With what (munificence) my Lord hath pardoned me and made me of the honoured ones!

36:28 We sent not down against his people after him a host from heaven, nor do We ever send.

36:29 It was but one Shout, and lo! they were extinct.

36:30 Ah, the anguish for the *BONDMEN*! Never came there unto them a messenger but *THEY DID MOCK HIM*!

36:31 Have they not seen *HOW MANY GENERATIONS WE DESTROYED BEFORE* them, which indeed returned not unto them;

36:32 But all, without exception, will be brought before Us.

36:33 A token unto them is the dead earth. We revive it, and We bring forth from it grain so that they eat thereof;

36:34 And We have placed therein gardens of the date-palm and grapes, and We have caused springs of water to gush forth therein,

36:35 That they may eat of the fruit thereof, and their hands made it not. Will they not, then, give thanks?

36:36 Glory be to Him Who created all the sexual pairs, of that which the earth groweth, and of themselves, and of that which they know not!

36:37 A token unto them is night. We strip it of the day, and lo! they are in darkness.

36:38 And the sun runneth on unto a resting-place for him. That is the measuring of the Mighty, the Wise.

36:39 And for the moon We have appointed mansions till she return like an old shrivelled palm-leaf.

36:40 It is not for the sun to overtake the moon, nor doth the night outstrip the day. They float each in an orbit.

36:41 And a token unto them is that We bear their offspring in the laden ship,

36:42 And have created for them of the like thereof whereon they ride.

36:43 And if We will, We drown them, and there is no help for them, neither can they be saved;

36:44 Unless by mercy from Us and as comfort for a while.

36:45 When it is said unto them: Beware of that which is before you and that which is behind you, that haply ye may find mercy (they are heedless).

36:46 Never came a token of the tokens of their Lord to them, but they did turn away from it!

36:47 And when it is said unto them: Spend of that wherewith Allah hath provided you, *THOSE WHO DISBELIEVE* say unto those who *BELIEVE*: Shall we feed those whom Allah, if He willed, would feed? Ye are in naught else than error manifest.

36:48 And they say: When will this promise be fulfilled, if ye are truthful?

36:49 They await but one Shout, which will surprise them while they are disputing.

36:50 Then they cannot make bequest, nor can they return to their own folk.

36:51 And *THE TRUMPET IS BLOWN* and lo! from the graves they hie unto their Lord,

36:52 Crying: Woe upon us! Who hath raised us from our place of sleep? This is that which the Beneficent did promise, and the messengers spoke truth.

36:53 It is but one Shout, and behold them brought together before Us!

36:54 This day no soul is wronged in aught; nor are ye requited aught save what ye used to do.

36:55 Lo! *THOSE WHO MERIT PARADISE THIS DAY* are happily employed,

36:56 *THEY AND THEIR WIVES, IN PLEASANT SHADE, ON THRONES RECLINING;*

36:57 Theirs the fruit (of their good deeds) and theirs (all) that they ask;

36:58 The word from a Merciful Lord (for them) is: Peace!

36:59 But avaunt ye, O ye guilty, this day!

36:60 Did I not charge you, O ye sons of Adam, that ye worship not the devil - Lo! he is your open foe!

36:61 But that ye worship Me? That was the right path.

36:62 Yet he hath led astray of you a great multitude. Had ye then no sense?

36:63 *THIS IS HELL WHICH YE WERE PROMISED* (if ye followed him).

36:64 *BURN THEREIN THIS DAY FOR THAT YE DISBELIEVED.*

36:65 This day We seal up their mouths, and their hands speak out to Us and their feet bear witness as to what they used to earn.

36:66 And had We willed, We verily could have quenched their eyesight so that they should struggle for the way. Then how could they have seen?

36:67 And had We willed, We verily could have fixed them in their place, making them powerless to go forward or turn back.

36:68 He whom we bring unto old age, We reverse him in creation (making him go back to weakness after strength). Have ye then no sense?

36:69 And We have not taught him (Muhammad) poetry, nor is it meet for him. This is naught else than a Reminder and *A LECTURE MAKING PLAIN,*

36:70 To warn whosoever liveth, and that the word may be fulfilled against the *DISBELIEVERS.*

36:71 Have they not seen how *WE HAVE CREATED FOR THEM OF OUR HANDIWORK THE CATTLE*, so that *THEY ARE THEIR OWNERS,*

36:72 And *HAVE SUBDUED THEM* unto them, so that some of them they have for riding, some for food?

36:73 Benefits and (divers) drinks have they from them. Will they not then give thanks?

36:74 And they have taken (other) gods beside Allah, in order that they may be helped.

36:75 It is not in their power to help them; but they (the worshippers) are unto them a host [army] in arms [weapons].

36:76 ~~So let not their speech grieve thee (O Muhammad). Lo! We know what they conceal and what proclaim.~~ [Cancelled by verse 9:5, i.e. violence replaces indifference][557]

36:77 Hath not man seen that We have created him from a drop of seed? Yet lo! he is an open opponent.

36:78 And he hath coined for Us a similitude, and hath forgotten the fact of his creation, saying: Who will revive these bones when they have rotted away?

36:79 Say: He will revive them Who produced them at the first, for He is Knower of every creation,

36:80 Who hath appointed for you fire from the green tree, and behold! ye kindle from it.

36:81 Is not He Who created the heavens and the earth Able to create the like of them? Aye, that He is! for He is the All-Wise Creator,

36:82 But His command, when He intendeth a thing, is only that He saith unto it: Be! and it is.

36:83 Therefor Glory be to Him in Whose hand is the dominion over all things! Unto Him ye will be brought back.

Chapter 72 - The Jinn

72:1 Say (O Muhammad): It is revealed unto me that a company of the jinn gave ear, and they said: Lo! we have heard a marvellous Qur'an,

72:2 Which guideth unto righteousness, so we *BELIEVE* in it and we *ASCRIBE NO PARTNER UNTO OUR LORD.*

72:3 And (we *BELIEVE*) that He - exalted be the glory of our Lord! - *HATH TAKEN NEITHER WIFE NOR SON,*

72:4 And that the foolish one among us used to speak concerning Allah an atrocious lie.

72:5 And lo! we had supposed that humankind and jinn would not speak a lie concerning Allah -

72:6 And indeed (O Muhammad) individuals of humankind used to invoke the protection of individuals of the jinn, so that they increased them in revolt (against Allah);

72:7 And indeed they supposed, even as ye suppose, *THAT ALLAH WOULD NOT RAISE ANYONE (FROM THE DEAD) -*

72:8 And (the jinn who had listened to the Qur'an said): We had sought the heaven but had found it filled with strong warders and meteors.

72:9 And we used to sit on places (high) therein to listen. But he who listeneth now *FINDETH A FLAME IN WAIT FOR HIM;*

72:10 And we know not whether harm is boded unto all who are in the earth, or whether their Lord intendeth guidance for them.

72:11 And among us there are righteous folk and among us there are far from that. We are sects having different rules.

72:12 And we know that we cannot escape from Allah in the earth, nor can we escape by flight.

72:13 And when we heard the guidance, we *BELIEVED* therein, and whoso *BELIEVETH* in his Lord, he feareth neither loss nor oppression.

72:14 And there are among us some who have surrendered (to Allah) and there are among us some who are unjust. And whoso hath surrendered to Allah, such have taken the right path purposefully.

72:15 And as for those who are unjust, *THEY ARE FIREWOOD FOR HELL.*

72:16 If they (the *IDOLATERS*) tread the right path, We shall give them to drink of water in abundance

72:17 That We may test them thereby, and whoso turneth away from the remembrance of his Lord; He will thrust him into ever-growing torment.

72:18 And *THE PLACES OF WORSHIP ARE ONLY FOR ALLAH, SO PRAY NOT UNTO ANYONE ALONG WITH ALLAH.*

72:19 And when the slave of Allah stood up in prayer to Him, they crowded on him, almost stifling.

72:20 Say (unto them, O Muhammad): I *PRAY UNTO ALLAH ONLY, AND ASCRIBE UNTO HIM NO PARTNER.*

72:21 Say: Lo! I control not hurt nor benefit for you.

72:22 Say: Lo! none can protect me from Allah, nor can I find any refuge beside Him

72:23 (Mine is) but conveyance (of *THE TRUTH*) from Allah, and His messages; and *WHOSO DISOBEYETH ALLAH AND HIS MESSENGER, LO! HIS IS FIRE OF HELL, WHEREIN SUCH DWELL FOR EVER.*

72:24 Till (the day) when they shall behold that which they are promised (they may doubt); but then they will know (for certain) who is weaker in allies and less in multitude.

72:25 Say (O Muhammad, unto the *DISBELIEVERS*): I know not whether that which ye are promised is nigh, or if my Lord hath set a distant term for it.

72:26 (He is) the Knower of the Unseen, and He revealeth unto none His secret,

72:27 Save unto every messenger whom He hath chosen, and then He maketh a guard to go before him and a guard behind him

72:28 That He may know that they have indeed conveyed the messages of their Lord. He surroundeth all their doings, and He keepeth count of all things.

Chapter 7 - The Heights

7:1 Alif. Lam. Mim. Sad.

7:2 (It is) a Scripture that is revealed unto thee (Muhammad) - so let there be no heaviness in thy heart therefrom - that thou mayst warn thereby, and (it is) a Reminder unto *BELIEVERS*.

7:3 (Saying): Follow that which is sent down unto you from your Lord, and follow no protecting friends beside Him. Little do ye recollect!

7:4 *HOW MANY A TOWNSHIP HAVE WE DESTROYED! AS A RAID BY NIGHT, OR WHILE THEY SLEPT AT NOON, OUR TERROR CAME UNTO THEM.*

7:5 No plea had they, when Our terror came unto them, save that they said: Lo! We were wrong-doers.

7:6 Then verily We shall question those unto whom (Our message) hath been sent, and verily We shall question the messengers.

7:7 Then verily We shall narrate unto them (the event) with knowledge, for We were not absent (when it came to pass).

7:8 *THE WEIGHING ON THAT DAY IS THE TRUE (WEIGHING)*. As for those whose scale is heavy, *THEY ARE THE SUCCESSFUL.*

7:9 And as for those whose scale is light: those are they who lose their souls because they used to wrong Our revelations.

7:10 And We have given you (mankind) power in the earth, and appointed for you therein livelihoods. Little give ye thanks!

7:11 And We created you, then fashioned you, then told the angels: Fall ye prostrate before Adam! And they fell prostrate, all save Iblis, who was not of those who make prostration.

7:12 He said: What hindered thee that thou didst not fall prostrate when I bade thee? (Iblis) said: I am better than him. Thou createdst me of fire while him Thou didst create of mud.

7:13 He said: Then go down hence! It is not for thee to show pride here, so go forth! Lo! thou art of those degraded.

7:14 He said: Reprieve me till *THE DAY WHEN THEY ARE RAISED (FROM THE DEAD).*

7:15 He said: Lo! thou art of those reprieved.

7:16 He said: Now, because Thou hast sent me astray, verily I shall lurk in ambush for them on Thy Right Path.

7:17 Then I shall come upon them from before them and from behind them and from their right hands and from their left hands, and Thou wilt not find most of them beholden (unto Thee).

7:18 He said: Go forth from hence, degraded, banished. As for such of them as follow thee, surely *I WILL FILL HELL WITH ALL OF YOU.*

7:19 And (unto man): O Adam! Dwell thou and thy wife in the Garden and eat from whence ye will, but come not nigh this tree lest ye become wrong-doers.

7:20 Then Satan whispered to them that he might manifest unto them that which was hidden from them of their shame, and he said: Your Lord forbade you from this tree only lest ye should become angels or become of the immortals.

7:21 And he swore unto them (saying): Lo! I am a sincere adviser unto you.

7:22 Thus did he lead them on with guile. And when they tasted of the tree their shame was manifest to them and they began to hide (by heaping) on themselves some of the leaves of the Garden. And their Lord called them, (saying): Did I not forbid you from that tree and tell you: Lo! Satan is an open enemy to you?

7:23 They said: Our Lord! We have wronged ourselves. If thou forgive us not and have not mercy on us, surely we are of the lost!

7:24 He said: Go down (from hence), *ONE OF YOU A FOE UNTO THE OTHER.* There will be for you on earth a habitation and provision for a while.

7:25 He said: There shall ye live, and there shall ye die, and thence shall ye be brought forth.

7:26 O Children of Adam! We have revealed unto you raiment to conceal your shame, and splendid vesture, but the raiment of restraint from *EVIL*, that is best. This is of the revelations of Allah, that they may remember.

7:27 O Children of Adam! Let not Satan seduce you as he caused your (first) parents to go forth from the Garden and tore off from them their robe (of innocence) that he might manifest their shame to them. Lo! he seeth you, he and his tribe, from whence ye see him not. Lo! We have made the devils protecting friends for those who *BELIEVE* not.

7:28 And when they do some lewdness they say: We found our fathers doing it and Allah hath enjoined it on us. Say: Allah, verily, enjoineth not lewdness. Tell ye concerning Allah that which ye know not?

7:29 Say: My Lord enjoineth justice. And set your faces upright (toward Him) at every place of worship and call upon Him, making religion pure for Him (only). As He brought you into being, so return ye (unto Him).

7:30 A party hath He led aright, while error hath just hold over (another) party, for lo! they choose the devils for protecting supporters instead of Allah and deem that *THEY ARE RIGHTLY GUIDED.*

7:31 O Children of Adam! Look to your adornment at every place of worship, and eat and drink, but be not prodigal. Lo! He loveth not the prodigals.

7:32 Say: Who hath forbidden the adornment of Allah which He hath brought forth for His *BONDMEN*, and the good things of His providing? Say: Such, on *THE DAY OF RESURRECTION*, will be only for *THOSE WHO BELIEVED* during the life of the world. Thus do we detail Our revelations for people who have knowledge.

7:33 Say: *MY LORD FORBIDDETH ONLY INDECENCIES*, such of them as are apparent and such as are within, and sin and *WRONGFUL OPPRESSION*, and that ye associate with Allah that for which no warrant hath been revealed, and that ye tell concerning Allah that which ye know not. [Note that it is only "wrongful" oppression which is forbidden.]

7:34 And every nation hath its term, and when its term cometh, they cannot put it off an hour nor yet advance (it).

7:35 O Children of Adam! When messengers of your own come unto you who narrate unto you My revelations, then whosoever refraineth from *EVIL* and amendeth - there shall no fear come upon them neither shall they grieve.

7:36 But *THEY WHO DENY OUR REVELATIONS AND SCORN THEM* - each are *RIGHTFUL OWNERS OF THE FIRE*; they will abide therein.

7:37 Who doeth greater wrong than he who inventeth a lie concerning Allah or denieth Our tokens. (For such) their appointed portion of the Book (of destiny) reacheth them till, when Our messengers come to gather them, they say: Where (now) is that to which ye cried beside Allah? They say: They have departed from us. And they testify against themselves that they were *DISBELIEVERS*.

7:38 He saith: Enter into *THE FIRE* among nations of the jinn and humankind who passed away before you. Every time a nation entereth, it curseth its sister (nation) till, when they have all been made to follow one another thither, the last of them saith unto the first of them: Our Lord! *THESE LED US ASTRAY, SO GIVE THEM DOUBLE TORMENT OF THE FIRE*. He saith: For each one there is double (torment), but ye know not.

7:39 And the first of them saith unto the last of them: Ye were no whit better than us, so taste the doom for what ye used to earn.

7:40 Lo! *THEY WHO DENY OUR REVELATIONS AND SCORN THEM*, **for them the gates of heaven will not be opened** *NOR WILL THEY ENTER THE GARDEN* **until the camel goeth through the needle's eye.** *THUS DO WE REQUITE THE GUILTY.*

7:41 *THEIRS WILL BE A BED OF HELL*, **and over them coverings (of** *HELL*). **Thus do We requite wrong-doers. [Unbelievers burn in Hell for their guilt.]**

7:42 But (as for) those who *BELIEVE* and do good works - We tax not any soul beyond its scope - Such are rightful owners of the Garden. They abide therein.

7:43 And We remove whatever rancour may be in their hearts. Rivers flow beneath them. And they say: The praise to Allah, Who hath guided us to this. We could not truly have been led aright if Allah had not guided us. Verily the messengers of our Lord did bring *THE TRUTH*. And it is cried unto them: *THIS IS THE GARDEN. YE INHERIT IT FOR WHAT YE USED TO DO.*

7:44 And the *DWELLERS OF THE GARDEN* **cry unto the** *DWELLERS OF THE FIRE*: **We have found that which our Lord** *PROMISED* **us (to be)** *THE TRUTH*. **Have ye (too) found that which your Lord promised** *THE TRUTH*? **They say: Yea, verily. And a crier in between them crieth:** *THE CURSE OF ALLAH IS ON EVIL-DOERS*, **[Obedient believers of Islam go to Paradise, others burn in Hell]**

7:45 *WHO DEBAR (MEN) FROM THE PATH OF ALLAH* **and would have it crooked, and who** *ARE DISBELIEVERS IN THE LAST DAY*.

7:46 Between them is a veil. And on the Heights are men who know them all by their marks. And they call unto the dwellers of the Garden: Peace be unto you! They enter it not although they hope (to enter).

7:47 And when their eyes are turned toward the *DWELLERS OF THE FIRE*, they say: Our Lord! Place us not with *THE WRONG-DOING FOLK*.

7:48 And the dwellers on the Heights call unto men whom they know by their marks, (saying): What did your multitude and that in which ye took your pride avail you?

7:49 Are these they of whom ye swore that Allah would not show them mercy? (Unto them it hath been said): Enter the Garden. No fear shall come upon you nor is it ye who will grieve.

7:50 And *THE DWELLERS OF THE FIRE CRY OUT UNTO THE DWELLERS OF THE GARDEN*: Pour on us some water or some wherewith Allah hath provided you. They say: Lo! Allah hath forbidden both to *DISBELIEVERS* (in His guidance),

7:51 *WHO TOOK THEIR RELIGION FOR A SPORT AND PASTIME, AND WHOM THE LIFE OF THE WORLD BEGUILED*. So this day We have forgotten them even as they forgot the meeting of this their Day and as they used to deny Our tokens.

7:52 Verily We have brought them a Scripture which We expounded with knowledge, a guidance and a mercy for a people who *BELIEVE*.

7:53 Await they aught save the fulfilment thereof? On *THE DAY* when the fulfilment thereof cometh, those who were before forgetful thereof will say: *THE MESSENGERS OF OUR LORD DID BRING THE TRUTH!* Have we any intercessors, that they may intercede for us? Or can we be returned (to life on earth), that we may act otherwise than we used to act? They have lost their souls, and that which they devised hath failed them.

7:54 Lo! your Lord is Allah Who created the heavens and the earth in six Days, then mounted He the Throne. He covereth the night with the day, which is in haste to follow it, and hath made the sun and the moon and the stars subservient by His command. His verily is all creation and commandment. Blessed be Allah, the Lord of the Worlds!

7:55 (O mankind!) Call upon your Lord humbly and in secret. Lo! He loveth not aggressors.

7:56 Work not confusion in the earth after the fair ordering (thereof). and call on Him in fear and hope. Lo! the mercy of Allah is nigh unto the good.

7:57 And He it is Who sendeth the winds as tidings heralding His mercy, till, when they bear a cloud heavy (with rain), We lead it to a dead land, and then cause water to descend thereon and thereby bring forth fruits of every kind. Thus bring We forth the dead. Haply ye may remember.

7:58 As for the good land, its vegetation cometh forth by permission of its Lord; while as for that which is bad, only the useless cometh forth (from it). Thus do We recount the tokens for people who give thanks.

7:59 We sent Noah (of old) unto his people, and he said: O my people! Serve Allah. Ye have no other Allah save Him. Lo! I fear for you *THE RETRIBUTION OF AN AWFUL DAY*.

7:60 The chieftains of his people said: Lo! we see thee surely in plain error.

7:61 He said: O my people! There is no error in me, but I am a messenger from the Lord of the Worlds.

7:62 I convey unto you the messages of my Lord and give good counsel unto you, and know from Allah that which ye know not.

7:63 Marvel ye that there should come unto you a Reminder from your Lord by means of a man among you, that he may warn you, and that ye may keep from *EVIL*, and that haply ye may find mercy.

7:64 But they denied him, so We saved him and those with him in the ship, and We drowned those who denied Our tokens. Lo! they were blind folk.

7:65 And unto (the tribe of) A'ad (We sent) their brother, Hud. He said: O my people! Serve Allah. Ye have no other Allah save Him. Will ye not ward off (*EVIL*)?

7:66 The chieftains of his people, who were *DISBELIEVING*, said: Lo! we surely see thee in foolishness, and lo! *WE DEEM THEE OF THE LIARS.*

7:67 He said: O my people! There is no foolishness in me, but I am a messenger from the Lord of the Worlds.

7:68 I convey unto you the messages of my Lord and am for you a true adviser.

7:69 Marvel ye that there should come unto you a Reminder from your Lord by means of a man among you, that he may warn you? Remember how He made you viceroys after Noah's folk, and gave you growth of stature. Remember (all) the bounties of your Lord, that haply *YE MAY BE SUCCESSFUL.*

7:70 They said: Hast come unto us that we should serve Allah alone, and forsake what our fathers worshipped? Then bring upon us that wherewith thou threatenest us if thou art of the truthful!

7:71 He said: *TERROR AND WRATH FROM YOUR LORD HAVE ALREADY FALLEN ON YOU*. Would ye wrangle with me over names which ye have named, ye and your fathers, for which no warrant from Allah hath been revealed? Then await (the consequence), lo! I (also) am of those awaiting (it).

7:72 And We saved him and those with him by a mercy from Us, and We cut the root of those who denied Our revelations and were not *BELIEVERS*.

7:73 And to (the tribe of) Thamud (We sent) their brother Salih. He said: O my people! Serve Allah. Ye have no other Allah save Him. A wonder from your Lord hath come unto you. Lo! this is the camel of Allah, a token unto you; so let her feed in Allah's earth, and touch her not with hurt lest painful torment seize you.

7:74 And remember how He made you viceroys after A'ad and gave you station in the earth. Ye choose castles in the plains and hew the mountains into dwellings. So remember (all) the bounties of Allah and do not *EVIL, MAKING MISCHIEF IN THE EARTH.*

7:75 The chieftains of his people, who were scornful, said unto those whom they despised, unto such of them as *BELIEVED*: Know ye that Salih is one sent from his Lord? They said: Lo! In that wherewith he hath been sent we are *BELIEVERS*.

7:76 Those who were scornful said: Lo! in that which ye *BELIEVE* we are *DISBELIEVERS*.

7:77 So they hamstrung the she-camel, and they flouted the commandment of their Lord, and they said: O Salih! Bring upon us that thou threatenest if thou art indeed of those sent (from Allah).

7:78 So the earthquake seized them, and morning found them prostrate in their dwelling-place.

7:79 And (Salih) turned from them and said: O my people! I delivered my Lord's message unto you and gave you good advice, but ye love not good advisers.

7:80 And Lot! (Remember) when he said unto his folk: Will ye commit abomination such as no creature ever did before you?

7:81 Lo! ye come with lust unto men instead of women. Nay, but ye are wanton folk.

7:82 And the answer of his people was only that they said (one to another): Turn them out of your township. They are folk, forsooth, who keep pure.

7:83 And We rescued him and his household, save his wife, who was of those who stayed behind.

7:84 And We rained a rain upon them. See now the nature of the consequence of *EVIL-DOERS*!

7:85 And unto Midian (We sent) their brother, Shu'eyb. He said: O my people! Serve Allah. Ye have no other Allah save Him. Lo! a *CLEAR PROOF* hath come unto you from your Lord; so give full measure and full weight and wrong not mankind in their goods, and work not confusion in the earth after the fair ordering thereof. That will be better for you, if ye are *BELIEVERS*.

7:86 Lurk not on every road to threaten (wayfarers), and to turn away from Allah's path him who *BELIEVETH* in Him, and to seek to make it crooked. And remember, when ye were but few, how He did multiply you. And see the nature of the consequence for the corrupters!

7:87 And if there is a party of you which *BELIEVETH* in that wherewith I have been sent, and there is a party which *BELIEVETH* not, then have patience until Allah judge between us. He is the Best of all who deal in judgment.

7:88 The chieftains of his people, who were scornful, said: Surely we will drive thee out, O Shu'eyb, and those who *BELIEVE* with thee, from our township, unless ye return to our religion. He said: Even though we hate it?

7:89 We should have invented a lie against Allah if we returned to your religion after Allah hath rescued us from it. It is not for us to return to it unless Allah our Lord should (so) will. Our Lord comprehendeth all things in knowledge. In Allah do we put our trust. Our Lord! Decide with truth between us and our folk, for Thou art the best of those who make decision.

7:90 But the chieftains of his people, who were *DISBELIEVING*, said: If ye follow Shu'eyb, then truly ye shall be the losers.

7:91 So the earthquake seized them and morning found them prostrate in their dwelling-place.

7:92 Those who denied Shu'eyb became as though they had not dwelt there. Those who denied Shu'eyb, they were the losers.

7:93 So he turned from them and said: O my people! I delivered my Lord's messages unto you and gave you good advice; then how can I sorrow for a people that rejected (truth)?

7:94 And We sent no prophet unto any township but We did afflict its folk with tribulation and adversity that haply they might grow humble.

7:95 Then changed We the *EVIL* plight for good till they grew affluent and said: Tribulation and distress did touch our fathers. Then We seized them unawares, when they perceived not.

7:96 And if the people of the townships had *BELIEVED* and kept from *EVIL*, surely We should have opened for them blessings from the sky and from the earth. But (unto every messenger) they gave the lie, and so We seized them on account of what they used to earn.

7:97 Are the people of the townships then secure from the coming of Our wrath upon them as a night-raid while they sleep?

7:98 Or are the people of the townships then secure from the coming of Our wrath upon them in the daytime while they play?

7:99 Are they then secure from Allah's scheme? None deemeth himself secure from Allah's scheme save folk that perish.

7:100 Is it not an indication to those who inherit the land after its people (who thus reaped the consequence of *EVIL-DOING*) that, if We will, We can smite them for their sins and print upon their hearts so that they hear not?

7:101 Such were the townships. We relate some tidings of them unto thee (Muhammad). Their messengers verily came unto them with *CLEAR PROOFS (OF ALLAH'S SOVEREIGNTY)*, but they could not *BELIEVE* because they had before denied. Thus doth Allah print upon the hearts of *DISBELIEVERS* (that they hear not).

7:102 We found no (loyalty to any) *COVENANT* in most of them. Nay, most of them We found wrong-doers.

7:103 Then, after them, We sent Moses with our tokens unto Pharaoh and his chiefs, but they repelled them. Now, see the nature of the consequence for the corrupters!

7:104 Moses said: O Pharaoh! Lo! I am a messenger from the Lord of the Worlds,

7:105 Approved upon condition that I speak concerning Allah nothing but *THE TRUTH*. I come unto you (lords of Egypt) with a *CLEAR PROOF* from your Lord. So let *THE CHILDREN OF ISRAEL* go with me.

7:106 (Pharaoh) said: If thou comest with a token, then produce it, if thou art of those who speak *THE TRUTH*.

7:107 Then he flung down his staff and lo! it was a serpent manifest;

7:108 And he drew forth his hand (from his bosom), and lo! it was white for the beholders.

7:109 The chiefs of Pharaoh's people said: Lo! this is some knowing wizard,

7:110 Who would expel you from your land. Now what do ye advise?

7:111 They said (unto Pharaoh): Put him off (a while) - him and his brother - and send into the cities summoners,

7:112 To bring each knowing wizard unto thee.

7:113 And the wizards came to Pharaoh, saying: Surely there will be a reward for us if we are victors.

7:114 He answered: Yes, and surely ye shall be of those brought near (to me).

7:115 They said: O Moses! Either throw (first) or let us be the first throwers?

7:116 He said: Throw! And when they threw they cast a spell upon the people's eyes, and overawed them, and produced a mighty spell.

7:117 And We inspired Moses (saying): Throw thy staff! And lo! it swallowed up their lying show.

7:118 Thus was *THE TRUTH* vindicated and that which they were doing was made vain.

7:119 Thus were they there defeated and brought low.

7:120 And the wizards fell down prostrate,

7:121 Crying: We *BELIEVE* in the Lord of the Worlds,

7:122 The Lord of Moses and Aaron.

7:123 Pharaoh said: Ye *BELIEVE* in Him before I give you leave! Lo! this is the plot that ye have plotted in the city that ye may drive its people hence. But ye shall come to know!

7:124 Surely I shall have your hands and feet cut off upon alternate sides. Then I shall crucify you every one.

7:125 They said: Lo! We are about to return unto our Lord!

7:126 Thou takest vengeance on us only forasmuch as we *BELIEVED* the tokens of our Lord when they came unto us. Our Lord! Vouchsafe unto us steadfastness and make us die as men who have surrendered (unto Thee).

7:127 The chiefs of Pharaoh's people said: (O King), wilt thou suffer Moses and his people to *MAKE MISCHIEF IN THE LAND*, and flout thee and thy gods? He said: We will slay their sons and spare their women, for lo! we are in power over them.

7:128 And Moses said unto his people: Seek help in Allah and endure. Lo! the earth is Allah's. He giveth it for an inheritance to whom He will. And lo! the sequel is for those who keep their duty (unto Him).

7:129 They said: We suffered hurt before thou camest unto us, and since thou hast come unto us. He said: It may be that your Lord is going to destroy your adversary and make you viceroys in the earth, that He may see how ye behave.

7:130 And we straitened Pharaoh's folk with famine and dearth of fruits, that peradventure they might heed.

7:131 But whenever good befell them, they said: This is ours; and whenever *EVIL* smote them they ascribed it to the *EVIL* auspices of Moses and those with him. Surely their *EVIL* auspice was only with Allah. But most of them knew not.

7:132 And they said: Whatever portent thou bringest wherewith to bewitch us, we shall not put faith in thee.

7:133 So We sent against them the flood and the locusts and the vermin and the frogs and the blood - a succession of clear signs. But they were arrogant and became a guilty folk.

7:134 And when the terror fell on them they cried: O Moses! Pray for us unto thy Lord, because *HE HATH A COVENANT WITH THEE*. If thou removest the terror from us we verily will trust thee and will let *THE CHILDREN OF ISRAEL* go with thee.

7:135 But when We did remove from them the terror for a term which they must reach, behold! they *BROKE THEIR COVENANT*.

7:136 Therefore We took retribution from them; therefore We drowned them in the sea: because they denied Our revelations and were heedless of them.

7:137 And We caused the folk who were despised to inherit the eastern parts of the land and the western parts thereof which We had blessed. And the fair word of thy Lord was fulfilled for *THE CHILDREN OF ISRAEL* because of their endurance; and We annihilated (all) that Pharaoh and his folk had done and that they had contrived.

7:138 And We brought *THE CHILDREN OF ISRAEL* across the sea, and they came unto a people who were given up to idols which they had. They said: O Moses! Make for us a god even as they have gods. He said: Lo! ye are a folk who know not.

7:139 Lo! as for these, their way will be destroyed and all that they are doing is in vain.

7:140 He said: Shall I seek for you a god other than Allah when He hath favoured you above (all) creatures?

7:141 And (remember) when We did deliver you from Pharaoh's folk who were afflicting you with dreadful torment, slaughtering your sons and sparing your women. That was a tremendous trial from your Lord.

7:142 And when We did appoint for Moses thirty nights (of solitude), and added to them ten, and he completed the whole time appointed by his Lord of forty nights; and Moses said unto his brother, Aaron: Take my place among the people. Do right, and *FOLLOW NOT THE WAY OF MISCHIEF-MAKERS.*

7:143 And when Moses came to Our appointed tryst and his Lord had spoken unto him, he said: My Lord! Show me (Thy Self), that I may gaze upon Thee. He said: Thou wilt not see Me, but gaze upon the mountain! If it stand still in its place, then thou wilt see Me. And when his Lord revealed (His) glory to the mountain He sent it crashing down. And Moses fell down senseless. And when he woke he said: Glory unto Thee! I turn unto Thee repentant, and I am the first of (true) *BELIEVERS*.

7:144 He said: O Moses! I have preferred thee above mankind by My messages and by My speaking (unto thee). So hold that which I have given thee, and be among the thankful.

7:145 And We wrote for him, upon the tablets, the lesson to be drawn from all things and the explanation of all things, then (bade him): Hold it fast; and command thy people (saying): Take the better (course made clear) therein. I shall show thee the abode of *EVIL-LIVERS*.

7:146 I shall turn away from My revelations those who magnify themselves wrongfully in the earth, and if they see each token *BELIEVE* it not, and if they see the way of righteousness choose it nor for (their) way, and if they see the way of error choose if for (their) way. That is because they deny Our revelations and are used to disregard them.

7:147 Those who deny Our revelations and the meeting of the Hereafter, their works are fruitless. Are they requited aught save what they used to do?

7:148 And the folk of Moses, after (he left them), chose a calf (for worship), (made) out of their ornaments, of saffron hue, which gave a lowing sound. Saw they not that it spake not unto them nor guided them to any way? They chose it, and became wrong-doers.

7:149 And when they feared the consequences thereof and saw that they had gone astray, they said: Unless our Lord have mercy on us and forgive us, we verily are of the lost.

7:150 And when Moses returned unto his people, angry and grieved, he said: *EVIL* is that (course) which ye took after I had left you. Would ye hasten on the judgment of your Lord? And he cast down the tablets, and he seized his brother by the head, dragging him toward him. He said: Son of my mother! Lo! the folk did judge me weak and almost killed me. Oh, make not mine enemies to triumph over me and place me not among the *EVIL-DOERS*.

7:151 He said: My Lord! Have mercy on me and on my brother; bring us into Thy mercy, Thou the Most Merciful of all who show mercy.

7:152 Lo! Those who chose the calf (for worship), terror from their Lord and humiliation will come upon them in the life of the world. Thus do We requite those who invent a lie.

7:153 But those who do ill-deeds and afterward repent and *BELIEVE* - lo! for them, afterward, Allah is Forgiving, Merciful.

7:154 Then, when the anger of Moses abated, he took up the tablets, and in their inscription there was guidance and mercy for all those who fear their Lord.

7:155 And Moses chose of his people seventy men for Our appointed tryst and, when the trembling came on them, he said: My Lord! If Thou hadst willed Thou hadst destroyed them long before, and me with them. Wilt thou destroy us for that which the ignorant among us did? It is but Thy trial (of us). Thou sendest whom Thou wilt astray and guidest whom Thou wilt: Thou art our Protecting Friend, therefore forgive us and have mercy on us, Thou, the Best of all who show forgiveness.

7:156 And ordain for us in this world that which is good, and in the Hereafter (that which is good), Lo! We have turned unto Thee. He said: *I SMITE WITH MY PUNISHMENT WHOM I WILL*, and My mercy embraceth all things, therefore I shall ordain it for those who ward off (*EVIL*) and pay the poor-due, and those who *BELIEVE* Our revelations;

7:157 Those who follow the messenger, the Prophet who can neither read nor write, whom they will find described in the Torah and the Gospel (which are) with them. He will enjoin on them that which is right and forbid them that which is wrong. He will make lawful for them all good things and prohibit for them only the foul; and he will relieve them of their burden and the fetters that they used to wear. Then those who *BELIEVE* in him, and honour him, and help him, and follow the light which is sent down with him: *THEY ARE THE SUCCESSFUL.*

7:158 Say (O Muhammad): O mankind! Lo! I am the messenger of Allah to you all - (the messenger of) Him unto Whom belongeth the Sovereignty of the heavens and the earth. There is no God save Him. He quickeneth and He giveth death. So *BELIEVE* in Allah and His messenger, the Prophet who can neither read nor write, who *BELIEVETH* in Allah and in His Words, and follow him that haply ye may be led aright.

7:159 And of Moses' folk there is a community who lead with truth and establish justice therewith.

7:160 We divided them into twelve tribes, nations; and We inspired Moses, when his people asked him for water, saying: Smite with thy staff the rock! And there gushed forth therefrom twelve springs, so that each tribe knew their drinking-place. And we caused the white cloud to overshadow them and sent down for them the manna and the quails (saying): Eat of the good things wherewith we have provided you. They wronged Us not, but they were wont to wrong themselves.

7:161 And when it was said unto them: Dwell in this township and eat therefrom whence ye will, and say "Repentance," and enter the gate prostrate; We shall forgive you your sins; *WE SHALL INCREASE (REWARD) FOR THE RIGHT-DOERS.*

7:162 But those of them who did wrong changed the word which had been told them for another saying, and We sent down upon them wrath from heaven for their wrongdoing.

7:163 Ask them (O Muhammad) of the township that was by the sea, how they did break the Sabbath, how their big fish came unto them visibly upon their Sabbath day and on a day when they did not keep Sabbath came they not unto them. Thus did We try them for that they were *EVIL-LIVERS.*

7:164 And when *A COMMUNITY AMONG THEM SAID: WHY PREACH YE TO A FOLK WHOM ALLAH IS ABOUT TO DESTROY OR PUNISH WITH AN AWFUL DOOM,* they said: In order to be free from guilt before your Lord, and that haply they may ward off (*EVIL*).

7:165 And when they forgot that whereof they had been reminded, We rescued those who forbade wrong, and *VISITED THOSE WHO DID WRONG WITH DREADFUL PUNISHMENT BECAUSE THEY WERE EVIL-LIVERS.*

7:166 So when they took pride in that which they had been forbidden, We said unto them: Be ye apes despised and loathed!

7:167 And (remember) when thy Lord proclaimed that He would raise against them till *THE DAY OF RESURRECTION* those who would lay on them a cruel torment. Lo! verily thy Lord is swift in prosecution and lo! verily He is Forgiving, Merciful.

7:168 And We have sundered them in the earth as (separate) nations. Some of them are righteous, and some far from that. And We have tried them with good things and *EVIL* things that haply they might return.

7:169 And a generation hath succeeded them who inherited the scriptures. They grasp the goods of this low life (as the price of *EVIL*-doing) and say: It will be forgiven us. And if there came to them (again) the offer of the like, they would accept it (and would sin again). Hath not *THE COVENANT OF THE SCRIPTURE* been taken on their behalf that they should not speak aught concerning Allah save *THE TRUTH?* And they have studied that which is therein. And *THE ABODE OF THE HEREAFTER IS BETTER,* for those who ward off (*EVIL*). Have ye then no sense?

7:170 And as for those who make (men) keep the Scripture, and establish worship - lo! We squander not the wages of reformers.

7:171 And when We shook the Mount above them as it were a covering, and they supposed that it was going to fall upon them (and We said): Hold fast that which We have given you, and remember that which is therein, that ye may ward off (*EVIL*).

7:172 And (remember) when thy Lord brought forth from the Children of Adam, from their reins, their seed, and made them testify of themselves, (saying): Am I not your Lord? They said: Yea, verily. We testify. (That was) lest ye should say at *THE DAY OF RESURRECTION*: Lo! of this we were unaware;

7:173 Or lest ye should say: (It is) only (that) our fathers ascribed partners to Allah of old and we were (their) seed after them. Wilt Thou destroy us on account of that which those who follow falsehood did?

7:174 Thus we detail the revelations, that haply they may return.

7:175 Recite unto them the tale of him to whom We gave Our revelations, but he sloughed them off, so Satan overtook him and he became of those who lead astray.

7:176 And had We willed We could have raised him by their means, but he clung to the earth and followed his own lust. Therefor his likeness is as the likeness of a dog: if thou attackest him he panteth with his tongue out, and if thou leavest him he panteth with his tongue out. Such is the likeness of the people who deny Our revelations. Narrate unto them the history (of the men of old), that haply they may take thought.

7:177 *EVIL AS AN EXAMPLE ARE THE FOLK WHO DENIED OUR REVELATIONS,* and were wont to wrong themselves.

7:178 *HE WHOM ALLAH LEADETH, HE INDEED IS LED ARIGHT, WHILE HE WHOM ALLAH SENDETH ASTRAY - THEY INDEED ARE LOSERS.*

7:179 Already have We urged unto *HELL* many of the jinn and humankind, having hearts wherewith they understand not, and having eyes wherewith they see not, and having ears wherewith they hear not. *THESE ARE AS THE CATTLE - NAY, BUT THEY ARE WORSE*! These are the neglectful.

7:180 Allah's are the fairest names. Invoke Him by them. And leave the company of those who blaspheme His names. They will be requited what they do. [Retreat cancelled by violent verse 9:5][558]

7:181 And of those whom We created there is a nation who guide with *THE TRUTH* and establish justice therewith.

7:182 And those who deny Our revelations - step by step We lead them on from whence they know not.

7:183 I give them rein (for) lo! My scheme is strong. [Tolerance of unbelief cancelled by verse 9:5][559]

7:184 Have they not bethought them (that) there is no madness in their comrade? He is but a plain warner.

7:185 Have they not considered the dominion of the heavens and the earth, and what things Allah hath created, and that it may be that their own term draweth nigh? In what fact after this will they *BELIEVE*?

7:186 Those whom Allah sendeth astray, there is no guide for them. He leaveth them to wander blindly on in their contumacy.

7:187 They ask thee of the (destined) Hour, when will it come to port. Say: Knowledge thereof is with my Lord only. He alone will manifest it at its proper time. It is heavy in the heavens and the earth. It cometh not to you save unawares. They question thee as if thou couldst be well informed thereof. Say: Knowledge thereof is with Allah only, but most of mankind know not.

7:188 Say: For myself I have no power to benefit, nor power to hurt, save that which Allah willeth. Had I knowledge of the Unseen, I should have abundance of wealth, and adversity would not touch me. I am but a warner, and a bearer of good tidings unto folk who *BELIEVE*.

7:189 He it is Who did create you from a single soul, and therefrom did make his mate that he might take rest in her. And when he covered her she bore a light burden, and she passed (unnoticed) with it, but when it became heavy they cried unto Allah, their Lord, saying: If thou givest unto us aright we shall be of the thankful.

7:190 But when He gave unto them aright, *THEY ASCRIBED UNTO HIM PARTNERS* in respect of that which He had given them. High is He Exalted above all that they associate (with Him).

7:191 Attribute they as partners to Allah those who created naught, but are themselves created,

7:192 And cannot give them help, nor can they help themselves?

7:193 And if ye call them to the Guidance, they follow you not. Whether ye call them or are silent is all one for you.

7:194 Lo! those on whom ye call beside Allah are slaves like unto you. Call on them now, and let them answer you, if ye are truthful!

7:195 Have they feet wherewith they walk, or have they hands wherewith they hold, or have they eyes wherewith they see, or have they ears wherewith they hear? Say: Call upon your (so-called) partners (of Allah), and then contrive against me, spare me not!

7:196 Lo! my Protecting Friend is Allah Who revealeth the Scripture. He befriendeth the righteous.

7:197 They on whom ye call beside Him have no power to help you, nor can they help you, nor can they help themselves.

7:198 And if ye (*MUSLIMS*) call them to the guidance they hear not; and thou (Muhammad) seest them looking toward thee, but they see not.

7:199 Keep to forgiveness (O Muhammad), and enjoin kindness, and turn away from the ignorant. [Cancelled by verse 9:5, i.e. violence replaces forgiveness and kindness][560]

7:200 And if a slander from the devil wound thee, then seek refuge in Allah. Lo! He is Hearer, Knower.

7:201 Lo! those who ward off (*EVIL*), when a glamour from the devil troubleth them, they do but remember (Allah's Guidance) and behold them seers!

7:202 Their brethren plunge them further into error and cease not.

7:203 And when thou bringest not a verse for them they say: Why hast thou not chosen it? Say: I follow only that which is inspired in me from my Lord. This (Qur'an) is insight from your Lord, and a guidance and a mercy for a people that *BELIEVE*.

7:204 And when the Qur'an is recited, give ear to it and pay heed, that ye may obtain mercy.

7:205 And do thou (O Muhammad) remember thy Lord within thyself humbly and with awe, below thy breath, at morn and evening. And be not thou of the neglectful.

7:206 Lo! those who are with thy Lord are not too proud to do Him service, but they praise Him and prostrate before Him.

Chapter 38 - Sad

38:1 Sad. By the renowned Qur'an,

38:2 Nay, but *THOSE WHO DISBELIEVE* are in false pride and schism.

38:3 *HOW MANY A GENERATION WE DESTROYED BEFORE THEM*, and they cried out when it was no longer the time for escape!

38:4 And they marvel that a warner from among themselves hath come unto them, and the *DISBELIEVERS* say: This is a wizard, a *CHARLATAN*.[Most contemporaries scoffed at Mohammed, and the most authoritative Muslim biographies of Mohammed show he had his critics murdered.]

38:5 Maketh he the gods One Allah? Lo! that is an astounding thing.

38:6 The chiefs among them go about, exhorting: Go and be staunch to your gods! Lo! this is a thing designed.

38:7 We have not heard of this in later religion. *THIS IS NAUGHT BUT AN INVENTION.*

38:8 Hath the reminder been unto him (alone) among us? Nay, but they are in doubt concerning My reminder; nay but they have not yet tasted My doom.

38:9 Or are theirs the treasures of the mercy of thy Lord, the Mighty, the Bestower?

38:10 Or is the kingdom of the heavens and the earth and all that is between them theirs? Then let them ascend by ropes!

38:11 A defeated host are (all) the factions that are there.

38:12 The folk of Noah before them denied (their messenger) and (so did the tribe of) A'ad, and Pharaoh firmly planted,

38:13 And (the tribe of) Thamud, and the folk of Lot, and the dwellers in the wood: these were the factions.

38:14 Not one of them but did deny the messengers, therefor My doom was justified,

38:15 These wait for but one Shout, there will be no second thereto.

38:16 They say: Our Lord! Hasten on for us our fate before *THE DAY OF RECKONING*.

38:17 Bear with what they say, and remember Our *BONDMAN* David, lord of might, Lo! he was ever turning in repentance (toward Allah).

38:18 Lo! We subdued the hills to hymn the praises (of their Lord) with him at nightfall and sunrise,

38:19 And the birds assembled; all were turning unto Him.

38:20 We made his kingdom strong and gave him wisdom and decisive speech.

38:21 And hath the story of the litigants come unto thee? How they climbed the wall into the royal chamber;

38:22 How they burst in upon David, and he was afraid of them. They said: Be not afraid! (We are) two litigants, one of whom hath wronged the other, therefor judge aright between us; be not unjust; and show us the fair way.

38:23 Lo! this my brother hath ninety and nine ewes while I had one ewe; and he said: Entrust it to me, and he conquered me in speech.

38:24 (David) said: He hath wronged thee in demanding thine ewe in addition to his ewes, and lo! many partners oppress one another, save such as *BELIEVE* and do good works, and they are few. And David guessed that We had tried him, and he sought forgiveness of his Lord, and he bowed himself and fell down prostrate and repented.

38:25 So We forgave him that; and lo! he had access to Our presence and a happy journey's end.

38:26 (And it was said unto him): O David! Lo! We have set thee as a viceroy in the earth; therefor judge aright between mankind, and follow not desire that it beguile thee from the way of Allah. Lo! those who wander from the way of Allah have an awful doom, forasmuch as they forgot *THE DAY OF RECKONING*.

38:27 And We created not the heaven and the earth and all that is between them in vain. That is the opinion of those who *DISBELIEVE*. And woe unto *THOSE WHO DISBELIEVE*, from *THE FIRE*!

38:28 Shall We treat *THOSE WHO BELIEVE AND DO GOOD WORKS* as *THOSE WHO SPREAD CORRUPTION IN THE EARTH*; or shall We treat the pious as the wicked?

38:29 (This is) a Scripture that We have revealed unto thee, full of blessing, that they may ponder its revelations, and that men of understanding may reflect.

38:30 And We bestowed on David, Solomon. *HOW EXCELLENT A SLAVE*! Lo! he was ever turning in repentance (toward Allah).

38:31 When there were shown to him at eventide lightfooted coursers

38:32 And he said: Lo! I have preferred the good things (of the world) to the remembrance of my Lord; till they were taken out of sight behind the curtain.

38:33 (Then he said): Bring them back to me, and fell to slashing (with his sword their) legs and necks.

38:34 And verily We tried Solomon, and set upon his throne a (mere) body. Then did he repent.

38:35 He said: My Lord! Forgive me and bestow on me sovereignty such as shall not belong to any after me. Lo! Thou art the Bestower.

38:36 So We made the wind subservient unto him, setting fair by his command whithersoever he intended.

38:37 And the unruly, every builder and diver (made We subservient),

38:38 And others linked together in chains,

38:39 (Saying): This is Our gift, so bestow thou, or withhold, without reckoning.

38:40 And lo! he hath favour with Us, and a happy journey's end.

38:41 And make mention (O Muhammad) of Our *BONDMAN* Job, when he cried unto his Lord (saying): Lo! the devil doth afflict me with distress and torment.

38:42 (And it was said unto him): Strike the ground with thy foot. This (spring) is a cool bath and a refreshing drink.

38:43 And We bestowed on him (again) his household and therewith the like thereof, a mercy from Us, and a memorial for men of understanding.

38:44 And (it was said unto him): Take in thine hand a branch and smite therewith, and break not thine oath. Lo! We found him steadfast, how excellent a slave! Lo! he was ever turning in repentance (to his Lord).

38:45 And make mention of Our *BONDMEN*, Abraham, Isaac and Jacob, men of parts and vision.

38:46 Lo! We purified them with a pure thought, remembrance of the Home (of the Hereafter).

38:47 Lo! in Our sight they are verily of the elect, the excellent.

38:48 And make mention of Ishmael and Elisha and Dhu'l-Kifl. All are of the chosen.

38:49 This is a reminder. And lo! for those who ward off (*EVIL*) is a happy journey's end,

38:50 *GARDENS OF EDEN*, whereof the gates are opened for them,

38:51 Wherein, *RECLINING, THEY CALL FOR PLENTEOUS FRUIT AND COOL DRINK* (that is) therein. [Paradise]

38:52 And with them are those of modest gaze, companions.

38:53 *THIS IT IS THAT YE ARE PROMISED FOR THE DAY OF RECKONING.*

38:54 Lo! this in truth is Our provision, which will never waste away.

38:55 This (is for the righteous). And lo! *FOR THE TRANSGRESSORS THERE WILL BE AN EVIL JOURNEY'S END,* [Those who don't practise Islam go to Hell.]

38:56 *HELL, WHERE THEY WILL BURN, AN EVIL RESTING-PLACE.*

38:57 Here is a boiling and an ice-cold draught, so let them taste it,

38:58 And other (torment) of the kind in pairs (the two extremes)!

38:59 *HERE IS AN ARMY* **rushing blindly with you. (Those who are already in** *THE FIRE* **say): No word of welcome for them. Lo!** *THEY WILL ROAST AT THE FIRE.*

38:60 They say: Nay, but you (misleaders), for you there is no word of welcome. Ye prepared this for us (by your misleading). Now hapless is the plight.

38:61 They say: Our Lord! Whoever did prepare this for us, oh, *GIVE HIM DOUBLE PORTION OF THE FIRE*!

38:62 And they say: What aileth us that we behold not men whom we were wont to count among the wicked?

38:63 Did we take them (wrongly) for a laughing-stock, or have our eyes missed them?

38:64 Lo! that is very truth: the wrangling of *THE DWELLERS IN THE FIRE*.

38:65 Say (unto them, O Muhammad): I am only a warner, and *THERE IS NO ALLAH SAVE ALLAH, THE ONE, THE ABSOLUTE,*

38:66 Lord of the heavens and the earth and all that is between them, the Mighty, the Pardoning.

38:67 Say: It is tremendous tidings

38:68 Whence ye turn away!

38:69 I had no knowledge of the Highest Chiefs when they disputed;

38:70 It is revealed unto me only that I may be a plain warner. [Persuasion replaced by verse 9:5][561]

38:71 When thy Lord said unto the angels: Lo! I am about to create a mortal out of mire,

38:72 And when I have fashioned him and breathed into him of My Spirit, then fall down before him prostrate,

38:73 The angels fell down prostrate, every one,

38:74 Saving Iblis; he was scornful and became one of the *DISBELIEVERS*.

38:75 He said: O Iblis! What hindereth thee from falling prostrate before that which I have created with both My hands? Art thou too proud or art thou of the high exalted?

38:76 He said: I am better than him. Thou createdst me of fire, whilst him Thou didst create of clay.

38:77 He said: Go forth from hence, for lo! thou art outcast,

38:78 And lo! *MY CURSE IS ON THEE TILL THE DAY OF JUDGMENT,*

38:79 He said: My Lord! Reprieve me till the day when they are raised.

38:80 He said: Lo! thou art of those reprieved

38:81 Until *THE DAY OF THE TIME APPOINTED.*

38:82 He said: Then, by Thy might, I surely will beguile them every one,

38:83 *SAVE THY SINGLE-MINDED SLAVES* among them.

38:84 He said: *THE TRUTH IS, AND THE TRUTH I SPEAK,*

38:85 That *I SHALL FILL HELL* with thee and with such of them as follow thee, together.

38:86 Say (O Muhammad, unto mankind): I ask of you no fee for this, and I am no simulating.

38:87 Lo! it is naught else than *A REMINDER FOR ALL PEOPLES*

38:88 And ye will come in time to know the truth thereof. [Cancelled by verse 9:5][562]

Chapter 54 - The Moon

54:1 The hour drew nigh and the moon was rent in twain.

54:2 And if they behold a portent they turn away and say: Prolonged illusion.

54:3 *THEY DENIED (THE TRUTH)* and followed their own lusts. Yet everything will come to a decision.

54:4 And surely there hath come unto them news whereof the purport should deter,

54:5 Effective wisdom; but warnings avail not.

54:6 So withdraw from them (O Muhammad) on the day when the Summoner summoneth unto a painful thing. [Cancelled by verse 9:5, i.e. violence replaces patience][563]

54:7 With downcast eyes, they come forth from the graves as they were locusts spread abroad,

54:8 Hastening toward the summoner; the *DISBELIEVERS* say: This is a hard day.

54:9 The folk of Noah denied before them, yea, they denied Our slave and *SAID: A MADMAN*; and he was repulsed.

54:10 So he cried unto his Lord, saying: I am vanquished, so give help.

54:11 Then opened We the gates of heaven with pouring water

54:12 And caused the earth to gush forth springs, so that the waters met for a predestined purpose.

54:13 And We carried him upon a thing of planks and nails,

54:14 That ran (upon the waters) in Our sight, as a reward for him who was rejected.

54:15 And verily We left it as a token; but is there any that remembereth?

54:16 Then see how (dreadful) was My punishment after My warnings!

54:17 And in truth We have made the Qur'an easy to remember; but is there any that remembereth?

54:18 (The tribe of) A'ad rejected warnings. Then *HOW (DREADFUL) WAS MY PUNISHMENT AFTER MY WARNINGS*.

54:19 Lo! We let loose on them a raging wind on a day of constant calamity,

54:20 Sweeping men away as though they were uprooted trunks of palm-trees.

54:21 Then see how (dreadful) was My punishment after My warnings!

54:22 And in truth *WE HAVE MADE THE QUR'AN EASY TO REMEMBER*; but is there any that remembereth?

54:23 (The tribe of) Thamud rejected warnings

54:24 For they said; Is it a mortal man, alone among us, that we are to follow? Then indeed we should fall into error and madness.

54:25 Hath the remembrance been given unto him alone among us? Nay, but he is a rash liar.

54:26 (Unto their warner it was said): To-morrow they will know who is the rash liar.

54:27 Lo! We are sending the she-camel as a test for them; so watch them and have patience;

54:28 And inform them that the water is to be shared between (her and) them. Every drinking will be witnessed.

54:29 But they call their comrade and he took and hamstrung (her).

54:30 Then see how (dreadful) was My punishment after My warnings!

54:31 Lo! We sent upon them one Shout, and they became as the dry twigs (rejected by) the builder of a cattle-fold.

54:32 And *IN TRUTH WE HAVE MADE THE QUR'AN EASY TO REMEMBER*; but is there any that remembereth?

54:33 The folk of Lot rejected warnings.

54:34 Lo! We sent a storm of stones upon them (all) save the family of Lot, whom We rescued in the last watch of the night,

54:35 As grace from Us. Thus We reward him who giveth thanks.

54:36 And he indeed had warned them of Our blow, but they did doubt the warnings.

54:37 They even asked of him his guests for an ill purpose. Then We blinded their eyes (and said): Taste now My punishment after My warnings!

54:38 And in truth the punishment decreed befell them early in the morning.

54:39 Now taste My punishment after My warnings!

54:40 And in truth *WE HAVE MADE THE QUR'AN EASY TO REMEMBER*; but is there any that remembereth?

54:41 And warnings came in truth unto the house of Pharaoh

54:42 Who denied Our revelations, every one. Therefore We grasped them with the grasp of the Mighty, the Powerful.

54:43 Are your *DISBELIEVERS* better than those, or have ye some immunity in the scriptures?

54:44 Or say they: We are a host *VICTORIOUS*?

54:45 *THE HOSTS [ARMIES] WILL ALL BE ROUTED AND WILL TURN AND FLEE.*

54:46 Nay, but *THE HOUR (OF DOOM)* is their appointed tryst, and the Hour will be more wretched and more bitter (than their earthly failure).

54:47 Lo! the guilty are in error and madness.

54:48 On *THE DAY WHEN THEY ARE DRAGGED INTO THE FIRE* upon their faces (it is said unto them): *FEEL THE TOUCH OF HELL.*

54:49 Lo! We have created every thing by measure.

54:50 And Our commandment is but one (commandment), as the twinkling of an eye.

54:51 And verily We have destroyed your fellows; but is there any that remembereth?

54:52 And every thing they did is in the scriptures,

54:53 And every small and great thing is recorded.

54:54 Lo! *THE RIGHTEOUS WILL DWELL AMONG GARDENS AND RIVERS,*

54:55 Firmly established in the favour of a Mighty King.

Chapter 86 - The Morning Star

86:1 By the heaven and the Morning Star
86:2 - Ah, what will tell thee what the Morning Star is!
86:3 - The piercing Star!
86:4 No human soul but hath a guardian over it.
86:5 So let man consider from what he is created.
86:6 He is created from a gushing fluid
86:7 That issued from between the loins and ribs.
86:8 Lo! He verily is Able to return him (unto life)
86:9 On the day when hidden thoughts shall be searched out.
86:10 Then will he have no might nor any helper.
86:11 By the heaven which giveth the returning rain,
86:12 And the earth which splitteth (with the growth of trees and plants)
86:13 Lo! this (Qur'an) is a conclusive word,
86:14 It is no pleasantry.
86:15 Lo! they plot a plot (against thee, O Muhammad)
86:16 And *I PLOT A PLOT (AGAINST THEM).*
86:17 ~~So give a respite to the *DISBELIEVERS*. Deal thou gently with them for a while.~~ [Cancelled by verse 9:5, i.e. command to violence replaces indifference and patience][564]

Chapter 90 - The City

90:1 Nay, I swear by this city -
90:2 And thou art an indweller of this city -
90:3 And the begetter and that which he begat,
90:4 We verily have created man in an atmosphere:
90:5 Thinketh he that none hath power over him?
90:6 And he saith: I have destroyed vast wealth:
90:7 Thinketh he that none beholdeth him?
90:8 Did We not assign unto him two eyes
90:9 And a tongue and two lips,
90:10 And guide him to the parting of the mountain ways?
90:11 But he hath not attempted the Ascent -
90:12 Ah, what will convey unto thee what the Ascent is! -
90:13 (It is) to free a slave,
90:14 And to feed in the day of hunger.
90:15 An orphan near of kin,
90:16 Or some poor wretch in misery,
90:17 And to be of those who *BELIEVE* and exhort one another to perseverance and exhort one another to pity.
90:18 Their place will be on the right hand.
90:19 But *THOSE WHO DISBELIEVE OUR REVELATIONS, THEIR PLACE WILL BE ON THE LEFT HAND.*
90:20 Fire will be an awning over them.

Chapter 50 - Qaf

50:1 Qaf. By the Glorious Qur'an,
50:2 Nay, but they marvel that a warner of their own hath come unto them; and the *DISBELIEVERS* say: This is a strange thing:
50:3 When we are dead and have become dust (shall we be brought back again)? That would be a far return!
50:4 We know that which the earth taketh of them, and with Us is a recording Book.
50:5 Nay, but *THEY HAVE DENIED THE TRUTH* when it came unto them, therefor they are now in troubled case.

50:6 Have they not then observed the sky above them, how We have constructed it and beautified it, and how there are no rifts therein?

50:7 And the earth have We spread out, and have flung firm hills therein, and have caused of every lovely kind to grow thereon,

50:8 A vision and a reminder for every penitent slave.

50:9 And We send down from the sky blessed water whereby We give growth unto gardens and the grain of crops,

50:10 And lofty date-palms with ranged clusters,

50:11 Provision (made) for men; and therewith We quicken a dead land. Even so will be *THE RESURRECTION* of the dead.

50:12 The folk of Noah denied (*THE TRUTH*) before them, and (so did) the dwellers at Ar-Rass and (the tribe of) Thamud,

50:13 And (the tribe of) A'ad, and Pharaoh, and the brethren of Lot,

50:14 And the dwellers in the wood, and the folk of Tubb'a: every one denied their messengers, therefor My threat took effect.

50:15 Were We then worn out by the first creation? Yet they are in doubt about a new creation.

50:16 We verily created man and We know what his soul whispereth to him, and We are nearer to him than his jugular vein.

50:17 When the two Receivers receive (him), seated on the right hand and on the left,

50:18 He uttereth no word but there is with him an observer ready.

50:19 And the agony of death cometh in truth. (And it is said unto him): This is that which thou wast wont to shun.

50:20 And the trumpet is blown. *THIS IS THE THREATENED DAY.*

50:21 And every soul cometh, along with it a driver and a witness.

50:22 (And unto the *EVIL*-doer it is said): Thou wast in heedlessness of this. Now We have removed from thee thy covering, and piercing is thy sight this day.

50:23 And (unto the *EVIL*-doer) his comrade saith: This is that which I have ready (as testimony).

50:24 (And it is said): Do ye twain *HURL TO HELL EACH REBEL INGRATE,*

50:25 Hinderer of good, transgressor, doubter,

50:26 Who setteth up another god along with Allah. Do ye twain hurl him to the dreadful doom.

50:27 His comrade saith: Our Lord! I did not cause him to rebel, but he was (himself) far gone in error.

50:28 He saith: Contend not in My presence, when I had already proffered unto you the warning.

50:29 The sentence that cometh from Me cannot be changed, and I am in no wise a tyrant unto the *SLAVES.*

50:30 *ON THE DAY WHEN WE SAY UNTO HELL*: Art thou filled? and it saith: Can there be more to come?

50:31 And *THE GARDEN IS BROUGHT NIGH FOR THOSE WHO KEPT FROM EVIL*, no longer distant.

50:32 (And it is said): This is that which ye were promised. (It is) for every penitent and heedful one,

50:33 Who feareth the Beneficent in secret and cometh with a contrite heart.

50:34 Enter it in peace. This is *THE DAY OF IMMORTALITY*.

50:35 There they have all that they desire, and there is more with Us.

50:36 And *HOW MANY A GENERATION WE DESTROYED BEFORE THEM*, who were mightier than these in prowess so that they overran the lands! Had they any place of refuge (when the judgment came)?

50:37 Lo! therein verily is a reminder for him who hath a heart, or giveth ear with full intelligence.

50:38 And verily We created the heavens and the earth, and all that is between them, in six Days, and naught of weariness touched Us.

50:39 ~~Therefor (O Muhammad) bear with what they say, and hymn the praise of thy Lord~~ before the rising and before the setting of the sun; [Tolerance cancelled by command to violence in verse 9:5][565]

50:40 And in the night-time hymn His praise, and after the (prescribed) prostrations.

50:41 And listen on the day when the crier crieth from a near place,

50:42 The day when they will hear the (Awful) Cry in truth. That is *THE DAY OF COMING FORTH* (from the graves).

50:43 Lo! We it is Who quicken and give death, and unto Us is the journeying.

50:44 On the day when the earth splitteth asunder from them, hastening forth (they come). That is a gathering easy for Us (to make).

50:45 We are Best Aware of what they say, ~~and thou (O Muhammad) art in no wise a compeller over them. But warn by the Qur'an him who feareth My threat.~~ [Compulsion is commanded, verse 9:5][566]

Chapter 77 - The Emissaries

77:1 By the emissary winds, (sent) one after another
77:2 By the raging hurricanes,
77:3 By those which cause earth's vegetation to revive;
77:4 By those who winnow with a winnowing,
77:5 By those who bring down the Reminder,
77:6 To excuse or to warn,
77:7 Surely that which ye are promised will befall.
77:8 So when the stars are put out,
77:9 And when the sky is riven asunder,
77:10 And when the mountains are blown away,
77:11 And when the messengers are brought unto their time appointed -
77:12 For what day is the time appointed?
77:13 For the Day of Decision.
77:14 And what will convey unto thee what *THE DAY OF DECISION* is! -
77:15 Woe unto the repudiators on that day!
77:16 Destroyed We not the former folk,
77:17 Then caused the latter folk to follow after?
77:18 Thus deal We ever with the guilty.
77:19 Woe unto the repudiators on that day!
77:20 Did We not create you from a base fluid
77:21 Which We laid up in a safe abode
77:22 For a known term?
77:23 Thus We arranged. How excellent is Our arranging!
77:24 Woe unto the repudiators on that day!
77:25 Have We not made the earth a receptacle
77:26 Both for the living and the dead,
77:27 And placed therein high mountains and given you to drink sweet water therein?
77:28 Woe unto the repudiators on that day!
77:29 (It will be said unto them:) Depart unto that (doom) which ye used to deny;
77:30 Depart unto the shadow falling threefold,
77:31 (Which yet is) *NO RELIEF NOR SHELTER FROM THE FLAME.*
77:32 Lo! it throweth up sparks like the castles,
77:33 (Or) as it might be camels of bright yellow hue.
77:34 Woe unto the repudiators on that day!
77:35 This is a day wherein they speak not,
77:36 Nor are they suffered to put forth excuses.
77:37 Woe unto the repudiators on that day!
77:38 This is *THE DAY OF DECISION*, We have brought you and the men of old together.
77:39 If now ye have any wit, outwit Me.
77:40 Woe unto the repudiators on that day!
77:41 Lo! *THOSE WHO KEPT THEIR DUTY ARE AMID SHADE AND FOUNTAINS,*
77:42 And fruits such as they desire.
77:43 (Unto them it is said:) Eat, drink and welcome, O ye blessed, in return for what ye did.
77:44 *THUS DO WE REWARD THE GOOD.*
77:45 Woe unto the repudiators on that day!
77:46 Eat and take your ease (on earth) a little. Lo! ye are guilty.
77:47 Woe unto the repudiators on that day!
77:48 When it is said unto them: Bow down, they bow not down!
77:49 Woe unto the repudiators on that day!
77:50 In what statement, after this, will they *BELIEVE*?

Chapter 104 - The Traducer

104:1 Woe unto every slandering traducer,

104:2 Who hath gathered wealth (of this world) and arranged it.
104:3 He thinketh that his wealth will render him immortal.
104:4 Nay, but verily he will be flung to the Consuming One.
104:5 Ah, what will convey unto thee what the Consuming One is!
104:6 (It is) *THE FIRE OF ALLAH, KINDLED*,
104:7 Which leapeth up over the hearts (of men).
104:8 Lo! it is closed in on them
104:9 In outstretched columns.

Chapter 75 - The Rising of the Dead

75:1 Nay, I swear by *THE DAY OF RESURRECTION*;
75:2 Nay, I swear by the accusing soul (that this Scripture is true).
75:3 Thinketh man that We shall not assemble his bones?
75:4 Yea, verily. We are Able to restore his very fingers!
75:5 But man would fain deny what is before him.
75:6 He asketh: When will be this *DAY OF RESURRECTION*?
75:7 But when sight is confounded
75:8 And the moon is eclipsed
75:9 And sun and moon are united,
75:10 On that day man will cry: Whither to flee!
75:11 Alas! No refuge!
75:12 Unto thy Lord is the recourse that day.
75:13 On that day man is told the tale of that which he hath sent before and left behind.
75:14 Oh, but man is a telling witness against himself,
75:15 Although he tender his excuses.
75:16 Stir not thy tongue herewith to hasten it.
75:17 Lo! upon Us (resteth) the putting together thereof and the reading thereof.
75:18 And when We read it, follow thou the reading;
75:19 Then lo! upon Us (resteth) the explanation thereof.
75:20 Nay, but *YE DO LOVE THE FLEETING NOW*
75:21 *AND NEGLECT THE HEREAFTER.*
75:22 *THAT DAY WILL FACES BE RESPLENDENT,*
75:23 Looking toward their Lord;
75:24 *AND THAT DAY WILL OTHER FACES BE DESPONDENT,*
75:25 Thou wilt know that some great disaster is about to fall on them.
75:26 Nay, but when the life cometh up to the throat
75:27 And men say: Where is the wizard (who can save him now)?
75:28 And he knoweth that it is the parting;
75:29 And agony is heaped on agony;
75:30 Unto thy Lord that day will be the driving.
75:31 For he neither trusted, nor prayed.
75:32 But he denied and flouted.
75:33 Then went he to his folk with glee.
75:34 Nearer unto thee and nearer,
75:35 Again nearer unto thee and nearer (is the doom).
75:36 Thinketh man that he is to be left aimless?
75:37 Was he not a drop of fluid which gushed forth?
75:38 Then he became a clot; then (Allah) shaped and fashioned
75:39 And made of him a pair, the male and female.
75:40 Is not He (Who doeth so) Able to bring the dead to life?

Chapter 101 - The Calamity

101:1 The Calamity!
101:2 What is the Calamity?

101:3 Ah, what will convey unto thee what the Calamity is!

101:4 *A DAY* wherein mankind will be as thickly-scattered moths

101:5 And the mountains will become as carded wool.

101:6 Then, as for him whose scales are heavy (with good works),

101:7 He will live a pleasant life.

101:8 But as for him whose scales are light,

101:9 A bereft and Hungry One will be his mother,

101:10 Ah, what will convey unto thee what she is! -

101:11 *RAGING FIRE.*

Chapter 106 - Winter or Qureysh

106:1 For the taming of Qureysh.

106:2 For their taming (We cause) the caravans to set forth in winter and summer.

106:3 So let them worship the Lord of this House,

106:4 Who hath fed them against hunger and hath made them safe from fear.

Chapter 95 - The Fig

95:1 By the fig and the olive,

95:2 By Mount Sinai,

95:3 And by this land made safe;

95:4 Surely We created man of the best stature

95:5 Then we reduced him to the lowest of the low,

95:6 Save *THOSE WHO BELIEVE AND DO GOOD WORKS, AND THEIRS IS A REWARD UNFAILING.*

95:7 So who henceforth will give the lie to thee about the judgment?

95:8 ~~Is not Allah the most conclusive of all judges?~~ [Cancelled by verse 9:5][567]

Chapter 85 - The Mansions of the Stars

85:1 By the heaven, holding mansions of the stars,

85:2 And by the Promised Day.

85:3 And by the witness and that whereunto he beareth testimony,

85:4 (Self-)destroyed were the owners of the ditch

85:5 Of the fuel-fed fire,

85:6 When they sat by it,

85:7 And were themselves the witnesses of what they did to the *BELIEVERS.*

85:8 They had naught against them save that they *BELIEVED* in Allah, the Mighty, the Owner of Praise,

85:9 Him unto Whom belongeth the Sovereignty of the heavens and the earth; and Allah is of all things the Witness.

85:10 Lo! *THEY WHO PERSECUTE BELIEVING MEN* and *BELIEVING* women and repent not, *THEIRS VERILY WILL BE THE DOOM OF HELL, AND THEIRS THE DOOM OF BURNING.*

85:11 Lo! *THOSE WHO BELIEVE AND DO GOOD WORKS*, theirs will be *GARDENS UNDERNEATH WHICH RIVERS FLOW* [Paradise]. That is *THE GREAT SUCCESS.*

85:12 Lo! the punishment of thy Lord is stern.

85:13 Lo! He it is Who produceth, then reproduceth,

85:14 And He is the Forgiving, the Loving,

85:15 Lord of the Throne of Glory,

85:16 Doer of what He will.

85:17 Hath there come unto thee the story of the hosts [armies]

85:18 Of Pharaoh and (the tribe of) Thamud?

85:19 Nay, but *THOSE WHO DISBELIEVE LIVE IN DENIAL*

85:20 And Allah, all unseen, surroundeth them.

85:21 Nay, but it is a glorious Qur'an.
85:22 On a guarded tablet.

Chapter 91 - The Sun

91:1 By the sun and his brightness,
91:2 And the moon when she followeth him,
91:3 And the day when it revealeth him,
91:4 And the night when it enshroudeth him,
91:5 And the heaven and Him Who built it,
91:6 And the earth and Him Who spread it,
91:7 And a soul and Him Who perfected it
91:8 And inspired it (with conscience of) what is wrong for it and (what is) right for it.
91:9 He is indeed successful who causeth it to grow,
91:10 And he is indeed a failure who stunteth it.
91:11 (The tribe of) Thamud denied (the truth) in their rebellious pride,
91:12 When the basest of them broke forth
91:13 And the messenger of Allah said: It is the she-camel of Allah, so let her drink!
91:14 But they denied him, and they hamstrung her, so Allah doomed them for their sin and razed (their dwellings).
91:15 He dreadeth not the sequel (of events).

Chapter 97 - Power

97:1 Lo! We revealed it on the Night of Predestination.
97:2 Ah, what will convey unto thee what the Night of Power is!
97:3 The Night of Power is better than a thousand months.
97:4 The angels and the Spirit descend therein, by the permission of their Lord, with all decrees.
97:5 (The night is) Peace until the rising of the dawn.

Chapter 80 - He Frowned

80:1 He frowned and turned away
80:2 Because the blind man came unto him.
80:3 What could inform thee but that he might grow (in grace)
80:4 Or take heed and so the reminder might avail him?
80:5 As for him who thinketh himself independent,
80:6 Unto him thou payest regard.
80:7 Yet it is not thy concern if he grow not (in grace).
80:8 But as for him who cometh unto thee with earnest purpose
80:9 And hath fear,
80:10 From him thou art distracted.
80:11 Nay, but verily it is an Admonishment,
80:12 So let whosoever will pay heed to it,
80:13 On honoured leaves
80:14 Exalted, purified,
80:15 (Set down) by scribes
80:16 Noble and righteous.
80:17 Man is (self-)destroyed: how ungrateful!
80:18 From what thing doth He create him?
80:19 From a drop of seed. He createth him and proportioneth him,
80:20 Then maketh the way easy for him,
80:21 Then causeth him to die, and burieth him;
80:22 Then, when He will, He bringeth him again to life.
80:23 Nay, but (man) hath not done what He commanded him.

80:24 Let man consider his food:
80:25 How We pour water in showers
80:26 Then split the earth in clefts
80:27 And cause the grain to grow therein
80:28 And grapes and green fodder
80:29 And olive-trees and palm-trees
80:30 And garden-closes of thick foliage
80:31 And fruits and grasses:
80:32 Provision for you and your cattle.
80:33 But when the Shout cometh
80:34 On the day when a man fleeth from his brother
80:35 And his mother and his father
80:36 And his wife and his children,
80:37 *EVERY MAN THAT DAY WILL HAVE CONCERN ENOUGH TO MAKE HIM HEEDLESS (OF OTHERS).*
80:38 *ON THAT DAY FACES WILL BE BRIGHT AS DAWN,*
80:39 Laughing, rejoicing at good news;
80:40 And *OTHER FACES, ON THAT DAY, WITH DUST UPON THEM,*
80:41 Veiled in darkness,
80:42 Those are *THE DISBELIEVERS, THE WICKED.*

Chapter 53 - The Star

53:1 By the Star when it setteth,
53:2 Your comrade erreth not, nor is deceived;
53:3 Nor doth he speak of (his own) desire.
53:4 It is naught save an inspiration that is inspired,
53:5 Which one of mighty powers hath taught him,
53:6 One vigorous; and he grew clear to view
53:7 When he was on the uppermost horizon.
53:8 Then he drew nigh and came down
53:9 Till he was (distant) two bows' length or even nearer,
53:10 And He revealed unto His slave that which He revealed.
53:11 The heart lied not (in seeing) what it saw.
53:12 Will ye then dispute with him concerning what he seeth?
53:13 And verily he saw him yet another time
53:14 By the lote-tree of the utmost boundary,
53:15 Nigh unto which is the Garden of Abode.
53:16 When that which shroudeth did enshroud the lote-tree,
53:17 The eye turned not aside nor yet was overbold.
53:18 Verily he saw one of the greater revelations of his Lord.
53:19 Have ye thought upon Al-Lat and Al-'Uzza
53:20 And Manat, the third, the other?
53:21 Are yours the males and His the females?
53:22 That indeed were an unfair division!
53:23 They are but names which ye have named, ye and your fathers, for which Allah hath revealed no warrant. They follow but a guess and that which (they) themselves desire. And now the guidance from their Lord hath come unto them.
53:24 Or shall man have what he coveteth?
53:25 But unto Allah belongeth the after (life), and the former.
53:26 And how many angels are in the heavens whose intercession availeth naught save after Allah giveth leave to whom He chooseth and accepteth.
53:27 Lo! it is *THOSE WHO DISBELIEVE IN THE HEREAFTER* who name the angels with the names of females.
53:28 And they have no knowledge thereof. They follow but a guess, and lo! a guess can never take the place of *THE TRUTH*.
53:29 ~~Then withdraw (O Muhammad) from him who fleeth from Our remembrance and desireth but the life of the world.~~ [Cancelled by verse 9:5, i.e. violence replaces indifference][568]

53:30 Such is their sum of knowledge. Lo! thy Lord is Best Aware of him who strayeth, and He is Best Aware of him whom goeth right.

53:31 And unto Allah belongeth whatsoever is in the heavens and whatsoever is in the earth, that *HE MAY REWARD THOSE WHO DO EVIL WITH THAT WHICH THEY HAVE DONE, AND REWARD THOSE WHO DO GOOD WITH GOODNESS,*

53:32 Those who avoid enormities of sin and abominations, save the unwilled offences - (for them) lo! thy Lord is of vast mercy. He is Best Aware of you (from the time) when He created you from the earth, and when ye were hidden in the bellies of your mothers. Therefor ascribe not purity unto yourselves. He is Best Aware of him who wardeth off (*EVIL*).

53:33 Didst thou (O Muhammad) observe him who turned away,

53:34 And gave a little, then was grudging?

53:35 Hath he knowledge of the Unseen so that he seeth?

53:36 Or hath he not had news of what is in the books of Moses

53:37 And Abraham who paid his debt:

53:38 That no laden one shall bear another's load,

53:39 And that man hath only that for which he maketh effort,

53:40 And that his effort will be seen.

53:41 And afterward he will be repaid for it with fullest payment;

53:42 And that thy Lord, He is the goal;

53:43 And that He it is who maketh laugh, and maketh weep,

53:44 And that He it is Who giveth death and giveth life;

53:45 And that He createth the two spouses, the male and the female,

53:46 From a drop (of seed) when it is poured forth;

53:47 And that He hath ordained the second bringing forth;

53:48 And that He it is Who enricheth and contenteth;

53:49 And that He it is Who is the Lord of Sirius;

53:50 And that He destroyed the former (tribe of) A'ad,

53:51 And (the tribe of) Thamud He spared not;

53:52 And the folk of Noah aforetime, Lo! they were more unjust and more rebellious;

53:53 And Al-Mu'tafikah He destroyed

53:54 So that there covered them that which did cover.

53:55 Concerning which then, of the bounties of thy Lord, canst thou dispute?

53:56 This is a warner of the warners of old.

53:57 The threatened Hour is nigh.

53:58 None beside Allah can disclose it.

53:59 Marvel ye then at this statement,

53:60 And laugh and not weep,

53:61 While ye amuse yourselves?

53:62 Rather prostrate yourselves before Allah and serve Him.

Chapter 112 - The Unity

112:1 Say: He is Allah, the One!

112:2 Allah, the eternally Besought of all!

112:3 He begetteth not nor was begotten.

112:4 And there is none comparable unto Him.

114:1 Say: I seek refuge in the Lord of mankind,

114:2 The King of mankind,

114:3 The God of mankind,

114:4 From the *EVIL* of the sneaking whisperer,

114:5 Who whispereth in the hearts of mankind,

Chapter 114 - Mankind

114.001 Say: I seek refuge in the Lord of mankind,

114.002 P: The King of mankind,

114.003 P: The God of mankind,
114.004 P: From the evil of the sneaking whisperer,
114.005 P: Who whispereth in the hearts of mankind,
114.006 P: Of the jinn and of mankind.

Chapter 113 - The Daybreak

113:1 Say: I seek refuge in the Lord of the Daybreak
113:2 From the evil of that which He created;
113:3 From the evil of the darkness when it is intense,
113:4 And from the evil of malignant witchcraft,
113:5 And from the evil of the envier when he envieth.

Chapter 105 - The Elephant

105:1 Hast thou not seen how thy Lord dealt with the owners of the Elephant?
105:2 Did He not bring their stratagem to naught,
105:3 And send against them swarms of flying creatures,
105:4 Which pelted them with stones of baked clay,
105:5 And made them like green crops devoured (by cattle)?

Chapter 109 - The Disbelievers

109:1 Say: O *DISBELIEVERS*!
109:2 I worship not that which ye worship;
109:3 Nor worship ye that which I worship.
109:4 And I shall not worship that which ye worship.
109:5 Nor will ye worship that which I worship.
109:6 Unto you your religion, and unto me my religion. [Tolerance cancelled by violent verse 9:5][569]

Chapter 107 - Small Kindnesses

107:1 Hast thou observed him who belieth religion?
107:2 That is he who repelleth the orphan,
107:3 And urgeth not the feeding of the needy.
107:4 Ah, woe unto worshippers
107:5 Who are heedless of their prayer;
107:6 Who would be seen (at worship)
107:7 Yet refuse small kindnesses!

Chapter 102 - Rivalry in Worldly Increase

102:1 Rivalry in worldly increase distracteth you
102:2 Until ye come to the graves.
102:3 Nay, but ye will come to know!
102:4 Nay, but ye will come to know!
102:5 Nay, would that ye knew (now) with a sure knowledge!
102:6 For ye *WILL BEHOLD HELL-FIRE,*
102:7 Aye, ye will behold it with sure vision.
102:8 Then, *ON THAT DAY*, ye will be asked concerning pleasure.

Chapter 108 - Abundance

108:1 Lo! We have given thee Abundance;
108:2 So pray unto thy Lord, and sacrifice.
108:3 Lo! it is thy insulter (and not thou) who is without posterity.

Chapter 100 - The Coursers

100:1 By the snorting courses,
100:2 Striking sparks of fire
100:3 And scouring to the raid at dawn,
100:4 Then, therewith, with their trail of dust,
100:5 Cleaving, as one, the centre (of the foe),
100:6 Lo! man is an ingrate unto his Lord
100:7 And lo! he is a witness unto that;
100:8 And lo! in the love of wealth he is violent.
100:9 Knoweth he not that, when the contents of the graves are poured forth
100:10 And the secrets of the breasts are made known,
100:11 *ON THAT DAY* will their Lord be perfectly informed concerning them.

Chapter 103 - The Declining Day

103:1 By the declining day,
103:2 Lo! man is a state of loss,
103:3 Save *THOSE WHO BELIEVE AND DO GOOD WORKS*, and exhort one another to truth and *EXHORT ONE ANOTHER TO ENDURANCE.*

Chapter 94 - Solace

94:1 Have We not caused thy bosom to dilate,
94:2 And eased thee of the burden
94:3 Which weighed down thy back;
94:4 And exalted thy fame?
94:5 But lo! with hardship goeth ease,
94:6 Lo! with hardship goeth ease;
94:7 So when thou art relieved, still toil
94:8 And strive to please thy Lord.

Chapter 93 - The Morning Hours

93:1 By the morning hours
93:2 And by the night when it is stillest,
93:3 Thy Lord hath not forsaken thee nor doth He hate thee,
93:4 And verily the latter portion will be better for thee than the former,
93:5 And verily thy Lord will give unto thee so that thou wilt be content.
93:6 Did He not find thee an orphan and protect (thee)?
93:7 Did He not find thee wandering and direct (thee)?
93:8 Did He not find thee destitute and enrich (thee)?
93:9 Therefor the orphan oppress not,
93:10 Therefor the beggar drive not away,
93:11 Therefor of the bounty of thy Lord be thy discourse.

Chapter 89 - The Dawn

89:1 By the Dawn
89:2 And ten nights,
89:3 And the Even and the Odd,
89:4 And the night when it departeth,
89:5 There surely is an oath for thinking man.
89:6 Dost thou not consider how thy Lord dealt with (the tribe of) A'ad,
89:7 With many-columned Iram,
89:8 The like of which was not created in the lands;
89:9 And with (the tribe of) Thamud, who clove the rocks in the valley;
89:10 And with Pharaoh, firm of might,
89:11 Who (all) were rebellious (to Allah) in these lands,
89:12 And multiplied iniquity therein?
89:13 Therefore thy Lord poured on them the disaster of His punishment.
89:14 Lo! thy Lord is ever watchful.
89:15 As for man, whenever his Lord trieth him by honouring him, and is gracious unto him, he saith: My Lord honoureth me.
89:16 But whenever He trieth him by straitening his means of life, he saith: My Lord despiseth me.
89:17 Nay, but ye (for your part) honour not the orphan
89:18 And urge not on the feeding of the poor.
89:19 And ye devour heritages with devouring greed.
89:20 And love wealth with abounding love.
89:21 Nay, but when the earth is ground to atoms, grinding, grinding,
89:22 And thy Lord shall come with angels, rank on rank,
89:23 And *HELL IS BROUGHT NEAR THAT DAY*; on that day man will remember, but how will the remembrance (then avail him)?
89:24 He will say: Ah, would that I had sent before me (some provision) for my life!
89:25 *NONE PUNISHETH AS HE WILL PUNISH ON THAT DAY!*
89:26 None bindeth as He then will bind.
89:27 But ah! thou soul at peace!
89:28 Return unto thy Lord, content in His good pleasure!
89:29 Enter thou among My *BONDMEN*!
89:30 *ENTER THOU MY GARDEN!*

Chapter 92 - The Night

92:1 By the night enshrouding
92:2 And the day resplendent
92:3 And Him Who hath created male and female,
92:4 Lo! your effort is dispersed (toward divers ends).
92:5 As for him who giveth and is dutiful (toward Allah)
92:6 And *BELIEVETH* in goodness;
92:7 Surely We will ease his way unto the state of ease.
92:8 But as for him who hoardeth and deemeth himself independent,
92:9 And *DISBELIEVETH* in goodness;
92:10 Surely We will ease his way unto adversity.
92:11 His riches will not save him when he perisheth.
92:12 Lo! Ours it is (to give) the guidance
92:13 And lo! unto Us belong the latter portion and the former.
92:14 Therefor have *I WARNED YOU OF THE FLAMING FIRE*
92:15 Which only the most wretched must endure,
92:16 He who denieth and turneth away.
92:17 Far removed from it will be the righteous
92:18 Who giveth his wealth that he may grow (in goodness).
92:19 And none hath with him any favour for reward,

92:20 Except as seeking (to fulfil) the purpose of his Lord Most High.
92:21 He verily will be content.

Chapter 87 - The Most High

87:1 Praise the name of thy Lord the Most High,
87:2 Who createth, then disposeth;
87:3 Who measureth, then guideth;
87:4 Who bringeth forth the pasturage,
87:5 Then turneth it to russet stubble.
87:6 We shall make thee read (O Muhammad) so that thou shalt not forget
87:7 Save that which Allah willeth. Lo! He knoweth the disclosed and that which still is hidden;
87:8 And We shall ease thy way unto the state of ease.
87:9 Therefor remind (men), for of use is the reminder.
87:10 He will heed who feareth,
87:11 But the most hapless will flout it,
87:12 He who will be flung to the great Fire
87:13 Wherein he will neither die nor live.
87:14 He is successful who groweth,
87:15 And remembereth the name of his Lord, so prayeth,
87:16 But ye prefer the life of the world
87:17 Although the Hereafter is better and more lasting.
87:18 Lo! This is in the former scrolls.
87:19 The Books of Abraham and Moses.

Chapter 81 - The Overthrowing

81:1 When the sun is overthrown,
81:2 And when the stars fall,
81:3 And when the hills are moved,
81:4 And when the camels big with young are abandoned,
81:5 And when the wild beasts are herded together,
81:6 And when the seas rise,
81:7 And when souls are reunited,
81:8 And when the girl-child that was buried alive is asked
81:9 For what sin she was slain,
81:10 And when the pages are laid open,
81:11 And when the sky is torn away,
81:12 And *WHEN HELL IS LIGHTED,*
81:13 And *WHEN THE GARDEN IS BROUGHT NIGH,*
81:14 (Then) every soul will know what it hath made ready.
81:15 Oh, but I call to witness the planets,
81:16 The stars which rise and set,
81:17 And the close of night,
81:18 And the breath of morning
81:19 That this is in truth the word of an honoured messenger,
81:20 Mighty, established in the presence of the Lord of the Throne,
81:21 (One) to be obeyed, and trustworthy;
81:22 And your comrade is not mad.
81:23 Surely he beheld Him on the clear horizon.
81:24 And he is not avid of the Unseen.
81:25 Nor is this the utterance of a devil worthy to be stoned.
81:26 Whither then go ye?
81:27 This is naught else than a reminder unto creation,
81:28 Unto whomsoever of you willeth to walk straight.
81:29 And ye will not, unless (it be) that Allah willeth, the Lord of Creation.

Chapter 111 - Palm Fibre

111:1 The power of Abu Lahab will perish, and he will perish.
111:2 His wealth and gains will not exempt him.
111:3 *HE WILL BE PLUNGED IN FLAMING FIRE,*
111:4 And his wife, the wood-carrier,
111:5 Will have upon her neck a halter of palm-fibre.

Chapter 1 - The Opening

1:1 In the name of Allah, the Beneficent, the Merciful.
1:2 Praise be to Allah, Lord of the Worlds,
1:3 The Beneficent, the Merciful.
1:4 Master of *THE DAY OF JUDGMENT,*
1:5 Thee (alone) we worship; Thee (alone) we ask for help.
1:6 Show us *THE STRAIGHT PATH,*
1:7 *THE PATH OF THOSE WHOM THOU HAST FAVOURED; NOT THE (PATH) OF THOSE WHO EARN THINE ANGER NOR OF THOSE WHO GO ASTRAY .* [A hostile reference to Jews and Christians].[570]

Chapter 74 - The Cloaked One

74:1 O thou enveloped in thy cloak,
74:2 Arise and warn!
74:3 Thy Lord magnify,
74:4 Thy raiment purify,
74:5 Pollution shun!
74:6 And show not favour, seeking wordly gain!
74:7 For the sake of thy Lord, be patient!
74:8 For when the trumpet shall sound,
74:9 Surely that day will be *A DAY OF ANGUISH,*
74:10 Not of ease, for *DISBELIEVERS*.
74:11 ~~Leave Me (to deal) with him whom I created lonely,~~ [Cancelled by verse 9:5][571]
74:12 And then bestowed upon him ample means,
74:13 And sons abiding in his presence
74:14 And made (life) smooth for him.
74:15 Yet he desireth that I should give more.
74:16 Nay! For lo! he hath been stubborn to Our revelations.
74:17 On him I shall impose a fearful doom.
74:18 For lo! he did consider; then he planned -
74:19 (Self-)destroyed is he, how he planned!
74:20 Again (self-)destroyed is he, how he planned! -
74:21 Then looked he,
74:22 Then frowned he and showed displeasure.
74:23 Then turned he away in pride
74:24 And said: This is naught else than magic from of old;
74:25 This is naught else than speech of mortal man.
74:26 Him shall I fling unto the burning.
74:27 - Ah, what will convey unto thee what that burning is! -
74:28 It leaveth naught; it spareth naught
74:29 It shrivelleth the man.
74:30 Above it are nineteen.
74:31 We have appointed only angels to be wardens of *THE FIRE*, and their number have We made to be a stumbling-block for *THOSE WHO DISBELIEVE*; that those to whom the Scripture hath been given may have certainty, and that *BELIEVERS* may increase in faith; and that those to whom the Scripture hath been given and *BELIEVERS* may not doubt; and that those in whose hearts there is disease, and

DISBELIEVERS, may say: What meaneth Allah by this similitude? Thus Allah sendeth astray whom He will, and whom He will He guideth. None knoweth the hosts [armies] of thy Lord save Him. This is naught else than a Reminder unto mortals.

74:32 Nay, by the Moon
74:33 And the night when it withdraweth
74:34 And the dawn when it shineth forth,
74:35 Lo! this is one of the greatest (portents)
74:36 As a warning unto men,
74:37 Unto him of you who will advance or hang back.
74:38 Every soul is a pledge for its own deeds;
74:39 Save those who will stand on the right hand.
74:40 *IN GARDENS THEY WILL ASK ONE ANOTHER*
74:41 *CONCERNING THE GUILTY:*
74:42 *WHAT HATH BROUGHT YOU TO THIS BURNING?*
74:43 *THEY WILL ANSWER: WE WERE NOT OF THOSE WHO PRAYED*
74:44 Nor did we feed the wretched.
74:45 We used to wade (in vain dispute) with (all) waders,
74:46 *AND WE USED TO DENY THE DAY OF JUDGMENT,*
74:47 Till the Inevitable came unto us.
74:48 The mediation of no mediators will avail them then.
74:49 Why now turn they away from the Admonishment,
74:50 As they were frightened asses
74:51 Fleeing from a lion?
74:52 Nay, but everyone of them desireth that he should be given open pages (from Allah).
74:53 Nay, verily. They fear not the Hereafter.
74:54 Nay, verily. Lo! this is an Admonishment.
74:55 So whosoever will may heed.
74:56 And they will not heed unless Allah willeth (it). He is the fount of fear. He is the fount of Mercy.

Chapter 73 - The Enshrouded One

73:1 O thou wrapped up in thy raiment!
73:2 Keep vigil the night long, save a little -
73:3 A half thereof, or abate a little thereof
73:4 Or add (a little) thereto - and chant the Qur'an in measure,
73:5 For we shall charge thee with a word of weight.
73:6 Lo! the vigil of the night is (a time) when impression is more keen and speech more certain.
73:7 Lo! thou hast by day a chain of business.
73:8 So remember the name of thy Lord and devote thyself with a complete devotion -
73:9 Lord of the East and the West; there is no God save Him; so choose thou Him alone for thy defender
73:10 ~~And bear with patience what they utter, and part from them with a fair leave-taking.~~ [Cancelled by verse 9:5, i.e. violence replaces indifference and patience towards unbelievers][572]
73:11 ~~Leave Me to deal with the deniers, lords of ease and comfort (in this life); and do thou respite them awhile.~~ [Cancelled by verse 9:5, i.e. Muslims to act in the face of unbelief, Kuffar][573]
73:12 Lo! with Us are heavy fetters and a raging fire,
73:13 And food which choketh (the partaker), and *A PAINFUL DOOM*
73:14 On *THE DAY WHEN THE EARTH AND THE HILLS ROCK*, and the hills become a heap of running sand.
73:15 Lo! We have sent unto you a messenger as witness against you, even as We sent unto Pharaoh a messenger.
73:16 But Pharaoh rebelled against the messenger, whereupon We seized him with no gentle grip.
73:17 Then how, if ye *DISBELIEVE*, will ye protect yourselves upon *THE DAY WHICH WILL TURN CHILDREN GREY,*
73:18 The very heaven being then rent asunder. His promise is to be fulfilled.
73:19 Lo! This is a Reminder. Let him who will, then, choose a way unto his Lord.

73:20 Lo! thy Lord knoweth how thou keepest vigil sometimes nearly two-thirds of the night, or (sometimes) half or a third thereof, as do a party of those with thee. Allah measureth the night and the day. He knoweth that ye count it not, and turneth unto you in mercy. Recite, then, of the Qur'an that which is easy for you. He knoweth that there are sick folk among you, while others travel in the land *IN SEARCH OF ALLAH'S BOUNTY*, and *OTHERS (STILL) ARE FIGHTING FOR THE CAUSE OF ALLAH*. So recite of it that which is easy (for you), and establish worship and pay the poor-due, and (so) *LEND UNTO ALLAH A GOODLY LOAN. WHATSOEVER GOOD YE SEND BEFORE YOU FOR YOUR SOULS, YE WILL FIND IT WITH ALLAH, BETTER AND GREATER IN THE RECOMPENSE*. And seek forgiveness of Allah. Lo! Allah is Forgiving, Merciful.[574]

Chapter 68 - The Pen

68:1 Nun. By the pen and that which they write (therewith),
68:2 Thou art not, for thy Lord's favour unto thee, *A MADMAN*.
68:3 And lo! thine verily will be *A REWARD UNFAILING.*
68:4 And lo! thou art of a tremendous nature.
68:5 And thou wilt see and they will see
68:6 *WHICH OF YOU IS THE DEMENTED.*
68:7 Lo! thy Lord is Best Aware of him who strayeth from His way, and He is Best Aware of those who walk aright.
68:8 Therefor *OBEY NOT THOU THE REJECTERS*
68:9 Who would have had thee compromise, that they may compromise.
68:10 Neither obey thou each feeble oath-monger,
68:11 Detracter, spreader abroad of slanders,
68:12 Hinderer of the good, transgressor, malefactor
68:13 Greedy therewithal, intrusive.
68:14 It is because he is possessed of wealth and children
68:15 That, when Our revelations are recited unto him, he saith: *MERE FABLES OF THE MEN OF OLD.*
68:16 *WE SHALL BRAND HIM ON THE NOSE.*
68:17 Lo! *WE HAVE TRIED THEM AS WE TRIED THE OWNERS OF THE GARDEN* when they vowed that they would pluck its fruit next morning,
68:18 And made no exception (for the Will of Allah);
68:19 Then a visitation from thy Lord came upon it while they slept
68:20 And in the morning it was as if plucked.
68:21 And they cried out one unto another in the morning,
68:22 Saying: Run unto your field if ye would pluck (the fruit).
68:23 So they went off, saying one unto another in low tones:
68:24 No needy man shall enter it to-day against you.
68:25 They went betimes, strong in (this) purpose.
68:26 But when they saw it, they said: Lo! we are in error!
68:27 Nay, but we are desolate!
68:28 The best among them said: Said I not unto you: Why glorify ye not (Allah)?
68:29 They said: Glorified be our Lord! Lo! we have been wrong-doers.
68:30 Then some of them drew near unto others, self-reproaching.
68:31 They said: Alas for us! In truth we were outrageous.
68:32 It may be that our Lord will give us better than this in place thereof. Lo! we beseech our Lord.
68:33 Such was the punishment. And verily the punishment of the Hereafter is greater if they did but know.
68:34 Lo! for *THOSE WHO KEEP FROM EVIL ARE GARDENS OF BLISS WITH THEIR LORD.*
68:35 Shall We then treat those who have surrendered as We treat the guilty?
68:36 What aileth you? How foolishly ye judge!
68:37 Or have ye a scripture wherein ye learn
68:38 That ye shall indeed have all that ye choose?
68:39 Or have ye *A COVENANT ON OATH FROM US* that reacheth to *THE DAY OF JUDGMENT*, that yours shall be all that ye ordain?
68:40 Ask them (O Muhammad) which of them will vouch for that!
68:41 Or have they other gods? Then let them bring their other gods if they are truthful,

68:42 On the day when it befalleth in earnest, and they are ordered to prostrate themselves but are not able,

68:43 With eyes downcast, abasement stupefying them. And they had been summoned to prostrate themselves while they were yet unhurt.

68:44 ~~Leave Me (to deal) with those who give the lie to this pronouncement. We shall lead them on by steps [punish] from whence they know not.~~ [Cancelled by verse 9:5][575]

68:45 Yet I bear with them, for lo! My scheme is firm.

68:46 Or dost thou (Muhammad) ask a fee from them so that they are heavily taxed?

68:47 Or is the Unseen theirs that they can write (thereof)?

68:48 ~~But wait thou for thy Lord's decree, and be not like him of the fish, who cried out in despair.~~ [Cancelled by verse 9:5, i.e. violence replaces indifference and patience towards unbelievers][576]

68:49 Had it not been that favour from his Lord had reached him he surely had been cast into the wilderness while he was reprobate.

68:50 But his Lord chose him and placed him among the righteous.

68:51 And lo! *THOSE WHO DISBELIEVE* would fain disconcert thee with their eyes when they hear the Reminder, and they say: Lo! he is indeed mad;

68:52 When it is naught else than a Reminder to creation.

Chapter 96 - The Clot

96:1 Read: In the name of thy Lord Who createth,

96:2 Createth man from a clot.

96:3 Read: And thy Lord is the Most Bounteous,

96:4 Who teacheth by the pen,

96:5 Teacheth man that which he knew not.

96:6 Nay, but verily *MAN IS REBELLIOUS*

96:7 *THAT HE THINKETH HIMSELF INDEPENDENT!*

96:8 Lo! unto thy Lord is the return.

96:9 Hast thou seen him who dissuadeth

96:10 A slave when he prayeth?

96:11 Hast thou seen if he relieth on the guidance (of Allah)

96:12 Or enjoineth piety?

96:13 Hast thou seen if he denieth (Allah's guidance) and is froward?

96:14 Is he then unaware that Allah seeth?

96:15 Nay, but if he cease not We will seize him by the forelock -

96:16 The lying, sinful forelock -

96:17 Then let him call upon his henchmen!

96:18 *WE WILL CALL THE GUARDS OF HELL.*

96:19 Nay, Obey not thou him. But prostrate thyself, and draw near (unto Allah)

NOTES

[1] "Obama in Cairo", *PBS*, 4 June 2009,
http://www.pbs.org/wnet/religionandethics/2009/06/04/june-5-2009-obama-in-cairo/3205/.

[2] On the myth of the tolerance of Islamic Spain see Emmet Scott, *The Impact of Islam*, London, 2014; Dario Fernandez Morera, *The Myth of the Andalusian Paradise: Muslims, Christians, and Jews under Islamic Rule in Medieval Spain*, Wilmington, 2016. The following are just a sample of the books refuting this lie that Islam is tolerant and peaceful: Paul Fregosi, *Jihad in the West: Muslim Conquests from the 7th to the 21st Centuries*, New York, 1998; Bat Ye'or, *Islam and Dhimmitude: Where Civilisations Collide*, Lancaster, 2002; Don Richardson, *Secrets of the Koran*, Ventura, California, 2003; Andrew Bostom (ed), *The Legacy of Jihad: Islamic Holy War and the Fate of Non-Muslims*, New York, 2005; Robert Spencer (ed), *The Myth of Islamic Tolerance: How Islamic Law Treats Non-Muslims*, New York, 2005; Robert Spencer, *Religion of Peace: Why Christianity Is And Islam Isn't*, Washington, 2007; Bruce Bawer, *Surrender: Appeasing Islam, Sacrificing Freedom*, New York, 2009. Andrew Bostom, *Sharia Versus Freedom: The Legacy of Islamic Totalitarianism*, New York, 2012.

[3] "O mankind! We have created you male and a female; and we have made you into nations and tribes so that you may know one another". From "Text: Obama's Speech in Cairo", *New York Times*, 4 June 2009,
http://www.nytimes.com/2009/06/04/us/politics/04obama.text.html#.

[4] In the Koran, peace is something only granted to Muslims, believers in Islam and only insofar as they are obedient Muslims, carrying out the commands of Allah. For example: "Allah was well pleased with the believers when they swore allegiance unto thee beneath the tree, and He knew what was in their hearts, and He sent down peace of reassurance on them, and hath rewarded them with a near victory; And much booty [slaves and loot] that they will capture" (Koran 48:18-48:19). See also "And if two parties of believers fall to fighting, then make peace between them. And if one party of them doeth wrong to the other, fight ye that which doeth wrong till it return unto the ordinance of Allah; then, if it return, make peace between them justly, and act equitably" (Koran 49:9).

[5] *Tafsir Al-Qurtubi: Classical Commentary on the Holy Qur'an*, translated by Aisha Bewley, London, 2003. As Christian Spaniards retook Spain from the Muslim invaders, the "tolerant" expert Qurtubi moved to Egypt (another land taken from Christians).
https://en.wikipedia.org/wiki/Al-Qurtubi/.

[6] *The Noble Qur'an : A New Rendering of its Meaning in English* [trans.] Abdul Haqq Bewley and Aisha Bewley, Norwich, 1999.

[7] *Tafsir Al-Qurtubi: Classical Commentary on the Holy Qur'an*, translated by Aisha Bewley, London, 2003, p.xvii.

[8] *Tafsir Al-Qurtubi: Classical Commentary on the Holy Qur'an*, translated by Aisha Bewley, London, 2003, pp.490-491.

[9] *Tafsir Al-Qurtubi: Classical Commentary on the Holy Qur'an*, translated by Aisha Bewley, London, 2003, p.496.

[10] In May 2013, after two Muslim converts murdered a soldier on the streets of London, Sheikh Bewley released the following video (saying "there is no justification whatsoever in Islam for this horrendous act of violence [...] it is quite clear these two men are suffering from serious mental illness"), https://youtu.be/p23Ai5y40yE?t=54#. In November 2015, after Muslims working for Islamic State organised multiple simultaneous attacks on Paris, Sheikh Bewley released the following video: https://www.youtube.com/watch?v=96hAkq9Y1LM. Following a further attack on the offices of the cartoon magazine *Charlie Hebdo*, Sheikh Bewley released another video (saying the attack was "a dreadful crime that has no justification under Islamic law"), https://youtu.be/lQLUFadhN5Q?t=18#.

[11] Dr. Patrick Sookhdeo quotes a 2006 study by the *Combatting Terrorism Center* which found that Qurtubi ranked fourth in all the Islamic commentators cited by Jihadi terrorists, the Jihadis believing themselves commanded by Allah to engage in the kind of warfare and

genocide that Mohammed and his Companions conducted in the seventh century (see *Global Jihad: The Future in the Face of Militant Islam*, London, 2007, p.309). Lest you think that the Jihadis have plucked a scholar like Qurtubi from obscurity, here is what *The Encyclopaedia of Islam* has to say about Qurtubi: "His commentary is of great richness and of great utility... all the authors... acknowledge it and insist on the benefit which may be derived from it" (see Andrew Bostom, *Sharia Versus Freedom: the Legacy of Islamic Totalitarianism*, New York, 2012, p.582). From this we can conclude that Ms. Bewley and Sheikh Bewley are not idiosyncratic in appreciating the importance of Qurtubi's scholarly interpretation. Qurtubi is precisely so significant for our exposition since his commentary on the Koran was translated by educated converts to Islam, people who could by no means be classed as "Jihadi", "Salafi" or "Wahhabi". That people whom no-one would regard as extremist should spend their time translating a scholar that Muslim terrorists take as their inspiration shows how meaningless are all these attempts to separate off "Muslim extremists" from "moderate Muslims". Whilst the Wahhabi movement dates from the eighteenth century and the Salafi movement dates from the early twentieth century (see Hamid Enayat, *Modern Islamic Political Thought*, Austin, Texas, 1982, pp.41-42), both movements hark back to the Islam of the seventh century. Thus, the same "Islamic fundamentalism" is propounded from the seventh century to the thirteenth century, and from the eighteenth century to the twenty-first century. Moreover, the warfare, sieges, genocide and slave-taking of Muslims between the thirteenth century and the eighteenth century shows that there are has really never been any significant length of time in which Islam could be regarded as peaceful or tolerant.

[12] The United Nations Convention on Genocide makes it clear that the destruction of a religion is genocide: "intent to destroy, in whole or in part, a national, ethnical, racial or religious group" (see https://treaties.un.org/doc/publication/unts/volume %2078/volume-78-i-1021-english.pdf). Qurtubi says that with the Koran "the goal is to abolish disbelief and that is clear", that is, to wipe out all that is not Islam. This makes it clear that Islam is genocidal.

[13] Ibn Warraq, *The Islam in Islamic Terrorism: The Importance of Beliefs, Ideas, and Ideology*, London, 2017, p. 133)

[14] Allah "hath sent His messenger with the guidance and the religion of truth, that He may make it conqueror of all religion however much idolaters may be averse" (*Koran* 61:9).

[15] *Dictionary of the Middle Ages*, Volume 7, New York, 1986, p.110. This thirteen-volume encyclopaedia was produced under the auspices of the American Council of Learned Societies, and the articles were written by hundreds of experts from the world's top universities.

[16] The volumes of the first edition of the *Encyclopaedia of Islam* appeared between 1913 and 1936, and despite being prohibitively expensive, it was so popular that it sold out and became a collector's edition. In 1953, the thousands of pages were condensed down to a six-hundred-page *Shorter Encyclopaedia of Islam*. It is to this condensed version which we refer in this book. The entries in the *Shorter Encyclopaedia of Islam* are the same entries as in the full encyclopaedia. This shorter version of the Encyclopaedia is 650 A4 pages, whilst the full version has over 6,000 pages. The current edition of the full encyclopaedia costs around $25,000. There can be no doubt about the authoritative status of this reference book.

[17] This passage is taken from H.A.R. Gibb and J.H.Kramers, *Shorter Encyclopaedia of Islam: Edited on Behalf of the Royal Netherlands Academy*, London, 1953, p.89. The actual entry in the Encyclopaedia is listed as "Djihad", so the spelling of this word in English has obviously changed in recent years. That the spelling has changed means that when one is looking back into even the recent past, it can be difficult to find what our own experts were warning us of about Islam in our lifetime. The immediate definition of Jihad in this encyclopaedia is "holy war", not the deceitful concept of "inner struggle" which has been used by our politicians and journalists to confuse the public in recent decades.

[18] In 2007, just a couple of years after Muslims detonated bombs on the London Underground, a professor at the University of London named Efraim Karsh published a book entitled *Islamic Imperialism: A History* (Yale University Press, London). The book

contains chapters with titles such as "The Warrior Prophet", "The House of Islam and the House of War". Here's how Prof. Karsh shows that Islam was not about simply fighting off oppressors:

> Expelling occupiers from one's patrimony is an act of self-liberation. Conquering foreign lands and subjugating their populations is pure imperialism [... Yet] this is precisely what Muhammad asked of his followers once he had fled from his hometown of Mecca (in 622) to the town of Medina to become a political and military leader rather than a private preacher: not to rid themselves of foreign occupation but to strive for a new universal order in which the whole of humanity would embrace Islam or live under its domination. As he told his followers in his farewell address: "I was ordered to fight all men until they say 'There is no god but Allah'". (p.3)

For further examples see the two dozen items published before the end of the twentieth century and listed in the "Recommended Books" at the end of the book you are reading.

[19] Sam Harris, *The End of Faith: Religion, Terror and the Future of Reason*, London, 2004, p.123.

[20] Unbeknownst to us, in her 2013 book *American Betrayal* (on communist infiltration at the heart of American politics), Diana West not only drew attention to the key principle of abrogation and how this principle negates any peace or tolerance found in the Koran. but she also goes on to describe the claim that Islam is a religion of peace as "The Big Lie" (p.344).

[21] For some strange reason, there are people who balk at any mention of the idea of an elite group in our democracies, which shows how well the brainwashing has worked. Quite simply, someone is a member of the elite if they have more political influence than an ordinary voter. For instance, at the most trivial level, those to whom television programmes turn repeatedly for opinion on current affairs are members of the elite. You will notice that this group includes anyone but representatives of the single biggest class in Western democracies: the white working class. If you still think this concept of an elite is bogus, search the politics section of any newspaper website for the word "elite" and you will find that in the last few years this has become a common term. Before the concept became vogue in recent years there were many books in politics which attempted to wake the public up to the power of elite groups, for example Christopher Lasch, *The Revolt of the Elites and the Betrayal of Democracy*, New York,1995; Rodney Atkinson, *Europe's Full Circle: Corporate Elites and the New Fascism*, Compuprint, 1996; Peter Oborne, *The Triumph of the Political Class*, London, 2007. In the late nineteenth century and early twentieth-century there were many academics who demonstrated how the elite manipulated democracy in their interest. Probably the most famous was anarchist and academic Roberto Michels, in his 1915 study *Political Parties*. Most of those who studied this book were on the Left, but by the 1960s these Leftists had mostly fallen silent on the power of the elite, perhaps an indication that they saw their political agenda was holding sway among the elites across Western democracies. With European peoples turning against the European Union (the deceptive, anti-democratic, elitist project *par excellence*), journalists appear to have been left with no choice but to discuss how the electorate are turning against the elite.

[22] You can see from the table in Appendix 1, that whilst most modern websites discussing the Koran agree on the order, Rodwell's Koran from 1861 is rather discrepant. However, even Rodwell agreed that Chapter 5 and Chapter 9 are among the last three chapters of the Koran when arranged chronologically. For a fuller discussion of the chronology of the Koran from the perspective of Islamic scholars, see Allamah Abu Abd Allah al-Zanjani, *History of the Quran*. A copy of this book can be found on the tanzil.net website, one of the best websites explaining the chronology of the Koran. http://www.webcitation.org/query?url=http://tanzil.net/pub/ebooks/History-of-Quran.pdf&date=2011-05-13 Al-Zanjani cites other Muslim scholars who put Chapter 9 and Chapter 5 as the last "revelations" of Mohammed. When the English scholar Sell wrote his account of the chronology of the Koran (1905), he offered three different chronologies (see Edward Sell, *The Historical Development of the Qur'an* [1906], 4th edition, London, 1923, p.203). In all three of the

alternative chronologies offered by Sell, Chapter 9 is either the last chapter or the penultimate chapter of the Koran. There is thus an immense amount of scholarship showing that the Koran ends with commands to wage war against non-Muslims. To our knowledge, there is no scholarship that places Chapter 9 anywhere other than at the end of the chronological Koran.

[23] *Koran* 2:256.

[24] W. Montgomery Watt, *Bell's Introduction to the Qur'an* (completely revised and enlarged), Edinburgh, 1970, pp.108-120. Bell notes that the German scholar Theodor Nöldeke was the most important nineteenth-century scholar with regard to the chronological ordering of the Koran (see Bell, p.109). Nöldeke's book was published in 1860, 1909, 1913 and 1938, attesting to the importance of this book, and to the widespread knowledge among educated Germans about the chronological order of the Koran. By contrast, Bell's own works on the chronological Koran have been almost entirely forgotten since the 1960s. Bell also lists other scholars who preceded him in their interest in the Koran, most notably Rodwell (1861) and Sir William Muir (1858,1861) in English; Hartwig Herschfeld (1878, 1886, 1902) and Hubert Grimme (1895) in German; Regis Blanchere in French (1947, 1949, 1951). See Bell, p.111-112.

Bell's *Introduction to the Qur'an* was reissued in 1970, edited by one of the twentieth-century's most notable apologists for Islam, W. Montgomery Watt. The Foreword to this "revised edition" makes it clear that Watt has adopted the position of Dhimmi, saying that he has altered the way that Bell talks of the Koran, removing references where Bell had referred to it as "Mohammed's Koran". Watt explains the dhimmitude of his scholarship thus:

> One major change in the form of expression has seemed desirable. Bell followed his European predecessors in speaking of the Qur'an as Muhammad's own [...] With the greatly increased contacts between Muslims and Christians during the last quarter of a century, it has become imperative for a Christian scholar not to offend Muslim readers gratuitously, but as far as possible to present his arguments in a form acceptable to them. (p.vi)

Thus, the position of critical and independent scholar Bell was subjected to the revisionism of an apologist for Islam. It should perhaps come as no surprise that it is extremely difficult for a reader in the twenty-first century to locate an original copy of Bell's *Qur'an*, or Bell's *Introduction to the Qur'an*. The revisionists have been extremely thorough, to the extent that few people interested in the critical interpretation of Islam are even aware of the necessity to understand the chronological ordering of the Koran.

[25] W. Montgomery Watt, *Bell's Introduction to the Qur'an*, Edinburgh, 1970, pp.205-213. For a general readership, rather than worry about the vagaries of when to use "kafirs" and "kuffar", we prefer to use just a single term throughout this book. For us the word "Kuffar" means "the individual unbeliever" or "a group of unbelievers". Also, we use the word "Kuffar" to mean "any and all of those beliefs which are opposed by Islam". This is because the single most important lesson the non-Muslim can learn (be he Buddhist, atheist, Christian, Jew, Hindu, nationalist or Communist) is that Islam is violently opposed to him, simply on the basis that his beliefs as a non-Muslim are not Islamic. Thus, we group all these belief systems and any associated identities under the word "Kuffar" (Islam groups all unbelievers together into a world of unbelief). It is immaterial to us whether or not Muslims or Arabic speakers tell us this is inaccurate. Combatting the idea that Islam is peaceful and tolerant is the single most vital lesson for all non-Muslims to learn, and this is an idea which almost the entire infrastructure of our own society is committed to concealing from the public.

[26] For a discussion of the word "kuffar" and comparison with the word "nigger" see this article: "The Worst Word", *The Centre for the Study of Political Islam*, 17 Jun 2017, https://www.politicalislam.com/the-worst-word/.

[27] Of the post-WW2 scholars, in 1961 the great Islamic scholar Maxime Rodinson had this to say about the difficulties in writing his biography of Mohammed: "How can one distinguish what is basically authentic from what is not, the true from the false? [...] We still

have the text of the Koran. It is very hard to use, being generally extremely enigmatic, and requiring lengthy labours to get it into chronological order..." (Maxime Rodinson, *Mohammed* [1961], trans. Anne Carter, New York, 1971, p.xi). A decade after he first wrote his biography of Mohammed, Rodinson was lamenting that all critical accounts of Islam had become unthinking apologism for Islam: "the anti-colonialist left... often goes so far as to sanctify Islam... to number among the conceptions permeated with imperialism, any criticism of the Prophet's moral attitudes... Understanding has given way to apologetics pure and simple." See Maxime Rodinson, "The Western Image and Western Studies of Islam", in Joseph Schacht (ed.) *The Legacy of Islam*, Oxford, 1974.

[28] *Reliance of the Traveller: A Classic Manual of Islamic Sacred Law*, trans. Sheikh Keller, 1997, section h8.17.

> The seventh category [of Charity] is those fighting for Allah, meaning people engaged in Islamic military operations [...] They are given enough to suffice them for the operation, even if affluent [...] Though nothing has been mentioned here of the expense involved in supporting such people's families during this period, it seems clear that they should also be given it...

[29] Dr. Sookhdeo lists various different kinds of Jihadi violence. Among these is the violence inflicted by Jihadis against other Muslims whom the Jihadi thinks have become apostates or dissenters. Patrick Sookhdeo, *Understanding Islamic Terrorism*, 2004, Pewsey, p.59. A prime example of this in the UK was a Jihadi who drove across Britain to kill a Muslim he had never even met but whom the Jihadi concluded was not sufficiently Muslim. "Man who murdered Glasgow shopkeeper Asad Shah in sectarian attack jailed", *The Guardian*, 9 Aug 2016, https://www.theguardian.com/uk-news/2016/aug/09/tanveer-ahmed-jailed-for-murder-glasgow-shopkeeper-in-sectarian-attack. At the same time, another example in the UK was an imam in Rochdale who was murdered by other Muslims because they thought some of his religious behaviour was un-Islamic. "Jalal Uddin murder: Syeedy guilty over Rochdale imam death", *BBC*, 16 Sept 2016, http://www.bbc.co.uk/news/uk-england-manchester-37388073/.

[30] See Koran 4:56.

[31] In the *Koran* there are over one hundred references to gardens of Paradise, which are almost always contrasted with the fires of Hell. "A similitude of **the Garden** which those who keep their duty (to Allah) are promised: Therein are **rivers of water** unpolluted, and **rivers of milk** whereof the flavour changeth not, and **rivers of wine** delicious to the drinkers, and rivers of clear-run honey; therein for them is every kind of fruit, with pardon from their Lord. (Are those who enjoy all this) like those who are immortal in the Fire and are given boiling water to drink so that it teareth their bowels?" *Koran* 47:15. See also 9:21, 5:85, 48:5, 57:12, 4:56, 3:15, 30:15, 42:7, 25:10, 7:44, 7:50, 85:11.

[32] Koran 9:111. See also Koran 8:15 and 8:16, where it is stated than any believer who runs from a battle with an unbeliever is going to Hell. Koran 57:19 says that those who are in Paradise are the martyred believers; the disbelievers are burning in Hell. Koran 47:4, which is explicitly about beheading unbelievers in war with Muslims, states: "those who are slain in the way of Allah, He rendereth not their actions vain". We see here that "the way of Allah" is connected to Jihad, and that those Jihadis who are martyred are rewarded for their death. If you doubt our interpretation, here is what Professor Rudolph Peters has to say: "The most important function of the doctrine of Jihad is that it mobilizes and motivates Muslims to take part in wars against unbelievers, as it is considered to be the fulfilment of a religious duty. This motivation is strongly fed by the idea that those who are killed on the battlefield, called martyrs [...] will go directly to Paradise". Rudolph Peters, *Jihad in Classical and Modern Islam*, Princeton, 1996 (from Andrew Bostom (ed.) *The Legacy of Jihad: Islamic Holy War and the Fate of Non-Muslims*, New York, 2005, p.323). Peters was Professor at the University of Amsterdam and director of the Netherlands Institute in Cairo.

[33] Every day when Muslims gather to pray they collectively recite Surah One of the Koran, a seven line verse which culminates in the denunciation of Jews and Christians.

[34] Ernest Renan, "L'Islam et la science", quoted in Christopher Caldwell, (2009) *Reflections on the Revolution in Europe*, London, p.93.

[35] Christopher Caldwell, (2009) *Reflections on the Revolution in Europe*, London, p.232.

[36] In 1965 the publishing company Routledge of London, one of the most famous publishers in the English-speaking world, issued a book by J.J.Saunders, *A History of Medieval Islam*. Saunders was an academic historian. The first few chapters of the book have titles such as "The First Conquests", "The Civil Wars", "The Arab Empire", clearly indicating that top publishers were displaying the mainstream academic opinion that Islam was anything but "a religion of peace". Moreover, the first page of the text by Saunders shows that the Islamic State is a fundamental part of Islam:

> the memorable struggles of Church and State, from which emerged the Western theory and practice of civil and political liberty, had no counterpart in Islam, which knows no distinction between secular and ecclesiastical, and [Islam] is puzzled by our concepts of representative government and a free society. (p.vii)

In the decades since Saunders' book was published, America and Europe have been struggling with an ever-growing Muslim population, a very significant number of whom do not want any separation between Islam and the State. Yet at the end of this book from the 1960s Saunders says:

> Spiritually and intellectually, the future of Islam remains doubtful. The efforts [...] to re-formulate Islamic law and doctrine in a manner more acceptable to the modern world have won little support or favour from the *ulama* [the Islamic clerical scholars...] Some social reforms have been achieved: slavery and concubinage, both sanctioned by the Koran, have vanished over a large part of the Muslim world, and here and there the veil has been discarded... (p.203)

Saunders' pessimistic view on the lack of reform in Islam might as well have been written in 2015 rather than 1965. Not only is it exceptional in the West to meet a Muslim woman who is not veiled in some way, but we have seen the return of sex-slavery with the rise of Boko Haram in Nigeria and of Islamic State in Syria. Muslims are far more regressive now than in 1965.

In the same year that Saunders' book was published Hugh Trevor-Roper, an Oxford professor and one of Britain's most famous twentieth-century historians, had this to say in a book aimed at the general public:

> By the time of his death in 632, the Prophet of Islam had already conquered Arabia, and his successors, immediately afterwards, set out to conquer the rest of the East. This Moslem conquest first of Syria and Egypt, then of North Africa and Spain, cut Europe off from the Mediterranean [...] The old world had ended by the eighth century; a new world did then begin; and among the causes of the change we cannot exclude the Moslem invasions. — *The Rise of Christian Europe*, Norwich, 1965, pp.72-73.

The work of Belgian historian Charles Pirenne is the basis for Trevor-Roper's remarks: Pirenne's book *Mohammed and Charlemagne*, which blames the Dark Ages in Europe on the rise of Islam, was published in 1935, and translated into English in 1992.

[37] Tom Clancy, *Executive Orders*, New York, 1996, p.839.

[38] It is not even clear from this transcript of Bush's speech, taken directly from the White House archive, just which part of the Koran President Bush is supposedly quoting, nor where his claimed quotation ends and his propaganda begins. https://georgewbush-whitehouse.archives.gov/news/releases/2001/09/20010917-11.html/.

[39] See Lawrence Wright, *The Looming Tower: Al-Qaeda's Road to 9/11*, New York, 2006, pp.177-179.

[40] See Lawrence Wright, *The Looming Tower: Al-Qaeda's Road to 9/11*, New York, 2006, pp.296-300.

[41] Al-Baladuri's ninth century book on the rise of Islam was translated into English as *The Origins of the Islamic State* (Columbia University Press, London and New York, 1916). This

book tells of the wars and conquests of the Arabs from the time of Mohammed in seventh century Arabia to the wars and conquests in the ninth century across Europe, Africa and Asia. It covers the conquests of lands from Arabia to Egypt, North Africa, and Spain in the west, and in the east to Iraq, Iran, and Sind (the latter of which is part of Pakistan). *The Origins of the Islamic State* begins with Mohammed arriving in Medina (confirming that the Islamic calendar is coterminous with the attempts of Muslims to rule over non-Muslims everywhere). From this point in his life Mohammed was regarded by western experts as having transitioned from being "a prophet" to being "a statesman" ('statesman' is an overly-polite word for someone who set about robbing and killing, someone who in the twenty-first century we would expect to be executed for war crimes). Dr. Hitti, the translator of *The Origins of the Islamic State*, ended up as Professor of Semitic Literature at Princeton University until 1954. He was involved in several famous political exchanges with Albert Einstein, and Hitti played a role in setting up the United Nations. In 2015, nearly 100 years after Hitti's translation, Robert Hoyland, a professor at New York University, published *In God's Path: the Arab Conquests and the Creation of an Islamic Empire*, a book which reconfirms the history of wars and conquests as told in *The Origins of the Islamic State*. Yet as far as the discourse of journalists, politicians and clergy was concerned, Islam was still "a religion of peace", even as the reformed Islamic State in Syria and Iraq was issuing Koranic justifications for its war, for its obscene executions, and for the reintroduction of Islamic sex-slavery. As far as most public discourse in the West in the twenty-first century was concerned, it was as if books like *The Origins of the Islamic State* and *In God's Path* (and scores of scholarly books in between) had never been published. In the last three decades of the twentieth century Bat Ye'or published multiple books (translated from French into English and Russian) on the subjugation of Jews and Christians under Islam and in *Islam and Dhimmitude: Where Civilisations Collide (Lancaster, 2002)*, she discusses the rise of the Islamic State and the subsequence brutal conquests of the lands around Medina (pp.35-42). The return of the Islamic State in Syria and Iraq in the summer of 2014 could not have been seen by informed individuals as anything other than the latest implementation of the ideal of Islam the religion of war.

[42] This book can be found in the British Library. http://primocat.bl.uk/F/? func=direct&local_base=PRIMO&doc_number=001108593&format=001&con_lng=eng#.

[43] Peter Hopkirk, *On Secret Service East of Constantinople: The Plot To Bring Down The British Empire* (London, 1994) discusses the attempts by German agents to foment Jihad against the British in India, Iran, Caucuses, Afghanistan.

> As an infidel, of course, the Kaiser had no authority to summon Muslims to a Holy War [...] only the Ottoman Sultan himself, in his capacity of Caliph of all Islam, had the authority which was required to issue such an awesome order. It was essential, therefore, that Turkey should ally itself with Germany, regardless of the best interests of its [German] people. [...] Within three months of the outbreak of war, Turkey threw in its lot with Germany [...] and one week later the Sultan called upon Muslims everywhere to rise and slay their Christian oppressors "wherever you may find them". [...] In mosques and bazaars through the East rumours were circulated that the German Emperor had been secretly converted to Islam. 'Haji' Wilhelm Mohammed – as he was now said to call himself – had even made a pilgrimage, incognito, to Mecca [...] word was to be spread that the entire German nation had followed their emperor's example and converted to Islam *en masse*. (pp.3-4)

It might come as little surprise following victory in World War I that Britain decided that the Caliphate must be destroyed. See also Barry Rubin and Wolfgang Schwanitz, *Nazis, Islamists and the Making of the Modern Middle East*, Yale University Press, New Haven, 2014, p.52. For decades around the turn of the twenty-first century, Germany imported millions of Turkish immigrants. Before the end of the twentieth century, Chancellor Helmut Kohl said, "If we today give in to demands for dual citizenship, we would soon have four, five, or six million Turks in Germany instead of three million". See Philip Martin, "Germany: Managing Migration in the Twenty-First Century", in Wayne Cornelius, *Controlling*

Immigration: A Global Perspective, Stanford, 2004, p. 246. Germany's associations with the former Islamic State (the Ottoman Empire) are long and deep.

[44] Raymond Schults, *Crusader in Babylon*, University of Nebraska Press, Lincoln, 1972, pp.66-83.

[45] The three lions of Richard 1st are still the Royal arms of England. They are to be found on the currency of the realm and are even used as the emblem of the England football team.

[46] "Between the sixteenth and nineteenth centuries, over one million Europeans [...] became chattel [slaves] in Northern Africa [...] In 1786, John Adams and Thomas Jefferson, then the U.S. Ambassadors to Britain and France respectively, met in London with the Tripolitanian [Libyan] envoy to Britain and asked him why his pirates were preying on American ships; he explained [...] the pirates' actions were

> founded on the Laws of their Prophet, that it was written in their Koran, that all nations who should not have acknowledged their authority were sinners, that it was their right and duty to make war upon them wherever they could be found, and to make slaves of all they could take as Prisoners, and that every Musselman who should be slain in Battle was sure to go to Paradise.

In their own eyes, in short, as well as in the eyes of the Muslim governments of the day, the Barbary pirates were engaged not in criminality but in Jihad [...] once America had built up seagoing forces that were up to the job it sent in the Navy and Marines to put an end to this [...] thus the line in the Marine Corps hymn about 'the shores of Tripoli'..." All three of the above paragraphs are quoted from Bruce Bawer, *Surrender: Appeasing Islam, Sacrificing Freedom*, New York, 2009, p.4.

[47] Joseph Pitts, *A Faithful Account of the Religion and Manners of the Mahometans*. By 1731, a third edition of this book had been printed.

[48] Frederick Quinn, *The Sum of All Heresies: The Image of Islam in Western Thought*, Oxford University Press, Oxford, 2008, p.55. In 2012 a movie was released entitled "The Day of the Siege: September Eleven 1683", starring F. Murray Abraham. https://en.wikipedia.org/wiki/September_Eleven_1683 Sadly most people still do not understand the significance of the date chosen for the airplane attack on the World Trade Center.

[49] M.A.Khan, *Islamic Jihad: A Legacy of Forced Conversion, Imperialism, and Slavery*, Felibri, 2008, p.246. Almost every book on Cervantes mentions that the novelist was enslaved by Muslims.

[50] Frederick Quinn, *The Sum of All Heresies: The Image of Islam in Western Thought*, Oxford University Press, Oxford, 2008, p.53.

[51] "The First Crusade commenced in 1096 when Byzantine Emperor Alexius Comnenus appealed to the Pope and princes of Europe for assistance against the Seljuk Turks who had recently overrun the whole of Asia Minor and now threatened Constantinople itself [the heart of Orthodox Christianity]. The fall of Constantinople must have placed the safety of Europe in jeopardy." Emmet Scott, *The Impact of Islam*, London, 2014, p.86.

[52] Whilst deceiving the American population (and much of the rest of the Western world), President Bush's approval ratings in the US were at 80% (and peaked at 92%). See https://en.wikipedia.org/wiki/File:George_W_Bush_approval_ratings.svg/. This could so easily have been turned on its head if within America Muslims, journalists, academics, clergy and other politicians had contradicted Bush with what was common knowledge about Islam among the educated elite. No-one who looked back to texts on Islam written before World War II would have much trouble discovering that Bush was carrying out the most brazen lie. President Bush might as well have taken lessons in propaganda from Adolf Hitler: "in the big lie there is always a certain force of credibility; because the broad masses of a nation are always more easily corrupted in the deeper strata of their emotional nature than consciously or voluntarily; and thus in the primitive simplicity of their minds they more readily fall victims to the big lie than the small lie, since they themselves often tell small lies in little matters but would be ashamed to resort to large-scale falsehoods. It would never come into their heads to fabricate colossal untruths, and they would not

believe that others could have the impudence to distort the truth so infamously. Even though the facts which prove this to be so may be brought clearly to their minds, they will still doubt and waver and will continue to think that there may be some other explanation." Adolf Hitler, *Mein Kampf*, [trans. James Murphy, 1939], Jaico Publishing House, 2007, p.104. Whilst Hitler was claiming that he had learned this technique from observing Jews and Marxists, there seems no doubt that he not only believed it to be a true observation, but that the National Socialists would go on to use this technique themselves to devastating effect.

[53] The only part of that paragraph which comes from the Koran are the following sentences: "In the long run, evil in the extreme will be the end of those who do evil. For that they rejected the signs of Allah and held them up to ridicule." In the translation of the Koran from which these sentences come, they are not even two sentences, but one sentence. http://corpus.quran.com/translation.jsp?chapter=30&verse=10#. It is reported that Bush was advised by Karen Armstrong and by Professor Bernard Lewis.

> But Mr Bush was staking his bet on the assumption that the Islamists were not speaking for Islam; that the world's Muslims long for modernity; that they are themselves repelled by the violence of the terrorists; that, most significantly, Islam is in its nature a religion that can be "internalized", like the world's other great religions, and that the traditional Islamic aspiration to conjoin worldly political with otherworldly spiritual authority had somehow gone away. It didn't help that Mr Bush took for his advisers on the nature of Islam, the paid operatives of Washington's Council on American-Islamic Relations, the happyface pseudo-scholar Karen Armstrong, or the profoundly learned but terminally vain Bernard Lewis. Each, in a different way, assured him that Islam and modernity were potentially compatible.

The question, "But what if they are not?" was never seriously raised, because it could not be raised behind the mud curtain of political correctness that has descended over the Western academy and intelligentsia. The idea that others see the world in a way that is not only incompatible with, but utterly opposed to, the way we see it, is the thorn ever-present in the rose bushes of multiculturalism. "Ideas have consequences", and the idea that Islam imagines itself in a fundamental, physical conflict with everything outside of itself, is an idea with which people in the contemporary West are morally and intellectually incapable of coming to terms. David Warren, "Revisitation", *Real Clear Politics*, 12 March 2006, http://www.realclearpolitics.com/articles/2006/03/revisitation.html/. (This article is also archived at http://www.webcitation.org/6m3pXQPzT).

[54] "Blair statement in full", *BBC News*, 7 October 2001, http://news.bbc.co.uk/1/hi/uk_politics/1585238.stm/.

[55] Why the elite should have chosen to take this path is not something we have the space to discuss here. One explanation for what is going on is to be found in the following works: Bat Ye'or, *Eurabia*, Madison, 2005; Bat Ye'or, *Europe, Globalization and the Coming Universal Caliphate*, Madison, 2011. Suffice to say, that while academics, the Western media and the political class were talking up "the Arab Spring" (a laughable idea that across Muslim North Africa, popular liberal democracies would spring up), Bat Ye'or was predicting the return of the Caliphate, the Islamic State. The phenomenon of the Arab Spring fizzled out very quickly, with "Islamic fundamentalists" winning the elections. Thus, Bat Ye'or's explanation of where the world is headed (and why) seems to have predictive power which outweighs the cumulative thought of almost the entire Western world. Consequently, it would be foolish for anyone to dismiss her explanation.

[56] Mona Siddiqui, *How To Read The Qu'ran*, London, 2007, p.85. Significantly, this British academic cites no scriptural basis from the *Koran* to substantiate this meaning of Jihad which she claims. Moreover, she was writing years after Daniel Pipes had already exposed the deception around the definition of Jihad: "it is an intellectual scandal that, since September 11, 2001, scholars at American universities have repeatedly and all but unanimously issued public statements that avoid or whitewash the primary meaning of jihad in Islamic law and Muslim history" from "Jihad and the Professors", November 2002,

http://www.danielpipes.org/498/jihad-and-the-professors/.

[57] "He advocated that true Jihad was an inner struggle for peace not a violent war against unbelievers as had been popularised by fanatic clerics". *House of Commons Culture, Media and Sport Committee - Online Safety* Sixth Report of Session 2013-2014, http://www.publications.parliament.uk/pa/cm201314/cmselect/cmcumeds/729/729vw. pdf, p.120. See also the claims for "inner struggle" by this Canadian "Muslim reformer": "The basic meaning of Jihad is 'struggle' and this struggle is not necessarily an armed struggle. It can mean the struggle for truth and justice or good over evil". Raheel Raza, *Their Jihad... Not My Jihad!*, Ingersoll, Canada, 2005, p.18.

[58] "We saw the same mechanism at work with Islamic terrorism where the concept of jihad - an inner struggle to overcome weakness - was hideously distorted to justify something evil – the casual disregard of human life". Canon Dr Alan Billings, "Thought for the Day", *BBC Radio 4*, 25 July 2007, http://www.bbc.co.uk/programmes/p00jd5wy/.

[59] This deception was being practised at the level of both central government and local government. We can see this was also being taught in schools as part of the National Curriculum. *Challenging R.E. - The Buckinghamshire Agreed Syllabus For Religious Education*, Buckinghamshire County Council, 2006, p.99.

[60] Phillip Blond and Adrian Pabst, "The roots of Islamic terrorism", *New York Times*, 28 July 2005, http://www.nytimes.com/2005/07/28/opinion/the-roots-of-islamic-terrorism.html/. See also Theo Hobson, "Jihad for the Soul", *The Guardian*, 30 March 2008, https://www.theguardian.com/commentisfree/2008/mar/30/jihadforthesoul.

[61] "In my view, jihad does not equal terrorism. In a perversion of what Islam teaches, terrorists have misappropriated the concept of jihad from its true meaning – struggle. But jihad is not what happened on 9/11". Sadhbh Walshe, "Jihad, justice and the American way: is this a model for fair terrorism trials?", *The Guardian*, 17 July 2014, https://www.theguardian.com/commentisfree/2014/jul/17/jihad-justice-terrorism-trials-babar-ahmad/.

[62] Raymond Ibrahim (ed.) *The Al-Qaeda Reader*, New York, 2007.

[63] In criminal trials, even the close family of Muslim terrorists would start to exculpate themselves by claiming that they thought Jihad meant "inner struggle". See Andrew Norfolk and David Sanderson, "Daughter, 3, raised 'to be terrorist's wife'", *The Times* [England], 07 Feb 2008, p.27.

[64] See *The Concise Oxford Dictionary of Current English*, Oxford, 1982; *Reader's Digest Universal Dictionary*, London, 1986; *Chambers Dictionary of Etymology*, Edinburgh, 1988.

[65] See the Bukhari hadith "Book of Fighting for the Cause of Allah (Jihaad)", https://sunnah.com/bukhari/56/. This core text of Islam talks of Jihad as battles, killing, martyrdom, booty and the spoils of war (slaves and loot), mutilated bodies, swords and arrows and spears and shields, Muslims leaving Paradise for the pious joy of being killed in wars for Islam over and over and over, women giving birth to a hundred children who will grow up to die killing for Islam, bravery and cowardice in battle (with Mohammed being the bravest in battle), how even murderers are forgiven and can get to Paradise provided they die in wars for Islam, how Jihad is a life-long effort, how those who prepare a Muslim for martyrdom and then look after his offspring will be rewarded as if they were martyred themselves, of armies and even naval battles. Perhaps the only exception with regard to the command for Muslims to interpret Jihad as warfare, is in relation to Muslim women, where the best Jihad for them is to perform the pilgrimage to Mecca (although the women also nursed the injured in battle). The text says that those later generations who have an unbroken continuity of soldiers who can be traced back to those who fought in battle alongside Mohammed will be assured victory (Sahih al-Bukhari 2897). There is nothing in the entire book of hadiths on Jihad about struggle that is not about warfare, including letters being sent to peoples far away from Arabia (Rome, Constantinople) telling them to submit to Islam or face the armies of Islam.

[66] *Dictionary of the Middle Ages*, Volume 6, New York, 1985, p.582. In 1985 journalist Robin Wright published (in New York and London) the book *Sacred Rage: The Wrath of Militant Islam*, which says:

the Prophet preached holy war in his seventh-century campaigns to spread the faith and increase the territory under Muslim control. During his lifetime, he led the first Muslims to victories throughout the Arabian peninsula. Within one hundred years, Islamic crusaders had [...] the largest and fastest military victory purely in the name of religion in the history of the world. [...] In strict interpretation, jihad is no longer possible, except perhaps against Israel... (p.55)

As the subsequent decades and the thousands and thousands of Jihadi attacks have shown, this was assessment of Muslim-terrorism-as-Jihad against Israel in the 1970s and 1980s appears callous and naive. The cover of Wright's book contains rave reviews from *The New York Times, NBC News*, The Rand Corporation, West Point, *The Christian Science Monitor*, and staff at The University of Virginia.

[67] As we pointed out earlier, in 1953 the *Encyclopaedia of Islam* made no attempt to describe Jihad as an inner psychological struggle, stating boldly that Jihad was a religious obligation on Muslims in general to spread Islam using warfare. (*Shorter Encyclopaedia of Islam*, London, 1953, p.89). Moreover, in a fourteenth-century manual of sharia law, translated at the end of the twentieth century into many languages because of the renewed interest in sharia law among Muslims around the world, the manual makes it clear that the principle meaning of Jihad is "war against non-Muslims [...] to establish the religion" of Islam. See Ahmad al-Misri, (circa 1360) *Reliance of the Traveller: a Classic Manual of Islam's Sacred Law*, trans. Sheikh Nuh Ha Mim Keller, section o9.0. This section of the manual does not begin with any discussion of "inner struggle". It states outright and explicitly: Jihad is war. The translator is a convert to Islam, who studied philosophy and Arabic at a number of universities in the United States.

[68] Rudolf Peters, *Jihad in Classical and Modern Islam*, Princeton, 1996 (from Andrew Bostom (ed.) *The Legacy of Jihad: Islamic Holy War and the Fate of Non-Muslims*, New York, 2005, p.320).

[69] In *Eurabia*, Bat Ye'or shows how, in response to the oil crisis of 1973, the European political elite planned a union with the Arabic world, which meant the importation of Muslims into Europe. As with so many operations of the European Union, this plan was concealed in layers of meetings, bureaucracy and declaration. Only Bat Ye'or has explicated what was planned.

[70] https://en.wikipedia.org/wiki/Quisling_regime/.

[71] The *Koran* 9:20. Sometimes the concept is translated as "striving in the path of Allah", "striving in the cause of Allah" or "striving in the way of Allah".

[72] https://en.wikipedia.org/wiki/Murder_of_Lee_Rigby/.

[73] Many people are unaware of the precise details concerning the killing of Lee Rigby. The attackers only just failed to sever the soldier's head from his body: they "set about the unconscious man with a cleaver and knives in a 'serious and almost successful' attempt to saw off his head...". "'Butchered like a joint of meat': Jurors gasp as they are shown footage of Lee Rigby murder", *The Independent*, 29 Nov 2013, http://www.independent.co.uk/news/uk/crime/lee-rigby-murder-trial-hears-of-cowardly-callous-and-barbarous-attack-8972608.html/.

[74] https://en.wikipedia.org/wiki/Nick_Clegg/.

[75] http://www.bbc.co.uk/news/uk-politics-22652340/.

[76] You can see Clegg's full speech here: "Woolwich attack: 'As though he killed all mankind'", *BBC*, 24 May 2013, http://www.bbc.co.uk/news/uk-22655020/.

[77] In the Hebrew of the book of *Exodus*, the Sixth Commandment (*Exodus* 20:13) is "Thou shall not murder" and not "Thou shall not kill". See Ben-Tsiyon Segal and Gershon Levi, *The Ten Commandments in History and Tradition*, Jerusalem, 1990, p.70; Alan Berger (ed), *Post-Holocaust Jewish–Christian Dialogue: After the Flood, before the Rainbow*, London, 2015, p.87; Ron Rhodes, *Commonly Misunderstood Bible Verses*, Oregon, 2008, p.58; John Dickson, *A Doubter's Guide to the Ten Commandments*, Grand Rapids, 2016, p.121.

[78] Emphasis added. From the umpteen translations offered on this website

http://islamawakened.com/quran/5/32/ not one of the standard translations there matches key words in the Clegg translation. We opted for the translation by Pickthall, which we use throughout this book. However, the reader is invited to read through all the translations to see that they say roughly the same thing. The question remains from where Clegg got his misleading and partial translation.

[79] http://islamawakened.com/quran/5/33/. Emphasis added.

[80] Indeed, the further context of Koran 5:32 is that it stipulates at the start of the verse that it is a stricture imposed upon "the Children of Israel". It is thus arguable that the restrictions in this verse are not even to be taken as restricting Muslim violence in any way at all.

[81] https://en.wikipedia.org/wiki/Murder_of_Lee_Rigby#Attack .

[82] https://en.wikipedia.org/wiki/Murder_of_Lee_Rigby#Attack .

[83] What follows is an excerpt from one of the more detailed reports of what Michael Adebolajo (chosen Islamic name, Mujahid Abu Hamza), said in his police interviews. Note that he protests against the "corruption" of Britain's political leaders, claims that he and the other killer are soldiers of Allah, that Muslims are at war with us, and that what was done to Lee Rigby was an attempt at beheading (the form of execution commanded in *Koran* 47:4). Despite these two Muslim killers asking that they be referred to by their Muslim names, almost without exception the British media would not use these Muslim names (clearly trying to deceive the British public into thinking these killers were not really Muslims).

> Michael Adebolajo [...] told officers that he had tried to behead Army drummer Lee, 25, outside his barracks before declaring: "May Allah forgive me if I acted in a way that is displeasing to him. [...] He was struck in the neck with a sharp implement and it was sawed until his head, you know, became almost detached. May Allah forgive me if I acted in a way that is displeasing to him." [...] The court heard that Adebolajo demanded to be addressed as Mujahid Abu Hamza and described Adebowale as "Ismael," calling him his "Islam brother." He added: "This is a war between the people of Britain and the Muslim people. Your leaders rule over you in a very wicked, corrupt, selfish and oppressive manner, sadly." [...] "The reality of Muslim lands is that they are full of people like myself who are soldiers of Allah." He added: "The point I'm trying to make is that these are lands where you are sending working class men where the men there love death more than they love life. I genuinely want people to reflect on what I have been telling you." Adebolajo continued: "Allah calls them the Mujahideen [soldiers]. Allah loves them." [...] Consultant psychiatrist Tim McInerny told the court that he examined Adebolajo three times after his arrest and found him to be "fully compliant and co-operative".

The above extended quotation comes from "Lee Rigby trial: Murder accused Michael Adebolajo 'confessed he tried to behead soldier' in police interviews", *The Mirror*, 04 Dec 2013, http://www.mirror.co.uk/news/uk-news/lee-rigby-murder-trial-murder-2890496 (also archived here: http://www.webcitation.org/6pt159veA).

[84] "Lee Rigby murder: Killer Michael Adebolajo handed witness a note attempting to justify actions", *The Independent*, 19 December 2013, http://www.independent.co.uk/news/uk/crime/lee-rigby-murder-killer-michael-adebolajo-handed-witness-a-note-attempting-to-justify-actions-9015775.html/.

[85] The "quality" newspaper *The Telegraph* is one of those who claimed to publish the letter in full, but omitted this list of verses: 4:69-76, 4:84, 9:41, 9:24, 9:39, 9:46, 9:87, 9:93, 9:67, 3:173, 47:20, 9:86, 9:31, 9:51-5, 8:5-6, 2:170, 3:160, 9:119, 9:123, 9:37, 2:216, 3:142. See "Lee Rigby trial: full text of letter given by Michael Adebolajo to 'Angel of Woolwich'", *The Telegraph*, 29 Nov 2013, http://www.telegraph.co.uk/news/uknews/law-and-order/10484601/Lee-Rigby-trial-full-text-of-letter-given-by-Michael-Adebolajo-to-Angel-of-Woolwich.html/. For an analysis of these verses see "UK jihad murderer handed blood-stained note full of Qur'an quotes to

bystander", *Jihad Watch*, 28 Feb 2014,
https://www.jihadwatch.org/2014/02/uk-jihad-murderer-handed-blood-stained-note-full-of-quran-quotes-to-bystander
[86] This Muslim, a prospective Conservative Party candidate for the 2015 General Election, was later exposed by Tommy Robinson, leading to Afzal Amin's resignation. "Afzal Amin quits over claims he sought to play up racial tensions", *The Telegraph*, 23 March 2015, http://www.telegraph.co.uk/news/politics/conservative/11490357/Afzal-Amin-quits-over-claims-he-sought-to-play-up-racial-tensions.html/.
[87] "Cameron: 'This is not Islam; it's a perverted ideology and we must fight it'", *The Times of Israel*, 26 June 2015, http://www.timesofisrael.com/liveblog_entry/cameron-this-is-not-islam-its-a-perverted-ideology-and-we-must-fight-it/. One of the rare occasions when a journalist has questioned why politicians keep repeating this lie was when following this attack in Tunisia, Douglas Murray questioned why the British Home Secretary was claiming Islam is a religion of peace. Douglas Murray "Why is Theresa May pretending that Islam is a 'religion of peace'?", *The Spectator*, 30 Sept 2014, http://blogs.spectator.co.uk/2014/09/why-is-theresa-may-pretending-that-islam-is-a-religion-of-peace/ Of course, The Grand Lie did not stop her party from selecting her to be the next Prime Minister of Britain.
[88] See Dion Dassanayake, "PM: Not good enough to say Islam is religion of peace then deny any extremism connection", *Daily Express*, 17 Nov 2015, http://www.express.co.uk/news/politics/619912/David-Cameron-Islam-Muslim-religion-peace-Paris-terror-attacks.
[89] The established governmental and controlled media sources do not even keep a tally of the terrorist attacks by Muslims. Volunteers at this website keep their own tally, which is in excess of 30,000 attacks since 9/11. http://www.thereligionofpeace.com/pages/site/the-list.aspx/. The University of Maryland in the USA is "a Department of Homeland Security Center of Excellence", yet it buries information about Islamic terrorism. Remember: the Department of Homeland Security was set up in the wake of the 9/11 failures. Their experts seem more concerned with confusing the public rather than by providing any kind of assessment of the scale of Islamic terrorism. "More than 80,000 entries and 12 years later, Miller is still engaged in the enigma of the world's most comprehensive open-source database of terrorist attacks". http://www.start.umd.edu/news/fascinating-puzzle-gtd/. It is not unusual for the home page of this organisation's website to feature articles on "the far right" or terrorism in Colombia, despite the fact that most people in the English-speaking world are suffering from Islamic terrorism above all other kinds (indeed, what is so remarkable is that the indigenous people of Western countries do not retaliate to terrorism with terrorism, i.e. there are so little Islam-related terrorism by the Kuffar that it is effectively a deception by the authorities).
[90] "Full text: Blair speech on terror", *BBC*, 16 July 2005, http://news.bbc.co.uk/1/hi/uk/4689363.stm/.
[91] Where the Koran and the Sunnah are unclear on a subject, Muslims used interpretation, "ijtihad". However, the vast majority of Muslims who know anything about Islam have agreed that "the gates of ijtihad" have been closed since the tenth century A.D. See Abdullahi Ahmed An-Na'im, *Toward an Islamic Reformation*, Syracuse, 1996, p.27; Malise Ruthven, *Islam*, Oxford, 2012, p.90; Clinton Bennett, *Muslims and Modernity*, London, 2005, p.21.
[92] Quilliam lists a selection of the Muslim organisations in Britain who agree with "the Islamist" goal of an Islamic State, and those Muslim organisations who do not. Suffice to say, that the number who want Islamic State vastly out-number the examples of those who do not (bear in mind, this Quilliam document was printed several years before ISIS appeared). "Preventing Terrorism: Where Next For Britain", *Quilliam*, 14 Jun 2010, https://www.scribd.com/document/34834977/Secret-Quilliam-Memo-to-government/. Hizb ut Tahrir is listed as one of the leading organisations seeking a return to the Islamic State. Before ISIS came into being, the Hizb ut Tahrir website in Britain used to list their leaders. Hizb ut Tahrir was established by a Sheikh, and nearly all the principal officers are professionals in high positions in the UK (proving that those Muslims who are educated are

the vanguard who know well that Islam is inseparable from politics). In Britain, both Tony Blair and David Cameron promised to ban Hizb ut Tahrir. Neither Prime Minister followed through on his promise; the UK media simply stopped reporting on the existence of Hizb ut Tahrir, and by 2012 many educated people in Britain thought that Hizb ut Tahrir had been banned. Instead, the agenda for the creation of the Islamic State was just being put into place across the Middle East.

[93] See the Wikipedia entry on the bombing of the London transport system in 2005. https://en.wikipedia.org/wiki/7_July_2005_London_bombings/.

[94] en.wikipedia.org/wiki/21_July_2005_London_bombings/.

[95] "Full text: David Cameron speech", 24 Aug 2005, *BBC*, http://news.bbc.co.uk/1/hi/uk_politics/4179698.stm/.

[96] Almost no one doubts now that National Socialism was genocidal. However, the various forms of Communism which arose in Europe were also genocidal (indeed, Stalin was committing genocide years before Hitler). See Stephane Courtois et al., *The Black Book of Communism: Crimes, Terror, Repression*, Harvard University Press, 1999.

[97] Shmuel Bar, *Warrant for Terror: The Fatwas of Radical Islam and the Duty to Jihad*, New York, 2006, p.ix.

[98] See Koran 9:100 and 9:117.

[99] For the most shocking example, see Ibn Ishaq, *The Life of Muhammad*, p.464. The original biography was written shortly after Mohammed's death, by a Muslim named Ibn Ishaq. It is published by one of the most prestigious publishers in the world, publishers whose reputation for scholarship would mean they wouldn't go near a book that was "islamophobic". Moreover, the actual book from Oxford University Press on sale in the UK is not printed in Oxford, but is printed in Pakistan, a country where they have the death penalty for blasphemy against Islam. We can take it from these facts, that either before 1955 or after that date no Muslims have found blasphemous the details of the character and behaviour of Mohammed found in this most authoritative Muslim biography of Mohammed. Guillaume was a Professor at the University of London, who received awards across the Islamic world for his work. To get an understanding of the importance of Ibn Ishaq, Ibn Hisham and Tabari (whose work Guillaume weaved together into one narrative) see *Shorter Encyclopaedia of Islam*, London, 1953, pp.547-548. Even the enemies of Christianity or Buddhism do not write biographies saying that the founders of these religions were killers. Yet here we have the most authoritative Muslim biography of Mohammed recording that he executed up to 900 men and boys, with the mothers and sisters being sold by Mohammed as slaves.

[100] Shmuel Bar's book is devoted to the fatwas (legal decrees issued by recognized religious authorities in Islam) on Jihad.

> Fatwas have been employed by rebels and insurgents across the Muslim world against westernized regimes' presumed heresy and foreign domination. This was true, for example, of the Wahhabis in the Arabian Peninsula (1881-85), the Mahdi in Sudan (1881-1885), and by Muslims in India against the British (1881) and in Indonesia against the Dutch (1948). [...] The defendants in the first World Trade Center trial [1993] explained their reliance on Sheikh Omar 'abd el-Rahman... Shmuel Bar, *Warrant for Terror: The Fatwas of Radical Islam and the Duty to Jihad*, New York, 2006, pp.11-12.

See also "Bin Laden's 1998 Jihad Against Jews and Crusaders" in Terry McDermott, *Perfect Soldiers*, New York, 2005, pp.267-270. This document was signed by Sheikh Bin Laden, and the emir of the Jihad Group in Egypt, Sheikh Mir Hamzah of Pakistan, and the emir of the Jihad Movement in Bangladesh. Hardly ignorant Muslims.

[101] According to the *Encyclopaedia of Islam* "the Muslim dedicates himself to the djihad [Jihad] in the same way that, in Christianity, the monk dedicates himself to the service of god" (Ibn Warraq, *The Islam in Islamic Terrorism: The Importance of Beliefs, Ideas, and Ideology*, London, 2017, p. 106).

[102] Ibn Ishaq, *The Life of Muhammad*, p.vii.

[103] As Professor Crone says: "if everything was in order on the side of the warriors, the jurists were satisfied that the enterprise was in the best interests of the victims. The conquered peoples were being dragged to Paradise in chains, as a famous saying went." "'Jihad': idea and history", *Open Democracy*, 1 May 2007, https://www.opendemocracy.net/faith-europe_islam/jihad_4579.jsp/.

[104] Theodor Nöldeke, *Sketches from Eastern History* (translated by John Sutherland Black and revised by the author), London, 1892, p.65.

[105] "Full text: David Cameron's speech", *The Guardian*, 24 Aug 2005, https://www.theguardian.com/politics/2005/aug/24/conservatives.faithschools/.

[106] Sarah Khan and Tony McMahon, *The Battle for British Islam: Reclaiming Muslim Identity from Extremism*, London, 2016; Tahir Abbas, *British Islam: The Road to Radicalism*, Cambridge, 2009; "Is 'French Islam' Possible", *The Arab Weekly*, 25th Sept 2016, http://www.thearabweekly.com/Opinion/6504/Is-%E2%80%98French-Islam %E2%80%99-possible%3F/.

[107] See Christopher Caldwell, (2009) *Reflections on the Revolution in Europe*, London, pp.232-233.

[108] Bruce Bawer, (2009) *Surrender: Appeasing Islam, Sacrificing Freedom*, New York, pp.42-46.

[109] Peter McLoughlin, *Easy Meat: Inside Britain's Grooming Gang Scandal*, London, 2016, pp.195-199.

[110] For example, Pakistan's blasphemy laws. See Bat Ye'or, *Islam and Dhimmitude: Where Civilisations Collide*, Lancaster, 2002, p.230.

[111] When it comes to ISIS it is sufficient to note that in the thousands of news reports concerning this group, the public are not told that "Islamic State" was the name that twentieth-century scholars of Islam in the West gave to the first political-military entity created by the founder of Islam, which on his death came to be known as "the Caliphate". The connection with 1400 years of Islamic history is further concealed by the media (particularly the BBC) insisting on referring to the group as "so-called Islamic State". The BBC did not refer to the IRA as "the so-called Irish Republican Army", evidence that the problem with Islam and sectarian violence in the West has already surpassed Britain's problem with terrorism from Irish republicans that the terms of debate must be deformed: if the BBC had thought that it would offend Irish people or legitimize the IRA, they would have referred to the IRA as "the so-called Irish Republican Army". British MPs attempted to add a further level of disassociation between Islam and the Islamic State by getting the BBC to only refer to Islamic State as "Daesh" (see "BBC rejects MPs' calls to refer to Islamic State as Daesh", *The Guardian*, 2 Jul 2015, https://www.theguardian.com/media/2015/jul/02/bbc-rejects-mps-calls-to-refer-to-islamic-state-as-daesh).

The efforts to conceal that Islamic State is Islamic is not the only deformation of debate. The group known as "Boko Haram" do not call themselves by that name. The name they use is "Group of the People of Sunnah for Preaching and Jihad". It is virtually impossible to find a mainstream news source or even an anti-terrorism think tank which will disclose that this is the true name of this group. These three reports all give the name in Arabic: 1) "Is Islamic State Shaping Boko Haram Media?", *BBC*, 4 Mar 2015, http://www.bbc.co.uk/news/world-africa-31522469; 2) "Boko Haram: An Assessment of Strengths, Vulnerabilities, and Policy Options", *National Consortium for the Study of Terrorism and Responses to Terrorism*, Jan 2015, https://www.start.umd.edu/pubs/START_%20SMA-AFRICOM_Boko%20Haram %20Deep%20Dive_Jan2015.pdf; 3) Alex Thurston, "The Disease is Unbelief: Boko Haram's Religious and Political Worldview", *Brookings Institute*, Jan 2016. https://www.brookings.edu/wp-content/uploads/2016/07/Brookings-Analysis-Paper_Alex-Thurston_Final_Web.pdf. It shows the extent to which the elite will go to conceal the connection between contemporary Islamic terrorists and their claims that they are emulating the behaviour of Mohammed (the word 'Sunnah' in the real name of Boko Haram). Even when such a group puts their goal specifically in their name, they are given an unrelated name, and the experts who mention the proper name in Arabic will either then not translate it or will give it only a partial translation (for example, *The Brookings Institute* translates "Ahl al-Sunna li-l-Da'wa wa-l-Jihad" as "People of the Prophet's Model". Even someone with the smallest understanding of the tenets of Islam can recognise the words "Sunna" (behaviour) and "Jihad" in the Arabic name, yet *The Brookings Institute* seems quite content with concealing that these Muslims see Jihad as part of the behaviour of the exemplary model of Islam, Mohammed. Both *The Brookings Institute* and *National Consortium for the Study of Terrorism and Responses to Terrorism* claim to be educational research institutes conducting in-depth research into politics and terrorism. Yet they fail to fully explain the name that this Islamic terrorist group have chosen for themselves.

[112] "FGM affects 137,000 women in England and Wales, reveals shocking new study", *The Telegraph*, 22 Jul 2014, http://www.telegraph.co.uk/women/womens-politics/10980268/FGM-affects-137000-women-in-England-and-Wales-reveals-shocking-new-study.html/.

[113] Before the influx of Muslims into the West and the concomitant one-sided violence from them, people in the West were free to draw Mohammed or criticise Islam in any way they saw fit. By contrast, nearly a century before the Mohammed cartoon controversy erupted in Denmark, in 1929 in India a publisher was assassinated by a Muslim for publishing a cartoon about Mohammed. In the wake of the assassination of the staff of *Charlie Hebdo* by devout Muslim terrorists, the "progressive" *New Republic*, which claims to "challenge the status quo" reminded its readers how wrong it is to provoke Muslims. See "What Gandhi Understood About Inflammatory Depictions of Muhammad", *New Republic*, 22 Jan 2015, https://newrepublic.com/article/120819/muhammad-images-used-provoke-muslims-what-gandhi-understood/.

[114] Christopher Caldwell, "Islamic Europe?", *The Weekly Standard*, 4 Oct 2004, http://www.weeklystandard.com/islamic-europe/article/5901/.

[115] "France's Permanent Emergency State", *New York Times*, 25 July 2016, http://www.nytimes.com/2016/07/25/opinion/frances-permanent-emergency-state.html/.

[116] "The Return of the French National Guard", *The Atlantic*, 29 July 2016, http://www.theatlantic.com/news/archive/2016/07/french-national-guard/493595/.

[117] G. Whyte, *The Dreyfus Affair: A Chronological History*, New York, 2008, p.5.

[118] "'Europe is at war': Leaders speak out against deadly terrorists attacks in Brussels", *Russia Today*, 22 Mar 2016, https://www.rt.com/news/336696-europe-terrorism-leaders-attacks/.

[119] "Election candidate arrested over Churchill speech - European election candidate was quoting an anti-Islamic passage from Winston Churchill book when he was arrested", *The Telegraph*, 28 Apr 2014, http://www.telegraph.co.uk/news/uknews/crime/10792895/Election-candidate-arrested-over-Churchill-speech.html.

[120] Winston Churchill, *The River War - An Historical Account of the Reconquest of the Soudan* (vol.II), Longman, London, 1899, pp.249-250.

[121] Winston Churchill, *The River War - An Historical Account of the Reconquest of the Soudan* (vol.II), Longman, London, 1899, pp.249-250.

[122] Most of the British news media did not even report the arrest. Of those who reported it, most of them did not inform their readers concerning Churchill's opinion of Islam. "Arrested for quoting Winston Churchill: European election candidate accused of religious and racial harassment after he repeats wartime prime minister's words on Islam during campaign speech", *Daily Mail*, 28 April 2014, http://www.dailymail.co.uk/news/article-2614834/Arrested-quoting-Winston-Churchill-European-election-candidate-accused-religious-racial-harassment-repeats-wartime-prime-ministers-words-Islam-campaign-speech.html; "Election candidate arrested over Churchill speech", 28 April 2014, *Telegraph*, http://www.telegraph.co.uk/news/uknews/crime/10792895/Election-candidate-arrested-over-Churchill-speech.html ; Euro candidate Paul Weston arrested over Islam remarks, *BBC*, 28 April 2014, http://www.bbc.co.uk/news/uk-england-hampshire-

27186573/.

[123] See *Easy Meat: Inside Britain's Grooming Gang Scandal*, London, 2016.

[124] "Britain's coping classes at breaking point", *The Telegraph*, 10 October 2010, http://www.telegraph.co.uk/news/uknews/8054403/Britains-coping-classes-at-breaking-point.html/.

[125] As with Boko Haram and Islamic State today, the Mahdi army of the 1880s flew the black flag of Jihad; those who helped the Mahdi were known as the Ansar [Helpers], the same word used to describe those who helped the founder of Islam when he became a thief, slave-taker and killer on his move from Medina to Mecca. See https://en.wikipedia.org/wiki/Charles_George_Gordon#Mahdist_uprising .

[126] David Meir-Levi, *History Upside Down: The Roots of Palestinian Fascism and the Myth of Israeli Aggression*, New York, 2007, p.62, p.77.

[127] Somewhere between 200,000 and 2 million died in the process of partitioning India, and another 14 million were relocated, the largest movement of people in history. See https://en.wikipedia.org/wiki/Partition_of_India/. British politicians started importing Muslims from Pakistan and India in the 1950s, barely 10 years after this huge death toll in the partition of India. These politicians, civil servants, academics and journalists would have known the history of the Raj, and the refusal of Muslims to learn English, lest it would break down the barriers which Islam erects to integration with the Kuffar. These politicians, civil servants, academics and journalists would have known about the "communal violence" where Muslims and Sikhs and Hindus would kill each other. This elite would also have known about the 1400 years of Islamic war-mongering and slave-taking. And still Muslims were invited into the United Kingdom, without ever explaining to the people of Britain what this would entail. By the 1980s Islamic sex-slavery in the UK was already causing Sikhs to engage in "communal violence" (see *Easy Meat: Inside Britain's Grooming Gang Scandal*, pp.53-58).

[128] Winston Churchill, *The Second World War - The Gathering Storm* [1948], The Reprint Society, London, 1950, p.61.

[129] Ali Dashti, *Twenty Three Years: A Study of the Prophetic Career of Mohammad*, trans. F.R.C. Bagley, Costa Mesa, California, 1994, p13.

[130] http://www.thereligionofpeace.com/attacks/attacks.aspx?Yr=2014#.

[131] Bear in mind that Churchill considered the Koran to be verbose and shapeless, and this opinion was with Churchill having access to Rodwell's chronological translation of the Koran, which was published by a mass-market publisher from 1861 to 1937, an edition which not only gave the Koran shape by putting it into chronological order, but which also attempted to render each chapter as if it was a chapter of a novel, instead of breaking the chapters up into numbered verses. Thus, it seems likely that those Kuffar who have attempted to understand Islam from any of the score of jumbled-up translations of the last 70 years have struggled far more than Churchill in understanding Islam.

[132] "Transcript of press conference with Prime Minister, David Cameron at the European Council, 26 June 2015", https://www.gov.uk/government/speeches/european-council-june-2015-david-camerons-speech: "The people who do these things, they sometimes claim they do it in the name of Islam. They don't. Islam is a religion of peace. They do it in the name of a twisted and perverted ideology that we have to confront with everything that we have..."

[133] "Who is Islamic State leader Abu Bakr al-Baghdadi?", *BBC*, 8 Mar 2016, http://www.bbc.co.uk/news/world-middle-east-35694311/.

[134] "David Cameron extremism speech", *The Independent*, 20 July 2015, http://www.independent.co.uk/news/uk/politics/david-cameron-extremism-speech-read-the-transcript-in-full-10401948.html/.

[135] Chris Horrie and Peter Chippendale, *What is Islam*, London, 1990, p.25.

[136] There are many instances in the Leftist newspaper *The Guardian* of feminists defending the burka – see "So much for the sisterhood", *The Guardian*, 13 Oct 2006, https://www.theguardian.com/commentisfree/2006/oct/13/whathappenedtosisterhood1

and "Full-face veils aren't barbaric – but our response can be", The Guardian, 17 Sept 2013, https://www.theguardian.com/commentisfree/2013/sep/17/full-face-veil-not-barbaric-debate-muslim-women/. In 2013, the "Conservative" woman who was to become the Prime Minister of Britain also spoke out defending the burka as "a woman's right to choose":
"Wearing veil should be the woman's choice, says Theresa May", *The Guardian*, 17 Sept 2013, https://www.theguardian.com/world/2013/sep/17/veil-womans-choice-theresa-may/.

[137] Andrew Bostom, (2012) *Sharia Versus Freedom: The Legacy of Islamic Totalitarianism*, New York, p.544.

[138] In 2004, a year before the first major terrorist attack by Muslims in the UK, philosopher David Selbourne (who also writes for the Leftist *New Statesman* magazine) lamented how the major publishers (including those who had previously published his books) would not touch his book on Islam. "Terrified publishers won't print truth about Islam, says author", *The Telegraph*, 25 July 2004, http://www.telegraph.co.uk/news/uknews/1467789/Terrified-publishers-wont-print-truth-about-Islam-says-author.html/.

[139] "Prosecutors summing up in Geert Wilders hate speech trial", 16 Nov 2016, *Belfast Telegraph*, http://www.belfasttelegraph.co.uk/news/world-news/prosecutors-summing-up-in-geert-wilders-hate-speech-trial-35220017.html/.

[140] Mark Steyn, "State Department Advisory: Steer Clear of Steyn", 30 Sept 2015, http://www.steynonline.com/7203/state-department-advisory-steer-clear-of-steyn/.

[141] "One person has been killed and three police officers injured after armed men opened fire on a cafe in Copenhagen where a debate on Islam and free speech was being held". From "One dead and three injured in Copenhagen 'terrorist attack'", *The Guardian*, 14 Feb 2015, https://www.theguardian.com/world/2015/feb/14/copenhagen-blasphemy-lars-vilks-prophet-muhammad-krudttonden-cafe/.

[142] Following the attack on the USA in September 2001, Britain's internal security service (MI5) kept a public list of those convicted of "international terrorism". This was code for "Islamic terrorism" since the attacks all occurred in Britain and the vast majority of those convicted were citizens of Britain and the long list of hundreds of case summaries made it clear that in every single case the people convicted had Muslim names (when the population of the UK was less than 5% Muslim). MI5 started to move the page to different parts of their website every few months, then they started to update it with decreasing frequency. Finally, they removed the list of summaries. At the time of writing, without considerable effort no-one can discover how many people have been convicted of "international terrorism". The news media and politicians appear to have no interest and no concern that the electorate are being kept in the dark about the scale of this problem.

[143] For the extraordinary details concerning the decades in which the army of state-funded childcare professionals covered-up the industrial-scale entrapment, rape and prostitution of non-Muslim schoolgirls by Muslims gangs see Peter McLoughlin, *Easy Meat: Inside Britain's Grooming Gang Scandal*, London, 2016.

[144] "David Cameron extremism speech", *The Independent*, 20 July 2015, http://www.independent.co.uk/news/uk/politics/david-cameron-extremism-speech-read-the-transcript-in-full-10401948.html/.

[145] https://en.wikipedia.org/wiki/David_Irving/.

[146] We can find only one instance of Irving speaking at a British university: "Over the objections of British politicians, Holocaust survivors, anti-fascist groups and students, Oxford University's Oxford Union debating society hosted Irving during a forum on free speech on November 26, 2007.... Dr. Julian Lewis, a senior Conservative Party member of Britain's Parliament, resigned from the Oxford Union in protest, and Defence Secretary Des Browne withdrew from an Oxford Union speaking engagement." http://archive.adl.org/learn/ext_us/irving.html?LEARN_Cat=Extremism&LEARN_SubCat=Extremism_in_America&xpicked=2&item=irving
Moreover, it appears that on this one occasion there was widespread disruption by Leftists

trying to stop Irving from speaking at this event: "A debate on free speech at the Oxford Union descended into chaos last night after scores of demonstrators broke through a security cordon and staged a sit-down protest in the union's famous chamber. Scuffles broke out in the hall as the demonstrators - there to voice their opposition to the presence of discredited historian David Irving ... clashed with organisers and security guards." "Irving and Griffin spark fury at Oxford Union debate", *The Guardian*, 27 November 2007, https://www.theguardian.com/uk/2007/nov/27/highereducation.studentpoliticseducatio n. This account thus completely undermines Cameron's pretence that controversial figures like Irving are freely invited to these universities and that on these occasions he gets to put his case for revising the history of the Holocaust, when this is untrue. In this one instance where Irving was allowed to speak it was specifically in the context of a debate about freedom of speech, and even then, Members of Parliament (Members of an organisation supposedly dedicated to open debate) would not speak if Irving was allowed to speak. When it comes to his views on the Holocaust, Irving is not permitted to speak. The British Prime Minister once again purported that black is white. If David Irving converted to Islam, he would almost certainly face no trouble in getting into universities to speak.

[147] "Abu Usamah to appear at Brunel University", *Student Rights*, 20 Nov 2012, http://www.studentrights.org.uk/article/2000/peaceful_protest_planned_against_abu_usa mah_s_appearance_at_brunel/.

[148] "Mohammed Naveed Bhatti, convicted for his role in Dhiren Barot's 2004 'dirty bomb' plot, was studying at Brunel University and met Barot in the university's prayer room". "Roots of violent radicalisation", *House of Commons*, Feb 2012, http://www.publications.parliament.uk/pa/cm201012/cmselect/cmhaff/1446/1446.pdf

[149] This was a sufficiently notable phenomenon that it was discussed in Bruce Bawer, *While Europe Slept: How Radical Islam Is Destroying The West From Within*, London, 2006, pp.139-146. In the following years, the situation in Europe got worse, with Jihadis killing small Jewish children at school, or killing customers in Jewish shops, or killing tourists in Jewish museums. Even the Bataclan club which was the scene of slaughter Paris in November 2015 had been a Jewish-owned business which had reportedly received terrorist threats for years: "Paris's Bataclan, which until recently was under Jewish ownership, was target for threats by Islamic extremists for years before becoming a main target in coordinated terror attacks by ISIL" from "Under threat: Bataclan theater terrorized for years", *Ynetnews*, 15 Nov 2015, http://www.ynetnews.com/articles/0,7340,L-4725983,00.html/.

[150] To get a sense of the scale of the genocide conducted by Muslims, just consider the eighty million killed in India. See Koenraad Elst, *Negationism in India: Concealing the Records of Islam*, New Delhi, 1992 and François Gautier, *Rewriting Indian History*, New Delhi, 1996.

[151] David Meir-Levi, *History Upside Down: The Roots of Palestinian Fascism and the Myth of Israeli Aggression*, New York, 2007, p.43.

[152] "The Panorama investigation identified a book for 15-year-olds being used in the classes which teaches about Sharia law and its punishments. It says: 'For thieves their hands will be cut off for a first offence, and their foot for a subsequent offence.' There are diagrams showing children where cuts must be made. One passage says: 'The specified punishment of the thief is cutting off his right hand at the wrist. Then it is cauterised to prevent him from bleeding to death'. For acts of 'sodomy', children are told that the penalty is death and it states a difference of opinion whether this should be done by stoning, or burning with fire, or throwing over a cliff." "Sharia lessons for pupils aged six: BBC uncovers 'weekend schools' that teach pupils how to hack off thieves' hands", *Daily Mail*, 24 November 2010, http://www.dailymail.co.uk/news/article-1331789/Sharia-lessons-pupils-aged-BBC-uncovers-weekend-schools.html/. See also "BBC's Panorama claims Islamic schools teach antisemitism and homophobia", *The Guardian*, 22 November 2010, https://www.theguardian.com/media/2010/nov/22/bbc-panorama-islamic-schools-antisemitism/.

[153] http://www.channel4.com/info/press/news/c4-survey-and-documentary-reveals-what-british-muslims-really-think/.

[154] Koran 9:5, 9:29.

[155] Koran 5:51.

[156] Koran 5:33.

[157] *The Times*, 29 Nov 1934, pg. 7.

[158] Mark Steyn, *After America*, Washington, 2012, p.105, p.310.

[159] George Orwell, *1984* [1949], Penguin, London, 1989, p.37.

[160] "What Americans really think about Muslims and Islam", 9 December 2015, http://www.brookings.edu/blogs/markaz/posts/2015/12/09-what-americans-think-of-muslims-and-islam-telhami/.

[161] "The majority of voters doubt that Islam is compatible with British values", 30 March 2015, https://yougov.co.uk/news/2015/03/30/majority-voters-doubt-islam-compatible-british-val/.

[162] "Common Concerns About Islamic Extremism - Muslim-Western Tensions Persist", 21 July 2011, http://www.pewglobal.org/files/2011/07/Pew-Global-Attitudes-Muslim-Western-Relations-FINAL-FOR-PRINT-July-21-2011.pdf .

[163] "Most Europeans want immigration ban from Muslim-majority countries, poll reveals", *The Independent*, 8 Feb 2017, http://www.independent.co.uk/news/world/europe/most-europeans-want-muslim-ban-immigration-control-middle-east-countries-syria-iran-iraq-poll-a7567301.html

[164] "Common Concerns About Islamic Extremism - Muslim-Western Tensions Persist", p.13.

[165] "Common Concerns About Islamic Extremism - Muslim-Western Tensions Persist", p.17.

[166] "Common Concerns About Islamic Extremism - Muslim-Western Tensions Persist", p.23.

[167] Bernard Lewis, "Politics and War", in Joseph Schact (ed), *The Legacy of Islam*, Oxford, 1974, p.174.

[168] Bernard Lewis, "Politics and War", in Joseph Schact (ed), *The Legacy of Islam*, Oxford, 1974, p.178.

[169] Andrew Bostom, "Jihad Conquests and the Imposition of Dhimmitude", in Andrew Bostom (ed.), *The Legacy of Jihad*, New York, 2005, p.33.

[170] For example, the British government stipulates this requirement with typical British indirection: "If the MP wishes to swear on a sacred text [...] those books which may not be handled by non-believers are kept in slip-cases" (omitting to say that it is only with Islam that this is a requirement). http://www.parliament.uk/about/how/elections-and-voting/swearingin/. Even in Guantanamo Bay the guards dealing with the Muslim terrorists were made to wear gloves when they handled the Koran (see Mark Steyn, *America Alone*, Washington, 2006, p.xxvii). This kind of behaviour confirms to even Muslim criminals that governments confirm that non-Muslims guarding Muslim criminals are essentially inferior to the criminals.

[171] "'I Will Kill You, You Are Dirt': Egypt's Coptic Christians Live in Fear as Islamist Gov't Takes Control", *The Blaze*, 14 Mar 2012, http://www.theblaze.com/stories/2012/03/14/i-will-kill-you-you-are-dirt-egypts-coptic-christians-live-in-fear-as-islamist-govt-takes-control/.

[172] When the mainstream media in the West report on these things, they ignore the Islamic basis behind the treatment of Christians as "unclean" in Muslim societies. Thus, the highly-prestigious *Washington Post* offers this explanation for why the garbage collectors in Cairo are mostly Coptic Christians:

> Because garbage collection is seen by Muslims as "unclean" (garbage is fed to pigs), this work for untold generations has mostly been done by Christians, who labor in their gritty stalls surrounded by icons and crosses and posters of Jesus.

> --"Cairo's Christians worry about Egypt's next chapter", *Washington Post*, 8 Nov 2011, https://www.washingtonpost.com/opinions/cairos-christians-worry-about-egypts-next-chapter/2011/11/08/gIQAk3CI3M_story.html

Is there any culture on earth that does not see garbage as "unclean"? The Hudson Institute is just as guilty, quoting a Scandinavian journalist saying that violence towards the Christians is a social or class issue, because they do work that is "unclean" ("The Ongoing Attacks on Egypt's Coptic Christians", *Hudson Institute*, 10 Mar 2011, http://www.hudson.org/research/7785-the-ongoing-attacks-on-egypt-s-coptic-christians). The Hudson Institute's Senior Research Fellow on Religious Freedom seems to have no idea why it is that those who profess a religion which pre-dates Islam in Egypt should have adherents who do the dirtiest work, when Islam has laws going back centuries saying that Muslim must not clean up after a non-Muslim. See Bat Ye'or, *The Dhimmi: Jews and Christians under Islam*, New Jersey, 1985, p.187.

[173] See Andrew Bostom, (2005) editor, *The Legacy of Jihad: Islamic Holy War and the Fate of Non-Muslims*, New York, p.565.

[174] Andrew Bostom, "Why I Support Sen. Tom Cotton/the GOP 47 and Their Letter to Iran's Leaders", *Breitbart*, 11 Mar 2015, http://www.breitbart.com/national-security/2015/03/11/why-i-support-sen-tom-cottonthe-gop-47-and-their-letter-to-irans-leaders/.

[175] France has laws which make it a crime to "provoke discrimination, hatred, or violence toward a person or group of persons because of their origin or belonging to a particular ethnicity, nation, race, or religion". "Why French Law Treats Dieudonné And Charlie Hebdo Differently", *The New Yorker*, 15 Jan 2015, http://www.newyorker.com/news/news-desk/french-law-treats-dieudonne-charlie-hebdo-differently/. Brigitte Bardot has been found guilty of breaking such laws. Novelists have also faced prosecution for responses given to interview questions. One would assume that the *Koran 9:28* stating that we Kuffar are inherently and permanently unclean would fall foul of such laws, but no prosecutions arise.

[176] Following a secret vote in the European Parliament in 2013, the elite went so far as removing legal immunity from Marine Le Pen MEP so that she could be prosecuted for remarks which were perfectly legal for her to make when she made them in 2010. The use of retroactive criminality is a hallmark of totalitarian governments – see Juan Jose Linz, *Totalitarian and Authoritarian Regimes*, London, 2000, p.101; Robin White & Claire Ovey, *The European Convention on Human Rights*, 5th edition, Oxford, 2010, p.298. This action by the European Parliament was done at the behest of the elite in France. Le Pen did not say, for example, "that all Muslims are essentially filthy, and we demand that the rest of us be protected from them" (the inverse of the rule that Muslims in countries like the UK are to be protected from the dirty Kuffar). The elite tried to prosecute her for comparing the illegal praying of Muslims in public spaces (in secular France) as being like a National Socialist army occupying foreign territory. "Marine Le Pen faces court on charge of inciting racial hatred", 22 Sept 2015, *The Guardian*, https://www.theguardian.com/world/2015/sep/22/marine-le-pen-faces-court-on-charge-of-inciting-racial-hatred/.

[177] A city council in Britain sacked an employee who was part of an organisation which argued that Islam contravened universal human rights. "ICLA Member Chris Knowles Dismissed By Leeds City Council Without Due Process", *International Civil Liberties Alliance*, 6 Aug 2012, http://www.libertiesalliance.org/2012/08/06/icla-member-chris-knowles-dismissed-by-leeds-city-council-without-due-process/ He was summarily dismissed, and his trade union refused to give him any support.

[178] A married couple had their children removed in Rotherham, England simply because the couple were members of a political party which advocated the UK leaving the European Union. "Parents who had children removed over UKIP links to get new family", *The Express*, 31 Aug 2014, http://www.express.co.uk/news/uk/505306/Parents-children-removed-UKIP-new-family-Rotherham-sex-scandal. This was the same town whose childcare professionals subsequently came to be viewed as emblematic of the cover-up of organized rape of schoolgirls by Muslim gangs. See Peter McLoughlin, *Easy Meat*, London, 2016, pp.95-114.

[179] A Dutch film-maker was murdered by a Muslim for far less than making a film saying that "Dutch people needed to be protected from the essential filth of Muslims".

Van Gogh's murder was apparently sparked by a documentary he made earlier this year with Ayaan Hirsi Ali, a Somali-born woman politician who calls herself 'an ex-Muslim'. The provocative film, broadcast on national television, featured quotes from the Koran, which Muslims believe is the word of God, projected on to a naked female body with a commentary composed of the testimonies of abused Muslim women. "The murder that shattered Holland's liberal dream", *The Guardian*, 7 Nov 2004, https://www.theguardian.com/world/2004/nov/07/terrorism.religion/.

See Peter McLoughlin, *Easy Meat* (pp.195-199) for an account of the British government's attempts to pass a blasphemy law that would target those who said something which offended any Muslim. At one stage it was intended that this law should carry a penalty of up to seven years' imprisonment.

[180] See for example "Catholic school girl who refused headscarf for mosque trip labelled a truant", 13 May 2010, *Daily Mail*, http://www.dailymail.co.uk/news/article-1277744/Parents-outrage-children-told-dress-Muslim-mosque-trip—branded-truant.html. "Students Publicly Humiliated by School Because Parents Refused Permission for Mosque Visit", *Breitbart*, 29 April 2015, http://www.breitbart.com/london/2015/04/29/students-publicly-humiliated-by-school-because-parents-refused-permission-for-mosque-visit/ "Easton CE Academy in Bristol is one of several schools across the UK featured on the website showing children kneeling and/or praying, sometimes dressed in Islamic garb. The Diocese of Bristol Academies Trust declined to say whether or not its children were praying to Allah...", 5 Apr 2016, *Daily Gazette* [Essex], http://www.gazette-news.co.uk/news/14403321.Concern_after_website_describes_school_visit_to_mosque_as_abuse_of_white_children_/. "Holland: School children taken to mosque, forced to pray to allah", *Creeping Sharia*, 20 Oct 2016, https://creepingsharia.wordpress.com/2016/10/20/holland-schoolkids-pray-at-mosque/.

There are hundreds of such stories which do not make it into the news. We have spoken to feminists who pressured their reluctant daughters to wear headscarves on visits to mosques. Some families who object to such visits but who do not want any publicity have disclosed they simply say their children are ill on the days when such mosque visits are enforced.

One town in England became synonymous with the "industrial scale" rape of schoolgirls by gangs which consisted almost entirely of Muslim men (see Peter McLoughlin, *Easy Meat*, pp.95-114). The small town had seen at least 1400 schoolgirls entrapped into rape and prostitution by gangs using the same methods across England. A school in that town cancelled its visit to a mosque over a variety of parental concerns. A Muslim campaigning organisation, which had received considerable amounts of government funding, used this as an opportunity to purport Muslim victimhood. "Parents Refuse to Send Their Children to A Mosque Visit in Rotherham", 28 Feb 2015, http://tellmamauk.org/parents-refuse-send-children-mosque-visit-rotherham/.

Even when children are not taken to mosques and made to pray as if they were Muslims, inside state schools they can be made to pray like Muslims. "Fury as German primary school 'forces' children to chant 'Allahu Akbar' in Muslim prayer", *Daily Express*, 30 Oct 2016, http://www.express.co.uk/news/world/725651/germany-migrants-allahu-akbar-muslim-christmas-islam-primary-school-pupils-angela-merkel/. See also: "'There is no God but Allah'? School accused of Islamic indoctrination", *Fox News*, Dec 2015, http://www.foxnews.com/opinion/2015/09/10/there-is-no-god-but-allah-school-accused-islamic-indoctrination.htm/.

[181] Supposedly Islam prizes peace above those other religions, since neither Christianity nor Judaism gets described as "a religion of peace".

[182] In his book on the devout Muslims who destroyed the World Trade Center in September 2001, Terry McDermott says:

It is hard to appreciate how much time these young men spent thinking, talking, arguing, and reading about Islam. It became for some of them nearly the only thing they did. Some of the men in the group later met frequently in the backroom of a [Muslim] bookstore near Al Quds [Mosque in Hamburg]. There they listened to audiotaped sermons and jihad chants. One sample lyric: "When I die as a martyr, I die as a better human being". Terry McDermott, *Perfect Soldiers – The Hijackers: Who They Were, Why They Did It*, New York, 2005, p.49.

When one looks at the nationalities of those involved in the Hamburg group and the 9/11 attacks, one sees that the former came from around twenty different Islamic countries, whilst those who actually carried out the attacks were mostly from Saudi Arabia.

[183] Here are just a few examples from Muslims in a variety of countries and covering a range of years, all proclaiming they love death more than we love life. "The cars of death will not stop", *The Guardian*, 22 Nov 2003, https://www.theguardian.com/world/2003/nov/22/alqaida.politics2/, "Yemen is a lesson in the limits of Western power", *The Spectator*, 13 Jan 2010, https://www.spectator.co.uk/2010/01/yemen-is-a-lesson-in-the-limits-of-western-power/, "Families of Toulouse victims seek gag order on leaked recordings", *Jewish Journal*, 9 Jul 2012, http://jewishjournal.com/news/world/105947/ , "Lee Rigby trial: Murder accused Michael Adebolajo 'confessed he tried to behead soldier' in police interviews", *The Mirror*, 04 Dec 2013, http://www.mirror.co.uk/news/uk-news/lee-rigby-murder-trial-murder-2890496/, "Live Coverage of the Aftermath of the Paris Terror Attacks", *CNN*, 15 Nov 2015, http://transcripts.cnn.com/TRANSCRIPTS/1511/15/se.03.html/ , "ISIS 'slaughters five British spies' before threatening David Cameron in sick new video", *News.com.au*, 4 Jan 2016, http://www.news.com.au/world/middle-east/isis-slaughters-five-british-spies-before-threatening-david-cameron-in-sick-new-video/news-story/360e80eb71d454da863d9d43e77cd4ed/.

[184] "Channel 4 cancels controversial screening of Islam: The Untold Story documentary after presenter Tom Holland is threatened", *The Independent*, 11 Sept 2012, http://www.independent.co.uk/arts-entertainment/tv/news/channel-4-cancels-controversial-screening-of-islam-the-untold-story-documentary-after-presenter-tom-8125641.html/.

[185] http://www.amazon.com/Life-Muhammad-I-Ishaq/dp/0196360331#.

[186] Ibn Ishaq, *The Life of Muhammad* (trans. Guillaume), p.515.

[187] Ibn Ishaq, *The Life of Muhammad*, p.676.

[188] Ibn Ishaq, *The Life of Muhammad*, p.464-466

[189] Remember, "sunnah" means "behaviour", so hadiths like this are records of how other devout Muslims say that Mohammed behaved when he was alive. http://sunnah.com/abudawud/40/54# (archived here: http://www.webcitation.org/6pt43b5O6).

[190] Reuven Firestone *Jihad: The Origin of Holy War in Islam*, Oxford University Press, 1999, pp.128-129.

[191] Ibn Ishaq, *The Life of Muhammad*, p.166.

[192] For example, in Professor Robert Hoyland's eight-hundred page book *Seeing Islam As Others Saw It: A Survey And Evaluation Of Christian, Jewish And Zoroastrian Writings On Early Islam* (Princeton, New Jersey, 1997), there are no references to how the seventh-century Pagans and Jews of Arabia saw Mohammed's treatment of them. That is, there is no sign that any such views exist independent of the Muslim version of history.

[193] Ibn Ishaq, *The Life of Muhammad*, pp.118-119.

[194] Ibn Ishaq, *The Life of Muhammad*, p.118.

[195] Ibn Ishaq, *The Life of Muhammad*, p.132.

[196] Ibn Ishaq, *The Life of Muhammad*, p.204.

[197] *Koran* 8:41.

[198] Efraim Karsh (2007) *Islamic Imperialism: A History*, London, p.18. In 2012 when the British Museum had an exhibition on the pilgrimage to Mecca called 'the Hajj', many

shocked visitors were taking photographs of a huge motorway sign, which showed that only Muslims were allowed into the city of Mecca, with the Kuffar being directed to by-pass Mecca (the indigenous Pagans of Mecca cannot return, the Jews of Medina cannot enter that city, atheists, Buddhists, Christians are also banned from these cities). The exhibition contained several items relating to the explorer Richard Burton's covert trip to Mecca. Not one of the signs informed the public that if Burton had been caught and exposed as a Kuffar, he would have been executed.

[199] In "A special Christmas Thought for the Day recorded by His Royal Highness the Prince of Wales" on *BBC* radio on 22 Dec 2016, Britain's Prince Charles lamented the persecution of Christians saying, "We might also remember that when the prophet Muhammad migrated from Mecca to Medina, he did so because he too was seeking the freedom for himself and his followers to worship." "Prince Charles: rising intolerance risks repeat of horrors of past", *The Guardian*, 22 Dec 2016, https://www.theguardian.com/uk-news/2016/dec/22/prince-charles-rising-intolerance-risks-repeat-of-horrors-of-the-past/. With barely disguised glee, this newspaper reports that Prince Charles was implicitly equating the election of Donald Trump as President of the United States with Adolf Hitler becoming the Chancellor of Germany.

Prince Charles begins his speech by saying it is possible that within five years Christians will have been driven from Iraq, and goes on to list a number of minority faiths whose followers are increasingly under attack (see https://www.worldwatchmonitor.org/2016/12/4790960/ for a transcript of his speech). Whilst he does not mention Muslims as the people doing this persecution, there is no Christian, Jewish or atheist group who can be blamed for this. Yet he then goes on to lament the rise in "populist" political movements in the countries to which "refugees" are moving (these "refugees" are mostly Muslims and are not from the "minority faiths" he described as suffering persecution). Charles says the rise of these movements have "deeply disturbing echoes of the dark days of the 1930s". He then concludes his "Christmas message" by comparing the flight of the parents of Jesus to the (supposed) persecution of "the Prophet Mohammed". One could hardly find more muddled thinking, and this from a man who, if he ends up being the head of state, will also be the Supreme Governor of the Church of England.

Most of the "refugees" coming into Europe are from Muslim-majority countries, and there is no evidence to suggest that most of these people are non-Muslims. (see "European opinions of the refugee crisis in 5 charts", *Pew Research*, 16 Sept 2016, http://www.pewresearch.org/fact-tank/2016/09/16/european-opinions-of-the-refugee-crisis-in-5-charts/). Most of them are not even refugees (see "Most fleeing to Europe are 'not refugees', EU official says", *The Irish Times*, 26 Jan 2016, http://www.irishtimes.com/news/world/europe/most-fleeing-to-europe-are-not-refugees-eu-official-says-1.2511133). The rise of Jew-hatred in Europe is repeatedly connected to the rise in attacks on Jews by Muslims: "Jews are leaving France in record numbers amid rising anti-Semitism and fears of more Isis-inspired terror attacks", *The Independent*, 25 Jan 2016, http://www.independent.co.uk/news/world/europe/jews-are-leaving-france-in-record-numbers-amid-rising-anti-semitism-and-fears-of-more-isis-inspired-a6832391.html; "Jews fleeing Paris suburbs because of Islamic anti-Semitism", *Jihad Watch*, 01 Jun 2016, https://www.jihadwatch.org/2016/06/jews-fleeing-paris-suburbs-because-of-islamic-anti-semitism ; "Jewish population may flee Europe unless Islamic terror threat is tackled", 02 Oct 2016, *Daily Express*, http://www.express.co.uk/news/world/716786/Jewish-population-flee-Europe-unless-threat-islamic-terror-far-right-rabbi-Pinchas-Goldsch/. Neither the PVV in Holland nor the National Front in France support the persecution of any minority religion, and certainly not the persecution of Jews.

So, a Prince who has meddled in politics for decades uses the state broadcaster in Britain to claim that the rise of anti-establishment, pro-democracy political parties in Europe somehow echoes the rise of the National Socialists and their hostility towards democracy. The reality is in fact almost the exact opposite of what Prince Charles says in this much-publicised propaganda from the state broadcaster.

[200] The brackets and the word "Jihad" are to be found in the original translation.

[201] http://sunnah.com/bukhari/56/186#.

[202] https://sunnah.com/muslim/5/7#. We realise that these claims about the morality of terrorism and robbery for what you have been told is "a religion of peace" might seem utterly incredible. If so, we suggest that at the above website you use the "search" box and type in the world "spoils". You will see many other sayings attributed to Mohammed by sources considered authentic by almost every Muslim who knows anything about Islam.

[203] As you can see from this hadith from another "Book of Jihad", those who went with Mohammed to attack, rob and kill have gone down in the history of Islam saying that it was not even necessary to invite Kuffar to Islam before attacking and killing:

> I wrote to Nafi' inquiring from him whether it was necessary to extend (to the disbelievers) an invitation to accept (Islam) before meeting them in fight. He wrote (in reply) to me that it was necessary in the early days of Islam. **The Messenger of Allah**... made a raid upon Banu Mustaliq while they were unaware [...] *He killed those who fought and imprisoned others.* On that very day, he captured Juwairiya bint al-Harith. Nafi' said that *this tradition was related to him by Abdullah b. Umar who (himself) was among the raiding troops.* Sahih Muslim, Book 32, Hadith 1. https://sunnah.com/muslim/32. (Emphasis added).

[204] See *Koran* 7:4, 8:12, 8:57, 8:67, 33:26, 59:2.

[205] For example, W. Montgomery Watt, one of Britain's top experts on Islam in the latter half of the twentieth century, wrote a book entitled *Muhammad: Prophet and Statesman* (London, 1961). It is simply inconceivable that anyone could have written a book about Jesus or Buddha as a statesman: unlike Mohammed, the interests of the founders of those other religions were purely spiritual. Created a thousand years after the death of Buddha, five hundred years after the death of Jesus, Mohammed's new religion merged religion and politics and war (unlike those two real religions).

[206] Raymond Ibrahim (ed) *The Al Qaeda Reader*, London, 2007, p.43.

[207] At the end of 2016, a year which had seen dozens of terrorist attacks and plots by Muslims in Europe, often targeting Christian activities, the Catholic elite were quoting the Pope saying, "no religion is terrorist". See "The world needs politics of peace, says Pope", *Catholic Herald*, 12 Dec 2016, http://www.catholicherald.co.uk/news/2016/12/12/the-world-needs-politics-of-peace-says-pope/. Yet there is considerable doctrinal authority in the core texts of Islam justifying terrorism by Muslims. There is no excuse for the Catholic clergy and Catholic journalists not to understand that this is part of Islamic doctrine and that it permeates the history of Islam. Pope Francis ignores this and is doing a disservice to non-Muslims (and to those who might seek to leave Islam and convert to Christianity). In ensuring that non-Muslims do not understand Islam, Pope Francis might as well be on the side of Islam.

[208] Noah Feldman, *The Fall and Rise of the Islamic State*, Oxford, 2008.

[209] In the aftermath of "the Iranian Revolution" (1979) Hamid Enayat published a book entitled *Modern Islamic Political Thought* (Austin, Texas, 1982). Enayat was a Professor of Political Science at Tehran University and a Fellow of an Oxford college. Professor Enayat's book has a chapter entitled "The Concept of the Islamic State" which discusses the activism of The Muslim Brotherhood in Egypt and Jamaat e Islami in Pakistan, in the wake of the dissolution of the Caliphate and the success of the Iranian Revolution respectively. Abdulrahman Kurdi published a book entitled *The Islamic State: a Study based on the Islamic Holy Constitution* (London, 1984), published in a series called "Islamic Studies" and edited by Ziauddin Sardar. Of the five chapters in Kurdi's book, one is entitled "The Concepts of Peace and War in Islam", another is entitled "The Economy of the Islamic State". The book finishes with a document attributed to Mohammed and which is generally known as "The Constitution of Medina" (the town where Mohammed came to be considered a "statesman" by slaughtering Jews who resisted Islam). Here are the first words of Kurdi's book:

> Islam, usually viewed by most observers as a religion concerned only with
> Divine Services and personal statutes, is rather a complete system of life – a
> system concerned before its religious instructions with the social and
> governmental aspects.

The very first paragraph of the Constitution of Medina says that it applies to those who
undertake Jihad (Kurdi, p.131). Mohammed the statesman is inseparable from Mohammed
the Jihadi.

[210] See, for example, Kalim Siddiqui, *Stages of Islamic Revolution*, London, 1996.

[211] *Koran* 24:55.

[212] Shiri Ram Bakshi, *Gandhi and Khilafat*, New Delhi, 1985, p.63.

[213] "...during the Iraqi insurrection against the British in the 1920s, Gertrude Bell observed
that [...] the Shi'ites anticipated a theocratic state under Sharia law...". Ian Beckett, "Victory,
Counter-Insurgency and Iraq", in Jan Angstrom and Isabelle Duyvesteyn (eds.),
Understanding Victory and Defeat in Contemporary War, London, 2008, p.85.

[214] See Manzooruddin Ahmad, *Pakistan: The Emerging Islamic State*, Karachi, 1966; Syed
Maududi, *First principles of the Islamic state*, Lahore, 1967. By 1969 a Muslim student at
Durham University had submitted a thesis on "The Concept of the Islamic State as found in
the Writings of Maududi". Article 227 of the 1973 Constitution of Pakistan says, "All existing
laws shall be brought in conformity with the Injunctions of Islam as laid down in the Holy
Quran and Sunnah". http://www.pakistani.org/pakistan/constitution/part9.html.

[215] Dr. Kalim Siddiqui, was the editor of the Khilafat (Caliphate) newspaper in Pakistan in
the 1940s. He moved to Britain and founded "The Muslim Parliament" in 1989. In a
discussion between several Muslim academics on how to bring about an Islamic State,
Siddiqui said:

> Since the Revolution in [predominantly Shiite] Iran I have been moving
> around some of the Sunni countries – some of the most reactionary Sunni
> countries [...] If national boundaries were taken away, probably Ayatullah
> Khoemini [sic] would be elected by acclamation by the Ummah as a whole
> as the leader of the Muslim world today.

In response, Professor Algar (a British convert to Islam) says "Very definitely" (see Hamid
Algar, *The Roots of the Islamic Revolution*, London, 1983, p.67). We can see from this how
the concept of a pan-national Islamic State might even unify Shiite and Sunni Muslims
against the Kuffar world (that all Muslims would unite behind the Muslim leader who most
successfully conducts war against the Kuffar). In 1989 it was Siddiqui, the former Marxist
turned Muslim, who led the protests in Britain and the calls for Rushdie's murder. See
Kenan Malik, *From Fatwa to Jihad: The Rushdie Affair and its Legacy*, London, 2009, pp.7-8,
pp.185-186). Not only "the Iranian Revolution" of 1979 but also the death sentence
imposed upon Salman Rushdie, were events which united the Ummah (Sunni and Shiite
alike). The fatwa against Rushdie is still in force. It was the start of western writers and
publishers cowering in fear of Muslims and Islam. As Daniel Pipes says "The Satanic Verses
provided a rare issue on which the Sunnis and Shi'is [sic] could agree..." *The Rushdie Affair:
The Novel, the Ayatollah, and the West*, New York, 1990, p.134.

[216] The economics of the Islamic system can be found exemplified by the Islamic State, the
pan-national Islamic empire which existed from the death of Mohammed until just after
World War I. Most Muslim organisations in Britain have been seeking the return of this pan-
national Islamic State. There are Islamic political parties to be found all over the world,
which advocate the recreation of the Caliphate. For minor theological or opportunistic
reasons, Islamic political parties such as Hizb ut Tahrir ("Party of Freedom"), claim that
Islamic State in Syria is not really a proper Caliphate, despite this party's decades-long
encouragement to Muslims to create the Islamic State. We can see in this existing Islamic
State what the economic model of the Islamic State was in history: war, piracy, slave-taking
and slave-selling. This economy of war and slavery has existed throughout the entire
history of Islam. As we see from a leaked memo from the Muslim organisation Quilliam to
the British government in 2010, many of the prominent Muslim organisations in the UK

support the creation of this Caliphate, the Islamic State. "many will agree with [the] overall goal of create a single 'Islamic State' which would bring together all Muslims around the world under a single government and then impose on them a single interpretation of shari'ah law." Appendix A of *Preventing Terrorism: Where Next for Britain?*, June 2010, https://www.scribd.com/doc/34834977/Secret-Quilliam-Memo-to-government. Within four years, this universally-desired Islamic State was re-created in Syria and Iraq. Despite the Quisling politicians around Europe claiming that the Islamic State in Syria was not Islamic, these European countries had to put obstacles in the way of their Muslim citizens travelling to the Islamic State to fight for it and to profit from its economy based on robbery and slavery. "Islamic State crisis: '3,000 European jihadists join fight'", *BBC*, 24 September 2014, http://www.bbc.co.uk/news/world-middle-east-29372494. Less than two years later this number had doubled, despite the efforts in Europe to stop those with citizenship from going there to fight for Islam: "Between 27,000 and 31,000 people have traveled to Syria and Iraq to join the Islamic State [...] There are approximately 6,000 people from Europe - with the most fighters leaving France, Germany and the UK" ("Iraq and Syria: How many foreign fighters are fighting for Isil?", *The Telegraph*, 24 March 2016, http://www.telegraph.co.uk/news/2016/03/29/iraq-and-syria-how-many-foreign-fighters-are-fighting-for-isil/). The more that the Western media publicised that these Muslim warriors were taking young women and girls as slaves to rape, the more Muslims in the West seemed to want to evade the obstacles placed in front of them by the countries of which they claimed citizenship. It seems incontrovertible that more British Muslims have gone to join the slave-raping cult of Islamic State than are in the British Army. "Is Donald Trump right that more British Muslims fight for Isis than the UK army?", *The Guardian*, 11 December 2015, https://www.theguardian.com/news/reality-check/2015/dec/11/donald-trump-needs-check-facts-british-muslims-isis.

[217] *Shorter Encyclopaedia of Islam*, London, 1953, p.176. The last pages of the above book list the multitude of experts on Islam who contributed articles to this encyclopaedia of Western knowledge about Islam.

[218] According to the contemporary, online *Oxford English Dictionary*, it was only in 2002 that this modern term of "Islamism" as a political ideology comparable to Communism or National Socialism began to be used.

[219] That is how we would view his actions from the morality of the twentieth century. Muslims will not see anything wrong with their genocide against non-Muslims in any century. "For Turkey, denying an Armenian genocide is a question of identity", *Al Jazeera*, 24 April 2015, http://america.aljazeera.com/articles/2015/4/24/for-turks-acknowledging-an-armenian-genocide-undermines-national-identity.html/.

[220] Sex with slaves is sanctioned by *Koran* 4:24. In the most authoritative hadiths, Mohammed criticises his Companions for taking care not to get their slave girls pregnant when they had sex with them:

> Abu Sa'id al-Khudri (Allah be pleased with him) reported that mention was made of 'azl [coitus interruptus] in the presence of Allah's Apostle (may peace be upon him) whereupon he said: Why do you practise it? They said: There is a man whose wife has to suckle the child, and if that person has a sexual intercourse with her (she may conceive) which he does not like, and there is another person who has a slave-girl and he has a sexual intercourse with her, but he does not like her to have conception so that she may not become Umm Walad, whereupon he (the Holy Prophet) said: There is no harm if you do not do that, for that (the birth of the child) is something pre-ordained. Ibn 'Aun said: I made a mention of this hadith to Hasan, and he said: By Allah, (it seems) as if there is upbraiding in it (for 'azl). See Sahih Muslim 8:3377, http://quranx.com/Hadith/Muslim/USC-MSA/Book-8/Hadith-3377/.

[221] "Thousands of Yazidi women sold as sex slaves 'for theological reasons', says Isil", *The Telegraph*, 29 April 2014, http://www.telegraph.co.uk/ news/worldnews/islamic-state/11158797/Thousands-of-Yazidi-women-sold-as-sex-slaves-for-theological-reasons-

says-Isil.html. See also "estimates put the number of girls still being held by extremist fighters at up to 4,000" in "'Nine-year-old pregnant' after being raped by at least 10 Islamic State paedophiles", *Daily Express*, 10 April 2015, http://www.express.co.uk/news/world/569556/Islamic-State-Nine-year-old-pregnant-rape-torture/.

[222] Murray Gordon, *Slavery in the Arab World*, New York, 1992, p.79.

[223] Some tenth century Muslim rulers would have harems consisting of 12,000 sex slaves, but even lowly tradesmen might have several sex-slaves. Ronald Segal, *Islam's Black Slaves*, 2001, p.39. "[To] take their women as our sex slaves. In this, we felt we would be accurately following in the footsteps of our role-model, Mohammed..." (Tawfik Hamid, *The Roots of Jihad: An Insider's View of Islamic Violence*, 2005, p.56).

[224] "The unmarried female slave is at the disposal of her male owner as a concubine..." (Joseph Schacht, *Introduction to Islamic Law*, Oxford, 1964, p.127). "Sexual intercourse was allowed by virtue of a master's ownership of the slave's body and [the] right to deal with his property as he saw fit" (Jonathan Brockopp, *Early Maliki Law*, Leiden, 2000, p.195).

[225] Sultan Hussyn Tabandeh, *A Muslim Commentary on the Universal Declaration of Human Rights*, Guildford, 1970, p.25.

[226] "[T]he Quran not only gave him the right to rape her — it condoned and encouraged it, he insisted" from "ISIS Enshrines a Theology of Rape", *New York Times*, August 14, 2015, http://www.nytimes.com/2015/08/14/world/middleeast/isis-enshrines-a-theology-of-rape.html/.

[227] Bassam Timi, "War and Peace in Islam" (from Andrew Bostom (ed.) *The Legacy of Jihad: Islamic Holy War and the Fate of Non-Muslims*, New York, 2005, p.328).

[228] "Strong reaction to Obama statement: 'ISIL is not Islamic'", *CNN*, 11 Sept 2014, http://edition.cnn.com/2014/09/10/politics/obama-isil-not-islamic/; Mehdi Hasan, "How Islamic is Islamic State?", *New Statesman*, 10 Mar 2015, http://www.newstatesman.com/world-affairs/2015/03/mehdi-hasan-how-islamic-islamic-state/.

[229] Rudolph Peters, *Jihad in Classical and Modern Islam*, Princeton, 1996 (from Andrew Bostom (ed.) *The Legacy of Jihad: Islamic Holy War and the Fate of Non-Muslims*, New York, 2005, p.322). The manual of sharia law *Reliance of the Traveller* agrees with this idea of Jihad being a communal obligation (see section o9.1).

[230] Frederick Quinn, *The Sum of All Heresies: The Image of Islam in Western Thought*, Oxford, 2008, p.39.

[231] John Quincy Adams, *The American Annual Register*, New York, 1830, p.274.

[232] One of the rare exceptions to this is Richard Gabriel.

> The idea of a soldier motivated by religion in the certainty that he was doing God's work on earth seems to have been one of Muhammad's most important military innovations [...] no army before Muhammad ever placed religion at the centre of military motivation [...] the soldiers of Islam were usually extremely religious [...] A central part of the motivation of the Islamic soldier was the teaching of his faith that death was not something to be feared, but to be sought [...] those killed in battle would be welcomed immediately into a paradise of eternal pleasure [...] To die fighting in defense of the faith (*jihad*) was to become a martyr. *Muhammad: Islam's First Great General*, Oklahoma, 2007, p.47.

Whilst focusing only on Mohammed as a military leader rather than on the subsequent history of Jihad, at least Gabriel was one academic who was prepared to provide a narrative that went against The Grand Lie that Islam is a religion of peace.

[233] Daniel Pipes, "Jihad in the West", *Middle East Quarterly*, June 1999, http://www.meforum.org/1297/jihad-in-the-west/.

[234] One of the exceptions to this rule in the twentieth-century was the attack by Muslim terrorists on Israeli athletes at the 1972 Munich Olympics. In this case, there were so few

Muslims in the West that Muslims needed the assistance of German National Socialists to carry out the attack. As with the later attacks by Muslim terrorists on the Westgate shopping mall in Nairobi and the Bataclan concert hall in Paris, the Muslims in Munich castrated and tortured their victims. "Revealed: How Palestinian terrorists tortured Israeli hostages before 1972 Munich Olympic massacre - including castrating one athlete while others watched", *Daily Mail,* 1 Dec 2015, "http://www.dailymail.co.uk/news/article-3341784/New-horrifying-details-emerge-1972-Munich-Olympic-massacre-including-one-athlete-castrated-hostages-watched.html.

[235] Chris Blackhurst, "Publishers cave in to threat of Islam ban", *The Independent*, 12 April 1997.

[236] The Quisling leaders of the West vacillate between attempting to identify the problem and then covering it up. After three elections in which the Islam-promoting socialist party in Britain were elected, the electorate switched from Tweedledee to Tweedledum. The so-called "conservative" party came to power in 2010 pretending to oppose "non-violent extremism", but by 2015 had given up and were back being apologists for "the religion of peace".

> The change of government from Gordon Brown to David Cameron in May 2010 sped up the shift in counter-terrorism policies from collaborating with non-violent extremists to seeing them as part of the problem rather than as part of the solution. [...] David Cameron's new approach of confronting extremism rather than winning over so-called non-violent extremists was, however, soon losing momentum... "Violent and Non-Violent Extremism: Two Sides of the Same Coin?", *International Centre for Counter-Terrorism*, May 2014, https://www.icct.nl/download/file/ICCT-Schmid-Violent-Non-Violent-Extremism-May-2014.pdf, p.6.

By 2015, the British Prime Minister was claiming that it was only "violent Islamism" which posed a threat: "Speaking about the threat to the West posed by violent Islamism, David Cameron..." ("David Cameron has started a courageous dialogue about faith and society", *The Telegraph*, 19 Jun 2015, http://www.telegraph.co.uk/news/uknews/terrorism-in-the-uk/11684975/David-Cameron-has-started-a-courageous-dialogue-about-faith-and-society.html). By 2016, the Pope Francis who replaced the now-retired Pope Benedict XVI, was saying "Not all Muslims are violent..." (see "Pope Francis Reveals Why He Doesn't Discuss 'Islamic Violence'", *NBC News*, 1 Aug 2016, http://www.nbcnews.com/news/world/pope-francis-reveals-why-he-doesnt-discuss-islamic-violence-n620551/. We can be sure that within the hierarchy of the Catholic Church there are hundreds of experts on Islam, people who understand the doctrines of the religion of war and who know the history of Islamic genocide. See also these other discussions where the problem is "violent Islamism" and not the fiction of "Islamism" *per se*: "Terror in Paris", *The Economist*, 10 Jan 2015, http://www.economist.com/news/leaders/21638118-islamists-are-assailing-freedom-speech-vilifying-all-islam-wrong-way-counter/ ; "Violent Islamism Has Failed", *New York Times*, 4 Nov 2011, http://www.nytimes.com/2011/11/05/opinion/violent-islamism-has-failed.html ; "Debating Non-Violent Islamism", *Foreign Policy*, 24 June 2010, http://foreignpolicy.com/2010/06/24/debating-non-violent-islamism/.

[237] "People of no religion outnumber Christians in England and Wales – study", *The Guardian*, 23 May 2016, https://www.theguardian.com/world/2016/may/23/no-religion-outnumber-christians-england-wales-study/. Since shirk (associating other god figures with god) is the unpardonable sin in the Islamic value system, it is hard to see how even Christians are not classed as isolators, since they associate Jesus and the Holy Ghost in a tripartite god figure.

[238] *Koran* 9:122.

[239] Muhammed Marmaduke Pickthall, *The Meaning of the Glorious Koran*, Everyman, 1991, p.18.

[240] Michael Gove, *Celsius 7/7*, London, 2006, pp.12-13.

[241] Michael Gove, *Celsius 7/7*, London, 2006, pp.11.

[242] There are multiple examples from 1838 to 1842 in reports concerning Lebanon, Egypt, Syria and Turkey. The following remarks would barely seem out of place in the Bradford of 2015, or the Cairo of 700 AD.

> A thousand men of the National Guard of this town [in Egypt] have embarked for Syria, in order to strengthen the timid against the fear of battle [...] they were assembled in a confined space, where they were made to slaughter a number of sheep, and, having washed their hands in the hot blood of those animals, they were obliged to swear by the Koran that they would cheerfully shed their own blood for the defence of Islamism... "Eastern Intelligence", *The Times* (London, England), 18 July 1840, p.5.

The Times of the 1840s was even talking about Islamism in relation to married women being forcibly turned into sex-slaves of the Emir in Lebanon. "The wife was sent into the Emir's harem and made to embrace Islamism..." from "Syria As It Is", *The Times*, 27 June 1842, p.6. Here is another example where Islamism is clearly just Islam:

> Several days' imprisonment, and frequent beating, failed to return him to Islamism [...] At the place of execution he was exhorted to recant Christianity [...] the naked sword was shown him, but he persisted in his refusal [...] at last he was thrown down in the most brutal manner, and his head sliced and sawed off". "Private Correspondence", *The Times*, 20 Sept 1843, p.5.

For other early examples where there is no distinction in English between "Islam" and "Islamism" see "Private Correspondence", *The Times*, 31 Dec 1838, p.5. These are just four of the oldest articles in *The Times* archive where the word "Islamism" occurs, and we can instantly see the themes which have made the rise of ISIS so disgusting: fanatical preparedness to die fighting for Islam, Christians beheaded for blasphemy, non-Muslim women stolen from their husbands and turned into sex-slaves. Clearly the idea that Islamism is somehow separate from Islam and that it is a product of the twentieth-century is a brazen lie.

[243] The editor of a collection of articles on Islam and politics emphasised that even within this highly-specialised subject, the word "Islamism" was a new way of speaking about Islam in the 1990s. See Andrew Kimmens (ed.), *Islamic Politics and the Modern World*, New York, 1991, p.8.

[244] Until the 1990s experts on the history of political thought in the West had virtually no interest in "political Islam". In a book cataloguing 8,000 of the most important scholarly books and articles on political thought in the West in the fifty years between 1945 and 1995, there is only 1 article which refers to Islam (see Robert Eccleshall and Michael Kenny (eds.) *Western Political Thought: A Bibliographical Guide to Post-war Research*, Manchester, 1995, p.37). Further evidence comes from the world's most comprehensive full-text index of books, which is provided by Google (at books.google.com). Google provide a tool called "the ngram viewer" (books.google.com/ngrams) which allows one to search for specific words across this massive corpus of books and to chart the frequency with which a word is to be found relative to the date of publication. When one searches for the word "Islamist", this tool shows that between 1900 and 1950 the world "Islamist" occurred in virtually no books. Between 1950 and 1990 a small number of books use the word. From 1990 to 2008 there is nearly a 1000% increase in the number of books using this word. This is proof that the idea of an Islamist was basically invented after World War Two, and specifically after the 1990s: writers in English became almost frenzied in their use of this word following the Rushdie Affair. The worse the problem with Islam gets in the West, the more the public must be deceived by maintaining that Islam and Islamism are somehow different things.

[245] Bassam Tibi, *Islamism and Islam*, London, 2012, pp.139-141.

[246] Bassam Tibi, *Islamism and Islam*, London, 2012, p.201.

[247] Hamed Abdel Samed, *Islamic Fascism*, New York, 2016, p.187 (originally published in German in 2014). Interestingly, in 2011 when Professor Ekmeleddin Ihsanoglu, the head of the Organisation of Islamic Cooperation (the largest voting bloc at the United Nations) was

asked a question about the difference between Islamism and Islam he replied "I don't know anything called Islamism, I know Islam, in fact I don't know what Islamism is" (see video here https://youtu.be/QgXhlQqAHhQ). Professor Ihsanoglu has umpteen honorary doctorates and professorships from a wide range of universities. A Google search for the words "Ihsanoglu islamism" returns http://tundratabloids.com/2008/10/oic-sec-gen-ekmeleddin-ihsanoglu-in-helsinki-islamism-anti-semitism-where-where/ as the top hits, and that is the webpage containing the links to and discussion of the above video. Given the importance of the OIC in global politics and the world of Islam, and the relative obscurity of the Tundra Tabloids website, it seems likely that never before has this Secretary-General of the largest Islamic organisation in the world previously been involved in any discussion positing a difference between Islam and "Islamism". For an in-depth discussion of the OIC see Bat Ye'or, *Europe, Globalization and the Coming Universal Caliphate*, Madison, 2011.

[248] *The Shorter Encyclopaedia of Islam*, London, 1953, p.139. The starting date of the Islamic calendar was decided by the Caliph, the Muslim leader who took over after Mohammed's death.

[249] Any Muslim who wants to reject the latter half of Mohammed's life should (at the very least) refuse to accept the traditional Islamic calendar.

[250] "The date of this declaration of war was later chosen as the first day of the Muslim calendar..." (Chris Horrie and Peter Chippendale, *What is Islam*, London, 1990, p.21).

[251] See the case of Mahmoud Mohammed Taha in Farhad Khosrokhavar, *Inside Jihadism: Understanding Jihadi Movements Worldwide*, London, 2016, p.157.

[252] "Prophet Muhammad", *BBC*, http://www.bbc.co.uk/religion/religions/islam/history/muhammad_1.shtml/.

[253] According to French academic Maxime Rodinson, the number of Muslims who left Mecca for Medina was as few as seventy people. *Mohammed*, New York, 1971, p.144 (see also W. Montgomery Watt *Muhammad: Prophet and Statesman*, Oxford, 1961, p.70). Before "emigrating" to Medina, Mohammed had approximately seventy-five followers in that settlement (see Ibn Ishaq, *The Life of Muhammad*, trans. Guillaume, London, 1955, p.203). The settlement was called Yathrib before Mohammed created his Islamic State there, and afterwards the name became "Medina" (which means "the city of the Prophet").

[254] http://en.wikipedia.org/wiki/Muhammad_in_Medina#Conquest_of_Mecca#.

[255] The Islamic calendar does not begin until Mohammed moves to Medina to become a politician instead of a preacher, and this move to Medina did not occur until Mohammed had been given permission from "Allah" to wage war "against all and sundry" (see Ibn Ishaq, *The Life of Muhammad*, p.204).

[256] The following comes from a Muslim website:

> Nearly 40% of British Muslims blame the actions of the police and MI5 for radicalising the younger generation [...] Some 39% said the authorities were contributing to radicalising young people, with 29% saying they were not. The survey confirms the widespread anger in the community over harassment, spying and entrapment techniques that the security services seem to be deploying against Muslims. "Nearly 40% of British Muslims blame police and M15 for radicalisation", 10 April 2015, http://5pillarsuk.com/2015/04/10/nearly-40-of-british-muslims-blame-policem15-for-radicalisation/.

Another Islamic website hosts an article which is attributed to a Muslim academic at Liverpool University:

> as researchers have confirmed, the increase [in the Muslim population of the UK] is potentially greater than this as it is very likely that a large percentage of the 7% of the population who did not answer the optional question regarding religion are Muslims. "The Significance of Muslim growth in the UK", 14 Jan 2013, http://www.islam21c.com/islamic-thought/7984-the-significance-of-muslim-growth-in-the-uk/.

[257] As evinced by the abject failure of political surveys to correctly predict the referendum in the UK concerning the UK leaving the European Union. A few months later, American polling companies again (almost without exception) got the result of the US Presidential election wrong.

[258] "Poll reveals 40pc of Muslims want sharia law in UK", *The Telegraph*, 19 Feb 2006, http://www.telegraph.co.uk/news/uknews/1510866/Poll-reveals-40pc-of-Muslims-want-sharia-law-in-UK.html/.

[259] "Waiting for the Kettle to Boil: Culture and Consciousness" in John Hartley, *A Short History of Cultural Studies*, London, 2003, p.88.

[260] Soeren Kern, "Europe: Islamic Fundamentalism is Widespread", *Gatestone Institute*, 16 December 2013, http://www.gatestoneinstitute.org/4092/europe-islamic-fundamentalism/. The survey can be found here: "The Six Country Immigrant Integration Comparative Survey", Evelyn Ersanilli and Ruud Koopmans, *WZB Berlin Social Science Center*, July 2013, https://bibliothek.wzb.eu/pdf/2013/vi13-102.pdf .

[261] "Fundamentalism and out-group hostility - Muslim immigrants and Christian natives in Western Europe", Ruud Koopmans, WZB Mitteilungen, *WZB Berlin Social Research Center*, December 2013, https://www.wzb.eu/sites/default/files/u6/koopmans_englisch_ed.pdf .

[262] *C4/Juniper Survey of Muslims*, 2015, https://www.icmunlimited.com/wp-content/uploads/2016/04/Mulims-full-suite-data-plus-topline.pdf, p.25.

[263] The survey did not say if the control group contained Muslims or not, nor from what geographical regions the control group came (the Muslims came from only some urban areas). If the control group also contained Muslims, then that might account for a small amount of support for the Caliphate among the control group (it might have only been Muslims in the control group who were supportive towards the Caliphate).

[264] Almost a decade after the *Policy Exchange* survey of Muslim attitudes in the UK, a television channel commissioned a new survey, as part of a programme about the failures of multiculturalism and the divergence between the attitudes of Muslims and the rest of the country. "C4 Survey and Documentary reveals What British Muslims Really Think", *Channel 4*, 11 April 2016, http://www.channel4.com/info/press/news/c4-survey-and-documentary-reveals-what-british-muslims-really-think/. When one considers the context in which this survey was commissioned, then one would expect the people involved to be aware of the high number of Muslims in the 2007 *Policy Exchange* survey who wanted homosexuality criminalised. The 2007 survey showed that, in aggregate, 61% of Muslims wanted homosexuality criminalised, but that 2007 survey also showed that young adult Muslims were extremely anti-gay. In the 2016 survey the proportion of Muslims who wanted to criminalise homosexuals fell to 52%, rather than going above 61% as one might expect based on the 2007 survey (71% of 2007 survey in the 16-24 age bracket wanted gays criminalized). This unexpected divergence from the 2007 survey receives no mention in the 2016 *C4/ICM* survey, nor the trend shown in that 2007 survey; thus, no explanation is offered in the later survey as to why there is this discrepancy from 2007. A Gallup survey from 2009 showed that 99.5% of UK Muslims admitted they had no tolerance of homosexuality (see "Muslims in Britain Have Zero Tolerance of Homosexuality, Says Poll", *The Guardian*, 7 May 2009, https://www.theguardian.com/uk/2009/may/07/muslims-britain-france-germany-homosexuality.) Having no tolerance would not necessarily equate to wanting to see gays criminalized (and possibly killed), but the 2016 survey is also widely discrepant with this 2009 survey. It seems highly likely that, as shocking as the general public seemed to find the C4/ICM poll, the true scale of Muslim hatred of homosexuals is far higher than the news headlines from 2016 would lead one to believe.

[265] Here are the last three major democratic campaigns in Britain and America. The polling companies got the result wrong each time. "Why the polls were wrong about the Conservative campaign", *The Telegraph*, 8 May 2015, http://www.telegraph.co.uk/news/general-election-2015/11591779/Why-the-polls-were-wrong-about-the-Conservative-campaign.html; "Here's why pollsters and pundits got Brexit wrong", *The Washington Post*, 24 June 2016, https://www.washingtonpost.com/news/monkey-cage/wp/2016/06/24/heres-why-

pollsters-and-pundits-got-brexit-wrong/; "How wrong were the polls in predicting the US election and why did they fail to see Trump's win?", *The Telegraph*, 17 Nov 2016, http://www.telegraph.co.uk/news/2016/11/09/how-wrong-were-the-polls-in-predicting-the-us-election/.

[266] Shmuel Bar, Warrant for Terror: *The Fatwas of Radical Islam and the Duty to Jihad*, New York, 2006, p.110.

[267] Shmuel Bar, *Warrant for Terror: The Fatwas of Radical Islam and the Duty to Jihad*, New York, 2006, p.111. In saying that criminal law is "civil" not "religious", we take it that Bar is making a primary distinction between secular (man-made) laws and religious laws.

[268] Patrick Sookhdeo, *Global Jihad: The Future in the Face of Militant Islam*, London, 2007. pp.154-155. See also the statement from Osama Bin Laden in November 2001, quoted in Raymond Ibrahim (ed) The Al Qaeda Reader, London, 2007, p.282.

[269] William Kilpatrick, *The Politically Incorrect Guide to Jihad*, Washington, 2016, p.55.

[270] The Fiqh Council of Birmingham, an organisation purporting to be expert in sharia law, claimed that such attacks were un-Islamic. "This is a clear textual injunction for establishing the universal sanctity of innocent life taught by Islam", they claimed, citing Koran 5:32 (http://www.fiqhcouncilbirmingham.com/page/article/17 and see also http://www.webcitation.org/6ptMEC62V). The "quotation" they give of Koran 5:32 omits the central part of the phrase which permits killing and they give no indication that they have omitted the permission to kill from the verse. There is no sanctity of life in Islam and it is only by doctoring verses from the Koran that Muslims and their Quislings can pretend that there is such regard for life.

[271] *Koran* 4:56.

[272] "[E]veryone is born sinless and by becoming Muslim, the 'revert' return to this natural condition". Jan N. Bremmer, Wout J. van Bekkum and Arie L. Molendijk (eds.), *Cultures of Conversion*, Leuvan, 2006, p.161. See also Karin van Nieuwkirk (ed.), *Women Embracing Islam: Gender and Conversion in the West*, Austin, Texas, 2006, p.198; Alison Pargeter, *The New Frontiers of Jihad: Radical Islam in Europe*, Philadelphia, 2008, p.177. The hadiths which form the basis for this principle of Islam confirm just how supremacist and hateful Islam is towards any religious belief except Islam. These hadiths are accepted by virtually all Muslims (and by all of the Quisling apologists for Islam). One version has the founder of Islam say, "Every child is born with a true faith of Islam (i.e. to worship none but Allah Alone) but his parents convert him to Judaism, Christianity or Magainism, as an animal delivers a perfect baby animal. Do you find it mutilated?" Bukhari, Book 32, 441 http://www.mohammeds-koran.com/texts/hadith/bukhari/23/23.441/. So, according to "the religion of peace" for any parent to bring their child up in a religion other than Islam is like mutilating their child.

[273] According to Islamic scholarship, dying as a Jihadi wipes away the "martyr's" sins (see Ibn Warraq, *The Islam in Islamic Terrorism: The Importance of Beliefs, Ideas, and Ideology*, London, 2017, p. 117). Much was made of the 9/11 terrorists gambling, consuming alcohol and visiting strip clubs shortly before the attacks, as if these 'sins' are not wiped out by the 'good deed' of being 'martyred' as a Jihadi. See "Seedy secrets of hijackers who broke Muslim laws", *The Telegraph*, 6 Oct 2001, http://www.telegraph.co.uk/news/1358665/Seedy-secrets-of-hijackers-who-broke-Muslim-laws.html/.

[274] Ibn Kathir was one of the leading intellectuals of fourteenth-century Syria. He was educated in Damascus, his career culminating in 1366 "with a professorial position at the Great Mosque of Damascus" (*Merriam-Webster's Encyclopaedia of World Religions*, Springfield, Massachusets, 1999, p.489).

[275] http://www.qtafsir.com/index.php? option=com_content&task=view&id=786&Itemid=60.

[276] Patrick Sookhdeo, *Global Jihad: The Future in the Face of Militant Islam*, 2007, p.196.

[277] Patrick Sookhdeo, *Global Jihad: The Future in the Face of Militant Islam*, 2007, p.197-198.

[278] Patrick Sookhdeo, *Global Jihad: The Future in the Face of Militant Islam*, 2007, p.198.

[279] Patrick Sookhdeo, *Global Jihad: The Future in the Face of Militant Islam*, 2007, p.200.

[280] Patrick Sookhdeo, *Global Jihad: The Future in the Face of Militant Islam*, 2007, p.203.

[281] For a book-length study of the statements of just one Muslim see Caroline Fourest, *Brother Tariq: The Doublespeak of Tariq Ramadan* (translated by Ioana Wieder and John Atherton), London, 2008.

[282] See sections K32.1 to K32.4 of *Reliance of the Traveller: A Classic Manual of Islamic Sacred Law*, trans. Sheikh Keller, 1997. In the absence of "moderate Muslims" or academic experts in Arabic coming forward to remedy the deception of this translation, individuals have had their own translations of these sections made. This manual of Islamic law says things like: "Women and children of the land that has been conquered are considered booty of the war and they are considered slaves. [...] The master who owns a woman slave can use her in any way for his sexual pleasure (see http://www.webcitation.org/6ptMtFW6F and https://mdharrismd.com/2015/03/03/translation-of-the-manual-of-islamic-sacred-law/). No wonder the terrorists of ISIS believe they are following the word of god when they take women and girls as sex slaves.

[283] In 2005 a Muslim scholar named Mahmoud Muhammad Taha was executed for apostasy. His crime in sharia law had been to say that the message of the Koran could be divided into two parts: the (relatively tolerant) Meccan verses which were meant to have eternal and global applicability and the (genocidal discriminatory) Medinan verses which were only supposed to apply to that time and that place. See Andrew March, *Apostasy: Oxford Bibliographies Online Research Guide*, Oxford University Press, Yale, 2010, p.18.

[284] "Over the centuries many quarrels and dissensions have arisen between Christians and Muslims. The sacred Council now pleads with all to forget the past..." from "Second Vatican Council", 28 Oct 1965, *United States Conference of Catholic Bishops*, http://www.usccb.org/beliefs-and-teachings/ecumenical-and-interreligious/interreligious/islam/vatican-council-and-papal-statements-on-islam.cfm.

[285] The following passage is from a book that records the impact of Islam on the religious communities in the countries invaded by the armies of Islam.

> the only surviving seventh-century Coptic [Christian] texts are all hostile to the Arabs. And later observations [...] contrast strongly with the anguish in earlier accounts like the following: "When the Arabs heard of the festival [...] they appeared there and took captive a large number of men and women and innumerable boys and girls. The Christians who were left no longer knew what to believe. Some of them said: 'Why does God allow this to happen'?" Robert Hoyland, *Seeing Islam As Others Saw It: A Survey and Evaluation of Christian, Jewish and Zoroastrian Writings on Early Islam*, Princeton, 1997, p.23.

[286] From the first few pages of *The History of Spain* by Louis Bertrand and Sir Charles Petrie (2nd edition, London, 1954):

> It was Julian, a Christian, who had summoned the Musulmans to Spain; and it was Christian Spaniards who acted as guides to them and, on occasion, opened the gates of towns to them. This incorrigible blindness was an error which was to repeat itself indefinitely in the course of the centuries. What Visigoth Spain once done light-heartedly Musulman Spain was to do over and over again through a regular fatality of the conquest. At every turn the Caliphs and their successors, the little Moorish kings, called upon Africans to support them against a rival or a Christian prince, or simply to maintain their personal security. They thought that they were finding in them merely momentary allies; they let them establish themselves in their towns; and, when the wanted to get rid of them, they had to fight and expel them at the cost of great effort, or else submit to the conquerors. (pp.27-28)

[287] See Emmet Scott, *The Impact of Islam*, London, 2014, for a discussion of the astounding deception concerning the myth of Islamic tolerance in Spain.

[288] Muslims do not even consider any translation of the Koran from Arabic to be a real Koran. Thus, the UK courts have been advised that any Koran on which a Muslim swears to tell the truth must be in Arabic: "no oath taken by a Muslim is valid unless taken on a copy of the Koran in Arabic", Adrian Keane and Paul McKeown, *The Modern Law of Evidence*, 11th edition, Oxford, 2016, p.141.

[289] Ibn Warraq, *What the Koran Really Says: Language, Text and Commentary*, New York, 2002, p.24.

[290] *Shorter Encyclopaedia of Islam*, p. 279.

[291] "'The scattered fragments of the Koran were in the first instance collected by his immediate successor Abu Bekr, about a year after the Prophet's death, at the suggestion of Omar, who foresaw that, as the Muslim warriors, whose memories were the sole depositories of large portions of the revelations, died off or were slain, as had been the case with many in the battle of Yemâma, A.H. 12, the loss of the greater part, or even of the whole, was imminent. Zaid Ibn Thâbit, a native of Medina, and one of the Ansars, or helpers, who had been Muhammad's amanuensis, was the person fixed upon to carry out the task". *The Koran*, trans. J.M.Rodwell, Dent, London, 1937, p.1. Note that in contrast to Christianity, the original followers of this "religion" of Mohammed were not killed because they were being persecuted; they were being killed in battle as warriors.

According to the Islamic authorities, it was under Caliph Uthman (*circa* 650 A.D.) that variants of the Koran were brought into uniformity. The newly-standardized Koran being distributed to Medina, Basra, Damascus, Kufa (and possibly other Islamic centres e.g. Mecca):

> the new version must have driven out the variants because of its official authority and the general desire for uniformity. It was in this way that there came into being the authorised Kur'an, which has remained generally authoritative to the present day and in spite of all vicissitudes has formed, with the Sunna, the solid foundation for Muslim life and thought. -- *The Shorter Encyclopaedia of Islam*, London, 1953, p.280.

Modern scholars have questioned the very foundations of the history of Islam and even of the existence of Mohammed as a real, historical person (for example, see Robert Spencer, *Did Muhammad exist?: an inquiry into Islam's obscure origins*, Wilmington, 2012). Under the onslaught of evidence unearthed by Western scholars at the turn of the twenty-first century, even Islamic organisations admit that none of the manuscripts which were claimed to be the original copies distributed by Caliph Uthman are complete, are standard and date from 650 A.D. (see http://www.islamic-awareness.org/Quran/Text/Mss/#b). Thus, the idea of a standard Koran distributed by Caliph Uthman may be a myth. If it was not a myth then it seems strange that this first, standardised Koran was an artefact which through the ages was never treated by Muslims with the respect one might expect as the supposed unchanging cornerstone of their ideology.

[292] "[T]he messenger and those who believe with him strive with their wealth and their lives [Jihad]. Such are they for whom are the good things. Such are they who are the successful" (Koran 9:88). See also "Allah hath bought from the believers their lives and their wealth because the Garden [Paradise] will be theirs: they shall fight [Jihad] in the way of Allah and shall slay and be slain [kill and be killed]" (9:111).

[293] Most Kuffar have so little understanding of Islam that they do not even know that in Islam they are regarded as lesser beings, practically as sub-human.

[294] For a critique of the ridiculous and pernicious concept of "Orientalism" see Ibn Warraq, *Defending the West: A Critique of Edward Said's "Orientalism"*, New York, 2007.

[295] The scriptural basis for the principle of abrogation can be found in Koran 2:106, "Nothing of our revelation (even a single verse) do we abrogate or cause to be forgotten, but we bring (in place) one better..." See Anwarul Haqq, *Abrogation in the Koran*, Lucknow, India, 1926. Physical copies of this book are extremely rare; it can be found here: http://www.muhammadanism.com/Quran/abrogation_koran.pdf .

Haqq's book is so important, that it is cited in the explanation of abrogation in the

Koran in *The Shorter Encyclopaedia of Islam* (p.275). If one consults this major mainstream text, written by credentialed academics, one sees that use of the principle of abrogation was the central focus of Muslims in the decades following Mohammed's death:

> During the second half of the first century of the *Hijra* [i.e. the latter half of the first century of the Islamic calendar], the focus in Qur'anic Studies was shifted to other topics, such as abrogation, semantic ambiguities in the Qur'an, exegesis, and the Meccan and Medinan revelations. Muslim scholars were more interested in exegesis than anything else during the second century of the Hijra: their research culminated in the emergence of comprehensive exegesis on the whole Qur'an by a distinguished scholar known as Ibn Jarir al-Tabari (d. 924). -- Hussein Abdul-Raof, "Qur'anic Studies", *Encyclopaedia of Islam*, Oliver Leaman (ed.), London, 2006, p.522.

Tabari is one of Islam's great historians and scholars and one of his books was called *The Book of Jihad*. This major Islamic scholar's book on war lists the various ways in which the victims of Islam may be attacked, and even lists how the most vulnerable may be killed by this religion of war:

> Abu Hanifa and his companions said: "There is no harm in [having] night raids and incursions". They said: "There is no harm if Muslims enter the Territory of War (dar al-harb) to assemble the mangonel [catapults] towards the polytheists' [Pagans] fortresses and to shoot them using mangonels, even if there are among them a woman, child, elder, idiot (matuh), blind, crippled, or someone with a permanent disability (zamin)." *Al-Tabari's Book of Jihad: a Translation from the Original Arabic*, translated by Yasir Ibrahim, Lewiston, 2007 (quoted in Andrew Bostom, *Sharia Versus Freedom: the Legacy of Islamic Totalitarianism*, New York, 2012, p.62).

When one sees that the greatest scholars in Islam are saying things like this, it is no surprise when devout Muslims destroy the World Trade Center or detonate bombs on crowded trains or perform massacres of the disabled and of children (for example, the Beslan massacre).

[296] That the French have chosen this word might well be a sign that the rest of the world should use this word. Because suicide is forbidden in Islam those Muslims who kill themselves in the name of Islam clearly see that what they are doing is something other than suicide.

[297] It was not as if Japan had a history of using suicide attacks in battles. The word "kamikaze" is the Japanese word for a typhoon and was chosen by the Allies as the word to describe this phenomenon. Alan Axelrod, *The Real History of World War II*, London, 2008, p.271.

[298] "Palestinian terrorist who shot Kennedy denied parole 15th time", *Arutz Sheva*, 11 Feb 2016, http://www.israelnationalnews.com/News/News.aspx/207915/.

[299] See https://en.wikipedia.org/wiki/Self-immolation/.

[300] Remember that some twenty years ago Fregosi's publisher backed out of publishing his book on Jihad, partly through fears of violent reprisals by Muslims.

[301] Kecia Ali and Oliver Leaman, *Islam: The Key Concepts*, London, 2007, pg.3.

[302] For examples misrepresenting Islam as a tolerant religion see: Yushua Sodiq, *An Insider's Guide to Islam*, Trafford, 2011, p.1; Bassam Tibi, *The Challenge of Fundamentalism: Political Islam and the New World Order*, London, 2002, p.xxv; "The Key to Defeating ISIS is Islam", *Huffington Post*, 18 Nov 2014, http://www.huffingtonpost.com/salam-al-marayati/the-key-to-defeating-isis-is-islam_b_5844164.html; Gerhard Bowering and Patricia Crowe et.al (eds) *The Princeton Encyclopedia of Islamic Political Thought*, Oxford, 2013, p.589; Zahid Aziz, *Islam, Peace and Tolerance*, London, 2007, p.11.

[303] https://en.wikipedia.org/wiki/The_Satanic_Verses_controversy#Attacks/.

[304] "12 Die in Bombay in Anti-Rushdie Riot", *New York Times*, 25 Feb 1989, https://www.nytimes.com/books/99/04/18/specials/rushdie-riot.html/.

[305] Japanese Translator of Rushdie Book Found Slain", *New York Times*, 13 Jul 1991, https://www.nytimes.com/books/99/04/18/specials/rushdie-translator.html/.

> The Japanese translator of "The Satanic Verses," [...] was found slain today at a university northeast of Tokyo [...] he was stabbed several times on Thursday night and left in the hallway outside his office [...] the Italian translator of "The Satanic Verses," was stabbed in his apartment in Milan.

[306] A.Guillaume, *The Life of Muhammad : a Translation of Ibn Ishaq's Sirat Rasul Allah*, Oxford University Press, 1955, pp.165-167.

[307] Daniel Pipes, (1990) *The Rushdie Affair: The Novel, the Ayatollah, and the West*, New York, pp.58-59.

[308] "Salman Rushdie: Iranian state media renew fatwa on Satanic Verses author with $600,000 bounty", *The Independent*, 21 Feb 2016, http://www.independent.co.uk/news/people/salman-rushdie-iranian-state-media-renew-fatwa-on-satanic-verses-author-with-600000-bounty-a6887141.html

[309] Alexander Knysh, "Multiple Areas of Influence, in *The Cambridge Companion to the Qur'an*, Jane Dammen McAuliffe (ed), Cambridge University Press, 2006, p.217.

[310] Alexander Knysh, "Multiple Areas of Influence", in *The Cambridge Companion to the Qur'an*, Jane Dammen McAuliffe (ed), Cambridge University Press, 2006, p.218.

[311] For a discussion of the different qualities of various translations of the Koran into English see John Gilchrist, *Muhammad and the Religion of Islam*, Benoni, South Africa, 1986, pp.215-223.

[312] The Rodwell translation from 1861 was not the only translation of the Koran into English. In 1937 Richard Bell of Edinburgh University published his translation of the Koran, where he refined the work of questioning the chronological order of verses, with more thoroughgoing work on chronology undertaken in the preceding eighty years by many different scholars in Germany, France and Britain.

[313] Tucked away at the end of the Pickthall translation is an "Index of Legislation". This index of sharia laws is very short: less than two pages of topics. The only topic with more page references than the laws on "War and Fighting" is the entry on "Worship". See Muhammad Pickthall, *The Koran*, London, 1930, pp.692-693. Anyone who looked at this index with an open mind would conclude that Islam was a religion of war, and absolutely not a religion of peace. "Peace" is not even listed in the topics. Besides the topic of "War and Fighting" there is a separate topic of "Fighting" which lists additional laws; the number of entries under that topic is greater than the number under the topic of "Ramadan". Indeed, there is an entry for "Booty" (the things stolen by warriors) which has more page references than there are page references for "Honest-dealing". The law on "Slaves" has as many page references as the laws on "Divorce" or "Food". It is clear from this that the Koran is more about rules for war, fighting, slavery and robbery than it is about rules for the observance of halal food and Ramadan.

[314] One can compare a few verses from the Rodwell translation with those "improvements" which came later. Here is Rodwell:

> 9:28 O Believers! only they who join gods with God are unclean! Let them not, therefore, after this their year, come near the sacred Temple.

> 9:29 Make war upon such of those to whom the Scriptures have been given as believe not in God, or in the last day, and who forbid not that which God and His Apostle have forbidden, and who profess not the profession of the truth, until they pay tribute out of hand, and they be humbled.

> 9:30 The Jews say, "Ezra (Ozair) is a son of God"; and the Christians say, "The Messiah is a son of God." Such the sayings in their mouths! They resemble the saying of the Infidels of old! God do battle with them! How are they misguided!

Compare the above with the same verses from the later, "improved" Pickthall translation:

9.28 O ye who believe! The idolaters only are unclean. So let them [the non-Muslims] not come near the Inviolable Place of Worship [Mecca] after this their year.

9.29 Fight against such of those who have been given the Scripture as believe not in Allah nor the Last Day, and forbid not that which Allah hath forbidden by His messenger, and follow not the Religion of Truth, until they pay the tribute readily, being brought low.

9.30 And the Jews say: Ezra is the son of Allah, and the Christians say: The Messiah is the son of Allah. That is their saying with their mouths. They imitate the saying of those who disbelieved of old. Allah (Himself) fighteth against them. How perverse are they!

The Rodwell translation makes it clear that Christians (who believe Jesus is part of the trinity which composes their God) would be included among the idolaters (the unclean), whilst the Pickthall translation conceals this.

It should be immediately obvious that the translation by Pickthall. the convert to Islam who showed every sign of being a traitor to Britain, does what it can to conceal that Islam is a religion of war. For example, in 9:29 where Rodwell's Koran says "make war", the Muslim Pickthall's Koran says "fight".

[315] Muhammed Marmaduke Pickthall, *The Meaning of the Glorious Koran*, Everyman, 1991, p.18.

[316] A rare exception to the lack of chronological *Korans* is Nicholas Starkovsky, *The Koran Handbook: An Annotated Translation*, New York, 2004. Starkovsky puts the Koran in chronological order, ending with Chapter 9 as the penultimate chapter (with the final chapter being the insignificant Chapter 110). Starkovsky thus knows that Mohammed's career as a leader ended with the creation of "a powerful Islamic State" (p.515), but this does not stop Starkovsky from admiring Islam and Mohammed, with his hope that his translation of the Koran helps Muslims and Christians (p.xiii). At the end of his book Starkovsky prefaces Chapter 9 thus: "the return of the Prophet to Medina after his conquest of Mecca [...] The Prophet denounced the treaty with the Confederates [...] took Mecca, fought the remaining opponents and, later, Byzantium [...], preparing the territorial conquests that began after his death" (p.515). We assume Starkovsky thinks the attacks by Mohammed and the first Muslims on the Jews of Medina, the Pagans of Mecca, and the Christians of Byzantium were all justified. Perhaps Starkovsky is of the view that if only the entire world submitted to Islam then the world would be at peace (apart from the lethal doctrinal disputes between Sunnis and Shias, etc.) Whilst Starkovsky was writing this translation, his wife was simultaneously preparing a version of the Koran in Russian, presumably also with the penultimate chapter being Chapter 9.

[317] Hilary Clinton, November 2015. "Clinton under fire for earlier remark that Muslims had 'nothing' to do with terrorism", *Fox News*, 13 June 2016, http://www.foxnews.com/politics/2016/06/13/clinton-under-fire-for-earlier-remark-that-muslims-had-nothing-to-do-with-terrorism.html/.

[318] Going back centuries, no records of social history in the West document any single event where 49 people were slaughtered for being homosexuals (and since another 53 people survived with injuries in the attack in Orlando, it is clear the Muslim terrorist was attempting to kill more than 100 people for being gay). For example, even when gay people were gathering publicly in England 500 years ago, there were no attempts to kill them *en masse* (see Alan Bray, *Homosexuality in Renaissance England*, London, 1982). A wave of persecution swept through Holland in the eighteenth century, but over a period of 80 years only 269 men were convicted, and fewer than 30 convictions in that century resulted in execution (see Martin Duberman et.al, *Hidden from History: Reclaiming the Gay and Lesbian Past*, London, 1989, pp.145-149). In Germany under the control of the National Socialist Workers Party, one of the West's most repressive regimes, homosexuals were sent to forced labour camps where tens of thousands died over the years, but homosexuals were not targeted for execution *en masse* (see Heinz Heger, *The Men With the Pink Triangle*, London, 1972; see also Richard Plant, *The Pink Triangle: the Nazi War Against Homosexuals*,

Edinburgh, 1987). Thirty people died in an arson attack on a gay club in America in 1973, but no culprit was ever identified and there is no evidence that they were targeted because of their sexuality.

Just two years before the attack in Orlando, a Muslim man pleaded guilty to trying to burn down a gay club in Seattle containing 700 people. Robert Spencer, "The War at Home", *Frontpage*, Sept 2014, http://www.frontpagemag.com/fpm/240980/war-home-robert-spencer/. When one considers that surveys of Muslims in Britain show they have "zero tolerance" for homosexuality, it should be clear that an Islamic West will be one where homosexuals have been wiped out. "Muslims in Britain have zero tolerance of homosexuality, says poll", *The Guardian*, 7 May 2009, https://www.theguardian.com/uk/2009/may/07/muslims-britain-france-germany-homosexuality/.

[319] "Is It Time for the Jews to Leave Europe?", *The Atlantic*, April 2015, http://www.theatlantic.com/magazine/archive/2015/04/is-it-time-for-the-jews-to-leave-europe/386279/; "Jews are leaving France in record numbers amid rising anti-Semitism and fears of more Isis-inspired terror attacks", *The Independent*, 25 Jan 2016, http://www.independent.co.uk/news/world/europe/jews-are-leaving-france-in-record-numbers-amid-rising-anti-semitism-and-fears-of-more-isis-inspired-a6832391.html; "'Muslim shouting Allahu Akbar' stabs Jewish rabbi, 62, in horrifying street attack in French city of Strasbourg", *The Sun*, 19 Aug 2016, https://www.thesun.co.uk/news/1639189/muslim-shouting-allahu-akbar-stabs-jewish-rabbi-62-in-horrifying-street-attack-in-french-city-of-strasbourg/; "Teenager faces terror charges over Marseille Jewish teacher attack", *The Guardian*, 13 Jan 2016, https://www.theguardian.com/world/2016/jan/13/teenager-to-appear-in-court-over-marseille-jewish-teacher-attack/.

[320] "Syrian patriarch fears Christianity is being wiped out in Middle East", *Catholic Herald*, 31 Aug 2016, http://www.catholicherald.co.uk/news/2016/08/31/syrian-patriarch-fears-christianity-is-being-wiped-out-in-middle-east/; "Revealed: ISIS butcher, 19, was a convicted French terrorist who had fled to Syria twice and was fitted with an electronic tag - but it let him free to roam in the mornings", *Daily Mail*, 26 July 2016, http://www.dailymail.co.uk/news/article-3708877/One-two-ISIS-knifemen-beheaded-French-priest-convicted-terrorists-home-parents-electronic-tag.html/.

[321] The electoral triumph of Donald Trump in November 2016 might be the first sign that voters are going to punish leaders who lie for Islam. One of the few planks of Trump's programme that the media emphasized was the idea of banning Muslims from entering the US:

> half of all Americans supported Donald Trump's unconstitutional proposal to temporarily ban Muslims from entering the United States. Support for the ban ticked upward after the shooting at an Orlando nightclub in June in which the shooter claimed allegiance to the Islamic State. "Donald Trump is bringing anti-Muslim prejudice into the mainstream", *Washington Post*, 1 Aug 2016.

Even though the media fell over themselves to conceal or distort Trump's policies, it was clear that with other politicians having had no response to Islamic terrorism other than to go to war in foreign lands, the idea of "banning Muslims" appealed to a majority of voters and this issue among others resulted in Trump's win, despite the media's repeated and false insinuations that Trump was some kind of Nazi for supporting the right of gay people not to be exterminated.

[322] Other religions such as Hinduism or Buddhism cannot have this status. The only option for followers of those religious beliefs is to convert to Islam or be killed. This would also be the only option offered to atheists.

[323] Bat Ye'or, *Islam and Dhimmitude: Where Civilisations Collide*, Lancaster, 2002, p.316.

[324] Samuel P. Huntington, *The Clash of Civilisations and the Remaking of World Order*, London, 1998, p.32; Shmuel Bar, *Warrant for Terror: The Fatwas of Radical Islam and the Duty to Jihad*, New York, 2006, pp18-35.

[325] Robert Mantram, *Great Dates in Islamic History*, New York, 1996, p.8.

[326] Bernard Lewis, *The Muslim Discovery of Europe*, New York, 1982, p.61.

[327] Bernard Lewis, "The Rise of Islam", *Commentary*, 1 Jan 1976, https://www.commentarymagazine.com/articles/the-return-of-islam/.

[328] The call to prayer "is not only an announcement to the people to gather together for prayer; it is as well a declaration of the principles of Islam" (Maulana Muhammad Ali, *A Manual of Hadith*, Routledge, London, 1983 [first printing 1944], p. 89). The call to prayer says "Muhammad is the Messenger of Allah. Come to prayer, Come to prayer; Come to success, Come to success" (*A Manual of Hadith*, p.93). The *Koran* is suffused with verses equating Muslims getting into Paradise with success, victory and triumph, whilst those who are condemned to eternal torture are the "losers" (see 9:111, 48:1, 61:4, 61:12, 5:35, 3:149, 32:29). Engaging in Jihad (either through violence or finance) is the only guaranteed path to Paradise. Thus "come to success" is an injunction to Muslims to engage in Jihad.

[329] Bernard Lewis, *The Muslim Discovery of Europe*, New York, 1982, p.61-62.

[330] Deepa Kumar, *Islamophobia and the Politics of Empire*, Chicago, 2012, p.9.

[331] See Christopher Davidson, *After the Sheikhs: The Coming Collapse of the Gulf Monarchies*, Oxford, 2015, pp.100-103.

[332] In reporting the ban, the British media were routinely referring to Geller and Spencer using the dismissive term "bloggers", when Spencer has umpteen books to his name, he has appeared on dozens of American factual television shows, and his articles have appeared in dozens of newspapers. "US bloggers banned from entering UK", *BBC*, 26 June 2013, http://www.bbc.co.uk/news/uk-23064355/. Pamela Geller also has several books to her name. That the British media should uniformly adopt this denigrating description, shows how closely the British media are allied with Islam. One assumes that the British media would have found it harder to justify reporting that "best-selling critic of Islam is banned from entering the UK".

[333] "Full Speech: Theresa May Hails Globalism, Calls for Action on Climate Change", *Breitbart News*, 27 Jan 2017, http://www.breitbart.com/london/2017/01/26/full-speech-theresa-may-hails-globalism/.

[334] "I've made very clear that this policy [of President Trump] is divisive and wrong. It is not a policy that we would introduce" in "Theresa May Finally brands Donald Trump's Muslim ban 'divisive and wrong'", *Daily Mirror*, 1 Feb 2017, http://www.mirror.co.uk/news/uk-news/theresa-finally-brands-donald-trumps-9736549/.

[335] "Donald Trump branded a 'buffoon, demagogue and wazzock' by MPs - but Republican ignores UK ban debate", *The Telegraph*, 18 Jan 2016, http://www.telegraph.co.uk/news/worldnews/donald-trump/12105940/donald-trump-muslim-ban-uk-debate-live.html/.

[336] Jacqui Smith, "After the abuse, how should ministers treat Trump?", Total Politics, 14 November 2016, https://www.totalpolitics.com/articles/opinion/jacqui-smith-after-abuse-how-should-ministers-treat-trump:

> following Trump's comments on banning Muslims from entering the US, the House of Commons held a debate on whether he should, in turn, be banned from entering the UK. [...] There was no support for Trump's views although MPs took different positions on whether he should be banned. [...] It is, of course, for the Home Office not Parliament to determine whether [he] can be barred from entering the UK using provisions that I strengthened as Home Secretary. In responding to the petition, then Home Secretary Theresa May stopped short of a ban, but said that she found Trump's remarks 'divisive, unhelpful and wrong'.

Instead of banning Donald Trump from Britain, the Quisling politicians settled for hurling personal abuse at the future President of the United States.

[337] "MPs debated calls to Ban him from Britain and Boris joked he'd avoid New York to

steer clear of him: How British politicians ridiculed Trump just months before he won the White House", *Daily Mail*, 9 Nov 2016, http://www.dailymail.co.uk/news/article-3920054/I-wouldn-t-visit-parts-New-York-case-meet-Trump-Boris-Johnson-British-leaders-RIDICULED-Donald-just-year-won-White-House.html/.

[338] "David Cameron stands by attack on Donald Trump over Muslim 'ban'", *BBC*, 16 May 2016, http://www.bbc.co.uk/news/uk-politics-36300005/.

[339] "Dutch MP banned from entering UK", *BBC*, 12 Feb 2009, http://news.bbc.co.uk/1/hi/7882953.stm/. Interestingly the liberal politicians Lord Ahmed and Chris Huhne, quoted in that report in support of the ban, were subsequently imprisoned for other crimes.

[340] Ibn Warraq, *Why I Am Not a Muslim*, New York, 1995.

[341] For example, the closest *The Times* gets to acknowledging the existence of Ibn Warraq's book is in an article ten years later on the threat to apostates (see "Muslim apostates cast out and at risk from friends and family", *The Times*, 5 Feb. 2005, p.26. No trace of a review of any of the books by Ibn Warraq could be found in *The Times* archive.

[342] Peter McLoughlin, *Easy Meat: Inside Britain's Grooming Gang Scandal*, London, 2016, pp.195-203.

[343] Professor Watt of Edinburgh University said:

> From shortly after its establishment at Medina the Islamic state was expanding, and this expansion continued... for at least a hundred years after Muhammad's death. Because of this certain political concepts presuppose expansion, and indeed expansion that in the end will be world-wide. This is expressed by the distinction between 'the sphere of Islam' and the 'sphere of war' (*dar al-islam, dar al-harb*). W. Montgomery Watt, *Islamic Political Thought*, Edinburgh, 1968, p.91.

Before writing the above book, Professor Watt wrote a two-volume biography (*Muhammad at Mecca* in 1953 and *Muhammad at Medina* in 1956). In 1961 he compiled a shorter version of these books, uniting material from both: *Muhammed: Prophet and Statesman*, where it is at Medina that Mohammed moves from being a religious leader to being a political leader. Watt is counted among Britain's foremost writers on Islam in the twentieth century. Bearing in mind that his works come so close after the Holocaust in National Socialist Germany, Watt is extraordinarily glib about Mohammed's solution to "the Jewish question" (his phrase).

> The lack of fundamental unity among the Jews was a weakness which meant that it was easy for Muhammad to find Jews who were ready to help him. The Arab allies of the Jews, too, being attached to them chiefly by bribes, were easily detached, partly by fear of Muslim reprisals and partly by Muhammad's diplomatic skill. The fall of Khaybar and the surrender of the other Jewish colonies marked the end of the Jewish question during Muhammad's lifetime [...] they had been utterly crushed. (p.191)

The Jews of Medina had taken in Mohammed when, after putting up with Mohammed's new religion for fifteen years, the multicultural Pagans of Mecca had had enough of him and the problems he was causing. In Medina, Mohammed as the head of the new Islamic State, ultimately repaid the Jews by exterminating them. Just a few years before Watt wrote these books, in Europe the "Final Solution" to "the Jewish Question" had just been "solved" by the mass-extermination of Jews. From our perspective it is extraordinary that an esteemed figure such as Professor Watt should have been so approving of Mohammed finding a "solution" no different from that of Hitler. It's not as though people did not know about the Holocaust in the 1950s, as Gerald Reitlinger's *The Final Solution: the Attempt to Exterminate the Jews of Europe* was published in 1953 (see Walter Laqueur (ed) *The Holocaust Encyclopaedia*, Yale University Press, New Haven, 2001, p.142).

Muhammad: Prophet and Statesman ends with an assessment of the founder of Islam. Watt uses a relativist argument, measuring the treachery, robbery and genocide by Mohammed against the behaviour of Mohammed's contemporaries. But even Watt realizes that this argument has terrible implications for the future, since Muslims regard Mohammed's behaviour as the perfect exemplar of morality:

> **Muslims, however, claim that he is a model of conduct and character for all mankind.** In so doing they present him for judgement according to the standards of enlightened world opinion. Though **the world is increasingly becoming one world, it has so far paid scant attention to Muhammad as a moral exemplar. Yet because Muslims are numerous, it will sooner or later have to consider seriously whether from the life and teaching of Muhammad any principles are to be learnt which will contribute to the moral development of mankind.** (p.235, emphasis added).

Watt's books must have had a considerable influence on the understanding of Islam in Britain from the 1950s onwards. It is quite clear that Watt saw that Islam was successful as a religion of war rather than a religion of peace, and that the success of Islam was more about politics than religion. Yet instead of the West having any kind of discussion about a seventh century desert warlord serving as a moral guide to humanity in the twentieth and twenty-first century (as Watt expected), the public discourse about Islam and Mohammed turned into one of lies and deception. If one's understanding of Mohammed came from state-controlled education or from the complicit mass-media, one would assume that Mohammed was more like Buddha than he was like Hitler (as we pointed out earlier, some Muslim writers have claimed that Mohammed was a greater military leader than Hitler).

[344] Patrick Sookhdeo, *Global Jihad: The Future in the Face of Militant Islam*, 2007, p.70.

[345] "Radicals target young converts at Brixton mosque", *The Times*, 26 Dec 2001, p.5; "Theory One Team of British Bombers", *The Times*, 9 July 2005, p.9. Three of the reports were part of a single spread (and should thus count as one report): "Dividing the World" *The Times*, 17 Jan 2005, p.5; "Britain's online imam declares", *The Times*, 17 Jan 2005, p.4; "War as he calls young to jihad", *The Times*, 17 Jan 2005, p5. The only other time the phrase occurs, is in a letter to the Editor (and therefore should not count at all as journalism): "Palestinian question at the centre of global conflict", *The Times*, 5 Feb 2002, p.5.

[346] In 2005 Imams from Denmark provoked a global crisis concerning cartoons of Mohammed which appeared in a newspaper (see https://en.wikipedia.org/wiki/Jyllands-Posten_Muhammad_cartoons_controversy for a summary of the events). Here are the events which led to the Motoons crisis, where Imams forged inflammatory cartoons, to provoke Muslims around the world into murder, including assassination attempts on prominent artists in the West.

> Among those affected by the chill on free speech was a Danish author who, when he tried to find somebody to draw pictures of Muhammed for a children's biography, got turned down by one illustrator after another, because they were too scared of possible Muslim reprisal. [... On September 30 2005] Rose [...] invited all forty-odd members of the Danish Cartoonists' Association to submit drawings of the prophet Muhammed. Twelve sent in submissions [...] pretty pallid stuff...
>
> Bruce Bawer, *Surrender: Appeasing Islam, Sacrificing Freedom*, London, 2009, p.42.

Following the Motoons crisis, and the repeated assassination attempts on various artists, Muslims succeeded in scaring prominent writers and artists more than with The Rushdie Affair. As we saw earlier, the publisher withdrew from his contract for Fregosi's 1998 book on Jihad. Rushdie's *Satanic Verses* never appeared in paperback, as an attempt to assuage the cultural terrorism of the Islamic world. In 2008 a novel on Mohammed's six-year old bride Aisha was withdrawn from publication by Random House, one of the world's largest publishers, because they feared being slaughtered by devout followers of "the religion of peace" ("Novel on prophet's wife pulled for fear of backlash", *The Guardian*, 9 Aug 2008, https://www.theguardian.com/books/2008/aug/09/fiction.terrorism/). Interestingly, in the immediate aftermath of 9/11 the American publicly-funded broadcaster PBS produced

a documentary about Mohammed in 2002 (http://www.pbs.org/muhammad/). The (otherwise highly deceptive) documentary contains many paintings in the background which were produced by Muslims centuries ago. This fact shows us that:
a) Muslims have drawn Mohammed in the past
b) even if this was not so, Muslims should not be allowed to apply the strictures of their belief system to those of us who do not ascribe to those strictures, and even more so, should not be allowed to do this to us when Muslims are a small minority in our lands
c) by 2005 Muslims in the West managed to terrify us Kuffar into backing away further from any critique of Islam, such that after 2005 almost no Kuffar would dare to depict Mohammed (if PBS were to have made that documentary in 2006, it is highly unlikely that they would have used any of those paintings which depict Mohammed and the central aspects of his biography).
Whilst no more than 5% to 10% of the population of most Western countries, Muslim cultural terrorism has virtually silenced all discussion of the character of Mohammed and his rise to power. We Kuffar are living under the thumb of Muslims, a minority in our society.

[347] David Aaronovitch. "It's the latest disease: sensible people saying ridiculous things about Islam", *The Times*, 15 Nov 2005, p.19.

[348] Patrick Sookhdeo, *Global Jihad: The Future in the Face of Militant Islam*, 2007, p.100.

[349] When *The Times* deigned to write its only (sneering) review of Sookhdeo's work, they mocked him and Bat Ye'or, presenting them as "ridiculous" people. Sookhdeo's presentation of the permanence of Islam's attitude of war towards unbelievers is backed up in the work of Prof. Bernard Lewis, the West's pre-eminent twentieth-century expert on Islam: "Between the two [dar al-Islam and dar al-Harb] there is a morally necessary, legally and religiously obligatory state of war, until the final and inevitable triumph of Islam over unbelief" (from the chapter "War and Peace" in Bernard Lewis, *The Political Language of Islam*, University of Chicago Press, Chicago, 1988, p.73). This expert opinion from Prof. Lewis is even to be found two decades earlier, in his article "Politics and War", which appears in a collection of essays written by Western experts on Islam and published by the Oxford University Press. The esteemed editors of this collection clearly did not think that Prof. Lewis' view on the permanence of Islam's state of war with the world was anything other than mainstream scholarship. See Joseph Schacht and C.E. Bosworth (eds), *The Legacy of Islam*, Oxford, 1974, pp.156-209.

[350] T.P. Hughes, *Notes on Muhammadanism: Being Outlines of the Religious System of Islam*, London, 3rd edition, 1894, pp.208-211.

[351] Andrew Bostom, *Sharia Versus Freedom: The Legacy of Islamic Totalitarianism*, New York, 2012, pp.62-65.

[352] A.Guillaume, *The Life of Muhammad: A Translation of Ibn Ishaq's Sirat Rasul Allah*, Oxford University Press, 1955.

[353] A.Guillaume, *The Life of Muhammad: A Translation of Ibn Ishaq's Sirat Rasul Allah*, Oxford University Press, 1955, p.xvii.

[354] Fred Donner, *Early Islamic Conquests*, Princeton University Press, 1981.

[355] Reuven Firestone *Jihad: The Origin of Holy War in Islam*, Oxford University Press, 1999.

[356] Robert Mantram, *Great Dates in Islamic History*, New York, 1996. Substantial portions of this book were published in French in 1990. Mantram had been a professor at the University of Provence, France.

[357] There are scores of other significant events listed in the last chapter of the book which are not acts of violence. Nevertheless, given the thousands of terrorist incidents in the name of Islam since 1993, it is significant that this (intentionally massive) terrorist attack by a learned Muslim should be a feature of Islam, 1400 years after the violence of Mohammed and his Companions.

[358] Muhammad Hamidullah, *Battlefields of the Prophet Muhammad: A Contribution to Muslim Military History*. Published in French in *Etudes Islamiques*, Paris, 1939; published in Urdu in Hyderabad-Deccan, 1945; published in English in *Islamic Review*, London, 1952-

1953; published in Arabic in Cairo, 1954; published in Farsi, Tehran 1956; published in Turkish in Istanbul, 1962.

[359] S.K.Malik, *The Quranic Concept of War*, Lahore, 1979. Reprinted Delhi, 1992.

[360] A.Guillaume, *The Life of Muhammad: A Translation of Ibn Ishaq's Sirat Rasul Allah*, Oxford University Press, 1955, p.516. That it took Mohammed four years to die from the poisoning that occurred after the Muslim army's raid on Khaybar is rather strange (see Robert Mantram, *Great Dates in Islamic History*, New York, 1996, p.5). Perhaps Mohammed or his Companions blamed the earlier poisoning incident so that Mohammed could appear to die as the consequence of a battle, and therefore die as a Jihadi.

> Narrated Aisha: The Prophet in his ailment in which he died, used to say, "O Aisha! I still feel the pain caused by the food I ate at Khaibar, and at this time, I feel as if my aorta is being cut from that poison". *Sahih Bukhari*, Volume 5, Book 59, Hadith 713, http://quranx.com/Hadith/Bukhari/ByIndex/USC-MSA/Volume-5/Book-59/Hadith-713/.

[361] In France, philosophy teacher Robert Redeker told the truth about Islam, the truth according to the core Islamic texts. He ended up losing his job and having to disappear, under police protection. Despite being a member of the editorial board of the prominent Leftist literary magazine *Les Temps Modernes* (whose mission was to write "engaged" literature), Redeker received virtually no support from the intellectual elite nor the French State (see "French philosophy teacher in hiding after attack on Islam", *The Guardian*, 4 October 2006, https://www.theguardian.com/world/2006/oct/04/france.schoolsworldwide). In an opinion piece in the prominent mainstream newspaper *Le Figaro* (in response to the attacks on Pope Benedict for quoting a medieval Byzantine Emperor's view on Islam), Redeker contrasted Jesus and Mohammed and said that the latter was "a merciless warlord, a looter, a mass-murderer of Jews and a polygamist" (all thing substantiated by the most authoritative Muslim biography of Mohammed). Redeker also said the *Koran* was "a book of incredible violence" ("Teacher in Hiding After Attack on Islam Stirs Threats", *New York Times*, 30 Sept 2006 http://www.nytimes.com/2006/09/30/world/europe/teacher-in-hiding-after-attack-on-islam-stirs-threats.html). In an article entitled "Has the West been silenced by Islam?" (3 Oct 2006, http://www.independent.co.uk/news/world/politics/has-the-west-been-silenced-by-islam-5330785.html) *The Independent* made a show of appearing to support the right to free speech, provided that what was said should not offend anyone. This article proved that, with one or two exceptions in the subsequent decades, those with any position sanctioned by the institutions of the West, have indeed been silenced - not just from criticising Islam but from even being able to say (as Kuffar) what it is that the texts of Islam demand from believers (if any Kuffar critic of Islam was to convert to Islam, suddenly he would be able to say what the texts of Islam said without fearing assassination by Muslims). The irony of such a cowardly defence of free speech appearing in a newspaper proclaiming itself "The Independent" is rich beyond words. See also Bruce Bawer, *Surrender: Appeasing Islam, Sacrificing Freedom*, New York, 2009, pp.99-102.

In the decade that followed the French equivalent of The Rushdie Affair, one struggles to find anyone with a position sanctioned by the institutions of our society who will go against The Grand Lie. One of these is the Dutch MP Geert Wilders (see his book *Marked for Death: Islam's War Against the West*, Washington, 2012, p.33). Another rare exception was when *The Times* published an opinion piece by Melanie Phillips (see "It's pure myth that Islam is 'a religion of peace'", *The Times*, 29th June 2015, http://www.thetimes.co.uk/tto/opinion/columnists/article4482378.ece). It is hard to find any more mainstream examples than these. Many newspapers compartmentalize Wilders and his party, wrongly describing them as "far right" (see "Far-right party still leading in Dutch polls, despite leader's criminal guilt", *The Guardian*, 10 Dec 2016, https://www.theguardian.com/world/2016/dec/10/netherlands-geert-wilders-politics-far-right; Geert Wilders, "Dutch Far-Right Leader, Is Convicted of Inciting Discrimination", *New York Times*, 9 Dec 2016, http://www.nytimes.com/2016/12/09/world/europe/geert-wilders-netherlands-trial.html). Ludicrously Melanie Phillips gets castigated as "a jihadi", when she has never been known to encourage terrorism nor to engage in violence (see "The personal jihad of Melanie Phillips", *The Guardian*, 31 Oct 2009, https://www.theguardian.com/commentisfree/belief/2009/oct/31/melanie-phillips-islamism-spectator). Beyond these few individuals, the list of establishment figures who will challenge The Grand Lie is virtually empty.

In the aftermath of the second and most deadly attack on the offices and staff of the Leftist French satirical magazine Charlie Hebdo, Zineb El Rhazoui, a member of staff who was not killed in the attack (she was in another country) came out and said, "we need to stop saying Islam is a religion of peace". "Charlie Hebdo survivor, discusses why the world needs to 'Destroy Islamic Fascism'", *New York Times*, 18 Oct 2016, http://nytlive.nytimes.com/womenintheworld/2016/10/18/zineb-el-rhazoui-charlie-hebdo-survivor-discusses-why-the-world-needs-to-destroy-islamic-fascism/ She lives under permanent police protection, because of the death threats made to her by devout Muslims. As an ex-Muslim who worked for a Leftist magazine, El Rhazoui may escape being labelled as "far right".

[362] T.P. Schwartz-Barcott, *War, Terror and Peace in the Qu'ran and Islam: Insights for Military and Government Leaders*, Army War College Foundation Press, Carlisle, Pennsylvania, 2004, p.xxi.

[363] T.P. Schwartz-Barcott, *War, Terror and Peace in the Qu'ran and Islam: Insights for Military and Government Leaders*, Army War College Foundation Press, Carlisle, Pennsylvania, 2004, p.xxiv.

[364] T.P. Schwartz-Barcott, *War, Terror and Peace in the Qu'ran and Islam*, p.41.

[365] T.P. Schwartz-Barcott, *War, Terror and Peace in the Qu'ran and Islam*, p.54. Despite the title of the ex-Marine's book leading with the word "war" rather than the word "peace", elsewhere in the book the sociologist in him likes to lead with the word "peace" rather than "war".

[366] Schwartz-Barcott spends considerable time discussing the "ambiguities" of Koran verses 2:190 to 2:193, and how these can serve to moderate other war-mongering verses in the Koran. T.P. Schwartz-Barcott, *War, Terror and Peace in the Qu'ran and Islam*, pp.52-54. According to Haqq, verses 2:190 to 2:193 are cancelled by verse 9:5, one of the very verses Schwartz-Barcott hopes can be moderated by the verses which it cancels.

[367] We outlined earlier in our Introduction the books on Islam from mainstream academic publishers in the West which discuss the importance of grasping those verses which are abrogated and which verse does the abrogating. However, attempts by books on Islam from mainstream publishers which actually indicate the verses which have been abrogated are so rare that the highly-esteemed *Encyclopaedia of Islam* only refers to the short book *Abrogation in the Koran* by Haqq, which we used to indicate cancelled verses in our Koran.

[368] T.P. Schwartz-Barcott, *War, Terror and Peace in the Qu'ran and Islam*, 2004, p.361.

[369] Since Schwartz-Barcott's bibliography refers to Richard Bell's *Quran* (Edinburgh, 1952), it seems hard to believe that Schwartz-Barcott was unaware of the importance of understanding the chronology of the Koran (Bell is one of the Western scholars who discusses this subject). See Richard Bell, *Introduction to the Qur'an*, Edinburgh, 1953.

[370] T.P. Schwartz-Barcott, *War, Terror and Peace in the Qu'ran and Islam*, p.xxiii.

[371] As part of the Western media's collaboration with the religion of war, the 1979 siege of Mecca is virtually forgotten. Hundreds of devout Muslims from all over the world smuggled in huge amounts of armaments (hidden in coffins) into The Grand Mosque and commandeered the mosque. With 100,000 Muslims trapped inside the compound, the Jihadis held off the well-equipped Saudi military for weeks. See Yaroslav Trofimov, *The Siege of Mecca: The Forgotten Uprising*, London, 2007. The siege, and the killing of people by these devout Muslims in The Grand Mosque, were not condemned by the most senior Islamic clerics in Sunni Islam. Mohammed Qutb, brother of the violent and fascistic Muslim Brotherhood's principal ideologue, had been living in Saudi Arabia for years, along with thousands of other members of the Muslim Brotherhood.

[372] Bernard Lewis, "The Rise of Islam", *Commentary*, 1 Jan 1976,

https://www.commentarymagazine.com/articles/the-return-of-islam/.

[373] Bernard Lewis, *The Political Language of Islam*, Chicago and London, 1988, p.4-5 (emphasis added).

[374] See "Brief Guide to the Text", which immediately precedes the verses from the Koran.

[375] One of the most important political theorists of the 20th century argues that the concept of the Other, the enemy, is the fundamental distinction in all political doctrine and political action (Carl Schmitt, *The Concept of the Political*, University of Chicago Press, 1996, p.26). In its obsession with disparaging non-Muslims and in commanding that Muslims be viciously violent towards us, Islam becomes fundamentally political and not religious. What is truly astounding is that anyone would consider these doctrines of genocide and apartheid to be moral in any way at all.

[376] As Dr. Andrew Bostom says:

> The 1990 Cairo Declaration, or so-called Universal Declaration of Human Rights in Islam, was drafted and subsequently ratified by all members of the OIC. Both the preamble and concluding articles (24 and 25) make plain that the OIC's [Organisation of Islamic Conference] Cairo Declaration is designed to supersede Western Conceptions of Human Rights as enunciated, for example, in the US bill of Rights and the United Nation's 1948 Universal Declaration of Human Rights. The opening preamble to the Cairo Declaration repeats a Koranic injunction affirming Islamic supremacism... -- Andrew Bostom, (2012) *Sharia Versus Freedom: The Legacy of Islamic Totalitarianism*, New York, p.141.

The OIC represents all the Muslim countries in the world. The Cairo Declaration makes it clear that Muslims place sharia law above universal human rights. Sharia law systematically discriminates against non-Muslims and legalizes slavery (something rejected outright by the Universal Declaration). This means that for decades Muslims have been telling the world that they reject the concept that the rights of man are universal. When you look through our version of the *Koran* you can see that separating believers from unbelievers is endemic in Islam, and that unbelievers are to be killed unless they submit to Islam (which is clear from *Koran* 9:29).

The only people trying to draw your attention to the Muslim world having rejected and supplanted our concept of human rights is a group of independent researchers. See David Littman, (1999) "Islamism Grows Stronger at the United Nations", in Robert Spencer (ed), (2005) *The Myth of Islamic Tolerance: How Islamic Law Treats Non-Muslims*, New York,pp 308-316; David Littman, (1999) "Universal Human Rights And 'Human Rights in Islam'", in Robert Spencer (ed), (2005) *The Myth of Islamic Tolerance,* pp.317-325; Bat Ye'or, (2002) *Islam and Dhimmitude*, Lancaster, p.198; Bat Ye'or, (2011) *Europe, Globalization and the Coming Universal Caliphate*, Madison. See also Sultan Hussyn Tabandeh, *A Muslim Commentary on the Universal Declaration of Human Rights*, Guildford, 1970.

[377] Pope Benedict had quoted a medieval Christian Emperor's question to an Islamic scholar.

> A transcript of the Pope's remarks obtained by The Associated Press television network reads: "In the seventh (sura, or chapter of the Quran), the emperor comes to speak about jihad, holy war. The emperor certainly knew that Sura 2, 256, [sic] reads: 'No force in matters of faith'. It is one of the early suras, from a time – as experts say – in which Mohammed himself was still powerless and threatened. However, the emperor of course also knew the requirements about the holy war that were later formulated in the Quran. Without going into details like the handling of the owners of the scriptures, or non-believers, he (the emperor) turned to his interlocutors – in a surprisingly brusque way – with the central question after the relationship between religion and violence. He said, I quote, 'Show me just what Mohammed brought that was new, and there you will find things only evil and inhuman, such as his command to spread by the sword the faith he preached'". --"Pope's Islam comments condemned", *CNN*, 15 Sept 2006.

Around the time of The Crusades, in the early eleventh century Pope Benedict IX abdicated.
https://en.wikipedia.org/wiki/Pope_Benedict_IX

[378] *The Reliance of the Traveller*, section o8.1.

[379] George Walden, *Time to Emigrate?*, London, 2007, p.119.

[380] Boris Johnson, *Seventy-Two Virgins*, London, 2004, p.69. Johnson's book was
supposedly a comedic novel about a Muslim terrorist attack on Parliament. Within months
of the paperback edition being published, Muslims conducted the co-ordinated attack on
the London bus and underground network in July 2005. It is irrelevant whether or not
Johnson claims that the comments quoted by us were comments made by one of his expert
characters: that Johnson was able to have a character express these views shows that
Johnson is fully aware that Muslim terrorists claim their terrorism is sanctioned by the
Koran, and Johnson even summarises the most significant injunctions from the Koran.
Johnson's expert character in 2004 says nothing that differs from what Islamic State would
offer as justifications a decade later in 2014. In 2004 Johnson demonstrated (in summary
form) the evidence laid out most explicitly in the book you are holding in your hands:
namely, that Koran 9:5 is the pivotal verse explaining the motivation of Jihadis. The title of
Johnson's comedic novel (*Seventy-Two Virgins*) also betrays his knowledge of one of the key
rewards Jihadis claim await them in Paradise. His book also uses the concept of "Takfir",
showing his understanding of the way in which devout Muslims denounce the Muslims who
are wavering from the literal interpretation of the Koran.

In 2005, just weeks before Muslims killed and maimed travellers on the London
transport system, the future Prime Minister also raised in the British Parliament his
objections to the idea that Islam should be protected from criticism, citing some examples
of the ways in which the Koran denounces the follower of other religions.

> Here is the Koran on those with a lack of correct religious belief:"As for the
> unbelievers, for them garments of fire shall be cut and there shall be poured
> over their heads boiling water whereby whatever is in their bowels and
> skins shall be dissolved and they will be punished with hooked iron rods."
>
> On Christians, it says: "They surely are infidels who say god is the third of
> three; for there is but one god; and if they do not refrain from what they say,
> a severe punishment shall light on those who are unbelievers."
>
> On Jews... the Koran says: "Because of the wickedness of certain Jews, and
> because they turn many from the way of god we have forbidden them good
> and wholesome foods which were formerly allowed them; and because they
> have taken to usury, though they were forbidden it; and have cheated others
> of their possessions, we have prepared a grievous punishment for the
> infidels amongst them."
>
> On the subject of Jews and Christians, it says:"Why don't their rabbis and
> doctors of law forbid them from uttering sinful words and eating unlawful
> food? Evil indeed are their works. The hand of god is chained up cry the
> Jews. Their own hands shall be chained up and they shall be cursed for
> saying such a thing... Believers do not take Jews or Christians as friends.
> They are but one another's friends. If anyone of you takes them for his
> friends then he is surely one of them. God will not guide evil doers."
> *Hansard*,
> https://publications.parliament.uk/pa/cm200506/cmhansrd/vo050621/d
> ebtext/50621-29.htm

[381] Boris Johnson, "Just don't call it war", *The Spectator*, 16 July 2005,
https://www.spectator.co.uk/2005/07/just-dont-call-it-war/ .

[382] "Boris Johnson calls for new word to be used when describing Islamic extremists",
Evening Standard, 17 April 2015, https://www.standard.co.uk/news/mayor/boris-
johnson-calls-for-new-word-to-be-used-when-describing-islamic-extremists-

10186330.html .

383 It is no surprise that Holland should be one of these countries where this is most noticeable, since politicians there like Geert Wilders must live under constant police protection, whilst the state itself criminalizes them for speaking the truth.

> For the fifth year in a row, emigration from the Netherlands [in 2008] exceeded immigration last year, reaching 123,000 emigrants, which amounts to 7.5 emigrants per 1000 inhabitants. Dutch media has repeatedly reported this phenomenon because it caught demographic forecasters by surprise. The last emigration wave occurred fifty years ago, and at present the Netherlands is the only Western European country experiencing net emigration, although similar trends are visible in the UK [...]and to lesser extent in Germany. – "Exit, voice and loyalty in the Netherlands", 6 Oct 2008, http://voxeu.org/article/why-are-dutch-leaving-netherlands/.

"France has always been a country of immigration, but now increasing numbers of young people, usually from the upper middle classes, are going abroad" ("Increasing numbers of French young people are emigrating", 9 Aug 2013, *The Irish Times*, http://www.irishtimes.com/news/world/europe/increasing-numbers-of-french-young-people-are-emigrating-1.1488837). At the time of the Charlie Hebdo massacre, two books topped the best-seller list in France. One was a novel imagining a future where France is under the control of Muslims by 2022, whilst the other book was on the suicide of the French national culture. See "Do France's Intellectuals Have a Muslim Problem? Houellebecq, 'Charlie Hebdo,' and the French struggle to understand how 5 million citizens fit into the Fifth Republic", 8 Jan 2015, *Foreign Policy*, http://foreignpolicy.com/2015/01/08/do-frances-intellectuals-have-a-muslim-problem/ The Professor of the following pessimistic overview of the situation in France has himself left to live in the USA: Guy Millière, "France on the Verge of Total Collapse", *Gatestone Institute*, 24 Nov 2016, https://www.gatestoneinstitute.org/9363/france-collapse/. See also his overview of the situation in Germany: "The Suicide of Germany", *Gatestone Institute*, 26 Dec 2016, https://www.gatestoneinstitute.org/9645/germany-suicide/.

384 In Britain a Conservative government made a commitment in 2010 to reduce net migration to "tens of thousands" but six years later conceded that this reduction had not been achieved and would not be achieved until 2020. "Theresa May waters down immigration target AGAIN as she says her goal to cut net migration to under 100,000 is only her 'belief' and will 'take some time' to achieve", *Daily Mail*, 20 July 2016, http://www.dailymail.co.uk/news/article-3699359/Theresa-waters-immigration-target-says-goal-cut-net-migration-100-000-belief-time-achieve.html/. This was a government which was committed to Britain remaining in the EU (which would mean that the country would have no control over its borders and therefore could not possibly meet any guarantee about overall numbers of incoming immigrants).

385 Rafiq Zakaria, *Muhammad and the Quran*, Penguin, 1991, p.59.

386 We considered re-ordering the verses themselves but for readability, flow and understanding within each chapter we decided it best not to do so. It is our hope that this work shakes journalists, academics and clergy out of their Collaborationist slumbers, and the subject of the chronological ordering of the Koran's chapters and surahs becomes a major subject of discussion.

387 Here is an explanation from near the beginning of a book by H. Montgomery Watt. Professor Watt was very much an apologist for Islam, but even he made no bones about the fact that Mohammed was not just a religious leader, but that Mohammed and Islam were inextricably bound with politics and war.

> **The Jihad or 'holy war' was a fundamental part of the mechanism of Islamic expansion both within Arabia and in the wider world.** [...] The Qur'an now **exhorts all Muslims to take part in the fighting** against the Meccans; this is the best way to interpret 5.35/9, "O believers, fear God... and **strive in His way**". There are also verses, however, which distinguish the Emigrants from the Medinan Muslims precisely on the grounds that the

former are "those who believed and emigrated and strove with goods and person in the way of God" (8.72/3) or "those who emigrated after being persecuted and strove and endured (hardships) patiently" (16.110/1). The word for "strove" here is jahadu, to which **corresponds the verbal noun jihad, properly "striving" or "the expending of effort"**. – From "The Islamic State Under Muhammad", Chapter 1 of H. Montgomery Watt, *Islamic Political Thought*, Edinburgh, 1969, pp.14-16 [emphasis added].

[388] Anwarul Haqq, *Abrogation in the Koran*, Lucknow, India, 1926, p.37.

[389] Many translations of the Koran use the word "fight" as a translation of words derived from the root of the Arabic word "qatal". However, the word "qatal" and those words derived from it have connotations of "murder, slaughter, wage war", meanings which are absent from the English word "fight". "Thus, while qatala is 'to kill', qattala is 'to kill violently or on a large scale' (i.e. 'to slaughter', 'to massacre')..." (G.M. Wickens, *Arabic Grammar*, Cambridge University Press, 1980, p.164). At the website which accompanies *Mohammed's Koran* you can see that in five different translations of verses such as Koran 9:29 the translators use the word "fight" (see http://www.mohammeds-koran.com/Koran/9/9.29). In this way virtually every translation of the meaning of the Koran has been made to appear far more anodyne than it truly it is. Here is a transliteration of Koran 9:29:

Qātilū Al-Ladhīna Lā Yu'uminūna Billāhi Wa Lā Bil-Yawmi Al-'Ākhiri Wa Lā Yuḥarrimūna Mā Ḥarrama Allāhu Wa Rasūluhu Wa Lā Yadīnūna Dīna Al-Ḥaqqi Mina Al-Ladhīna 'Ūtū Al-Kitāba Ḥattá Yu`ṭū Al-Jizyata `An Yadin Wa Hum Ṣāghirūna

See https://sahih-bukhari.com/Pages/Quran/Quran_english_arabic_transliteration.php?id=9 Clearly the first word is derived from "qatal". The derivations from this root word ("kill") occur 170 times in the Koran, the fundamental text of "the Religion of Peace".

The English word "fight" connotes "struggle"; the Arabic word "qatal" instead connotes "massacre". Remember that the Koran is held up by Muslims as a pre-eminent work of poetry. When it comes to texts which are claimed to be poetic, the connotations matter immensely, and meanings can be easily obscured by the allegiance of the translator. When Professor Wickens' book on Arabic grammar (which often discusses words which are key concepts of Islam) spends 1/160th of the book discussing the meaning of the word "qatal", we should understand that these connotations of "kill, slaughter, massacre" are of considerable importance in the translation of words derived from "qatal".

[390] Anwarul Haqq, *Abrogation in the Koran*, Lucknow, India, 1926, p.38.

[391] Anwarul Haqq, *Abrogation in the Koran*, Lucknow, India, 1926, p.39.

[392] Anwarul Haqq, *Abrogation in the Koran*, Lucknow, India, 1926, p.39.

[393] Anwarul Haqq, *Abrogation in the Koran*, Lucknow, India, 1926, p.40.

[394] Anwarul Haqq, *Abrogation in the Koran*, Lucknow, India, 1926, p.40.

[395] Anwarul Haqq, *Abrogation in the Koran*, Lucknow, India, 1926, p.29.

[396] Anwarul Haqq, *Abrogation in the Koran*, Lucknow, India, 1926, p.30.

[397] In Islam "the straight path" is Sharia. See John Esposito, *Islam: The Straight Path*, 1988, p.103: "The supremacy of Islamic law as the eternally valid expression of the straight path of Islam for state and society..." Also see John Esposito, *The Islamic Threat: Myth or Reality?*, 1999, p.26: "The call to Islam was a call to turn away from the path of unbelief and return to the straight path (Sharia) or law of God."

[398] Anwarul Haqq, *Abrogation in the Koran*, Lucknow, India, 1926, p.30.

[399] Anwarul Haqq, *Abrogation in the Koran*, Lucknow, India, 1926, p.30.

[400] Anwarul Haqq, *Abrogation in the Koran*, Lucknow, India, 1926, p.49.

[401] Anwarul Haqq, *Abrogation in the Koran*, Lucknow, India, 1926, p.49.

[402] Anwarul Haqq, *Abrogation in the Koran*, Lucknow, India, 1926, p.49.

[403] Anwarul Haqq, *Abrogation in the Koran*, Lucknow, India, 1926, p.50.

[404] Anwarul Haqq, *Abrogation in the Koran*, Lucknow, India, 1926, p.50.

[405] Anwarul Haqq, *Abrogation in the Koran*, Lucknow, India, 1926, p.51.

[406] Anwarul Haqq, *Abrogation in the Koran*, Lucknow, India, 1926, p.51.

[407] Anwarul Haqq, *Abrogation in the Koran*, Lucknow, India, 1926, p.52.

[408] Anwarul Haqq, *Abrogation in the Koran*, Lucknow, India, 1926, p.52.

[409] Anwarul Haqq, *Abrogation in the Koran*, Lucknow, India, 1926, p.71.

[410] Anwarul Haqq, *Abrogation in the Koran*, Lucknow, India, 1926, p.72.

[411] Anwarul Haqq, *Abrogation in the Koran*, Lucknow, India, 1926, p.72.

[412] Anwarul Haqq, *Abrogation in the Koran*, Lucknow, India, 1926, p.42.

[413] Anwarul Haqq, *Abrogation in the Koran*, Lucknow, India, 1926, p.64.

[414] Anwarul Haqq, *Abrogation in the Koran*, Lucknow, India, 1926, p.64. Haqq cites 47:40 as being the abrogating verse, yet there is no 47:40. It is clear from the translation of the abrogating verse that he is referring to 47:38.

[415] Anwarul Haqq, *Abrogation in the Koran*, Lucknow, India, 1926, p.64. Haqq cites 47:40 as being the abrogating verse, yet there is no 47:40. It is clear from the translation of the abrogating verse that he is referring to 47:38.

[416] Anwarul Haqq, *Abrogation in the Koran*, Lucknow, India, 1926, p.27.

[417] Anwarul Haqq, *Abrogation in the Koran*, Lucknow, India, 1926, p.27.

[418] Anwarul Haqq, *Abrogation in the Koran*, Lucknow, India, 1926, p.27.

[419] Anwarul Haqq, *Abrogation in the Koran*, Lucknow, India, 1926, p.27.

[420] Anwarul Haqq, *Abrogation in the Koran*, Lucknow, India, 1926, p.28.

[421] Anwarul Haqq, *Abrogation in the Koran*, Lucknow, India, 1926, p.29.

[422] Anwarul Haqq, *Abrogation in the Koran*, Lucknow, India, 1926, p.29.

[423] Anwarul Haqq, *Abrogation in the Koran*, Lucknow, India, 1926, p.28.

[424] Anwarul Haqq, *Abrogation in the Koran*, Lucknow, India, 1926, p.28.

[425] Anwarul Haqq, *Abrogation in the Koran*, Lucknow, India, 1926, p.28.

[426] Anwarul Haqq, *Abrogation in the Koran*, Lucknow, India, 1926, p.28.

[427] See http://www.mohammeds-koran.com/Koran/4/4.102 .

[428] Shirk is "the sin for which God has no forgiveness". *Shorter Encyclopaedia of Islam*, p.542. See also the classic manual of sharia law, *The Reliance of the Traveller*, where funding Jihad in the form of paying for weaponry, expenses and financial support to the family of the Jihadis are listed as "charitable" actions (section h8.17, p.272).

[429] Zakat (the Islamic concept of "charity") was used "not to support the needy only but also, and **even preferably** when the necessity arose, **for his military enterprises** and other political purposes" (emphasis added). *Shorter Encyclopaedia of Islam*, p.655.

[430] Anwarul Haqq, *Abrogation in the Koran*, Lucknow, India, 1926, p.29.

[431] Anwarul Haqq, *Abrogation in the Koran*, Lucknow, India, 1926, p.68.

[432] Anwarul Haqq, *Abrogation in the Koran*, Lucknow, India, 1926, p.69.

[433] See the other translations here http://www.mohammeds-koran.com/Koran/33/33.6 .

[434] Anwarul Haqq, *Abrogation in the Koran*, Lucknow, India, 1926, p.55.

[435] Anwarul Haqq, *Abrogation in the Koran*, Lucknow, India, 1926, p.19.

[436] Anwarul Haqq, *Abrogation in the Koran*, Lucknow, India, 1926, p.19.

[437] Anwarul Haqq, *Abrogation in the Koran*, Lucknow, India, 1926, p.20.

[438] See http://www.mohammeds-koran.com/Koran/3/3.153 .

[439] Anwarul Haqq, *Abrogation in the Koran*, Lucknow, India, 1926, p.21.

[440] See http://www.mohammeds-koran.com/Koran/3/3.195 to observe how Pickthal merges those who fled with those who were aggressive Jihadis.

[441] Anwarul Haqq, *Abrogation in the Koran*, Lucknow, India, 1926, p.35.

[442] Other translations of 8.38 are far less deceitful than Pickthall. Thus Yusuf Ali translates this verse as "Say to the Unbelievers, if (now) they desist (from Unbelief), their past would be forgiven them; but if they persist, the punishment of those before them is already (a matter of warning for them)." That is, he inserts "from Unbelief" rather than "from Persecution". Other translations are more in keeping with Yusuf Ali than with Pickthall http://www.mohammeds-koran.com/Koran/8/8.38 .

[443] Anwarul Haqq, *Abrogation in the Koran*, Lucknow, India, 1926, p.36.

[444] Anwarul Haqq, *Abrogation in the Koran*, Lucknow, India, 1926, p.37.

[445] Anwarul Haqq, *Abrogation in the Koran*, Lucknow, India, 1926, p.37.

[446] Anwarul Haqq, *Abrogation in the Koran*, Lucknow, India, 1926, p.11.

[447] Anwarul Haqq, *Abrogation in the Koran*, Lucknow, India, 1926, p.11.

[448] Anwarul Haqq, *Abrogation in the Koran*, Lucknow, India, 1926, p.11.

[449] Anwarul Haqq, *Abrogation in the Koran*, Lucknow, India, 1926, p.12.

[450] Anwarul Haqq, *Abrogation in the Koran*, Lucknow, India, 1926, p.12.

[451] Anwarul Haqq, *Abrogation in the Koran*, Lucknow, India, 1926, p.12.

[452] Anwarul Haqq, *Abrogation in the Koran*, Lucknow, India, 1926, p.13.

[453] Anwarul Haqq, *Abrogation in the Koran*, Lucknow, India, 1926, p.14.

[454] Anwarul Haqq, *Abrogation in the Koran*, Lucknow, India, 1926, p.14.

[455] Anwarul Haqq, *Abrogation in the Koran*, Lucknow, India, 1926, p.15.

[456] Anwarul Haqq, *Abrogation in the Koran*, Lucknow, India, 1926, p.15.

[457] Anwarul Haqq, *Abrogation in the Koran*, Lucknow, India, 1926, p.15.

[458] Anwarul Haqq, *Abrogation in the Koran*, Lucknow, India, 1926, p.15.

[459] Anwarul Haqq, *Abrogation in the Koran*, Lucknow, India, 1926, p.15.

[460] Anwarul Haqq, *Abrogation in the Koran*, Lucknow, India, 1926, p.17. To see that other translations are more honest than Pickthall see the translations at http://www.mohammeds-koran.com/Koran/2/2.221 .

[461] Anwarul Haqq, *Abrogation in the Koran*, Lucknow, India, 1926, p.18.

[462] Anwarul Haqq, *Abrogation in the Koran*, Lucknow, India, 1926, p.18.

[463] Anwarul Haqq, *Abrogation in the Koran*, Lucknow, India, 1926, p.19.

[464] Anwarul Haqq, *Abrogation in the Koran*, Lucknow, India, 1926, p.54.

[465] Anwarul Haqq, *Abrogation in the Koran*, Lucknow, India, 1926, p.54.

[466] Anwarul Haqq, *Abrogation in the Koran*, Lucknow, India, 1926, p.54.

[467] Anwarul Haqq, *Abrogation in the Koran*, Lucknow, India, 1926, p.70.

[468] Anwarul Haqq, *Abrogation in the Koran*, Lucknow, India, 1926, p.70.

[469] Anwarul Haqq, *Abrogation in the Koran*, Lucknow, India, 1926, p.66.

[470] Anwarul Haqq, *Abrogation in the Koran*, Lucknow, India, 1926, p.66.

[471] Anwarul Haqq, *Abrogation in the Koran*, Lucknow, India, 1926, p.55.

[472] Anwarul Haqq, *Abrogation in the Koran*, Lucknow, India, 1926, p.50.

[473] Anwarul Haqq, *Abrogation in the Koran*, Lucknow, India, 1926, p.50.

[474] Anwarul Haqq, *Abrogation in the Koran*, Lucknow, India, 1926, p.48.

[475] Anwarul Haqq, *Abrogation in the Koran*, Lucknow, India, 1926, p.49.

[476] Anwarul Haqq, *Abrogation in the Koran*, Lucknow, India, 1926, p.49.

[477] Anwarul Haqq, *Abrogation in the Koran*, Lucknow, India, 1926, p.44.

[478] Anwarul Haqq, *Abrogation in the Koran*, Lucknow, India, 1926, p.44.

[479] Anwarul Haqq, *Abrogation in the Koran*, Lucknow, India, 1926, p.45.

[480] Anwarul Haqq, *Abrogation in the Koran*, Lucknow, India, 1926, p.45.

[481] Anwarul Haqq, *Abrogation in the Koran*, Lucknow, India, 1926, p.73.
[482] Anwarul Haqq, *Abrogation in the Koran*, Lucknow, India, 1926, p.73.
[483] Anwarul Haqq, *Abrogation in the Koran*, Lucknow, India, 1926, p.73.
[484] Anwarul Haqq, *Abrogation in the Koran*, Lucknow, India, 1926, p.63.
[485] Anwarul Haqq, *Abrogation in the Koran*, Lucknow, India, 1926, p.64.
[486] Anwarul Haqq, *Abrogation in the Koran*, Lucknow, India, 1926, p.62.
[487] Anwarul Haqq, *Abrogation in the Koran*, Lucknow, India, 1926, p.62.
[488] Anwarul Haqq, *Abrogation in the Koran*, Lucknow, India, 1926, p.62.
[489] Anwarul Haqq, *Abrogation in the Koran*, Lucknow, India, 1926, p.62.
[490] Anwarul Haqq, *Abrogation in the Koran*, Lucknow, India, 1926, p.60.
[491] Anwarul Haqq, *Abrogation in the Koran*, Lucknow, India, 1926, p.60.
[492] Anwarul Haqq, *Abrogation in the Koran*, Lucknow, India, 1926, p.61.
[493] Anwarul Haqq, *Abrogation in the Koran*, Lucknow, India, 1926, p.59.
[494] Anwarul Haqq, *Abrogation in the Koran*, Lucknow, India, 1926, p.58.
[495] Anwarul Haqq, *Abrogation in the Koran*, Lucknow, India, 1926, p.59.
[496] Anwarul Haqq, *Abrogation in the Koran*, Lucknow, India, 1926, p.59.
[497] Anwarul Haqq, *Abrogation in the Koran*, Lucknow, India, 1926, p.57.
[498] Anwarul Haqq, *Abrogation in the Koran*, Lucknow, India, 1926, p.57.
[499] Anwarul Haqq, *Abrogation in the Koran*, Lucknow, India, 1926, p.57.
[500] Anwarul Haqq, *Abrogation in the Koran*, Lucknow, India, 1926, p.57.
[501] Anwarul Haqq, *Abrogation in the Koran*, Lucknow, India, 1926, p.58.
[502] Anwarul Haqq, *Abrogation in the Koran*, Lucknow, India, 1926, p.58.
[503] Anwarul Haqq, *Abrogation in the Koran*, Lucknow, India, 1926, p.58.
[504] Anwarul Haqq, *Abrogation in the Koran*, Lucknow, India, 1926, p.58.
[505] Anwarul Haqq, *Abrogation in the Koran*, Lucknow, India, 1926, p.58.
[506] Anwarul Haqq, *Abrogation in the Koran*, Lucknow, India, 1926, p.56.
[507] Anwarul Haqq, *Abrogation in the Koran*, Lucknow, India, 1926, p.55.
[508] Anwarul Haqq, *Abrogation in the Koran*, Lucknow, India, 1926, p.57.
[509] Anwarul Haqq, *Abrogation in the Koran*, Lucknow, India, 1926, p.57.
[510] Anwarul Haqq, *Abrogation in the Koran*, Lucknow, India, 1926, p.32.
[511] Anwarul Haqq, *Abrogation in the Koran*, Lucknow, India, 1926, p.32.
[512] Anwarul Haqq, *Abrogation in the Koran*, Lucknow, India, 1926, p.32.
[513] Anwarul Haqq, *Abrogation in the Koran*, Lucknow, India, 1926, p.32.
[514] Anwarul Haqq, *Abrogation in the Koran*, Lucknow, India, 1926, p.33.
[515] Anwarul Haqq, *Abrogation in the Koran*, Lucknow, India, 1926, p.33.
[516] Anwarul Haqq, *Abrogation in the Koran*, Lucknow, India, 1926, p.33.
[517] Anwarul Haqq, *Abrogation in the Koran*, Lucknow, India, 1926, p.33.
[518] Anwarul Haqq, *Abrogation in the Koran*, Lucknow, India, 1926, p.33.
[519] Anwarul Haqq, *Abrogation in the Koran*, Lucknow, India, 1926, p.34.
[520] Anwarul Haqq, *Abrogation in the Koran*, Lucknow, India, 1926, p.34.
[521] Anwarul Haqq, *Abrogation in the Koran*, Lucknow, India, 1926, p.34.
[522] Anwarul Haqq, *Abrogation in the Koran*, Lucknow, India, 1926, p.34.
[523] Anwarul Haqq, *Abrogation in the Koran*, Lucknow, India, 1926, p.43.
[524] Anwarul Haqq, *Abrogation in the Koran*, Lucknow, India, 1926, p.43.
[525] Anwarul Haqq, *Abrogation in the Koran*, Lucknow, India, 1926, p.44.
[526] Anwarul Haqq, *Abrogation in the Koran*, Lucknow, India, 1926, p.44.

[527] Anwarul Haqq, *Abrogation in the Koran*, Lucknow, India, 1926, p.44.
[528] Anwarul Haqq, *Abrogation in the Koran*, Lucknow, India, 1926, p.42.
[529] Anwarul Haqq, *Abrogation in the Koran*, Lucknow, India, 1926, p.42.
[530] Anwarul Haqq, *Abrogation in the Koran*, Lucknow, India, 1926, p.42.
[531] Anwarul Haqq, *Abrogation in the Koran*, Lucknow, India, 1926, p.40.
[532] Anwarul Haqq, *Abrogation in the Koran*, Lucknow, India, 1926, p.40.
[533] Anwarul Haqq, *Abrogation in the Koran*, Lucknow, India, 1926, p.41.
[534] Anwarul Haqq, *Abrogation in the Koran*, Lucknow, India, 1926, p.41.
[535] Anwarul Haqq, *Abrogation in the Koran*, Lucknow, India, 1926, p.41.
[536] Anwarul Haqq, *Abrogation in the Koran*, Lucknow, India, 1926, p.41.
[537] Anwarul Haqq, *Abrogation in the Koran*, Lucknow, India, 1926, p.41.
[538] Anwarul Haqq, *Abrogation in the Koran*, Lucknow, India, 1926, p.45.
[539] Anwarul Haqq, *Abrogation in the Koran*, Lucknow, India, 1926, p.45.
[540] Anwarul Haqq, *Abrogation in the Koran*, Lucknow, India, 1926, p.46.
[541] Anwarul Haqq, *Abrogation in the Koran*, Lucknow, India, 1926, p.54.
[542] Anwarul Haqq, *Abrogation in the Koran*, Lucknow, India, 1926, p.53.
[543] Anwarul Haqq, *Abrogation in the Koran*, Lucknow, India, 1926, p.53.
[544] Anwarul Haqq, *Abrogation in the Koran*, Lucknow, India, 1926, p.53.
[545] Anwarul Haqq, *Abrogation in the Koran*, Lucknow, India, 1926, p.53.
[546] Anwarul Haqq, *Abrogation in the Koran*, Lucknow, India, 1926, p.48.
[547] Anwarul Haqq, *Abrogation in the Koran*, Lucknow, India, 1926, p.48.
[548] Anwarul Haqq, *Abrogation in the Koran*, Lucknow, India, 1926, p.47.
[549] Anwarul Haqq, *Abrogation in the Koran*, Lucknow, India, 1926, p.47.
[550] Anwarul Haqq, *Abrogation in the Koran*, Lucknow, India, 1926, p.47.
[551] Anwarul Haqq, *Abrogation in the Koran*, Lucknow, India, 1926, p.47.
[552] Anwarul Haqq, *Abrogation in the Koran*, Lucknow, India, 1926, p.47.
[553] Anwarul Haqq, *Abrogation in the Koran*, Lucknow, India, 1926, p.56.
[554] Anwarul Haqq, *Abrogation in the Koran*, Lucknow, India, 1926, p.52.
[555] Anwarul Haqq, *Abrogation in the Koran*, Lucknow, India, 1926, p.53.
[556] Anwarul Haqq, *Abrogation in the Koran*, Lucknow, India, 1926, p.53.
[557] Anwarul Haqq, *Abrogation in the Koran*, Lucknow, India, 1926, p.56.
[558] Anwarul Haqq, *Abrogation in the Koran*, Lucknow, India, 1926, p.35.
[559] Anwarul Haqq, *Abrogation in the Koran*, Lucknow, India, 1926, p.35.
[560] Anwarul Haqq, *Abrogation in the Koran*, Lucknow, India, 1926, p.35.
[561] Anwarul Haqq, *Abrogation in the Koran*, Lucknow, India, 1926, p.57.
[562] Anwarul Haqq, *Abrogation in the Koran*, Lucknow, India, 1926, p.57.
[563] Anwarul Haqq, *Abrogation in the Koran*, Lucknow, India, 1926, p.66.
[564] Anwarul Haqq, *Abrogation in the Koran*, Lucknow, India, 1926, p.72.
[565] Anwarul Haqq, *Abrogation in the Koran*, Lucknow, India, 1926, p.65.
[566] Anwarul Haqq, *Abrogation in the Koran*, Lucknow, India, 1926, p.65.
[567] Anwarul Haqq, *Abrogation in the Koran*, Lucknow, India, 1926, p.73.
[568] Anwarul Haqq, *Abrogation in the Koran*, Lucknow, India, 1926, p.66.
[569] Anwarul Haqq, *Abrogation in the Koran*, Lucknow, India, 1926, p.73.

[570] When Surah One refers to those with whom "Allah is angry" it refers to the Jews; those who "have gone astray" refers to the Christians. This is the most essential prayer in Islam (unless it is said, all other prayers are invalid). The meaning and importance of this verse

proves Islam renews this hatred on a daily, collective basis. Imagine the contemporary cries of "Islamophobia" if up to the modern-day Jews and Christians gathered five times a day to denounce those who behaved like Muslims. The leaders of those religions would be apologetic and would reform; the followers of Islam do neither. See the certified parallel text English/Arabic Koran from Saudi Arabia – *Interpretation and Meaning of the Noble Qur'an*, trans. Muhammad Hilali and Muhammad Khan, Riyadh, 1996, pp.14-15.

[571] Anwarul Haqq, *Abrogation in the Koran*, Lucknow, India, 1926, p.71.

[572] Anwarul Haqq, *Abrogation in the Koran*, Lucknow, India, 1926, p.70.

[573] Anwarul Haqq, *Abrogation in the Koran*, Lucknow, India, 1926, p.70.

[574] The chronology of this verse appears problematic. Considering that it talks of "fighting for the cause of Allah", and of people going in search of "bounty" (looting), it would appear to fit more with the later Koran than the earlier Koran.

[575] Anwarul Haqq, *Abrogation in the Koran*, Lucknow, India, 1926, p.69. The translations of this verse by Yusuf Ali and Sahih are clear that this refers to punishment. You can see multiple translations of this verse at http://www.mohammeds-koran.com/Koran/68/68.44 .

[576] Anwarul Haqq, *Abrogation in the Koran*, Lucknow, India, 1926, p.69.

RECOMMENDED BOOKS

Manzooruddin Ahmad, *Pakistan: the Emerging Islamic State*, Karachi, 1966.

Hamid Algar, *The Roots of the Islamic Revolution*, London, 1983.

Ahmad al-Baladuri, *The Origins of the Islamic State*, trans. Philip Khuri Hitti, London, 1916.

Ahmad al-Misri, *Reliance of the Traveller: a Classic Manual of Islamic Sacred Law*, trans. Sheikh Keller, 1997.

Abu Al-Qurtubi, *Tafsir Al-Qurtubi: Classical Commentary on the Holy Qur'an*, translated by Aisha Bewley, London, 2003.

Shmuel Bar, *Warrant for Terror: The Fatwas of Radical Islam and the Duty to Jihad*, New York, 2006.

Bruce Bawer, *Surrender: Appeasing Islam, Sacrificing Freedom*, New York, 2009.

Richard Bell, *Introduction to the Qur'an*, Edinburgh, 1953.

Andrew Bostom (ed), *The Legacy of Jihad: Islamic Holy War and the Fate of Non-Muslims*, New York, 2005.

Andrew Bostom, *Sharia Versus Freedom: the Legacy of Islamic Totalitarianism*, New York, 2012.

Christopher Caldwell, *Reflections on the Revolution in Europe*, London, 2009.

Fred Donner, *Early Islamic Conquests*, Princeton University Press, 1981.

Hamid Enayat, *Modern Islamic Political Thought*, Austin, Texas, 1982.

Reuven Firestone, *Jihad: The Origin of Holy War in Islam,* Oxford University Press, 1999.

Paul Fregosi, *Jihad in the West: Muslim Conquests from the 7th to the 21st Centuries*, New York, 1998.

Richard Gabriel, *Muhammad: Islam's First Great General*, Oklahoma, 2007.

H.A.R. Gibb and J.H.Kramers, *Shorter Encyclopaedia of Islam*, Edited on Behalf of the Royal Netherlands Academy, London, 1953.

Muhammad Hamidullah, *Battlefields of the Prophet Muhammad: A Contribution to Muslim Military History*. Published in French in Etudes Islamiques, Paris, 1939.

Anwarul Haqq, *Abrogation in the Koran*, Lucknow, India, 1926.

Robert Hoyland, *In God's Path: the Arab Conquests and the Creation of an Islamic Empire*, London, 2015.

Samuel P. Huntington, *The Clash of Civilisations and the Remaking of World Order*, London, 1998.

Ibn Ishaq, *The Life of Muhammad: a Translation of Ibn Ishaq's Sirat Rasul Allah*, by A.Guillaume, London, 1955.

Efraim Karsh, *Islamic Imperialism: a History*, London, 2007.

John Kelsey, *Islam and War*, Kentucky, 1993.

Abdulrahman Kurdi, *The Islamic State: a Study based on the Islamic Holy Constitution*, London, 1984.

Bernard Lewis, *The Muslim Discovery of Europe*, New York, 1982.

Bernard Lewis, *The Political Language of Islam*, London, 1988.

S.K. Malik, *The Quranic Concept of War*, Lahore, 1979. Reprinted Delhi, 1992.

Syed Maududi, *First Principles of the Islamic State*, Lahore, 1967.

Peter McLoughlin, *Easy Meat: Inside Britain's Grooming Gang Scandal*, London, 2016.

George Nafziger , *Islam at War: a History*, Westport, 2003.

Muhammad Pickthall (trans.), *Koran*, London, 1930.

Daniel Pipes, *The Rushdie Affair: the Novel, the Ayatollah, and the West*, New York, 1990.

Tommy Robinson, *Enemy of the State*, Batley, 2015.

J.M. Rodwell (trans.), *Koran*, Dent, London, 1861. Reprinted 1909.

J.J. Saunders, *A History of Medieval Islam*, London, 1965.

T.P. Schwartz-Barcott, *War, Terror and Peace in the Qu'ran and Islam: Insights for Military and Government Leaders*, Army War College Foundation Press, Carlisle, Pennsylvania, 2004.

Emmet Scott, *The Impact of Islam*, London, 2014.

Edward Sell, *The Historical Development of the Qur'an*, 1906 (4th edition, London, 1923).

Kalim Siddiqui, *Stages of Islamic Revolution*, London, 1996.

Patrick Sookhdeo, *Global Jihad: The Future in the Face of Militant Islam*, London, 2007.

Robert Spencer (ed), *The Myth of Islamic Tolerance: How Islamic Law Treats Non-Muslims*, New York, 2005.

Nicholas Starkovsky, *The Koran Handbook: an Annotated Translation*, New York, 2004.

Ibn Warraq, *Why I Am Not a Muslim*, New York, 1995,

W. Montgomery Watt, *Muhammad: Prophet and Statesman*, London, 1961.

W. Montgomery Watt, *Islamic Political Thought*, Edinburgh, 1968.

W. Montgomery Watt, *Bell's Introduction to the Qur'an*, 1953. Completely revised and enlarged), Edinburgh, 1970.

Bat Ye'or, *Islam and Dhimmitude: Where Civilisations Collide*, Lancaster, 2002.

Bat Ye'or, *Eurabia*, Madison, 2005.

Bat Ye'or, Europe, *Globalization and the Coming Universal Caliphate*, Madison, 2011.

Recommended Books (Date Order)

The reading list is here arranged with the oldest books first. The reason for this is to show the importance of Ibn Ishaq's biography of Mohammed, and how the concept of the Islamic State is nothing new. Furthermore, when arranged in chronological order one can see there were many books published in English since 1861 which made it clear to the educated elite that Islam was a political ideology and a religion of war, that the Koran needed to be understood in chronological order and that Islam has and would cause major conflicts with non-Islamic societies.

⌗

Ibn Ishaq, (circa 769) *The Life of Muhammad: a Translation of Ibn Ishaq's Sirat Rasul Allah*, by A.Guillaume, London, 1955.

Ahmad al-Baladuri, (circa 890) *The Origins of the Islamic State*, trans. Philip Khuri Hitti, London, 1916.

Abu Al-Qurtubi, (circa 1270) *Tafsir Al-Qurtubi: Classical Commentary on the Holy Qur'an*, translated by Aisha Bewley, London, 2003.

Ahmad al-Misri, (circa 1360) *Reliance of the Traveller: a Classic Manual of Islamic Sacred Law*, trans. Sheikh Keller, 1997.

J.M. Rodwell trans, (1861) *Koran*, Dent, London, 1909.

Edward Sell, (1906) *The Historical Development of the Qur'an*, 4th edition, London, 1923

Anwarul Haqq, (1926) *Abrogation in the Koran*, Lucknow, India.

Muhammad Pickthall trans., (1930) *Koran*, London.

Muhammad Hamidullah, (1939) *Battlefields of the Prophet Muhammad: A Contribution to Muslim Military History. Published in French in Etudes Islamiques*, Paris, 1939.

H.A.R. Gibb and J.H.Kramers, (1953) *Shorter Encyclopaedia of Islam*, Edited on Behalf of the Royal Netherlands Academy, London.

Richard Bell, (1953) *Introduction to the Qur'an*, Edinburgh

W. Montgomery Watt, (1961) *Muhammad: Prophet and Statesman*, London.

J.J. Saunders, (1965) *A History of Medieval Islam*, London.

Manzooruddin Ahmad, (1966) *Pakistan: the Emerging Islamic State*, Karachi.

Syed Maududi, (1967) *First Principles of the Islamic State*, Lahore.

W. Montgomery Watt, (1968) *Islamic Political Thought*, Edinburgh.

W. Montgomery Watt, (1970) *Bell's Introduction to the Qur'an* [1953] (completely revised and enlarged, 1970), Edinburgh.

S.K. Malik, (1979) *The Quranic Concept of War*, Lahore. Reprinted Delhi, 1992.

Fred Donner, (1981) *Early Islamic Conquests*, Princeton University Press.

Hamid Enayat, (1982) *Modern Islamic Political Thought*, Austin, Texas.

Bernard Lewis, (1982) *The Muslim Discovery of Europe*, New York.

Hamid Algar, (1983) *The Roots of the Islamic Revolution*, London.

Abdulrahman Kurdi, (1984) *The Islamic State: a Study based on the Islamic Holy Constitution*, London.

Bernard Lewis, (1988) *The Political Language of Islam*, London.

Daniel Pipes, (1990) *The Rushdie Affair: the Novel, the Ayatollah, and the West*, New York.

John Kelsey (1993) *Islam and War*, Kentucky.

Ibn Warraq, (1995) *Why I Am Not a Muslim*, New York.

Kalim Siddiqui, (1996) *Stages of Islamic Revolution*, London.

Paul Fregosi, (1998) *Jihad in the West: Muslim Conquests from the 7th to the 21st Centuries*, New York, 1998.

Samuel P. Huntington, (1998) *The Clash of Civilisations and the Remaking of World Order*, London.

Reuven Firestone, (1999) *Jihad: The Origin of Holy War in Islam*, Oxford University Press.

Bat Ye'or, (2002) *Islam and Dhimmitude: Where Civilisations Collide*, Lancaster.

George Nafziger (2003) *Islam at War: a History*, Westport.

T.P. Schwartz-Barcott, (2004) *War, Terror and Peace in the Qu'ran and Islam: Insights for Military and Government Leaders*, Army War College Foundation Press, Carlisle, Pennsylvania.

Nicholas Starkovsky, (2004) *The Koran Handbook: an Annotated Translation*, New York.

Andrew Bostom, (2005) editor, *The Legacy of Jihad: Islamic Holy War and the Fate of Non-Muslims*, New York.

Robert Spencer (ed), (2005) *The Myth of Islamic Tolerance: How Islamic Law Treats Non-Muslims*, New York.

Bat Ye'or, (2005) *Eurabia*, Madison.

Shmuel Bar, (2006) *Warrant for Terror: The Fatwas of Radical Islam and the Duty to Jihad*, New York.

Efraim Karsh (2007) *Islamic Imperialism: a History*, London.

Richard Gabriel (2007) *Muhammad: Islam's First Great General*, Oklahoma.

Patrick Sookhdeo, (2007) *Global Jihad: The Future in the Face of Militant Islam*, London.

Bruce Bawer, (2009) *Surrender: Appeasing Islam, Sacrificing Freedom*, New York.

Christopher Caldwell, (2009) *Reflections on the Revolution in Europe*, London.

Bat Ye'or, (2011) *Europe, Globalization and the Coming Universal Caliphate*, Madison.

Andrew Bostom, (2012) *Sharia Versus Freedom: the Legacy of Islamic Totalitarianism*, New York.

Emmet Scott, (2014) *The Impact of Islam*, London

Robert Hoyland, (2015) *In God's Path: the Arab Conquests and the Creation of an Islamic Empire*, London.

Tommy Robinson, (2015) *Enemy of the State*, Batley.

Peter McLoughlin (2016) *Easy Meat: Inside Britain's Grooming Gang Scandal*, London.

APPENDIX 1: EXPERT CHRONOLOGIES

Traditional	Tanzil.net	Rodwell	Qran.org	Traditional Name
1	**96**	96	96	The Opening
2	**68**	74	68	The Cow
3	**73**	73	73	The Family of Imran
4	**74**	93	74	Women
5	**1**	94	1	The Table Spread
6	**111**	113	111	Cattle
7	**81**	114	81	The Heights
8	**87**	1	87	The Spoils of War
9	**92**	109	92	Repentance
10	**89**	112	89	Jonah
11	**93**	111	93	Hud
12	**94**	108	94	Joseph
13	**103**	104	103	The Thunder
14	**100**	107	100	Abraham
15	**108**	102	108	Al Hijr
16	**102**	92	102	The Bee
17	**107**	68	107	The Children of Israel
18	**109**	90	109	The Cave
19	**105**	105	105	Mary
20	**113**	106	113	Ta Ha
21	**114**	97	114	The Prophets
22	**112**	86	112	The Pilgrimage
23	**53**	91	53	The Believers
24	**80**	80	80	Light
25	**97**	87	97	The Criterion
26	**91**	95	91	The Poets
27	**85**	103	85	The Ant
28	**95**	85	95	The Story
29	**106**	101	106	The Spider
30	**101**	99	101	The Romans
31	**75**	82	75	Luqman
32	**104**	81	104	The Prostration
33	**77**	84	77	The Clans
34	**50**	100	50	Saba
35	**90**	79	90	The Angels
36	**86**	77	86	Ya Sin
37	**54**	78	54	Those Who Set The Ranks
38	**38**	88	38	Sad
39	**7**	89	7	The Troops
40	**72**	75	72	The Believer
41	**36**	83	36	Fusilat
42	**25**	69	25	Counsel

43	**35**	51	35	Ornaments of Gold
44	**19**	52	19	Smoke
45	**20**	56	20	Crouching
46	**56**	53	56	The Wind-Curved Sandhills
47	**26**	70	26	Muhammad
48	**27**	55	27	Victory
49	**28**	54	28	The Private Apartments
50	**17**	37	17	Qaf
51	**10**	71	10	The Winnowing Winds
52	**11**	76	11	The Mount
53	**12**	44	12	The Star
54	**15**	50	15	The Moon
55	**6**	20	6	The Beneficent
56	**37**	26	37	The Event
57	**31**	15	31	Iron
58	**34**	19	34	She That Disputeth
59	**39**	38	39	Exile
60	**40**	36	40	She That Is To Be Examined
61	**41**	43	41	The Ranks
62	**42**	72	42	The Congregation
63	**43**	67	43	The Hypocrites
64	**44**	23	44	Mutual Dissillusion
65	**45**	21	45	Divorce
66	**46**	25	46	Banning
67	**51**	17	51	The Sovereignty
68	**88**	27	88	The Pen
69	**18**	18	18	The Reality
70	**16**	32	16	The Ascending Stairways
71	**71**	41	71	Noah
72	**14**	45	14	The Jinn
73	**21**	16	21	The Enshrouded One
74	**23**	30	23	The Cloaked One
75	**32**	11	32	The Rising of the Dead
76	**52**	14	52	Time or Man
77	**67**	12	67	The Emissaries
78	**69**	40	69	The Tidings
79	**70**	28	70	Those who Drag Forth
80	**78**	39	78	He Frowned
81	**79**	29	79	The Overthrowing
82	**82**	31	82	The Cleaving
83	**84**	42	84	Defrauding
84	**30**	10	30	The Sundering
85	**29**	34	29	The Mansions of the Stars
86	**83**	35	83	The Morning Star
87	**2**	7	2	The Most High
88	**8**	46	8	The Overwhelming

Traditional	Tanzil.net	Rodwell	Qran.org	Traditional Name
89	**3**	6	3	The Dawn
90	**33**	13	33	The City
91	**60**	2	60	The Sun
92	**4**	98	4	The Night
93	**99**	64	99	The Morning Hours
94	**57**	62	57	Solace
95	**47**	8	47	The Fig
96	**13**	47	13	The Clot
97	**55**	3	55	Power
98	**76**	61	76	The Clear Proof
99	**65**	57	65	The Earthquake
100	**98**	4	98	The Coursers
101	**59**	65	59	The Calamity
102	**24**	59	24	Rivalry in Worldly Increase
103	**22**	33	22	The Declining Day
104	**63**	63	63	The Traducer
105	**58**	24	58	The Elephant
106	**49**	58	49	Winter or Qureysh
107	**66**	22	66	Small Kindnesses
108	**64**	48	61	Abundance
109	**61**	66	62	The Disbelievers
110	**62**	60	63	Succour
111	**48**	110	48	Victory
112	**5**	49	5	The Unity
113	**9**	9	9	The Daybreak
114	**110**	5	110	Mankind

The first and last columns show the traditional number and name of the Surahs. The three middle columns show the variety of chronological orderings of the chapters. Whilst experts disagree slightly on this order, we can see that modern scholarly websites (committed to presenting the *Koran* in chronological order for Muslims) are in columns two and four (from tanzil.net and qran.org). **Rodwell's (1861) chronological ordering is the centre column, showing that for over 150 years educated English speakers have had the chronological ordering of the Koran available to them.**

Whilst there is obviously slight disagreement about where some chapters fit in the chronological ordering, we can see that for 150 years it has been agreed that **Chapter 9 and Chapter 5 (the chapters commanding genocide and apartheid) are chronologically among the last three chapters of the Koran.** That this is so, means the commands in those chapters abrogate any contradictory verses occurring in earlier chapters. When one knows that the most violent and discriminatory verses of the Koran occur at the end, this explains to everyone why the world is facing endless jihad. It explains why Muslims kill to subjugate non-Muslims.

We have taken the chronological ordering from tanzil.net (which is one of the world's best websites for studying the Koran), and we reversed it (to emphasize the importance of abrogation). Column two above is rendered in bold so that in crossing successive pages of this Appendix the reader can see which column is the tanzil.net ordering.

For those who still do not believe the chronological orders above, we suggest you acquire a copy of W. Montgomery Watt, *Bell's Introduction to the Qur'an*. Bell and Watt were two of Britain's foremost twentieth-century scholars of Islam. Bell's book first appeared in 1953, then was re-published by Professor Watt in 1970. The Table of Surahs at the end of that book shows the Koran in its traditional order and contrasts this order with the order in four other scholarly Korans (where the surahs are put in chronological order). In all four of these scholarly Korans, Chapter 9 (containing "The Verse of the Sword") is dated as either the last Chapter from Mohammed, or the next to last Chapter from Mohammed. This validates the chronology found on the Islamic websites listed above. We believe that our presentation (reverse chronological order) is the one which will most easily make sense of the Koran for the ordinary reader.

The book entitled *Bell's Introduction to the Qur'an* is still in print and has been republished and reprinted many times since the original 1953 version, particularly the edited Quisling version from 1970. Indeed, the frequency with which this book on an obscure topic by a forgotten author has been reprinted is extraordinary. According to WorldCat (a global publishing database) this book was reprinted by Edinburgh University Press in 1975, 1990, 1991, 1994, 1997, 2001, 2003, 2005, 2007, 2008, 2011, 2014, 2015 (the database from which the above information comes may not even have the complete record of the re-printing of this book). Mostly the books printed by university presses have very small print runs and would rarely ever be reprinted, let alone be reprinted every few years. For example, Bell's original two volume translation of the Koran (which questions the order of verses) was last printed in 1960 and has never been reprinted. Typically abstruse books have only a single print run.

The frequency with which the publisher has reprinted Dr. Bell's book on the way scholars put the Koran into chronological order leads one to conclude that the book has been a core text in theology departments across the West (the book is quite short, extremely expensive and covers a topic that was of interest only to specialists). We can infer that throughout the past 30 years those who study the Koran in universities in the West were well aware of the chronological order of the Koran and what effect abrogation has on the meaning of Islam. They understand how to decode the Koran, but they remain silent. The complicity of the Quisling elite is total.

APPENDIX 2: ENCRYPTED KORAN INDEX

This index shows the Koran chapters in their traditional order. Use this to compare our highlighted or cancelled verses with any standard Koran you have to hand. The chapters listed here are in the same order as you will find in the traditional (encrypted) Koran.

APPENDIX 3: DECRYPTED KORAN INDEX

This index is provided to enable you to find chapters in our reverse chronological Koran, tallying their traditional chapter numbers or names to their page number in our book.

Appendix 4: The Banning Of This Book

In Germany in the 1930s the state and big business collaborated to discriminate against Jews and to silence Jewish objections to this hatred. That's where we are now. The concentration camps were preceded by Jews being banned from universities and banned from journalism. When the Nazis occupied France, this discrimination was imposed by the Vichy regime on Jews there too. Only this time the victims of this discrimination are the citizens of Western democracies, who are prevented by the state and big business from expressing the truth about the history of Islam or the threat that Islam poses to non-Muslims. If the argument or evidence in *Mohammed's Koran* was flawed Muslims and academics would have refuted the book in reviews. If the argument was inconsistent, one expects even journalists would have been able to refute *Mohammed's Koran*. Instead, in our so-called "liberal democracies", the book was systematically censored.

For a long time we have warned that mass censorship is coming to the West. **Here's the story of censorship in relation to *Mohammed's Koran*, the first No.1 best-selling book to be banned in the age of tolerance and diversity.** *Mohammed's Koran* denounces the hatred found in the Koran and denounces the Koran's calls for Muslims to kill non-Muslims. It's as if we published an annotated edition of *Mein Kampf* where we highlighted and denounced the hatred and the call to kill Jews in Hitler's book, and this annotated edition of *Mein Kampf* was then banned whilst the original continued to be published.. The authors of *Mohammed's Koran* must be silenced because people cannot refute the evidence the book contains.

Amazon's actions in banning *Mohammed's Koran* have corroborated the main argument made in the book: the elite do not want the public to understand that the Koran commands Muslims to kill non-Muslims, and for over 1000 years it has been accepted by Islamic scholars that the commands to kill us cancel out (abrogate) any instructions in the Koran which appear to guide Muslims towards peace or tolerance. **The book Amazon banned provides the clearest illustration in history of the effects of abrogation on the meaning of the Koran. Those Korans which promote violence as moral behaviour (and which are regarded as the final and holy word of god) are still on sale.** Amazon banned the book which irrefutably decodes the Koran, the book which would assist the public in taking civilized action to curb the growth of this genocidal ideology. **The followers of Islam can freely distribute copies of their book which calls on Muslims to kill us; the victims of Islam are not permitted to know what this evil book has in store for us. Imagine if Jews were forbidden from selling books denouncing Nazism.**

It is clear that we non-Muslims are not permitted to criticise the ideology which has inspired over 30,000 terrorist attacks since 9th September 2001. Customers were extremely enthusiastic about *Mohammed's Koran* (as evidenced not only by the sales of a book ignored by the media, but also by the 1,000 "verified purchaser" reviews left by readers, almost all of which gave the book the maximum five stars). **Amazon are following orders from above, and what the customer wants is irrelevant when the crypto-fascist state demands the suppression of information. Imagine how delighted the KGB, the Stasi or the Gestapo would have been to have had a monopolist like Amazon doing their bidding, destroying any book that exposed the lies of the state.**

In July 2017 when *Mohammed's Koran* was first published, it went straight to No.1 on Amazon UK, and remained at the No.1 spot until the first print run of 5,000 copies had sold out five days later. Before Amazon would distribute the book through the Kindle programme or through print on demand they made it clear they would vet the content of the book. They did so, and it passed the first hurdle. In those first few weeks following publication Amazon contacted the authors to say that the book had been reported to them as "hate speech" and that Amazon were investigating these claims and if found to be true the book would be banned by Amazon. A week later Amazon informed us that despite the calls to have it banned, they were not going to ban it. Thus, *Mohammed's Koran* **was twice cleared by Amazon for distribution by them. From then on, every couple of months they would email the authors asking to put the book into a special category of Kindle promotion which would allow Amazon to gouge even more of the profits from the book** (Amazon kept most of the cover price of both the print on demand book and the Kindle ebook). So Amazon sought to profit as much as possible from the sale of the book which they had twice cleared as suitable for distribution. Back then **Amazon ignored the demands to ban the book which came from Communist newspapers.**

Eighteen months after the book first went to No.1, Amazon emailed us to say that the book was banned because it was "in violation of our content guidelines". Following the ban, repeated requests from us asking what they found offensive (and what had changed since they gave the book the all-clear in 2017) were ignored by Amazon. On more than one occasion Amazon staff have falsely reported to complaining customers that the authors had deleted the book from the Amazon website. When these Amazon customers informed us of this we pointed out that only Amazon has the power to delete entries from their database and we provided the email from Amazon where they stated they were banning the book. Amazon sent one customer a transcription of his interaction with them, showing that Amazon not only record conversations with customers but also automatically transcribe these conversations. **Having proved to these Amazon customers that Amazon staff were deceiving them about the disappearance of this book, one customer contacted Amazon a second time and complained about this deception. Amazon staff then responded by saying that *Mohammed's Koran* had been banned in the wake of Tommy Robinson exposing the BBC's lies in their flagship documentary series *Panorama*.** Just two days after Tommy released his documentary (entitled *Panodrama*), Amazon banned the only Koran which denounces violence. In the conversation with their angry customer about *Mohammed's Koran* being banned, **Amazon also said that the order to ban the book had come from above Amazon. As the Amazon customer asked in surprise: "What's above Amazon"?** The UK government? Significantly, this time Amazon did not send their customer a transcript of this second conversation. Being wise to the fact that Amazon were recording these conversations, the customer also recorded the conversation and sent us the recording. We thank him for his foresight.

Following Tommy's exposure of the extent to which the premier state broadcaster was prepared to fabricate material in order to destroy a man's life, **Tommy was then censored and permanently banned by companies such as Facebook, Instagram, Snapchat and others: more global corporations prepared to do the bidding of the British state.** The deputy leader of the socialist party in Britain wrote a public letter to Google, demanding that they ban Tommy from YouTube. **A few weeks later YouTube bowed to their political masters, hiding Tommy's videos from other users, ensuring that the media lies are the dominant account of what Tommy says and what he does. In Orwell's novel *1984*, Emmanuel Goldstein is branded an enemy of the state, and only Big Brother is allowed to present the views of Goldstein. In the 21st century the collusion between multinational corporations and the fascist state is more obvious now than it was during Hitler's time in government.** So much for "liberal democracy". A year after the BBC "documentary" was completed, the BBC refuses to answer Freedom of Information requests concerning the BBC's reluctance to broadcast it or about this waste of public money in making it.

That the British government would want *Mohammed's Koran* banned comes as no surprise. Since we had been publicly discussing the book in the months before publication, the Quisling elite had time to get their propaganda in place. **No sooner was this book published than state-funded organisations were taking out advertisements on Google's search results, intercepting any search for "Tommy Robinson's new book" or "Mohammed's Koran" with an advertisement for a series of expensive, professionally-made videos warning people not to read this book!** Google would not take advertisements from the publisher for key phrases relating to the book, but they would take advertisements for such phrases from people who wanted to stop the public reading the book. In this way these huge monopolies (who pay virtually no tax in the UK) work hand-in-glove with the state's efforts to shape what the public knows. So much for Google's slogan "do no evil".

As you might expect with Amazon following orders from on high to ban this book, Amazon is absolutely inconsistent about what they ban. **It is highly significant that Amazon still sells Hitler's *Mein Kampf* (a book which openly advocates the gassing of Jews, which doctrine was then put into practice in Auschwitz and other death camps).** It's not that

Amazon is merely allowing third parties to sell *Mein Kampf*: Amazon is the seller profiting from a book which was the foundation of the Nazi policy to exterminate the Jews. So much for Amazon's "content guidelines". **Amazon still sells *The Anarchist Cookbook*, a bomb-making manual which has resulted in people being jailed for terrorism** ("Publisher of Anarchist Cookbook convicted under Terrorism Act", *The Guardian*, 9th Mar 2011). **A few years ago Amazon famously refused to ban a book promoting paedophilia, with Amazon saying "Amazon believes it is censorship not sell [sic] certain books simply because we or others believe their message is objectionable"** (see "Amazon Under Pressure for Selling Pedophilia Book", *CNBC*, 10th Nov 2010). The only Koran Amazon has banned is also the only Koran which denounces violence. **All those Korans which promote the hatred of non-Muslims are still for sale.** Amazon is still selling those Korans which unequivocally tell Muslims they will go to Paradise if they become murderous Jihadis. What are those "content guidelines" Amazon? Before Amazon became a modern-day book-burner, our Koran which denounces violence was also the No.1 best-selling Koran in the UK. **Now you can't even sell a used copy of our book through Amazon's website, so extensive is this ban!** If there were any Korans which should have been banned it was all those Korans purporting to be the final word of god and which command that Muslims should kill us non-Muslims. Those tracts of violent hatred are permitted and promoted by Amazon (just as *Mein Kampf* extolls the mass-killing of Jews).

Under English law a company is assumed to be a monopoly if it controls 50% of a market (and if its competitors are much smaller, then the company is judged to be a monopoly with considerably less than 50% of market share). The book trade is not even able to estimate the size of Amazon's control of the book market (Amazon are highly secretive not only about why they ban books, but also about the scale of their monopolistic practices). In a 2010 submission to the British government opposing Amazon's purchase of a competitor, The Booksellers Association stated that between 2008 and 2010 the share of books sold over the internet rocketed from 17% to 44% of all sales in just two years (there is no reason to believe that a similar trajectory did not continue for the following decade). The same report states that in 2010 Amazon already had 70% of internet sales (before Amazon bought their small, but fast-growing competitor, The Book Depository). Still, **the British government, which purports to favour competition, permitted Amazon to buy up their fast-growing competitor (Amazon owns other "competitors", such as Abebooks).** The report by The Booksellers Association estimated that in 2010 internet sales accounted for approximately 50% of all sales of books outside of supermarkets, book clubs and bargain book shops. **There is every reason to assume that Amazon now totally dominates the market for serious books bought outside university bookshops. If their exploitation of this dominant position did not suit the state, then they would not be permitted to maintain their monopoly.**

When Amazon banned the only Koran which denounces Islamic terrorism, they also deleted around 1,000 five star reviews from very satisfied customers. Luckily many of those reviews were backed up on the website which accompanies the book (see inside front cover of the book for details). But don't think that Amazon is alone in banning this book. **In the UK we have had reports from customers that the largest chains of book-sellers (such as Waterstones and Foyles) have refused to supply *Mohammed's Koran* to customers (Muslim propaganda organisations are on record claiming they are responsible for this). In the US we have had reports of customers going to Barnes & Noble and Books-a-Million to order copies, only to be told that the book cannot be found in their databases and therefore cannot even be ordered (something the bookshop staff reported they had never seen happen before with a book that was still in print).** When the book was first published the British police threatened the launch venue with bankruptcy should they go ahead with the launch. All of these small details are part of a larger project. **When Professor Guy Millière left the toxic environment of France for the freedoms of the USA, he gave a speech where he noted that it was impossible to go into any bookshop in Paris and find a book that was critical of Islam (we'd already observed this fact in the major bookshops of London).** Such books are being driven off the internet too. Perhaps now it becomes clear why the UK government is proposing to censor the internet itself, making Britain as fascist as Saudi Arabia, Communist China and North Korea, places where no criticism of the orthodox truth is permitted. **In a few years we expect it will be illegal in the UK to criticise Islam (between 1997 and 2006 the UK government attempted over and over to covertly pass such a law and came within one vote of succeeding, as documented in Peter's book *Easy Meat*).**

Here's our promise to the fascists who ban books: when it becomes impossible to print *Mohammed's Koran* or impossible for us to get these printed copies into the hands of the public, then the book will be made public domain. In those circumstances anyone will then be able to distribute it for free or print it for themselves and others. When there are no publishers, printers or retailers blocking this book, then you fascists will have removed any obstacle in the way of anyone who wants to spread the truth about Islam. **You are not going to prevent the victims of Islam from understanding that we are offered two choices by Islam: submit or die. The British government and most of the publishing industry have chosen submission.**

Amazon have now set the precedent. In the West the Koran can be banned and journalists and politicians will applaud such a ban. The Index which follows demonstrates how the violent hatred of non-Muslims pervades the Koran. If anything is hate speech then the Koran is surely the foremost example of an ideology which promotes violence and hatred. The elite want to conceal this from you.

THEMATIC INDEX TO THE KORAN

Ideological Conflict (cont'd)

Ideological Conflict (cont'd)

Religion Of War (cont'd)

Subjugation (continued)